# Dictionary of Literary Biography

## *Documentary Series*

14 *Four Women Writers for Children, 1868-1918*, edited by Caroline C. Hunt (1996)

15 *American Expatriate Writers: Paris in the Twenties*, edited by Matthew J. Bruccoli and Robert W. Trogdon (1997)

16 *The House of Scribner, 1905-1930*, edited by John Delaney (1997)

17 *The House of Scribner, 1931-1984*, edited by John Delaney (1998)

18 *British Poets of The Great War: Sassoon, Graves, Owen*, edited by Patrick Quinn (1999)

19 *James Dickey*, edited by Judith S. Baughman (1999)

## *Yearbooks*

1980 edited by Karen L. Rood, Jean W. Ross, and Richard Ziegfeld (1981)

1981 edited by Karen L. Rood, Jean W. Ross, and Richard Ziegfeld (1982)

1982 edited by Richard Ziegfeld; associate editors: Jean W. Ross and Lynne C. Zeigler (1983)

1983 edited by Mary Bruccoli and Jean W. Ross; associate editor: Richard Ziegfeld (1984)

1984 edited by Jean W. Ross (1985)

1985 edited by Jean W. Ross (1986)

1986 edited by J. M. Brook (1987)

1987 edited by J. M. Brook (1988)

1988 edited by J. M. Brook (1989)

1989 edited by J. M. Brook (1990)

1990 edited by James W. Hipp (1991)

1991 edited by James W. Hipp (1992)

1992 edited by James W. Hipp (1993)

1993 edited by James W. Hipp, contributing editor George Garrett (1994)

1994 edited by James W. Hipp, contributing editor George Garrett (1995)

1995 edited by James W. Hipp, contributing editor George Garrett (1996)

1996 edited by Samuel W. Bruce and L. Kay Webster, contributing editor George Garrett (1997)

1997 edited by Matthew J. Bruccoli and George Garrett, with the assistance of L. Kay Webster (1998)

1998 edited by Matthew J. Bruccoli, contributing editor George Garrett, with the assistance of D. W. Thomas (1999)

## *Concise Series*

**Concise Dictionary of American Literary Biography,** 7 volumes (1988-1999): *The New Consciousness, 1941-1968; Colonization to the American Renaissance, 1640-1865; Realism, Naturalism, and Local Color, 1865-1917; The Twenties, 1917-1929; The Age of Maturity, 1929-1941; Broadening Views, 1968-1988; Supplement: Modern Writers, 1900–1998.*

**Concise Dictionary of British Literary Biography,** 8 volumes (1991-1992): *Writers of the Middle Ages and Renaissance Before 1660; Writers of the Restoration and Eighteenth Century, 1660-1789; Writers of the Romantic Period, 1789-1832; Victorian Writers, 1832-1890; Late-Victorian and Edwardian Writers, 1890-1914; Modern Writers, 1914-1945; Writers After World War II, 1945-1960; Contemporary Writers, 1960 to Present.*

**Concise Dictionary of World Literary Biography,** 20 volumes projected (1999-    ): *Ancient Greek and Roman Writers.*

# Chicano Writers
## Third Series

Dictionary of Literary Biography® • Volume Two Hundred Nine

# Chicano Writers
## Third Series

Edited by
Francisco A. Lomelí
*University of California, Santa Barbara*
and
Carl R. Shirley
*University of South Carolina*

A Bruccoli Clark Layman Book
The Gale Group
Detroit • San Francisco • London • Boston • Woodbridge, Conn.

Printed in the United States of America

The paper used in this publication meets the minimum requirements
of American National Standard for Information Sciences–Permanence
Paper for Printed Library Materials, ANSI Z39.48-1984. ⊚™

**Library of Congress Cataloging-in-Publication Data**

Chicano writers. Third series / edited by Francisco A. Lomelí and Carl R. Shirley.
    p. cm.–(Dictionary of literary biography: v. 209)
"A Bruccoli Clark Layman book."
Includes bibliographical references and index.
ISBN 0-7876-3103-5 (alk. paper)
1. American literature–Mexican American authors–Bio-bibliography–Dictionaries. 2. American literature–Mexican American authors–Dictionaries. 3. Mexican American authors–Biography–Dictionaries. 4. Mexican Americans in literature–Dictionaries. I. Lomelí, Francisco A. II. Shirley, Carl R., 1943–   .
III. Series.
PS153.M4C485  1999
810.9'86872'03–dc21                         99–27671
[B]                                            CIP

10 9 8 7 6 5 4 3 2 1

*For*
*Yazmín Sofía Lomelí*
*Carlos Francisco Lomelí*
*and Natasha Gabriela Lomelí*

# Contents

# Contents

# Plan of the Series

*... Almost the most prodigious asset of a country, and perhaps its most precious possession, is its native literary product—when that product is fine and noble and enduring.*

Mark Twain*

The advisory board, the editors, and the publisher of the *Dictionary of Literary Biography* are joined in endorsing Mark Twain's declaration. The literature of a nation provides an inexhaustible resource of permanent worth. We intend to make literature and its creators better understood and more accessible to students and the reading public, while satisfying the standards of teachers and scholars.

To meet these requirements, *literary biography* has been construed in terms of the author's achievement. The most important thing about a writer is his writing. Accordingly, the entries in *DLB* are career biographies, tracing the development of the author's canon and the evolution of his reputation.

The purpose of *DLB* is not only to provide reliable information in a convenient format but also to place the figures in the larger perspective of literary history and to offer appraisals of their accomplishments by qualified scholars.

The publication plan for *DLB* resulted from two years of preparation. The project was proposed to Bruccoli Clark by Frederick G. Ruffner, president of the Gale Research Company, in November 1975. After specimen entries were prepared and typeset, an advisory board was formed to refine the entry format and develop the series rationale. In meetings held during 1976, the publisher, series editors, and advisory board approved the scheme for a comprehensive biographical dictionary of persons who contributed to North American literature. Editorial work on the first volume began in January 1977, and it was published in 1978. In order to make *DLB* more than a reference tool and to compile volumes that individually have claim to status as literary history, it was decided to organize volumes by

*From an unpublished section of Mark Twain's autobiography, copyright by the Mark Twain Company*

topic, period, or genre. Each of these freestanding volumes provides a biographical-bibliographical guide and overview for a particular area of literature. We are convinced that this organization—as opposed to a single alphabet method—constitutes a valuable innovation in the presentation of reference material. The volume plan necessarily requires many decisions for the placement and treatment of authors who might properly be included in two or three volumes. In some instances a major figure will be included in separate volumes, but with different entries emphasizing the aspect of his career appropriate to each volume. Ernest Hemingway, for example, is represented in *American Writers in Paris, 1920–1939* by an entry focusing on his expatriate apprenticeship; he is also in *American Novelists, 1910–1945* with an entry surveying his entire career, as well as in *American Short-Story Writers, 1910–1945, Second Series* with an entry concentrating on his short stories. Each volume includes a cumulative index of the subject authors and articles. Comprehensive indexes to the entire series are planned.

Since 1981 the series has been further augmented by the *DLB Yearbooks*, which update published entries and add new entries to keep the *DLB* current with contemporary activity. There have also been *DLB Documentary Series* volumes which provide biographical and critical source materials for figures whose work is judged to have particular interest for students. One of these companion volumes is devoted entirely to Tennessee Williams.

We define literature as the *intellectual commerce of a nation:* not merely as belles lettres but as that ample and complex process by which ideas are generated, shaped, and transmitted. *DLB* entries are not limited to "creative writers" but extend to other figures who in their time and in their way influenced the mind of a people. Thus the series encompasses historians, journalists, publishers, book collectors, and screenwriters. By this means readers of *DLB* may be aided to perceive literature not as cult scripture in the keeping of intellectual high priests but firmly positioned at the center of a nation's life.

*DLB* includes the major writers appropriate to each volume and those standing in the ranks behind them. Scholarly and critical counsel has been sought in deciding which minor figures to include and how full their entries should be. Wherever possible, useful references are made to figures who do not warrant separate entries.

Each *DLB* volume has an expert volume editor responsible for planning the volume, selecting the figures for inclusion, and assigning the entries. Volume editors are also responsible for preparing, where appropriate, appendices surveying the major periodicals and literary and intellectual movements for their volumes, as well as lists of further readings. Work on the series as a whole is coordinated at the Bruccoli Clark Layman editorial center in Columbia, South Carolina, where the editorial staff is responsible for accuracy and utility of the published volumes.

One feature that distinguishes *DLB* is the illustration policy–its concern with the iconography of literature. Just as an author is influenced by his surroundings, so is the reader's understanding of the author enhanced by a knowledge of his environment. Therefore *DLB* volumes include not only drawings, paintings, and photographs of authors, often depicting them at various stages in their careers, but also illustrations of their families and places where they lived. Title pages are regularly reproduced in facsimile along with dust jackets for modern authors. The dust jackets are a special feature of *DLB* because they often document better than anything else the way in which an author's work was perceived in its own time. Specimens of the writers' manuscripts and letters are included when feasible.

Samuel Johnson rightly decreed that "The chief glory of every people arises from its authors." The purpose of the *Dictionary of Literary Biography* is to compile literary history in the surest way available to us–by accurate and comprehensive treatment of the lives and work of those who contributed to it.

The *DLB* Advisory Board

# Introduction

A reader just embarking on the study of Chicano literature might have the impression that it is a rather recent phenomenon. While it is true that Chicano writing has only been flourishing since the 1950s, Chicanos and their creative works have long been a part of the American landscape. The antecedents of Chicano literature date to the earliest Spanish presence in the New World. Chicanos have contributed to all aspects of contemporary American life, and their literature is but one artistic manifestation of their increasingly significant place in modern America.

In 1600 the area that later became northern Mexico and now comprises the states of Texas, Arizona, New Mexico, California, Nevada, Utah, and Colorado, was controlled by Spain. In addition to the Native Americans, other groups living in what is now the southwestern United States included Spaniards, Creoles (Spaniards born in the New World), and mestizos (people of mixed Spanish and Native American descent). Moving north from what is now Mexico, they established towns and built missions and roads; they carried with them the Spanish language, the Catholic religion, Spanish laws, and new forms of agriculture, food, livestock, art, and architecture, as well as oral and literary traditions. As the Anglo settlements in the eastern United States expanded westward and the unstable Mexican government suffered a great financial crisis in the mid nineteenth century, a conflict emerged in which land interests, power bases, social traditions, and worldviews clashed, resulting in the Mexican-American War of 1846–1848. Mexico, weakened by internal strife, reluctantly gave up 50 percent of its territories in the Treaty of Guadalupe Hidalgo in 1848. The treaty stipulated that after one year, all who chose to remain in the region would automatically become United States citizens. From that time to the present, Anglo-American culture, language, traditions, and values have been combined with or superimposed on the previous Hispanic ones to form what has become Chicano culture.

Hispanic ways have continuously been reinforced by immigration, both legal and illegal; the long (approximately two thousand miles) land border with Mexico has also facilitated the perpetuation of Hispanic culture and customs in the region. Thus, the majority of Chicanos have never been fully Americanized in quite the same way as other immigrant ethnic groups. They have assimilated elements from Native American, Anglo, and Hispanic cultures to form a separate, distinct one of their own. Most of the more than 30 million people who can be classified as Chicanos live in the Southwest, but there are large concentrations in other places, notably the Midwest.

Scholars have offered several theories concerning the origin of the word *Chicano;* the most widely accepted is that it is derived from *mexicano,* which comes from *mexica* (pronounced "meschica"), the term the Aztecs used to refer to themselves. *Chicano* was in widespread use by the 1950s, replacing the old designation of *Mexican* or the sociological-sounding *Mexican-American.* The older generation sometimes resented the word *Chicano* because it had historically been viewed as pejorative, but beginning in the 1960s it increased in use and popularity to the point that for most Chicanos today it symbolizes pride and cultural revival. Most literary critics and formal literary studies employ the term, usually with an historical and cultural explanation.

Many Chicanos speak both standard Spanish and English and the vernacular within each language, while some speak only English and others mostly Spanish. Most are adept enough in both Spanish and English to employ among themselves a practice called "code-switching"—alternating the use of both languages, with some verbs, nouns, and expressions in Spanish and some in English. Many, especially the young, speak and understand what is variously called "caló," "pocho," or "pachuco." This variant is a mixture of Spanish and English grammars, vocabularies, and syntactical structures that is more than a hybrid: it is a separate language that combines borrowings from each of its ancestors with new words and structures. Some contemporary Chicano literature is written in English, Spanish, and caló in varying combinations. While the blend may pose difficulties for the person who does not speak Spanish, it is a source of literary strength for Chicano writers because it enables them to reflect three sometimes different realities: Anglo, Mexican, and Chicano. (For a more extensive discussion of the topic, see "Chicano Language," by Erlinda Gonzales-Berry and Shaw N. Gynan, in *Dictionary of Literary Biography* volume 82.)

Chicano literature comes from three major sources. The first is the Indian past, embodied in the concept of *Aztlán,* named after the mythical home of the

Aztecs prior to 1519, the date of the Spanish explorer Hernán Cortés's invasion of Mexico. *Aztlán* frequently refers to the entire American Southwest, which constituted the northwestern part of Mexico before the Mexican-American War, but it has also become a symbol for a homeland or a spiritual nation of Chicanos. The second source is the Spanish and Mexican heritage; the third is the Anglo overlay dating from the early and mid nineteenth century. Chicano scholars have concluded that the roots of their literature can be said to extend as far back as 1542, with the Spanish explorer Alvár Núñez Cabeza de Vaca's *Relaciones* (Accounts). There is a rich history of folklore, poetry, prose, and theater from that time to the present. Until the 1950s most of this literature–much of which had appeared in newspapers–remained forgotten or ignored.

Following World War II, Chicano literature began to appear in places where it was noticed by the establishment, especially during what has been termed the "Chicano Renaissance," starting around 1965. The themes and subjects of Chicano literature throughout its history have been those common to all literatures. Since the Chicano Renaissance, however, some distinct Chicano topics have frequently appeared in all genres. Among them are social protest and exploitation; the migratory experience; self-exploration or self-definition, which includes the exploration of myths and legends; and life in the barrio, the traditional Chicano district of a city. There is also *La Raza* (The People), which, like Aztlán, has a spiritual connotation that links all Spanish-speaking peoples of America. Beginning in the mid 1960s, much Chicano literature became a reflection of a social and political movement with attitudes ranging from the advocacy of complete separation from Anglo society to a call for a Mexican-American cultural identification within the framework of the larger society. After about 1975 the focus shifted to technique and style, while the issues became more personal and less social. The 1980s offered a great diversification of theme and content and more exploration of issues pertinent to families and women.

Chicano prose can be traced to the chronicles of the early explorers. In the nineteenth century many histories, diaries, and memoirs appeared, and short narratives were published in newspapers. Toward the end of the nineteenth century several novels appeared in print. Prose written by Chicanos was not published in sources readily accessible to the majority population, however, until 1947. The short stories by Mario Suárez published in the *Arizona Quarterly* that year mark the beginning of contemporary Chicano prose. He is sometimes dismissed as just another local colorist, but he is the first truly Chicano writer because he was comfortable using the term *Chicano* in its modern connotation. Moreover, his characters are not stereotypical or comical, nor are

they treated as eccentric members of a cultural minority performing for the amusement of Anglos. They are normal people, capable of existing comfortably in either the majority culture or in their own world. They possess a psychological depth that Mexican characters in American periodicals before 1947 generally lacked.

Chicano literature has undergone various phases of development without abandoning its past. New experimental themes have emerged since the 1980s, but older ones persist; the most common social equality and sovereignty, gender issues, barrio and rural life, family structures, migration patterns, economic disparities, cultural rediscovery, political enfranchisement, and language. While the more modern writers pursue an agenda of diversifying expression, readers are discovering that writings of the past possessed some of the same verve and determination decades and even centuries earlier.

The history of the publication of contemporary Chicano literature is mostly one of neglect by mainstream publishing houses. Prior to the mid 1960s, only a handful of works had been published, including such recognized classics as José Antonio Villarreal's *Pocho* (1959). Not many of the hundreds of Chicano works that have appeared since then have been published by mainstream firms, and relatively few have been reviewed in mainstream journals. The literature, nonetheless, has continued to grow rapidly. It has reached the point that most American universities west of the eastern Texas border–and in other enclaves, such as Illinois and the Northeast–incorporate Chicano works into their curricula. A new attitude toward what socially and ethnically constitutes an "American" has generated greater interest in the Hispanic elements of American society and what those elements imply culturally. Chicano literature seems to address dimensions that have been largely ignored by mainstream society.

Chicano literature can no longer be described as burgeoning. It has come of age and continues to blur borders, challenge traditional genres, and create linguistic pyrotechnics as it makes its way into an international arena, including Bordeaux and Paris in France, Amsterdam and Utrecht in the Netherlands, Mexico City, Madrid and Barcelona in Spain, San José in Costa Rica, Bremen and Germersheim in Germany, Milan and Rome in Italy, New Delhi, Montreal, Vienna, and Havana. These cities are places where international literary conventions dedicated to Chicano literature have been held or where major scholars have published books or journals with a principal focus on Chicano literature. The militant 1960s and 1970s demands for social justice have been replaced by the desire to unearth voices and experiences that had been silenced or repressed. For example, the quotidian and mundane is now subject matter for much literature by Chicanos, especially by women, whose high-quality writings have dominated the 1980s and 1990s. The historically significant epics, with their dramatic heroes, have given way to stories of common folk and their everyday lives.

Despite these new trends and styles, including a postmodern influence, Chicano literature cannot escape a past that, only a quarter of a century ago, few knew it had. Most readers of Chicano literature in the 1970s believed that they were dealing with a phenomenon dating back perhaps only to the 1960s. But Herminio Rios-C. and Lupe Castillo's bibliography in *El Grito: A Journal of Mexican-American Thought* (1970), Philip D. Ortego's "Backgrounds of Mexican American Literature" (a 1971 dissertation), Luis Leal's "Mexican American Literature: A Historical Approach" (1973), and Francisco A. Lomelí and Donaldo W. Urioste's *Chicano Perspectives in Literature: A Critical and Annotated Bibliography* (1976) established historical landmarks proving that Chicano literature had a definite past closely aligned with Mexico and the American Southwest and had not just recently emerged. Historical amnesia had set in to such a degree that Chicanos had lost sight of their past, resulting in their being labeled recent immigrants with no real place in the American Southwest matrix. In *Chicano Perspectives in Literature* Lomelí and Urioste presented excerpts and texts from a variety of epochs and genres, including subgenres such as the oral tradition in print and *literatura chicanesca*, texts with Chicano characters and situations but created by non-Chicanos and providing a view from the outside. The 1976 volume included 127 entries; a similar list compiled in 1997 would have easily comprised more than 1,500 entries. Despite all the pressures and criticism for its sui generis nature–including critics' difficulty in classifying some works–this literature has continued to grow. Many Chicano journals have come and gone, but Chicano writers continue to delve into unexplored realms of human experience with American and universal implications.

*Chicano Writers, Third Series,* like the previous volumes, includes contemporary writers as well as those from the past. We have also attempted to include well-known and lesser-known authors from a variety of geographical regions. If a particular author does not appear in this volume or the previous ones, it is probably because we were unable to locate a contributor willing to write the entry.

At the end of the twentieth century, as the culture of America rapidly changes from traditional Anglo domination and fragments itself into a diverse array of minicultures, Chicano literature, as one of the oldest and perhaps the most prominent of the ethnic literatures, enjoys a wealth of talented writers. Chicano literature has, indeed, come of age and is deserving of greater critical attention. With the three series of *Chicano*

*Writers* volumes we hope to fill some of that void by bringing these writers and their texts to wider notice.

–*Francisco A. Lomelí and Carl R. Shirley*

## Acknowledgments

This book was produced by Bruccoli Clark Layman, Inc. Karen L. Rood is senior editor for the *Dictionary of Literary Biography* series. Tracy Simmons Bitonti was the in-house editor. She was assisted by Charles Brower.

Production manager is Philip B. Dematteis.

Administrative support was provided by Ann M. Cheschi, Tenesha S. Lee, and Joann Whittaker.

Accountant is Sayra Frances Cox. Assistant accountant is Angi Pleasant.

Copyediting supervisor is Phyllis A. Avant. Senior copyeditor is Thom Harman. The copyediting staff includes Ronald D. Aiken II, Brenda Carol Blanton, Worthy B. Evans, Melissa D. Hinton, and William Tobias Mathes. Freelance copyeditors are Brenda Cabra, Rebecca Mayo, Nicole M. Nichols, Raegan E. Quinn, and Jennie Williamson.

Editorial trainee is Carol A. Fairman.

Indexing specialist is Alex Snead.

Layout and graphics supervisor is Janet E. Hill. Graphics staff includes Zoe R. Cook.

Office manager is Kathy Lawler Merlette.

Photography editors are Margo Dowling, Charles Mims, Scott Nemzek, Alison Smith, and Paul Talbot. Digital photographic copy work was performed by Joseph M. Bruccoli.

SGML supervisor is Cory McNair. The SGML staff includes Tim Bedford, Linda Drake, Frank Graham, and Alex Snead.

Systems manager is Marie L. Parker.

Database manager is Javed Nurani. Kimberly Kelly performed data entry.

Typesetting supervisor is Kathleen M. Flanagan. The typesetting staff includes Karla Corley Brown, Mark J. McEwan, Patricia Flanagan Salisbury, and Kathy F. Wooldridge. Freelance typesetters include Deidre Murphy and Delores Plastow.

Walter W. Ross and Steven Gross did library research. They were assisted by the following librarians at the Thomas Cooper Library of the University of South Carolina: Linda Holderfield and the interlibrary-loan staff; reference-department head Virginia Weathers; reference librarians Marilee Birchfield, Stefanie Buck, Stefanie DuBose, Rebecca Feind, Karen Joseph, Donna Lehman, Charlene Loope, Anthony McKissick, Jean Rhyne, and Kwamine Simpson; circulation-department head Caroline Taylor; and acquisitions-searching supervisor David Haggard.

# Chicano Writers
## Third Series

# Dictionary of Literary Biography

# José Acosta Torres
## (13 December 1925 –    )

### Luis Leal
*University of California, Santa Barbara*

BOOKS: *Ortografía comparativa* (Austin, Tex.: Southwest Educational Development Laboratory, 1972);

*Composición creativa* (Austin, Tex.: Southwest Educational Development Laboratory, 1972);

*Spanish/English Bilingualism* (Austin, Tex.: Southwest Educational Development Laboratory, 1972);

*Spanish/English Publications* (Austin, Tex.: Southwest Educational Development Laboratory, 1972);

*Cachito Mío,* with English translation by Herminio Ríos-C. (Berkeley, Cal.: Quinto Sol Publications, 1973).

José Acosta Torres is one of several fiction writers whose work was introduced in the literary review *El Grito: A Journal of Contemporary Mexican-American Thought,* published in Berkeley by Octavio I. Romano-V. and Herminio Ríos-C. from 1967 to 1974. His first story, "Dormir es vivir" (To Sleep is to Live), appeared in the spring of 1972, and his second, "Sinfonía" (Symphony), appeared in the summer of 1973, the year his entire collection of fifteen stories was published by Quinto Sol Publications under the title *Cachito Mío* (My Little One).

The storytelling technique used by Acosta Torres is an old and popular one: *relatos ejemplares* (exemplary stories) are especially designed with the purpose of teaching morals or imparting knowledge. In Spain the technique goes back to the Middle Ages; one of the earliest books of this nature is *Libro de los enxiemplos del conde Lucanor et de Patronio* (Book of the Tales of Count Lucanor and Patronio), a book by Don Juan Manuel that was completed in 1335. In Mexico this type of story has been popular since the sixteenth century in prose and also in the popular *romances* (ballads). Some of these stories are still found among the Chicano people

in the late twentieth century and have even been passed to other art forms, such as motion pictures.

Acosta Torres was born on 13 December 1925 in Martindale, Texas, where he attended elementary and high school. In 1944 he was drafted into the United States Army; he was wounded in action, and he received the Purple Heart in 1945. After the war he enrolled in Southwest Texas State University, where he received a B.S. in 1950 and an M.Ed. two years later. In 1965 he completed his Ph.D. at Universidad Interamericana, Saltillo, Coahuila, Mexico. He attended three National Defense Education Act Spanish Language Institutes: one in 1963 at Lady of the Lake College in San Antonio, Texas, and the others in 1967 and 1968 at the University of Texas, Austin. He had been teaching since 1950 in the elementary and high schools of San Antonio, where he also held several administrative positions. From 1965 to 1970 he taught at San Antonio College, San Antonio, Texas. In August 1970 he married Patricia Resch; the couple has three children: Gregory, Maruca, and Angela. He spent two years (1970 to 1972) at the Southwest Educational Development Laboratory in Austin, Texas, where he published three books on education and one on Spanish and English publications. He has since held several positions in education in Crystal City, Texas; in Austin at St. Edward's University; and in Kingsville, at Texas A & I, as professor of bilingual education. He also served as project coordinator for the U.S. Office of Education.

One of the important influences on Acosta Torres's work is the contemporary Spanish writer Juan Ramón Jiménez, the author of the now-classic *Platero y yo* (Platero and I, 1914). In his "Words to the Reader," which serves as an introduction to *Cachito Mío,* Acosta Torres states that though his stories are

*Cover for José Acosta Torres's 1973 collection of stories, in which the narrator, Don Pepe, offers various lessons to his son*

Don Pepe's qualities can be observed in "Dormir es vivir," a meditation about the importance of sleeping and dreaming. In a statement preceding the story Acosta Torres tells the reader that "Don Pepe likes to read a great deal. One of his favorite plays is a work by the Spanish author, Calderón de la Barca. Cachito learned the meaning of the words quoted by Don Pepe." The composition ends with a reference to "a great Spanish writer," who said that "Life is but a dream . . . and dreams are made of dreams." The source of that thought is, of course, the Spanish playwright Pedro Calderón de la Barca's *La vida es sueño* (Life is a Dream, 1635).

Dreams, however, can have another function: they are a refuge from the reality of everyday life, as can be seen in the story "Un cuete encendido" (A Bomb With a Lighted Fuse), which addresses the destructive possibilities of the H-bomb. Its existence makes Don Pepe sad, and he advises Cachito to sleep "and dream while you still can." The reader does not know how old Cachito is, or whether he understands the philosophical meaning and implications of what his father is telling him.

Not all the stories, however, have philosophical themes. Several of them are derived from traditional sources; they are stories handed down from generation to generation. The source for "Animales compestres" (Wild Animals), for example, is a tale told to Don Pepe by his father. Don Pepe begins by saying, "Your grandfather has an extraordinary ability to know and appreciate the things of nature." This grandfather has transmitted the oral history of his people, preserved in his memory, to Don Pepe, who is now transmitting it to Cachito. Although there is no reaction from Cachito, it is assumed that he is learning all about nature as interpreted by his people. The story ends with an experience of Don Pepe's that now will be added to the store of knowledge preserved by Cachito's family.

Another source for the stories is old newspapers, which also contribute information worth transmitting to future generations. In "Sucedió ayer" (It Happened Yesterday), Cachito receives a lesson in history taken from newspapers published early in the century. Don Pepe has saved a newspaper published in 1913, the same year Cachito's grandmother was born; he uses this resource to tell his son about the principal events of the period.

In "Ranas y enacuajos" (Frogs and Tadpoles), Cachito learns about natural history by studying the changes a tadpole goes through in order to become a frog. Scientific information is also offered in "Alpha Centauri," which provides a lesson in astronomy in terms Cachito can understand. More than imparting factual knowledge, here Don Pepe's purpose is to make his son realize the vastness of the universe. "Mira la

original, he does "not make the slightest claim to presenting something which has never been seen nor heard. This is but a small and modest book of short stories. . . . I do not have the slightest presumption of placing myself in the same plane as the author of *Platero y yo*." There is, however, a similarity in the structure of the two works. Both narrators address their comments to a silent recipient: Jiménez's narrator to his donkey, Platero, and Acosta Torres's Don Pepe to his son, Cachito.

As Acosta Torres explains, "The fifteen short stories were selected for their variety of content. They deal with war and peace; the sky and the earth; angels and animals; life and death." More than true *cuentos* (short stories), *Cachito Mío* is a collection of fifteen meditations on philosophical themes told by Don Pepe to Cachito. As Charles M. Tatum points out in *A Selected and Annotated Bibliography of Chicano Studies* (1979), "Don Pepe proves to be a person with a lucidity and perception akin to that of a wise man."

hormiga" (Look at the Ant) is a description of an ant colony and serves to give Cachito a lesson in entomology. Don Pepe urges Cachito to "study the ants and learn all you can from them" because the ants, "without teachers, can teach us many things."

One of the stories, "Un angelito nuevo" (A New Little Angel), is derived from the death of Cachito's baby brother, a loss deeply felt by Don Pepe. The lesson here seems to be the power of grief to help people understand the nature of life and death. "Yes, Cachito, it is true," Don Pepe says, "that we can see more clearly with tears in our eyes." This sad story is in contrast to the one titled "Sinfonía," in which Don Pepe tries to arouse Cachito's interest in music. The story is interesting because of its structure, since the point of view shifts. Music, personified as a woman, relates, in idealistic terms, her own life. Cachito learns that Music was born before the earth was created and is eternal. "Don't forget," Music tells Cachito, "that my symphony is the voice of the angels, the art of the prophet, the poet's manna and the celestial and universal sound that can be yours, too . . . if you study me, appreciate me, and wish to love me as I love you."

Cachito learns about a related subject, poetry, while listening to the story "Rimas y reumas" (Rimes and Rims). In the short synopsis that precedes the story, readers learn that Cachito has told his father that he knows only one poem. (Cachito does not speak in this story, or in any of the others.) Don Pepe quotes three so-called poems, the last two based on traditional jokes. There is little in the story, however, that could inspire Cachito to become a poet.

The closest that Acosta Torres comes to the true short story is the selection titled "La vida en ruedas" (Life on Wheels), made up of three anecdotes related to driving a car. Focused more on narrative elements than on didactic ones, the piece ends with the remark, "That's the way it is, Cachito, life on wheels!" Although this story lacks the lesson implicit in the other stories, Cachito perhaps subconsciously learns not to cross intersections with his eyes closed; to study English in order not to be misunderstood; and to believe that other people do not appreciate help, so giving it to them is useless (a message that strikes an anomolous note in the collection).

In the last stories Cachito receives lessons in linguistics: the origin of language, according to popular beliefs; the use of phonetics; and the nature of cognates. The reader learns that Cachito is bilingual. In the final story, appropriately titled "Fin del año escolar" (End of the School Year), Don Pepe, who is a teacher, relates to Cachito some anecdotes to illustrate human foibles. The story ends when Don Pepe asks Cachito to tell him about some of the experiences he has had in his school. This closing suggests that the author may have planned to write another group of stories, this time narrated by Cachito.

In general Acosta Torres's stories show his desire to teach the younger generation to be kind to their fellow men, to appreciate life and nature, and to try to understand reality. Since the stories are directed to young readers who can identify with Cachito, they are told in a plain style, have a simple structure, and include popular anecdotes in order to create interest. Since they are told in both Spanish and English, these stories are ideal for the bilingual classroom. They are not presented in the form of a textbook, however, but as a collection of stories for the general reading public, stories that "come from the heart," Acosta Torres says, although "they are only the reflection of other's thoughts and other's feelings." As Francisco A. Lomelí and Donaldo W. Urioste remark in *Chicano Perspectives in Literature* (1976), his book is a "refreshing contribution to Chicano literature in balancing simplicity and deep human concerns."

## Reference:

Charles M. Tatum, *A Selected and Annotated Bibliography of Chicano Studies,* second edition (Lincoln, Nebr.: Society of Spanish and Spanish-American Studies, 1979), p. 101.

# Justo S. Alarcón

*(10 March 1930 –  )*

Cida S. Chase
*Oklahoma State University*

BOOKS: *Chulifeas fronteras: Cuentos* (Albuquerque, N.Mex.: Pajarito Publications, 1981);

*Crisol: Trilogía* (Madrid: Editorial Fundamentos, 1984);

*Los siete hijos de la Llorona: Novela* (Mexico City: Alta Pimería Pro Arte y Cultura, 1986);

*Técnicas narrativas en Jardín umbrío de Valle-Inclán* (Mexico City: Alta Pimería Pro Arte y Cultura, 1990);

*Poemas en mí menor* (Mexico: Alta Pimería Pro Arte y Cultura, 1991);

*Los dos compadres: Cuentos breves del barrio* (Mexico: Alta Pimería Pro Arte y Cultura, 1993);

*El espacio literario de Juan Bruce-Novoa: Un estudio metacrítico del texto/Juan Bruce-Novoa's Theory of Chicano Literary Space: A Metacritical Analysis of the Text,* by Alarcón and Lupe Cárdenas, translated by Cárdenas (San Diego: Marín, 1994);

*La teoría de la dialéctica de la diferencia en la novela chicana de Ramón Saldívar: Un análisis metacrítico del texto* (Phoenix: Editorial Orbis Press, 1997).

OTHER: *La Palabra: Revista de Literatura Chicana,* edited by Alarcón, 1979–1985;

*Canto al pueblo: Antología/Anthology,* edited by Alarcón, Juan Pérez Aldape, and Lupe Cárdenas (Mesa: Arizona Canto al Pueblo, 1980);

*Flor y Canto IV and V: An Anthology of Chicano Literature from the Festivals held in Albuquerque, New Mexico, 1977, and Tempe, Arizona, 1978,* edited by Alarcón, José Armas, and others (Albuquerque, N. Mex.: Pajarito Publications, 1980);

"El político," in *Hispanics in the United States: An Anthology of Creative Literature,* volume 2, edited by Gary D. Keller and Francisco Jimenez (Ypsilanti: Bilingual Press/Editorial Bilingüe, 1982), pp. 141–148;

"El 'Río' como tema y figura en tres obras chicanas," in *Proceedings of the Rocky Mountain Council for Latin American Studies* (Glendale, Ariz., 1983), pp. 398–404;

"El substrato ideológico en la literatura chicana," in *Acta del XX congreso del Instituto Internacional de literatura iberoamericana,* edited by Horanyi Matyas

*Justo S. Alarcón ( from* Crisol: Trilogía *[Crucible: Trilogy], 1984)*

(Budapest: Eotvos Lorand University Press, 1984), pp. 257–264;

"La violencia en *LA: The Sacred Spot* de Javier Alva," *Proceedings of the Rocky Mountain Council for Latin American Studies* (Las Cruces, N.Mex., 1987), pp. 113–119;

"El autor como narrador en . . . *y no se lo tragó la tierra* de Tomas Rivera," *Proceedings of the Rocky Mountain*

6

*Council for Latin American Studies* (Fort Collins, Colo., 1988), pp. 67–74;

"La teoría saldivariana de la 'dialéctica de la diferencia' en la novela *Pocho*," *Proceedings of the Rocky Mountain Council for Latin American Studies* (Las Cruces, N.Mex., 1989), pp. 96–106.

## SELECTED PERIODICAL PUBLICATIONS–UNCOLLECTED:

POETRY

"Los niños III," "Los niños IV," "Los niños V," "Los niños VI," "Los niños VII," "Los niños IX," and "Los niños X," *Confluencia,* 6, no. 1 (1990): 197–201.

FICTION

". . . y diente por diente," *Semana de Bellas Artes* (UNAM, Mexico, 1979): 2–4;

"Recuerdos elementales I & II," *De Colores,* 5, nos. 3–4 (1981): 3–15;

"Recuerdos elementales III," *Borderlines Journal,* 3, no. 2 (1981): 115–120;

"El coyote," *Revista Chicano-Riqueña,* 9, no. 3 (1981): 22–30;

"Aquí se habla English Only," *Ave Fenix,* 1, no. 2 (1987): 2;

"El parque San Lázaro," *Ave Fenix,* 1, no. 5 (1987): 10;

"Las palabras malentendidas," *La voz del norte* (Sonora, Mexico), 30 December 1989, p. 10;

"Los dibujos animados," *La voz del norte* (Sonora, Mexico), 4 January 1990, p. 10;

"Los salones de baile," *La voz del norte* (Sonora, Mexico), 5 January 1990, p. 11;

"Los que prometen mucho y . . . ," *La voz del norte* (Sonora, Mexico), 9 January 1990, p. 10.

NONFICTION

"El pre-esperpento en Valle-Inclán," *Explicación de textos literarios,* 6, no. 2 (1976): 95–105;

"Hacia la nada . . . o la religión en *Pocho,*" *Minority Voices,* 1, no. 2 (1977): 17–27;

"Under a Never Changing Sun o el determinismo chicano," *Revista Chicano-Riqueña,* 6, no. 1 (1978): 33–43;

"Consideraciones sobre la literatura y crítica chicanas," *La Palabra: Revista de Literatura Chicana,* 1 (1979): 3–21;

"La metamorfosis del diablo en *El diablo en Texas,*" *De Colores,* 5, nos. 1–2 (1980): 30–44;

"Miguel Méndez M.: Entrevista," *La Palabra: Revista de Literatura Chicana,* 3, nos. 1–2 (1981): 3–17;

"La metacrítica chicana," *Revista Chicano-Riqueña,* 1, no. 3 (1982): 47–52;

"La nueva poesía en *Bajo cubierta,*" *Third Woman,* 2, no. 1 (1984): 52–60;

"Estructuras narrativas en *Tata Chasehua* de Miguel Méndez," *Confluencia,* 1, no. 2 (1986): 48–54;

"La búsqueda de la identidad en la literatura chicana: tres textos," *Confluencia,* 3, no. 1 (1987): 137–144;

"La aventura del héroe como estructura mítica en *Tata Casehua* de Miguel Méndez," *Explicación de Textos Literarios,* 15, no. 2 (1987): 77–91;

"Introducción al cuento chicano," *La Palabra: Revista de Literatura Chicana,* 6–7, no. 1–2 (1988): 1–14;

"De cómo algunos chicanos ven a sus hermanos mexicanos," *Ave Fenix,* 1, no. 12 (1988): 9;

"Silueta I: Amanecer," *Ave Fenix,* 1, no. 13 (1988): 11;

"Silueta II: Atardecer," *Ave Fenix,* 1, no. 14 (1988): 19;

"Los salones de baile," *Ave Fenix,* 1, no. 15 (1988): 19;

"Peculiaridad de los personajes en *Tunomás Honey* de Jim Sagel," *Confluencia,* 3, no. 2 (1988): 83–89;

"Entrevista a Miguel Méndez M.," by Alarcón and Lupe Cárdenas, *Confluencia,* 4, no. 1 (1988): 151–157;

"Entrevista con Aristeo Brito," by Alarcón and Cárdenas, *Confluencia,* 4, no. 2 (1989): 97–103;

"Lo esperpéntico en Miguel Méndez M.," *Americas Review,* 17, no. 1 (1989): 84–100;

"El espacio brusnovoence de la literatura chicana," *Review of Latin American Studies,* 2, no. 1–2 (1989): 81–95;

"La teoría saldivariana y su 'dialéctica de la diferencia': primeros esbozos," *Discurso literario,* 7, no. 1 (1989–1990): 25–50;

"Entrevista con Alberto Ríos," by Alarcón and Cárdenas, *Confluencia,* 6, no. 1 (1990–1991): 119–126;

"Miguel Méndez y sus influencias literarias españolas," *Entorno: Revista Cultural,* no. 30 (1993): 49–56.

The poet, fiction writer, and critic Justo S. Alarcón was born on 10 March 1930 in Río Gordo, a small town in the province of Málaga, Spain. His father was a schoolteacher. After Alarcón completed his primary education in his hometown, his father placed him in a Franciscan boarding school. He received his bachelor's degree in philosophy in 1951 at the Seráfica of Santiago. He earned his master's degree in theology at the same institution in 1954. Traveling to Canada to pursue further studies, he received a master's degree in sociology from L'Université Laval in Quebec in 1959. He began to explore the American Southwest at this time and decided to settle in Arizona. He enrolled at Arizona State University at Tempe, where he received a master's degree in Spanish in 1966. He entered the graduate Spanish program at the University of Arizona in Tucson and in 1974 obtained his Ph.D. with a specialization in twentieth-century Spanish literature.

While still pursuing his doctorate, in 1968 Alarcón became professor of Spanish, Southwestern

*Cover for Alarcón's first book, a 1981 collection of stories that depict cultural clashes on either side of the border between the United States and Mexico*

culture, and Chicano literature and civilization at Arizona State University. He was instrumental in the founding of the Chicano Faculty and Staff Association at Arizona State, serving as president of the organization for several terms. Moreover, he was responsible for the creation of the Chicano Studies department accomplishing the latter by teaching pilot courses during the summers to demonstrate to the administration that such a program was necessary and feasible. Additionally, Alarcón served as the faculty advisor of MECHA (Movimiento Estudiantil Chicano de Aztlán [Southwestern Hispanic Student Movement]) from 1972 through 1975 and from 1984 through 1987. His activism on behalf of the Hispanic students at Arizona State University twice gave rise to severe reprimands from the upper administration. He said in an unpublished 5 February 1995 interview that he considers Leñero, the main character of his novel *Crisol: Trilogía* (Crucible: Trilogy, 1984), his alter ego. Leñero is a former college professor who lost his job because he embraced the Chicano

cause on campus. Scenes of student unrest on American and Mexican college campuses also appear in his short story "El puente" (The Bridge), included in his collection *Chulifeas fronteras: Cuentos* (Borders Fair and Foul: Stories, 1981).

Alarcón's first short story, "Ojo por ojo y . . ." (An Eye for an Eye and . . .), also included in *Chulifeas fronteras,* was inspired by an incident that occurred in Arizona near the Mexican border: an Anglo father and his two sons captured four illegal Mexicans, tied them to cactus stalks, and used them for target practice. The other stories in *Chulifeas fronteras* are "Contaminación," "Despojo" (Dispossession), "Rotación solar" (Rotating Sun), "Reconocimiento" (Recognition), "El mercado" (The Market), and "Resbaladero" (Slippery Climb). The stories are set in the United States–Mexican border area and depict cultural conflicts. "Contaminación" emerged from a personal experience of Alarcón's: he and some friends were returning to the United States after a brief visit to Mexico; at the border the customs official harassed all of them except a blue-eyed blonde with questions about their residence–and she was actually the only person in the group who was not a United States citizen (she was Canadian). In "Contaminación" the customs official, Roy Bunker, considers the presence of dark-skinned people a menace to the purity of Caucasian Americans; he believes that any mixing of dark- and fair-skinned people contradicts the laws of nature and is an act of contamination. Bunker looks tenderly at the Canadian blonde, fondly gazing at her lovely yellow hair and her "dos luceritos azules" (two sky-blue eyes); but when he looks at the dark face of the group's spokesman, his glance turns fierce as "la púa de un puercoespín" (a porcupine's thorn). The omniscient narrator views Bunker with contempt, portraying him through decadent, disgusting imagery. He is compared to a piece of raw meat and to an ill-humored, mistrusting dog who seeks refuge in his "cuchitril" (hole, den). His right hand, which he uses at the denouement to murder a dark-skinned individual, is likened to a monstrous spider with tentacles for legs. Bunker loses his mind when he learns that he has a Mexican great-grandmother and that his immaculate, fair-skinned wife has fallen in love with a dark-skinned man.

Ethnic unity between Mexican nationals and the inhabitants of the "México de afuera" (outside Mexico) is the central theme of "Reconocimiento," which portrays people who look at each other through the "alambrada enjauladora" (wire net of a cage) at the border. The reader sees these people as hundreds and thousands of eyes, some of which gaze toward the south while the others look north. Although they are divided by a physical barrier, they maintain emotional ties and find solace in recognizing each other. The text is punctuated with exclamations such as "Hola, Johnny" and "Hi, Juan."

*Crisol* is divided into three sections: "Realidad," "Reminiscencia," and "Realización." The first section consists of a series of dialogues between Miguel Torres, a Chicano journalism student, and Leñero, a sort of bum philosopher, who spends his days on a bench in San Lázaro Park in the Barrio Las Pencas. Leñero is an enigmatic figure. People in the barrio wonder who he is and whether he may have committed a crime or whether he is insane. Miguel, however, believes that there is much more to Leñero than meets the eye. The young man insists on interviewing Leñero repeatedly, although it is difficult to communicate with him. Leñero resorts to riddles and parables to express his ideas, but Miguel gradually comes to understand him. Leñero believes that America is a pseudo-democracy because it allows the marginalization of large segments of the population. Nevertheless, Leñero is not totally pessimistic: he adheres to José Vasconcelos's idea of the "raza cósmica" (cosmic race) that will emerge in the new world. He explains that a weak, sterile race will allow the rise of another young, virile, and fruitful race; that is the law of history, the law of empires, and the cyclical law of humanity. This universal, cosmic race will be a mixed race in which individuals will not suffer discrimination on account of their ethnic origins. "Realidad" ends with Leñero's death and the clearing up of the mystery of his identity: he was the former college professor Dr. Lázaro Villa, who had refused to tolerate the injustices committed against Chicano students; he was also Miguel's father.

"Reminiscencia" offers glimpses into Leñero's childhood. Here Alarcón brings forth the failures of the American system of public education in regard to Chicano children. School personnel systematically discourage young people from learning and from pursuing professional careers, and teachers are ignorant about their students' culture and home environment. This ignorance is revealed in an exchange between a teacher and her students:

> "Do you like Halloween, children?"
> "Yes, Ms. Fairchild."
> "Why?"
> "Because of trick or treat."
> "I'm scared, teacher."
> "Why?"
> "Because La Llorona will get me."
> "Who?"

Ms. Fairchild is a recurrent figure in Alarcón's fiction. She is the prototype of the ignorant teacher who intentionally or unintentionally inflicts harm on her Chicano students. Ms. Fairchild's reaction to the child's fear of

"La Llorona" (The Wailing Woman)—in Chicano folklore, the spirit of a woman who supposedly drowned her children and wanders searching for their souls—is evidence of her ignorance about a Chicano child's world. That night, the fearful child dreams that Ms. Fairchild is La Llorona.

Don Braulio Quezada, a blind man, emerges as a dominant character in "Reminiscencia." Like Leñero, Don Braulio is fond of spending his days in San Lázaro Park. Don Braulio's conversations with his friends and an abundance of hallucinatory images pointing at a state of blindness and danger form the nucleus of "Reminiscencia." Through Don Braulio it becomes evident that Anglo material progress and technology provide minimal benefit to the Chicano people. In fact, construction undertaken for the convenience of the Anglo population seems to be planned to isolate the barrios. Since Don Braulio is blind, the new structures pose a serious danger to his safety; he is finally killed by a train.

"Realización" dramatizes the creation of the cosmic race through a dream Miguel has while recovering from a concussion in which an enormous army of insects, frogs, moles, and birds advances. The novel ends with mythological figures converging in the cataclysm that results in the creation of "la raza cósmica."

Alarcón's second novel, *Los siete hijos de la Llorona* (The Seven Children of The Wailing Woman, 1986), posits that the crime committed against La Llorona's children symbolizes the dispossession and exploitation that the Chicanos have suffered at the hands of others. Seven young Chicanos from the Barrio Las Pencas, four boys and three girls, gather in a cave in the hills, form a mystical covenant, and conjure up the folkloric figure's spirit. As they sit in a circle with their heads bowed, they hear the voice of La Llorona in a gust of wind:

> Ay . . . de mis hijos, yo no fui. Por decenios y
> centenios me vinieron acusando. Yo no fui.
> Una madre no puede matar a sus hijos. Le
> faltarían fuerzas a mis brazos para hundirlos
> bajo el agua.
>
> (Oh . . . my unfortunate children, it was not I. For decades and
> centuries they have accused me. It was not I.
> A mother could not kill her children.
> My arms would not have the strength
> to sink them in the water.)

Moved by the lamenting words of the ghostly voice, the seven children make a solemn commitment to La Llorona: "Madre Nuestra [Our Mother], tus [your] complaints will be avenged!" One by one, the children bring those whom they identify as guilty to the cave, submit-

*Cover for Alarcón's 1984 novel, which includes the character Leñero, whom Alarcón has called his "alter ego"*

ting them to rigorous tortures before killing them. The reader is shown seven individuals who symbolize prominent social institutions or belong to a class of people who have inflicted harm on the descendants of La Llorona, the Chicanos: the archbishop, whose institution stole the Chicanos' indigenous nature and enslaved them; Ms. Fairchild, the teacher, under whose care generations of children have suffered; and a judge whose sentences have been unjust to Chicanos; a *coyote* (smuggler of illegal aliens) whose activities have resulted in a multitude of deaths; a *político vendido* (betraying politician) who forgot his people as soon as he was elected; a doctor whose contempt for Chicanos led him to sterilize

Nellie López, one of the seven children; and a banker, identified as "el mero chingón" (the worst of all), for he controls the money and, therefore, holds people in his hands as if they were puppets.

In 1991 Alarcón published *Poemas en mí menor* (Poems in E Minor). The first part, "Juveniles" (Youthful Poems), centers on reminiscences of his childhood. The other sections of the book are "Sonámbulos" (Sleepwalking Poems), "Sociales" (Poems of Social Content), and "Gráficos" (Vivid Poems). In the first poem, "Autorretrato" (Self-Portrait) Alarcón depicts himself as a man of varied tastes who loves children and women and whose peaceful nature does not prevent him from fighting injustice. In his most tender stanzas he recalls a loving family and a father who sacrificed his own well-being for the welfare of others. He introduces "Los caracoles" (The Snails) with an image of his father:

Recuerdo . . .

en mi frágil memoria de niño
que mi cansado padre,
por convicciones honestas,
como hacen los caracoles,
andaba con la casa a cuestas.

(I remember . . . . . . . . . . . . .

in my fragile child memory
my weary father
who, for his just convictions,
such as the snails do,
carried his dwelling on his back.)

The majority of the poems in "Sonámbulos" are lyrical descriptions of nature and of the poet's emotional identification with the creatures of nature. In "Las dos tórtolas" (The Two Turtledoves) the poet discovers someone's love for him when he observes two amorous birds on his window sill:

Fue ayer. A las once de la mañana.
Dos tórtolas, anidando en la ventana.
Y que no me daba cuenta
de que alguien me decía
que me amaba . . . . . . . .

(It was yesterday. At eleven.
Two turtledoves, nesting on my window.
And I could not see
that someone was telling me
that she loved me . . . . . . . . )

The compositions included in "Sociales" center on Alarcón's concern for the Chicano people's undeserved lot. This aspect is evident in the *corridillos* (little ballads) I, II, III, and IV, which have, respectively, the subtitles "La peregrinación" (The Pilgrimage), "La persecución," "La usurpación," and "La destrucción." Each *corridillo* begins with a chorus that explains the purpose of the poem and continues with diverse types of small animals who explain what has happened to them and to the Chicanos. "Corridillo I" begins:

Nosotros los oprimidos
en esta marcha obligada
dejaremos consignada
la historia de lo sufrido.

(We the oppressed
in this forced march

shall leave the story
of our suffering.)

The moles then say:

No queda en la tierra vena
que no hayamos perforado
pa' que otros se hayan chupado
nuestra sangre a boca llena.

(There is no vein left on earth
that we have not perforated
for others to suck dry
our blood by the mouthful.)

The Chicano theme continues in the last section of the book, "Gráficos," in which the desert is a frequent motif.

Two years after *Poemas en mí menor* Alarcón published *Los dos compadres: Cuentos breves del barrio* (The Two Comrades: Stories of the Barrio, 1993). The stories are closely related, and the two old men of the title are present in each. The stories are set in San Lázaro Park at various times of the year, with the first and last taking place when the first signs of autumn are appearing; the work thus has a circular structure. The two old men begin their dialogue with smiles, reminiscing about the past, but they become alarmed when Don Epifanio brings up the chaotic situation of their people. As Don Epiceno blames all of the problems that plague the Chicanos on the people's laziness and lack of initiative, Don Epifanio makes it his mission to educate his friend in regard to the origin of those problems.

He comments in regard to the Anglos, who have the local government in their hands:

es que no nos tienen respeto, y esa es la mera pelona verdad. Mire nomás, aquí nos encasqueta hasta el cuello el aeropuerto, las cárceles, los almacenes de cosa y media, y otras muchas cosas y, pues, tanto ruido y tanto negocio sucio, que parece como si los barrios pos fueran resumideros de agua empuercada y montes de basura.

(The fact is that they have no respect for us and that is the plain truth. Look, here they force us to put up with the airport, the prisons, the cheap businesses and, then, so much noise and so many dirty stores; it seems as if the barrios were reservoirs of filthy water and mountains of trash.)

He is even more fearful of Chicano politicians, however, because once they are in office, they turn into shameless *vendidos* (betrayers) who have little use for Chicanos and their troubles.

The theme of the *vendidos* emerges frequently in *Los dos compadres.* One sees them in all walks of life, but

*Alarcón in 1997 with a copy of his 1993 collection of interrelated tales,* Los dos compadres *[The Two Comrades] (courtesy of Alarcón)*

they appear most often as used-car salesmen. These individuals disguise themselves as Chicanos in their advertisements. Some of the more humorous passages in the book involve a used-car salesman who calls himself "El Charro" but whose ethnic background neither Don Epifanio nor Don Epiceno can identify. He advertises his business by saying "vengan, vengan, vengan" (come, come, come), while wearing a huge black mustache that appears to be fake.

Another theme is that the Chicanos, on losing the land that was the patrimony of their ancestors, also lost their historical space in the United States; hence, they have lost and continue to lose their own identity. Don Epiceno does not understand why young Chicanas, wishing to have light skin, avoid exposure to the sun, while *gringas* (Anglo girls) long to be tanned and lie for hours in the sunshine. Don Epifanio explains that "la chicanita" (the young Chicano girl), having an identity crisis, truly wishes that she could be Anglo; the Anglo girl, however, knowing well who she is, only wants to be brown on the surface.

Another prominent theme discussed by the two old men is the disintegration of the family, whose members are pressured to acquire a value system that is foreign to their native culture. The characters also discuss the violence that arises when the Chicanos are subjected to a system of laws that they do not understand. Superstitions, *la Migra* (immigration officers), *los coyotes,* and United States–Mexican policies in regard to Mexican laborers and illegal aliens are also discussed.

Don Epifanio instructs Don Epiceno on all these topics by posing leading questions until the latter arrives at the desired conclusions. His teaching method is much like the one Socrates is supposed to have used with his disciples. In addition to the dialogues of the two main characters, *Los dos compadres* features a third-person narrator who introduces each of the short narratives. These introductions are frequently lyrical passages that temper the harshness of the themes discussed.

Alarcón has also offered significant contributions to literary criticism of Chicano writing. His *El espacio lit-*

*erario de Juan Bruce-Novoa: Un estudio metacrítico del texto* (The Literary Space of Juan Bruce-Novoa: A Metacritical Study of the Text, 1994) offers insightful comments on Bruce-Novoa's concept of the literary space of Chicano literature.

Alarcón has in preparation a children's book titled "Corridos de animales para jóvenes y niños" (Animal Ballads for Children and Young People), which will be made up of *corridos* featuring the adventures of small mammals, birds, and insects. The poem "El corrido del gatito" (Ballad of the Kitty) begins:

> Aquí les cuento la historia
> de un gatito secuestrado.
> Era bueno y cariñoso
> y se perdió por confiado.
> Año de mil novecientos
> ochenta y cuatro cumplidos
> Fue por el mes de las flores.
> Me compraron un gatito.
>
> (Here I'll tell you the story
> about my abducted kitty.
> He was good and loving
> but got lost for being too trusting.
> The year was
> eighty four.
> When in the month of flowers
> my kitty I received.)

These compositions follow the traditional pattern of the Mexican folk ballad: the setting of the story and the year in which it occurred serve as the introduction to the narrative event; the stanzas that follow tell the story; and in the last lines the poetic voice usually takes leave of the reader, offering some sound advice about avoiding uncomfortable situations. Alarcón's contributions to Chicano children's literature will likely be as highly regarded as his other creative endeavors.

While Justo S. Alarcón is not of Mexican descent and was born in Spain rather than in the United States, the birthplace of those classified as Chicano writers, his creative works are permeated with the Chicano spirit and are, therefore, said to belong to *literatura chicanesca* (Chicanoesque literature). *Chulifeas fronteras, Crisol, Los siete hijos de la Llorona, Poemas en mí menor,* and *Los dos compadres* are valuable additions to the growing corpus of Hispanic literature written in the United States.

**Interview:**

Lupe Cárdenas, "Entrevista con Justo S. Alarcón," *Confluencia,* 8, no. 1 (1993): 199–210.

**Reference:**

Margarita Cota-Cárdenas, "La creación-protesta en *Crisol: Trilogía,*" *Confluencia,* 1, no. 2 (1986): 66–72.

# Miriam Bornstein

*(19 February 1950 – )*

Alfonso Rodríguez
*University of Northern Colorado*

BOOKS: *Bajo cubierta* (Tucson, Ariz.: Scorpion Press, 1976);

*Donde empieza la historia* (Sacramento, Cal.: Spanish Press, 1993).

OTHER: "Nacimiento," in *Window Rock,* edited by Raymond Quintanar (Tucson, Ariz.: Tucson Poetry Center, 1975), pp. 35–36;

"Toma de nombre," "Perspectiva," "Media vuelta y un poema," "Ineptitud," "Directorio," "Para el consumidor," "Celebrando el bicentenario," "Psico-Fem," "Historia de todas," and "Ellos," in *Siete poetas,* edited by Margarita Cota-Cardenas and Eliana S. Rivero (Tucson, Ariz.: Scorpion Press, 1978), pp. 1–10;

"Por un solo momento," "Pequeña declaración de fe," and "Inventando los días," in *Flor y Canto IV & V: An Anthology of Chicano Literature,* edited by José Armas, Bernice Zamora, Michael Reed, and Justo Alarcón (Albuquerque: Pajarito, 1980), pp. 32–33;

"El lugar de la mujer," in *Nosotras: Latina Literature Today,* edited by María del Carmen Boza, Beverly Silva, and Carmen Valle (Binghamton, N.Y.: Bilingual Review/Press, 1986), p. 60;

"Toma de nombre," "Para el consumidor," in *Infinite Divisions: An Anthology of Chicano Literature,* edited by Tey Diana Rebolledo and Eliana S. Rivero (Tucson: University of Arizona Press, 1993), pp. 79, 282;

"On Becoming Round," in *Daughter of the Fifth Sun: A Collection of Latina Fiction and Poetry,* edited by Bryce Milligan, Mary Guerrero Milligan, and Angela de Hoyos (New York: Riverhead Books, 1995), p. 42;

"Toma de nombre," "Media vuelta y un poema," "Un saludo," "Afirmación culinaria," "Homenaje," and "Recogiendo recuerdos," in *La voz urgente: Antología de literatura chicana en español,* edited by Manuel M. Martín-Rodríguez (Madrid: Editorial Fundamentos, 1995), pp. 211–217;

*Miriam Bornstein (courtesy of Bornstein)*

"Una pequeña contribución," "To a Linguist Studying Discourse Strategies of Bilingual/Bicultural Students," in *Floricanto Sí: A Collection of Latina Poetry,* edited by Bryce Milligan, Mary Guerrero Milligan, and Angela de Hoyos (New York: Penguin, 1998), pp. 37–38.

SELECTED PERIODICAL PUBLICATIONS– UNCOLLECTED: "Herencia intangible," *Letras Femeninas,* 2, no. 1 (1976): 14–15;

"Másallá de los días," "Desde otro mirador," and Rebeldía," *Revista Chicano-Riqueña,* 5, no. 4 (1978): 30–31;

"Afirmación culinaria" and "Evaluación," *La Palabra,* 1, no. 1 (1979): 25;

"El templo mayor," "La señora del aseo de la biblioteca," and "Nicaragua," *Areíto,* 1, no. 25 (1981): 52;

"Media vuelta y un poema," *Hora de poesía,* 48 (November–December 1986): 11.

Miriam Bornstein is a Chicana feminist poet whose work is an exploration of the diverse facets of womanhood, an affirmation of identity, and a search for communion with the "other." It evokes feelings of tenderness and anguish, and at times it offers an indictment of the ills that plague modern society. It begins with personal existential concerns, and from there it strives toward identification with a collective entity represented by those sectors of society who have suffered deprivation or who struggle for a moral good. In her work, the personal extends toward the social.

Miriam Mijalina Bornstein was born on 19 February 1950 in Puebla, Mexico. Her mother, Cristina Gómez Sánchez, a homemaker and hairstylist, was Mexican; her father, Abraham Bornstein, a medical sales representative and writer, was an immigrant from Poland. Bornstein has lived in the United States since 1964 and is a naturalized citizen. She studied at the University of Arizona, earning her bachelor's degree in 1973, her master's degree in 1976, and her Ph.D. in 1982, all in Spanish. Since her early days as a graduate student, Bornstein has been a teacher of Spanish language and Chicano and Latin American literatures. She is presently a tenured faculty member at the University of Denver. Bornstein is married to Oscar Somoza, director of Latin American Studies at the university, and they have two children: Armando and Melina.

Bornstein's first book, *Bajo cubierta* (Under Cover, 1976), was published while she was a graduate student. Its thirty-two poems constitute a thematic whole and are written in standard Spanish—not Chicano Spanish, which shows the strong influence of English and is enriched by barrio expressions. She expresses the hope that women will be able to overcome the barriers imposed by men and achieve fulfillment.

Bornstein speaks of the housewife who yearns to undertake intellectual endeavors, the wife who neglects household chores to write poetry, the writer who suppresses her creative voice because her husband or lover fails to acknowledge her poetic gifts, the woman who surrenders all and sees herself abandoned by the man, the lover who searches for genuine communion with the man with whom she has cast her lot, and the wife who loses her husband and is forced to make greater sacrifices for her children.

"Otra concepción" (Another Conception) imagines a new period in history in which every person will acquire attributes of both sexes, thus attaining greater mutual understanding. This new person would be "evadánico," that is, would have characteristics of both Eve and Adam:

a veces
me parece que va a llover
...................
    una manada arrasadora y profunda
...........................
    negando la existencia y la forma
entonces regresamos
    no a ser Eva o Adan
sino
    un ser evadánico
    que quizá
    no sea mas viejo
      pero sí más sabio.

(At times
it seems it's going to rain
..................
    an equalizing and profound herd
...........................
    denying existence and form
only then do we return
    not to be Eve and Adam
rather
    an evadamized being
    which perhaps
    might not be older
      but certainly wiser.)

Two of the poems take the creative process as their theme. "Más allá de los días" (Beyond the Days) describes a woman whose love of poetry provides the courage she needs to give expression to the images that are stirring inside her:

triturando las noches en letras
caminando por días sinónimos
    voy pasando por tumbos
      y tumbos
pensando que llego
    pero no
    pero sí
esfuerzos de mujer que se atreve
sí
se atreve
    a vivir
    a soñar
    a crear
      en un nicho
      una imagen
      un instante
diluido en signos
    reflejando metáforas en vela.

(grinding nights into letters
walking through synonymous days
    I keep going through roller coaster
      rides

thinking I'm getting there
    but no
    but yes
efforts of a woman daring
yes
daring
    to live
    to dream
    to create
        in a niche
        an image
        an instant
diluted in signs
    reflecting metaphors sleepless.)

The second poem, "Para la conciencia" (For the Conscience), establishes a contrast between the speaker's real life, which is full of burdens, because she is partnered with a man who ignores the value of poetry and the poetic experience of the speaker, which transports her to a higher dimension:

Tu mundo
lleno de método y máscaras en fila
pesado se me cuelga de los hombros
(que mal me queda)
no puedo vivir contigo
porque he sentido un cálido beso
    unitivo y sudoroso
porque me he sumido en un abismo de voces
    interminable al pasar la noche
porque he esperado las letras en rosario
    embriagadas al salir
porque dentro de lo que llaman vida
    he comprendido la eternidad
    en un poema.

(Your world
full of rationale and masks in single line
weighs heavily on my shoulders
[it fits me poorly]
I can't live with you
because I have felt a warm kiss
    bonding and sweaty
because I have plunged into an abyss of voices
    never-ending in the passing of night
because I have waited for the letters in sequence
    intoxicated upon leaving
because within that which is called life
    I have understood eternity
    in a poem.)

Treating her material without stridency, Bornstein expresses woman's yearning for liberation from the various forms of oppression imposed by man. This objective can be reached by collaboration on equal terms with the opposite sex; through a genuine communion with the husband or lover; or through poetic creation.

*Donde empieza la historia* (Where History Begins, 1993) is a much longer collection, comprising fifty-four poems with greater thematic variety than the first collection. In the prologue Bornstein outlines the ideological foundations of her poetry and explains the significance of her book:

*Donde empieza la historia* surge como respuesta aunque parcial, a la pregunta ¿La historia de quién? ¿Qué voz representa esta palabra? De alguna manera, poco a poco se fue perfilando no solamente una voz simplemente personal íntima sino múltiples voces que apuntan a una colectividad esencialmente femenina, a la dimensión insólita de la expressión relacionada al poder. Es la voz que sale de las rajaduras de una sociedad que se empecina en desnaturalizar, son las voces de la mujer por fin convertida en sujeto a cargo de la representación de su propia experiencia.

(*Where History Begins* originates as a response, although a partial one, to the question, Whose history? What voice represents this word? In some way, not only did a simply intimate personal voice come to manifest itself but many multiple voices that signal an essentially feminine collectivity and an uncommon dimension of the expression related to power. It is the voice that emerges from the cracks of a society that insists on divesting [women] of citizenship. They are the voices of woman finally turned into a subject in charge of the representation of her own experience.)

Bornstein quotes *Borderlands/La Frontera: The New Mestiza* (1987) by Chicana writer Gloria Anzaldúa: "Ethnic identity is twin skin to linguistic identity–I am language." Writing poetry in Spanish is fundamental to Bornstein's identity as a writer because, she believes, each language has its own ideologies:

Para mí, el escribir en español representa una lucha contra la autocensura que hemos sufrido al ver que nuestro lenguaje, a pesar de nuestra larga historia literaria, no es aceptado como conducto expresivo; como aventura comercialmente gratificable. En busca de la integración al 'mainstream' hemos ido entregando una manera más de entendernos. El uso del español posibilita un balance entre todas las demás formas de expressión literaria; facilita el acceso a otros puntos de referencia.

(For me, writing in Spanish represents a struggle against the self-censureship that we have suffered upon seeing that our language, despite our long literary history, is not accepted as an expressive vehicle; as a commercially gratifying enterprise. In search of integrating into the mainstream we have given up one more way of understanding ourselves. The use of Spanish permits a balance among all the other forms of literary expression; it facilitates the access into other points of reference.)

The book is divided into four sections. The first, "MUJER: ASI DICE EL POEMA" (Woman: The Poem States It Thus), connects *Bajo cubierta* and *Donde empieza la historia* thematically. It is the longest of the parts, composed of twenty-four poems addressing topics such as the struggle of women to erase the negative images perpetuated by men; the problem of communication with "the other"; the lower status in marriage to which women have been relegated; Central American women who have made a commitment to revolutionary and social change; women's efforts to create and affirm their own identity; the difficult task of creating poetry; and the liberating qualities of the creative process. Some of the poems are characterized by a sober tone, others by restrained rage, and still others by irony. For example, "Las aventuras de la muñeca barbie" (The Adventures of the Barbie Doll) is an ironic statement of men's objectification of women:

¡Ah, ser tu hermosa cosita!
Siempre fui uno de tus esplendorosos trofeos
durante una larga noche de suburbio
me guardaste por ahí tan bien
que ni siquiera yo me he podido encontrar.

(Oh, to be your beautiful, darling thing!
I always was one of your magnificent trophies
during a long suburban night
you put me away so well on the shelf
that not even I could find me.)

"Haciendo guardia en Nicaragua" (Guard Duty in Nicaragua), is dedicated to a "mujer sandinista" (Sandinista woman):

Inclinada sobre tu carta
contemplo ese jirón que es tu firma
y que quizás de alguna manera te define.

Pienso en el lugar
donde estarás indomable
con la noche caída sobre tu sombra
con tu pueblo sobre el hombro
y las arrugas del combate entre los dedos.
Como leona agredida
acecharás al enemigo
y defenderás tu necesario tiempo humano.

(Bent over your letter
I gaze at that scribble that is your signature
and that perhaps somehow defines you.

I think of the place
where you must be untamable
with night hanging over your shadow
with your people over your shoulder
and the wrinkles of combat between your fingers.
Like a cornered lioness

Cover for Bornstein's 1993 collection of fifty-four poems focusing on women's experiences

you will ambush the enemy
and defend your inalienable human time.)

In "Poeta" (Poet) Bornstein expresses part of the price a woman has to pay to be a poet: the endurance of a solitary struggle that drives her to physical and emotional exhaustion:

así le llaman a esta extension de mujer
          a este cuerpo desvencijado
      insistente en inventar espacios
                  alzar tejidos
y amanecer de espalda al silencio.

(that's what they call this extension of woman
          this shattered body
      insistent in inventing spaces
                  lifting fabrics
and waking up with your back against silence.)

The second part of *Donde empieza la historia,* "HOMBRE: PARA VERTE MEJOR" (Man: The Better to See You), extends a bridge of understanding to men. These thirteen poems constitute an effort to reach out to the "other." "Viejito haciendo su cama" (Little Old Man Making His Bed) is a picture of destitution and hopelessness representing a man at the end of his journey, awkwardly continuing his inexorable march toward the grave with no consoling vision of a better life beyond it. "Pintor" (Painter), on the other hand, is a tribute to a Chicano muralist, celebrating his firmness of character, his special way of seeing reality, and his artistic gifts, which defy logical explanations. In "En estos tiempos" (Nowadays) the poet reinvents fragments of the past and reconstructs an image of her father. The rest of the poems in this second part refer to woman's search for communion with man in an encounter in which physical and spiritual love merge to create poetry. Poetry becomes a vehicle toward the attainment of a deeper understanding of the "other" in "Para verte mejor":

Si de pronto te ocuparas de mis sueños
y encararas toda su verdad
ocuparías el nexo a la locura
y cayeran a mi mundo ordinario
tus demolidos huesos
tu discutible cara;
seguramente
vivirías sin preguntar a nadie
en qué poema existes pedazo a pedazo
algo se desgasta
en cada gota de silencio
algo se disuelve
ante estas manos
germinando signos
para verte mejor.

(If you would suddenly take charge of my dreams
and confront all their truth
you would occupy the link to insanity
and your demolished bones
your questionable face
would fall into my ordinary world;
most certainly
you would live without asking anyone
in what poem you exist piece by piece
something wastes away
in each water drop of silence
something becomes dissolved
before these hands
this populated skin
germinating signs
with which to see you better.)

The third part of *Donde empieza la historia,* "RECLAMO DE LA TIERRA" (Claim on the Land), includes seven poems of political commitment to oppressed peoples of Mexico and Central America, whose history of colonization and degradation links them to Chicanos in the United States. "Dejes coloniales" (Colonial Inflections) uses the image of women to represent the land to the south of the Rio Grande, which was raped by the Colossus of the North. "Nota para dos" (Note For Two), dedicated to the people of Guatemala and El Salvador, contrasts the freedom fighter, who dies valiantly to defend the land, leaving a legacy of honor to his children, to the oppressor, who usurps the land, causing bloodshed and death. "En plan de guerra" (On the Verge of War) poses a question with regard to the future of Third World children:

¿Dónde podrán los niños
nacer como las flores
que soñaron desde un mundo fresco
como espejo de mañana?

Ahora llegan
y de nube son sus manos
su estómago
es la culpa del presente

¿En qué lugar podrán
los niños terminar en algo más que cenizas?

(Where might children
be born like flowers
which dreamed from a renewed world
like a morning mirror?

They now arrive
and their hands are of clouds
their stomach
is the fault of the present.

In what place might children
end up in something other than ash?)

Part four, "TODO ESTA EN TI" (Everything is Within You), was inspired by the death of the poet's mother. "Ya no estás" (No Longer There) expresses the desolation death leaves behind. The separation of mother and daughter is abrupt and definitive. No hope is expressed in an afterlife:

envuelta en tu sombra
parada en tu Día de las Madres
ya no estás
pendiente del que llega
ni del arroz compartido

y yo escribo poema tras poema
para hurtarte un rato de ese frío
y mis manos rotas
ya no te alcanzan
mis palabras caen rendidas
sobre tu pecho duro y polvoriento

se van cayendo las capas
se va quedando irremediablemente
un solitario murmullo entre mis huesos.

(wrapped in your shadow
standing on your Mother's Day
you are no longer
awaiting for whomever arrives
nor the shared rice

and I write one poem after another
to spare you awhile from that cold
and my broken hands
can no longer reach you
my words drop exhausted
on your hard and dusty chest

the layers are falling
a solitary whisper between my bones
hopelessly remains behind.)

The creative process is an attempt to cope with the hurt. In "Registros" (Registers) recurring visitations of the lost loved one in the poet's memory engender a desire for poetic expression as a way to gain a deeper insight into the life of the deceased: "Ya ver / de nuevo he vuelto a la palabra / a esta manera especial de entenderte" (As you can see / I have once again returned to the word / to this special way of understanding you). Poetry is the daughter's only hope to heal her pain: "mas ahora / regresas con tus labios / próximos a la ternura de este poema" (but now / you return with your lips / next to the tenderness of this poem). The mother's memory becomes an irresistible force that impels the author to write: "Eres constante / puntual en tu presencia / insistente en caber otra vez / en el hueco de esta hoja" (You are consistent / punctual in your presence / insistent in fitting once again / in the gap of this leaf).

No poem expresses more anguish than "Día de guardar" (A Day to Behold). The central question, "¿Dónde está tu amor / sellado contra el tiempo?" (Where is your love / sealed against time?), conveys the poet's feeling of abandonment. The poem ends on a note of despair:

No quiero pensar
que ya no llegas
aunque mis raíces enloquecidas
aún necesitan tanto de tus ríos
como hoy
cuando arrojé un clavel
contra mi propia fosa.

(I don't want to believe
that you won't get here
although my maddening roots
still need as much of your rivers
like today
when I hurled a carnation
against my own grave.)

The poetry of Miriam Bornstein is concerned with questions of gender and feminine identity, political and economic inequality, and the quest for meaning in a world of separation and spiritual distress. She is part of an important movement among Chicana poets who exhibit simila r thematic tendencies, but her poetry stands out for its impressive use of language and imagery.

# Ronnie Burk
## (1 April 1955 – )

Inés Hernández-Ávila
*University of California, Davis*

BOOKS: *En el Jardín de los Nopales: Poems 1976–1977* (San Jose, Cal.: Mango Publications, 1979); revised as *En el Jardín de los Nopales* (San Antonio, Tex.: Ganesha Head Stand, 1983);

*The Single Hand Alphabet Collage Poem* (New York: MontanaPrinnerz, 1981);

*Father of Reason, Daughter of Doubt* (San Francisco: Saturn's Clock, 1996);

*Scrolls of White Cabbage* (San Francisco: Centaur Productions, 1997);

*Mutations* (San Francisco: Centaur Productions, 1998);

*Indios Verdes* (San Francisco: Centaur Productions, 1998);

*Man-of-War* (San Francisco: Hekate's Gallery, 1999);

*Mandragora* (San Francisco: Hekate's Gallery, 1999);

*The History of America* (San Francisco: Hekate's Gallery, 1999).

OTHER: "En el Jardín de los Nopales," "Ogre Woman's Song," and "Garden Song," in *Flor y Canto IV and V: An Anthology of Chicano Literature from the Festivals held in Albuquerque, New Mexico, 1977, and Tempe, Arizona, 1978,* edited by José Armas, Justo S. Alarcón and others (Albuquerque: Pajarito Publications, 1980), pp. 40–41;

"Untitled," "Drop Poems for Peace: A Collage Poem," "Untitled," "The Anatomy of Love," and "Semen," *The Stiffest of the Corpse: An Exquisite Corpse Reader,* edited by Andrei Codrescu (San Francisco: City Lights Books, 1989), pp. 34, 56, 67, 104, 220;

"Dear Anne," in *Iovis,* by Anne Waldeman (Minneapolis: Coffee House Press, 1993), p. 200;

"En el Jardín de los Nopales" and "Millie," translated in *Recent Chicano Poetry/Neueste Chicano-Lyrik,* edited by Heiner Bus and Ana Castillo (Bamberg, Germany: Universitätsbibliothek Bamberg, 1994), pp. 42, 44–46;

"Untitled" and "Que Viva Mexico," in *First World Ha Ha Ha,* edited by Elaine Katzenberger (San Francisco: City Lights, 1995), pp. 218–222;

*Ronnie Burk in New York City, 1994 ( photograph by Richard Kern)*

"Retablo," in *Goddess of the Americas: Writing on the Virgin of Guadalupe,* edited by Ana Castillo (New York: Riverhead Books, 1996), pp. 151–152.

SELECTED PERIODICAL PUBLICATIONS–UNCOLLECTED: "I Miss An Invitation To A Sufi Wedding Visiting The Camarillos," "135 Miles From Corpitos," "Tibetan New Year," "Tonantzin/Los Chicanos/Guadalupe," and "A Big Woman In A Dream," *Caracol,* 3 (February 1977): 16;

"Tattoo Bone Scar" and "Dream on a Bus on Way Back from Houston into Galveston in the Chair," *Revista Chicano-Riqueña,* 3 (Summer 1979): 25;

"In the Park," *Maize,* 3 (Fall/Winter 1979–1980): 77;

"Upon Seeing Scenes" and "Postcard," *Revista Chicano Riqueña,* 3 (Summer 1980): 25–26;

"Heatwave," *Baltimore City Paper,* 30 April 1982, p. 1;

"La Merced," *Maize,* 6 (Spring/Summer 1983): 48;

"A Day in the Life: Collage Poem," *Open 24 Hours,* no. 3 (1984): 21;

"Mictlan," *Revista Chicano-Riqueña,* 11 (Summer 1984): 35;

"The Nineties Glimpsed," *Exquisite Corpse,* 4 (September–October 1985): 3;

"Dreamland" and "Semen," *Exquisite Corpse,* 5 (June–August 1987): 1;

"Quality of Life More than Dollars," *Maui News,* 2 September 1987, p. A9;

"Letter to Miguel Piñero," "Hazards of the Day," "NYC Collage," and "The Getaway," *Americas Review,* 16 (Fall/Winter 1988): 39, 42–44;

"2 Surrealists of the Century" and "Poem," *Calibán,* 4 (1988): 113–114;

"Millie," "NYC Collage," and "Decalcomania," *Calibán,* 5 (1988): 67–69;

"Pluto 23 Libra Retrograde (after Kabir)," *Calibán,* 6 (1988): 122;

"The Children of Paradise," *Calibán,* 8 (1988): 23;

"Collage: Transfigured Head," *City Lights Review,* 4 (1990): 63;

"Mad Sonnet," *Calibán,* 9 (1990): 36;

"In a Void" and "Invisible World," *Night,* no. 19 (1990): 13;

"Día de los Muertos, 1990," *Cold-Drill* (1990): 13;

"Untitled," *Red Dirt: Crosscultural Poetry,* 1 (Spring 1991): 37;

"The War in San Francisco," *Exquisite Corpse,* 9 (January–April 1991): 2;

"Another Superstar's Diet Plan," *Exquisite Corpse,* no. 36 (1991): 3;

"Elegy for My Brothers," *Calibán,* 11 (1992): 33–36;

"Sol y Luna" and "L'Amour Fou," *Cover* (August 1992): 19;

"Some Notes on the Discovery of the New World," *Revista Paralax,* 1 (October 1992): 13;

"At the Gallery Paule Anglim" and "Neon Life," *Exquisite Corpse,* 39 (November–December 1992): 19;

"Magic Squares," *Cover,* 6 (December 1992): 21;

"The Forces of Imperialism as Seen in the Cracked Mirror of Time," *City Lights Review: War After War,* 5 (1992): 171;

"Mineral Life," "The Hanged Man," "Genesis," and "Wednesdays," *Calibán,* 13 (1993): 38;

"Flat with no Rules," *Fritz,* 3 (1993): 23;

"The Three Fold Origami Prayer For World Peace" and "Untitled," *15 Minutes,* 12 (1993): 9;

"Advent of the Real" and "For Ana," *Exquisite Corpse,* 45 (1994): 30;

"Militarism Beggars Country," *Corpus Christi Caller Times,* 14 January 1994, p. A11;

"Invisible World (song for the ancestors)," "Datura," and "United States Immigration Law," *Crossroads,* 38 (February 1994): 26;

"In Praise of Sun-Ra" and "The Illustrated Story of Desire," *Verbal Abuse,* 3 (1994): 35;

"Sinton, Texas," *Io,* 2 (1994): 14;

"Cuauhtemoc" and "Excavations," *Calibán,* 14 (1994): 71–72;

"Ronnie Burk Dancing: 25 April 1994," *Radical History Review,* 60 (Fall 1994): 177;

"Farewell Texas Poem," *Exquisite Corpse,* 50 (1994–1995): 18;

"I Don't Care If Jack Kerouac Wiped His Ass With the American Flag, Don't Forget the Indians" and "Interstellar Sighting," *Exquisite Corpse,* 51 (1995): 5, 19;

"Untitled" and "Dream," *Dream Machinery,* 4 (May 1995): 1, 5;

"Untitled," "Valerie Solanas," "Untitled," and review of *Out of the Labyrinth (Selected Poems)* by Charles Henri Ford, *Cafe Review,* 7 (Summer 1996): 26, 32, 35, 72–75;

"Deep in the Bowels of the Cast Iron City" and "Mirror of Water," *MESECHABE,* no. 14–15 (Spring 1996): 12, 13;

"Leo Ford," *MESECHABE,* no. 17 (Spring 1998): 27;

"Yves Tanguy," "Tarantual," and "Max Ernst, 1928," *Cafe Review,* 9 (Spring 1998): 23, 25, 29;

"The Racist Cliché in the USA," "collage from The History Of America," and review of *The Forecast is HOT!* edited by Franklin Rosemont and others, *Race Traitor,* no. 9 (Summer 1998): 70, 98, 126–127;

"Medusa," "Black Mermaid," "Beast-Star," and review of *Loba* by Diane di Prima, *Cafe Review,* 9 (Fall 1998): 2, 3, 63, 70–71;

"Fever," *MANTICORE,* 3 (Autumn 1998): 1;

"My Life, My Abandoned House," "Sacred Heart," and "High Frequency," *Orpheus Grid,* no. 2 (Winter 1998): 19–20;

"Compass Rose," *Orpheus Grid,* no. 3 (Winter 1999): 99.

Renegade artist, surrealist, collagist, poet, and activist, Ronnie Burk is a Tejano-Chicano-Mexicano who voices what he feels is the crisis in civilization at the end of the twentieth century. Burk believes that the role of the artist is to find the trapdoor out of this oppressive society; his contribution to Chicano literature is his synthesis of surrealism, Tibetan Buddhism, indigenous (particularly Mexican) iconography and indigenous American landscapes, Mexican politics, gayness, and a critique of "world orders." His poetry and his collages chronicle a process of intuiting, seeking and then discovering validation for an intuition each time more informed by the experience of the search.

In the 1970s, Burk's initial impulse was toward a surrealist vision, even though at the time he had no orientation toward surrealism philosophically. His predisposition toward exploring and unearthing often unlikely correspondences reflects a certain mindfulness and a play of consciousness that come about, as he says, when "you live in one society and are of another—the humor, the language, the kind of absurdist quality of our lives that lends itself to surrealism—the kind of collage reality of living in an Anglo society." Burk is, in effect, a traveling correspondent; through his poems, his essays, his letters (both his "Open Letters" and his letters to his friends), he offers distilled cartographies of the body, mind, and spirit, revealing the terrain he has covered in puzzles that emerge in poetic shorthand.

Burk was born on April Fool's Day, 1955, in Sinton, Texas, to Everett Burk and Frances Serda Burk, from Anglo sharecropping and Mexican campesino backgrounds, respectively. Coming from an Anglo-Mexican working-class family, Burk believes, contributed in a major way to his working-class consciousness and his solidarity with workers, as well as to his understanding of issues of race and ethnicity. The censure his parents faced because of their mixed marriage, including the enforced invisibility his mother experienced when she was pregnant with him, have caused him to note, "I suspect even in the womb I had [a] social consciousness." By the tenth grade, Burk's coming out as gay added another important dimension to his critique of the repressive and racist nature of Texas society in the 1950s and 1960s. In Sinton, by the age of seventeen, an "out" Burk was growing his hair long, wearing androgynous clothes, leafleting against the Vietnam War, reading the French Symbolists, and beginning to write. Of those early years growing up in South Texas, Burk said in an 12 May 1994 unpublished interview:

> When I joke about it I used to say that I was Jesus
> Christ and they were going to nail me to the cross
> because up until my teen-age years I thought I was the
> only one in terms of being a visionary, being involved
> as a revolutionary, having the dispensation of a poet.
> The isolation was very extreme. Texas to me was like
> Hell.

Remembering an alienating landscape made harsher by corporate farming, Burk refers to his early years as a prison and recalls that even as a child he knew he would at some point break out to see the "free world."

In what became his modus vivendi, Burk's first foray out of South Texas happened in 1971 when he dropped out of high school and left home to be more closely involved in the antiwar movement. In 1972 he made his way to the Republican Convention in Miami, where he took part in demonstrations against President Richard Nixon and the Vietnam War. Upon his return to Texas, he became involved in the *Movimiento* (Movement) through familial ties to his activist cousin from Robstown, Guadalupe Youngblood, a leader of the Chicano movement and in particular of the *Raza Unida* (United People) party in Texas. Because the *Raza Unida* political experiment demonstrated the futility of electoral victories without economic bases, Burk quickly developed a disdain and a distrust for the electoral process. The phenomenon of the movement itself, however, including the Texas Farmworkers Union activities, and the flourishing Chicano literary, artistic, and cultural scene, proved to be invaluable to Burk's evolution as a writer.

Burk has lived a nomadic, and for the most part, underground bohemian life, working in the unskilled labor market in order to be able to move around. He has worked as a waiter, a painter, a constructor of sets, and even briefly as a professional tarot card reader and astrologer. Where he has lived has coincided with the times when living was inexpensive in a particular place and/or when his quest for poetry has guided him to a certain locale or ambience. His trajectory has included San Antonio, Galveston, Houston, Zacatecas (Mexico), New York City, Boston, Cambridge (Massachusetts), Guadalajara, Mexico City, Memphis, Honolulu, Maui, and San Francisco. From 1974 through 1982 Burk lived in downtown San Antonio, an experience that informed his politics and gave him a sense of urgency not only about being a Mexican but also about needing to embrace being a Mexican, a theme that appears consistently in his work.

In a characteristic movement for him, back and forth between communities, Burk left San Antonio in the summers of 1974 through 1976 to study Buddhist philosophy and literature at the Naropa Institute in Boulder, Colorado. In Boulder he says he noticed middle-class white students who had to be convinced that magic was a part of reality. His Mexicanness gave him an acceptance of serpents that could fly, *diablos* (devils) that come out of the water, *La Llorona* (The Wailing Woman, a mythical figure), and snakes and dogs that could transform—in effect, an understanding of a natural world where magical things could happen (they could be brutal, but still magical). The Tibetan Buddhists did not have to convince him about magic.

Floating Gallery
Ronnie Burk
1983

inez,

    as always your poetry moves me to thought and towards communication.
i saw your poems in las Americas (review) spring '87. oops o mean fall
winter 86. that night of nights the 1st tuesday of nov. election night
i was in guadalajara in a trance overcoming the dread of Mien Fuhrer
Victory at the box or is it the ballot box office. politics.
    and had to ask myself is this all just a nightmare?
    but your poems stimulate me to think about all of this.
    once at a painters friends house outside mexico city i came to a
sudden deep realization as to why. the why of things.
    i had wanted so much to live in Mexico but always the hand off ate
pushed me off towards some other direction. finally on a conscious
level i understood. in a room full of artists i realized i was born
north of the border to achieve something within the walls of that country.
the differecne between being born north of the rio bravo and south is
very simple. north of theborder we incarnate in a country that has no
morals no grace no sense of atunement to the earth and universe. so
we are hymn hungry for such sustenence. south of the border the hunger is
simply food. simply a place to sleep and love and bring a family up with
food and books and hope. Even thepoorest of us Notte Americanos even the
most oppressed live high on the hog of amreican imperalism as opposed to
our fellow brothers and sisters suth of Yanquiville U.S.A. and so we are
mirror images of the same person. one side we yearn for spiritual wholeness
the other side feeds itself nourishing food to fill the flesh body with strength
for what has to bedone. one side we can afford the luxury of a poem or a
dream the other side has to consider the machinegun or a cracked skull to
overturn history by the throat. one day we will merge into one dream.flesh
body and it will be that moment that the poem and the meal are one.
    until then we have the schizophrena of the split person and the nightmare
of reality.
    thank your for the poetry and for your presence. You are wisdom and
youm are love. 1988 will have to be a better year. but wait till 1992!
when all dreams will become real!
Merry X-Mas Happy New Year Inez Hernandes!

*Ronnie Burk*
*Dec. 13th '87*
*maui*

*Letter from Burk to friend and fellow poet Inés Hernández-Ávila (Collection of Inés Hernández-Ávila; by permission of Ronnie Burk)*

Taking the literature classes being taught by Diane di Prima, Allen Ginsberg, George Quasha, and Anne Waldman, and moving in a milieu that included such writers as William S. Burroughs, Amiri Baraka, Gregory Corso, and John Cage, Burk began to take his writing more seriously. Di Prima, in particular, became a lasting influence on Burk, their relationship developing through the practice of Buddhism as well as through the support she has given Burk for his work. The avant-garde techniques di Prima taught at Naropa, using dreams, chants, and collage, as well as teaching visualization and ways of working with guided imagery, were as important to Burk's development as his (re)searching his indigenous and revolutionary Mexican roots. In a telling moment, Burk remembers, he was in Boulder in a formal hall in June 1974, sitting on a *zafu* (meditation cushion) and practicing Buddhist techniques. Suddenly he heard, outside, the chanting of "Que Viva la Raza!" (Long Live Our People), "Sal Si Puedes!" (Get Out If You Can), and other slogans. When he walked outside to see, he discovered people marching by the university to protest the bombing of Denver Chicano Rodolfo "Corky" Gonzales's premises. Burk joined the march, then later returned to sit on his *zafu* and meditate, with the feeling of having achieved an epiphany of sorts. He said in the 1994 interview, "I was straddling two worlds again, only this time it wasn't the gringo world and the Mexican, but the Chicano/American and the Asian worlds. That was a moment when I realized that you could do both [protest and meditate]. That it was OK to do both and in fact that it was necessary to do both."

After his summertime stints in Boulder, Burk returned to San Antonio to participate in the cultural and political activities in the Chicano community. In 1977 Burk published his first poems in the San Antonio-based magazine *Caracol: La Revista de la Raza* (Snail: The Magazine of the Race), which was founded and edited by Cecilio García-Camarillo and Mia Kirsi Stageberg. The latter became a good friend and influenced Burk's writing with her use of dreams and of traveling worlds to make breakthroughs in reality. In 1987, in *Exquisite Corpse: A Monthly of Books and Ideas,* Burk published a prose poem called "Dreamland," which he dedicated "to Mia Kirsi Stageberg and the language of the dream." In "Dreamland" the speaker swims upstream with the salmon, discusses a Claes Oldenberg sculpture with the artist in Cuernavaca, is mute in the face of a Guatemalan woman whose son is dead, finds himself with no money to buy "Buddha Oil" in a Texas border Botánica, and ends up in Maui with a Catholic gentleman with whom he discusses God. "Dreamland" concludes with Burk playfully blurring the edges of dreams and waking moments; as he noted in 1994, a "rainbow

appears several yards away and intensifies in color. Moves toward us and finally dissolves at our feet. This was not a dream but actually happened and I took it for a sign that everything would be alright."

In 1977 Burk traveled with García-Camarillo, Stageberg, and Max Martínez to the fourth Floricanto Festival (a national festival of Chicano literature) in Albuquerque, New Mexico, where he met poet and editor Lorna Dee Cervantes. She later published Burk's chapbook, *En el Jardín de los Nopales* (In the Garden of Prickly Pear Trees, 1979), as a Mango Publication. The collection came out of the experience of the Chicano barrio; the poems are rooted in Texas, they are involved with the Mexican quality of the Texas landscape, and they represent a grounding for Burk during a period when he was developing his poetic style. Because of his English last name and because he writes in English, Burk has often felt that he has to prove he is Mexican. The publishing of *En el Jardín de los Nopales* was fulfilling to him because of the acceptance and comradeship he felt from the Chicano community, in what he calls the "unique situation in the mid 1970s" that launched him into other worlds. He remembers that the poems came first and then he went to Mexico; the poems such as "Cihuacóatl" and "En el Jardín de los Nopales" intuitively led him to places such as Tula. Like so many other Chicanos and Chicanas at the time, he went to Mexico to recover the ancient Mexican poetic and philosophical traditions and to discover, as he said in the interview, "Yes, I am in fact an Indian, despite everything I've been told—essentially I have the soul of an *indígena* [indigenous person]."

Contributing with his voice and his work to the decolonization process that inevitably emerged as a result of the social struggles of the 1960s and 1970s, Burk is painfully aware of the institutional distortion, if not erasure, of ethnic identity that non-whites face in American society. He tells the story of being in a coffee shop once, where a gay Irish-American woman, out of her innocence and affection for him, said, "Your hair is so beautiful, so thick, it's like Indian hair, . . . you're Indian," and Burk answered, "Yes." She went on, "That means Chicanos are Indians," and Burk again answered, "Yes." He relates that he was amazed at the interchange, that the woman would see as obvious something that is denied by the educational system as well as by many Chicanos themselves. In the poem, "Invisible World (song for the ancestors)," Burk extends this image of his hair, his physical appearance, as he makes an offering:

See this hair?
You can have this hair
Long, black, Indian hair
If you take this hair

All those dead Indians
Will come back
To live inside you
Here! take this hair
and may it give you enough strength
to live a million lives.

In 1979 Burk initiated a correspondence with the poet and photographer Charles Henri Ford (of *Blues Magazine*) that has continued and strengthened into a rewarding friendship. Burk went to New York in 1979 to meet Ford, who has been instrumental over the years in Burk's publishing his poetry in the avant-garde magazines. Through Ford, Burk met poets Ira Cohen, G. T. Dickenson, Gerard Malanga, Valery Oisteanu, the Nepali collagist and photographer Indra Bahadur Tamang, and filmmaker Kenneth Anger. At the turn of the decade, moving into the 1980s, Burk suffered bouts of depression; yet, even though his poetry production was sparse, the poems that he created during that time were strong in their visual imagery and wit. In the poem "Heat Wave—for Ira Cohen" (1980), Burk creates an image that is at once him and the cosmos: "A skull peers over the horizon of yet another day. / At dawn the sky is a desert of blue. / The shadows of birds fly out between the eye-sockets / of morning." The poet/cosmos speaks to Cohen: "Midnight is a fandango of 1100 skeletons / Doing the medicine jig to the tune / Of that ever popular hit: / 'I may not be Himalayan Blue / But I sure am yearnin / for something cool.'"

Both male and female friends and colleagues have figured critically in Burk's life. At the beginning of the 1980s he met and established a lasting friendship with poet and novelist Ana Castillo. In the winter of 1981–1982 Burk moved to the Lower East Side of Manhattan, where he lived with the artist, writer, and musician Montana Houston. Through Houston, he met the filmmaker Tommy Turner. Ginsberg introduced him to Miguel Algarín and Miguel Piñero. Burk worked at the Nuyorican Poets' Cafe, where, collaborating with Algarín and Eileen Myles of the St. Mark's Poetry Project, he organized a poetry reading series. In 1982 Burk also took the Kalachakra Empowerment course taught by the Very Venerable Kalu Rinpoche at Columbia University. Shortly afterward he returned to San Antonio, settling there as a base but once again spending much of his time in Mexico City. In 1983, while living in Cambridge, Burk attended an eight-day Buddhist retreat in Barre, Massachusetts. Ruth Dennison, a German woman and a strict meditation teacher, helped him to clear away much of his depression. He started to write more, made plans to move to Hawaii, and spent time in and out of New York.

In 1984 Burk went to see performances of Julian Beck and Judith Malina's Living Theater; they had been in Europe for several years, and so upon their return, Burk made it a point to see them, attracted as he was to Beck's philosophy: the ideas that "the work of the theatre is the work of summoning the spirit" and that "we need a free rationale: a bounding mathematics of the mind, and freeing ecstatic transformation." When Beck passed away in 1985, Burk and Cohen suggested that the *Exquisite Corpse* publish an homage to Beck. In collaboration with Living Theater artist Rain-House, Burk organized and took part in a poetry theater tribute to Beck performed by a group of actors and jazz musicians at the Cambridge jazz club Charlie's Tapp in January 1986.

In 1982 Burk began to publish and exhibit his collages in venues such as *Exquisite Corpse*. In the first issue of that journal, Codrescu (a prolific poet, essayist, and well-known commentator for *All Things Considered* on National Public Radio), explains the derivation of the term *cadavre exquis* as "a collaborative method invented and practiced by the French Surrealists." He adds, "We believe both in an unfolding and in an end to this century. Our aim in *Exquisite Corpse* is to encourage the vigorous activity necessary to bring it to an end. To this purpose we encourage lucidity, seriousness, wickedness, and profound laughter." Burk's collages and his poetry are in keeping with the general principles of the project, which can be demonstrated by his consistent publications in the journal.

By the time *The Stiffest of the Corpse: An Exquisite Corpse Reader* appeared in 1989, it was clear that Burk was part of the "*Corpse* community" of writers and artists, and the *Reader* (which spans the publication years 1983 through 1988) includes four of his collages. Among them is "Drop Poems for Peace," which emerged from a newspaper clipping about Charlie Chaplin—a "Today in History" segment announcing the fact that on 17 May 1978 Chaplin's body was stolen from its grave in Switzerland, abandoned, then found in a cornfield eleven weeks later. Using the clipping as his base, Burk draws a halo around Chaplin's head, and incorporates the newspaper article into a drawing of the Little Tramp, giving him a shepherd's staff in his left hand and a parachute dropping hearts in his right hand. Beginning in the upper right corner, in a letter to Codrescu that critiques what the poet feels is an increasing manifestation of Nazism in the American media and mind-set, Burk asks, "Is nothing sacred?"

Burk's art work has appeared not only in periodicals but also in several exhibitions. "April Fool's Birthday Cake" was part of a group show in New York City in March and April 1982. Two-color pasteups titled "Alchemy of the Image" were displayed at the Museum of Modern Eating, Buddy's Ize Box, in San Antonio, Texas, in February 1984. The following month,

"Dream Poem Which Provides the Possibility of Being in Three Places at Once," a poem in codice format, was hung as a painting in the San Antonio Museum of Art. "The Seven Planets," a series of photo collages, was exhibited at the Artful Dodger Bookshop in Maui in November 1988. Two collages with assemblage were part of *Art Against War,* a group show at the Artist Television Access Gallery in San Francisco in March 1991, and five PhotoMantic collages with assemblage were displayed at the Venusian Gallery of Dreams in San Francisco in January and February 1992. Burk has also published three collections of collages: *Scrolls of White Cabbage* (1997), *Mandragora* (1999), and *The History of America* (1999).

In February 1987 Burk moved into a meditation center in Paia, Hawaii, where for the first time he established a formal relationship with a Tibetan Buddhist teacher. Lama Tenzin had been a monk for the Panchan Lama (second to the Dalai Lama) in Chigatze, Tibet, at his monastery in Tashilungpo, and had come to Hawaii after the invasion of Tibet. Burk was able to practice Tibetan Buddhism on a daily basis, seeking the "inner religion," the inner life, taking initiations and engaging in deeper study. He stayed in Paia for two years, after which he moved to San Francisco, following the need to regain contact with old poet friends; also, because many friends were dying of AIDS, he wanted to see those who were close to the ones who had died and to be with the ones who were dying. After he lost several lovers and friends to AIDS, it was more of an anticlimax than a shock to Burk when he was diagnosed HIV-positive in April 1992. At the suggestion of Sakya Jetsunma Chimmey and with the blessing of Lama Kunga Rinpoche, Burk traveled to Maui to Lama Tenzin's retreat center to do a thirty-day White Tara, Long Life retreat; he has continued alternative treatment for his health. The years since 1984 have been difficult for Burk because of losing friends to AIDS, suicide, drug overdoses, and motorcycle accidents, and because Reaganism and inflation made it harder to live a bohemian lifestyle; but the most difficult part has been seeing friends die.

At the beginning of the 1980s, during a bitter cold December week in South Texas, Burk wrote a poem called "Mictlan," which, in its expression of sorrow and loss, surprised him and caused him to wonder where it came from. He says, "I knew it came from the wind, . . . from a harsh wind." By the end of the decade, he realized the poem had augured the eventual demise of those friends and loved ones he lost over that ten-year period. In "Mictlan" the poet, interrelating images of the Aztec and Egyptian underworlds, presages the "rumor of Holocaust," envisioning a place "where ice winds / gleam / with obsidian knives / that sever / the heart / of everything / you ever / loved" and foretelling "the loneliness / that aches / thru the bones." The poem is one of his major early pieces, and as a companion piece to "Elegy for My Brothers," which he wrote in 1992, it encompasses more than a decade of intense pain and grief.

Burk dedicates "Elegy for My Brothers" to "Jack Parsons, Bob Marley, John Lennon, Julian Beck, Jackson Allen, Miguel Piñero, Abbie Hoffman, Huey Newton, Lama Karma Dundrup, Montana Houston, Alan Marlowe, Osel Tenzin, Cameron Chick, Johnny Hernandez, Carlos Gonzalez, Leo Ford, and for my sisters who endure the madness." The death by motorcycle accident of Ford, a young gay actor known for his incandescent presence, prompted the writing of the poem, which Burk begins with a passage from "The Angelic Manuscripts of John Dee" (written by the court astrologer to Queen Elizabeth I, circa 1582): "and they gathered themselves together / and became the house of death." Burk asks the brothers who died, "Did the hawk faced ones come for you / at the end of the sky?", and throughout the four sections of the poem he elaborates the deaths within the context of the times, the wars upon the people, and the wars against the land.

However, whereas in "Mictlan" the poet says to Kali, the Hindu goddess of destruction, "Take me too! . . . take me to where spirits dance," in "Elegy" he says of Anubis, the Egyptian jackal-headed god who judges the souls of humans, "He beckons me to follow / Oh! but soon enough I will follow." In the last section, addressing Ford and the others as well, the poet ends with affirmation, saying, "I see you traversing galaxies / a distant star in the blackening space / a light tho distant flickers brightly / tho burned out years ago still flickers / brightly." With "Elegy," Burk says he "formally put an end to grief" and was able to go on to another cycle of poems.

Upon his move to San Francisco, Burk met Nancy Joyce Peters of City Lights Books and Philip Lamantia, whose work is said by Jody Norton in an article in *American Poetry Review* (November–December 1992) to be "perhaps closer in spirit and style to the first generation of French surrealists than that of any other American poet." Burk credits Lamantia as being the biggest influence on his returning to write, desiring to write, and shedding old forms. Lamantia introduced Burk to the work of André Breton—to his proletariat politics, his kinship with Leon Trotsky, and to his surrealist agenda not only for poetry but for love and revolution, for life itself. Lamantia encouraged Burk to take up the practice of automatism, and as a teacher, an ally, and a comrade of sorts, he gave Burk an understanding of poetry as a way of life and as an end unto itself, an exalted state of mind and being. This understanding allowed Burk to break through his death obsession to create poems that were vivid and that had a fantastic, visionary quality, aimed at a certain beauty that he had been trying to achieve.

It might seem unusual that Burk would find himself at ease with the surrealist philosophy, given the tendency of surrealism to produce what Anna Balakian, in her *André Breton: Magus of Surrealism* (1971), calls "a *de*nationalization of the artist who comes within its magnetic field, . . . [causing] an obliteration of ethnic differences" and a rejection of nationalisms and regionalisms, since "the surrealist's concern and subject was the condition of man, his reception of the data of his senses, in the face of the colossal enigma of his ageless, non-historical identity." Reading Breton, however, Burk was inspired by the ideas that surrealism creates art and a political agenda, and that the liberation of the human spirit and the liberation of people from oppression could be the soul and cause of poetry—themes that Breton explored in a revolutionary way. Breton, for his part, was known to be attracted to and affirming of the indigenous voices in countries such as the United States and Mexico. According to Balakian, Breton

> was drawn to writers who like himself achieved a mystical intimacy with nature, who were easily aroused to wonder by simple manifestations of the dynamism of the physical world, who gave love and sensuality a high place in their existence, and who had been able to deliver themselves from the self-torture of an inherited code of sins, who loved the immediacy of life and in the name of liberty were not afraid to use the pen as others used the sword.

There are some completions of cycles evident in Burk's life and work, and certainly consistencies with respect to his social and political analyses and his racial/ethnic, class, and gay consciousness. In "Ronnie Burk Dancing: 25 April 1994," Burk writes of the time he protested the Vietnam War in 1972, citing a litany of charges against Nixon: "1950's G-man for JUAC, persecutor of free thought, advocate of drug-war hysteria, author of the notorious Hate List." He remembers yelling at Nixon that he would dance on his grave, and asks, on the day of Nixon's death, "Would anyone care to join me?" Burk has kept his activist stance, serving as commentator on events such as the Persian Gulf War, through protests and through poems such as "Día de los Muertos 1990" and "Millenial Missive." In the latter poem, the poet bears witness to a "disposable world we inhabit a jewel encrusted island mandala / set upon a seething ocean of misery," while at the same time he foresees "a golden age" that "cries out to be born / An age of wisdom, generosity, loving kindness, and compassion / Not this catastrophe to lay low all illusion."

*Cover for a 1999 collection of Burk's collages*

In 1994 Burk wrote "Farewell Texas Poem," which he designates "(after di Prima)"; the poem takes as its model di Prima's "Take Off, Flight 347" (from her collection *Pieces of a Song: Selected Poems,* 1990). By acknowledging her (his first major influence) and his roots in Texas, Burk comes full circle and brings to bear upon the Texas landscape the benefit of his learning over the years since he was a child who thought of himself in prison:

> Man-of-war filled beaches sticky
> with black gold, teach me
> to sing! grackles in the treetops
> of Matagorda St.
> saffron prayer flag from Tsurphu
> turning in March wind may your
> blessings fall on this harsh
> inhospitable land, turn old
> hardened sorrows of regret & dismay
> into spontaneous joy of each
> new beginning. . . .

Growing up Chicano and gay in South Texas taught Burk early on that moving back and forth among many worlds gave him a sense of options, of possibilities. Coming into an internationalist viewpoint about the need for a world socialist economy is not incompatible with his first awareness of the inequities of Chicano life in Texas. Also, he knows now that if the Texas land is harsh and inhospitable, it is because the land has been besieged and crudely, violently exploited. In asking the "Man-of-war filled beaches sticky / with black gold" for lessons in song, the poet finds forgiveness, and unites what has come to be sustenance for his spirit, the "saffron prayer flag from Tsurphu," with the inherent spirit rhythms of the homeland of his birth.

While many Chicanos have downplayed or denied any indigenous connection to Mexico, other than perhaps acknowledging it as a distant (often mystical) component to contemporary *mestizaje* (mixture), Burk has welcomed it and brought it into the forefront. In one of his essays, "Que Viva Mexico" (Long Live Mexico, a title recalling the Russian filmmaker Sergei Eisenstein's unfinished epic of the same name), Burk discusses the subject of the 1994 armed uprising of the Mayan people in Chiapas against the Mexican government. He predicts, "The conditions exist in Mexico for a true workers' state to emerge out of the ongoing crisis. At the end of this mad century of revolutions, Mexico might very well show the world how it's done." For Burk, the face of the Mexican revolution continues to be an indigenous one, affirming once again his early definitions of "Mexican." He also finds correspondences between Native peoples throughout the Americas and internationally, given his affinity with the Tibetans. There are times when the place where he locates himself interlocutes with another, as in "Poem," which he writes from Maui: "I was eating a mango under the banyan tree and had to blink / my eyes to make sure I was not dreaming Coyoacan mercado."

Burk's work has been basically ignored by literary critics. Having been published mostly in avant-garde magazines, he is known, in his words, "in a peripheral underground cliqueish group of initiated readers." He is in distinguished company, and the "group" is not so small, given the circles in which he has moved and continues to move. Burk's inclusion in *The Stiffest of the Corpse*, in particular his collages, and his publications in avenues such as *City Lights Review* and *Calibán*, establish him as a member of a critical mass of provocative contemporary intellectuals who chronicle the outrage, the sorrows, and the hope of an age that is ending, calling forth with their works a new time of transformation.

After living in Hawaii, where he worked with the Buddhist center and supported the Hawaiian sovereign rights movement, Burk moved to San Francisco. He has gathered his most recent work, as well as previously published poems, in an as-yet-unpublished collection titled "Inventory." While his new work is derivative of Breton and Lamantia, he is exploring, with his own voice and language, in poems obsessed with fire, burning, flames, explosions, and stars, a search for new life out of destruction. He continues to elaborate his own Mexicanness in his work, at the same time exploring critically the interrelatedness of new associations and new territories that bear upon definitions of self, of Mexico, and the world.

# Daniel Cano

*(1 August 1947 – )*

Nuria Bustamante
*Los Angeles Harbor College*

BOOKS: *Pepe Rios* (Houston: Arte Público, 1991);
*Shifting Loyalties* (Houston: Arte Público, 1995).

With his 1991 novel *Pepe Rios* Daniel Cano has contributed to and further expanded the narrative of the Mexican immigrant experience established by José Antonio Villarreal in 1959 with the novel *Pocho*. In *Pepe Rios* Cano gives voice to the ordeals and tribulations undergone not only by the hundreds of Mexican immigrants who came to the United States at the time of the 1910 Mexican Revolution but also by the thousands who have subsequently left their Mexican homeland under difficult circumstances in hopes of improving their lot. Thus, the saga of the struggles of young Pepe Rios before and after his immigration to the United States may be a mirror to some readers, an inspiration to others, and an entertaining book of history and adventure to most. In his second and most recent book, *Shifting Loyalties* (1995), Cano explores a subject of which few Chicano authors have written: the Chicano community and the Vietnam War.

Born in Santa Monica, California, on 1 August 1947, Daniel Raymond Cano was the first of five children of Raymond Cano, a construction worker, and Esther Gonzalez Cano. Although his mother was the only woman of her generation in the neighborhood to receive an associate of arts degree from a community college, Daniel Cano disliked studying and confesses that in his early adolescent years the only things he liked about school were baseball, lunch, and recess. Despite this disinterest, he said in an unpublished 13 June 1995 interview, "I always wanted to write and always wrote stories, poems and song lyrics. . . . always writing something, but I didn't have the skills."

Cano graduated from high school in 1965. The following year he enlisted in the army and went to Vietnam. When he returned at the age of twenty-one, he enrolled in Santa Monica College, but he lacked interest and dropped out shortly afterward.

Coming from a family of storytellers, Cano listened especially to the fascinating tales that his grandfa-

*Daniel Cano (courtesy of Cano)*

ther Maximiano Cano, following a Latino custom, told at weddings, funerals, and family reunions. Later, Cano felt the need to bridge the gaps between the many fragments of stories he remembered from his grandfather's repertory. He realized, however, that he had neither the vocabulary nor the skills to do it. Thus, more highly motivated than before, in 1973 he re-enrolled in Santa Monica College and stayed until he completed a master's degree in English in 1985.

Pepe Rios P. 148 draft

Pepe had been about 8 years old. His father told him not to pick the mangoes that
grew ~~of~~ *from* the branches that ~~grew~~ *reached* out over the fast moving river. But Pepe could not
help himself. The beautiful mango hung innocently on the forbidden branch. Miranda,
climbing in ~~one of the other~~ *a* tree**s** downstream, saw Pepe and hollered for him to be
careful. Pepe straddled the branch and inched his way to the mango. He reached ~~with~~ *and*
*brushed the mango with his fingertips.*
~~his arm but could not grab the mango.~~ He reached again but ~~this time didn't even touch~~ *could not grab*
the fruit. ~~Somehow his~~ *his* legs slipped and he fell ~~out of~~ *from* the tree. He latched onto a
clump of branches, but they were not strong enough to support him. Pepe ~~refused to~~ *did not* scream
fearing ~~he'd get~~ *his father would* punish**ed** *him* for his disobediance. The branches broke, and ~~Pepe~~ *he* fell into
the swift current.
~~Frankly,~~ *Out of desperation,*
He tried to scream, ~~but~~ *each* time he opened his mouth a rush of water entered. He tried
to swim but the current was too strong. ~~He finally~~ *finally, he* reached a spot where the river slowed,
~~done. Pepe feet reached for~~ *Pepe stretched his legs to grip* the sand below, but ~~he~~ felt nothing except rock as slick
as wet marble. He could not walk, and he was too tired to swim. He looked over his shoulder
and saw ~~that~~ more *rocks and jagged rocks. Exhausted, he gave up.* ~~rapids awaited him, and large boulders protruded from the river. He could~~
~~do nothing so~~ He let himself go limp, and ~~allowed~~ *whisked* the water ~~to take~~ him away, ~~and smash~~
~~his body against the rocks downstream. Suddenly, as if he'd been plucked from the devil's~~
~~grasp, He~~ felt himself being pulled from the river by his hair. Pepe lifted his eyes
upwards and ~~caught a glimpse of~~ *saw* Miranda's face.

Miranda had looked over at the mango tree where Pepe had been *climbing.* Not seeing his little
brother in the tree and knowing he'd been there a second ago, Miranda ~~panicked and~~
quickly began searching the river. He saw Pepe bobbing in and out of the water. Miranda
ran downstream ~~and~~ *and* crawled out on ~~the~~ ~~branch o~~ *the* low hanging branch of a sycamore tree.
Luckily the current slowed where Miranda waited. He reached down, grabbed his brother
by the hair and yanked him from the swirling torrent.

It was one of the only times Miranda had allowed a younger brother to cry. Miranda
hugged Pepe tightly. Both boys shivered  not from the cold but from fright.

"Tonto! Tonto!" Miranda kept saying to Pepe, as he kissed his little brother all over
the face. Miranda never told anybody what had happened that day.

164

*Page from the revised typescript for* Pepe Rios *(Collection of Daniel Cano)*

In college he was introduced to great literature, especially novels. John Steinbeck's *Tortilla Flat* (1935) opened new perspectives because it was the first time Cano read something with a Latino protagonist. He also read Villarreal's *Pocho,* and *Macho!* (1973) by Victor Villaseñor, but he could not find many books in American literature with Latinos as main characters. Nevertheless, these readings reawakened Cano's memories of the family tales, and his decision to become a writer took shape. He wanted to tell his stories from the Chicano point of view. To that end he practiced by imitating the styles of the writers he most admired: Steinbeck, Ernest Hemingway, and Hermann Hesse.

A single parent with joint custody of his three children, Diane, Danny, and Reina, Cano worked as a gardener, a custodian, a truck driver, and later as an administrator at the University of California at Los Angeles, the University of California at Davis, and California State University at Dominguez Hills. He also taught English at Santa Monica College for nine years before becoming dean of admissions.

About his motivation for writing *Pepe Rios,* Cano said in the 1995 interview: "I wanted to dedicate the book to my grandparents and to all the grandparents who came to the U.S. at the time of the 1910 Mexican Revolution. They got very little thanks for all they did. They worked hard and suffered a lot. For me, it was like trying to understand what our grandparents went through in those days. It's still going on." The novel is based on Cano's grandfather's life before and during the Mexican Revolution. "I wanted to portray the Mexican Revolution the way a Chicano sees it," Cano explained, "and to create a reader for Chicanos who wanted to know about the Mexican Revolution but don't want to read history books. A book that would educate and entertain at the same time."

To familiarize himself with the area in which the events in his ancestors' lives took place, Cano traveled to Juchipila, a small town in the state of Zacatecas. "I stayed there doing my research because I wanted to get the feel of the land, the atmosphere, and the landscape; to observe life on the ranch so as to describe it accurately," Cano said in 1995. From Juchipila he went to Mexico City to visit his aunt, Francisca Meireles, the oldest living family member, who recalled many stories about Maximiano Cano. Cano transformed his grandfather into the title character. "I like the name Pepe Rios because of *ríos* [rivers] like running waters that don't stop but keep moving," Cano said in 1995. Because of Cano's jobs and family responsibilities, the book took him seven years to write.

According to Cano, the narrative is about 30 percent biographical and 70 percent fiction. "The politics are accurate," Cano said. "I had to do a lot of research and learn about the complex history of the revolution. I went by the different battles and characters, and by the different generals in command at the time. The description of the last battle, for instance, is very accurate."

The story is told by an omniscient narrator; the plot is fast paced, uncomplicated, and full of action. "I just wanted to tell a story, to create something that even a fifteen-year old would pick up and not want to put down." Cano has created a strong protagonist whose appeal lies in a combination of admirable traits: keen intelligence, integrity, high moral principles, courage, ambition, and the daring of youth.

As the novel opens, seventeen-year-old Pepe Rios initially is leading a placid existence on his parents' hacienda with his eight brothers and sisters. Pepe decides to leave the ranch when his mother, Susana, marries the suspected killer of Pepe's father, Toribio. He joins the revolutionary forces against the regime of the dictator Porfirio Díaz. At the end of the novel Pepe is full of personal grief and no longer cares about the outcome of the revolution. Leaving his native country behind in political turmoil, he crosses the Rio Grande and enters the United States at El Paso, Texas.

Other than a few details about Pepe's appearance—his height and his hair color—Cano does not present a clear picture of his protagonist's physical features. His thoughts, feelings, actions, and reactions are portrayed so vividly, however, that Pepe looms larger than life. An example is the passage in which Pepe is first introduced:

Someday he would go. He would wander through the world tasting his dreams and touching his thoughts. A sadness came over him. He loved this ranch, the mountains and the people. And there lay his contradictions. How could he ever leave the land and family that were a part of him? Were dreams stronger than blood? Generations of Ríos had given their dreams to his land. Their ghosts had made permanent homes in the depths of his heart. Would the ghosts hold or release him? Was the longing in his heart so great that he would go against all tradition?

The physical descriptions of the other significant characters such as Isabel, Pepe's girlfriend; El Estudiante (The Student), a rebel leader; and Perico, the overseer of the hacienda, are also neglected. This lack of detail contrasts with the often elaborate descriptions of attire, actions, settings, and landscapes:

Dark, grey clouds crept over the mountains swallowing the last patches of blue sky. In the distance a thin screen of fog fell and touched the earth. The pointed leaves of the manzanita and mesquite bushes fluttered as the rain released a warm breeze. The rugged needle leaves of

*Cover for Cano's 1995 collection of interrelated stories about Chicano soldiers in World War II and Vietnam*

the cactus and the long armed maguey, like solitary centurions, stood rigid against the mountain side.

At the foot of the tallest mountain in the range sat the home of the Ríos family. On one side of the adobe house a long rolling plateau stretched to the base of the mountain. To the opposite side tiny leaves of corn sprouted on a large parcel of land. When the stocks grew sturdy, the beans would be planted, and the vines would climb, clinging to the thick, green stocks.

Throughout *Pepe Rios* the reader has the sensation of viewing an accelerated motion picture in which one animated scene rapidly follows another. This effect is achieved by Cano's use of short descriptive sentences that capture light and shadow, movement and passion. For example, he economically renders the action on a battlefield:

Pepe screamed as if he'd been shot. He stumbled towards the river bank and collapsed to the earth. The rifle flew out of his hands and struck another man on the side of the head. One man was shot through the neck. The body of the dead rebel splashed into the

water and floated downstream. The others rushed to get out of the water. El Estudiante led the crawl up the bank. Once the men reached the top of the embankment, they began firing at the federal outpost. The night turned into a blizzard of screaming rifles and loud explosions.

*Pepe Rios* has not received a great deal of critical attention. The few reviews have, however, been enthusiastic.

Cano intended *Pepe Rios* as the first part of a trilogy. While taking a respite from work on the second volume he was encouraged by his friend Ernesto Padilla, editor of the Lalo Press, to put together some stories he had written about the Vietnam War for publication in chapbook form. A six-month project turned into a three-year obsession, and the work became too large for the Lalo Press. Cano sent the manuscript to Nicolás Kanellos, editor of the Arte Público Press, which published it in 1995 as *Shifting Loyalties*, which is a collection of interrelated stories. Cano had begun writing some of these stories as early as 1974. He had watched on television as the last helicopter to leave the U.S. embassy in Saigon carried the last American soldiers out of Vietnam. "We had lost the war. It was a very emotional moment for me," Cano said. "I felt betrayed, lied to. What a waste of lives and effort!" Because of his emotional involvement in the war, and because most of the material in *Shifting Loyalties* is autobiographical, it was, as he said in an unpublished 9 October 1997 interview, "a very difficult book to write." Altogether, it took him nearly twenty-one years to complete it.

*Shifting Loyalties* consists of nineteen stories depicting the dreams, disillusions, hopes, fears, and despair of a group of young Chicano soldiers in the Vietnam War. For many of them, the decision to enlist was inspired by the heroic and somewhat exaggerated war sagas their fathers, mostly World War II veterans, recounted during family gatherings. As children, these Chicanos had heard their elders glorify their war experiences and tell how "they were there to do a job, do their duty, do the things men do." The uncle of one of the soldiers, bragging about the Bronze Star he "should have received on D-Day," said: "Yup, I guess war was exciting. Never did much before the Army took me. Home wasn't ever the same after that!"

More than a dozen main characters appear in the work, but none of them dominates the action or occupies center stage for long. Yet, the characters are memorable. Charley Yáñez, while on guard duty, fatally shoots his best friend, Beto, and has to be restrained from taking his own life. Joey Serrano is approached by a Vietnamese girl who hands him a beer laced with drain cleaner; he dies from internal bleeding. Danny

Rios stands night watch and sees one helicopter after another unload its dismal cargo, the bodies of dead American soldiers, so many that they have to be stacked in a pyramid. Rudy Medrano, the outstanding pointman who refused to take off his wide-brimmed sombrero, is mangled and killed by a mine. Jesse Peña is a radio technician whose sudden disappearance leaves behind a trail of stories and speculations: is he dead, or has he joined the enemy? Their pain and the precariousness of their existence stay with the reader long after the book is put down.

David Almas, a character who is present in most of the stories, serves as the narrator, who remembers the war twenty years after it ended. The narrative moves backward and forward in time, covering a thirty-year period. It begins in the 1990s in a quiet Santa Monica residence, where David is writing a letter and recalling the events. The setting shifts to the school playground where some of the characters played as children, moves to the jungles of Vietnam, goes back to the Los Angeles suburbs and highlights the gatherings of the storytelling World War II veterans, and ends with David visiting a friend's grave in Pennsylvania—the friend whose death motivated David to communicate with the friend's parents by writing the letter that initiates the collection.

Throughout the apparently haphazard organization of the various episodes there are several common threads that link the stories. These threads include the characters, the settings (the Los Angeles suburbs and the jungles of Vietnam), and the themes of duty, pride, and loyalty. The concept of loyalty is probed at several levels: loyalty to country; to family, especially to one's father; to community and cultural values; and even to friends.

Cano's ability to engage the reader's senses enables him to create tense prose packed with sharp images. Once again, he vividly depicts battlefield scenes:

> he remembered one night when the wind had whipped the jungle and a trip flare had ignited . . . a shrill, piercing sizzle, lighting up the thick foliage. A shadow had darted across the perimeter. Grenades pounded the jungle and machine guns chattered. The howitzers exploded, shooting bright flares into the sky. The firing stopped as the flares burned brilliant, descending, oscillating beneath white parachutes. Seconds later the darkness had returned and the world, again, rumbled.

Drawing on his war experiences and his ability to conjure powerful, realistic images, Cano has created an eloquent portrayal of the frequently overlooked presence of the Chicano community in the Vietnam War.

**References:**

Juan R. Palomo, "A Colorful Story About Coming of Age and War," *Houston Post,* 10 March 1991, p. C4;

Rich Seeley, "SMC Teacher Writer Brings Characters to Life Again," *Daily Breeze,* 18 July 1993, pp. B1, B3.

# Norma Elia Cantú

*(3 January 1947 – )*

Ellen McCracken
*University of California, Santa Barbara*

BOOK: *Canícula: Snapshots of a Girlhood en la Frontera* (Albuquerque: University of New Mexico Press, 1995).

OTHER: "Se me enchina el cuerpo al oír tu cuento," in *New Chicano/a Literature,* edited by Charles M. Tatum (Tucson: University of Arizona Press, 1992), pp. 101–102;
"Decolonizing the Mind" and "Trojan Horse," in *Floricanto Sí: A Collection of U.S. Latina Poetry,* edited by Bryce Milligan, Mary Guerrero Milligan, and Angela de Hoyos (New York: Penguin, 1998), pp. 44–47.

SELECTED PERIODICAL PUBLICATIONS–UNCOLLECTED: "Untitled," *Huehuetitlan,* no. 2 (November 1982): 4;
"Unemployed," *Huehuetitlan,* nos. 3–4 (February 1984): 2;
"Action, Thought, Spirit" and *Canícula* chapters 42–44, *Prairie Schooner,* 68 (Winter 1994): 163–169;
"Nebraska Family: A Triptych," *Nebraska Humanist* (Spring 1995);
"Bailando y Cantando," "Las Diosas," and "Fiestas de Diciembre," *Blue Mesa Review,* no. 9 (1997): 53–54, 71–75;
"El luto," *Ventana Abierta,* 1 (Spring 1998): 46–51;
"Farewell in Madrid," in *Proyecto Sherezade* [on-line journal] (June 1999).

The refreshing variety that characterizes the creative and scholarly writing of Norma Elia Cantú stems from her intimate connection to a crucial series of literal and figurative borders. Born on 3 January 1947 in the border community of Nuevo Laredo, Mexico, she moved with her family across the river to Laredo, Texas, shortly thereafter. The rich culture of the U.S./Mexican border region strongly underlies Cantú's creative and scholarly work, which itself crosses many figurative borders between genres, prescribed conventions, and subject matter. Her identity as a writer pivots on

*Norma Elia Cantú (photograph by Michael Short)*

the border hybridism so central to the age of postmodernism in the late twentieth century.

Cantú, the oldest of eleven children of Virginia Ramón Becerra and Florentino Cantú Vargas, was the beneficiary of the rich heritage of her ancestors' long presence on both sides of the border. Even though her maternal grandfather was born in Texas, he and his family were repatriated to Mexico in 1935 after he quit his job with the railroads in protest against the way in which the company treated Mexicans. Cantú's mother, who was born in Corpus Christi in 1925 and repatriated with the rest of the family, had a difficult time adjusting to the new school, where she was expected to read and write in Spanish. In 1945 she married Cantú

Vargas, who was born in Allende, Coahuila, and raised in Nuevo Laredo and Anahuac, Nuevo Leon. Opposed to the marriage, his father finally gave approval on the condition that the couple stay in Mexico to work on the family ranch. Although Cantú's mother wanted her to be born on the American side, the child was one year old before the family was able to settle in Laredo.

Cantú experimented with writing poetry as early as the age of seven, while she was a student at Saunders Elementary School; she remembers her teacher, Mrs. Treviño, acknowledging her youthful intelligence. One of the few stories she wrote as a child won an honorable mention in a television contest when she was eight or nine. Since the age of thirteen she has kept a journal in which she writes poems, ideas, stories, even science fiction. But apart from publishing a few pieces in high school and junior college newspapers in the early 1960s and winning a prize for a poem about nature when she was sixteen, she was reluctant for her writing to enter the public sphere. In an unpublished 17 February 1999 interview she noted, "To me, writing is like eating or breathing; it's not something for other people; I do it for myself, to nourish me." She notes that her book, *Canícula: Snapshots of a Girlhood en la Frontera* (1995), represents a coming of age for her as a writer as she reveals personal details about her life and includes private family photographs.

Against her high-school counselor's advice, Cantú applied for and won a one-year Rotary Club tuition scholarship for a community college. Despite the financial assistance, attending college was a hardship; she held a part-time job and sometimes had to walk five miles home from school instead of taking the bus. After a year and a half she left college and took a full-time job at Central Power and Light Company, where she was a clerk for seven years, supporting her parents and siblings.

Later, after resuming her studies, she earned a B.S. in education, English, and political science from Texas A&I University–Laredo in 1973 and a master's degree in English from Texas A&I University–Kingsville in 1976. Cantú remembers reading the literary review *El Grito: A Journal of Contemporary Mexican-American Thought* in the college library and being moved to tears by Isabel Flores's "I Remember" (September 1973), a poem about a family picking crops. In this poet's honor, the first piece in *Canícula,* titled "Las Piscas" (Cotton Picking), is devoted to the grueling labor of farmworkers. Other of Cantú's works that discuss similar issues are the 1982 story "Se me enchina el cuerpo al oír tu cuento" (I Get Goosebumps When I Hear Your Story), which points to a way out of the dehumanizing conditions of migrant workers, and the 1984 poem "Unemployed," which captures the despera-

tion of a man and his family in the parallel growing darkness of an evening and a period of unemployment. Another literary influence on Cantú during the Chicano movement was the Flor y Canto Festival in Corpus Christi that she attended in 1978; the readings of Inés Hernández Tovar and Lorna Dee Cervantes at the festival particularly impressed her.

In 1980 Cantú became a professor at what is now Texas A&M International University in Laredo, where she continued her scholarly and creative writing along with teaching, administrative duties, and community service. She earned a Ph.D. in English from the University of Nebraska in 1982. Politics is an essential part of Cantú's life and, as she describes in *Canícula,* something she and her family lived as she was growing up. In the 1960s she participated in *Raza Unida* (United People) party activities such as voter registration and in the early 1970s worked in a group called Action League of Laredo for the election of Sissy Farenthold as governor. She helped to found a women's political action group in 1982 that established an adult literacy program. From 1993 to 1995 she worked as a senior arts specialist for the National Endowment for the Arts in Washington, D.C., which awarded grants to communities and traditional-arts organizations.

Cantú's varied writing displays a creative conjoining of cultural criticism and literary creativity that erodes the standard borders between genres. In her 1983 doctoral dissertation she studies the tradition of the *pastorela,* or shepherd's play, focusing on a version that has been performed each Christmas for many years in Laredo. A second scholarly study to be published by Texas A&M University Press, "Soldiers of the Cross: Los Matachines de la Santa Cruz," examines the popular tradition of the *Matachines,* the dancers in Indian dress who venerate the Holy Cross in Laredo during religious festivals on 3 May, 12 December, and Christmas Eve. Her essay "La Quinceañera: Towards an Ethnographic Analysis of a Life-Cycle Ritual," part of a book project on traditional celebrations in Laredo, examines the tradition of the *quinceañera* celebration, the rite of passage ceremony for fifteen-year-old girls, as a communal and individual performance with religious and social elements. In all of these scholarly works, Cantú includes her own experiences of these cultural rituals in her scholarly analysis. In her study of the *quinceañera,* for example, she describes, with both insiders and outsiders in mind, her own *quinceañera* Mass years earlier: "The aisle seemed interminable, my knees were shaking and I was trying not to hobble, for that day I wore high heels for the first time. After Mass, we went home to hot chocolate and *repostería,* a kind of pastry that is traditional for the Christmas season, which in Mexican tradition extends until February 2,

*Dust jacket for Cantú's fictionalized autobiography*

the Feast of Candlemas, or *el día de la Candelaria*." She is both author and subject in these ethnographic studies, one of the local informants whose experience openly shapes the scholarly narrative she writes.

In August 1993 the author Ana Castillo lent Cantú her house in Albuquerque so that Cantú could concentrate on finishing her study of the *Matachines*. As Cantú worked on the scholarly study, however, she found that various personal stories emerged, and she decided instead to focus on writing these. Later, after giving them an order and a narrative frame based on the motif of photographs randomly selected from a storage box, Cantú published her first major work of creative writing, *Canícula,* which joins the tendencies of her scholarly and poetic writing in an experimental, partially fictional, ethnographic account of her own life and family traditions. Transcending standard generic classifications, this collage of eighty-five vignettes and twenty-three interspersed photos is a hybrid of the visual and verbal, fiction and autobiography, the novel and the short story, and ethnography and creative writing. Cantú settles on the neologism "fictional autobioethnography" to classify the book, a creative new genre

that merges this fictional and veridical account of the self and community.

Two creative autobiographical works by contemporary women, Rita Mae Brown's *Six of One* (1978) and Maxine Hong Kingston's *Woman Warrior: Memoirs of a Girlhood Among Ghosts* (1976), inspired Cantú to attempt to write an experimental narrative about her life on the Texas/Mexican border. Cantú tells her own story from the late 1940s to the mid 1960s in the "land in between," the single geographic unit now known as the border area around the cities of Laredo and Nuevo Laredo, depicted in the hand-drawn map that opens the book. Inextricably connected to the lives of her family and community, this self-narration recounts the daily life, work, traditions, fiestas, and history of her family, friends, and the larger Mexicano population of the borderlands. Using the real names of those who have died and fictional names for those still living (the names of eight flowers stand in for the eight girls in her family), Cantú describes the everyday and the extraordinary—from the repaying of *mandas* (promises) at the Santo Niño de Atocha church in Nuevo Laredo to the death of her brother Tino in Vietnam. The disturbing memories of repatriation, the poll tax, and picking cotton under the hot summer sun join the pleasant remembrances of performing *declamaciones* (recitations) on special occasions, watching Hopalong Cassidy on television, memorable outings, and fiestas.

Celebrating the epistemological questioning common in postmodernist experimentation in the late twentieth century, *Canícula* intentionally blurs the border between fact and fiction from the beginning. Undermining the reader's expectation of "truth" in autobiography, the text is open fabrication from its first sentence, as Cantú situates the book as the second part of a nonexistent trilogy she pretends to have written. In a disquieting paradoxical statement, she notes: "In *Canícula* the story is told through the photographs, and so what may appear to be autobiographical is not always so." The authorial "I" asks readers to question the presumed truth value of both photographs and first-person accounts; just as viewers may incorrectly interpret photographs as truthful representations of one's past life, so too must readers be wary of that other representational strategy in the book, verbal autobiography, which readers might falsely trust as completely truthful.

The book challenges readers to discern what the French theorist Roland Barthes has termed "the photographic paradox" at work in the pictures Cantú carefully integrates into the text. Despite the ostensible documentary level of photographs, Barthes notes, several hardly visible techniques add the highly subjective code of connotation to the denotative level. To emphasize this subjectivity, Cantú sometimes deliberately mismatches photographs and narratives, reverses a photograph, or omits, retouches, or lies about them. She reverses one family photograph, for example, to emphasize her sense of standing apart from and outside of the family unit at that time. She forges her fictional name (one of the eight flowers), "Azucena Cantú," on retouched immigration and citizenship documents in order to call into question facile markers of identity and to deconstruct the veridical aura of documents and photographs. And the avowed photographic impetus of the book turns out also to be a lie, since Cantú first wrote the stories and then later decided upon the motif of photographs randomly selected from a box as the frame to hold the stories together.

Cantú's insistence on the continuum between fiction and reality that is so often celebrated by postmodernist writers is one of several levels of hybridism in the book involving linguistic, religious, cultural, generic, disciplinary, and geographic border-crossing. In an unpublished essay, "How I Wrote *Canícula*: Musings on Writing, Reading and Life," Cantú summarizes her own intriguing hybrid identity as a literary critic, an ethnographer, and a creative writer with respect to the book: "All in all, the critic had to write *Canícula,* and the novelist had to be the soul for the mind. . . . How can someone who does all these things: write literary criticism, folklore, ethnography and fiction—separate these into neat little boxes labeled and set aside?" Her 1997 poem "Fiestas de Diciembre" similarly mixes ethnography and creative writing in a poetic space, focusing on the hybridism of the "border navidad all our own."

In earlier creative writing, Cantú merged disciplinary concerns more subtly by developing an ethnographic overlay in fiction. Because a cousin on her father's side of the family had settled in Omaha, Nebraska, years earlier, Cantú's father allowed her to leave home to attend graduate school there, assured that his relatives would watch over her. Based on that experience, she wrote "Nebraska Family: A Triptych" (1995), which implicitly patterns itself on the visual model of a three-paneled painting. It recounts three tales of life in Nebraska, focusing on a daughter who is just turning fifteen, her mother, and her grandmother. Cantú views the three women as versions of a single story and through the triptych form presents three key feasts—Thanksgiving, a *quinceañera,* and a wedding—that represent, respectively, a secular American celebration, a tradition that emphasizes Mexican roots, and an official church ceremony marking the union of an Anglo and a Mexican. Through this narrative, Cantú notes, she came to know her "other" family.

Revisionist readings of historical women and goddesses underlie several of her poems. In "Trojan Horse" (1998) the speaker imagines herself as the active rescuer of others and as one who changes the world and "bears the power of triumphant entry." Beyond beauty and betrayal, she is neither the figure of Helen of Sparta nor Malinche (mistress and guide of Hernán Cortés), but the bearer of a gift that may or may not last forever. She invites the reader to "take my skeletal hand, / look into the eyes of night, / Come into the blinding light / Storm the fortress, / rescue those who need rescuing / offer the proper offerings." The social message of the poem works as a countermodel to traditional images of both ideal and negative femininity, suggesting that women's power is connected to helping those in need with the gift of oneself.

In the 1994 poem "Action, Thought, Spirit" Cantú argues that Santa Teresa is to be celebrated not only for her mysticism but also for her action; contemporary women, whether working with "test-tubes or computers," should imitate either Teresa's commitment to action or the warrior goddess Coyoxaquhui, who led the attack against Coatlicue in Aztec mythology. Cantú focuses on the practical side of Teresa, who perhaps "was a woman just trying to get things done" as she traveled throughout Spain to various sacred sites. St.

purposes of acctg, she wld average it all out
and so it was between $25-30 that she
claimed in the books. When ppl wntd to pay c/
or cards she upped it $5⁰⁰ and w/ checks $10.
No one seemed to mind & no one had ever complained
until one day Cuca, la secretaria del Dr. Saliz
insisted on a receipt & when Diamond charged her
$20 for a cut, perm & tint she became enraged.
Claimed I was stealing & overcharging. Even after
I explaind that she was getting 3 $40 jobs she
wouldn't be placated. Accusing I of overcharging
her most loyal customers she stormed out. After
writing a ch that I knew wld bounce — ah well, she
thought alcabo q todos se paga. And went on to her
next customer, wondred wtt was going on for she never
pd more than $20 no matter wht. $10 for cuts or trim
and $10 for perm or tint — she'd pd that years ago
on her 1st visit when she came for a
quick cut & at one late Sat evening. She knew
Cuca well Cuca's children had been her students at
Martin High & Dr. I. had taught chemistry for over 40 years &
now she was retired and came in regularly. Every
Sat for her set & once a mo. for color & every 3 mos
for a perm. Her reddish brown coif framed
paper thin skin wrinkled over bright blue eyes & brows
a mo she drew on every morning. She joked
w/ her friends at the Retired Teachers' meetings
once a mo how even her face was fading.

*Page from the manuscript for the unpublished "Hair Matters," a novel told in short short stories (Collection of Norma Elia Cantú)*

John of the Cross, Cantú suggests, could have learned a lesson from Teresa, as should young women today. The 1997 "Las Diosas" (The Goddesses), written entirely in Spanish, functions as a modified litany to deities such as Tonantzin, Coatlicue, Shiva, Gaia, and the Virgin Mary; instead of the usual repeated supplications of the litany, Cantú's poem chants affirmative statements about an alternate pantheon of female goddesses who suffer with women today, crying for their daughters who suffer on earth.

In the 1998 short story "El luto" (Mourning) Cantú divides the narrative into a Spanish and an English section to represent the separate worlds of a mother and daughter. Offering an updated version of the Biblical narrative about Ruth, "El luto" suggests that the contemporary Ruth will engage in filial piety while at the same time breaking with traditional expectations for women in Mexican culture. Unwilling to follow the prescribed mourning rituals after the death of her father, who had deserted her and her mother and plunged them into greater poverty, Ruth nonetheless continues to live at home and care for her mother while her sisters pursue exciting careers elsewhere. As wide a gap exists between mother and daughter culturally as between the Spanish and English sections of the story, but Ruth's sensible rejection of public mourning for the father who was not a father suggests that she successfully negotiates the tradition of the Biblical Ruth's goodness and her own contemporary need for identity and autonomy.

Cantú's story "Farewell in Madrid" was published in June 1999 on the Internet as part of *Proyecto Sherezade,* an on-line journal edited by Enrique Fernández and devoted to stories in Spanish from all over the world. "Farewell in Madrid" deploys the central motif of equivalencies–linguistic and generational–to work through a woman's pain as loved ones pass in and out of her life. The technique of the crossword puzzle, whereby one set of signifiers is substituted for an equivalent set, frames the story: the title, "Farewell in Madrid," is the clue seeking the answer "adios," while the ending word, "father," is the answer not only for the crossword query but for the larger question that the story as a whole subtly poses. The narrative about the imminent departure of the protagonist's son for college is superimposed on the memory of her own painful separation from a lover in Spain a generation earlier; the revelation of an equivalent for the lover's identity at the end is the answer to the story as a metaphorical crossword puzzle. Cantú deliberately includes ambiguity so that the reader must move sometimes confusingly back and forth between signifiers that highlight the homologous structure and the overlay of the two key moments in the protagonist's life. Just as the six-letter word "father" substitutes by fitting exactly in the crossword puzzle space, so does the story substitute for the mother's telling her son about her private memories of her time with his father.

Cantú's creative writing has been anthologized in several collections of poetry and short stories, and *Canícula,* winner of the 1996 Premio Aztlán Literary Prize (established by Rudolfo and Patricia Anaya), has been reviewed in *The New York Times, The Washington Post, Southwestern American Literature, Voices of Mexico,* and *Ventana Abierta* (Open Window). Cantú's innovative scholarly and creative writing–two parts of a continuum–provide seminal information about Chicano identity, the border, hybridism, and postmodernism at the close of the twentieth century and point enticingly to new directions for the next century.

# Rafael C. Castillo

*(30 December 1950 – )*

Jesús Rosales
*Texas A & M University–Corpus Christi*

BOOK: *Distant Journeys* (Tempe, Ariz.: Bilingual Press/ Editorial Bilingüe, 1991).

SELECTED PERIODICAL PUBLICATIONS– UNCOLLECTED: "A Variation on a Dostoevski Theme," *Arizona Canto al Pueblo* (Summer 1980): 44–47;

"The Old Man's Revenge," *Arizona Quarterly* (Summer 1984): 142–146;

"Interview with Ricardo Sánchez," *Imagine: International Journal* (January 1985): 22–33;

"The Battle of the Alamo," *Southwestern American Literature* (Fall 1992): 51–57;

"The Penitent of Guadalupe Street," *New Growth 2 Contemporary Texas Writers* (Fall 1993): 17–28.

*Rafael C. Castillo (courtesy of Castillo)*

Rafael C. Castillo's narrative provides many exciting possibilities for the new generations of Chicano short-story writers interested in craft and the expansion of Chicano themes. Blended with subtle humor, parody, and challenging philosophical concepts (or "games" as Castillo calls them), his short stories explore the inner selves of men and women in an effort to better understand their human complexities. Castillo's work, in particular *Distant Journeys* (1991), is indicative of the desire of a young generation of Chicano writers to explore a wide range of literary themes without limiting their creativity to the social demands of past Chicano cultural needs.

Essayist, editor, poet, and short-story writer Rafael Cruz Castillo was born on 30 December 1950 in San Antonio, Texas, more specifically in the west side of the city, where he is proud to have lived most of his life. His mother, Rosa, was a housewife, and his father, José, was a notary public. Castillo received his early education at Lorenzo de Zavala Elementary, Cooper Junior High, and at the most popular West Side high school, Sidney Lanier. He began his formal academic training at St. Mary's University, where he received a B.A. in English and political science in 1975. In 1977 he received an M.A. from the University of Texas at San Antonio, where he majored in English and bicultural studies. Not interested in pursuing a Ph.D., Castillo nonetheless has often participated in summer programs in the English departments of the University of Texas at Austin and at Trinity University in San Antonio. At present, Castillo is professor of English at Palo Alto Community College in Texas, where he has taught American and British literature since 1985. Castillo has been recognized repeatedly by his academic peers for his stimulating teaching. Among the many awards he has received for his dedication to teaching and to community service are the 1987 Palo Alto College Teaching Excellence Award, the 1990 Certificate of Outstanding Achievement from the Palo Alto College Board of Trustees, and the 1991 Palo Alto College President's Award for Teaching.

Castillo spent his early years under the care of his paternal grandparents. His childhood and adolescence were difficult times as he struggled to survive in two different worlds: the nurturing world of his grandparents and the unstable world of his parents, whose marriage eventually ended in divorce. The separation deeply hurt Castillo. As a result of this family breakup, Castillo affirms that he became a private and isolated individual–not in a negative sense but in a positive one, since the isolation provided him with added inspiration to write. He shares his life with Esperanza Castillo, a writer of children's literature, whom he married on 20 November 1992.

In a November 1993 unpublished interview, Castillo shared an early recollection of his childhood years, and talked about his first encounter with the written word at the age of nine. At that time his grandparents were living on the second floor of a two-story house. The first floor of the house was used as a mortuary and as a notary public office. The man who worked downstairs, Manuel Donovan, was a prolific womanizer who had twenty-seven children and fifty-seven grandchildren. More important for Castillo was the fact that Donovan possessed a great collection of books that he did not allow anyone to touch. That prohibition made the young Castillo want to explore the mysteries that surrounded these books. The smell of the pages, the roughness of the covers, and "the caterpillar of words" that he found printed in endless lines fascinated him.

Castillo's first significant literary experience, however, came as a result of a written poetry assignment in his ninth grade English class at Lanier. He recalled how at that time he and his friend Raymond Sánchez were watching afternoon cartoons while discussing the assignment. Castillo, the more intense and academic student, remembers that he was struggling to create a perfect literary piece and mocked Sánchez, who was planning to incorporate Popeye's cartoon theme song as an integral part of his poem, for not taking the assignment seriously. Castillo recalled that when they read their poems in class, Sánchez "read his poem in a very serious tone, relating it to the barrio experience. At the end of every stanza Ray would recite solemnly and in a deep and tragic voice: 'I - am - what - I - am - and - I'll - die - like - I - am.' I struggled not to laugh out loud for I could not believe the tremendous impact that the poem had created on the teacher." This teacher, Castillo continued, "became very emotional and began to cry. She

told Ray that it was the best thing that he had ever done." Castillo's poem, on the other hand, was criticized severely for being too academic and difficult to understand. From this experience Castillo discovered the power of parody, and he became obsessed with being a creative writer.

Castillo considers Philip D. Ortego, Fyodor Dostoyevsky, and Ignacio García to have played important roles in his development as a writer. He asserts that Ortego provided him with the guidance and the maturing he desperately needed to perfect his craft. Dostoyevsky, says Castillo, "writes like a mexicano for when he writes about St. Petersburg I recall images of my barrio and its struggles to survive." Castillo considers the novel *The Brothers Karamazov* (1880) a major influence in his life, because he could relate the story of the alcoholic father and his three sons to his personal experience. Castillo maintains that this novel helped him to crystallize his ambiguous feelings of the time since it instilled in him the desire to write his problems out on paper. García, a close friend from high school and one-time editor of *Saguaro: Journal of Fiction and Contemporary Thought*, encouraged him to submit his creative work to literary journals.

Castillo's first published work was an essay titled "Chicano Philosophy," written in 1975 and included in the now-legendary Chicano journal *Caracol* (Snail). This essay discusses the theme of human understanding from a Chicano's point of view, using, as Castillo affirms, the "typical recipe of the late 1960s and early 1970s–Ernesto 'Che' Guevara, Karl Marx, etc." Also in these early years he toyed with poetry, writing parodies in verse on how he saw the Chicano Movement and also on the unscrupulous abuse of power by the political establishment. In 1980 his epic poem "A Variation on a Dostoevski Theme" was published in the *Arizona Canto al Pueblo* (Song to the People). After these early experiments with poetry Castillo decided not to continue in this genre, concentrating instead on the writing of essays and Chicano theater reviews for various newspapers, including the *San Antonio Express News*.

Castillo edited the *ViAztlán Journal* from 1984 to 1987. From 1986 to 1991 he served as a contributing editor of *Saguaro*, originating at the University of Arizona. Currently, Castillo is chairman of the editorial board for the *Palo Alto Review* at Palo Alto College. During the years he worked for *ViAztlán* he began to publish many of the short stories that eventually became part of *Distant Journeys*. Among the literary journals that published his stories were the *Arizona Quarterly, Frank: International Journal of Writing*, and *Saguaro*.

*Distant Journeys* is a collection of eighteen short stories written between 1980 and 1988. Castillo views the stories as allegorical pieces in which life is seen

*Cover for Castillo's 1991 collection of short stories that explore being a Chicano*

through the paradigm of a journey. According to the definition given by Castillo, a journey symbolizes "a looking within oneself." Castillo considers this journey to be as far or as close as one needs to explore. The three parts of the book—"Distant Journeys with Strange People," "Distant Journeys to Faraway Places," and "Distant Journeys to Other Cultures"—explore themes that place the Chicano in a larger context. "A Chicano can be anything he wants to be and be anywhere he wants to be," says Castillo, adding, "He could be in a barrio of San Antonio, sitting by a bonfire in an empty parking lot narrating stories of yesteryear, or he could be strolling in the streets of Paris or Prague, bathing himself with intelligence." The representation of the journey, with its constant movement provides Castillo with the needed paradigm that helps him explore the essence of being a Chicano.

Death, "something that is accidental, a part of fate that is intertwined with human emotions," is a prevalent theme in the nine stories that make up the first sec-

tion of *Distant Journeys*. Castillo also frequently uses the word *strange*—which he defines as anything that is not part of the mainstream—to explore the reactions of his main characters to this "ultimate journey." The journey to the self, according to Castillo, shows that the only hope of understanding the complexity of life is through confrontation with death.

Death as a theme is best represented in "Hugo's Diary," "Icicles," and "The Accident." In the first story, Hugo, a deformed hunchback, suffers because the woman he loves continually ignores him. She eventually dies of an abortion attempt, and Hugo, feeling that his life was "one huge melodramatic lump of absurdity," kills himself on April Fool's Day. His foolishness lies in his inability to cope with the death of a loved one, an experience that most people have to face during their lifetimes.

In "Icicles," a story that touches on lesbianism, Lilith decides not to abandon her husband for the love of her friend, Eva, who was recently widowed. Lilith has opportunities to let death take her husband—at one point a sharp icicle hangs dangerously over his head, and later a truck almost runs him over—but she decides not to let it happen. Instead, Lilith decides to end her relationship with Eva, her possible lover.

Of particular interest is "The Accident," in which Castillo deftly experiments with magical realism and surrealism to present his theme. The story depicts a man who feels a tremendous guilt for the drowning of his wife and her unborn child in a recreational vehicle accident. Emotionally disturbed by the incident, the man eventually kills himself by drowning in a bathtub. As he slowly submerges his head under the water he begins to hear the distant voices of his wife and child calling him. His journey, through the process of dying, seems to be the only way of escaping his sorrow.

Castillo's characters in this first section are strange only in the sense that they possess certain characteristics that distinguish them from other people. In "The Goy from Aztlán" Roberto Guzmán-Levine, a highly educated Chicano writer "with an upper-class Welsh accent," changes his name to Nahum Goldstein in order to be recognized by the mainstream readership; in "Fortuna" the title character, a *curandera* (healer), drives away evil spirits by sprinkling bodies with *bálsamo* (balsam) and branches of *pirul* (pepper tree); in "Doris González," the title character is an obese woman who heals her sorrow over the death of her Chicano lover in Greece by eating forty boxes of Lady Godiva chocolates; and in "Emilio," the protagonist is a farm worker who abandons a campsite to journey into the night where a blond *fantasma* (ghost) comes to lead him through the mist of a dark forest into the shadows of another world. All of these characters, though brushed with humor, nevertheless capture poignantly the seriousness of the message.

Castillo leads readers into the world of his characters in order to show that they are not at all as strange as the title of the section labels them to be. Many readers will see themselves in one or two of these characters that range from the *campesino* (farmworker) who envisions sexual encounters with the boss's wife to the arrogant Chicano intellectual who is rapidly losing his identity. Obscure desires and unpredictable reactions are well represented in these individuals. Through his stories Castillo shows that all people are strange and share a common journey, each one clinging to his or her own peculiarities.

In the section titled "Distant Journey to Faraway Places" Castillo addresses social concerns with the purpose of broadening the Chicano experience. Using religious motifs, Castillo depicts men suffering from poverty and dying from drug overdoses in Paris in "Jesús is Dead" and suffering torture in Central America in "El Coronel." Castillo thus shows that human suffering is present everywhere. Although the stories that are included in this section take place in "faraway places" such as Paris, Chile, and El Salvador, the violence and the exploitation generated by man are in reality not too far from one's own territory.

Two of the four short stories included in the second section show opposite searches for salvation. In "Gregorio's Dilemma" Gregorio Sosa, the main character, tries to save himself by selling his soul. Held as a political prisoner along with other men, he makes a pact with a mysterious man named Devlin (who clearly symbolizes the Devil) out of a selfish desire to seek eternal life. He betrays his fellow inmates in exchange for his salvation but ends up dying with the rest of the prisoners in a tavern symbolically named "Pinochet's Bar and Grill"—a reference to the cruel and notorious dictator of Chile.

The second story, "Conoro: A Tale," depicts a man who gains salvation through faith and hope. Conoro was a relatively quiet village surrounded by the dense jungle of El Salvador until "men of guns upset the nature of things." The people are forced to seek refuge in the mountains until an old man, a Jesus figure, comes down to encounter the colonel who is threatening the village. The colonel imprisons the old man, and just as a firing squad is about to kill him the earth trembles, devouring the colonel and his men. The old man then returns to the mountain, never to be seen again. The people return from the mountain and live a life of peace and tranquility. A ray of hope thereby shines in a part of the world that has perpetually witnessed violence and death.

In the third section, "Distant Journeys to Other Cultures," Castillo deals more specifically with Chicano concerns. One of these concerns is the recuperation of Chicano culture and history. The club in the story "The Poetry Club" is made up of Chicanos who are strongly influenced by Anglo American poets and are detached from Chicano themes and social commitment. The club is disturbed when Hugo García, whose poems are full of cultural messages that create a strong impression on most of the members, seeks admission. "His words remained a cultural testimony to their lost ancestral roots," writes Castillo; "Hugo's poetry had purged them of that cataclysmic sin their fathers had committed of anglicizing their Spanish names." Hugo is accepted, and the group's ideology changes until those who do not like Hugo invite an Anglo poet to the club to renew the assimilation process. Thus the group once again falls, for this new poet "struck at the vulnerabilities of the new generation engulfed with the fantasies of appearance." Castillo holds out hope for the members of the club by introducing another poet, Macario, who, like Hugo, preaches cultural awareness.

Read collectively, the short stories in this section provide a sense of the *ambiente* (ambiance) of a barrio in San Antonio. In "Grandfather's Tale," for example, the grandfather gathers the kids and tells them anecdotes of his childhood. He describes the street of his youth, Guadalupe Street–"an eyesore, a cancerous ligament, an enigma"–and the people who live in it. The grandfather proceeds to tell a story of the legendary *curandera* Sister Fortuna, a cultural icon of the barrio. The story is important because of the impact that it has on the children who hear it and are able to document it for future generations. Castillo sees this story as a warning for Chicanos to protect their culture.

In "The Miracle" Castillo uses the image of the Virgin of Guadalupe to demonstrate how deeply this image has penetrated into the hearts and souls of Mexicans and Chicanos. An old lady, who sees the image of the Virgin on the bumper of a car, also sees the image in the birthmark on a child's buttocks and wants the people believe that the Virgin, in fact, did appear. Castillo wrote the story cautiously, providing a humorous touch to a delicate subject. In the end he lets the reader decide whether the image of the Virgin is real or if the old lady is a full-fledged *alcahueta* (intermediary). The story shows the desire for faith amid a chaotic technological background that is trying to dehumanize people.

With this last section of *Distant Journeys* Castillo reveals his preoccupation with Chicano culture. He feels that the Chicano stands at a vulnerable cultural crossroads. On the one hand, his culture is dangerously fading away, and on the other, the culture that he might want to assimilate into is uncomfortably out of reach. Castillo believes that the Chicano should not have to sacrifice cultural identity. In the five stories in this section the author evaluates Chicano cultural icons in order to keep them from disappearing.

Castillo has finished another collection, "Dwarfs and Penitents," which includes twelve short stories and is under consideration for publication. Castillo says that in this collection the dominant themes deal with human isolation and discovery. He covers issues such as the cultural dichotomy of Chicano experience (Anglo and Mexican) and the question of how to proceed in accomplishing the difficult goal of negotiating between the two sides of the dual heritage.

Castillo has also finished writing a novel in collaboration with his friend Rogelio Gómez. The novel (presently untitled) deals with a World War II veteran who is so disillusioned with life in the United States that he decides to reside in a foreign country once the war has ended. Among Castillo's other publications are "The Penitent of Guadalupe Street" and "The Battle of the Alamo," a short story written to honor those Chicano soldiers who died in Vietnam.

Though Castillo's work has not been studied seriously, his work is regarded highly by those who know it well, as indicated by Philip D. Ortego's description of his poetry: "His pieces are like finely crafted works of glass–clear, reflective and wrought with considerable care." Robert Sosa, chairman of the board of the Guadalupe Cultural Arts Center, also admires Castillo, whom he considers "among the best writers San Antonio has produced." Castillo's original and stimulating short stories, narrated always with a delicate touch of humor and grace, promise a significant literary career.

### References:

Philip D. Ortego, "The Book of the People Sets the Tone of the '80s," *San Antonio Express News,* 21 February 1982;

Robert Sosa, "Castillo's Writing Wears the Signature of Life," *San Antonio Light,* 20 August 1990.

# Carlos Cortéz

*(13 August 1923 – )*

Marc Zimmerman
*University of Illinois at Chicago*

BOOKS: *Crystal-Gazing the Amber Fluid & Other Wobbly Poems,* introduction by Eugene Nelson (Chicago: Kerr, 1990);

*De Kansas a Califas & Back to Chicago: Poems & Art,* foreword by Joel Climenhaga (Chicago: MARCH/Abrazo Press, 1992);

*Where are the Voices? & Other Wobbly Poems,* introduction by Archie Green (Chicago: Kerr, 1997);

*Fanning the Flames,* edited by Tere Romo (Chicago: Mexican Fine Arts Museum, forthcoming 2000).

OTHER: "Where are the Voices?" and "Digging the Squares at Jack London Square," in *Rebel Voices: An IWW Anthology,* edited by Joyce L. Kornbluh (Ann Arbor: University of Michigan Press, 1964), pp. 392, 395;

"Outa Work Blues," in *Poets of Today: A New American Anthology,* edited by Walter Lowenfels (New York: International Publishers, 1964), p. 36;

"May Song," in *Arrangement in Literature,* edited by Edmund J. Farrell, Ovida H. Clapp, James L. Pierce, and Raymond J. Rodrigues (Glenview, Ill.: Scott, Foresman, 1979), p. 597;

"This is the Land," in *The United States in Literature,* edited by James E. Miller, Carlota Cárdenas de Dwyer, Robert Hayden, Russell J. Hagan, and Kerry M. Wood (Glenview, Ill.: Scott, Foresman, 1979), p. 574;

"Peregrinaje en Hannibal, Missouri" and "Calabria," in *Canto al pueblo: antología / Anthology,* edited by Justo S. Alarcón, Juan Pérez Aldape, and Lupe Cárdenas (Mesa: Arizona Canto al Pueblo, 1980), p. 48;

"Prelude to the Moment of Truth," "Empty House Blues," "Quo Vadisimus," and "Yosemite," in *Emergency Tacos: Seven Poets con Picante,* edited by Carlos Cumpián (Chicago: MARCH/Abrazo Press, 1989), pp. 16–19.

SELECTED PERIODICAL PUBLICATIONS–UNCOLLECTED: "Eulogy" and "Napa Night Bit," *Beatitude/East,* no. 17 (1961): 9;

*Carlos Cortéz ( photograph by Alejandro Galindo)*

"Sun Chant," "Buon Giorno," and "Who's Vanishing?" *Smith,* no. 7 (1966): 16–18;

"I. F. Blues," "Wagon Driver," and "La Verité Cose," *Quixote,* 55, no. 1 (1969–1970): 1–3;

"Macuilhaikuh," and "Cinco Haiku Chicano," *Revista Chicano-Riqueña,* 4, no. 3 (1975): 5;

"Untitled," *Nit & Wit* ( January–February 1981): 43;

"Puridad" and "Aztlan Aik Ixpoliziv," *Notebook: A Little Magazine,* 4, no. 2 (1985): 24–28;

"Sunday Night in Morelia," *Pittsburgh Quarterly,* 1, no. 3 (1991): 18.

While Carlos Cortéz may ultimately be better remembered for his linocut and woodcut graphics than for his verse, he exhibits some of the same virtues in the visual and the verbal media; it may indeed be said that in some ways Cortéz translates radical Mexican traditions into populist verse. His graphics, often augmented with words, are striking, bold, and direct, as are his poems. In an unpublished January 1988 interview he said, "The social forces of repression and the consequent forces of rebellion have long influenced my writing as well as . . . other forms of expression."

Parental influence and early experience during the Depression and World War II led to his joining the Industrial Workers of the World (IWW). An awareness of Cortéz's participation in the IWW, or "Wobblies," is central to understanding his graphics, his poetry, and above all his contribution to Chicano and Latino cultural life through the Movimiento Artístico Chicano (MARCH) in Chicago, with which he has been identified since the mid 1960s. As Cortéz noted in the 1988 interview, the IWW was "the initial force motivating my expression, and participation in any other type of movements were but a logical extension of that." As a popular working-class Wobbly poet, Cortéz was not without a certain recognition even prior to his connection with a specifically Chicano or Latino group or movement.

Cortéz's radical vision and art were not simply the organic outgrowth of standard Midwestern Mexican migration processes; rather, they stemmed from a broader evolution of international worker migrations and their convergences with syndicalist and political struggle. His father, Alfredo Cortez (Carlos Cortéz added the accent to his surname), was born in Mazatlan, Sinaloa, to a mestiza mother from Jalisco and a Yaqui father from northern Mexico. Around 1916 Alfredo, having worked in the vineyards and on the railroads, joined the IWW as that organization began to reach out toward immigrant workers. He quickly became a traveling delegate, and in 1918 he was sent to organize the growing numbers of Mexican and the already vast numbers of German immigrant workers in the Milwaukee area. There, in 1920, he met a second-generation German woman, Augusta Ungerecht, a domestic worker and a pacifist/Socialist follower of Eugene Debs and Norman Thomas. She soon joined the Wobblies, and she and Alfredo Cortez became honorary members of the Young Peoples Socialist League (YPSL). They married in 1923, and Carlos Alfredo Cortez was born on 13 August of that year.

Cortéz drew his initial social and minority consciousness, his radicalism, and his artistic bent from his parents, who were working class, poor, socially conscious, and artistic at a time of racial and labor strife. Ethnic confusion and tension were part of the context into which Cortéz was born. His father was a dark-skinned Mexican in a period when all Mexicans were subjects of discrimination and prejudice in Wisconsin. Although an intellectual radical, Alfredo Cortez had never finished primary school and was, therefore, even less attractive to Augusta Ungerecht's assimilating relatives. Her immediate family accepted the marriage, but distant cousins cut her off.

Both parents spoke fluent English, but they also retained elements of their original cultures. In an unpublished 1994 interview Cortéz recalled that when he was young his mother spoke to him in her "immigrant German kinder-deutsch"; and his father, an orator and singer, peppered his English with a Mexican Spanish inflected by his Italian-speaking days as a Napa Valley worker. Augusta Cortez also wrote pacifist and socially conscious English-language poetry for the local newspapers.

Cortéz attended public schools in Milwaukee and in the rural southern part of Milwaukee County. Growing up mainly in the township of Oak Creek, halfway between Milwaukee and Racine, he heard German constantly but English predominated. He was taunted and jeered by schoolmates, though his mother told him that because of his father's Native American blood he was not "foreign" at all. In 1994 he recalled, "It was my German mother who put the seed of Chicano identity in my brain. It was the support of my parents that put me through the traumas of being the only Mexican kid in school." For a while, he said, "I considered myself a German, but the German kids made fun of me as a Mexican." Yet, he was aware of not being quite Mexican, either, of sharing little with the Mexican migrant children. Never fully a member of either Mexican or German groups, he would eventually identify with and be critical of both—and of others, as well. His initial reaction was a heightened awareness and sensitivity that opened him to artistic creation in the footsteps of his parents.

His parents encouraged the early interest he showed in the visual arts, and he took two years of high-school art classes. They also wanted him to go to college, "but I wasn't the academic type." He loved learning, "but not in the academic way." His real love was drawing, sketching, and painting, though he did not think of art as a career. Instead, he became a construction worker. His father belonged to the hod carriers union and had served as the union representative, retaining enough influence to get his son admitted. His father also urged him to join a radical group, and

Cortéz chose to join the YPSL. In the early 1940s he took classes at the Layton Art Gallery in Milwaukee.

The fundamental influence of these years was World War II. Cortéz's German grandfather thought that Adolf Hitler was going to save Germany, while his mother was firmly pacificist—and so was Cortéz. He refused to respond to a draft notice and was sentenced to prison. "I'm anti-militarist and anti-authoritarian," he explained. "If I could've been guaranteed a shot at Hitler, you wouldn't have had to draft me." He never regretted his decision. During two years at Sandstone Federal Prison near Duluth, Minnesota, he did artwork and came into contact with a variety of ethnic groups, religious sects, and literary texts.

Out of prison, he joined the IWW in 1947, traveled for the first time to Mexico and California, and held a wide range of jobs, including factory worker, janitor, book and record salesman, journalist, and illustrator. In the 1950s he began to contribute to the cultural section of the IWW's publishing organ, *The Industrial Worker*. At first he wrote movie reviews, then he began to do cartoon work in the style for which he became best known. By the time his mother died in 1959, he had begun to follow her lead by publishing political poems on an almost weekly basis. Many of the poems in his collections were first published in *The Industrial Worker*.

By 1965 Cortéz and his wife, Mariana, had sold their Milwaukee house to pay back taxes; and since *The Industrial Worker* was published in Chicago, it seemed logical to move there. Coupled with his trips to California, the Chicago move intensified his identification with the emerging Chicano Movement. At first he saw the United Farm Workers struggle and the overall Chicano Movement in terms of his IWW-related principles of unionism and cultural solidarity. Nevertheless, the Chicano vision, which melded with his views on the Vietnam War, civil rights, and the IWW critique of capitalist domination, and ecological devastation soon grew to become more central to his thinking.

Cortéz participated in the first Chicago artists coalition, involving painters such as Efraín Martínez, a member of the budding MARCH organization, and John Weber, a key member of the politically progressive Chicago Mural Group, which included and often worked closely with Latino artists and organizations. In the early 1970s Martínez introduced Cortéz to activist painters and cultural workers such as José Nario, Ray Patlán, Victor Sorrell, Antonio Zavala, and MARCH founder José Gamaliel González. Cortéz and his wife started attending MARCH meetings in 1972 or 1973; they were considered members after three sessions. Cortéz was still unsure what the outcome of this involvement would be, as he explained in 1994:

*Cover for a 1997 printing of Cortéz's first book (1990), with a 1985 woodblock self-portrait by the author*

Would I be completely accepted or not because I wasn't fully Mexican or fully involved in Mexican art? They didn't know about the poetry, but they did like my visual work. And of course there were influences of Posada, Orozco and Diego. But I was also strongly influenced by Art Young and the Wobbly cartoonists, Kathe Kollwitz and the German expressionists. My art was social-minded and so was my poetry. But the fact was that I hadn't done many Mexican themes.

Over the years the doubts faded, and Cortéz began to put an assertive (perhaps anarchist-inspired) Spanish accent mark over his name in autographs and artwork signings. His process of identification was slow, and only in the early 1980s did he come to accept himself as fully involved in the Chicano cultural movement. In 1994 he said: "I'm a poet and visual artist first. My background is an accident of birth. . . . if you're really proud of your own identity, you're forced to look at others. And if you're really into your own identity, you realize how much of it comes from somewhere else."

*Cover for Cortéz's second collection of poetry (1992), inspired by a 1991 road trip*

Influenced by Cortéz and his young disciple, Carlos Cumpián, MARCH modified its emphasis on painting to highlight poetry performance and publishing, with Cortéz's graphics as the primary visual-arts component. As Mexicans came to constitute the vast majority of an ever-growing Latino cultural world in Chicago, Cortéz became involved with such emergent entities as the Mexican Taller del Grabado and the Chicago Mexican Fine Arts Museum. He illustrated many books and became a figure on the national Chicano art scene. He presented one-man shows and participated or exhibited at a variety of festivals and exhibits. He also taught and held writing and arts workshops at various institutions, including the Field Museum of Natural History, the Mexican Fine Arts Museum, the Chicago Art Institute, and the Children's Museum in Chicago; the University of California at Santa Cruz; and the Summer Art Camp at the University of Wisconsin at Green Bay. In addition, his poetry appeared in non-Wobbly multicultural and general anthologies and in Latino and Chicano journals, including *Revista Chicano-Riqueña.*

While Cortéz sometimes uses *corrido* (popular ballad) and other Mexican forms, he also is comfortable with Indian storytelling patterns, blues, and white folk forms. He writes in Spanish only occasionally. "All forms of literature of whatever ethnicity have influenced me," he said in 1988. "I happen to be one who uses poetry as a means of expressing certain strong feelings; and had I been born of different parents, resulting in an entirely different frame of identification, I no doubt would still be expressing myself as strongly with whatever ethnic pride that I may have." His poetic models include Robert Burns, Jack London, Robert Service, and the early Wobbly poets. He was also influenced by Beat Generation writers such as Lawrence Ferlinghetti, Jack Kerouac, and perhaps his biggest writer-hero, Kenneth Patchen.

As a Wobbly, Cortéz's perspective is ultimately internationalist. His specifically Latino and Indian identifications, especially in his overtly Wobbly poems, must be considered in light of this international orientation. Indeed, the Mexican references emerge as part of a pattern involving many cultures. Most of Cortéz's early work remains distanced from a Mexican verbal medium and more tied to Anglo traditions.

Nevertheless, his first collection, *Crystal-Gazing the Amber Fluid & Other Wobbly Poems* (1990), gives a somewhat misleading impression of his early production. Left out are his best-known panoramic poems, such as his comprehensive hymn for the oppressed, "Where are the Voices?" (1960), and one of his most important expressions of Indian roots, "This is the Land" (1979), as well as his haiku and haikulike forms. Most significant is the exclusion of almost all of his African American and Latino-inflected poems, so that this focus seems far less crucial than a concern with working-class Swedes or Italians.

Cortéz's earliest work draws on the blues and has at least some specific African American historical reference—even if he tends to subordinate issues of race to those of class. The first poem he published in *The Industrial Worker* (September 1958) was "Blues for a Busdriver," which includes the lines:

> The driver takes a weary glance
> In the overhead mirror
> Seeing for the thousandth time
> His equally weary load
> Of wage slaves.

Other blues poems include "Late Evening Working Stiff Blues," "Blues for a Fisheater," "Outa Work Blues," and "More Blues by C Red." The poems are uneven; Cortéz often does not keep to the rhythm or pattern, and making a political point sometimes seems more important than creating graceful lines.

Cortéz tends to emphasize the Indian aspect of his identity more than the Spanish and mestizo dimensions. This emphasis emerges in "Adios Tecopita" in *Crystal-Gazing the Amber Fluid & Other Wobbly Poems,* which is more Indian than Mexican in tone and orientation, and in the cumulative impression gained from reading the work as a whole. Cortéz adopts the role of a pithy, bemused, and rueful Indian sage looking on the actions of the white bosses, both locally and globally. At times he uses Indian pen names: C. C. Redcloud as early as 1962 and later Carlos Cortéz Koyokuikatl, or "Song of the Coyote"–the "spirit name" given him by a Spanish- and Nahuatl-speaking Indian in the early 1980s. *Coyote* has taken on negative connotations for Mexicans, as it is used to refer to the smugglers of illegal immigrants and contraband across the border; but for the Native Americans, Cortéz insisted in 1994, the coyote is a positive figure, expressive of freedom and other laudable qualities.

Cortéz notes that he had this Indian identification from childhood but adds, "My generation played down our Indian side. Getting by was getting by white. Spanish sounds better than Mexican or Indian." Emphasizing his Indianness is Cortéz's way of critiquing both the racism of his own ethnic group and European imposition in the New World in general. This critique emerges especially in the second half of *Crystal-Gazing the Amber Fluid & Other Wobbly Poems,* in such poems as "Requiem Chant for a Half-breed Warrior," "Three Spirits," and "The Downfall of a Disease-Giver."

Some of the technical flaws in Cortéz's early poems, such as awkward rhythm or lack of tonal unity, can be attributed to rapid composition and to his greater concern with what he communicates than with how he communicates it. Sometimes the broken rhythms or diction patterns are intentional, when he is writing from his Indian sage persona and wants to create dissonance with the rhythms and norms of urban modernity. While some of his best poems are relatively long, Cortéz generally does better with fragments or short, pithy forms.

In the 1960s Cortéz studied Japanese culture and experimented with haiku and haikulike forms, some of which capture a moment or make a succinct political or cultural point. An example is "Springtime Haiku" (1961):

Wise little pigeons
they know
   How to decorate
The courthouse.

Other vignettes express working-class feelings or establish a sense of place, such as "Windy City Christmas" (1961):

In a chilly alleyway
Off West Madison Street,
Santa Claus is an old man
With a dirty beard
Passing a bottle of cheap Muscatel
To his buddies.

The absence of Cortéz's haiku-influenced works from *Crystal-Gazing the Amber Fluid & Other Wobbly Poems* prevents that book from being an adequate representation of his poetic capacity and breadth. He righted this imbalance in 1997 with *Where are the Voices? & Other Wobbly Poems.*

Cortéz is concerned with ecological issues such as smog, acid rain, and radiation as well as with the racism and pretensions of his contemporaries–including those Latinos who attempt to deny their Indian or African blood. Such concerns are treated in his second collection, *De Kansas a Califas & Back to Chicago: Poems & Art* (1992), a tour of the American waste- and wonderland. The poems were drafted on a trip Cortéz took with his friend Joel Climenhaga and Climenhaga's wife and deaf dog at the end of 1991. The main themes are the destruction of the environment and a reaffirmation of an idealized relationship between Native Americans and nature. The poems conjure up lost nature, evoking the buffalo, the California condor, the Mojave Desert, the high Sierras, and Machu Picchu in the Andes. The technique is close to that of his early haikus; most of the poems draw on short lyric jabs, with punchlines sometimes in bold caps and with exclamation marks, such as "**NOW!**" or "**THERE!**" The poems are sprinkled with phrases in Spanish, as well as some Indian phrases; there are almost as many Mexican as Indian references. The collection closes with "Día de la Raza" (Day of the People), a jeering trilingual evocation of Christopher Columbus's so-called discovery.

Writing about this volume, Cortéz's old friend Zavala points to the poet's evocation of "the solitude and beauty of the desert, the Tenachapi Mountains and the Chicano culture of California." Zavala particularly praises the haikus in the text. "I can't recall a small press book as beautiful as this one," he writes. "It is a perfect book from a great poet and artist. From cover to cover you can tell that it was a labor of love."

Cortéz's third volume, *Where are the Voices? & Other Wobbly Poems,* includes several of the early Wobbly newspaper poems left out of *Crystal-Gazing the Amber Fluid & Other Wobbly Poems* and a few haiku-inflected and Latino-centered poems along with some newer material. The book includes a generous selection of graphics and

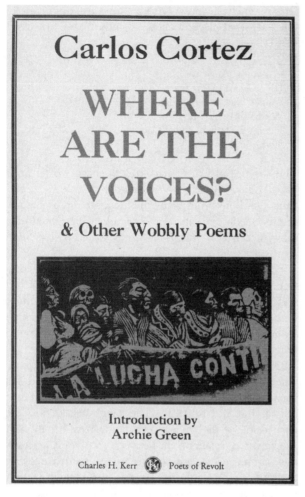

# Carlos Cortez

# WHERE ARE THE VOICES?

## & Other Wobbly Poems

### Introduction by
### Archie Green

Charles H. Kerr        Poets of Revolt

*Cover for Cortéz's 1997 collection of poems, which includes several early works that had appeared in* The Industrial Worker, *the newspaper of the Industrial Workers of the World*

inspirations: cultural, ecological, revolutionary." E. Donald Two-Rivers says that Cortéz's work "has always been a source of inspiration for younger native poets." Chicana author Ana Castillo writes: "Cortéz is the better half of the twentieth century walking. Through his words and woodcuts Cortéz is a delightful and important chronicler of labor movements, Chicano history and, of course, *la vida.*"

Rosemont's view is developed in Green's introduction, which is perhaps the clearest exposition to date of Cortéz's aesthetic. Green notes the lack of any "study attempting to frame Wobbly artistry with questions of origin, form utility, and meaning. In short, in what physical setting, and out of what inner impulse did a miner, logger, waitress, or weaver compose a poem or draw a cartoon to be shared with fellow workers?" He adds that the IWW transformed the verbal slurs hurled against them into an ironic affirmation of their identity and eventually of their distance from dogmatic communists. Noting that Cortéz "built upon the achievements of José Guadalupe Posada, Art Young, Kathe Kollwitz, Edvard Munch and other artists involved in social movements," Green observes that Cortéz perfected his linocut skills "because the *Industrial Worker*'s old flatbed press could not handle electroplate." He reads "this pragmatic turn to linoleum as a metaphor for much IWW expression–close to the bone." Acknowledging Cortéz's debts to Whitman, Patchen, and Carl Sandburg, Green notes that Cortéz's poetry also has ties to a Wobbly tradition of "songsters and word smiths"–adding to Rosemont's mention of T-Bone Slim such names as Ralph Chaplin, Harry McClintock, Arturo Giovannitti, Joe Hill, Ralph Winstead, Jim Seymour, and Vera Moller.

Green posits that the work of Cortéz and his predecessors offer an informal Wobbly aesthetic: "Together, they favored the vernacular voice but rejected the stereotyped dialect and stilted portraiture of elite approaches to a romanticized underclass. Realism won out over abstraction in most IWW expression, but not to the extent that its creative souls failed to experiment with the modernism of [James] Joyce or [Pablo] Picasso." Green argues that Wobblies, who rejected Communist Party/Popular Front politics in the 1930s and 1940s, did not find "midbrow" nationalism or patriotism in art appealing; nor did their definition of socially tuned art lead them into some kind of socialist realism aesthetic. This freedom, Green suggests, helps explain the openness to varied forms in Cortéz's work. It also helps to explain how Cortéz the Wobbly could simultaneously contribute to Native American developments and, above all, to the rise of the Chicano cultural-political movement in the United States.

offers some of Cortéz's sharpest topical poems on mine disasters, Vietnam, corrupt police, and labor heroes, as well as some poems in a panoramic, epic vein, such as the well-honed "And the Buzz of the Flies Grows Louder" and the title poem–a Walt Whitmanesque/Wobbly articulation of social history first published on 2 May 1960 and frequently republished. In his introduction to the volume Archie Green says that the title poem "stands today as an elegy for class-war dead, intensely sad at constant loss by worker partisans"; it is one of the great achievements of Cortéz's work as a Wobbly and "people's poet."

The back cover and opening page of *Where are the Voices? & Other Wobbly Poems* carry praise from other writers. Penelope Rosemont notes: "The art of . . . Cortéz draws from the same springs as that of José Guadalupe Posada and George Grosz, his poetry from the same roots as Robert Burns and T-Bone Slim, but all that he does is uniquely his own–a 'One Big Union' of diverse

Looking back at his relation to the Chicano cultural movement and its development, Cortéz concluded in the 1994 interview:

> Of course, there's no such thing as a modest artist, we're all exhibitionists and self promoters. But I must've brought something to the movement to help it to grow. I'm optimistic about its future, it's going great guns. And I guess it's rather fortunate that so many of us worked so long in obscurity from the dominant culture so that we didn't become trapped in commercialism. We've had to grow by ourselves, but now we can take on, be influenced by, but also influence the rest of the world.

Recovering from a heart attack in 1993 and facing his mortality, Cortéz stepped up his production and arranged to leave his visual and literary work to the Mexican Fine Arts Museum and Harold Washington Library in Chicago. In 1994 Cortéz was featured in an article by William Miller in an issue of Montgomery Ward's trade magazine; he was invited by the Smithsonian Institution to discuss his work; and he was the subject of a poem in Cumpián's *Latino Rainbow: Poems about Latino Americans* (1994). His days of obscurity and, apparently, his heart trouble behind him, he celebrated his seventieth birthday with a new creative outburst. "I believe now is the most productive phase of my life," he commented to Miller. In the summer of 1997 he was honored by the Mexican Fine Arts Museum with a well-organized retrospective. *Fanning the Flames,* a catalogue of his artwork, is to be published in 2000 in conjunction with a national and international tour of the retrospective.

Writing of his friend and fellow Wobbly, Eugene Nelson says in the introduction to *Crystal-Gazing the Amber Fluid & Other Wobbly Poems:*

> This man is a genius at living, and his face is a poem, his whole being is a poem. For there are few people, a fortunate few (Walt Whitman was another) whose vivid lively love of life and all the world is so great that it overflows through their eyes and glows from their face. . . . If there were a position as chief advisor and arbitrator for the world I would nominate him for the post. For he loves the world and living things more than any one I know.

Zavala asserts that the "Latino-Chicano art scene" in Chicago is "hard to imagine without the presence and contributions of Carlos A. Cortéz." Resisting the passage of time, Cortéz is preparing new drawings, new poems, and new contributions to Chicago and national Chicano and Latino cultural development.

**Interview:**

Jennifer Sprull, "Interview with Carlos Cortéz," *Pittsburgh Quarterly,* 1, no. 3 (1991): 19–27.

**References:**

Alan G. Artner, "Arte de un activista: Los imágenes atrevidas y urgentes del poeta y pintor Carlos Cortéz," *¡Exito!* 26 June 1997, p. 46;

Carlos Cumpián, "Carlos A. Cortez, Chicano Artist and Poet," in his *Latino Rainbow: Poems about Latino Americans* (Chicago: Childrens Press, 1994), pp. 32–33;

Shifra Goldman, *Dimensions of the Americas: Art and Social Change in Latin America and the United States* (Chicago: University of Chicago Press, 1994), pp. 295–297;

William Miller, "Star Focus: Genius at Living. Carlos Cortéz and His Poetry," *Vantage: Better Living for Less from Montgomery Ward* (May/June 1994): 24–25;

Andrew Patner, "A Labor of Creativity: Artist Supports Working Class," *Chicago Sun Times,* 23 June 1997, pp. 25, 28;

Antonio Zavala, "Carlos Cortéz tiene un nuevo libro sobre arte y poesía / Carlos Cortéz Has a New Book of Art and Poetry," *Chicago Lawndale News,* 28 January 1993, pp. 3–4;

Marc Zimmerman, "Transplanting Roots and Taking Off: Latino Poetry in Illinois," in *Studies in Illinois Poetry,* edited by John E. Hallwas (Urbana, Ill.: Stormline Press, 1989), pp. 77–116.

# Carlos Cumpián

*(22 August 1953 –     )*

Marc Zimmerman
*University of Illinois at Chicago*

BOOKS: *Coyote Sun* (Chicago: MARCH/Abrazo Press, 1990);

*Latino Rainbow: Poems about Latino Americans* (Chicago: Childrens Press, 1994);

*Armadillo Charm* (Chicago: Tía Chucha Press, 1996).

OTHER: "Poem for a Puerto Rican Policeman," in *The Banyon Press Anthology 1,* edited by Daniel Campion (Chicago: Banyon Press, 1977), p. 11;

"Cuento," in *Fiesta in Aztlán: An Anthology of Chicano Poetry,* edited by Toni Empringham (Santa Barbara: Capra Press, 1982), p. 114;

*Cosecha Aztlán,* special issue of *Ecos: A Latino Journal of People's Culture and Literature,* edited by Cumpián, 3, no. 1 (Spring 1985);

"Understanding My Feet All Day," in *Third World,* edited by Jim Villani (Youngstown, Ohio: Pig Iron Press, 1988), p. 57;

"No Deposits No Returns," in *Emergency Tacos: Seven Poets con Picante,* edited by Cumpián (Chicago: MARCH/Abrazo Press, 1989), p. 21;

"Once Was Enough" and "La Migra for tú," in *Chicago Uptown Indian Poetry Anthology,* edited by William Oandasan (Chicago: Chicago Indian Center, 1996), pp. 22–23;

"With Only Smoke to Cover Me" and "The Circus," in *El Coro: A Chorus of Latino and Latina Poetry,* edited by Martin Espada (Amherst: University of Massachusetts Press, 1997), pp. 53–55;

"Recuerdos for Those of the First Wave" and "The Ninth Level of Death," in *Shards of Light / Astillas de Luz,* edited by Olivia Maciel (Chicago: Tía Chucha Press, 1998), pp. 28–30.

SELECTED PERIODICAL PUBLICATIONS–
UNCOLLECTED: "Culture cul-de-sac: Save Chicano Cryptograms," *Revista Chicano-Riqueña,* 5, no. 3 (1977): 15;

"The After Dinner Dent," *R.A.M. Collective,* 2 (June 1977): 3;

*Carlos Cumpián in Chicago at the release party for his 1990 collection,* Coyote Sun *(photograph by Phil Moloitis)*

"The New Left Shoe" and "The Migra for Two," *Rocky Mountain Arsenal of the Arts,* 1 (August 1986): 6–7;

"Evocación planetaria," *Rocky Mountain Arsenal of the Arts,* 2 (October 1987): 13;

"America Necesita Operación Trabajo: Lee Treviño desaparecido o Pancho Villa, donde estás ahora cuando te necesito / America Needs Operation Jobs: Vanished Lee Treviño or Pancho Villa, Where Are They Now When You Need Them,"

52

*Underground Forest / La selva subterránea,* 10 (1991): 24–25.

Carlos Cumpián followed the poets Carlos Cortéz, Ana Castillo, and Carlos Morton as pioneering Mexican and Mexican American writers who identified themselves as Chicano and who began reading and publishing their work in Chicago during the 1970s. Born and mainly raised in Texas, he brought a Southwest Chicano perspective to the post-1968 political and cultural world of the city.

Carlos Jerónimo Cumpián was born on 22 August 1953 in San Antonio to Texas-born parents. His mother was the daughter of a Texas-born railroad worker, though one of her grandmothers was from Zacatecas, Mexico; his father was a Korean War veteran who, even though college educated, worked as a migrant laborer in Texas, Illinois, and California. The family left Texas when Cumpián was two and spent some years in Sacramento and San José, California. In 1954 his father had contacts with labor leader César E. Chávez in the San José branch of a nationwide community activist organization headed by Saul Alinsky; when they returned to Texas, the father had contacts with key families involved with *La Raza Unida* (The United People's Party) in Crystal City. The job market forced him to leave the Southwest and seek a new future in the burgeoning labor market of Chicago; he found work with Amvets and sent for his family in late 1967.

During his family's Texas years Cumpián attended school in Crystal City, Carrizo Springs, and Harlingen. He recalled in a 1992 television interview that his mother "liked reading stories and enjoyed telling me *dichos* [Spanish-language sayings]. She found some old Grimm brothers books in a barn and read them to me as I was growing up." Perhaps that practice is what saved him from the segregated and mediocre education he received in South Texas and the harsh, racially conflicted urban educational experience he had in Chicago.

Cumpián has frequently expressed his surprise at the black/white racial polarization he found in Chicago. He was not sure where Latinos fit on that spectrum, and the Mexican community in the city was relatively distant from the militancy stirring within Southwest Chicano movement circles. Cumpián was moved by the work of Dr. Martin Luther King Jr. and grew to identify with African American and countercultural modes of life and art.

Cumpián attended public school from seventh through tenth grades but dropped out at sixteen to explore the streets, experimenting with drugs, damaging his health, and losing a few friends along the way—victims of "their excesses and traffic accidents," as he said in 1992. By age seventeen he was a troubled adolescent who had "faced the specter of mortality" and was beginning to ask fundamental questions about life and death. Attaining his general education degree at this time, he stopped watching television for five years and dedicated his waking hours to exploring Chicago rhythm and blues scene (he even worked in a blues club to hear local performers). He also increasingly read Beat and other avant-garde poets, including a few Chicano writers.

Describing Cumpián during this period, Cathleen Schandelmeier, a reporter for *Letter eX: Chicago's Poetry Newsmagazine,* says that he

> quickly became bored with what he was learning. A bright and impatient young man, he didn't feel that they were teaching him the "relevant material." This was during the days of the Vietnam war. He wanted to better understand what was going on with the war from both sides. He didn't feel that the "sound bites" the media was feeding the public were the whole story, so he sought truth within the pages of books and the practice of Buddhism.

Cumpián said in 1992: "I didn't decide to become a poet. My parents told me stories, I was bilingual, I felt the need to struggle with words in English and Spanish." He told Michael K. Johnson in 1994, however: "It wasn't until I started reading a number of books by different writers of poetry, and people who wrote poems to read before an audience, that it dawned on me how interesting poetry was."

Among the key figures with whom he identified were Beat and "marginal" poets such as Diane di Prima, Allen Ginsberg, Charles Bukowski, Lawrence Ferlinghetti, Gregory Corso, and Andrei Codrescu (especially the Romanian writer's pseudo-Puerto Rican collection, *License to Carry a Gun,* 1970); but he was also interested in the rabble-rousing proto-rap groups such as "The Last Poets" of New York. As Johnson notes, Cumpián remembers being especially drawn to "writers such as Ferlinghetti because 'they were funny, they were full of absurdities and they had a humorous element that I liked. They addressed issues like what it means to be an American.' Their frank openness on topics that were traditionally taboo pushed middle class norms to their limits."

He remembers being told in his early years that "Spanish was a foreign language." Even as he read non-Latino writers, he found himself interested in bilingual and bicultural approaches. After all, he thought, "They were speaking Spanish here first, in what was to become America." By the early 1970s Cumpián "was already getting some Chicano awareness," and he "even wanted to become a social worker or counselor."

*Cover for Cumpián's 1990 collection of his early poems, with artwork by Cumpián and Carlos Cortéz*

He worked as a volunteer for Centro de la Causa and then for BASTA, the Brotherhood Against Slavery to Addiction. Nevertheless, his interests continued to veer toward Mexican and Chicano culture and art. In 1972 he traveled to Mexico to learn about pre-Columbian cultures, as well as about contemporary issues in the Mexican youth movement. Around this time he joined with the singer/guitarist Chuy Negrete and the artist Aurelio Díaz, as well as Negrete's singer sisters and Juana Guzmán (a close friend of Ana Castillo and a major Chicana arts facilitator), in developing El Teatro del Barrio in south Chicago. They worked up skits to present in theaters, schools, and churches, as well as in the streets, "touring Midwest barrios and colonias, and participating in endless discussions and study groups about Chicano/Mexican cultural life and history." He also worked in the budding Chicago Latino arts movement, which involved Díaz, Cortéz, and such visual artists as Ray Patlán and José Gamaliel González. His

wide reading and the impression made on him by Negrete's dramatic presentation of Rodolfo "Corky" González's classic 1967 poem, *I am Joaquín / Yo Soy Joaquín,* led him to turn increasingly toward "poetry with a Chicano theme." During his theater days he began to perform Chicano *actos* (skits), reading other people's poems between the *actos*–until, as he put it in 1992, "I finally decided I had my own story to tell."

Cumpián fell under the sway of the Chicago Puerto Rican poet David Hernández, whom he admired and with whom he gave joint readings in the early 1970s. "I'm a graduate of the David Hernández School of poetry," Cumpián has often said, referring primarily to Hernández's oral-presentation skills. By this time African American pre-rap rhythms were becoming evident in Cumpián's work, along with English-language Native American inflections drawn mainly from writers such as Simon Ortiz, Lonnie Poco, William Oandasan, and Ray Young Bear.

Around the same time, working in an Industrial Workers of the World (IWW, or "Wobbly") unionized warehouse, Cumpián met the Wobbly graphic artist and poet Cortéz, who brought him into the organization and came to serve as perhaps his most important mentor. Another local influence was Castillo, whose early chapbook, *Otro Canto* (Another Song, 1977), Cumpián helped to promote on a trip to a Texas Chicano cultural festival in 1978. Still another was the critic Nicolás Kannellos, a young professor at the University of Indiana in Gary and editor of *Revista Chicano-Riqueña* (later renamed *Américas Review*), for whose proliferating Latino cultural projects Cumpián voluteered his time and talents. Other influences included such national figures as Ernesto Galarza, Raúl Salinas, Juan Felipe Herrera, Ricardo Sánchez, and Abelardo "Lalo" Delgado.

In the late 1970s Kannellos and the art critic Victor Sorrell enlisted Cumpián to head up the poetry section of *Abrazo* (Embrace), a tiny cultural journal they had established as an outlet for the *Movimiento Artístico Chicano* (MARCH), founded by José González with Cortéz and others. Cumpián joined MARCH and quickly emerged as the leading literary force in this group, helping to edit the poetry section of *Abrazo* and performing at the first annual Canto Al Pueblo festival of Chicano/Latino arts and literature in Milwaukee. He participated increasingly in Chicano cultural events in the Midwest and Southwest, serving over the years as MARCH secretary, promoter, editor in chief, and president. In these capacities he arranged poetry readings and was responsible for the final selection and editing of every volume of a series of books published by MARCH/Abrazo Press that helped place Chicago on the national Chicano/Latino literary map, after Morton, Kannellos, Sandra Cisneros, and Castillo left the city to make their names in the Southwest.

Cumpián married Rosalyn Ayala when he was twenty-two; they had two children, Camilo and Mía. Divorced by the early 1980s, he made his living working in bookstores, restaurants, and health-food stores. Also in the early 1980s, after taking classes at several community colleges, he entered the English program at the University of Illinois at Chicago ("on the eight year plan," as he told Schandelmeier). He became the editor of the university's Latino cultural center journal, *Ecos: A People's Journal of Latino Culture and Literature,* in which capacity he prepared a special national Chicano issue titled *Cosecha Aztlán* in 1985. After graduating from the university, he married the poet Cynthia Gallaher, with whom he had a third child, Julián. Taking a position in the public relations unit of the Chicago Public Library, he continued his work at MARCH, coordinating the publication of *Emergency Tacos: Seven Poets con Picante* (1989), a mini-anthology including his own work along with that of Cortéz, Cisneros, Gallaher, Raúl Niño, Margarita López, and Beatriz Badikian. From the early 1980s through the 1990s he led workshops and gave individual and group readings while promoting readings and workshop presentations by local and national Latino and Latina writers, both through his library job and his role as MARCH cultural worker. When the library job came to an end in 1993, he increased his teaching work, giving classes on Latino literature and poetry at Columbia College in Chicago and taking a position as a high-school English teacher.

Some of Cumpián's friends grew worried about his development because he had given so much to promoting Latino arts and the work of other writers and because he was struggling to make a living while pursuing an art that rarely pays. Yet, it was during this period that he emerged as a nationally recognized Chicano poet.

Cumpián's poetry began appearing in local and national journals and anthologies in the late 1970s. In 1990 he published some of the key poems from his early oeuvre in the volume *Coyote Sun.* In the fall of 1994 he published a high-school-level illustrated book, *Latino Rainbow,* with twenty poems on Latino historical events and figures including Chávez, politician Henry Cisneros, activist Reies López Tijerina, NASA astronaut Ellen Ochoa, ballplayer Roberto Clemente, and musicians Tito Puente, Joan Baez, and Linda Ronstadt, as well as his mentor, Cortéz. In 1996 he published a collection of his humorous, surrealistic, and political poems written since the late 1980s, *Armadillo Charm.*

Most of Cumpián's early poetry evokes barrio street sound and fury, and almost all his work to date is strongly urban in its irony, cynicism, and sarcasm.

There is also a strong current of ecological and "New Age" concerns in Cumpián's work that grew out of his early jobs and friendships. He had championed indigenous precapitalist culture and had worked closely with the artists Ray Vázquez, José González, Marcos Raya, and Cortéz in the development of these tendencies within the framework of MARCH. The blending of these currents creates contradiction and tension within the urban patter and verbal twists and turns that dominate Cumpián's poetic style. The breadth of his concerns, as well as his extensive interaction with mainstream and radical Chicago and Latino writing circles, leads to a body of work that ranges widely over such themes as ecological destruction, presidential bungling, the arms race, economic and racial discrimination, Indian mysticism, popular fads and fashions, Chicago street crimes, and, perhaps above all, to Anglo cultural hegemony resistance.

Josh Sparbeck, writing about one of Cumpián's presentations in the mid 1980s, gives a representative view of his work:

> Much of Cumpián's poetry deals with social and political issues of the day. The problems in El Salvador and Nicaragua crop up often in his work, as does the plight of the American Indian. In addition, popular culture and advertising are often lampooned. But his work is generally as humorous as it is biting, and he is adept at drawing in his audience rather than putting them off.

As a performance poet, Cumpián frequently presents his work to audiences who have never read it and for whom multilayered complexity can lead to waning interest and even rejection. He draws in his listeners by offering explanations and quips, creating an atmosphere of fun that leads to a sense of shared assumptions and complicity. He is often able to help his listeners "hear" things that they would not understand if they simply read the poem. But his poetry is not necessarily simple or fully accessible. It makes demands on readers who have not witnessed his performances. Cumpián embeds deep structural patterns in his poems that can best be grasped through hearing them and that will only emerge fully for a reader through careful attention that goes beyond the surface of the text.

One of the poems in *Coyote Sun,* "Cuento" (Story), provides an example of the complexity of a seemingly simple poem. The speaker, in an effort to "call home," asks the telephone operator to connect him to Aztlán, the symbolic Chicano homeland, but she and her supervisor deny any knowledge of its existence. The speaker tells them, "You'll hear more / about it soon!" Readers may be as ignorant about Aztlán as are the operators, but Cumpián chooses not to explain its meaning. His message seems to be that Aztlán is not com-

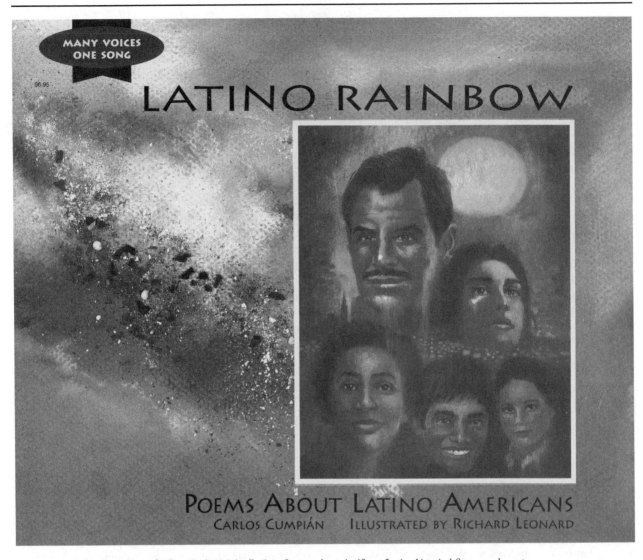

MANY VOICES ONE SONG

$6.95

# LATINO RAINBOW

### POEMS ABOUT LATINO AMERICANS
CARLOS CUMPIÁN    ILLUSTRATED BY RICHARD LEONARD

*Cover for Cumpián's 1994 collection of poems about significant Latino historical figures and events*

municable in one poem or by one poet, but that the growing Chicano presence will make it clear soon enough.

Cumpián, like Cortéz, sees the world as a harmonious cycle disrupted by European, and subsequently, American Anglo conquest—in other words, by history, which is perceived as the enemy. His poems deal with significant dates and events: 1492, 1521, the battle of Puebla in 1862, the American attack on Veracruz in 1914, the dropping of the atomic bomb in 1945, and the Cuban Revolution of 1959. Through it all, the basic scenario is his mythified history of the rape of Indian land and culture. He presents scene after scene of destruction; yet, his sense of humor is always present as he seeks the recovery of spiritual wholeness.

In some of Cumpián's poems signs of hope and rebirth appear. In "El Arbolito" (The Little Tree), he writes to Cortéz of a new compact with the Midwest—a symbolic effort to create, from Mexican transplanting in the Midwest, a transformational process that will bear fruit:

> After a long absence
> you wanted to see
> the green sapling
> planted in the yard
> by the hands which once
> carried you as a child.
> Standing under its mature shade
> you and your bride to be
> gathered around its
> full trunk and
> embraced,
> rain and sun

soil and wind
winter and summer
father and mother . . .
past and present meeting in one flesh.
El arbolito
still stands, now a tree in Wisconsin
years after the planters
have gone, leaving
a reminder
of what cariño [affection] can mean.

Many of Cumpián's poems involve totemic or mythical animals. While for Mexicans the term *coyote* has come to refer to one who profits from illegal immigration, to Cumpián the coyote represents Chicano/Indian identity, perseverance, and survival by wits at the margins of society. Encroached upon and endangered, the coyote is a magician, a trickster, a poet, and a public-transportation-riding beggar who draws on the devices of the modern world (telephones, book publishing) to maintain his connection with nature.

The poems of *Armadillo Charm* address further mutations in the relationships between nature and history, magic and technology, and Chicanos and "the other." Most striking in this work are the extended range; the broader, more confident poetic voice; and the deeper ironies. The first two poems in this collection serve as a kind of a double overture for the overall work. The title poem portrays that survivor of ancient evolutionary patterns, the armadillo, which is now in danger of extinction. Like marginalized urban inhabitants, these armadillos are smart: they have resisted the numbing zoo of the American working world inhabited by life-threatening "two legged foreigners." They want to be around when the cycle of nature-destroying civilization comes to an end, but in the meantime they resist extinction and are "skinning themselves / raw while roaming hungry in the dark."

Having escaped the meteor that left the world a dinosaurless desert wasteland that could be inhabited and cultivated by two-legged mammals, the armadillo survived only to be discovered by mid-nineteenth-century independence-clamoring gringos as part of the takeover of the American Southwest. Meat for nouvelle cuisine tacos, the armadillo survives once again, sticking to a worm-based diet and becoming a hardened tourist walking backwards across the Mexican-Texas borderland. The reader is invited to try the creature's diet (food is one of the main themes throughout the book) but is urged not to be like the "schmucks" who buy armadillo kitsch in airports on impulse. Cumpián's point may be that kitsch collectors have appetites as undiscriminating as a young adult's sexual drive left to its own devices. But the poet clearly wants to resurrect

the armadillo's connection to preconquest Indian identity and its survival in the postmodern world.

In the final stanza the poet notes how the "armadillo prefers his original Nahuatl name" and seems to say "don't touch me." Do not trivialize armadillos into extinction, says Cumpián; save individual armadillos in the good old American way by adopting one.

The other overture poem, "Don't Wanna Peso Much," anticipates subsequent pieces dealing with ecological destruction, Thanksgiving turkeys, the transformation of the American Eden into a golf course, relations between Mexicans and Chicanos, new immigration policies, and the anti-Mexican backlash. The domestication and suburbanization of Aztlán and the reduction of nature to a gringo-dominated recreational space is not a new theme in Chicano literature: it is portrayed in Alberto Ríos's short story of Chicano boyhood heaven as a golf course, "The Secret Lion" (1987), and a related trope emerges in John Nichols's novel *The Milagro Beanfield War* (1974). Both of these works are favorites of Cumpián's.

What is at least relatively new in "Don't Wanna Peso Much" is the expansion of Cumpián's satiric style as he organizes his poem as a kind of performance skit. The writer and performance artist Guillermo Gómez Peña is clearly the major influence on this new Cumpián style, with its rapid-fire geographies and its play with new communications technologies, collage, parody, and multivoiced techniques.

The poem starts with a gibe at the contemporary penchant for novelty, the commodification of news coverage, and, above all, the push for privatization and social amnesia. Thanksgiving, originally a ceremony of immigrant Anglos and Native Americans, is converted into an all-out attack on undocumented Mexican border-crossers. The Mexico City performance artist Superbarrio is watching it all on his "tiny Tenochitlán tele," as the roads to occupied Mexico are sealed. A newscaster describes the border crackdowns, and Superbarrio hears how the American employers of Mexican waiters, grocery boys, Kelly Girl office clerks, gardeners, and groundskeepers suddenly miss their brown workers. The poetry grows rhapsodic and Whitmanesque:

From burning beaches where ice blue raspas are shaved into cones,
to the dark apple orchards after the fall dumps its lonely pickers,
to the gravel pits of sorrow, where ruined bruised backs once gathered,
is there no one conducting an underground railroad to save
targeted people, who lack the empire's proper papers for staying this side of the fence.

The poet moves on to a vision of a football stadium full of Spanish-speaking Los Angeles natives being deported, as Brown Berets defend East Los Angeles and a Los Lobos concert is canceled. This scene is followed by a talk-show discussion of the Mexican effort to take over Anglo-California. The gringos are afraid of losing their parking spaces and golf courses; the worst fear of all is that the Mexicans are "pushing for a permanent shift in our values." A telephone call rather bizarrely takes the reader from Los Angeles golf courses to a Dallas grassy knoll—a reference to the assassination of President John F. Kennedy. The poem closes with three stanzas about Cumpián's generic Mexican, Juan, beginning with a litany of his multicultural food experiences and going on, in the second stanza, to his capture by the *migra* (agents of the Immigration and Naturalization Service). Meanwhile, Chicago has been renamed Chicano, Illinois, and the majority of Americans use more hot salsa than ketchup. In the final stanza the Gómez Peña references appear, as Californians are portrayed as rabidly eager to attack the new immigrants.

Other poems in the collection reveal some of Cumpián's major concerns. "Before the Great Gorge" goes back to the first Thanksgiving and speaks facetiously of Indian displacement in the expansion of European domination and the Indian contribution to American life. "Eighteen Holed Dreams Gotta Go" bemoans the gringo destruction of nature in the form of golf courses, which the poet would like to miniaturize or eliminate entirely. "El Comandante" is a whimsical look at the Argentinian revolutionary leader Che Guevara in relation to a possible resolution to Western spoliation, exploitation, and commodification. But did Guevara understand the indigenous world in which he sought to move? Did he misrepresent the people he sought to lead? What of Latino poets such as Cumpián? The poet questions his own function in relation to the Latinos and Chicanos he wishes to represent. In "Getting Closer" he satirizes those who live and breathe their ethnic identifications. "Soon it's Robots" addresses questions of economic restructuring, displacement, and loss, as corporate heads make millions. In "Are the Tacos Taking Over?" Cumpián amusingly conjures the rising Anglo fear of a Chicano takeover.

"Beto and Oso" portrays Oso (Bear), a Chicago Mexican, cajoling his boss, Beto, into telling of his exploits as a Marine in the invasion of the Dominican Republic in 1965. This piece reveals Latino complicity in the Anglo conquest ideology. Without any overt criticism or commentary, Cumpián shows envy of the adventures of Oso's boss and the values implicit in the story he has to tell: military jingoism, racism, chauvinism, and American contempt for the poor and "underdeveloped." The poem portrays an attitude frequently found in the barrio. The theme of barrio blindness recurs in the next poem, "Armadillo's Diagnosis," as the title character, a world-weary participant-observer of barrio life, watches a birthday party at which a piñata is featured and comments on how the persistence of Mexican customs leads to dietary imbalance. But, the poet defends the happiness produced by the piñata by describing Armadillo's birthday-party-less, sour-grapes life.

"Hermanas guapas" (Handsome Sisters) is one of the odd poems in this volume that plays with food smells, hygienic habits, and eroticism. In "The Eighth Commandment & Uranium 235" Cumpián points to the relationship between the emergent American Latino world and the atomic age—a theme at the heart of Rudolfo A. Anaya's *Bless Me, Ultima* (1972) and Ana Castillo's *So Far from God* (1993). He starts with a note from the Native American poet Ortiz about the involvement of a Navajo named Martínez in the discovery of the uranium that was used in atomic bombs and in electricity projects in the Southwest. Clearly, Cumpián is not proud of the achievement of his Spanish-surnamed Native American brother; thinking of the ruined land, of those working in radioactive mines, the further development of the Southwest, and the concomitant uprooting of Chicanos and Mexicans, he tells his fellow poet, "Simon, I wish these veins were never discovered," and conjures up a vision of Anglo developers as so many "sharks . . . with eyes like their makers, / eyes that never close, but instead, / continuously cast a fixed gaze on all they will devour."

"Tejas Ode" is a poem in questionable Spanish about the Alamo as seen from a vulture-filled sky. "On the Bus" is a ride through ethnic Chicago, with White Castles, pierogi, lottery tickets, and much more as the bus moves from stop to stop. In "Atrocity in the Assassin/nation" Cumpián satirizes computer industry technocrats who "take Bill Gates as guide" and participate in the pollution and desecration of the planet. "Appendectomy" is a rambling reverie weaving in references to ethnic hostilities in Yugoslavia and the United States, studies of mythology by "ol' Joe Campbell," Cumpián's IWW-influenced view of capitalist politics and Midwest Chicano life in comparison to the lives of Texas outdoor workers and Mexican Harvard or Yale graduates. "Estrellitas" (Little Stars) is an exercise in imagery, with two Chicanos, "their chins lifted / like moon-struck coyotes," watching "heaven's sparklers." In "Tochtli Luna and Cuauhtli" white men do not contemplate the skies but go beyond them to the moon—only to find Mexican sandals in the lunar sand.

In "Premonition" Cumpián projects a vision of vast upheaval extending from Africa to the western shore of America, from Europe to the Caribbean to Rio

Cover (with art by Camilo Cumpián) for Cumpián's 1996 collection of poems, in which the armadillo is a symbol of survival

de Janeiro to the Mexican border, and from Los Angeles to the Ganges by way of Las Vegas, Nevada, and Pueblo, Colorado. In the middle of it all are the armadillos, now penitent, trekking their way up from border areas to Oklahoma, to Iowa, and finally to Chicago and the termite- and rat-infested housing projects of urban sloth and mismanagement. "Singing Armadillo" (the title refers to a bar in Chicago) expresses Chicano identification with Caribbean immigrants as a dreadlocked Jamaican Rastafarian truck driver meets the "word dealer" poets Cumpián and Cortéz as they wait for a train to take them back to Chicago from a Kenneth Patchen poetry festival in Ohio. He offers to give them a ride if they write a poem for the Ethiopian emperor Haile Selassie. "Bout to Leave the Barrio" portrays two Mexican club boxers battling to see who will get the chance to rise out of the barrio world.

In "Loco Chuy Raps with Tony Atole" Loco Chuy tells his friend that he has worked all week and is not interested in health food but in good-tasting, munchable hot dogs, bloody steaks, and milkshakes.

The poem is a ghastly catalogue of junk-food carcinogens, detailing the most baleful aspects of one of the major American gifts to a globalizing world—although one has a sense that Cumpián sometimes cannot resist the fat-and-salt attractions of the ghoulish products he conjures up.

In "He Still Makes House Calls" Cumpián writes of Dr. Jack Kevorkian's misunderstood mercy killings and suggests a better approach in which death applicants would be taken to gang-infested Chicago neighborhoods in attire that will guarantee their rapid liquidation. This poem is followed by "Our Evil Empire," a meditation on the Watts, California, race riots of 1965 as seen in the context of Beirut, the failed coup against Mikhail Gorbachev, and, implicitly, the race riots in 1990s Los Angeles, all pointing to the racist evil indicated in the title. "Estás Invitado y" (You Are Invited And) celebrates some excellent Mexican cooking, including a soup that allegedly helped Mexican boxer Julio César Chávez to defeat the Puerto Rican Hector "Macho" Camacho.

In the final poem, "Armadillo's Aquí Buey of Knowledge," Oso and Armadillo are living the good urban life, sharing a sloppy bachelor pad while they await a long-delayed trial resulting from a bar fight that broke out when Armadillo tried to defend Oso after his friend's flirtation with a woman. This playful, sexy poem ends with a portrayal of Armadillo's transformations through "four stages of tequila." He is an acculturated Chicago Mexican who is keeping his feet in the old culture, a carpenter scarred by nails and screws that have religious as well as erotic implications.

In Cumpián's images of urban displacement, barroom brawls, ghetto riots, and boxing bouts, from one end of the United States to another, through all the dimensions of the American "evil empire," the key theme is that the struggle for Chicano culture and identity is important not just to Latino but to all human identity, redemption, and rebirth. Musing about his life and work, Cumpián has noted that his continuing problems in finding a way to make a living while developing his work are an extension of the problems his father and many other Chicanos and Latinos have encountered, even when they have had considerable formal education. "It is as if the so-called American dream has been a trickster's joke on us," he says. "We've had to be improvising tricksters our whole lives just to hold our own." His high-school and college teaching have taken priority over his work as an arts and literary promoter, publisher, and performer. Cumpián, however, has continued his work and is well into new writing projects. He has been invited to give readings at the Guadalajara Book Fair in 1992 and the Latin American Studies Association Conference in 1998. Selections from a recording of satirical improvisations he developed with other poets and spoken-word artists in local radio workshops led by Gómez Peña on his MacArthur Foundation trips to Chicago were played on National Public Radio. One piece, Cumpián's interpretation of a funda-mentalist preacher, is reproduced in Gómez Peña's *Warrior for Gringostroika* (1993).

*Armadillo Charm* shows Cumpián still struggling, like other Chicanos, to find his own space, his own contemporary Aztlán, in a changing transnational world of ever-shifting and difficult-to-determine identities. In these contexts, Cumpián forges new dimensions of his own identity struggle and, more than most Chicano writers, he goes beyond his group's particular concerns to those of the wider global community. Still developing and finding his way through the maze of a post-NAFTA United States, Cumpián is a transnationalized Chicago Chicano poet making every effort to understand and confront, with courage and humor, the transforming and dangerous times in which he has lived.

**References:**

"Carlos Cumpián," *Drumvoices Revue: A Confluence of Literary, Cultural and Vision Arts,* 6 (Fall–Winter–Spring, 1996–1997): 14–17;

Guillermo Gómez-Peña, *Warrior for Gringostroika: Essays, Performance Texts, and Poetry* (St. Paul, Minn.: Graywolf Press, 1993), p. 170;

Michael K. Johnson, "Teacher Pens a Rainbow of Poetry," *Columbia College Chronicle,* 28, no. 11 (1994): 10;

Maureen McLaine, "Poetry in Motion: The Varied Voices of Artists in Our Midst," *Chicago Tribune,* Books, 20 April 1997, pp. 1–2;

Cathleen Schandelmeier, "Poetry Profile: Carlos Cumpián," *Letter Ex: Chicago's Poetry Newsmagazine,* no. 95 (August/September 1994): 8–9;

Josh Sparbeck, "Poetry Series Features Chicago's Cumpián," *Wayne State University South End,* 16 October 1986, p. 2;

Marc Zimmerman, "Transplanting Roots and Taking Off: Latino Poetry in Illinois," in *Studies in Illinois Poetry,* edited by John E. Hallwas (Urbana, Ill.: Stormline Press, 1989): 77–116.

# Barbara Brinson Curiel

*(11 December 1956 – )*

Ramón Sánchez
*Olivet College*

BOOKS: *Nocturno* (Berkeley, Cal.: University of California, Chicano Studies, 1978);
*Vocabulary of the Dead* (Oakland, Cal.: Nomad Press, 1984);
*Speak To Me From Dreams* (Berkeley, Cal.: Third Woman Press, 1989).

PLAY PRODUCTIONS: *Guadalupe,* Oakland, Cal., Mills College and the Latin American Library, April 1978;
*Tongues of Fire,* Oakland, Cal., Oakland Museum, 1981.

OTHER: "Fire" and "María la O," in *A Decade of Hispanic Literature,* edited by Nicolás Kanellos (Houston: Chicano-Riqueña, 1982), pp. 36–41;
"Winter," "Drought: San Joaquín Valley, Winter," "Remnants," "Dying," "María la O," and "The Warehouse of the Hungry," in *Contemporary Chicano Poetry: An Anthology,* edited by Wolfgang Binder (Erlangen, West Germany: Verlog, Palm & Enke, 1986), pp. 21–30;
"Pearl," "Recipe for Sand," and "Recipe for Salt," in *Early Ripening: American Women Poets Now,* edited by Marge Piercy (London: Pandora, 1987), pp. 16–17;
"Roads" and "Drought: San Joaquín Valley, Winter," in *Infinite Divisions: An Anthology of Chicana Literature,* edited by Tey Diana Rebolledo and Eliana S. Rivero (Tucson: University of Arizona Press, 1993), pp. 175, 183, 344;
"Sonora Ghazal," "Self-portrait," and "Tú eres como yo," in *Vous Avez Dit Chicano: Anthologie Thématique de Poésie Chicano,* translated and edited by Elyette Benjamin-Labarthe (Bordeaux: Editions de la Maison des Sciences de L'Homme D'Aquitaine, Centre de Recherches Sur L'Amerique Anglophone, 1993), pp. 69, 73, 209.

SELECTED PERIODICAL PUBLICATIONS-
UNCOLLECTED: "Tlaxcala," *De Colores Journal,* 4, no. 1–2 (1978): 45–47;

*Barbara Brinson Curiel (courtesy of Curiel)*

"The Hair," *El Tecolote Literario,* 6 (December 1985): 3;
"Heteroglossia in Ana Castillo's *The Mixquiahuala Letters,*" *Discurso Literario: Revista de Estudios Iberoamericanos,* 7, no. 1 (1990): 11–23.

Barbara Brinson Curiel's poetry has strong roots in the oral and written folklore traditions of Chicano-Mexican and Anglo-American cultures. Her complex, yet accessible, literary work confronts issues such as gender, the search for identity, and affirmation of community.

Born on 11 December 1956 in San Francisco, California, Barbara Brinson grew up in the Mission District at a time when the previously middle-class neighborhood was becoming a more working-class environment. Her mother, Dolores Pineda Brinson, did clerical work in doctors' offices, and her father, Wilkin Brinson, worked as a laborer, eventually becoming a salesman. The eldest of three children, Brinson has a sister, Linda, and a brother, William. Until the seventh grade she attended public school. Then she attended St. James Girls School and Immaculate Conception Academy, both Catholic schools run by Dominican nuns.

Brinson recalls that at the age of eight she was composing poems and stories and was encouraged by her teachers to write. In the fourth or fifth grade she began to read voraciously. She was enthralled by Charlotte Brontë's *Jane Eyre* (1847), a novel about a woman in conflict with her natural desires and the restraints of her social condition. Louisa May Alcott's *Little Women* (1868–1869)–a novel based on Alcott's recollections of her modest New England childhood–was also an important literary influence.

Both Brinson's parents were born in San Francisco. On her father's side, her grandfather was Anglo Texan and her grandmother was a Mexican American from Tucson. The issue of mixed ancestry appears in Brinson's *Nocturno* (1978), in which the themes of identity and the search for a poetic voice dominate. "The collection," Brinson said in a 13 January 1994 telephone interview, "was an effort to claim my experience and cultural self." The poem "Tú eres mi otro yo" (You Are my Other Self) stands out in addressing the mixed-ancestry issue.

The impact of the civil-rights movement made Brinson conscious of the dialogic role of art in giving people political power. By 1972 she had a sense of the power an individual could have to change things. She remembers seeing a performance of El Teatro Campesino (The Farmworkers' Theater), which made her realize that art could empower people socially and politically, that art could convey a message. These experiences and the challenges to cultural norms and personal values typified by events such as the "Summer of Love" in 1967 had an impact on her attitudes. Brinson credits her high-school teacher Paul Shuttleworth, a poet who was involved in the artistic movements of the San Francisco area, with introducing her to modern American poetry. From 1975 through 1979 Brinson attended Mills College, a private women's liberal-arts college in Oakland, California, where she earned her B.A. with a double major in English and Spanish. She later worked there as a lecturer in ethnic studies and received a Mellon Grant for Curriculum Development at the college in 1983. While she was still an undergraduate student she wrote and arranged the poems in her *Nocturno* chapbook. In 1978 her play *Guadalupe* was performed at

Mills College, and in 1981 *Tongues of Fire* was staged at the Oakland Museum.

*Nocturno* begins with "Back Home: Winter, Johnson's Island, Calif.," which sets the tone of re-identification. The speaker describes a place where "I catch my reflection in the glass: / the face of my mother / . . . I begin to number / the years by their rainfall." The symbolic return is to "Home," where reflection and reevaluation occur. In this collection of English, Spanish, and code-switching (alternating Spanish and English) poems, the motifs of sleep, dreams, and night are important, and the various personas of the poems act out self-discoveries. The final poem, "Waking Up: Feeling Soft Breathing in My Ear," leaves the reader with an awareness of the poet's acquisition of a lyric voice: "A chorus of red birds / shatters the frailty of my sleep / The ground sighs in content: / morning rain fills the pockets / of its thirst."

At Mills College, Brinson became conscious of her own experience as a Chicana and grew increasingly aware of her community, ethnic issues, and the intellectual environment. As she came in contact with the Chicano studies program her understanding about why she was in undergraduate school increased in conjunction with her sense of being an outsider, being the "other," as she became involved in the dialogues about class, race and ethnicity, and eventually gender.

In 1979 Brinson received a National Hispanic Scholarship and went to Stanford University, where she earned her M.A. in Spanish in 1981. In 1979 she also received a prize for her poetry from the Ina Coolbrith Circle in California. Her college experience brought her in touch with the works of poets such as James Wright, Marge Piercy, and Sylvia Plath–whom she credits with giving her a sense of the aesthetic. She acknowledges the strong influence of Wright, noting that his *The Branch Will Not Break* (1963), a collection of poems that avoid traditional meter, rhyme, and discursive reasoning, was especially important in her development as a poet. From reading Wright, Piercy, and Plath, Brinson learned to build on the poetic image and not the narrative structure.

Her university studies led Brinson to read texts in Spanish by writers such as Gabriel García Márquez, which affirmed her cultural experience and gave value to her Hispanic heritage. Latin American writers became literary examples of means to express her Latino heritage and showed her how to present a discourse that described an experience–a Chicana experience–that was outside the literary canon of the dominant culture.

In the early 1980s Brinson worked as a higher-education student-support counselor and as a part-time instructor at California State University at Hayward. In 1982 she was awarded third prize in the Chicano Liter-

ary Contest at the University of California at Irvine,
and she won the Third Woman Poetry Prize in 1986.
Her verse began appearing in poetry anthologies. In
1986 Brinson married Anthony Curiel, a professional
stage director who teaches in the Theater Department
at the University of California, San Diego. He was also
associate artistic director at El Teatro Campesino from
1985 to 1993. The couple has two children, María
Allegra and Alejandro.

Curiel describes *Vocabulary of the Dead* (1984), her
second chapbook, as a "meditation on spirituality." It
includes still-life illustrations by Jos. Sances, primarily of
everyday items such as flowers, teapots, or a trunk, but
also a skeleton. Lucha Corpi's poem "Caminando a
solas" (Walking Alone, 1979) sets the stage for Curiel's
poetry with its theme of journey into the dark side of
memory: "bajar / al sótano / de la memoria" (to go
down / to the cellar / of memory). This collection
begins with "Vocabulary of the Dead," the opening line
of which—"Ship without compass, ocean of blindness"
—introduces a journey filled with anxieties, that nevertheless becomes a voyage of self-discovery. Curiel
republished several of the poems from this collection—
including "Yerma," "Dirge," "Digging a Grave," "Bonds,"
and "Letanìa peregrina" (Pilgrimage Litany)—in *Speak
To Me From Dreams* (1989).

In *Speak To Me From Dreams,* for a persona to find
herself, she must articulate the pain, anger, lust, and
losses that turn out to be those of the community. At
times the persona seems to be unconsciously acting out
rituals that are part of the struggle with an alienating
world. Curiel reveals her literary influences by using
epigraphs from Wright, Gary Soto, T. S. Eliot, and
Níkos Kazantzákis. For instance, in "Ya pa' qué quiero
adornos" (Who Wants Adornments Now), an epigraph
from Wright ("have you been holding the end of a /
frayed rope / For a thousand years?") interplays with
the burden described in the poem. The first poem in
the collection, "María la O," narrates the forced journey
that will test and transform the persona, María. By
establishing the need to give meaning to human suffering and to the inexplicable beauty encountered in life,
this poem sets the stage for the rest of the collection.
Thus, María says, "Mario grinds his teeth in his sleep; /
dreams of hell, / doesn't see our wood fence / splinter
into the road / Looking for a wedding ring, / I found an
incomplete circle of brass," though earlier she comments, "Wake up marido [husband] / Fields of dark
flowers / bloom beneath your hair." The persona not
only attempts to understand the suffering and the sense
of beauty but also tries to express them. Meso-Ameri-
can influences appear in the work, as in "Xquic": Xquic
is the mother of Xbalanqué and Hunahpú, the hero
twins of the sixteenth-century Mayan holy book, the

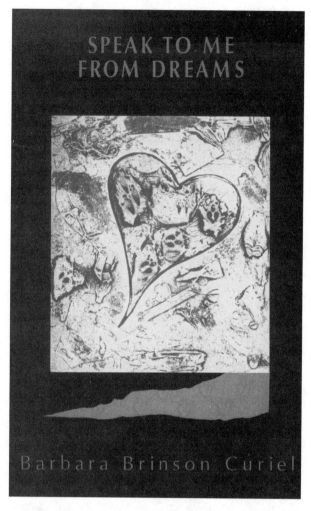

Cover for Curiel's 1989 book, poems exploring issues
of identity, gender, and ethnicity

*Popol Vuh.* These allusions echo an indigenous heritage
that is both oral and literary.

In addition to poems in English *Speak To Me From
Dreams* includes several poems in Spanish—such as "Tu
pelo" (Your Hair), "Aquí venimos a pasar hambre y
amarguras" (Here we Come to Pass Hunger and Bitterness), and "Letanía peregrina"—demonstrating the heritage that allows the writer to draw from two cultural
environments. The code-switching presents a Chicano
community reality of language. Code-switching occurs
mainly in poems that have Spanish titles and English
text, but in some poems Curiel code-switches within the
text, in "Diez libras de masa" (Ten Pounds of Dough),
for example, she uses code-switching to demonstrate
the overlapping cultural influences in verse. She shows
her ethnic consciousness by alluding to folk oral narratives in "El Cucuy" (The Bogeyman) in lists of items
and through "the Chicano Scavenger Hunt."

Curiel's awareness of both ethnic and gender issues is evident in "Recipe: Chorizo con Huevo [Sausage with Egg] / Made in The Microwave," "Diez libras de masa," "María Yo" (I María), and "My Name." In "Diez libras de masa" the persona goes through a process of socialization. A journey for food becomes a ritual of passage into a new identity, one that does not come easily and causes the persona to be "careful not to disturb / such a hard-won / kernel of my life." Here and in other food poems, the reader encounters the down-to-earth act of naming, selecting, and cooking food. The process is intimate and nonintellectual, but it makes one aware of how such a common activity roots a person in ethnicity and reveals junctions and disjunctions. This type of exploration presents old roles and defines new ones through contrast—all leading the personas to identify themselves in the context of a community. In a blurb on the back cover of *Speak To Me From Dreams*, Ana Castillo notes how Curiel's poetry "has conjured a María to speak to us from the smokey days of Tenochtitlán, through the Mexican Revolution, and the U.S. fields and railroads that have soaked up the sweat of our labor; finally she has given us a María who microwaves tortillas . . . the María who is the sum of us all." Individual identity cannot be separated from community.

Published in the anthology *Early Ripening: American Women Poets Now* (1987), Curiel's poems "Pearl," "Recipe for Sand," and "Recipe for Salt" are among the works that cause Marge Piercy to comment: "we should look at the women's landscape and realize how densely populated and beautifully planted it is with designs beginning to emerge as the trees come of age, and bear cones and fruit and make good hard wood." Tey Diana Rebolledo and Eliana S. Rivero, editors of *Infinite Divisions: An Anthology of Chicana Literature* (1993), offer Curiel's poem "Roads" as an example of "shifting spaces of Chicana reality, from private spaces of the house to public spaces." The freeway, they add, "also symbolizes freedom, the ability to travel, to return to one's roots, or to travel to find new ones." The theme of journey is employed in dealing with identity and community once more in "Roads," in which the persona says, "I migrate into my history / these cool mornings / I return weekly / to the first graders, / expecting to yank them / from these fields / with ditto sheets and chalk."

Curiel completed her Ph.D. in American literature at the University of California at Santa Cruz in 1995. Her dissertation, "Sex and the Spirit: The Authorization of Narrative in the Work of Three Women Writers of Color," explores the writings of Castillo, Sandra Cisneros, and Sara Lawrence Lightfoot. The hours spent on her dissertation and with her children left her with little time for creative writing. Yet, in 1994 she was anticipating "resurrecting as a prose writer." She has published short stories and two children's stories: "Un traje nuevo" (A New Suit, 1987) and "Suberopa, bajaropa" (Clothes Lifter, Clothes Lowerer, 1990). The prose narrative has begun to attract her interest, she says, because she wants to reach a wider audience, and prose can convey complicated tales that present the possibilities of a multivoiced culture. Domestic themes and cookbooks also have caught her attention, for she believes they are powerful reflections of ethnicity that engage nonliterary and literary worlds. She sees the prose poem as influential in allowing cultural criticism. She finds that the plasticity of prose, demonstrated in short-story writing, presents her with rich possibilities for creative expression.

Curiel's poetry has been anthologized along with works by poets such as Corpi, Lorna Dee Cervantes, and Bernice Zamora. The inclusion of Curiel's poetry in anthologies that compile a literary and cultural history of Chicana poetic production acknowledges her work as notable and significant. Her writing continues the discourse of the individual's struggles with issues of identity, gender, ethnicity, and humanization especially in the context of the Chicano community.

# Celso A. De Casas

(9 June 1944 - )

## Ramón Sánchez
*Olivet College*

BOOK: *Pelón Drops Out* (Berkeley, Cal.: Tonatiuh International, 1979).

OTHER: "And Another Piece of Litter Is Thrown on the Junk Heap," in *Literatura chicana: texto y contexto/ Chicano Literature: Text and Context,* edited by Antonia Castañeda Shular, Tomás Ybarra-Frausto, and Joseph Sommers (Englewood Cliffs, N.J.: Prentice-Hall, 1972), pp. 133–138.

A strong mocking tone dominates Celso A. De Casas's work, which employs wit to expose the contradictions of life. The satire is harsh and coarse when dealing with the horror and corruption of the times. For De Casas, satire serves as a survival kit that can help a people endure through laughter.

The sixth of nine children, Celso Alfred De Casas was born on 9 June 1944 in Atwood, an unincorporated area of Orange County, California. His grandparents, who had left Mexico during the revolution, had settled there after years of working for the railroads and as migratory agricultural laborers. De Casas recalls that his grandfather, Ricardo De Casas, was a founder of a mutual aid society, La Sociedad Progresista Mexicana (The Progressive Mexican Society); De Casas remembers his father, Celso Sandoval De Casas, carrying out organizational duties. In 1999 his mother, Guadalupe Gonzalez, was still involved with the organization as treasurer of one of its lodges. The society was incorporated in California in 1927 and became one of the largest of its type in the Southwest. De Casas recalls being taken to meetings of the organization when he was six or seven and traveling extensively because of the family's ties to it. The activities of his parents introduced him to many areas of Southern California and to issues involving Mexican Americans, especially education, a primary concern of the Sociedad, which awarded scholarships. De Casas said in an unpublished interview on 22 January 1994 that because of this background, from an early age he "became aware of a bigger world and of social issues."

Entering school in La Jolla, California, De Casas experienced the prohibition of Spanish—including corporal punishment for speaking it—in both elementary and high school. During the summers of his fifth- and sixth-grade years he walked three or four miles to the nearest public library, in Placentia. He became an avid reader. At Valencia High School in Placentia a journalism class revealed to him that he could write; he calls the instructor Emily Disen "a catalyst" to his writing. At that time he began reading sports columnist Jim Murray in the *Los Angeles Times,* as well as James Michener stories.

De Casas attended Fullerton Junior College from 1962 to 1965, then transferred to California State University in Fullerton. He was in his second semester there when he was drafted into the army in 1966; he describes his military experience as "a shattering one that hardened me" and says that it took him a "long time to soften." His brother Bob, eighteen months younger than he, was also drafted, served in Vietnam, and was awarded two Purple Hearts.

After being discharged from the military, De Casas returned to California State in 1969 and received his B.A. in political science. He entered the Ph.D. program in the political science department at Stanford University with a fellowship in 1970. Feeling "burned out," he left in 1972.

During his university studies De Casas became acquainted with the works of several writers who had an impact on him. One was the novelist Carlos Fuentes, whose work uses cinematographic techniques, flashbacks, interior monologues, and language from many non-Spanish literatures. Khalil Gibran's writings which deal with themes of love, death, nature, and longing for the homeland, were another influence, especially *The Prophet* (1923). The philosopher Georg Wilhelm Friedrich Hegel's *Phänomenologie des Geistes* (The Phenomenology of Mind, 1807) also influenced De Casas's intellectual development. After discontinuing his graduate studies, De Casas taught Chicano Studies at Fuller-

*Cover for Celso A. De Casas's antidrug satire*

awareness. People in the Chicano movement were acknowledging their pre-Columbian narrative legacy and denouncing social injustices; a demand for equality set the context for Chicano writers to channel these concerns through literature. De Casas was part of a movement of Chicano authors who began to express themes and viewpoints that until then had been considered unworthy of artistic representation. In "And Another Piece of Litter Is Thrown on the Junk Heap" (1972), he says:

> The subject of this pseudo-intellectual work is intended as a basis for the beginnings of a course in the historical philosophy of the world. The course (no catalogue number or course code will be required for registration), will deal with the History of Philosophy, consisting in three distinctive yet similar approaches encompassing the Spanish, the Indian and the Mestizo (being the dialectic of the Chicano) and the respective contributions to the sum total of this reality in its entirety as it prepares to do away with itself.

This parody of the language and assumptions of an academic priestly caste is done in the voice of an outsider. At the same time a new dimension is being proclaimed as legitimate and worthy of exploration.

After leaving Stanford in 1972, De Casas began writing a novel to affirm what he had done socially and politically. The work proved difficult; then, what started out as an addendum to the novel became *Pelón Drops Out*. He shifted to the added section in 1973, and the writing came to him easily. The manuscript was accepted for publication in 1974 but was not published until 1979. The work is a satire of Carlos Castaneda's *The Teachings of Don Juan: A Yaqui Way of Knowledge* (1968).

De Casas aimed the book at a junior-high-school audience; although he considers the antidrug message the moral core of the novel, the theme of search for identity stands out. This theme is explored with humor, starting with the chapter titled "What it am?" Francisco A. Lomelí points out that the "internal structure of the novel is dictated by an ardent search to find a place where Pelón might achieve self-actualization through either dreams or visions." Lomelí notes that the overcoming of fear by the character means understanding "his Indian part, his Chicano consciousness and his freedom from ignorance."

Humor is a major part of the narrator's attempt to find truth and identity. At one point he says: "A lot of people pay good money for junk. Trash of all sorts is on the market. It has been said that if you promote something enough, spend a good deal of money advertising and keeping a product in front of the public's face, it will sell." This observation questions the validity of an

ton College. Leaving the post in 1973 because of political tensions, he went to work as a cement mason.

De Casas says that several factors made him "hyper politicized." The civil rights and Chicano movements affected him; he was involved in MECHA (Movimiento Estudiantil Chicano de Aztlán, Chicano Student Movement of Aztlán). Through Chicano Studies courses he became familiar with such writers as Alurista, whose verse communicates sociopolitical themes and links Chicano literature to mestizo heritage. De Casas and his brother Bob also became involved in the antiwar movement. De Casas was at the 29 August 1970 national Chicano moratorium march in Los Angeles. Between twenty-five thousand and thirty thousand people attended the march, which stressed resistance against the draft and a commitment to social justice within the United States. A riot broke out; fires and disturbances continued into the night. Three people were killed, including *Los Angeles Times* columnist Rubén Salazar, and four hundred were arrested.

De Casas's writing thus developed during a period of heightened ethnic, social, and historical

innate identity, since people will accept something as what advertisers say it is.

The young pseudo-streetwise narrator, who hints that he has seen a lot, cynically mocks the established social system. A sense of the absurd runs through the narrative; the narrator claims that he "sent this book to a disc jockey and bribed him with a promise of one million ears as a pledge to convince him people were listening to his show. He became very angry because the book ruined his record players and totalled-out his needles." The references of the novel to Castaneda's work are obvious: the Castaneda character Don Juan aims to gain power over the demonic world through the ritualized ingestion of peyote and other hallucinogenic plants. An echo of this theme is seen when Pelón goes through a humorous ritual:

> The master moaned in ritualistic communion with the spirit of spirits. Handing the thermos to Pelón with practiced movements, he whispered with closed eyes. "Drink it quickly. Do not stop until it is all gone." The spirit of the chilepuro slashed its way down his throat, meeting his terrified heart halfway on its trip towards Pelón's adam's apple.

The word *chilepuro* adds an ethnic element to the parody that is important. It is composed of *chile,* a pepper that can be hot and spicy, and *puro,* meaning either "chaste" or "a cigar" and having sexual connotations. The satire is multileveled and depends on cross-cultural references.

The narrative uses prose and poetic conventions to communicate various states or perceptions. The code-switching between Spanish and English in the work expresses the complex history of Chicanos and the variety of perspectives that inform their responses. This complexity can be detected even in mundane warnings: "'Don't stay out too late, mi'jo [my son]. Don't talk to the pachucos [gang members] and watch out for the cu-cui [bogeyman]. Que Dios te bendiga [God bless you],' she said."

Despite echoes of a Don Juan desert landscape, the sense of an urban environment dominates in the work. At times the language has a countercultural tone; De Casas admits the influence of Frank Zappa on the style of the text. The narrative presents a youth who finds himself surrounded by symbols that construct his reality; yet, he realizes that he can construct a reality of his own. Language and myth are intertwined. The drawings in the book, by New Mexico artist Dennis Martínez, add to the humor and to the sense of rebelling against the norms that deny the characters' identities. In his hit-and-run reaction to life Pelón, and by implication the narrator, seek to obliterate the gap between object and subject, making art not an act of imitation but of discovery of reality.

Although De Casas's work is intended as didactic, the search for identity touches on many issues from a pseudo-streetwise youthful perspective. "Being Chicano, I talk-off-the-wall," the narrator tells the reader at the end, adding, "Language is the ingredient and we the cooks, / creating a recipe not found in any books." The work shows barrio humor, ritualized in such a manner that it comments on a multileveled environment in which people react to various cultural pressures that affect not only an individual's identity but also a community's. Consequently, externally imposed and unsympathetic standards in the novel are questioned and broken through the use of humor. The process forces characters to reassess Chicano reality.

De Casas and his wife, Lucy, were divorced in 1995; they have a son, José Andres, and two daughters, Asia and Katrina. In 1996 De Casas left the construction field and became a teacher at an elementary school in Ontario, California. Because of the demands on his time, De Casas has not had much chance to continue his writing in a consistent and concentrated manner. He has been channeling some of his creative energy into his musical interests. He is continuing to research his family roots, and is interested in studying people in isolated regions. For some years a novel, tentatively titled "Lágrimas y semilla" (Tears and Seed), based on historical, sociological, and political material, has been gestating in his mind. De Casas's fiction reflects the struggle of Chicanos for a place in an antagonistic culture—a struggle against alienation at both the social and the personal level.

**Reference:**

Franciso A. Lomelí, "Internal Exile in the Chicano Novel: Structure and Paradigms," in *European Perspectives on Hispanic Literature of the United States,* edited by Genevieve Fabre (Houston: Arte Público, 1988), pp. 107–117.

# Ramón Del Castillo

*(25 May 1949 – )*

David Conde
*Metropolitan State College of Denver*

BOOKS: *Broken Concrete* (Oakland, Cal.: Unity Publications, 1988);

*From the Corazón of a Bato Loco* (Denver: Rubén Sosa Villegas Publications, 1994);

*When the Owl Can't See at Night,* edited by Brenda Romero (Denver: Printed by Denver School Press, 1994).

OTHER: Preface to *Reflections of an Aztlaneco,* by J. L. Navarro (Oakland, Cal.: Unity Publications, 1988);

"A Silent Martyr," in *Urania,* edited by Jane C. Schaul (Denver: Mile High Poetry Society, 1989);

"Please Don't Send Me to Nicaragua," in *Parnassus,* edited by Schaul (Denver: Mile High Poetry Society, 1991);

"Doubt," in *Thalia,* edited by Schaul (Denver: Mile High Poetry Society, 1992);

"Bato Loco!" in *Cool Salsa: Bilingual Poems on Growing Up Latino in the United States,* edited by Lori M. Carlson (New York: Columbia University Press, 1994);

"The Life History of Diana Velázquez: La Curandera Total," in *La Gente: Hispano History and Life in Colorado,* edited by Vincent C. de Baca (Denver: Colorado Historical Society, 1998), pp. 223–240.

SELECTED PERIODICAL PUBLICATIONS–UNCOLLECTED:

POETRY

"Los Soldados de la Gente," *El Universal* (Denver), March 1983;

"The Prison in my Mind," *El Perico* (Wichita), January 1984;

"The Veteran Sleeps Tonight," *El Perico* (Wichita), February 1984;

"La Familia," *El Perico* (Wichita), April 1984;

"Images," *El Perico* (Wichita), July 1984;

"Green Card Carriers," *La Voz Hispana de Colorado* (Denver), 11 July 1984;

"The Lies of Yesterday," *El Perico* (Wichita), August 1984;

*Ramón Del Castillo (photograph by Virginia García)*

"Nuestro Trabajo" and "The Falling Apart of Age," *La Voz Hispana de Colorado* (Denver), August 1984;

"Viet Nam Veterans" and "The Falling Apart of Age," *El Perico* (Wichita), September 1984;

"Porque Hoy?" and "The Simpson Mazzoli Bull," *La Voz Hispana de Colorado* (Denver), 16 September 1984;

"Día de los Muertos," *La Voz Hispana de Colorado* (Denver), October 1984;

"Somos Hermanos Iguales," *El Perico* (Wichita), October 1984;

"Veteranos Elegantes" and "A Thanksgiving Prayer," *La Voz Hispana de Colorado* (Denver), 7 November 1984;

"Chicano Christmas," *La Voz Hispana de Colorado* (Denver), 19 December 1984;

"Wichita, Mi Tierra," *El Perico* (Wichita), December 1984;

"War is the Enemy of Peace," *El Perico* (Wichita), February 1985;

"For Whom the Bell Tolls" and "Why Are You My Valentine?" *La Voz Hispana de Colorado* (Denver), 20 February 1985;

"The Creative Spirit," *La Voz Hispana de Colorado* (Denver), 6 March 1985;

"Why a Chicano Studies Department," *El Perico* (Wichita), June 1985;

"The Reunion of Old Comps," *El Perico* (Wichita), August 1985;

"Los de Kansas," *El Perico* (Wichita), October 1985;

"La Plática," *El Perico* (Wichita), May 1986;

"Answered Prayers," *El Perico* (Wichita), October 1986;

"It is the Children Who Suffer," *El Perico* (Wichita), April 1987;

"Frightened Children" and "Only Time Will Tell," *El Perico* (Wichita), June 1987;

"El Mercado," *El Perico* (Wichita), February 1988;

"The Showdown," *El Perico* (Wichita), March 1988;

"Contradiction," *El Perico* (Wichita), April 1988;

"Inside the Walls," *El Perico* (Wichita), July 1988;

"If Only She Could Talk," "Trilinguality," "The Aluminum Can Collector," and "El Machete or El Molcajete?" *Confluencia: Revista Hispanica de Cultura y Literatura,* 4 (Fall 1988): 175–177;

"Sanctuary," *El Perico* (Wichita), November 1988;

"The Echo From the Summit," *La Voz Hispana de Colorado* (Denver), June 1990;

"Anthropomorphic Spanglish," "the token mannequin," and "technological deviance," *Confluencia: Revista Hispánica de Cultura y Literatura,* 6 (Spring 1991): 193–195;

"Too Much!" *El Perico* (Wichita), August 1991;

"Visiones," *Southwest Magazine* (October 1992).

NONFICTION

"Viet Nam Veterans," *El Universal* (Denver), March 1983;

"Viva Nuestra Historia," *La Voz Hispana de Colorado* (Denver), March 1985;

"Lessons Learned in Viet Nam," *La Voz Hispana de Colorado* (Denver), February 1986;

"16th of September, Why Today?" *La Voz Hispana de Colorado* (Denver), September 1987;

"Bienvenido Compadre," *La Voz Hispana de Colorado* (Denver), November 1988;

"Global Challenges Call for New Voices in U.S. Economy," *Denver Rocky Mountain News,* 29 April 1993;

"Faith is What Keeps Leaders Moving Forward," *Denver Rocky Mountain News,* 27 May 1993;

"Many Latinos Looking Beyond Catholic Church," *Denver Rocky Mountain News,* 24 June 1993;

"Changing Nation Demands That We Drop Our 'isms,'" *Denver Rocky Mountain News,* 22 July 1993;

"Ending Violence Should Be Shared Responsibility," *Denver Rocky Mountain News,* 19 August 1993;

"True Freedom: A Concept We've Yet to Achieve," *Denver Rocky Mountain News,* 16 September 1993;

"Immigration: A Two-Edged Sword in Uncertain Times," *Denver Rocky Mountain News,* 21 October 1993;

"Many Who Fight for Justice Do Not Find it Themselves," *Denver Rocky Mountain News,* 11 November 1993;

"La Familia: The Latino/Chicano Family in Transition," *Denver Times Journal* (November 1993);

"Soldier of Peace Falls to Evil Force that Threatens All," *Denver Rocky Mountain News,* 9 December 1993;

"Youth Performers Focus Healing Ways on Others in Pain," *Denver Rocky Mountain News,* 6 January 1994;

"Indian Uprising Draws Attention to 'Other Mexico,'" *Denver Rocky Mountain News,* 10 February 1994;

"Scapegoating of Latino Men," *Visiones: Colorado's Only Hispanic Magazine* (February/March 1994);

"Chicano Literature Deserves Respect–It's Earned It," *Denver Rocky Mountain News,* 24 March 1994;

"Farmworkers: Twentieth Century Slavery," *Visiones: Colorado's Only Hispanic Magazine* (April 1994);

"From Parrot to Perot: The Third Party Politics of Richard Lamm, *El Semanario* (Denver), 11 July 1996;

"Fiesta politics is on the move," *El Semanario* (Denver), 15 August 1996;

"Bilingual Education: Speaking with Forked Tongues," *El Semanario* (Denver), 10 October 1996;

"Advocate for Latinos," *El Semanario* (Denver), 31 October 1996;

"Viva Josie Acosta!" *El Semanario* (Denver), 16 January 1997;

"Politics of Bilingual Education," *El Semanario* (Denver), 13 February 1997;

"Who Are the Real Pundits," *El Semanario* (Denver), 13 March 1997;

"Reveille for La Raza," *El Semanario* (Denver), 27 March 1997;

"Violence Comes in Many Forms, *El Semanario* (Denver), 10 April 1997;

"From Revolution to Reform," *El Semanario* (Denver), 1 May 1997;

"Unveiling the myths of the undocumented worker," *El Semanario* (Denver), 12 June 1997;

"Healing America's Racism," *El Semanario* (Denver), 10 July 1997;

"Let's reclaim the children," *El Semanario* (Denver), 11 September 1997;

"The time has arrived to heal," *El Semanario* (Denver), 18 September 1997;

"Battles for Veterans Continue," *El Semanario* (Denver), 13 November 1997;

"Welcome Home, Viet Nam Veterans," *El Semanario* (Denver), 14 November 1997;

"Adding sabor to educational curriculum," *El Semanario* (Denver), 11 December 1997;

"Who Really Stole Christmas?" *El Semanario* (Denver), 12 December 1997;

"When Treaties Are Broken," *El Semanario* (Denver), 15 January 1998;

"Cruising Is an American Tradition," *El Semanario* (Denver), 12 February 1998;

"Nonviolence and Social Change," *El Semanario* (Denver), 12 March 1998;

"When the Sage Burns," *El Semanario* (Denver), 2 April 1998;

"A time for celebration and lamentation," *El Semanario* (Denver), 30 April 1998;

"Who Are the Real Protagonists?" *El Semanario* (Denver), 11 June 1998;

"Bridge into Las Americas," *El Semanario* (Denver), 16 July 1998;

"The Passing of the Baton," *El Semanario* (Denver), 23 July 1998;

"Who Are the Real Turncoats: A Critical View at Partisan Politics," *El Semanario* (Denver), 13 August 1998;

"Una Despedida to Ana Maria Sandoval," *El Semanario* (Denver), 10 September 1998;

"When Ghosts Are Summoned," *El Semanario* (Denver), 8 October 1998;

"Who's really the boss?" *El Semanario* (Denver), 10 December 1998;

"You can serve only one master," *El Semanario* (Denver), 14 February 1999;

"El Alma de la Raza becomes a reality," *El Semanario* (Denver), 11 March 1999.

Because Ramón Del Castillo grew up in western Kansas, the Chicano Movement of 1965 did not influence him as strongly as it did Chicanos living in the great urban centers of the Southwest. The Vietnam War and the tragedies it brought to his family and community were the first influences on his creative work.

After moving to Colorado in 1972, Del Castillo became involved in the Chicano Movement, exploring issues of Chicano identity, the Chicano family, the education of Chicano children, the life of the *vato* (barrio dude) in the cities in the Southwest, and the activities of Chicano leaders on behalf of their community.

Ramón Rosalio Del Castillo was born on 25 May 1949 in Newton, Kansas, a railroad town some twenty miles from Wichita. The Santa Fe Railroad had brought his grandfather Rosalio Lopez Del Castillo from Mexico City to work in Newton. Ramón Del Castillo was raised in a close-knit Catholic family. His father, Adolpho Constantino Del Castillo, was a Marine Corps veteran who encouraged traditional values and a Catholic education. Del Castillo graduated from high school in 1967, was drafted, and served in the military in 1969, but he was not sent to Vietnam.

In 1972 Del Castillo entered the University of Northern Colorado, where he earned a B.A. in sociology and Mexican American Studies in 1976. He earned two master's degrees at the University of Colorado at Denver: one in social sciences in 1983, and the other in public administration in 1994. Five years later he completed his Ph.D. at the Graduate School of Public Affairs at that university. Married in 1974 and later divorced, he has one son, Andrés Vicente. While in college Del Castillo sat on the board of directors of the United Mexican American Student Organization (1973–1976), helping to implement a local boycott of California lettuce in support of César Chávez and the United Farmworkers. Among Del Castillo's odes to Chicano role models is "Una Despedida to César Chávez" (A Farewell to César Chávez), which first appeared in *La Voz Hispana de Colorado* (The Spanish Voice of Colorado) on 28 April 1993 to mark the occasion of the labor leader's death. At the University of Northern Colorado, Del Castillo also worked with organizations such as the Apostles for Justice, later known as El Frente de Lucha (The Front Line), and the Weld County Concilio.

In Colorado, Del Castillo had many opportunities to read and listen to the poetry of writers such as Abelardo "Lalo" Delgado, Alurista, Ricardo Sánchez, and Len Avila. Reflecting on their work and posing questions to himself about the significance of being Chicano, he discovered his own gift for writing. Three collections of his poetry have been published: *Broken Concrete* (1988), *From the Corazón of a Bato Loco* (From the Heart of a Crazy Dude, 1994), and *When the Owl Can't See at Night* (1994). His works have also appeared in anthologies and periodicals. Del Castillo's unpublished collections include "The Journey to Galena: A Community Healing Experience," sponsored by the Colorado Outward Bound School (1989), and "Lagrimas en las

# Broken Concrete

Poetry and a Short Story by
**Ramon Del Castillo**

*Cover for Del Castillo's 1988 collection, which includes "Primos Hermanos" (First Cousins),
a story about two young men who serve together in Vietnam*

calles del barrio" (Tears in the Streets of the Barrio, 1993).

A long-standing community activist, Del Castillo has written motivational poems for many community events. His professional career has included jobs in drug- and alcohol-abuse treatment and in community mental health. He also has taught in interdisciplinary Chicano Studies programs at colleges and universities.

Del Castillo's poetry is lyrical and intense, revealing his feelings about the Chicano condition in a distinctive style. One of his earliest published poems is "Las Fuerzas de Malo" (The Forces of Evil), written in 1976, first published in 1985 in *El Perico* (The Parakeet), and later included in "The Many Faces of El Vatocrat," a section of *Broken Concrete*. Somewhat influenced by Rodolfo "Corky" Gonzales's *I Am Joaquín / Yo Soy Joaquín* (1967), Del Castillo's poem addresses the dehumanizing effects on the Chicano condition of imperialism, technology, racism, oppression, and injustice, as

well as the lack of equality, freedom, and educational opportunities. Yet, "Las Fuerzas de Malo" also includes a note of optimism, a willingness to see the possibility of positive change in the future. At important moments in the poem Del Castillo writes in Spanish, as if attempting to recapture elements of the Chicano home language lost in the onslaught of oppression.

Also in "Many Faces of El Vatocrat" is "La Cucaracha" (The Cockroach), written in 1976 and first published in *The Mirror,* a newspaper of the University of Northern Colorado, in 1980. ("La Cucaracha" is also the title of a popular song of Mexican and Chicano epic history beginning in the Mexican Revolution of 1910.) In a sense the subject of Del Castillo's poem becomes a role model for Chicanos; cockroaches are depicted as perhaps smarter, more humane, and better at surviving than people.

*Broken Concrete* collects many works published separately in the 1970s and 1980s, recording the history of

Del Castillo's concerns during those decades. The collection is divided into four parts: "War and Peace," "Los Ancianos" (The Aged), "Children of the World" (which includes a poem by Del Castillo's son, Andrés), and "The Many Faces of El Vatocrat."

"Primos Hermanos" (First Cousins) which opens "War and Peace," is based on the experiences of Del Castillo's brother and cousin during the Vietnam War. The story takes place in 1966, as cousins Javier Del Castillo and Rogelio Ramírez complete their Marine Corps basic training. They leave for Vietnam, where both are wounded within a short time. Rogelio comes home first, only to die in a car accident. "Wounded" again by the news of his cousin's death, Javier returns home. Narrated by Javier in the first person, the story is intense and poetic in tone. It begins, "Rogelio's spirit visited me again this beautiful Spring morning. He flew through the open window, fluttered his speckled wings, glided three times around the room, and landed on the window sill." The tale ends with a bugle playing taps.

The most moving of the five poems in "War and Peace" is "If Only She Could Talk," first published in the 16 July 1986 issue of *La Voz Hispana de Colorado* and dedicated to the Statue of Liberty. In this poem the silent Statue of Liberty appears as an incarnation of *La Llorona* (The Wailing Woman), a mythic figure who has abandoned her children to pollution, political games, disharmony, corruption, and decadence. If she could talk, the poem suggests, she would speak against the growing antagonism toward immigrants, who in the past have helped to make the country great.

Of the five poems in "Los Ancianos," the short, simple piece "A Cultural Exchange" is impressive for the way it presents respect for the elderly. A woman offers her seat to a *viejito* (little old man) because she respects his age, not to demonstrate her liberated condition. The old gentleman accepts it out of need, not because of a sense of male superiority.

"Children of the World" comprises six poems. The most dramatic is "The Dropout," which depicts a school dropout as a dropout from an uncaring society.

"The Many Faces of El Vatocrat" is the most dynamic section of *Broken Concrete*. Besides "Las Fuerzas de Malo" and "La Cucaracha," this section includes "El Machete or el Molcajete?" (The Machete or the Grindstone?), "La Curandera" (The Healer), "Vatocrats,"

"Santo Niño de Atocha," and "Celebración." In "El Machete or el Molcajete?" the poet plays the two title images against one another. The grindstone represents the wife's traditional role, while the machete represents the husband's. The challenge is to bring equality between the two, to strengthen the marital unit without the distractions associated with machismo. "La Curandera" is an ode to Diana Velázquez, a healer who taught the poet many of her skills. "Vatocrat" is a powerful piece about the *vato* who does well economically but can never change who he is or where he came from. "Santo Niño de Atocha" creates a magical place that endures history and the human condition. "Celebración" is an ironic view of people celebrating Cinco de Mayo (The Fifth of May) in grotesque solitude.

In 1988 "If Only She Could Talk" and "El Machete or el Molcajete?" were published in *Confluencia* with "Trilinguality" and "The Aluminum Can Collector," two poems not included in *Broken Concrete*. A reaction to the "English Only" movement of the period, "Trilinguality" defends the use of English, Spanish, and Spanglish as a means of constructing Chicano identity. "The Aluminum Can Collector" depicts a street person in the early morning gathering cans left after a night of activity in the barrio. It is a striking view of a character who is part of everyday life in the city but is unseen or ignored by most people. In 1991 Del Castillo contributed three additional poems to *Confluencia*: "Anthropomorphic Spanglish," which revisits the theme of "Triinguality" from an historical perspective that goes back to Cuauhtémoc (the last Aztec emperor) and the Náhuatl language (spoken by the Aztecs); "the token mannequin," a depiction of a Chicano who betrays his people and culture for a piece of the so-called American dream; and "technological deviance," a powerful portrayal of dehumanization.

In a preface to *Broken Concrete* Abelardo Delgado calls Del Castillo's poems "slices of Chicano life" that "show a concern with issues which affect Chicano communities." In the same preface Irene Blea calls Del Castillo "an important poet" who "crafts his poems with the skill of a person rooted in their reality." Ramón Del Castillo is a master of lyrical poetry whose themes and techniques make him worthy of a place in the history of Chicano literature.

# Jason Flores-Williams

## (16 November 1969 – )

### Eddie Tafoya
#### New Mexico Highlands University

BOOKS: *A Postmodern Tragedy* (Prague: Orpheus Press, 1991);

*The End of the West* (San Francisco: Caught Inside Press, 1996);

*The Last Stand of Mr. America* (San Francisco: Caught Inside Press, 1998).

The novels of Jason Flores-Williams ignore virtually every theme that has come to be associated with the Chicano novel since the publication of José Antonio Villareal's *Pocho* in 1959. His protagonists come neither from the farmlands nor from the barrio, and they are much more involved in questions of ontology, nihilism, and existentialism than in those of oppression, racism, economic opportunity, and cultural identity. While artistic and personal fulfillment are of some concern in the Flores-Williams world, political equality is hardly an issue. Instead, the Flores-Williams protagonist is a pensive antihero, an artist and philosopher with a bad attitude who hurls himself headlong into the depths of the postmodern abyss, a world in which technology is deified and in which, as a result, the individual has become isolated from both himself or herself and his or her world. Flores-Williams sees himself as being much more directly affected by the contributions of the philosophers Martin Heidegger and Friedrich Nietzsche than those of the labor leader César Chavez or the activist Reies López Tijerina; he is a young man deeply devoted to his all-out search for meaning—even when that quest demands an extended examination of ugly truths.

Jason Drake Flores-Williams was born on 16 November 1969 in Los Angeles and raised in Houston, Albuquerque, and Santa Fe. Grandson of League of United Latin American Citizens founder William Flores, whom he considers one of his greatest influences, Flores-Williams has exhibited remarkable ambition and confidence for such a young writer. He completed his first novel, the unpublished "Harlem," at nineteen, and he earned a bachelor's degree from Hunter College in New York in 1991, the same year his second novel, *A Postmodern Tragedy,* was published.

Another novel, *The End of the West,* appeared in 1996, followed by *The Last Stand of Mr. America* in 1998. While his work has not found its way into the mainstream publishing houses, Flores-Williams has begun to develop a consistent following in the San Francisco Bay Area and has been a featured performer at the Capp Street Project in San Francisco and the Naropa Institute in Boulder, Colorado. He has also been invited to read in Mexico, the Netherlands, Czechoslovakia, and Spain and at the Paris bookstore Shakespeare and Company.

Flores-Williams says a turning point in his artistic development came in 1986 when he dropped out of Albuquerque High School, earned his GED, and boarded a Greyhound bus bound for Washington, D.C. On that thirty-six-hour bus ride, on which he spent the great majority of the time in the seat next to the restroom, he was first exposed to the underside of the American Dream, that part of society that rarely finds its way into literature or television. He saw none of the promise he had heard so much about all through elementary and high school; the freedom and romance of Jack Kerouac's life on the road had evaporated. This disillusionment was crystallized, he said in an unpublished April 1997 interview, when he watched a "nineteen-year-old mother of three spanking her children at three in the morning." He continued, "This was my first experience of confronting things that totally disgusted me. You see this and you realize that America is not a beautiful place. I didn't see the dignity that I was looking for."

Within three years of that initial venture from home, and after dropping out of the philosophy program at the University of New Mexico, Flores-Williams found himself at St. Mary's University in San Antonio, a six-hundred-student institution where, through the "Prose Blast," a genre he created, he quickly earned a reputation as a writer. Although he stayed at St. Mary's for only one semester, the Prose Blast readings that began as five-person gatherings in Flores-Williams's dormitory room soon developed into school-sanctioned readings in the campus auditorium.

*Jason Flores-Williams (courtesy of Flores-Williams)*

The Prose Blast utilized elements of poetry, performance art, political commentary, song, and stand-up comedy to explore a variety of issues, from the deeply philosophical to the absurd, from the brooding to the outrageous. Among Flores-Williams's more than one hundred Prose Blasts, which have been performed in New York, San Francisco, Prague, Albuquerque, and Santa Fe, are "Apologies of a Child Molester," "Surfing," "Suspicion," and "Charlie Sheen," the last of which argues tongue in cheek that the actor Charlie Sheen—because he is a young, rich, handsome, and famous product of Hollywood sensationalism—is a postmodern god.

Flores-Williams's first novel, "Harlem," draws on the ten months the writer lived in Harlem while a student at Hunter College in uptown Manhattan. The story of Zach Flores, an upper-middle-class Santa Fe native who transplants himself to an apartment near the cross streets of Martin Luther King Boulevard and Malcolm X Avenue (an intersection that takes on symbolic importance in the novel), "Harlem" questions the modern liberal agenda as Zach attempts to translate that rhetoric into action. While the initial concern of the work is hypocrisy regarding racial issues, the story quickly establishes a more far-reaching question: has

modern America constructed its own version of the caste system, one in which the great majority of people are trapped within certain psychological boundaries? Even going into the twenty-first century, is America still more invested in assigned seating than equal opportunity?

Zach's ten-month spell of loneliness in his new environment is broken only by two meaningful conversations. He is rejected by his neighbors, pummeled with snowballs, and deserted by his downtown friends, who are afraid to visit him in Harlem. He finds himself trapped in a solitary existence, one in which he can establish communion for only short periods of time, and then usually within the context of the local playground basketball court. The book ends with Zach's return, hardened and increasingly cynical, to his old life, indicating that the shallowest of American social classifications endure despite all the attention that has surrounded racial issues since the days of the civil-rights movement.

Flores-Williams said in 1997 that he considers "Harlem" a "weak effort" but an important step in the development of his narrative voice. Many of the questions raised in "Harlem," especially those concerning loneliness and the individual versus society, surface again in *A Postmodern Tragedy,* which was written in Prague—

where he had gone hoping to find, he says, "a Paris of the '20s expatriate scene" but was sorely disappointed—over the course of six months. Like Zach Flores, the writer/artist/philosopher Ivan Brown is a Santa Fe native transplanted to New York; but his extended isolation results from a conscious choice. Within the depths of his solitude Ivan pursues *Sorge*, the Heideggerian notion of concern for the "mystery of being itself," as George Steiner puts it in his *Martin Heidegger* (1991). Ivan consequently begins to forge his own moral and aesthetic matrix in a chaotic world of unstable demands. Heidegger believed that modern human beings had become insulated from themselves, that they were relying for their identity on what they did rather than who they were; Ivan thus embarks on an inward journey of severe self-questioning to produce art that he believes is both authentic and necessary.

Ultimately, the core of the book becomes "I" versus "They," and this postmodern quest ends when Ivan's loneliness gets the best of him and his personal contentment begins to erode. He finds himself in the midst of a Zarathustrian downfall: he must, despite the wisdom of Nietzsche that he knows so well, abandon his noble cause and return to the "herd." *A Postmodern Tragedy* concludes with Ivan rejoining friends in a New York coffeehouse, and the ending asks the question: "What good is truth if truth is only pain?"

Ivan Brown is also the protagonist of *The End of the West*, which was written over the course of a month and edited twice during the next two years (1994–1995), while Flores-Williams sought a publisher. The majority of the action takes place in San Francisco, where Ivan has secured a tryout with a newspaper. Although the novel finds Ivan at the peak of his artistic and physical vitality, any stature he attains is sharply contrasted with the world he enters, which is filled with teenage male prostitutes, ranting psychotics, shallow yuppies, and unemployed MBAs.

Yet, unlike Richard Rubio of *Pocho*, Antonio Mares of Rudolfo A. Anaya's *Bless Me, Ultima* (1972), or Esperanza of Sandra Cisneros's *The House on Mango Street* (1983), who struggle against external pressures and limitations, Ivan struggles with internal conflicts, to which the bleakness and rampant psychosis of San Francisco are only a backdrop. Ivan is granted multiple opportunities for professional, financial, social, and romantic success. Within weeks of his arrival in San Francisco he has achieved most of what he desired: he has secured a good job, a girlfriend, and a social life. Even a seemingly ominous venture into a Tijuana gambling den and a hundred-dollar bet on the Pittsburgh Steelers turn out well, as Ivan ends up doubling his money. Yet, his achievements seem unchallenging and shallow.

Just as his new environment reveals a world of lost dignity, once his job as journalist is secured, Ivan begins to feel that he is sacrificing his Heideggerian "I" to the external "They" and that he has more in common with the prostitutes that surround him than he would care to admit. While walking out to get dinner one evening Ivan observes "a red-headed sixteen-year-old kid from Omaha" engaged in cheap prostitution with "two overweight, married city workers," and he concludes, "there is really no legitimate appreciation or sympathy that can be evinced toward the kid, the men, society or anything—so I just lower my head and walk past them."

Perhaps the most apt metaphor for Ivan's plight is the Polk Street residential hotel in which he lives, an environment that appears to be an extension of the vision afforded Flores-Williams from the backseat of the Greyhound bus. Located above a gay bar along a strip known worldwide as a hub of gay life and male prostitution, the hotel is filled with a variety of shattered lives: a gay couple who has become resigned to living within that temporary environment, a man who has been saying for years that he will be moving out in a month, a pimp upstairs who is constantly beating his women, and a paranoid neighbor who accuses Ivan of stealing his medication. The novel presents America in all its ugliness, portraying California as a destructive, rather than nurturing, environment, the residential hotel signifies the exact opposite of what the West stood for in the days of the frontier. Through repeated exposure to such horrors, Ivan realizes that the West is near its end. It has become the land of the sellout and the person who could have been but never was, and the Promised Land now holds much more risk than promise.

His position at the edge of success leads Ivan to ask the troubling questions that have haunted artists and thinkers throughout the ages. Is being a big-shot reporter enough, if it means writing fluff pieces on Alcatraz Island as a tourist trap or on the gay chief garbage man? Is it enough simply to go through the motions, performing each assigned task with admirable deftness? The answer to such questions is a resounding "no." Thus, Ivan's frustration with life, combined with his meaningless success, leads to a final round of drunkenness and his suicide in his tiny room in the residential hotel.

Flores-Williams's style and confidence have evolved to the point that he is apt to employ Kerouac's method of "first thought, best thought." Consequently, his prose often comes at the reader in waves without transitions and with minimal punctuation:

As expected, the bunk room is a total piece of crap. Seven squeaky, smelly bunks with half-inch, foam mat-

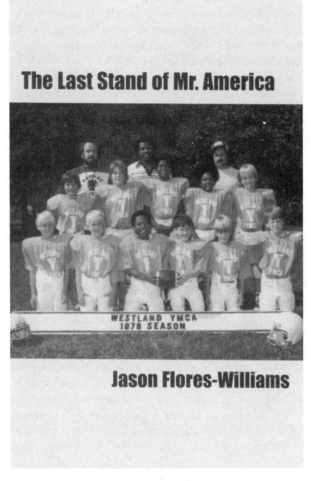

# The Last Stand of Mr. America

**WESTLAND YMCA 1978 SEASON**

## Jason Flores-Williams

*Cover for Flores-Williams's third novel, in which the protagonist alternates between his "respectable" public-relations job and his visits to a sex-and-drug club*

tresses that look like they were pulled out of a garbage dump and a horrible looking cot that can't weigh more than two pounds placed in the middle of the tiny room for good measure. There is a small window that needs to be kept open to keep the place from smelling like stinky European feet but the price to pay is a freezing room.

In *The Last Stand of Mr. America*, which was also published by the San Francisco writers' collective Caught Inside Press, Flores-Williams refines the vision of America he offers in *The End of the West*. Sam, the protagonist of the novel, has less of an artistic and philosophical bent than Ivan Brown but is equally angst-ridden. Sam is a public-relations specialist for Liberty Telecomm International, a company so nondescript that it could be any major corporation. Sam's rise to the top seems to be ensured, as long as he continues the sycophantic charade of which he has become a master. In contrast, Sam's off-work hours are split into two distinct

spheres. The first is the tiny, bleak residential-hotel apartment where his attempts to watch television are continually interrupted by sounds of the lawyer next door beating his wife. The second—and the setting for the most violent, disturbing, explicit, and distinctive scenes in the book—is Rockets and Missiles, a sex-and-drug haven Sam frequents to find relief from the ennui that threatens to swallow him whole. Within these walls, in a place teeming with homosexual, transsexual, group, and sadomasochistic liaisons, Sam begins to grapple with the meaning of his existence. He observes:

> I'm drawn to this place. I tell myself that I come to Rockets and Missiles in the name of sexuality, but I'm starting to think that the real cause is to force myself to think.
>
> Funny, when I was in class in college all I could think about was getting laid. Now that I'm in a sex club all I can think about is whether or not god exists. . . .

The parallels are clear, and the symbolism is unmistakable: the "respectable" modern world, full of bigotry, provincialism, and brutality, is separated from underworld iniquity by little more than a thin membrane of denial and sanctimonious decorum, in much the way Sam's workaday persona, with its well-placed smiles, nods, and handshakes, conceals his tendencies toward misogyny, brutality, and extreme hedonism, which grow out of his frustrated urge toward authenticity. Perhaps this personality split is nowhere more pronounced and revealing than in the scene in which Sam meets with the chief executive officer of Liberty Telecomm International, who is considering commissioning Sam to write his biography. As the CEO asks why there is no American flag in Sam's office and announces that he is a born-again Christian and that being a good American equals being a good Christian, Sam barely manages to conceal his disgust, as his running internal commentary indicates:

> "Free will is indeed one of the Lord's most wondrous gifts to mankind," he says as though he's the one who thought of it. "That being what it is," he says haughtily, "we are put into a position of having to direct mankind to the way of the Lord. Put him back on track, as it were. This nation, the United States of America, is mankind's greatest hope insofar as realizing the godlike potential that is within us." He pauses, "We are, after all, God's country."
>
> Some dipshit in Iran is probably saying the exact same thing right now about his godforsaken nation.
>
> He continues. "God has a plan for mankind. The plan consists of evolving man toward greater freedom. It is only through greater freedom that man can accept responsibility for himself . . . God is about taking charge of our lives and our own destiny. . . . There are indeed people in our government who would seek to limit our freedoms, who would seek to make us depen-

dent upon them and therefore ungodlike in our weakened state. This is why welfare and lack of patriotism are the greatest evils we face."

A depiction of Sam as brutal, self-absorbed, and misogynistic emerges during the three chapters set at Rockets and Missiles. When, for instance, he encounters an apparently innocent young woman who has ventured into the bar, his automatic impulse is to dominate her:

There's only one way to handle these youngsters, and that's to get to the point. "Lets do it, then," I say hungrily. "Let's go in that room together. . . . "
Her little nose twitches, she shifts her weight back and forth, all for naught. I move in closer, corner her further. There's only six inches between our lips. I flick out my tongue and get a little lip.
"Get your ass in there," and pull back and take a swig. All day drinking lends little toleration of bullshit. ". . . Don't go home empty handed. . . . Let's get down and dirty. . . ."
She is now faced with the real deal, the guy who will pull the trigger and make her call him daddy. . . . with these hetero chicks I'm as confident as Deion Sanders. This is prime time, baby. Let's get those sweat pants off and get something going.

This Sam, too, however, proves to be just another persona, raising the question: which is the authentic Sam? Or is there anything authentic about him at all? Soon this exterior also melts away, and Sam finds himself vulnerable and diffident as he is smitten with Lady California, an alluring transvestite who initially rejects him—the shock of which is so traumatic that consolation only comes via liquor and the repeated affirmation to himself that the object of his affection is anatomically male. Although he finally does have sex with Lady California, Sam discovers himself to be ultimately unsalvageable, a conclusion that is reinforced by his inability to step up to the defense of the brutalized wife next door until it is too late. Thus, Sam becomes a metaphor for the American male, whom Flores-Williams has described in a 1998 interview with Michelle Goldberg as "already dead" and so "abjectly lost" and "foolish" that to depict him in any way that does not involve sodomy and animalistic sex for its own sake would be tantamount to lying.

Flores-Williams is aware that, despite his cult following, he has been called arrogant, misogynistic, and self-aggrandizing, but these labels do not seem to bother him. "If someone wants to label me with something," he says, "I am not going to waste my energy defending myself." Rather, he is concerned with carrying the mantle that he sees as having been passed down to him from Nietzsche, Leo Tolstoy, and Herman Melville. "I have decided that I am a genius," he says. "I have come to that. Anyone who claims to be a writer who has the output I have and faces the issues that I have is a genius. I am just going to believe in myself, and if that's going to be construed as arrogance, that's all right with me." As of the spring of 1999 he had completed the manuscript for a novel titled "The Incarceration of Ivan Brown" and was looking for a publisher for it.

Flores-Williams may indeed be Chicano literature's answer to the nihilism of Generation X, and perhaps even to the political conservatism of the late 1990s. As Chicanos, if even only to a small degree, have begun to assert their presence on the American landscape, as they continue to carve their place in the corporate world, in popular movies, and especially in higher education, and as they become a larger segment of the population, Flores-Williams sees a disturbing question looming in the not-too-distant future: what comes next?

**Interview:**
Michelle Goldberg, "Shock Talk: Jason Flores-Williams' Will to Power," *San Francisco Metropolitan,* 2–15 November 1998.

# Montserrat Fontes

*(5 September 1940 – )*

Roberto Cantú
*California State University, Los Angeles*

BOOKS: *High Contrast,* by Fontes and Norine Dresser, as Jessie Lattimore (Tallahassee, Fla.: Naiad Press, 1988);

*First Confession* (New York: Norton, 1991);

*Dreams of the Centaur: A Novel* (New York: Norton, 1996).

SELECTED PERIODICAL PUBLICATIONS–
UNCOLLECTED: "Saga of an Indomitable Mexican Family," review of *Rain of Gold,* by Victor Villaseñor, *Philadelphia Inquirer,* 8 September 1991, p. J3;

"A Bedeviled Life in the City of Angels," review of *The Miraculous Day of Amalia Gomez,* by John Rechy, *Philadelphia Inquirer,* 3 November 1991, p. K2;

"At Home on the Range," review of *All the Pretty Horses,* by Cormac McCarthy, *Philadelphia Inquirer,* 10 May 1992, p. F1;

Review of *Silk Hope,* by Laurence Naumoff, *Philadelphia Inquirer,* 19 May 1994, p. K3;

"Prop. 187 Created a U.S. Sarajevo," *Philadelphia Inquirer,* 13 December 1994, p. A21;

"Mama's Third Street,–1947–1950, A Memoir," *Westways Magazine* (September 1998): 72.

*Montserrat Fontes at the time of* Dreams of the Centaur
*( photograph by Arnold Rubinoff )*

Montserrat Fontes will, in time, be known as a writer who helped to redefine the Chicano historical novel. Among the themes developed in her novels are the class and racial differences in Mexico, the frontier culture on the United States–Mexico border, the search for personal meaning in an economically stratified society, and the impact of modernity on the traditional roles assigned to Mexican men and women.

Fontes was born on 5 September 1940 in Laredo, Texas, to a Mexican family with a history of land dispossession, political executions, and exile. Native to Sonora for more than two hundred years, both branches of the Gómez/Fontes clan represented the independent and rebellious Mexicans of the northern frontier, who fought against native Yaqui Indians or, when unhappy with national politics, against the Mexican government. In Fontes's family a military tradition became inseparable from a frontier culture that posed an ideological conflict–dating back to colonial times, but exacerbated in the late nineteenth century–between civilization and barbarism; such conflict was used often to rationalize Mexico's own "manifest destiny" in its northern frontiers. There were exceptions: in the Battle of Mazocoba, a granduncle took arms on the side of the Yaquis against the army of Porfirio Díaz.

When asked in an unpublished 1997 interview how her family background has left an historical imprint on her narrative, Fontes responded: "I'm fortunate that both sides of my family have led raucous, wild, dangerous lives. They've also suffered and dared a great deal. All of us grew up with the Fontes/Gómez clan talking about the revolution, the exiles, the suicides, the love affairs, the battles, the history, the executions."

Fontes's maternal great-grandfather, Abundio Elías, was related to the Elías family, one of the biggest cattle-ranch families in northern Sonora. At the outbreak of the Mexican Revolution both of Fontes's grandfathers spearheaded military forces against Díaz. Her paternal grandfather, Col. Paulino Fontes, a railroad promoter and advocate of national progress, became a member of President Venustiano Carranza's elite guard; after witnessing Carranza's assassination in Tlaxcalantongo in 1920 he went into exile in Spain. Colonel Fontes had given his house on Calle Lerma in Mexico City to President Carranza; it became the Carranza Museum. According to Fontes, "My father was educated in Barcelona because my grandfather was exiled after the assassination of President Venustiano Carranza. Grandfather fled with enough money to support his large family of eight in a grand manner." Her father lived most of his youth in exile, either in Spain or in the United States.

Fontes's maternal grandfather, Gen. Arnulfo R. Gómez, was a presidential candidate in 1927, running against Alvaro Obregón and, because of opposing postrevolutionary alliances, against his wife's cousin Plutarco Elías Calles. Gómez's execution in Veracruz on 4 November 1927 made international headlines and partly inspired a modern Mexican literary masterpiece: *La sombra del caudillo* (The Shadow of the Caudillo, 1929), a novel by Martín Luis Guzmán. Prior to these events Fontes's grandmother's ranch in Sonora had been burned to the ground by Pancho Villa's troops at least three times. As a child Fontes visited this ranch during summer vacations, learning at an early age to ride a horse and to recognize the hard work required in ranch life. Her parents, Paulino Fontes Jr. and Aida Gómez de Fontes, were teachers and writers who instilled in their children a consciousness of Mexican history and culture. Fontes's early religious education at the Ursuline Academy in Laredo had a secular supplement: "My mother taught us to love literature, but our childhood stories were classical stories: Greek myths, Shakespeare, opera librettos, and biographies of writers, painters and composers. Father taught us history—from his point of view." She has two younger sisters, Angela and María Cristina, and a younger brother, Paulino, who is also a writer.

Her family history served as fertile terrain for Fontes's narrative fiction; it also manifested itself in a temperamental personality that triggered expulsions from various private boarding schools for misbehaving. In 1995 Fontes recalled that before her tenth birthday she had gone through all the Catholic elementary schools in Texas: "My parents, both highly literate peo-ple, grieved tremendously." She graduated in 1959 from the American High School in Mexico City with a 1.75 grade-point average—the result, she said, of youthful hyperactivity, distraction with sports, and undiagnosed dyslexia. Made physically fit by summer horseback riding and ranch life in Sonora, Fontes trained for the PanAmerican Games in the javelin and the sprints, but she pulled a hamstring in the semifinals.

Fontes's graduation yearbook, *The Anáhuac,* includes the revelation that she wanted to write a book. In the 1997 interview, Fontes commented on the generating forces behind her 1991 novel, *First Confession:* "My secret ambition was to write a book that said ALL I had felt and seen as a child no matter how horrible."

Fontes's early experiences took place largely in a post–World War II Mexican economy modeled after the United States. During the 1950s industrialization and rich oil reserves in Mexico produced economic diversification and social progress, creating a rising middle class and promoting political stability. These historical transformations are incorporated into *First Confession.*

Fontes had attended costly private schools in Laredo and in Mexico City; in California she attended relatively inexpensive public colleges, enrolling at Los Angeles City College and at California State University, Los Angeles. At the university she majored in English, earning a bachelor's degree in 1966 and a master's degree with honors a year later with a focus on Russian literature. In a 1992 interview with Janet Wiscombe, Fontes said that she awakened intellectually at California State and had remained a "voracious reader" ever since. Her literary interests, rooted in her mother's readings of William Shakespeare and world myths, turned to Fyodor Dostoyevsky, Edgar Allan Poe, Albert Camus, and William Faulkner; she observed: "Dostoyevsky taught me that we are a divided species. Camus agreed with that. I looked inward and saw myself as a series of contradictions." This sense of self developed into what she calls a fascination with cultural and religious frailties. In the 1980s Fontes discovered points of affinity with Flannery O'Connor, Harper Lee, and Carson McCullers, authors who are known for their critical representation of the South—the racism, the class differences, the violence—and who are close to Fontes's worldview. Among Mexican American writers, Fontes's personal "soul favorites" are Rudolfo A. Anaya, Ana Castillo, and John Rechy.

After earning her master's degree Fontes began her teaching career at the University of California, Los Angeles, as a composition instructor from 1969 to 1970. She was an English teacher at Rio Hondo College from 1969 to 1977 and at Markham Junior High School from 1968 to 1973 and taught advanced placement and honors English, ethnic literature, and journalism at Univer-

*Fontes's grandfathers, Colonel Paulino Fontes and General Arnulfo R. Gómez, in Mexico City, circa 1926 (courtesy of Montserrat Fontes)*

sity High School from 1974 through 1995. Under her mentorship students have been honored with more than four hundred journalism awards and have received recognition from *Who's Who, Literary Cavalcade,* and the Association of City Librarians Short Story Contest.

Fontes sold the idea for a television movie of the week, *Murder is a Confidential Matter,* in 1972. With Norine Dresser and Kay Hardman she wrote the treatment for a movie titled *Moscow Finish Line* in 1979; the project was shelved when the United States boycotted the Moscow Olympics the following year. Fontes worked with Dresser again in 1988 when they published *High Contrast,* a novel about an exotic dancer, under the joint pseudonym Jessie Lattimore.

In the summer of 1980 Fontes enrolled in a creative writing extension course at the University of California, Los Angeles, where she established friendships that turned into El Carmen's Third Street Writers. "We all wrote different types of fiction," she recalled in the

1997 interview, "and our only commitment was to improve each other's work. We worked every first and third Tuesday (including Christmas and birthdays), for 12 years and wrote well over a dozen novels, several screenplays, short stories. Some never saw the light, but they were written."

The first draft of *First Confession* was completed in 1984. Fontes said in the 1997 interview that "despite some fictional aspects, much of what goes on in the novel really did happen. Our families were affluent and I learned about class differences as I was growing up. The gap between the haves and have-nots is so vast; their worlds might as well be different planets." In the 1995 interview she said that since her youth she had felt drawn to the people who lived by the edge of the Rio Grande, and she supposed that her social consciousness developed while she hung around with the "river kids." Fontes added, "People have always said, '*A la Montserrat le gusta la plebe*' [Montserrat likes to hang around with the rabble]." Fontes believes that traumatic experiences in one's early childhood take a lifetime to heal. "We design our adult lives as children," she asserts. "Isn't life spent trying to decode ourselves?"

Writing *First Confession* became a healing tool after a lifelong friend committed suicide in 1971. Fontes said in the 1995 interview, "My life seemed to hit a wall when I found out about his death," adding:

> Victor was very much like the beautiful man in the novel. Life seemed harder for him than for the rest of us. If it is possible to ever meet one's higher self, I guess he would have been mine. His dealings with the world were non-negotiable. In the end he could not continue to live by the standards he set for himself. . . . He remains the love of my life. Ours was never an erotic love. It was fuller–without points or punctures.

Publishing *First Confession* was not easy; after several rejections by major publishing houses, Fontes's agent returned the manuscript and never contacted her again. Dresser suggested that Fontes send the manuscript to Amy Cherry, an editor at W. W. Norton; she did, and Cherry loved it. When *First Confession* was published in 1991 the reviews, for the most part, were positive. *The Los Angeles Times* (20 January 1991) voiced the general enthusiasm:

> This is a novel with a dark undercurrent of drama, one in which questions of sin and redemption are raised, and issues of class and cultural difference examined. Borders of all kinds are explored–the literal border dividing Mexico and the United States, the border between wealth and poverty, between Indian mysticism and Catholicism, and, perhaps most important, the border between innocence and knowledge, childhood and the adult world, naiveté and the awareness of carnal sin.

Other reviewers, such as the novelist Erlinda Gonzales-Berry in the *Albuquerque Journal* (23 June 1991), although impressed with the characterization and narrative voice in the novel, raised questions about its organization, in particular the epilogue. This section takes place in 1968, twenty-one years after the penultimate chapter, and illustrates Fontes's premise that "We design our adult lives as children."

The novel begins in 1947 in a Mexican town on the border with Texas. The story is centered on two nine-year-olds, Andrea Durcal and her friend Victor Escalante, and is narrated by the adult Andrea. Andrea is an assertive girl and Victor is a vulnerable, sensitive boy. The narrative is an historical reconstruction of an era of postwar prosperity and material expectations created by Miguel Alemán, president of Mexico from 1946 to 1952. According to Andrea, "our parents were pretty people who laughed daily and had big dreams of mov-

*Fontes (second from left) and her younger sister Angela with two of the "river kids." The boy in the striped shirt inspired the character of Beto in Fontes's 1991 novel,* First Confession *(courtesy of Montserrat Fontes).*

ing to Mexico City when they had made their fortune in our small border town."

*First Confession* thus depicts a frontier river–the Rio Grande, here called the Río Bravo–and its contrasting socioeconomic worlds: that of the laboring masses and that of the rising professional and entrepreneurial "Americanized" Mexican class. The social and economic rifts dividing Mexican society in the 1940s became visible chasms by 1968, the year that closes *First Confession*. The contrast is made evident from the beginning of the novel:

> The banks of the Río Bravo were lined with tiny shacks inhabited by people from the interior of Mexico who came hoping for a better life on the American side. They had no other place to live; the Mexican side of the river could not employ the hundreds who left their homes for the border. They made it to the river and got stuck there. The river spawned disease and violence, and Victor and I and other children from our side of town had been warned to stay away.

Of course, this warning only serves as an enticement to the children, thus setting a well-structured plot on a course that leads downward to the social hell of the "River People."

Andrea and Victor realize that their first communion requires the confession of sins, and not having any to tell, they agree to do "fifty bad things before

*Dust jacket for Fontes's 1996 novel, for which she won an American Book Award from the Before Columbus Foundation*

Andrea as an adult. Similar devices can be found in works by other Mexican American writers, such as *Bless Me, Ultima* (1972), by Anaya, and *Hunger of Memory* (1983), by Richard Rodriguez. These works are adult confessions either to the reader or to an audience inside the text.

Fontes's next novel, *Dreams of the Centaur* (1996), required interviews and several trips to libraries and to her grandmother's ranch in Sonora. The review in the *Denver Post* of *Dreams of the Centaur* (3 March 1996) quoted Fontes as saying that her initial purpose in writing the novel was not to produce an historical narrative but "to write about the psychic connection between a mother and son." Her reading of Jane Holden Kelley's *Yaqui Women: Contemporary Life Histories* (1978), with its descriptions of the Yaqui exodus, however, brought memories of the granduncle who fought beside the Yaquis at the Battle of Mazocoba. Fontes's historical imagination was thus stimulated. In the 1995 interview, when asked about the partiality of the point of view of the novel toward the Yaquis, Fontes commented:

> My concern was focusing on the clash and injustices perpetrated by the powerful upon the indigenous peoples, especially the Yaquis who have survived *because* they have refused to be Mexican. *First Confession* focused on the clash of two cultures: American and Mexican. *Dreams of the Centaur* focuses on the clash of Mexicans with Yaqui Indians who suffered enslavement in their own land. The pattern I saw emerging as I researched *Dreams of the Centaur* was that no dream is fulfilled without hostages, without victims, without blood.

Reviews of *Dreams of the Centaur* were for the most part positive. *The San Francisco Review* (May/June 1996) judged the story a "picaresque of the grotesque, an exposé of the genocidal system." The time covered by the narrative is the period between 1885 and 1900.

A *corrido* or border ballad written by Fontes and titled "El Corrido de José Durcal" serves as a kind of overture to the novel. The ballad tells the story of two friends who covet the same horse, followed by the murder of one and concluding with a son's revenge. The two friends, José Durcal and Esteban Escobar, represent, respectively, the enterprising Mexican farmer and the old ranching elite of Sonora allied to international interests of the United States (represented in the novel by Billy Cameron, "the smiling American"). The Escobar family symbolizes both the collaboration of the Mexican elite with American capital and the lineage of the conquering Spaniards on horseback (the "centaurs" of the New World) dating back to the conquest of Mexico.

José Durcal is an orphan who never knew his father's identity; moreover, he is not native to Sonora

lunch." Petty transgressions soon turn to voyeuristic games that lead to their witnessing of acts of prostitution by Armida, the wife of a local grocer. Shaken by their glimpses of the adult world, which include the murder of one of the Durcals' maids, Andrea and Victor agree on a transaction in which "bad money" stolen from the grocer's wife is invested in a "good cause": they give it to the River People.

The plot rapidly shifts from the children's initial need for something to confess to their resolution to keep secrets. "I had lied at my First Confession, lied without remorse. My major sin was to Armida; that was my greatest sin and I deposited it in the vessel we carry inside our souls, the cold lonely vessel that holds pain and secrets that cannot be shared with anyone." These sins and secrets take their toll on Victor; twenty-one years after that summer, he commits suicide. To cleanse herself from the pain of his death, Andrea takes all of their childhood mementos to the beach and burns them. Severing all ties to the past, she frees herself to begin her regeneration.

The "first confession" in the novel is not the one in the summer of 1947 but the self-revealing narration by

and carries another's surname. José represents the Romantic hero as well as the rising "new man" of the frontier, a social category most likely to establish alliances with the Yaqui Indians. His wife, Felipa–daughter of the Spanish-born Octavio Robles–is a Mexican from Sonora who fears and hates Yaquis. Her mother was murdered by Yaquis, and her marriage to José becomes a personal test, first when he brings Yaquis to the ranch as hired hands, then when the Yaqui daughters become the object of his sexual interest. The novel begins with Felipa's premonition of José's untimely death; the first narrative image of José shows him chasing Rosario, a young Yaqui woman who nine months later gives birth to Charco, who has blue eyes and a scythe-shaped birthmark similar to José's.

Sonora is undergoing rapid economic change fostered by a developing global market:

> José warned against foreign investors from the United States coming into Sonora to colonize Yaqui lands. He pushed for a Mexican-owned railroad to link Alamos to Guaymas and Hermosillo.... His stand for Yaqui autonomy drew angry criticism from friends. Felipa never argued with his long tirades, but it was clear she could never be convinced of Yaquis coexisting peacefully with Mexicans. José refused to cooperate with government orders that miners, ranchers, and farmers count and report the number of Yaquis they had working for them. He urged fellow ranchers not to obey the authorities.

Felipa emerges as one of the strongest characters in the narrative, particularly in her resolve to confront her prejudices against Yaquis. Near the end of the novel she wants an Indian wife for her son:

> I wished a good *Indian* woman–to serve him. Ashamed of her disloyalty to her son and to Carmen, Felipa makes a rushed sign of the cross, vows to the sky to let her sons marry who they want. . . .Vows can't change this ugly rejection of people like me and those whom José called Mexico's primera gente. José was a better person. . . . People like me allow the Mazocobas that maimed my son.

José and Felipa's son, Alejo, decides to avenge his father's murder, resulting in his being sent to the *bartolinas,* the infamous prison caves that passed as jails during the Díaz era. From the beginning, the narration centers on Alejo, rapidly moving in time in the first sixty pages of the novel (covering 1885 through 1899), then abruptly slowing to cover only one year (1900) in almost three hundred pages. The avenger's maturation and trials–incarceration, military conscription, and journeys–represent the main story line of the novel. Shortly after his father's murder, Alejo undergoes a quasi-mythical journey composed of tests and rites of

initiation, symbolically coming into the world as an adult ready to take his father's place. There are three tests or initiatory rites, one for each part of the novel: the taming of Moro (the horse over which Alejo's father was murdered) under the guidance of Tacho, an old Yaqui friend and mentor of the father; the Yucatán rite of Pan-Mexican Indian "solidarity," overseen by Anginas, an old Mayan survivor of persecution by the *hacendados* or landholders; and the Battle of Mazocoba, a test of fire that unifies the previous two.

The ending of the novel, however, turns against the reader's expectations of a romance. The heroic quest is set aside, and seventeen-year-old Alejo quietly settles down across the Mexican border, dreaming of breeding horses and of spending his life with Ana María, the wife of Rafael Castillo, Alejo's protector and father figure. Alejo, seeing his mother "for the last time," is transformed into an incarnation of his father, carrying on his father's dreams.

Fontes has been working on a novel titled "The General's Widow," to take place in the Los Angeles of the 1920s and 1930s. Asked in 1995 about the content of the novel, she responded: "It's about three single women trying to make a life for themselves when L.A. was still part of the Wild West. Again, I will turn to my family stories to start and then wait for the possession seizure to begin and then my characters will take over and go bounding off into a horizon which I hope will be sexy and full of heat." She has not finished with the characters from *Dreams of the Centaur:* some of them–Charco, Alejo, Felipa, and perhaps Moro–will appear in this novel.

Fontes teaches advanced placement English and journalism at Marshall High School in Los Angeles. In 1996 she was invited by the English Department at California State University, Los Angeles, to teach a course in creative writing. In March 1999 Fontes said that she is ready "to reverse my priorities: write full time and teach part-time. After teaching for 31.5 years, I realize I must direct my energies to writing; I must tap the unwritten history of Mexicans in the creation of what is loosely referred to as 'The West.'" She added, "The focus will be the widows and orphans of the Mexican Revolution who sought refuge in Los Angeles." As before, she will have her rich family background from which to draw inspiration.

**Interviews:**

Janet Wiscombe, "A Look Behind 'Confession,'" *Long Beach* (California) *Press-Telegram,* 1 February 1992, pp. D1, D5;

Roberto Cantú, "Without Points or Punctures: An Interview with Montserrat Fontes," *(untitled),* 4 (Summer–Fall 1995).

# María Magdalena Gallegos

*(12 July 1935 –   )*

## David Conde
*Metropolitan State College of Denver*

## SELECTED PERIODICAL PUBLICATIONS–UNCOLLECTED:

### FICTION

"The Swallowtail Butterfly," *Colorado Heritage,* no. 2 (1985): 21–26;

"An Old Fashioned Christmas," *Urban Spectrum,* 2 (December 1987): 14.

### NONFICTION

"The Forgotten Community: Hispanic Auraria in the Twentieth Century," *Colorado Heritage,* no. 2 (1985): 5–20;

"The Sounds of Salsa: KUVO Carves a Niche in Denver Radio," *Odyssey West,* 5 (March/April 1986): 30–31;

"Educational Opportunity Center VS. Gramm-Rudman: A Battle of Priorities," *Odyssey West,* 5 (July/August 1986): 25–27;

"Caution: Labels Ahead," *Odyssey West,* 5 (September/October 1986): 30–34;

"Las Posadas: A Mexican Tradition," *Odyssey West,* 5 (November/December 1986): 17–18;

"Cinco de Mayo: Then and Now," *Denver Journal,* 1 (24 April 1987): 7;

"Florence Hernández-Ramos, A Tiny Giant" and "KUVO: Past, Present and Future," *Urban Spectrum,* 2 (26 June 1987): 4, 7;

"Bringing 'The Arts' to 5-Points," *Urban Spectrum,* 2 (August 1987): 4;

"Servicios de la Raza and Asian Pacific: Providing Help When You Need It," *Urban Spectrum,* 2 (October 1987): 6, 14;

"Diana Velásquez, Curandera: 'They Said I was Unique,'" *Urban Spectrum,* 3 (April 1988): 4, 20;

"Nita Gonzales, Making Dreams Come True," *Urban Spectrum,* 3 (May 1988): 4–5;

"History of Cinco de Mayo, an Inspiration to all," *Urban Spectrum,* 3 (May 1988): 6, 10;

"Doctor Justina Jones: A Medical Legacy Continues," *Urban Spectrum,* 3 (September 1988): 4–5;

"Flor Saiz: Education Paid the Way," *Urban Spectrum,* 3 (January 1989): 4, 9;

*María Magdalena Gallegos (courtesy of Gallegos)*

"El Centro Su Teatro: The Dream is now a Reality" and "A Taste of Jazz," *Urban Spectrum,* 4 (May 1989): 14;

"Percy Howard Lyle: Doing What Comes Naturally," as Florence Tower, *Odyssey West,* 8 (May/June 1989): 23–24;

"League of United Latin American Citizens: Past, Present and Future," *Urban Spectrum,* 4 (May 1989): 12;

"Bernard Valdez: The Old Master," *Urban Spectrum,* 4 (September 1989): 4, 14;

"NY Director to Direct *Soldier's Play*," "Nickelson Says 'Don't Take Any Wooden Nickels,'" and "A Taste of Jazz, Part II," *Urban Spectrum,* 4 (September 1989): 5, 10, 11;

"John Hancock: In Denver to Play Key Role in *Fences,*" *Urban Spectrum,* 4 ( January/February 1990): 18;

"Hispanic Life in Auraria, Colorado: The Twentieth Century," *U.S. Catholic Historian,* 9 (Spring 1990): 195–208;

"Dr. Evie G. Dennis: Breaking the Barriers," "Fences Tell Hard-hitting Stories," and "My One and Only Taps into Audience's Favor," *Odyssey West,* 9 (March/April 1990): 12–14, 15;

"Billy Anders: Setting a Trend For Computer Technology," "Local Theatre Troupe Revives *Huck Finn* Controversy," and "Su Teatro Throws a Party," *Odyssey West,* 9 (May/June 1990): 16–17, 25, 27;

"Denver Drama Critics Circle Awards to be Held October 15" and "Angelo 'Angel' Méndez-Soto: Activist to Actor," *Urban Spectrum,* 5 (September 1990): 15, 22, 28;

"Playwright García Gets What He Wants in Su Teatro Revival" and "Studio E Casts Theatrical Spell," *Odyssey West,* 9 (September/October 1990): 6–7;

"Theatre Scene," *Odyssey West,* 9 (November/December 1990): 28–29;

"The Colorado Black Chamber of Commerce: Getting Down to Business," by Gallegos and Prudencio Gallegos, *Odyssey West,* 10 ( January/February 1991): 4–9;

"Spotlight on CBCC's Herman Malone," *Odyssey West,* 10 ( January/February 1991): 7, 10, 29;

Review of a production of *Ludlow, El Grito de las Minas* by Anthony J. García, "World Premier of Ludlow Set for April 9," and "Su Teatro, A New Era," *Urban Spectrum,* 6 (April 1991): 17, 18;

"Denver Mexican History: Casa Mayan Style," *Urban Spectrum,* 6 ( July 1991): 8–9;

"The Other Side of History: Roberto Trujillo, the Happy Communist," *Urban Spectrum,* 6 (November 1991): 6.

OTHER: "Florence and the New Shoes," in *Southwest Tales: A Contemporary Collection in Memory of Tomas Rivera,* edited by Alurista and Xelina Rojas-Urista (Colorado Springs: Maize, 1986), pp. 71–78;

*Auraria Remembered,* edited by Gallegos (Denver: Community College of Denver, 1991).

María Magdalena Gallegos's life is an example of the change in the world of the Chicana from being primarily a daughter, wife, and mother to being in the vanguard of the social, business, and intellectual communities. She was brought up in the traditional neighborhood of Auraria in Denver, Colorado. Her articles on Auraria, published in 1985 and 1990, and *Auraria Remembered,* an oral-history collection she edited in 1991, address that way of life and its destruction by a governmental decision to raze the neighborhood in the early 1970s and allocate the land to the Auraria Higher Education Center so that it could build a campus for three schools: the Community College of Denver, the Metropolitan State College of Denver, and the University of Colorado at Denver. The desire to preserve the folklore and the collective memory of the customs and traditions of her community has led Gallegos to exercise an expanding leadership as well as to write creatively of that way of life.

María Magdalena Gallegos was born on 12 July 1935 in Denver, Colorado. Her father, Felix Gallegos, worked for the Ace Box Company; her mother, Florence Torres Gallegos, was a homemaker. Gallegos received a traditional upbringing and a Catholic education. She married in 1955, had four children, and stayed at home to raise the family for the next seventeen years. Gallegos was divorced in 1975 while still in the process of raising her two youngest children. In 1980 she was admitted to the University of Colorado at Denver. She enrolled in 1981 in an oral-history course and wrote a research paper on the former residents of Auraria, including herself. In 1984 one of her history professors asked Gallegos to expand on the paper, and the result was the publication in 1985 of "The Forgotten Community: Hispanic Auraria in the Twentieth Century" in *Colorado Heritage* magazine. With this publication, Gallegos began her career as an author; later she became a publisher and drama critic.

Also in 1985 Gallegos published her first short story, "The Swallowtail Butterfly," in *Colorado Heritage.* She went on to publish "Florence and the New Shoes" in the anthology *Southwest Tales* (1986) and "An Old Fashioned Christmas" (1987) in *The Urban Spectrum,* a magazine serving the African American and Chicano communities. Gallegos is a founder and editor of *The Urban Spectrum,* which is committed to the artistic community in which she participates. Along with short stories, Gallegos has published many articles about life, people, and events in her community in *Colorado Heritage, The Urban Spectrum,* and *Odyssey West,* another regional magazine. Especially important are her theater reviews, which give the reader a sense of her cosmopolitan perspective as well as an awareness of what is important in Chicano theater. In October 1992 Gallegos became the publisher and editor in chief of *Southwest Magazine,* a culturally diverse quarterly publication.

Setting the tone for Gallegos's work, *Auraria Remembered* features a series of interviews with former members of the Auraria community. Throughout the

*Cover for an issue of the multicultural magazine that Gallegos has published since 1992*

interviews there is a poetic sense of nostalgia and loss as the subjects talk about their life in the community and how things used to be. Gallego's introduction traces the beginning of Auraria to 1859 with the gold rush in Cherry Creek and goes on to describe the first wave of Mexicans and New Mexicans who established residence in Auraria in 1916. It relates how the community achieved permanency in 1926 with the construction of St. Cajetan's Catholic Church. Life revolved around the church for almost fifty years, and when the state government proposed the removal of the people of Auraria to make way for the construction of a college campus in the early 1970s, the community organized itself to fight against the loss of their neighborhood. Their fight appeared successful until the church that had united them betrayed their effort to stay together by publicly supporting the government project. "The Forgotten Community: Hispanic Auraria in the Twentieth Century" (1985) and "Hispanic Life in Auraria, Colorado: The Twentieth Century" (1990) supplement *Auraria Remembered* and cover the same period. These articles concentrate on Auraria families, their history, their lifestyles, and especially their customs, traditions, and folklore.

Gallegos's story "The Swallowtail Butterfly" is an autobiographical work narrated in the first person. The narrator awakens to a phone call from her sister, who informs the narrator that their mother, Florence, has leukemia. On the way to the hospital, the narrator begins to think of a series of occasions that illustrate what a beautiful person her mother is. These little stories demonstrate Florence's acceptance of the realities of the world around her, her love of hats, her youthfulness, her pragmatism, her faith in the church, her excellent cooking, her generosity, her creativity, her common sense, and her love of children. The narrator tells the final story—one that Florence told her when she was little—to the rest of the family as her mother lies on her deathbed in the hospital. It depicts Florence as a young girl rushing home from work to get ready for a dance. Along her way she stops at church for a hurried prayer, and a multitude of butterflies rises to the ceiling and disappears into the dusty rays of the sun. Later, Florence tells the story to her mother, and her mother says that the butterflies were a group of startled angels. The short story ends with Florence's burial service, during which a swallowtail butterfly rises out of a flower bed and alights on her coffin.

Echoing the theme of Cinderella, "Florence and the New Shoes" is also biographical, dealing with Florence's first pair of shoes, which she gets in order to attend school for the first time. She expected to get beautiful, black, shiny shoes like the ones she had seen in the Montgomery Ward catalogue, but instead she got boys' work boots. That night she thinks of the Cinderella story and the slippers that fit perfectly and create a miracle for Cinderella. Like Cinderella, however, Florence must suffer before the magical resolution of her plight. In addition to having to wear the boots, she experiences the further embarrassments of having to take a burrito to school for lunch and not knowing English. She is ridiculed by her fellow students not only because of her shoes but also because she is a Mexican. Florence comes home in despair and decides that she does not want to go to school any more. Then the miracle happens: her family exchanges the boots for shiny new black shoes. Florence returns to school with her new shoes and finds that her fellow students' attitudes change. They even like her burritos and offer to exchange lunches with her.

Another story about Florence, "An Old Fashioned Christmas," deals with the merging of two Christmas traditions: the family's Mexican tradition of celebrating Christmas with food, singing, and rejoicing at the birth of the baby Jesus and the American tradition of Santa Claus and gifts. Midway through the preparation for their Mexican-style Christmas celebration, Florence looks out the window into the dark and sees a man coming to the door. She automatically assumes it is Santa Claus bringing gifts, but it turns out to be Mr. Burger, the owner of the farmhouse where the family lives. He does play the role of Santa Claus, however, as he gives Florence's mother two keys to a shed in back of the house. On opening the shed and a trunk inside, the family finds many beautiful old things that become Christmas presents for them, including dolls for Florence and her sister, Margaret. Thus the Torres family combines the two ways of celebrating Christmas.

The Florence stories are simple but powerful representations of a way of life. They deal with important moments in the lives of a Mexican family and a little girl as they attempt to maintain their cultural heritage and traditions. Transforming elements of family history into mythical events with transpersonal implications, the short stories are prose poems that seek to bring the concrete and the universal together. Through Florence, the family appears to connect their Mexican tradition with the American way of life, raising the descriptions of family history and community life found in *Auraria Remembered* to mythical proportions.

Although Gallegos is a prominent critic, her writing has not received the attention and commentary necessary to establish its significance to the body of Chicano literature. Yet, it can be said that she participated in the great wave of literary production by women in the 1980s.

**References:**
Judith L. Gamble, "Introduction to Historic Auraria," *Colorado Heritage,* no. 2 (1985): 2–4;

Christopher J. Kauffman, "About This Issue," *U.S. Catholic Historian,* 9 (Spring 1990): iii.

# Andrew García
### *(1854? – 1943)*

## Luis Leal
### *University of California, Santa Barbara*

BOOK: *Tough Trip through Paradise, 1878–1879,* edited by Bennett H. Stein (Boston: Houghton Mifflin, 1967).

PERIODICAL PUBLICATION–UNCOLLECTED: "Graves and Grizzlies," *American Heritage,* 18 (June 1967): 36–39, 97–103.

Andrew García is known because of his colorful adventures as a Western pioneer, which he relates in his memoir, *Tough Trip through Paradise, 1878–1879* (1967). In his later years, perhaps motivated by his reading of Western adventure stories and his desire to present what he believed to be a truer view of life on the frontier, he recorded his memories of his eventful youth. According to García, the novelist "always manages to cover up the trail on the Indians or villains who are pursuing the hero with the red-headed maiden in his arms on horseback. I never had such luck. They could always find my trail dead easy and run the hell out of me. . . . I am sorry to have to dispell [*sic*] the beautiful hallucination and tell, in most cases, that is B.S. In the many years that I have lived I have seen more heroes get it in the neck from the villain than were left to go around."

García was born, by his account, on the border between Texas and Mexico, in the region near El Paso, and was "raised on the Rio Grande and among the Apaches of Arizona." Later he reiterates that he spent his early years "down on the Rio Grande in southwest Texas and near the New Mexico line, being of Spanish-American extraction." A reference to "old Isaleta on the Rio Grande" might allude to the town of his birth. *Isaleta,* however, does not appear among the names of towns in that region of the borderlands. Similarly, the year of his birth cannot be determined with precision. He reports that he took up trapping in Montana during the summer of 1878, when he was "just coming twenty-three years old," which indicates that he was born around 1854.

*Andrew García*

García had originally gone north on a cattle drive; enchanted by the Montana scenery and the open spaces, he never returned to the region of his birth. He often refers to Texas and its people in his memoirs, however, although he does so ironically: "Like all Texans, I knew what most people thought and said behind our backs. Mainly, that it was just as natural for a Texan to take up stage-robbing and horse stealing as it was for a duck to take to water." At times he recalls useful lessons from his upbringing: "I . . . had been taught down on the Rio Grande never to ask a man his name, religion or politics, and as long as he left you alone and did not injure you, it was none of your business where he came from or what he did."

In 1876 García was working for the U.S. Army at Fort Ellis, near Bozeman. Following the soldiers throughout the area, he became acquainted with the Yellowstone and Musselshell regions, where he spent the rest of his life and became known as the "Squaw Kid." In the summer of 1878, after a year and a half with the Second Cavalry as a herder and sometimes as a packer, he decided to leave the army and take up trapping on the advice of a drunken eccentric, Beaver Tom. Tom was reputed to be the best beaver trapper in the Yellowstone country, as well as a good buffalo hunter, and García was swayed by his stories about trappers and life among the Indians. Although the soldiers of Fort Ellis advised him that he "was a damn fool to leave and go running off through the country with that locoed whiskey soak," he maintained his resolve: "I was a woolly Texan from Spanish America and did not believe in doing any more work with plow or shovel than I could help." The decision was a monentous one: "Little did I know that day that . . . I was leaving the white man and his ways forever, and that I would become inoculated with the wild life of the old-time Indian and be one of them, to live and run with them, wild and free like the wild mustang, and do what few white men can do—that is to gain the respect and confidence of the Indian." His ready acceptance of the Indian way of life is, perhaps, explained by his former acquaintance with Apaches in Arizona.

García invested all his savings and borrowed money from a storekeeper at Bozeman to buy horses (or cayuses, as he calls them) and trapping supplies, since Tom's only equipment was a .45-120 Sharps buffalo gun. As they prepared to leave Bozeman, they were joined by a group of men who claimed to be trappers as well. They insisted on accompanying García and Tom and left with them for the Yellowstone River. Soon García discovered that the men were horse thieves and murderers; their leader, the Canadian Hypolite La Brie, later tried to kill him. García's experiences with La Brie and his four companions provide an additional level of interest in the first part of the book; his account offers an authentic perspective on a type of man commonly romanticzed in Western stories.

When García refused to continue the journey in the company of La Brie and his men, there was a confrontation between the Texan and the Canadian. García had the chance to kill La Brie but did not. Red Murphy, a member of La Brie's gang, "wanted to know what kind of a damn fool I was for not plugging La Brie when I had the chance. I ought to know, said he, that La Brie would do it to me the first chance he got." García, however, justifies his action:

> When we were packing up, I knew that I should have shot him down while I had the chance. What Red said was so; when La Brie got the chance, he would have shot me in the back if he had to. But I had not the heart to do it that way. This killing business may seem easy to do on paper, but no one whose heart is any good wants to stain his hands with human blood if it can be avoided. I know that according to blood and thunder writers, who write from a deranged brain back East, and manufacture such stuff, that I ought to have pulled my gun at the start, and at the crack of both our guns, the villain La Brie would lay dead on the ground.

With the help of Murphy and other members of La Brie's gang, García and Tom finally broke away and reached the Musselshell River. Tom, however, was more trouble than help because of his drinking. For Tom, whiskey was "as necessary as it was for the sun to rise and shine." García, on the other hand, had a "deadly hatred of whiskey and of them that used it" because of the lessons taught him by his father. He remembers that when he was a boy, he and his father met some drunkards in El Paso. His father grabbed him by the arm and told him, "Say it, *muchacho,* that you will never be like those vile men, for I would rather see you lying dead at my feet." As he explains it, he "had all the chances in the world to be a crook," but he always resisted the temptation and "always turned down anything that was not on the square."

The editor of *Tough Trip through Paradise,* Bennett H. Stein, attributes García's honesty to the rigid discipline to which he was submitted by his family and the church: "The padres on the border had instilled into him a keen sense of hell, and as he succumbed to the beauties of primitive life, he fairly smelled the brimstone. He continually weighed himself in the balance of good and evil." As García recalls, his mother had even prophesied that he was going to be "a pillar of the church, and no less than a Bishop someday." He was conscious that, as he says, "crookedness and honesty cannot travel together in the same outfit without mixing." His strong character, however, helped him to keep them separate without the help of organized religion. Whenever he visited Bozeman, the ladies of the town would urge him to attend church, but he declined, saying that he had no Bible.

García made the acquaintance of the Pend d'Oreille tribe in 1878 and was closely associated with them until 1887. Those years in Montana, during which García became a trader rather than a trapper, and his acculturation to the Indian way of life forms the bulk of

*García's first wife, In-who-lise, one of the few survivors of the U.S.
Army massacre of the Nez Percé Indians at the
Battle of Big Hole, 9 August 1877*

rest among the blizzard-swept crags of the wild Marias Mountains. . . . All of my associates of those rough and ready years have crossed the Great Divide, and the Squaw Kid wanderer awaits the final journey."

García abandoned the Indian life in the 1880s, and in 1899 he married Barbara Voll, with whom he settled on a sixty-seven-acre ranch west of Missoula, Montana; he remained there with his wife and four sons the rest of his life, writing at night about his adventures as the Squaw Kid.

His return to American society, however, did not buy him a greater degree of happiness. Four decades later he reflects on his decision to leave Indian life: "Though I now follow the white man's ways and have a good home, and many will tell you I ought to have no kick coming, still I am a leopard in a cage." García joined the Society of Montana Pioneers and dutifully attended its meetings through the 1930s. He was often consulted by historians and corresponded with several over a period of years. Most of the historians were interested in his knowledge of the Battle of Big Hole. It was these conversations that led García to write his memoirs. In a letter to a friend in 1939 he wrote: "I have been trying to put enough of my ravings together, to send them to you. . . . But as most of this stuff has been written with a hard No. 4 lead pencil, over ten years ago . . . it is now badly faded and hard to make out."

In 1948, five years after García's death, Stein came across his manuscript, which consisted of "several thousand pages of legal-size paper, both handwritten and typed." The manuscript was well preserved, "stored in dynamite boxes, packed solid in the heavy waxed paper that powder comes in." At the time of his death García was a rancher and guide. In 1967 Stein edited and published part of the manuscript under the title *Tough Trip through Paradise, 1878–1879*.

Although the book is mainly an account of García's adventures in 1878 and 1879, he gives a view of his entire life by means of frequent references to years before and after the trip through the Musselshell region. His story offers, as Stein observes, "a truer feeling of Indian life than anything I had ever read." Although he decries the stereotypical accounts of the Old West in the dime novels of his time, García uses some of the techniques of fiction, thus giving the book the flavor of an adventure story. His portrayal of himself as a character—thus distancing himself from the events he describes—is one such device. The opening of chapter 20 is not far from the style of the writers of dime novels:

> The foolish In-who-lise and Squaw Kid, instead of keeping their eyes and ears open, kept on dreaming and like all sweet dreams that are too good to be true,

his story. He had three Indian wives: Squis-squis and Mal-lit-tay-lay, both of the Pend d'Oreille tribe, and In-who-lise, a Nez Percé girl whose original name was White Feather. Christened Susan by the missionaries, she had survived the annihilation of her tribe and had been given shelter by the Pend d'Oreille. She had been shot in the shoulder at the Battle of Big Hole in August 1877, and a soldier had hit her with the butt of his gun and broken one of her teeth, accounting for her name. García vividly recaptures his relationship with this strong-willed girl.

Most of the adventures García relates took place during the trip to Musselshell and in the camp of the Pend d'Oreille, where he lived for about a year. Eventually forced to leave their camp, he and In-who-lise traveled to Big Hole in Idaho to visit the burial grounds of In-who-lise's father. From there they went to the Marias Mountains, where In-who-lise died. The book ends with the words: "It has been more than half a century since I laid my beloved Susie, my In-who-lise, to

theirs had a cruel and rude awakening. Suddenly, like a silent evil spirit, Spel-a-qua sneaked out of the brush and stood before us. It was a good thing that we saw him in time to stand up and face him, for he was mad as peccary.

The change in point of view from third to first person, with its suggestion of a sudden shift from the historical to the fictitious, is typical of García's writing style. Some passages indicate that García still thought of himself as the Squaw Kid even as he wrote his memoirs. Recalling how the Pend d'Oreille chief and his warriors saved him and In-who-lise from Spel-a-qua, he writes: "There is no doubt if they had let them have their way they would have made short work of the both of us, and the Squaw Kid would not be writing this today." Further complicating the matter of García's identity, he sometimes refers to himself as An-ta-lee, a name given to him by the Pend d'Orielle: "I said, 'See An-ta-lee has his gun, and Spel-a-qua's knife will make him sorry. He will be in the land of the dead before tonight.'"

One of the attractions of García's narrative is his use of Western terms and a conversational tone that is akin to an oral history. His style is enriched by the use of Mexican words, learned in southwest Texas, such as *cayuses, aparejos* (packsaddle), and *camas* (bedroll), and colloquialisms such as "to buffalo," meaning to bluff. In looking back on some of his adventures he sees the humor in them, as when he had to kill a bear that threatened to attack him and his wife: he whimsically describes In-who-lise's wild exhortations as he struggled with the bear.

Another device García uses is that of delegating the narration to another character, as in chapter 25, where In-who-lise tells her story in a discourse in which images of nature predominate: "We will leave and go through to the land of the buffalo. . . . Next day before the sun was in the middle of the sky, the warriors who went to powwow with the Salish chief came back. . . . The chiefs asked the warrior, 'Did you see the Salish chief and is he well?' The warriors said, 'Yes, he is well, but alas for us, he is mad and like the rattlesnake when he is blind, now strikes at the sound of our voice, and does not see or know his friends of the Nez Percé any more.'" Her narrative also provides insights into relationships among various Native American tribes.

García is interested in correcting historical inaccuracies. For example, in a letter written in 1941 to L. V. McWhorter, historian of the Nez Percé–quoted by Stein in the introduction to *Tough Trip through Paradise*–he says that the real leader at the Battle of Big Hole was not Joseph,

*García in Montana, circa 1930s*

whom he refers to as subchief, but Chief Looking-Glass, who, until he was killed at the Battle of Bear Paws, "was the brains of the whole outfit, with White Bird no slouch either. Still yet they are never given credit by Joseph himself."

García's memoirs are written in the language of the period; the terms he uses to refer to Native Americans, such as *bucks* and *injuns,* were popular among settlers and in Western novels. Yet, his sympathy for the Indians is undeniable and, as García writes, not without a price: "Unscrupulous white men might make me pay dearly for saying that the Indian is one of God's creatures and is entitled to live and have a square deal–something he never received from the white man."

In assessing García's narrative voice the critic is compelled to consider the extent to which Stein edited García's manuscript. According to Stein, he "attempted to preserve the author's manner of expression. . . . I have punctuated and cut, and re-ordered the material somewhat, but the words are all his." Stein observes that García's greatest success was in depicting a dynamic social interchange between representatives of different cultural groups.

# Richard García
*(5 August 1941 –    )*

## Miguel R. López
*Southern Methodist University*

BOOKS: *Selected Poetry* (Berkeley, Cal.: Quinto Sol, 1973);

*My Aunt Otilia's Spirits/Los espíritus de mi tía Otilia,* with translation into Spanish by Jesús Guerrero Rea (San Francisco: Children's Book Press, 1978; revised, 1987);

*The Flying Garcías* (Pittsburgh: University of Pittsburgh Press, 1993).

OTHER: "Me and My Shadow Animal," in *Beatitude Anthology,* edited by John Kelly (San Francisco: City Lights Books, 1960), p. 101;

"L" and "N," in *Thread Winding in The Loom: California Poets in the Schools, 1987 Statewide Anthology,* edited by Duane BigEagle and others (San Francisco: California Poets in the Schools, 1987), p. 77.

SELECTED PERIODICAL PUBLICATIONS– UNCOLLECTED: "Untitled Poem," *El Grito,* 4 (Winter 1971): 75;

"Danza de los huesos," *Vuelta,* 20 (July 1978): 27;

"Curb Your Cloud," *Cricket* (June 1985);

"Holding Cell" and "Visiting the Old Neighborhood," *Americas Review,* 17 (Summer 1989): 40, 41;

"Dennis and the Headless Ranger," *Cricket,* 20 (October 1992): 56.

*Richard García (photograph by Dinah Berland)*

As a young poet Richard García was several years ahead of his time. His first book, *Selected Poetry* (1973), charted a new direction for Chicano poetry when hardly anyone was listening. Throughout the late 1960s and early 1970s Chicano poets attracted audiences with a powerful mix of social narrative and personal lyricism, combining Chicano oral tradition with English and Spanish vernacular idioms. *Selected Poetry* was written in English and introduced a sophisticated symbolic and metaphysical aesthetic that read more like magical realism than Chicano movement poetry. Nevertheless, the editors of *El Grito* claimed in the Winter 1971 issue that "Richard García is without question one of the finest young Chicano poets in the country." García's inno-

vations did not, however, win popular approval. For several years his poetic path seemed to be the road not taken by the majority of Chicano authors. Nor was the editors' enthusiasm shared by readers who considered the function of Chicano literature to be the unequivocal defense of Chicano communities. *Selected Poetry* is a clear example of the literary merit of a Chicano text being overlooked for reasons of poor distribution, political bias, or lack of critical study. García's next book of poetry, the long overdue *The Flying Garcías* (1993), is a welcome companion text that allows reassessment of the work of a poet who has been neglected for too long.

The youngest of six children and a full generation younger than most of his siblings, Richard Louis García was born in San Francisco, California, on 5 August 1941. His mother, Mary Ballesteros García, was born in Mexico; his father, John García, a butcher and formerly a chef on a cruise ship, was born in Puerto Rico. García's upbringing in a Latino household is reflected in his children's story, *My Aunt Otilia's Spirits/Los espíritus de mi tía Otilia* (1978), a bilingual tale based loosely on his childhood experiences. The narrator is a boy who, like García, has a dual cultural identity. In the book, the author comments: "The Puerto Rican and Mexican sides of my family are very different. The Mexicans seem more somber, and the Puerto Ricans tend to be better dancers. I grew up thinking of myself as Mexican-American, and am only recently beginning to think of myself as a Mexi-Rican." The poet claims that the only book in his house when he was growing up was a much-consulted guide to dream interpretation. A fascination with dreams and archetypal images has persisted throughout García's adult life. It led him to the work of the Swiss psychoanalyst Carl Gustav Jung, whose ideas have continued to influence García's poetry.

García traveled extensively prior to the publication of *Selected Poetry*. He also lived for extended periods in Colorado, Mexico, New York, and Israel. By the mid-1980s he was once more writing poetry and working in the state-sponsored California Poets in the Schools program in San Francisco. In 1989 he moved to Los Angeles, and in 1990, under a grant from the California Arts Council, he was named poet in residence at the Long Beach Museum of Art. In 1991 he received a fellowship in poetry from the National Endowment for the Arts, and in 1993 he was the recipient of the Cohen Award from *Ploughshares* for the best poem published by the magazine in 1992. In January 1994 García completed an M.F.A. degree in creative writing at Warren Wilson College. In 1995 he received the Greensboro Prize from the *Greensboro Review* for his poem "Note Folded Thirteen Ways," which was also awarded a 1997 Pushcart Prize. Also in 1997 García received the Mudfish Prize from *Mudfish* magazine and the Georgetown Poetry Prize from the *Georgetown Review*. He is currently poet in residence at the Children's Hospital in Los Angeles and is married to poet Dinah Berland.

In their 1976 analysis of *Selected Poetry* Francisco Lomelí and Donaldo Urioste note the polished craftsmanship exhibited in the work. This collection of forty-six poems conveys a mythical, synoptic history of the poetic subject's quest for knowledge and maturity. This quest develops in three stages. First, by means of subjective visions and dream states, the first half of the book presents an archetype of primordial chaos out of which the text gradually develops a hierarchy of value. In the second stage, which encompasses the remaining half of the book, with the exception of the final poem, García explores the lower levels of the hierarchical system founded in the first stage. The subject's ascent is compromised, then reversed, becoming at last a long descent through history and various levels of earthly experience at which the value of places, things, and people (specifically, women and political authorities) is inverted and made to represent the nadir of the scale of values. As the subject experiences hell on earth, he also learns about the redemptive power inherent in the poem as magical artifact. The final stage of the text consists of a single poem, "Gregorio Cortez," in which Chicano history and the author's personal experience are presented as the latest evolutionary stage of human history. The poem summons up the spirit of the legendary Gregorio Cortez, who eluded pursuit of Texas lawmen at the turn of the century.

These three stages present a mythopoetic narrative that recovers popular beliefs and a premodern understanding of reality that are often in conflict with Western scientific knowledge. *Selected Poetry* confronts such canonic antecedents as the Homeric epics, Dante's *Inferno* (early fourteenth century), William Shakespeare's *Hamlet* (written ca. 1601) and *Macbeth* (written ca. 1606), John Milton's *Paradise Lost* (1667), and Johann Wolfgang von Goethe's *Faust* (1808, 1832) in which mythical structures, ghosts, witches, and the devil intervene in the course of human history. García's text also engages contemporary influences including surrealism, the poetry of the Beat Generation, and the Chicano *pinto* (convict) poets.

The first stage of *Selected Poetry* situates the poetic discourse within the chaotic interaction of natural, social, and supernatural phenomena. Images of the sea, the earth, and the sky flow in and out of the subjective states of sleep and sensual awareness, dreamscapes, and memories. The initial poem, "You Walk Through the Dead House of My Sleep," provides an immediate entry into the archetypal imagery of this section:

> You walk through the dead house of my sleep
> Someone knocks, you let in the sea
> A whisper of foam hisses over your skin
> And my face rolls in the fold of a wave
> We float through twisted moans of night
> We are bruised by the laughter of fish.

In the next piece, "It is always morning," a dazed sleepwalker awakens to the reality of dreams, and a sense of oneiric submersion is repeated in the poems "Return" and "Arrival." "When They Told Her" recalls the anguish of a sibling's death, and "The Soul" reveals a conscious-

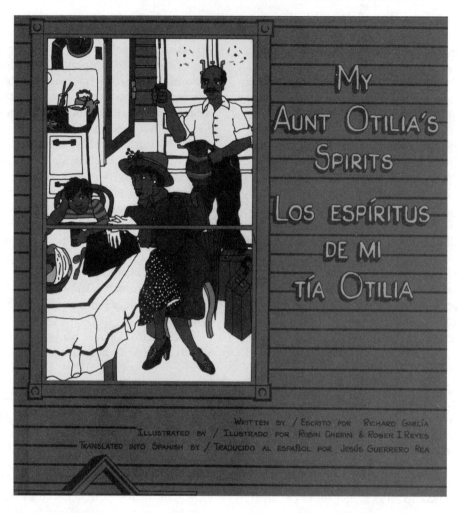

*Printed cover for the revised version (1987) of García's 1978 story for children*

ness haunted by war, violence, and personal loss. In the latter poem ghostlike figures persist in obedience to a sort of dream logic. They transgress normal categories of space and time in search of values that establish the human need for justice and moral satisfaction. "Ascending Song" confirms the moral hierarchy that structures this section:

> It is an ascending song
> The pain of the just
> And what descends is rain
> A sudden kindness in the desert
> Releasing flowers we have never seen
> And will never see again.

Images of motion, especially of flight, characterize García's poetry. In "Ascending Song" these images are consistent with the vertical hierarchy that structures the section, although they acquire different meanings in subsequent stages and texts. In this poem the prayer or

song is answered by the healing rain, which is a stage in a natural cycle that flows from the sky to the earth, then to the sea, and, finally, back to the sky. When the vertical dynamic is thus linked to a natural cycle, the text produces its mythological meaning. But the poem confirms that individual beings, like the flowers, are not lost in the recurring cycle. It recognizes the distinctiveness inherent in their incommensurable life and death. In the hierarchy of vital elements—air, earth, and water—the first and highest is air, symbolized by the flight of birds and spirits, by the wind, and by poetry itself in its capacity to elevate and inspire.

These dynamic elements are part of a consciousness that is in constant flux. Even while sleeping and dreaming, this consciousness rises heavenward and flies inward to the soul, extending the boundaries of psychic space in quest of meaning. Several of the poems in this stage evoke the epic of Gilgamesh and cities—Pompeii, pre-1906 San Francisco, and ancient Jerusalem—that were destroyed in mythic time but that are, nevertheless, present as ruins and as texts that preserve both memory and meaning.

The second stage of the text presents the subject in a gradual attitude of decline as he grows increasingly bound to contemporary man-made artifacts. The mythic cycle describes an inexorable downward plunge, as in "I Set Dead Wood Free," in which the subject abandons the possibility of ascent, saying "I live in a flying house / Dropping like a plane through fog." The text gradually abandons the mythical level established in the first stage and enters an historical one. "In The Market Places" presents the subject's arrival in Jerusalem, and in the poems that follow, a series of sites—"The Old Man's Store," "Clown Alley," and a jail from which the subject must escape in "The Master of Disguise"— are evidence of a chilling fact: "The City is So Big. . . . And people disappear." After this denunciation, the book proceeds to document the contention that this environment ("The City") is responsible for the suppression of human nature. Urban civilization stands accused of crimes against humanity, and the poet collects evidence and develops the argument. In an extended metaphor that links several of the poems in this section, medieval castles symbolize the military and political powers of a microcosmic city where relationships between men and women are distorted and destroyed.

In "The American Witch" the subject's descent reaches the stratum of contemporary American society as it recalls a figure of the military expansion that founded Western Civilization in ancient Greece and Asia Minor: "Her face inspires armies / And calls the sailors toward her." These Homeric epithets were assigned to Helen of Troy in the *Iliad* and to the Sirens in the *Odyssey*. In García's poem they belong to "The American witch / With her smile of a hundred dollars . . .Turning out cars boats stereos / And trips to Hawaii . . . She is tall she is fair / And streamlined for flight." The images of flight and of womanhood are reduced to commercial and industrial ends that glorify American consumer culture. The adjective *streamlined* implies that the ideals of poetic flight and of feminine beauty have been degraded by their association with aerodynamics, a science responsible for aircraft in general and for war planes in particular. In this poem America presents a hellish scene in which the poet's highest value—the love of beauty—becomes rubbish.

The poem continues with fragments of broken syntax that alternate with flowing rhythms, thus engaging the reader in a struggle for meaning in the face of loss. The descent into the hellish, mechanized city goes on "Until there was nothing there / And I was alone in the city dump / Strangling mops and stomping on tin cans / And throwing rocks at unbreakable televisions / While the scavengers with an eye for value / Were carting them away." The fall culminates in the nadir of a trash heap despoiled of value, where the subject is condemned to serve an indefinite sentence. Fearing that this place will be a final one from which there can be no escape, the subject desperately casts through an inventory of personal things that may provide meaning.

At this point a series of poems presents a collection of signifiers-as-artifacts that are the personal/impersonal accessories of modernity: "Newspaper," "My New Shoes," "The Things in My Room," "My New Watch," "My New Wallet," "My New Pipe." These artifact-poems establish an intertextual relationship with the nonrepresentational works of the French Surrealists. For example, René Magritte's famous painting of a pipe is accompanied by the legend "Ce n'est pas une pipe" (This is not a pipe). Magritte was attempting to release the artistic image from conventional perceptions so as to explore its suppressed and hidden properties. With his series of artifact-poems, García dramatizes this notion that the poetic image is not the thing itself. If it is not a pipe, then what is it? García's answer is that poetic art goes beyond representation to bridge the void between subjective and objective reality. It goes beyond the practical, political, and normative to the talismanic value of the image. The poetic subject, like the child and the Surrealist artist, transforms found objects, rubbish, and other mere "things" into charmed artifacts that become vessels of personal and collective meaning:

With my seven league boots
A wishing wallet, a dreaming pipe
And a watch with a tiny mirror
That shows the future
By the glow of windows filled with light
And ready to sail, I am the prince of whales.

The poetic imagination becomes the medium that recovers this art from the dump and gives it value in the present. Of course, this magical art is on a lower plane of experience when compared to the mythical art of flight that characterizes the first stage of *Selected Poetry*. This second stage is about more human and earthbound experience. Nevertheless, the text demonstrates the poetic capacity to recover both myth and magic from their banishment and suppression and to make them imaginative tools in the present.

The final stage of development in *Selected Poetry* consists of "Gregorio Cortez," the last and also the longest poem in the collection. It is made up of five numbered parts that recall the legend of Gregorio Cortez as a collective memory and as an historical record preserved in the newspapers of the period. Cortez's confrontation with the Texas lawman who shot his brother at the turn of the century, his flight and pursuit by the Texas Rangers, and his capture have been the subject of books and scholarly studies as well as of popular ballads. Just as the poet recovered the arts of myth and magic from oblivion in previous stages, in his rendition of Cortez's story he becomes the medium through which the ghost of Cortez speaks.

This poem also transforms the mythical flight of the earlier stages. No longer is flight a metaphor of elevation, power, and movement through the realm of gods and angels; nor is it the degrading descent of the second stage. The image becomes one of persecution—movement and escape along a metonymic borderland that divides two cultures and can be mapped on the surface of the earth in a specific place called Texas. It is the persecution of man by man: "the chase / That never ends, the great american chase . . . Of escaped slaves . . . Of escaped convicts . . . As they follow the last poet / into the desert." This flight is one that histories, ballads, and moving pictures record and that the poet links to his own identity and personal history.

The first two parts of "Gregorio Cortez" conjure up a desert setting "along the border . . . By a dry river," where the poet finds the ghost of Cortez and recites his story in a rhythmic, second-person narrative: "And the sheriff shot your brother / And you put a hole through his star / And so the chase began." In the third numbered section the poet establishes a link between Cortez and his own youthful persona:

> When I was a boy
> Richard García was the only
> Desperado in the neighborhood
>
> They caught up with me
> Many years later and took me to jail.

(García's real-life entanglements with the law were fairly minor. On a few occasions in his early twenties he was arrested, and spent several days in jail for misdemeanors. During one of these episodes he escaped from custody.) The poem dramatizes the exchange of stories and personal histories between two fugitives, the poet and Cortez, who are bound together as the subjects of the poem and branded as "desperados"–Cortez by the Anglo authorities and press, and García by the poem itself. In the final section the poem again dramatically brings to life Cortez and the desert night that forms the setting of his eternal flight:

> You just keep riding
> Pursued by six dead horses
> And a posse always a day behind
> Riding towards the border
> Where even the stillness of dry creek beds
> Has the sound of hooves.

"Gregorio Cortez" captures a moment of Chicano history and links it to the poet's own exaggerated history as a fugitive and a prisoner. The figure of the prisoner reappears in other García poems. It is present in "The Master of Disguise" in the same collection, in the uncollected poem "Holding Cell," and in "The Defiant Ones" in *The Flying Garcías*. In these poems the archetype of the prisoner is in ironic relation to the metaphor of flight, thereby establishing an intertextual link with the subgenre of contemporary Chicano poetry known as *pinto* poetry: autobiographical prison poetry that presents the *pinto* as a victim of state oppression; by doing so, it produces a universal metaphor of political oppression, the shackling of poetic flight. García's rendition of the *pinto* poet deflates the original model by presenting a plausible but ironic view of the *pinto* as *pocho* (a person between cultures). That is, his Chicano prisoner is a "non-movement" Hispanic boy, an Americanized loner who is the exact opposite of the canonical view of the *pinto* as pachuco as seen in the works of such writers as Ricardo Sánchez and Raúl Salinas.

The poem says that "Richard García was the only / Desperado in the neighborhood"; in other words, not only was he not a member of a gang of pachuco youths but he self-identifies as a desperado, thus internalizing the Anglo-American term of reprobation that is used to stereotype the Mexican as a bandit or outlaw. Yet, the term *desperado* simultaneously represents the subject's rebellion against the society that brands him with such a stereotype. Thus the reader sees the psychic scission characteristic of the *pocho* who is torn between two cultures, represented, on the one hand, by the English language and, on the other, by a Chicano history of struggle. Because his loyalty belongs to no gang, the García in the poem must venture out alone, and by so doing he defines the *pocho's* individuality as the border between collective identities. On the Anglo side is institutional power; on the Chicano side are the compelling social and historical claims of that culture. If the *pocho* is scorned as a Mexican on one side and persecuted as a traitor on the other, to survive he will tend to abandon allegiance to either nationality and forge a loyalty to individual identity.

From its inception the Chicano movement has valued the idea of the group over the individual. Thus, the sacred image of pachucos as victims of police authority that considered them nothing more than teen rebels who, because of their organization into groups or gangs, their eccentric dress (the zoot suit), and their hybrid English-Spanish vernacular (*caló*), were branded as hoodlums and troublemakers who must be dealt with accordingly. The legacy of the pachucos lived on in the *vatos locos* and *cholos* (other categories of barrio youth) of subsequent generations, but in the 1940s and

1950s it was the pachucos who attained notoriety in cities such as El Paso and Los Angeles and were emulated as far north as San Jose, California.

When García was coming of age in San Francisco, however, the city was the home of a different group of cultural rebels. These were the Beat Generation poets and artists, many of whom had migrated from the East Coast and established themselves in the relatively tolerant atmosphere of San Francisco. García's poetic experimentation and his youthful rebellion against a paranoid Cold-War America emerged out of a blend of cultural influences that included his *mexicano/boricua* heritage, the cosmopolitan diversity of his native city, and his readings and travels in the United States and abroad. In high school García had read the Beats and had published his first poems in *Beatitude Anthology* (1960), a collection that included contributions by Allen Ginsberg, Lawrence Ferlinghetti, Jack Kerouac, and Peter Orlovsky. Obviously, the rhetoric of the Chicano movement did not overcome these earlier influences, nor did García's poetry embrace the Chicano origin myth of Aztlán because, as a poet, García was actively exploring the possibilities of myth and of shaping a poetic language from his own particular experience. García did not attempt to represent the pachuco worldview, nor did he address the cause of the migrant farmworkers who were led by César Chávez. These cultural constructs were the sacred vessels of the Chicano movement of the 1970s, and as some critics have noted, García was not a devotee of the movement. He was, and continues to be, a poet who works within a variety of traditions.

Other "non-movement" writers include José Antonio Villarreal, the author of the novel *Pocho* (1959). Villarreal was a generation older than the Chicano poets of the 1970s; like García, however, he was a first-generation Californian. His most famous character, Richard Rubio, becomes a maverick, the archetypal *pocho* who rejects the Chicano group identity. Many experts consider Villarreal's novel one of the founding texts of contemporary Chicano literature; yet, *Pocho* remained forgotten and out of print for years before the editors of Quinto Sol Publications alerted Chicanos to its existence. Quinto Sol attempted, unsuccessfully, to label García and Villarreal as members of the movement. The publisher certified García's poetry as "Chicano," while the critics and perhaps even the Chicano reading public considered it "non-movement" poetry. The standard for movement literature had been set some time earlier by influential writers of García's generation—Sánchez, Salinas, Luis Valdez, and José Montoya—who were responsible for the *pinto* and pachuco mythos. By this standard, the *pocho* was a *vendido* [sellout]. If a Chicano intellectual or activist chose to remain

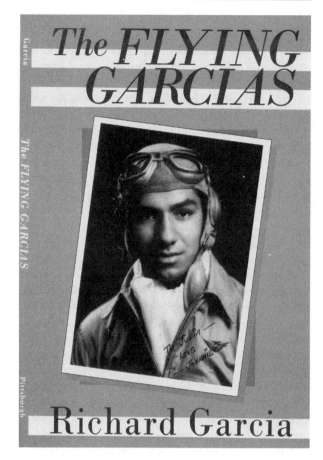

*Cover for García's 1993 collection of poetry incorporating family lore and the theme of flight*

aloof from the movement, he revealed the characteristic inauthenticity of the *pocho* who was neither gringo nor Chicano.

Lomelí and Urioste describe *Selected Poetry* as "Highly polished, low-key, non-Movement poetry" in which "Realities float as in dreams." The work of Lomelí and Urioste was an early effort to establish the professional analysis of Chicano literature as an academic discipline. In the 1960s and early 1970s a body of analysis and critical opinion had yet to develop around the growing output of Chicano poetry, drama, narrative, and film. There was virtually no one with critical training and expertise in these areas, nor were there critical standards that defined Chicano literature as an artistic movement distinct from the social and political struggles of the day. On the contrary, art and politics were connected in the minds of many Chicano authors and their audiences. In oppressed communities literature and art were seen either as luxuries that required practical justification or as useful ideological instruments. Only later, when Chicano Studies programs had been established in schools and universities, did critical analysis begin to suggest distinctions and to define what Juan Bruce-Novoa called "the space of Chicano literature." The fact that García's *Selected Poetry* was described as "non-movement poetry" suggests the extent to which a movement bias influenced the critical reception of Chicano literature. The critical description of the work as "low key" suggests that García avoids strident polemics and partisanship; indeed, the disturbing—sometimes nightmarish—images in the book are far from timid or sluggish. Nevertheless, the collection received few reviews, and by the mid-1970s García's poetic career was dying of neglect.

The disappointing response to the book was a blow that affected García for years. The failure to reach an audience left him literally incapable of writing poetry. He made no attempt to read at the Flor y Canto or Canto al Pueblo poetry festivals at which Chicano authors presented their work to the public. Instead, he remained silenced by self-doubt and frustration as he tried to examine the cultural and linguistic bases of his poetry. In this respect, García's experience was not unusual and reflected the internal struggle and analysis that characterized Chicano and Chicana poetry during the late 1970s. In the 1980s marginalized groups such as Chicana writers, feminists, and gays were reclaiming their voices with direct calls for renewal and empowerment. During this period García ended his silence and was able once again to communicate through poetry.

García acknowledges the important role that the Mexican poet Octavio Paz played in his recovery. Paz, who published a literary journal, *Vuelta*, had seen a copy of *Selected Poetry* five years after it came out, and, as García revealed in an unpublished 1993 interview:

> he then wrote to me . . . asking for some new poems to publish in *Vuelta*. He had never published me before. In fact, it was Paz's letter and the need to produce some new work to send him, that brought me out of my silence. The poem he published was an early draft of "Los Amantes" [from *The Flying Garcías*]. It started me trying again although it took some years before I was getting more poems worth keeping.

Paz's vote of confidence helped to resolve the doubts that had silenced García's creativity. New poems by García began to appear in journals such as *The Kenyon Review, The Americas Review, Ploughshares,* and *Parnassus.* In 1993, twenty years after the publication of *Selected Poetry,* García was back with *The Flying Garcías,* his second collection of poetry.

*The Flying Garcías* is filled with wit, wisdom, and hard-won truths. Whereas *Selected Poetry* uses myth and history to represent a quest for cultural and individual values, *The Flying Garcías* seems to chronicle and evaluate the outcome of that quest. It does not exhibit the

rigid structural development of *Selected Poetry,* though it does refer to the mythical hierarchy and the imagery of flight in that book. The poems grow out of the symbolic order and the technical sophistication of García's earlier work and allow him to extend the social and artistic implications of that work more freely; he is liberated from the crises of youth but is confronting the uncertainties and loneliness of aging. It is written primarily in English, although there are words and phrases in Spanish.

In the irreverent "Pancho Villa in the Land of Forever" García continues to disrupt the pantheon of cultural icons and ironically appropriates the Dantean technique of historicizing eternity. Several poems take satiric aim at movies or refer to contemporary events such as elections and the Persian Gulf War. "The Defiant Ones" takes its title from a popular 1958 movie starring Tony Curtis and Sidney Poitier as escaped convicts who are shackled together. As they fight and quarrel, "In the distance you hear the baying / of the bloodhounds." García has fun replotting and miscasting his version of the movie, which becomes another irreverent take on the prisoner/fugitive archetype. One of his substitute fugitives is Leslie Howard's title character in the 1934 motion-picture version of *The Scarlet Pimpernel,* and the other is "a tattooed language poet / from East L.A." This odd couple, shackled together, yields a composite of the García desperado in "Gregorio Cortez": fugitive fop plus *pinto* poet equals *pocho* poet. The formula satirizes the dialectics of contemporary cultural relations while also lampooning the movies and the *pinto* mystique.

A concern for social problems and the exploration of personal subjectivity remain central preoccupations that demonstrate García's undiminished range and versatility. The metaphor of flight reappears in several poems, including "The Book of Dreams," as well as the title poem. "The Book of Dreams" recalls the manual of dream interpretation that the speaker consulted as a child—a book with "pages / that stretch out like wings." Several poems, such as "Pen," comment on the void of silence that followed the publication of the author's first collection.

*The Flying Garcías* is a mature, self-assured compilation of family anecdotes, customs, and tall tales of ghosts in the sky and in the corners of the house. One ghost story, "Fly Fishing in England," attempts another odd match, this one between the seventeeth-century English poet John Donne and a contemporary of García's, Beat poet and novelist Richard Brautigan, author of *Trout Fishing in America* (1967). Donne's resonant voice and the imagery of the piece are testimony to García's commitment to the poetic tradition in English that connects the metaphysical poets to the Beat Generation. García is imaginative and edifying but never didactic.

While mainstream reviewers have generally been delighted by the linguistic and conceptual gamesmanship of the collection, acceptance by Chicanos has not been universal. Some will continue to view García's poetic agenda as a rejection of Chicano aesthetics, despite the fact that the collection implicitly develops a cultural *mestizaje* (mixture) that is relevant to much of contemporary Chicano experience. For instance, several of the poems address a personal struggle against silence and the void created by labels and cultural icons. Gender, ethnic identity, and nationality are compartments from which the subject must flee to escape the confining walls that threaten to restrain his flight. The poetic persona remains an outsider and a stubbornly unintegrated misfit who, like the *pocho,* belongs to no community. Unlike Villarreal's Richard Rubio, he does not judge himself from a Chicano perspective. His ironic and self-deprecating references, as in "I was a Teenage Zombie," are always in English.

In "Why I Left the Church" a young space cadet is dismissed for wearing his helmet to Sister Mary Bernadette's catechism class. He exits via the roof and ascends to such an incredibe altitude that he becomes a human satellite, gathering data "in the blackness / and brightness of outer space, / my body cold on one side and hot / on the other." The young apostate must overcome his fears and fly, because his mission is to reclaim the mysteries of metaphysical speculation from the thrall of science, science fiction, and institutionalized religion.

García still confronts moments of doubt, as in "Sadness and the Movies":

> Sometimes you take it personal.
> The pressure of the wind
> against your eyes that feels like crying.
> The sign on the road
> that says Go Back
> You Are Going The Wrong Way.

But the subject sees things in a positive light "when he gets his sword back / slicing the air into fifty pieces." His "sword" is, of course, the pen, symbolizing the recovery of a poetic vision that gives unity to the fifty pieces of air that are the poems of this collection.

For García, the ancient flight of Pegasus continues to be the course that the poet must chart to transcend the walls and borders of this life and communicate with both the living and the dead. In the touching elegy "Mi

Mamá, the Playgirl," the lonely vocation of the poet is relieved by the company of family, both living and deceased:

> After she died, she came to see me as she had promised. My father came, too. We sat around in the kitchen drinking coffee as if nothing had happened. My father looked great, said he'd been working out. . . . When they left it was nothing dramatic. They just walked out the door and up a street that seemed to reach into the night sky. How beautiful, I thought, as I was walking, the stars shining in my mother's hair.

In the title poem readers learn that "My sister Mary Cucha / was the first of the Garcías to fly." In one of the poems in *Selected Poetry* the subject says, "I live in a flying house." It is poignant to hear, twenty years later, the approach of a melancholy milestone:

> They are old now and have retired.
> I am almost old, but I still fly.
> People think I'm brave because I fly alone.
> But I admit—I'm afraid.
> I don't like to fly alone. And I miss the slap,
> the reassuring slap of my palms against the forearms
> of my brother Memo, against the forearms of my brother
>     John.

The poetic imagination unfolds, airy, humorous, yet in earnest, like a trapeze artist who consents to risk his neck as he soars and twirls from one end of the circus tent to the other.

Although García never uses the term *Chicano, The Flying Garcías* addresses again the fundamental questions of Chicano identity posed by *Selected Poetry.* Chicano literature reveals that each generation and each individual must struggle for a sense of self. Garcia has participated not only in that struggle but also in the debate over what constitutes poetry. While there may never be a definition capable of resolving that problem, Richard García is a poet who continues to raise difficult and provocative questions and who tries to fill the silence.

**References:**

"The Authors in This Issue," *El Grito,* 4 (Winter 1971): 7–8;

Juan Bruce-Novoa, "The Space of Chicano Literature," *De Colores: A Journal of Emerging Raza Philosophies,* 1, no. 4 (1975): 22–24;

Francisco A. Lomelí and Donaldo Urioste, *Chicano Perspectives in Literature: A Critical and Annotated Bibliography* (Albuquerque, N. Mex.: Pajarito Publications, 1976), p. 24.

# Cecilio García-Camarillo

(*12 September 1943 –   )

Enrique R. Lamadrid
*University of New Mexico*

BOOKS: *Get Your Tortillas Together,* by García-Camarillo, Carmen Tafolla, and Reyes Cárdenas (San Antonio: Cultural Distribution Center, 1976);

*Hang a Snake* (Albuquerque: Mano Izquierda Books, 1981);

*Ecstasy and Puro Pedo* (Albuquerque: Mano Izquierda Books, 1981);

*Winter Month* (Albuquerque: Mano Izquierda Books, 1982);

*Calcetines embotellados* (Albuquerque: Mano Izquierda Books, 1982);

*Double-Face* (Albuquerque: Mano Izquierda Books, 1982);

*Carambola* (Albuquerque: Mano Izquierda Books, 1982);

*Cuervos en el Río Grande* (Albuquerque: Mano Izquierda Books, 1983);

*Burning Snow* (Albuquerque: Mano Izquierda Books, 1984);

*Borlotes mestizos* (Albuquerque: Mano Izquierda Books, 1984);

*The Line* (Albuquerque: Mano Izquierda Books, 1984);

*Soy pajarita* (Albuquerque: Mano Izquierda Books, 1986);

*Black Horse on a Hill* (Albuquerque: Mano Izquierda Books, 1988);

*Zafa'o* (Albuquerque: Mano Izquierda Books, 1992);

*Crickets* (Albuquerque: Mano Izquierda Books, 1992);

*Fotos* (Albuquerque: Mano Izquierda Books, 1993);

*Dream-Walking* (Albuquerque: Mano Izquierda Books, 1994).

PLAY PRODUCTIONS: *Vista del Puente,* adaptation of *A View from the Bridge,* by Arthur Miller, Albuquerque, La Compañía de Teatro de Albuquerque, 1 November 1983;

*Tartuffe Tafoya,* adaptation of *Tartuffe,* by Molière, Albuquerque, La Compañía de Teatro de Albuquerque, 17 May 1985;

*Puente Negro,* adaptation of the play by Estela Portillo Trambley, Albuquerque, La Compañía de Teatro de Albuquerque, Winter 1985;

*Spanish Fly,* adaptation of *Manrágola,* by Niccolò Machiavelli, Albuquerque, La Compañía de Teatro de Albuquerque, 17 March 1989;

*Bienvenido! Don Goyito,* adaptation of the play by Manuel Méndez Ballester, Albuquerque, La Compañía de Teatro de Albuquerque, 14 June 1990;

*La Virgen de Tepeyac,* by García-Camarillo and Ramón Flores, Albuquerque, La Compañía de Teatro de Albuquerque, 11 December 1992;

*A Chicano Christmas Carol,* adaptation of *A Christmas Carol,* by Charles Dickens, Albuquerque, La Compañía de Teatro de Albuquerque, 19 December 1991, 1 December 1994.

VIDEO: *Flow of the River,* script by García-Camarillo, Miguel A. Gandert, and Sabine R. Ulibarrí (Albuquerque: Hispanic Culture Foundation, 1988).

OTHER: *Magazín,* edited by García-Camarillo, 1971–1972;

*Caracol: La Revista de la Raza,* edited by García-Camarillo, 1974–1977, 1980;

"Noche de Aquellas," in *Festival Flor y Canto II: An Anthology of Chicano Literature, from the Festival Held March 12–16, 1975, Austin, Texas* (Albuquerque: Pajarito Publications, 1975?, p. 67;

"Cartero," "A La Edad de 35 Años," "Quetzalcóatl," "Mujer/Quetzalcóatl," "Ojo," "Por Tus Ojos," and "Suroeste," in *El quetzal emplumece,* edited by García-Camarillo, Carmela Montalvo, and Leonardo Anguiano (San Antonio: Mexican American Cultural Center, 1976), pp. 103–107;

"un bato con las manos abiertas," in *Trece Aliens,* edited by Alurista (San Diego: University of California, 1976), cover;

*Nahualliandoing: Poetry in Español/Nahuatl/English,* edited by García-Camarillo (San Antonio: Caracol, 1977);

"Periquiando en Aztlán," in *Dale Gas: Chicano Art of Texas: An Exhibition of Contemporary Chicano Art,* edited by Santos Martínez (Houston: Contemporary Arts Museum, 1977), p. 7;

*Rayas,* edited by García-Camarillo, 1977–1979;

"The Lake" and "Las 4 direcciones del mundo y el centro," in *Canto al Pueblo: An Anthology of Experiences* (San Antonio: Penca Books, 1978), pp. 22–25;

"The Woman Who Came in at Six," translation of "La mujer que volvió a las seis," by Gabriel García Márquez, in *Mestizo: An Anthology of Chicano Literature,* edited by José Armas (Albuquerque: Pajarito Publications, 1978), pp. 99–108;

"Juvencio," "Rancho," "Compassionate Heart," and "Chivo," in *A Decade of Hispanic Literature: An Anniversary Anthology,* edited by Nicolás Kanellos, *Revista Chicano-Riqueña,* 10 (Winter–Spring 1982): 73–76;

"tejiendo," in *Ceremony of Brotherhood,* edited by Rudolfo A. Anaya and Simon J. Ortiz (Albuquerque: Academia Publications, 1981), p. 92;

"Víbora Energía" and "Hombre Mariposa," by García-Camarillo and Itzolín V. García, in *Resiembra,* edited by Jim Sagel (Española, N. Mex.: Conjunto Cultural Norteño, 1982), pp. 42–43;

"Portrait," "Hormigas," and "Eagle," in *And the Ground Spoke: Poems and Stories by Cecilio García-Camarillo, Joy Harjo, E. A. Mares, and Jim Sagel,* edited by Bryce Milligan (San Antonio: Guadalupe Cultural Arts Center, 1986), pp. 5–14;

"Le bouc (Chivo)," "Origines (Orígenes)," "Album de famille (Family photographs)," "Cloture ancestrale (Ancestral fence)," and "Retour (Going home)," in *Vous avez dit Chicano: Anthologie thématique de poésie chicano,* edited and translated by Elyette Benjamin-Labarthe (Bordeaux: Editions de la Maison des Sciences de l'Homme d'Aquitaine, 1993), pp. 128–129, 196–199, 202–205.

## SELECTED PERIODICAL PUBLICATIONS– UNCOLLECTED:

### POETRY

"cuentista," "espíritu," "el embrujo del frijol," "correr," "página," "abuelo," "mano," "dientes de la noche," "crimen," "calles," "fingersliquid," "cabeza," "domingo," "haikus," and poemas concretos: "lluvia marxista," "frío," "winter," "hormiguero," "aire triste," and "naturaleza es cadáver," *El Grito–La Voz Poética del Chicano,* 7 (March–May 1974): 29–45;

"Alma," *Maize: Cuaderno de Arte y Literatura Xicana,* 1 (Winter 1977): 14–15;

"y la cólera aplastante . . .," "viendo un lago," "nopal y piedras," "silenciosi," and "medianoche," *Maize: Cuaderno de Arte y Literatura Xicana,* 1 (Summer 1978): 39–42;

"el ex-pinto todo contento," "el chavo de west tejas," and "sapos," *Revista Río Bravo,* special García-Camarillo issue, 1 (Winter 1981): 6;

"peculiar smile," *Blue Mesa Review,* 3 (1991): 57;

"Rectángulos Carcomidos: Es Absurda," "The Consuming Power of Guilt," "Sonriendo Me Dices que con Besos You'll Drive Away My Evil Thoughts," "Dudo Seriamanete the Goodness of the Heart," "El Nuevo Deseo de Odiar Es tan Viejo," and "Huir Otra Vez del Contacto Humano," *Puerto del Sol,* special caló supplement, 27 (1992): 111–116.

### NONFICTION

"Poesía: un anti-essay," *Magazín,* 1 (November 1971): 42;

"Writing that Poem for a Chicano Magazine," *Rayas,* 5 (September–October 1978): 3;

"Poesía Chicana," *Revista Río Bravo,* special García-Camarillo issue, 1 (Winter 1981): 7.

Poet, publisher, editor, literary journalist, textual artist, scriptwriter, radio personality, and cultural attaché, Cecilio García-Camarillo is a Chicano Renaissance man whose cultural activism has transfigured Chicano literary culture. With seventeen bilingual chapbooks to his credit, he writes poetry that is brash and playful, resonant with dream imagery, pulsating with dialogic orality, and passionately involved with the personal dimensions of social struggle and the tortuous inner quest for self-understanding. His command of the *poema breve* (brief poem) and affinity with the highly visual imagery of the haiku has also led him to explore *poemas concretos* (concrete poems) and to create more than five hundred *poemas visuales* (visual poems)—poster-sized panels of text swirled into rivers and patterns that graphically recall the forces that created them. He founded and edited two influential reviews, *Magazín* and *Caracol: La Revista de la Raza,* which provided forums for scores of new Chicano writers. His newsletter, *Rayas* (Lines), evolved into a weekly public radio show, *Espejos de Aztlán* (Mirrors of Aztlán), the longest-running cultural-affairs program at radio station KUNM in Albuquerque, New Mexico. His long-term association with La Compañía de Teatro de Albuquerque has also earned him a place in the history of bilingual community theater.

In an editorial in a 1981 special issue of *Revista Río Bravo* dedicated to García-Camarillo, editor Carlos Nicolás Flores offers a qualified indication of the esteem the poet-activist enjoys in the Chicano literary community:

*Cecilio García-Camarillo with one of his* poemas visuales *(visual poems), a tribute to philosopher Jiddu Krishnamurti (photograph by Delilah Montoya)*

Though unknown in his home town [Laredo], he is loved within the movement. Max Martínez described him in *Carta Abierta,* a literary newsletter circulated nationally among Chicano writers and artists, as "one of the most respected figures in the Chicano movement." Everywhere I have been in my recent travels as editor–Austin, Houston, San Antonio, Albuquerque, and so forth–I have found the same sentiments expressed towards him, affection and respect. . . . Laredo, despite its fashionable contempt for Chicanos and the Chicano movement in general, has produced in Cecilio García-Camarillo an important Chicano leader and thereby has contributed significantly (although unconsciously) to the development of this movement.

Although his family always lived in Laredo, Texas, Cecilio García-Camarillo was delivered on 12 September 1943 by a *partera* (midwife) in the nearby village of Big Wells, where Julia Camarillo was kept during the traditional forty-day *cuarentena* (quarantine) period following childbirth. The oldest of five children, he has two brothers and two sisters. His father, Mónico García, was in the army in France and did not meet Cecilio until the boy was four years old. His relationship with his father was strained by alcohol and was ultimately severed because of disagreement over the Vietnam War, to which García-Camarillo was passionately opposed. The retention of his mother's last name is an indication of her redemptive significance in García-Camarillo's life.

With the exception of his maternal grandfather, who was from Zacatecas, Mexico, both sides of García-Camarillo's family have been *Tejanos* (Texans); as he said in an unpublished 27 February 1995 interview, "It's not in our memory that we came from anywhere else." Both of his parents were migrant agricultural workers before World War II; after the war his father got a job with the Texas Mexican Railroad. Among García-Camarillo's earliest recollections is

> traveling by train always running into Mexicanos that needed help, porque no dominaban el inglés [because they could not handle English]. Ever since I can remember we would always be helping the Mexicanos to make phone calls, to ask for the food that they wanted to eat when we would get to the train stations.

Decades later, García-Camarillo continues his advocacy work for Mexicans as a caseworker and cultural attaché in the Mexican Consulate of Albuquerque. His memories of a border childhood in the Barrio del Trompezón of Laredo also center around language:

> One of the things that I remember about those days was the great *amistad* [friendship] that existed before between the guys. And this great awareness of language, because there was so much joking back and forth. Everything had double meaning. You had to defend yourself verbally. . . . And so I consider all that as an apprenticeship for later on developing an appreciation for poetry.

García-Camarillo majored in English at the University of Texas at Austin from 1967 to 1971. In 1970 his poem "The Bomb/La Bomba" won the American Academy of Poets contest.

The Vietnam War and the rift it caused with his father spurred García-Camarillo's creative impulses. He protested the war by going on an extended hunger strike, the physical consequences of which he still endures. His 1971 poem "Canción" (Song) included in *Carambola* (Billiards, 1982), is an incantation for peace and for the strength to resist:

> con 122 libras de conciencia
>     contra la guerra
>         de los gringos
>            en vietnam
>
> camina en sí
> camina en sí . . .
>
> cargando
>     las gruesas contradicciones

*García-Camarillo (left) with fellow poets Carmen Tafolla and Reyes Cárdenas (photograph from the back cover of their joint publication,* Get Your Tortillas Together, *1976)*

> de chavo colonizado
>     en su huelga de hambre. . .
>
> (with 122 pounds of consciousness
>     against the
>         gringo's war
>           in Vietnam
>
> he travels on himself
> he travels on himself . . .
>
> carrying
>     the thick contradictions
>         of a colonized dude
>            in his hunger strike . . . )

During this period he read poetry of surrealist anguish and social commitment by Pablo Neruda and by post–World War II Japanese poets. He dedicated several poems to labor leader César Chávez, who was also engaging in fasts at that time.

In San Antonio in 1971 García-Camarillo founded *Magazín,* a pioneering Chicano literary review that had a run of fourteen issues. As he recalled in 1995:

> I was always combining *literatura* with politics. It was very important and it served as an organizing tool. A

HANG A SNAKE

Cecilio García-Camarillo

*Cover for a 1981 collection of poems written in the early 1970s at García-Camarillo's family ranch in Texas*

used IBMs and took it to a big printing company there in San Antonio. . . . It was just a small rag, but we were sending it to every major university in this country.

The journal had a literary impact that far surpassed its regional base and its circulation of one thousand copies. According to García-Camarillo, some of those copies ended up traveling around the world to Mexico, Nicaragua, Cuba, Chile, Argentina, and even to Europe (primarily Germany, France, and Spain): "We don't know how they got ahold of those, but they would subscribe. . . . We didn't print that many, but it just went all over." A trilingual English/Spanish/Náhuatl (the language spoken by the Aztecs) poetry contest announced in the magazine in the fall of 1976 resulted in the anthology *Nahualliandoing* (1977). The title is *Nahual,* a Náhuatl term for animal spirit guide, transformed with Spanish and English suffixes into a gerund. In his trilingual prologue, García-Camarillo notes:

> Parece que anda pegando fuerte la onda de consciencia lingüística. Parece que ya le andamos escarbando más ondo a la raíz pa' tratar de conocernos mejor. Chicano acceptance of Náhuatl es dirección positiva. It's a good way to pegarle de aquellas a algo más íntimo, más netamente Chicano. Chanza que con 3 idiomas le estamos siendo más fieles a nuestro espíritu y a nuestra compleja realidad Chicana.

> (It appears that the new wave of consciousness is a big hit. It seems we are digging deeper into our roots in order to get to know ourselves better. Chicano acceptance of Náhuatl is something in the right direction. It's a good way to really get something more intimately and purely Chicano. It's a greater chance with three languages that we can be more faithful to our spirit and complex Chicano reality.)

lot of awareness was spreading, el concepto de Aztlán, la identificación con la raíz indígena [the concept of (the mythical Chicano homeland) Aztlán, the identification with the indigenous roots]. . . . People were demanding that education be relevant to their own experiences. . . . It was like a new level of awareness of who we were. . . . Our job is to create a solid foundation of literatura, something that will not disappear tomorrow or the day after, but something that is big and solid and strong. And something that will endure.

After a brief sojourn in Toronto, García-Camarillo returned to San Antonio and began publishing *Caracol,* the successor to *Magazín.* This endeavor lasted from 1974 to 1980, and many Chicano poets and critics published their first pieces in *Caracol.* García-Camarillo said in the 1995 interview:

> *Caracol* became an important forum for a lot of things. . . . We were open to everything and everyone. Always supporting *las mujeres también* [women too]. . . . There's no university that could give you a tenth of the education that it did. . . . It was difficult to put out a monthly magazine, it was no easy task, it was very draining, but we were young and reckless and full of energy. . . . Everyone was such a great supporting cast. . . . We

*Get Your Tortillas Together* (1976), García-Camarillo's first book of poems, also includes work by his fellow *Tejano* poets Carmen Tafolla and Reyes Cárdenas. García-Camarillo's poems in *Get Your Tortillas Together* display the clever dramatic irony that characterizes much of his subsequent work. The lead poem, "Sala" (Living Room), equates the labor of poetry with the labor of the fields: "la sala es como un acre / de tierra harada, / lista pa la siembra" (the living room is like an acre / of plowed land / ready for seeding). The seeds to be sown for the harvest of poetry are a sunny table, three enigmatic figures in peaked hats, a lamp, and a necklace of "deer's eyes" (a large black and red seed used in Mexico for cures and good luck charms). The speaker notes, "se asoma mi ruca / y me trai el sombrero / / voy a regar / la sala" (my old lady peeks in / and brings my hat / / I'll go water / the room). The conversational diction (*pa, trai*) and caló jargon (*ruca*) are trademarks of García-Camarillo's colloquial style.

Other "tortillas" by García-Camarillo in the collection include a series of ten numbered "Event" poems that place the poetic persona in a series of situations and dilemmas. "Event 5" humorously connects mundane Chicano reality to the mythic dimension of the Aztec world at the time of European conquest:

> make some instant coffee
> and sit on the porch
>
> pretend you are
> Moctezuma and that
> the mailman is a
> messenger from
> your friend the King of Texcoco . . .

"Event 7" was inspired by the 5 August 1975 birth of García-Camarillo's first child, his son Itz-Ollín, and is a chronicle of a new father's sense of joy and self-sacrifice. In his early work García-Camarillo revels in the symbols and syntax of Chicano cultural nationalism—revolutionary heroes, Aztec indigenism, English/Spanish code-switching, and barrio slang.

Late in the same year that *Get Your Tortillas Together* appeared García-Camarillo co-edited a landmark encyclopedic collection of Chicano writing in Texas. *El quetzal emplumece* (The Quetzal Bird Grows Feathers, 1976) includes a broad sampling of the writings of schoolteachers, church activists, community organizers, and some emerging Chicano authors whose names remain prominent decades later.

In the summer of 1977 García-Camarillo moved to Albuquerque with his wife, Mia Kirsi Stageberg, and Itz-Ollín. García-Camarillo edited the journal *Rayas* for two years before turning to *Espejos de Aztlán,* a weekly radio show devoted to the Chicano and Latino cultural and political scene in Albuquerque. The program continued for fifteen years.

García-Camarillo's long association with La Compañía de Teatro de Albuquerque began in 1983 with *Vista del Puente,* a bilingual translation and adaptation of Arthur Miller's *A View from the Bridge* (1955). Other writers whose works were adapted for bilingual Chicano productions include Molière, Niccolò Machiavelli, Charles Dickens, Manuel Méndez Ballester, and Estela Portillo Trambley. García-Camarillo's most significant dramatic work is *La Virgen de Tepeyac* (1992), a humorous political thriller that he wrote with Ramón Flores, a director of the theater. In the *Albuquerque Journal* (19 December 1992) the theater critic Catalina Reyes noted that the play offers

some particularly snappy writing, especially in scenes where the Aztec characters interact. Here the co-writers delightfully achieve that elusive balance of idea and whimsy that communicates strong messages without the viewer feeling clubbed. Among those messages is one about the history of oppressed people undermining their own battle to survive by fighting among themselves; and another about how only through the end of such infighting can people support each other enough to stand up to the social results of oppression.

Over the years García-Camarillo has worked in hospitals and nonprofit associations; driving a truck for a community food bank did not interfere with his poetic endeavors, since he could write a haiku "even while shifting gears. I wrote a lot of haiku in the streets of Albuquerque." His work with cultural organizations included positions with Pajarito Publications, the Hispanic Culture Foundation, and the Mexican consulate. Recognition of his ongoing poetic career came in 1982 with a National Endowment for the Arts fellowship, which allowed him to buy a house in Atrisco, his favorite barrio of the South Valley Albuquerque.

García-Camarillo's daughter Cielo Rojo, whose name derives from the Mayan calendar, was born on 7 March 1978; his daughter Oraibi, named for an ancient Hopi village, was born on 22 August 1980. Then after a ten-year relationship, Stageberg and García-Camarillo went their separate ways, leaving him a single father.

In 1981 García-Camarillo established Mano Izquierda Books, a series of chapbooks illustrated with original and clip-art line drawings and offset-printed in successive limited editions of one hundred. They are distributed locally at bookstores, by mail order, at book fairs and poetry readings, and by the poet personally to a large circle of friends, family, and literary allies. The imprint was thus named because the *mano izquierda* (left hand) usually knows what the right is doing.

All three of the García children began exploring their dreams with their father and illustrating with fanciful line drawings his poetic response to their imaginations. At age four, Itz-Ollín collaborated with his father on a children's story that became *Cuervos en el Río Grande* (Crows on the Rio Grande, 1983), a mythic encounter with migrating crows on the banks of the same river that the father knew as a child in Laredo. Itz-Ollín went on to publish several other bilingual children's stories, including *El volcán de la dragona* (The Volcano of the Dragon, 1982), *El perro fiero de la acequia* (The Wild Dog of the Irrigation Ditch, 1982), *Una mañana extraña* (A Strange Morning, 1982), *La casa del brujo* (The House of the Sorcerer, 1984), and *Pepe el piano* (1986), all with his father's imprint, Mano Izquierda Books. He finished his first novel at the age of fifteen, although it is unpublished. García-Camarillo's collaboration with Cielo

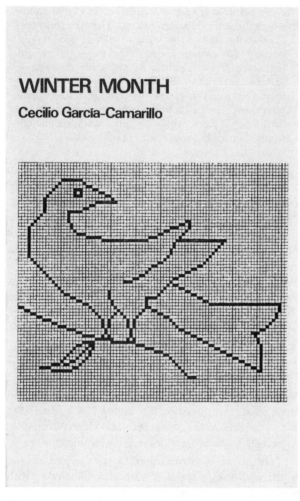

WINTER MONTH

Cecilio García-Camarillo

*Cover for the second edition of a 1982 collection in which García-Camarillo experiments with the haiku form*

Rojo produced *Soy pajarita* (I am a Little Bird, 1986), a bilingual story with whimsical drawings designed to teach a child to read Spanish. The protagonist dreams that she is a many-colored bird who flies above the world to understand it better through her extraordinary senses. The moral of the story is to trust in the power of the imagination. In 1994 Cielo published a collection of poems, *Blue Innocence,* which tempers lyrical themes with the worldly realities of betrayal, abortion, gang warfare, and death. At age seven Oraibi told García-Camarillo the story that became *Black Horse on a Hill* (1988), a tale of a solitary horse visited by five pesky crows.

García-Camarillo has said of his chapbooks:

Two currents run through my work. One is experimental stuff that continues traditions that started around the turn of the century that I think was one of the most fertile periods in terms of global creativity. It's interesting how a lot of these things are related to wars. But the works that the surrealists, that the dadaists, all

those things, I kind of inherited those things. . . . Then at the same time doing social realism. I'm able to do both things.

García-Camarillo writes his own notes for the back covers of his books. He has written most of them in an authoritative third-person voice, though for *Fotos* (1993) and *Dream-Walking* (1994) he takes off the mask and comments in the first person.

Although all of the chapbooks were published in Albuquerque, the first six—*Hang a Snake* (1981), *Ecstacy and Puro Pedo* (Ecstasy and Bull Crap, 1981), *Winter Month* (1982), *Calcetines embotellados* (Bottled Socks, 1982), *Double-Face* (1982), and *Carambola* (1982)—were written in Texas in the early 1970s. All of these poems share an experimental vanguard spirit, a short line structure, visual imagery, and an ambiguous first-person poetic voice.

The author's back-cover notes for *Hang a Snake* indicate that the twenty poems were written at his family ranch, El Quiote, near Laredo. He explains:

The Chicano spiritual crisis in a rural context is the explicit theme of this text which actually reads as a lengthy, bilingual poem. García-Camarillo utilizes the technique of hallucination as the basis for his portrayal of a self-doubting voice, fractured cultural traditions and a pain-inflicting South Texas environment.

In an ironic pastoral mode, the poet returns to the *campo* (country) in a vain search for his origins. Urban anxieties unwind, only to reveal another level of bleakness and desperation. In the poem "rancho" the poet asks himself:

a qué le tiras
crouching todo el día
[what are you good at
crouching all day long]
on this sandpapered land
of malnutritioned shrubs

la luna
parece una tuerca
de plastic
[the moon
resembles a plastic
screw]

my soul
well
there's plastic in it too

city acid has galloped
through veins
and you've let a few books
curdle your mind cells. . . .

Intense introspection leads, through hallucination, to fragmentation of the poetic self in "Presence of a Poem": ". . . your eyes / are a grasshopper that jumps around / and lands on an ashbrown shrub."

*Ecstacy and Puro Pedo* is a Dionysian invitation to poetic excess and linguistic sacrifice. In the notes on the back cover of this collection García-Camarillo explains:

> *Ecstasy and Puro Pedo* is a viaje estrambólico [bizarre trip] in which Chicano relaje [madness], Aztlán rural existentialism, dadaist poetic irreverence, haiku compactness, and radio splicing techniques are twisted together to create a knotted, introverted portrait of the Chicano experience in the States. In this collection of 12 poems written between 1970–71, the experimental underlying tissue in García-Camarillo's poetry really comes into focus.

A *flor y canto* (flower and song) Chicano poetics is fully developed in this collection, which includes allusions to classical Náhuatl themes such as the hummingbird as a warrior spirit who brings blessings down from heaven: "hummingbird baila / en árbol de la vida / / hummingbird / picotea / 2 canciones / 2 acroirises / de la máscara" (hummingbird dances / in a genealogical tree / / hummingbird / picks at / 2 songs / 2 rainbows / of the mask).

The next collection steps away from the ecstatic into a more severe and hard-bitten minimalism set in the same disenchanted pastoral setting as *Hang a Snake;* these poems were also written at El Quiote. *Winter Month* is a bleak thirty-poem chronicle that reflects the season as well as the anguish and nausea that have overcome the poet. In his back-cover notes García-Camarillo explains:

> *Winter Month* may very well be the first collection of haiku published by a Chicano poet. García-Camarillo immerses himself in the spirit rather than the traditional form of haiku in an attempt to pull together his center, fragmented by the harsh South Texas environment and the brutalizing forces of American culture. Using psychiatric jargon, he struggles to transcend his own alienated and cynical voice.

A certain grayness, tedium, and despair overcome these poems, as in the haiku dated 29 November 1970: "a photograph-stillness / if the poem doesn't move / all is dead."

*Calcetines embotellados* is a revision of poems written a decade earlier, alongside responses or extended glosses written later. These poems are almost entirely in Spanish. The curious image of bottled poems and bottled socks appears several times. In his notes García-Camarillo says that the book has a "haunting,

internal landscape reminiscent of the poetry of post-war Japan," adding:

> Lyrically, los unsuppressed cucuys tienen la rienda suelta para danzar por todos los [the unsuppressed monsters have free rein to dance over all of the] parameters of his poetic vision. The integrity lies in the acceptance of these feelings projected mostly in chicano-type Spanish que fueron escritos en [that was written in] 1970–71. *Calcetines embotellados* is an experiment of transformations: the original (left side) poems, years later, became the right side animals that look, smell and behave somewhat like the sombras originales [original shadows].

Empty streets, red light bulbs, dogs dragging their entrails, rivers of filth, plastic skin, and a pen seen as a wriggling cockroach combine and recombine in a panoply reminiscent of the bleak surrealism of Pablo Neruda's *Residencia en la tierra* (Residence on Earth, 1933, 1935). The book is a virtual journal of nightmares.

The technique of revision and response is used again in *Double-Face,* in which the poet reaches the depths of cynicism and despair over the Vietnam War. The original poems were written in 1970, the companion poems in 1975; the collection was rediscovered by García-Camarillo in 1980. In his notes he calls this book his "most spiritually disturbing collection of poems," adding:

> Doubt and isolation son las inquietudes que [are the restlessness that] his haunting, bilingual voice dibuja en una configuración que es [sketches in a configuration that is] distressful as it is compelling. There is no escape from his godless universe, and one is condemned to alienation from the environment and from oneself.

In one poem he writes:

> en pozos
> donde descanzan víboras
> se mutilan estrellas
>
> lo negro
> de noche
> tiene cuernos que raspan
> sensibilidad endrogada
> . . . . . . . . . . . . . . . . . .
> desde túnel
> le ladro a gente
> con dientes de azufre
> con cuervo
> en espalda
> con espuma
> en boca
> muerdo canción
> que no se puede terminar

SOY PAJARITA
Cecilio García-Camarillo

Dibujos de Cielo Rojo

*Cover for a children's story inspired and illustrated by García-Camarillo's elder daughter*

(in wells
where snakes rest
stars are mutilated

the blackness
of night
they have horns that scratch
a drugged sensibility
. . . . . . . . . . . . . . . .
from the tunnel
I bark at people
with sulphur teeth
with a crow
on your back
with foam
in the mouth
I bite a song
that is endless)

The poems in *Carambola* span the entire decade of the 1970s. The feverish poetic production of 1970 and 1971 gives way to a more measured pace that carries clear signs of maturation. In these pages the poet emerges from his despair, identifies its source, and joins with others to combat it. In his notes for the volume García-Camarillo calls the collection "a serious billiard game" and explains (in the third person) that "García-Camarillo plays with the various levels of Chicano language in an attempt to get to the heart of the two major movements in his life: the oneiric and the socio-political. Se vale [That's it]."

The poem "Canción" is a good example of the uplifting strength that the poet summons to confront and overcome the forces pitted against him. He curses the gringos' war in Vietnam as he challenges it with his fasting and his spiritual "diet" of words. "Preparándonos pa la marcha de Muleshoe a Austin, Tejas 1.27" (Preparing Ourselves for the March from Muleshoe to Austin, Texas, 1–27) is a chronicle of the Texas farm workers' 1976 march on the state capital to demand their rights. The poem ends with shouts of "ya basta / ya basta" (enough is enough / enough is enough). Yet, even the most political of García-Camarillo's poems are playfully revolutionary. This playful element is especially evident in "Sapos" (Toads), in which the entire landscape comes alive with toads; the poet himself ends up turning into a *sapo* and hopping down an alley.

The first poems García-Camarillo wrote in New Mexico are published in *Burning Snow* (1984), a collection of haiku that stands in sharp contrast to the *Winter Month* haiku set in south Texas. In this collection the dreary gray landscapes of the southern Rio Grande valley are replaced by the dazzling snowy landscapes of the headwaters of the river. The poet's notes explain:

Written around the Christmas holidays in 1983, *Burning Snow* is García-Camarillo's second collection of published haiku. Once again he opts for the Japanese poetic form of economy of words, focus on a particular season, depth of image and clarity of vision to portray his inner landscape and this time not his ancestral land at the Mexican border near Laredo, Texas, but the landscape around the D. H. Lawrence Ranch, north of Taos, New Mexico. García-Camarillo's feelings are the protagonist that journey from being nauseously trapped in the city, brooding over the decaying body and crumpled spirit, detesting the aloneness of the aging process, to the rural, open spaces where acceptance of fate and communion with the sun and snow is accessible. In-between these two poles of the soul, his children, several women, animals and even insects visit with García-Camarillo, and he draws them all with the finesse and honesty that is his distinctive style.

There is less desperation in these northern landscapes than in the southern ones of *Winter Month*. Somehow pain is more completely integrated or absorbed into them; in one haiku the speaker says: "the snow falling from the trees / makes me feel / like i'm not alone." The anguish of distant urban landscapes is quelled by the mountain stillness. Reminders of the barrio are softened: "the drunk's eyes / are redder / than a rose." García-Camarillo's New Mexico poems are longer than his earlier works; they are characterized by increasingly lengthy poetic lines and by incantatory structure and poetic dialogues.

With *Borlotes mestizos* (1984) the social vein of García-Camarillo's poetry reaches its apex. *Alborotar* means to rile up or infuriate; *borlote* is a caló expression denoting an occasion for outrage. The book is the impassioned complaint of the mestizo, the marginalized underdog of a racist society. In his notes García-Camarillo says:

> At a time when Chicano academicians are making their move to put bureaucratic suits and ties on carefully crafted poetry with near to nothing content, García-Camarillo's *Borlotes mestizos* reasserts la meta fundamental de nuestra literatura: opinar concretamente sobre nuestra realidad [the fundamental goal of our literature: to concretely give opinions about our reality]. García-Camarillo's voice cruises powerfully through the plight of laborers, the contradictions of Reagan's politics, police brutality, la concientización de los pintos [the of prisoners], colonialism in Texas agribusiness, la amargura de [the bitterness of] stereotyping, the business of torturing in El Salvador, personal weaknesses and the everpresent dangers of being a Chicano in the USA. It is a voice that consciously reaches back to the oral tradition of storytelling pa contarnos trozos de la vida que nosotros conocemos tan bién [to relate bits and pieces of the life that we know so well].

In "Cuerpo humano" (Human Body) the poet links his own body to the suffering of the victims of torture in Central America and launches incantations of protest: "como duele al cuerpo humano / cuando el enemigo / corta una cruz en el estómago / con una botella quebrada de coca cola . . . " (how the human body hurts / when the enemy / cuts a cross in one's stomach / with a broken Coca-Cola bottle . . . ). Gone is the hallucinatory anguish brought on by the war in Vietnam. These poems display a clarity fueled by rage and a desire to enlist and empower language to resist the oppression.

In "Ojos de Rata" (Rat Eyes) the poet refuses to take the compassion of the reader for granted. Ojos de Rata is a barrio dweller who becomes a victim of police brutality. In a kind of Brechtian alienation effect, Ojos de Rata is distanced from any easy sympathy. His story is told in barrio slang as an animal fable. As he cruises the South Valley of Albuquerque, he is stopped and killed by a pack of dogs with badges.

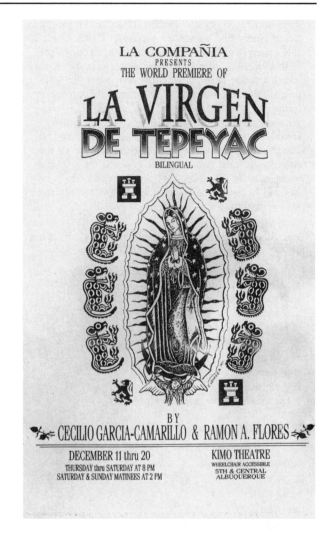

*Advertisement for a 1992 play that was a collaboration between García-Camarillo and one of the directors of La Compañía de Teatro de Albuquerque*

The lengthy poem *The Line* occupies an entire 1984 chapbook. It is a chronicle of humiliation, solidarity, and frustration, a compendium of impressions and emotions felt by the poet while getting food stamps. García-Camarillo summarizes the strengths of the work in his notes:

> Written in the winter of 1981, *The Line* is to date García-Camarillo's longest poem. It represents a general statement on the problem of hunger in the U.S., and more concretely, an on the spot poetic portrayal of typical bureaucratic foul-ups that literally leave the poor, old and unemployed out in the cold with empty stomachs. García-Camarillo, as a participant of the food stamp line, narrates with succinct immediacy the tragi-comic raw energy of los de abajo [the underdogs]. The voice is haikulike, bold and conversational in its strokes that cut out a vision of a group's will to survive. Literatura social y comprometida: García-Camarillo

logra superar el yo que escribe solamente lo que yo siento [Social and committed literature: García-Camarillo manages to overcome the I that only writes what I feel]. Conscious of his own socio-economic status, se atreve a tomar la responsabilidad de recoger [he dares to take the responsibility of gathering] the collective feelings of los marginados [marginal people]. The freezing winter day is as much a participant in this drama of controlled violence and transcendence as are the real and memorable characters that move up and down the strangely formed food stamp line. But if there is one protagonist in *The Line,* it is el sentimiento de compasión [the feeling of compassion] that permeates the very soul of the poem.

"Scene 5" describes an encounter that can occur in the barrio any day of the week:

a 60 year old pachuco
with greased hair combed back
and a centipede-looking scar on his forehead
offers a 2 year old giggly girl some candy

but the mother
with the nicest smile
says no sir
it's just too early for that garbage

After the people in line wait for hours and almost freeze to death, the poet receives enough food stamps for another month:

i take a deep breath
and head home
through the lines of my people
still waiting it out
shoving
cussing
laughing
joking
refusing to surrender to the deadly cold
in this our daily struggle for survival

In *Zafa'o* (1992) García-Camarillo paints a frenetic series of poetic portraits, tributes, and snapshots of important people and portentous moments in his life. In his notes the author explains that the work

explores through a 7 year tour de force the configurations of life's disillusionments as well as the enigmatic strength that propels us on. The 11 English/Spanish/ bilingual imagistic poems are drawn with unparalleled intensity, not in his usual compact style, but in broader conversational strokes. García-Camarillo's mature voice is less cynical than accepting of the new and recurring pains that visit and oftentimes stay to haunt us. *Zafa'o,* slang for crazy, unbalanced, free, may be García-Camarillo's most compelling and intimate poetry chapbook to date.

As his life enters into a period of crisis with the breakup of his marriage, the poet uses the power of his art on himself, confronting the demons of his past and present. All the decisive moments are recalled and lamented in *Zafa'o.* The collection also includes a touching tribute to the poet's mother and a memorial for a friend, the New Mexico activist and graphic artist Rini Templeton.

*Zafa'o* is an anticipation of the throes of loss that burst forth in the next book, *Crickets.* In his notes García-Camarillo calls this work

an experimental literary collage where social realism is woven with dream and metaphor to create a complex drama of probing ontological/social/spiritual anxieties. An interview with a barrio philosopher published years ago in "Caracol," a car conversation with an old hitch-hiker, a letter never mailed to a professor of sociology, a taped counseling session with a Chicano political theoretician, and a monologue written on the banks of the Río Grande form the five narrative threads that García-Camarillo interlaces around the central theme of the text: the disintegration of his intense ten year relationship with his wife.

In these selections of narrative prose the speaker seeks solace in revelation, the sage advice of strangers, and a conversation with his strongest mythical and personal link to New Mexico: the Rio Grande. "Talking to the Río Grande," written in 1983, expresses García-Camarillo's connection to the river:

Siempre regreso a ti [I always come back to you], my source, you gnarled piece of liquid leather. When I feel good or reventado [exhausted] you're always there for me. Solamente [Only] your indifference tiene la capacidad de entender [has the capacity to understand] the outpourings of my soul. . . . I swam in you and your dark waters mixed with my blood. Toda mi vida he permanecido cerca de ti [All my life I have remained close to you] cause I have the need to reveal myself to you so that I can cope con todas las chingaderas de la vida [with the screwups of my life]. Listen to me old one, and help me make her love me once again.

The title of the book comes from a nightmarish boyhood episode on the family farm, re-created in "Talking to the Rio Grande." A group of boys finds a dry well with snakes at the bottom; the boys kill the snakes with their .22 rifles and force the poet to descend on a rope to get the bodies. On the way down he discovers that the walls of the well are crawling with thousands of crickets. The imagery of this episode echoes in several poems from different periods in the poet's life.

García-Camarillo's subsequent poetic development reveals the effects of the catharsis he achieves in *Crickets.* Beyond pain, the maturing poet finds his fullest expressive voice. In *Fotos,* published in 1993, personal pain and desire are detached from anecdote, abstracted from memory, and explored in allegory and metaphor. In his notes for the back cover García-Camarillo recalls:

> empezó con las notas que escribí después de haber visto un libro de fotografía contemporánea de España [it all started with the notes I wrote after having read a book of contemporary Spanish photography]. En el transcurso de 2 años [In the course of two years] I "layered" los textos [the texts] with personal dreams and with influences from movies, Jung, the I Ching, Krishnamurti, and with work I've done for Chicano theatre. No estoy seguro si conozco a las mujeres de los poemas, pero me imagino que existen [I am not sure if I know the women in the poems, but I assume they exist]. I understood recently that what I was trying to do all along was to photograph desire, that oftentimes dark force that moves and shapes our existence.

In these poems desire moves between the opposite poles of objectification and subjectification. Its correlatives are sex, addiction, obsession, devotion, manipulation, and, ultimately, death. "Foto 9" is a study in black on black:

> negro que se teje en negro
>
> las palabras fácilmente pueden ser
> un remolino de cuchillos
>
> es difícil penetrar superficies cuadradas
> donde ni siquiera existen sombras
> pero sé que estás allí
> derrotada
> tatuaje en tus pechos
> tu mirada ahogada en alcohol . . .
>
> [black that weaves itself with black
>
> words can easily be
> a whirlwind of knives
>
> it is difficult to penetrate square surfaces
> where not even shadows exist
> but I know you are there
> beaten down
> tattoos on your bosom
> your glance drowned in alcohol . . . ]
>
> in the total darkness there's a river
> with the black waters of fate
> slowly maneuvering to consciousness
> fragments of illusions . . .

The dreamlike images dissolve into a raucous no-win lover's argument after which the only solace is a solitary walk on a dark street. The last poem, "foto 10," depicts an armed stand-off between deranged lovers in

*Cover for García-Camarillo's 1994 collection of poems inspired by his dreams during a difficult period in his life*

a leafless cottonwood forest. The speaker watches the sunlight glinting off the barrel of his lover's gun as three blue jays swoop around them.

In *Dream-Walking* (1994) García-Camarillo returns to the automatic symbolic language and integrative power of dreams, as he says in the back-cover notes:

> Dreams taste like the purest form of metaphor. To dream is to walk a journey of renewal where the oppressive, rational censor in all of us is irrelevant. *Dream-Walking* es una colección de [is a collection of] 14 bilingual poems I originally recorded in my journal as the remembered dreams de un periódo muy intenso y controversial en mi vida [of a very intense and controversial period in my life]. . . . Sospecho que siempre conservaré la necesidad de tejer imágenes soñadas [I suspect that I will always conserve the need to weave dreamed images] in the texture of my poems. I need this liberating movida que nomás no puedo encontrar [movement that I just cannot find] anywhere else.

Exploring his dreams, the poet heals some of the wounds of his past, including his relationship with his father. After a lifetime of struggle with the anguished family dynamics that shaped his inner life, the mature poet exorcises the source of his pain in dream poem "4," in which the thirty-year-old speaker, stands by his father's deathbed and recalls excruciating scenes of drunkenness and violence from his adolescence. The father "wants to have a final talk," but the speaker says they cannot, "porque no sabemos conversar" (because we don't know how to converse). In dream "6," with his father in a burning house that has horses running through it, the poet finally sees the route of his deliverance:

> and i try to understand
> why the bedroom window
> por donde entra
> y sale mi mundo
> [where my world
> goes in and out]
> hasn't burned
>
> it hangs there
> surrounded by fire
>
> i wonder what kept me
> from seeing it before

*Dream-Walking* is a psychotropic catalogue of wishes, fears, obsessions, and desires, covering the entire range of the poet's social and interior poetic universe. In dream "7" the poet contemplates the source of his song and reaffirms his commitment to sing it:

> but it doesn't matter
> cause i'm listening to the voice
> that can't be bought or stolen
> but must be earned
> with a clarity of mind
> and patience
> . . . . . . . . . .
> i can hardly think now
> but i understand

> and i will sing
> till the end of my days
> i promise

There are dreams of pursuit, violence, and death. Oneiric imagery has always been a part of García-Camarillo's poetry, but in earlier phases of his work this imagery often lacked the extraordinary resonance and narrative control that it has here. Although he claims in his notes that he wishes he could interpret his dreams better, his dream poems are masterfully rendered, saturated with symbol, significance, and feeling. They impart a sense of integrated equilibrium.

Many lesser poets have won praise and celebrity, but few poets have worked through and experimented as much, with as much persistence, as has Cecilio García-Camarillo. Although relatively few critics and readers have read his work, those who have realize that García-Camarillo has one of the most evolved and expressive voices in the broadening range of Chicano literature.

## References:

Evangelina Vigil, "Una mordida de *Get Your Tortillas Together,* poesía de Cecilio García-Camarillo, Reyes Cárdenas, and Carmen Tafolla (an analytic poem)," *Caracol,* 3 (May 1977): 17;

Max Martínez, "Max-y-más," *Carta Abierta,* 15 (Summer 1979): 8–9;

Martínez, "Los Mejores Escritores de Aztlán," *Rayas,* 2 (March–April 1978): 3;

Salvador Rodríguez del Pino, "La poesía chicana: una nueva trayectoria," in *The Identification and Analysis of Chicano Literature,* edited by Francisco Jiménez (New York: Bilingual Press/Editorial Bilingüe, 1979), pp. 68–89;

Carlos Nicolás Flores, "A Tribute to Cecilio García Camarillo," *Revista Río Bravo,* special García-Camarillo issue, 1 (Winter 1981): 17, 19.

## Papers:

Cecilio García-Camarillo's papers are in the Special Collections Department of the Zimmerman Library, University of New Mexico, Albuquerque.

# Erlinda Gonzales-Berry

*(23 August 1942 – )*

## Angie Chabram-Dernersesian
*University of California, Davis*

BOOK: *Paletitas de guayaba* (Albuquerque: El Norte Press, 1991).

OTHER: "Excerpts from El Tren de la ausencia," in *Voces: New Mexican Hispanic Writers,* edited by Rudolfo A. Anaya (Albuquerque, N.Mex.: El Norte Publications, 1987), pp. 151–152;

"Rosebud" and "(Más) Conversaciones con Sergio," in *Las mujeres hablan: An Anthology of Nuevo Mexicana Writers,* edited by Gonzales-Berry, Tey Diana Rebolledo, and Teresa Márquez (Albuquerque: El Norte Publications, 1988), pp. 27–31, 187–191;

*Pasó por aquí: Critical Essays on the New Mexican Literary Tradition, 1542–1988,* edited by Gonzales-Berry (Albuquerque: University of New Mexico Press, 1989);

"Carlota Gonzales," in *Nuestras mujeres: Hispanas of New Mexico, Their Images and Lives, 1582–1992,* edited by Rebolledo, Millie Santillanes, and Gonzales-Berry (Albuquerque: El Norte Publications/Academia, 1992), pp. 35–36;

"Malinche Past: Selections from Paletitas de guayaba" (translation), in *Infinite Divisions: An Anthology of Chicana Literature,* edited by Rebolledo and Eliana S. Rivero (Tucson: University of Arizona Press, 1993), pp. 207–212;

*Recovering the U.S. Hispanic Literary Heritage,* volume 2, edited by Gonzales-Berry and Chuck Tatum (Houston: Arte Público, 1996).

SELECTED PERIODICAL PUBLICATIONS–UNCOLLECTED: "Burque," *Revista Chicano-Riqueña,* 3, no. 3 (1975): 18;

"Queriéndote," *San Marcos Review* (Spring 1983): 13.

*Erlinda Gonzales-Berry in 1992 ( photograph by Miguel Gandert)*

In a 1993 interview with Manuel de Jesús Hernández and Michael Nymann, Erlinda Gonzales-Berry described her professional life: "I am first and foremost an academician. I write literary criticism, and I dabble in creative writing. I hope to change that order in the near future." Her early creative output is limited–she published a few poems in 1975 and 1984 and excerpts from a promising novel, "Rosebud," which explores the lives of five New Mexican sisters living on a ranch, in 1988. The 1991 publication of *Paletitas de guayaba* (Guava Popsicles), written after her return from taking students on a study trip to Mexico in 1980–1981, firmly established Gonzales-Berry as an important New Mexican writer.

Erlinda Viola Gonzales-Berry was born on 23 August 1942 in Roy, New Mexico, to Carlota and Canuto Gonzales. Her mother was a rural schoolteacher, her father a rancher. She completed a B.S. in education (1964), an M.A. in Spanish (1971), and a Ph.D. in Romance languages (1978) at the University of New Mexico. She was a professor of Spanish there from 1979 through 1996. In 1992 she became the first Chicana to head a department in the College of Arts and Sciences, serving until 1996, when she became chair of the ethnic-studies department at Oregon State University, Corvallis. Gonzales-Berry several times won the Outstanding Teacher of the Year Award at the University of New Mexico (1983, 1984, and 1991) and was named an Eminent Scholar in 1989 by the New Mexico Council on Higher Education. As a critic Gonzales-Berry has published several articles on Chicano language and literature and is widely respected for her contribution to Southwestern cultural studies. She has also edited three important anthologies that target New Mexico: *Las mujeres hablan: An Anthology of Nuevo Mexicana Writers* (1988), *Pasó por aquí: Critical Essays on the New Mexican Literary Tradition, 1542-1988* (1989), and a forthcoming collection edited with David Maciel: *The Chicano Experience in Nuevo Mexico, 1840s-1990s.*

*Paletitas de guayaba* has received critical praise in works such as *Multiculturalism: A Critical Reader* (1994) and Tey Diana Rebolledo's *Women Singing in the Snow: A Cultural Analysis of Chicana Literature* (1995). The novel is also the topic of several dissertations and articles. Portions of the novel have been published in periodicals and anthologies. Excerpts were published under the original title of the novel, "El tren de la ausencia" (The Train of Absence), in *Voces: New Mexican Hispanic Writers* (1987); other selections have appeared as "(Más) Conversaciones con Sergio" in *Las mujeres hablan* (1988), "Conversaciones con Sergio" in *Third Woman Press* (1989), and "Malinche Past: Selections from *Paletitas de guayaba*" in *Infinite Divisions: An Anthology of Chicana Literature* (1993).

*Paletitas de guayaba* attempts to set the record straight about Chicanos and New Mexicans, two groups that have been subject to a great deal of misrepresentation in the United States and Mexico. Gonzales-Berry attributes the pedagogical thrust of the novel to her life experience: in Mexico she found herself explaining "who we are"; in the United States her life's work involves instructing Chicano and New Mexican students about their history. Some of the commentary on *Paletitas de guayaba* has emphasized a Mexican connection, interpreting the novel as part of an important and timely dialogue with Mexico, especially its youth and intellectuals. Links to widely circulated Mexican works such as Octavio Paz's collection of essays *El laber-*

*into de la soledad* (The Labyrinth of Solitude, 1950, revised 1959) are indisputable.

Gonzales-Berry's novel reverses the geographical and cultural movement that frames Paz's first essay, "The Pachuco and Other Extremes," in which the Mexican national encounters his "questioning image" in the United States. That is, Paz wrote, whenever he "attempted to examine North American life, anxious to discover its meaning," he learned instead something about himself. In addition, Gonzales-Berry alters the gender orientation of Paz's Mexican/pachuco border identity by having as her protagonist a young, bohemian Chicana traveler named Mari. Throughout the novel Mari irreverently chain smokes, frequently curses, and boldly encounters her questioning image in unlikely places in Mexico City as she moves from the train to city streets, political forums, the bedroom, and the fantastic.

Mari's trip to Mexico is partially rendered as a way of "making sense" of her apparently disparate regional (New Mexican) and transnational (Mexican/ U.S. and Mexican/Chicana) identities and coming to terms with the way in which American and Mexican societies have constructed gender and race relations within a heterosexual, patriarchal context. Although *Paletitas de guayaba* does not follow a chronological sequence, it is also a bildungsroman. The novel captures the protagonist's movement from childhood (innocence) to womanhood (self-consciousness).

The contrast between the child's world and the adult's is graphically displayed in the photographs on the front and back covers of the novel, which feature the author at different points in her life. On the front cover, a small child dressed in traditional Mexican garb is positioned in front of a Juárez background with her older sister Consuelo. In the 1991 photograph on the back cover, a solitary, grown-up Chicana has abandoned the reserved pose of her childhood and confidently smiles at the camera from a 1963 automobile. In contrast to the reserved, serious pose of the childhood photograph taken in the 1950s, the adult photograph is intended to break with convention. In a 1993 unpublished interview, the novelist admitted to selecting the car picture (taken by her husband, Ed Berry) because her sister urged her to use an "outrageous" picture for the book. As Gonzales-Berry explained, "what could be more ridiculous" than a nearly fifty-year-old college professor in a "low rider" Plymouth Valiant that had belonged to her great-aunt.

Much of the innovation of *Paletitas de guayaba* lies in its particular mode of recovering and transforming Chicano Movement narratives. While the novel incorporates many of the artistic sensibilities associated with the Chicano Renaissance of the 1960s–including the reaffirmation of Mexican roots—it is also a postmodern text. Gonzales-Berry captures the complexities of global cultures in the twentieth century through a fragmented style, the strategic de-centering of Chicano and Mexican identities and subjectivities, and her purposeful mixing of diaries, memories, short stories, tabloid-magazine articles, and ethnographic portraits.

The narrator's carefully placed interventions regarding the production of the text and character definition also suggest a definitive break with the realistic impulses of earlier Chicano identity narratives. *Paletitas de guayaba* incorporates the rebellious spirit of widely read Chicana novels and autobiographies. However, it diverges from this body of work—much of which is primarily written in English or is bilingual—in terms of language. Gonzales-Berry's bold-spirited Chicana novel is written in Spanish, rivaling the best of Chicano literature in Spanish because of its lively prose and its rich linguistic repertoire. Gonzales-Berry credits her interest and abilities in the Spanish language to her early exposure to the oral tradition; however, in this novel the Spanish language is marked by a contemporary sensibility and has strong writerly or essayistic overtones.

At times the language of the novel approaches verbal combat; at times it is playfully self-conscious, humorous, and ironic; and at times it is filled with the seriousness and rhetorical maneuvers of an academic or political discourse. As Gonzales-Berry admitted to Rebolledo in 1992: "My Spanish persona has a certain flair, it's a risk taker, it is a game player, it is wily." This quality permits the author to establish a critical distance from the different Chicana and Mexican identities she scrutinizes and to maintain the reader's attention throughout, even though Mari's voice prevails. Mari is the subject and narrator of her text from beginning to end.

*Paletitas de guayaba* is also replete with "forbidden" expressions that are rarely counted among Chicano and Mexican "linguistic" differences as a result of what Gloria Anzaldúa has called "the culture of silence." Gonzales-Berry breaks with this culture in a dramatic, original, and highly effective manner. She flaunts the forbidden languages of sexuality, politics, and gender relations and incorporates a feminist intent. For example, the female protagonist rebuffs unwanted sexual advances, including a male gaze: "And you, dirty old man, what are you looking at?" In order to underscore the prevalence of this type of behavior, Gonzales-Berry immediately turns her reader's attention to another scenario: "And on this side, another one. At least this one cleans his spittle with the napkin. Maybe his wife is blind. If I were her I'd slap him: Here you pig, you shameful fool, quit eyeballing that girl and eat your breakfast." As Rebolledo explains in *Women Singing in the Snow,* by seizing language in this manner, the female speaker reclaims her body, re-creates the particular sexual encounter as a disgusting spectacle, and symbolically punishes the behavior by imagining a few choice words from the offender's partner. This passage illustrates one of the ways in which Gonzales-Berry consciously reverses the rules of the game: the reader's participation is enlisted in the condemnation of heterosexist cultural practices.

Gonzales-Berry extends her critical analysis of situations involving gender relations or sexuality to instances of racial, class, and linguistic discrimination partially because of the way she defines feminism. In her interview with Hernández and Nymann she explained:

> *Feminism* is, for me, a state of consciousness which makes one aware of how structures of domination affect the lives not only of women but all colonized peoples. But that is not enough; it is also a state of consciousness that makes one openly oppose and combat practices, discourses, codes, language, etc. that treat/mark women and people of color as inferior, or less than. . . . That I am a Chicana means that my feminism will necessarily be affected by that fact. What is most important to me is to feel free to write whatever it is I want and need to write. All of that will come from my experience as a Chicana.

When Gonzales-Berry writes what she "wants and needs to write" in *Paletitas de guayaba,* she travels through aspects of female identity that are contested, fragmented, and not easily reconciled.

In the tradition of the best Chicana fictional autobiographies, Gonzales-Berry in *Paletitas de guayaba* is committed to a purposeful definition of a new type of Chicana identity that is not "fixed-once and for all." The terms of this Chicana identity change as the author variously positions her Chicana subject within the discourses of Mexican, New Mexican, and American history, culture, and society. The dynamic is played out as the protagonist narrates her travel experiences and recalls instances of national, racial, gender, and heterosexual oppression.

*Paletitas de guayaba* follows the designs of American Latina autobiographies, which have been outlined by Lourdes Torres. The narrative breaks down "the unitary aspects of . . . prescriptive paradigms" directed to the marginal in society. Typical of the complexity of the novel, the narrator refuses to attribute the reason for her journey, associated with rupture and loss, to any single event. She travels to escape the pressures of assimilating to American society; to deal with with her boyfriend's rejection; to recover a Mexican dimension or desire lacking in the New Mexican imagination; to

*Cover for Gonzales-Berry's 1991 novel, with a retouched photo of the author and her sister Consuelo*

dispute claims of New Mexican/Chicano whiteness; to encounter the Chicano Movement, albeit belatedly; and to satisfy her desire for "guayaba (guava) popsicles."

Above all, the trip is motivated by Mari's need to reclaim her cultural, ethnic, political, racial, and sexual identities. She can do so only by submitting to "an obsessive necessity to give voice to her frustrations, her doubts, her anger" and by reordering her world. Her process of reordering is facilitated by the writing of the travel narrative itself, which the protagonist confesses to elaborating years after her return. Finding her journal allows her to recover a part of her past that she thought was lost, and her notes open the door to memory, starting a flow of images and voices that had long been repressed.

The novel thus affords Mari the opportunity to "analyze the realities and complexities" of her life and, as Gonzales-Berry stated in an unpublished 1993 inter-

view, to "say any damn thing she wants." Mari mixes present with past, ingenuity with critical analysis, and alienation with self-consciousness. Like the female subjects of Chicana Latina autobiographies examined by Torres, Mari constructs a politics of personal and collective transformation that is built on the strength of difference and is also bent on disentangling the contradictions that form parts of her multiple identities.

Gonzales-Berry's response to Hernández and Nymann's question of how the discourse on sexuality and the body in *Paletitas de guayaba* contributes to Chicana liberation is instructive:

I see my own discourse on sexuality as necessary for breaking through so many layers of cultural (and I use this word very broadly here) repression. I think this tendency in the work of Chicana writers stems from the urgent need to decolonize our minds. But how can we decolonize our minds, if our bodies remain sites of colonization and domination? Unfortunately, male discourse on sexuality so often is constructed over the passive bodies of females. If Chicana discourse on sexuality is in opposition to male discourse, it is to show that we are more than passive females whose raison-de-être is to assume the missionary wife's position for males.

Gonzales-Berry's response is particularly important given the context of her discussion: widespread masculine constructions of Mexican national culture. According to Claudio Lomnitz-Adler, within these constructions sexual relations are often a metaphor of domination and women are seen as being intrinsically open, a position that is reserved for the dominated. Given this scenario, Gonzales-Berry's choice to launch Mari's trip to Mexico with a "Dear Steve" letter to her boyfriend, in which her sexual liberation and freedom from subservient roles are the central issues, is highly significant. Through the letter Mari explains to the reader how she was seduced by her boyfriend, who fabricated a fantasy, assuring her that he would liberate her of her cultural baggage and convincing her to enter into an erotic, yet childlike, state.

While Mari experienced pleasure, the sexual act has not liberated her of her baggage, because she intends to have a baby; her boyfriend's plan to remain commitment-free is disrupted by her plans to reproduce. Armed with intuition, she echoes in her letter his subconscious thoughts, imagining that he tells her that her juicy skin is not enough, that she does not have land, a name, or well-placed relatives. Mari exposes Steve's deceit and sexual privilege. His call for sexual liberation was just a line. As a professor, he has most likely seduced other students. Most important, she discovers his double standard—Steve has not shed his own cultural baggage. She links him to the "I told you so's" of his friends who stereotype brown women by suggesting that they devour men with their primitive instincts only to demand respect, a home, and a family afterward.

This powerful letter, which admonishes Steve not to respond, confirms that the practice of sex does not guarantee sexual liberation or an independent sexual identity. The lessons here are many: sexuality is bound up with society, social institutions such as marriage and religion, ideology, class privilege, and gender roles. Mari's desire to embark on an adventure that will erase Steve's presence in her life "once and for all" is also a longing for a different kind of location within society and another kind of control over her body and sexuality. By the end of the letter, she is already questioning the sexual mores—"the minds"—that led to her deception and Steve's possession of her body.

In the course of the novel Mari develops another discourse on sexuality, one that is not constructed over the passive bodies of females but over that of a male: Sergio, her Mexican lover. In their relationship Mari is critical of socially prescribed roles and gender relations and rejects the mandated connection between sex and marriage to which she succumbed with Steve. She takes control of her sexuality and directs sexual activity between them, telling him in Spanish: "There, No, No, further up. There. . . . Perfect. No, not so hard. . . . Now it's right, yes, yes, yes."

Mari teases her Mexican lover about his sexual appetite, delivers several theories on the superiority of the female orgasm, and poses the sarcastic question of who else would she belong to if not him, which underscores her desired independence from him. Mari overturns the social and sexual positions mandated for Mexican women in Chicano culture; she appropriates the male public language of sexuality and assumes the male privilege of naming the body. Mari critiques the heterosexist doublespeak that claims the value of a woman is not in her body but her mind while upholding the opposite in practice.

Mari must also redefine the national and ethnic identities that mark her body (as well as other social bodies) across a fractured national space—*el México de adentro* (inside), or Mexico proper, and *el México de afuera* (outside), or Aztlán/New Mexico. She must reckon not only with her gender difference but also with her Mexican difference: although she speaks Spanish and is brown, she is from "the other side." Significantly, Mari's reaction to her glaring geopolitical difference is to adopt an ultranationalist position: she wants to be Mexican again, to "renacer Mexicana; be A BORN AGAIN MEXICAN: a New *Mexican*." In Mexico, however, she is identified as a brown female assimilated half-breed: a *pochita*. This term is associated with *pocho,* a pejorative label used to refer to those Chicanos who have lost their cultural identity as Mexicans and to refer to "white" Mexican Americans. Invariably this label carries a negative judgment about the way Chicanos speak Spanish and denies Chicanos an intimate share of the Mexican national identity.

This scenario is played out in Mexico at El Centro, the foreign-language program in which Mari embarks on a course of study. Her dreams of connecting to Mexicans are dashed by the fact that her program is geared to Anglo students who barely speak Spanish. Mari also encounters Mexican prejudice. Although she understands and speaks Spanish perfectly well, she is placed in a beginning language class in order to remove her "*pocho* accent." The Mexican families who are affiliated with the program prefer not to house "*pocho* students." Mari underscores the effects of this exile by asking Sergio to imagine how it hurt her to know that Mexicans prefer Anglos to Mexicans, and this pain is doubled because she lives in a society where Anglos are privileged.

Mari finds housing with a group of young liberal students (the Cordovas and Julie). She then meets Sergio, who has ties to the Chicano Movement and is committed to politics as a matter of living. With Sergio, Mari begins an alternative education through which she gains consciousness of her ethnic and political identity and makes the all-important transition from the *pochita* (brown female other identity) to the Chicana. This passage is not without tension, however; just as Mari's sexual identity is not a given, her political identity is not automatic either. In fact, at the beginning she is antagonistic to the term *Chicana,* as she recalls when describing her encounter with Sergio:

> Do you remember Sergio, the day we met? I was waiting for Julie in front of the bookstore. It started to rain and you invited me to wait inside. Psssss, come in here, you're going to get wet, you told me, and I had barely entered when you asked if I was a Chicana. How did you know that? Don't tell me that by how I walked and dressed. . . . you had it stamped on your forehead you said. I answered you that I might be from the other side but that I wasn't a Chicana, that I didn't like that word, that where I came from Chicanos were a bunch of communists and rowdy opportunists. So you don't like communists? you asked me with a big spark in your eyes. Then you must be from New Mexico. From what I've heard, New Mexicans are very conservative and they don't affiliate themselves with the rest of the Chicano people. What do I know about politics I told you; for the moment I'm only concerned about surviving within this jungle.

Sergio assumes the role of the political mentor. He explains to Mari that she should know about politics, that their lives are politics, and that it is her "moral" responsibility to learn about the Chicano Movement. He gives her several articles and Rudolfo Acuña's *Occupied America: The Chicano's Struggle Toward Liberation* (1972) so that she can decide for herself whether or not she is a Chicana, and he offers the necessary stereotypes about New Mexicans and communists that will challenge her not only to pair Mexican and Chicano history but to establish a progressive New Mexican connection to both and to factor in a class analysis as well.

Hernández and Nymann suggest that Mari is locked into a student/teacher relationship with Sergio, an observation shared by some feminist critics who are troubled by Sergio's position as privileged interlocutor within a novel that claims to respond to a canon that silences the female voice. Gonzales-Berry has suggested

that this problematic scenario is linked to the predicament of women, such as herself, who did advanced study before the heyday of feminism: "How we struggled to maintain some sense of self and dignity, but had no mirrors to look at except male eyes and texts."

Yet, while the literary and political vision is mediated by Sergio and his political rhetoric is filled with paternalism, he is also the butt of Mari's humor. She makes him her sounding board on Chicano Mexican identities even when he is tired and is interested only in sex. In addition, he is a mysterious and enigmatic figure whose speech is deliberately curtailed in the text. As Gonzales-Berry suggested in 1993: "Sergio's voice occasionally peeps through. . . . Occasionally, but I didn't want to give him too much space. I didn't want to give his voice too much to do." Although Sergio is one of the few men in the novel who does not call Chicanas *pochitas* or resort to vulgar, sexist street talk, the reader's knowledge of him is limited because he must remain silent about his involvement with an underground guerrilla movement that fights for "bread and justice" and has met with political repression.

While Sergio's political activity demands silence, Mari wants to be an open book for him; she has a profound need to tell him everything, to speak her doubts, her frustrations, and her anger. The contrast reflects important differences in the narratives of liberation that target Chicano Mexican communities. Sergio's political narrative attends to racial and class differences without critiquing gender dynamics within a patriarchal, capitalist system or incorporating female political identities. Mari translates, engages, critiques, edits, and often disrupts Sergio's masculine narrative of liberation (and the narratives of Chicanos) through her imaginary conversations with male characters. She challenges Sergio and the Chicanos at Casa Aztlán in Mexico City to complement their Marxist and nationalist analyses with a social critique that features the woman question and recognizes the politics of heterosexuality. She challenges them to extend their focus by incorporating a fuller range of human experience.

Mari also supplies the female reader with a narrative that reflects on the nature of ethnic and class marginalization. Armed with the insights of the newfound political identity that she gains as a result of her association with Casa Aztlán and a meeting with Dolores Huerta, a leading advocate for farm workers, Mari talks back to Mexican nationals, questioning faulty, prejudiced views of Chicanos. She elaborates her position to Sergio: "I don't know why they can't give us credit for something. For over a century we've lived under the North American flag where English is the dominant language and every attempt has been made to eradicate Spanish."

*Gonzales-Berry in her 1963 Plymouth Valiant (photograph by Ed Berry; from the back cover for* Paletitas de guayaba)

Whereas in Mexico, Chicano Spanish is associated with *pochismo* (betrayal and voluntary cultural loss), Mari associates Chicano Spanish with resistance, national pride, and cultural retention. She targets the stereotypes that fault individuals for language loss, connecting the linguistic situation of Chicanos to their social position: "What they don't understand here is that Spanish is stigmatized in the U.S. because the people who speak it are stigmatized, second class citizens. They put down our culture and language; they treat us like animals." The cruelty of this situation is captured by her recollection of an infamous sign reading:

NO DOGS
NEGROS
MEXICANS

Because it is her objective to provide an analysis of the situation, she deliberately emphasizes the "class base" of this type of racial discrimination with her devastating observation that Chicanos are not put into the ovens because their cheap labor is needed.

Mari also "talks back" to New Mexicans on the other side of the border when she critiques their faulty perceptions of Mexicans as violent, distrustful job takers. In the process she strays from the representations of New Mexicans as impenetrable, or *gachupín* (Spaniard-centered), or conservative. Mari disputes a presumedly singular Spanish New Mexican heritage by offering linguistic and historical refutations of this mode of creating an ethnic connection. She vigorously promotes a Mexican identification and provides a social analysis for the preponderance of Spanish genealogies in the New Mexican imagination. She proposes that this Spanish grounding of local identities is a way of gaining acceptance into Anglo society and suggests that the gesture is destined to fail with these rhetorical questions:

When will we understand that they will never accept us as equals? And it is not only a question of brown skin... If they educated our children. . . . Who would be the beasts of burden? Who would harvest the crops, work in the mines . . . wash the dirty dishes. . . . Who?

With this line of questioning the narrator proposes a kind of consciousness-raising that is transnational and offers a more integrated analysis of the social conditions of Mexicans on both sides of the regional and national borders.

Mari presents a Chicano identity that is neither Anglo nor Mexican. However, her work is not complete until she incorporates women into another narrative of Chicano liberation. Mari implements the cross-cultural feminist analysis of Chicano subjects by negotiating crucial political transitions between race, class, and gender that are not available in any singular discourse of liberation. Mari also provides an all-important female genealogy, and her mother serves as an important role model for this type of feminist project.

Mari remembers her mother as a self-made woman who rose up from poverty, became a rural schoolteacher, worked alongside her husband to support the family, and eventually became the sole bread-winner of the family. Mari describes her mother in much the same way that Gonzales-Berry did in her interview with Hernández and Nymann—as "a deeply complex, wise and admirable woman, trapped in sexist constructs." In spite of this entanglement, Mari's mother emerges as the bedrock of the family, as the Chicana woman whose image imposes itself on the landscape of her life. Mari chronicles her mother's incredible inner strength and legacy—her ability to function in a hostile environment. Her mother has also provided important feminist lessons by nurturing a creative outlet: teaching herself to play the piano. Through her lone song, all of "her life can pass in front of her in slow motion," and she can claim something in the world that belongs to her. Mari's writing also provides her with a pathway to self-affirmation and ownership.

While Mari inherits her thirst for knowledge and creative spirit from her mother, it is from Malintzin Tenepal/Doña Marina (Hernán Cortés's translator and lover) that Mari discovers the power of the word and her kinship with Mexican women. In the fashion of Chicana nationalism, Mari's encounter with her symbolic Mexican birth mother, who bears her name, appears as a dream sequence that forecasts the fall of Tenochtitlán (the original Mexico City as the Aztecs knew it). Malintzin enthusiastically welcomes Mari to the race and marvels at her presence.

Malintzin accepts the value of *mestizaje* (miscegenation) and defines herself as Mari's foremother in feminist writing. She urges Mari to chronicle her (Malintzin's) story, to clarify her social motivations for collaborating with Cortés, and to set the record straight about her lack of desire for this beastly man. Most important, she urges Mari to connect words with voices and to connect with the words of other women; to write about the abuses women have endured through time; and to assist them in plotting voices and turning them "against the world of the great masters."

In the same way that Mari seeks to liberate identities from the structures of domination, her foremother, Malintzin, uses language to imagine a more equitable society in which men and women could all be in charge of nurturing their children so that they could learn to act with "grace, honor and creativity." Malintzin breaks with the Lencho's definitive assertion that Mexicans do not care about the other side of Mexico. Malintzin confirms who Mari is—she is a subject of "her-story," not an object of "his-story." Rather than being a *malinchista* (sellout), she is the product of her own creations.

The novel ends with a good-bye letter in which Sergio tells Mari that he must leave the country for political reasons. He admits to being sustained by the dream of a new world and her beautiful image, leaves open the possibility of encountering her once again, and hints that he will tell her the details of his political activity. With this ending, Gonzales-Berry suggests that the dialogues between the narratives of Chicano Mexican liberation are ongoing, that they require more negotiations if coalitions are to be made. Mari's attempt to connect Mexican Marxism and Chicana feminism also confirms the fact that there is much ground to be covered on both sides if class and gender are to be united in a broader critical analysis.

Sergio's departure can also be read as a feminist statement. Now that Mari has assumed control of discourse and her body, he is no longer needed; he has served his intended purposes by acting as a sounding board and "opening up the door to other issues," as Gonzales-Berry told Hernández and Nymann. In the end it can be stated that Mari's mother and Malintzin provide the element of subversion necessary for survival in hostile environments. As Gonzales-Berry indicates, they are both "more of a teacher to Mari than Sergio or *el gavacho*" (the white guy—Steve). They illustrate to Mari how women write, teach, and dream. This function is precisely what makes *Paletitas de guayaba* such an important novel: Mari struggles to assimilate this lesson and instructs her readers along the way.

*Paletitas de guayaba* delivers the powerful lesson of how multiple identities and subject positions can be constructed from opposite sides of various international, inter-ethnic, and sexual borders. By combining this lesson with humor and presenting it in wonderfully executed language, the novel instructs at the same time that it entertains, sealing its connection to the best of the Chicano oral tradition.

**Interview:**

Manuel de Jesús Hernández-G. and Michael Nymann, Interview with Gonzales-Berry, *Mester,* special double issue: *Chicana/o Discourse* 22, no. 2 / 23, no. 1 (Fall 1993–Spring 1994): pp. 135–149.

**References:**

Norma Alarcón, "Chicana Feminism: In the Tracks of the 'Native' Woman," *Cultural Studies* (October 1990): 248–255;

Gloria Anzaldúa, *Borderlands / La frontera: The New Mestiza* (San Francisco: Spinsters/Aunt Lute, 1987);

Arthur Brackel, "Paletitas de guayaba: Mujer Chicana y la ardiente otredad," *Bilingual Review/La Revista bilingüe,* 20 (May–August 1995): 128–134;

Angie Chabram-Dernersesian, "And Yes . . . The Earth Did Part: On the Splitting of Chicana/o Subjectivity," in *Building with Our Hands: New Directions in Chicana Studies,* edited by Adela de la Torre and Beatriz M. Pesquera (Berkeley: University of California Press, 1993), pp. 34–56;

Chabram-Dernersesian, "Chicana? Rican! No Chicana-Riqueña: Refashioning the Transnational Connection," in *Multiculturalism: A Critical Reader,* edited by David Theo Goldberg (Oxford: Blackwell, 1994), pp. 269–295;

Claudio Lomnitz-Adler, *Exits from the Labyrinth: Culture and Ideology in the Mexican National Space* (Berkeley: University of California Press, 1992);

Octavio Paz, "The Pachuco and Other Extremes," in his *The Labyrinth of Solitude: Life and Thought in Mexico,* translated by Lysander Kemp (New York: Grove, 1961), pp. 9–28;

Tey Diana Rebolledo, "Erlinda Gonzales-Berry," in *Nuestras mujeres: Hispanas of New Mexico, Their Images and Lives, 1582–1992,* edited by Rebolledo, Millie Santillanes, and Gonzales-Berry (Albuquerque, N.Mex.: El Norte Publications/Academia, 1992), pp. 86–87;

Rebolledo, "The Problematics of Writing in Spanish," in her *Women Singing in the Snow: A Cultural Analysis of Chicana Literature* (Tucson: University of Arizona Press, 1995), pp. 171–181;

Manuel M. Martín Rodríguez, "En la lengua materne: Las escritoras Chicanas y la novela en español," *Latin American Literary Review,* 23, no. 4 (1995): 64–84;

Lourdes Torres, "The Construction of the Self in U.S. Latina Autobiographies," in *Third World Women and the Politics of Feminism,* edited by Torres, Chandra Talpade Mohanty, and Ann Russo (Bloomington: Indiana University Press, 1991), pp. 271–287.

# Armando P. Ibáñez

*(26 June 1949 –    )*

Jesús Rosales
*Texas A&M University–Corpus Christi*

BOOKS: *Midday Shadows* (New York: Vantage, 1980);
*Mesquites Never Die–A Theology of Poetry* (Oakland, Cal.:
Pluma Productions, 1993);
*Wrestling with the Angel: A Collection of Poetry* (Los Angeles:
Pluma Productions, 1997).

VIDEOS: *Mesquites Never Die* (Pluma Productions,
1995);
*Sea* (Pluma Productions, 1995);
*My Angel* (Pluma Productions, 1995);
*Creating Sacred Space–Reaching Out to the Artist* (Pluma Pro-
ductions, 1995);
*A Moment of Silence* (American Film Institute, 1998).

SELECTED PERIODICAL PUBLICATIONS–
UNCOLLECTED: "Queen Bee," *Canto al Pueblo: An
Anthology of Experiences* (1978): 87–88;
"The Afternoon of the Jackass," *Aciendo Arte*, 2, no. 1
(Winter 1987): 42–43;
"In Search of Nakedness," *Double Dealer Redux*, 2, no. 4
(1995): 11;
"Never on a Sunday or Ever, Ever," *Double Dealer Redux*,
3, no. 1 (1996): 50–51.

*Armando P. Ibáñez (courtesy of Ibáñez)*

Armando P. Ibáñez is a poet who writes passionately about man and his physical and spiritual existence. Though Ibáñez's poetry tends to explore
existential universal themes, his constant use of the
Spanish language and of Mexican American images distinctly associated with the Southwest identifies his
poetry as regional and deeply connected to his Chicano
roots. By combining universal themes with regional
characteristics, Ibáñez intends to prove that, as a Chicano poet, he is capable of writing about universal
human concerns without sacrificing his cultural individuality.

Armando Perez Ibáñez was born on 26 June 1949
in San Diego, Texas, to Gerónimo and Vicenta Ibáñez,
both of whom have deep cultural ties to South Texas.
On his father's side, his great-grandfather came to the
United States from Mexico during the 1860s to fight
alongside the Union army in the Civil War. His
mother's family came from Ciudad Mier, Tamaulipas,
early in the nineteenth century, years before Mexico
became a republic. When Ibáñez was ten, he and his
family moved to Alice, a small city south of Corpus
Christi.

In 1969 Ibáñez entered Texas A&I University
(later renamed Texas A&M University–Kingsville), where
he studied journalism. After a brief stay at this institu-

tion, he attended the University of Houston but returned to Alice in 1971 to help support this mother, whose financial situation had worsened after the death of his father in 1968. In Alice he worked for the Welfare Department for five years before continuing graduate school and dedicating himself to writing.

In 1977 Ibáñez decided to attend the University of Texas undergraduate program in journalism. His stay at the university was brief, for he was soon given the opportunity to work for a Public Broadcasting System (PBS) children's bilingual program called *Sonrisas* (Smiles). After spending time writing children's dramas (one of which was nominated for a Peabody Award), Ibáñez returned to Alice and took a job with the *Alice Echo-News* as a staff writer. From there, he worked for seven years at the *Corpus Christi Caller Times,* covering South Texas life. During his tenure at the *Caller Times,* Ibáñez won several writing awards, including the sweepstakes award for the top story of the year in the Harte-Hanks newspaper chain.

At this period of his life Ibáñez felt the "call" to the religious life. "God has a way to make his presence known," Ibáñez said in an unpublished December 1993 interview, adding, "God's call is different for every vocation but He is where truth is in our lives." Eventually Ibáñez earned two master's degrees, in theology and divinity, at the Dominican School of Philosophy and Theology, Graduate Theological Union, at Berkeley, California, in 1993. That same year he was ordained a priest in the Order of Preachers (Dominican Order) of the Southern Dominican Province in San Diego, Texas. Currently Ibáñez resides in Los Angeles, California, where he is a filmmaker. He earned an M.F.A., specializing in producing, from the American Film Institute in 1998. There he was awarded the Colin Higgins Screenplay Production Award for his screenplay *A Moment of Silence* (1998). He also serves as the chaplain for a group of Dominican cloistered nuns at the Monastery of the Angels.

The first published works of Ibáñez appeared in *El carnal* (The Brother), a student journal at Texas A&I University, and in other regional periodicals of South Texas. His poetry has been published throughout the United States in journals such as *Aciendo Arte* (Making Art) in Corpus Christi, *Canto al pueblo* (Song to the People) in San Antonio, *Ruah* in Berkeley, and *Preachers' Exchange* in New Orleans. In 1995 three of his poems, "Mesquites Never Die," "Sea," and "My Angel," have been made into poetry videos, which he produced, directed, and edited. According to him, the poetry video communicates poetry to a society that is increasingly visually oriented. At the same time he believes that the conglomeration of music, sound, and image in a video captures effectively the art of the poet narrating stories around a campfire.

Ibáñez's first book of poetry, *Midday Shadows,* was published in 1980. He considers this collection a summary of existential concerns that date back to his childhood. In defining his work Ibáñez believes that poems, like any other form of art, exist to comfort and inspire, depending on each individual's personal interpretation. *Midday Shadows* is divided into four parts—"Opening Our Eyes, We Eventually See The Light," "We Walk Unknown Paths and Never See The Trees," "We Landed On The Moon but Failed To Capture Its Light," and "Closing Our Eyelids, We Are Surrounded By Darkness and Sleep"—each comprising twenty-one poems that emphasize the image of light as one overflowing with sentimental (lyrical) and spiritual (mystical) symbolism. All four parts explore humankind's relationship with nature, particularly with the concept of light as a source of life and existential meaning. The poems as a whole seem to suggest that man is illuminated by the physical nature of light but fails to understand its symbolic meaning.

Ibáñez has emphasized that the one concern he wanted to present in this book was "humanity's inhumanity to nature." He feels that even though God has provided humans with a wonderful place to live (witnessed daily by the magic of nature—the warmth of the sun, a fragile drop of water, or the cycle of life), humankind is frequently responsible for disturbing its beauty. In his poetry Ibáñez personifies nature, providing it with feelings of anger over those elements (including people) that intend to disrupt its harmony. For the most part, the imposing physical presence of nature is depicted as a dynamic and powerful force. One senses nature's superiority over humanity as it is represented through images that demonstrate its overwhelming power. "Rayos of the Sun," for instance, provides examples of the raw power of nature and its demand on society to acknowledge it. Humans seem to have been capriciously insensitive to the strength of nature, leaving nature with no alternative but to warn them of the possible consequences that may result from this negligence:

> The sun's rays
> accompanied by the wind
> brush every blade of grass
> that stands or bows.
> people with multi-faces
>     laugh and go throughout the world
> making codes and proclamations
>     thanking God for life.
> the clouds in the sky
> release their anguish
>     on every plant and person.

*Cover for Ibáñez's 1997 book, in which he explores man's relationship with God*

a furious wind roars
through the trees
shouting in the ears of every person:
    "Look at me! And Beware!"

Existential questions are also part of Ibáñez's thematic priorities. Ibáñez writes about man's purpose in life and the anguish that results from the possibility of not finding answers that justify his existence. Life presents a constant struggle between the mind and the soul. His faith and the presence of a supreme God provide him with the courage to overcome this anguish. Yet, to Ibáñez, humankind will always be searching for existential purpose and meaning, both in this world and the one that exists after death. In "Just Wondering" Ibáñez's use of the Spanish language suggests an intent to search the most intimate corners of his being for meaning, hoping that in this cultural dichotomy he may find possible solutions:

I often wonder
what it's all about.
Our reason for being here
has been asked
a million times over
the years of our existence
*Para qué es todo?*
[What is everything all about?]
The human mind
and soul two different
things yet running in unison
debate over it!
*Padre de mis padres*
*te ruego*
*que me oigas.*
 [Father of my parents
 I beg
 That you hear me.]
If there is no heaven
then at least let there be peace of mind.

"Nacer" (To Be Born) explores the mystery of birth, which is identified as a fleeting experience that will intrigue humankind throughout life. People seem incapable of grasping the true essence of life, for it presents itself as a ubiquitous shadow, luring one to believe that life, in reality, is not made up of a series of tangible events and experiences but a series of constant dreams, "dreams to be born again" over and over. As a result, death is also presented as surreal. It "creeps" and "dances" over people, moving stealthily over them, torturing mercilessly, forcing them ultimately to utter: "We are the walking dead."

Several poems deal with the process of maturation, stressing the fast-paced lifestyle of an individual coming of age. Life is to be enjoyed at any cost, without regard to any negative consequences that might result from the experiences lived. Images of racing cars speeding through country roads ("Highway 44"), excessive intoxication ("On a Binge"), and erotic fantasies ("Enticement") are examples of the situations and growing insecurities that face a young man. For many, some of these experiences represent a brief but difficult phase of a normal life. Ibáñez, however, introduces them to complement the existential questions that are expressed throughout the book.

An important characteristic of *Midday Shadows* is Ibáñez's use of various cultural images to provide essential Mexican-American elements in his universal themes. Two of these are *la lechuza* (the barn owl) and *la llorona* (the wailing woman), both appearing at night, causing fear among those who believe in their powers. *La lechuza* is said to be an evil witch armed with curses and tragic spells, while *la llorona* prowls through the night searching for her dead children. Ibáñez understands the distinctiveness of the cultural interpretation of this "barn owl" and this "wailing woman" among Mexican Americans, and does not translate their meaning. *La lechuza* and *la llorona* are not only ominous popular icons for Mexican Americans but also represent a set of values (good versus evil) for many Mexican Americans.

There are other cultural images—such as *mestizos* (people of half-Indian, half-European descent), *quelites* (pigweeds), *las piscas* (the harvests), and *las labores* (the working fields)—that identify a particular Mexican American cultural experience (many having to do with working in the cotton fields). None is more present in this collection than the mesquite tree. Long associated with the terrain of the Southwest, the mesquite is portrayed as possessing human qualities. For the Mexican American the mesquite is a positive entity that is strongly identified with Chicano culture. The poem "Mestizo" offers an example of the symbolic connection that exists between the Chicano and the tree. The mesquite acknowledges the mestizo as essential to the cycle of life and acts responsibly to perpetuate the world by offering the mestizo to the gods:

> The mesquites
> in offering
> lifted the mestizos
>
> Taking 'em to the altar of the sun
> they prayed for the brown faces
> sons of the sun
>
> The moon smiled,
> embracing and cuddling 'em
> she gave them a kiss.

The images in this poem suggest the powerful pre-Columbian rituals in which human beings were sacrificed for the purpose of prolonging life. The "altar of the sun" and the reference to the smiling moon could well refer to the Pyramid of the Sun and the Pyramid of the Moon in the ancient city of Teotihuacán in Mexico. The mesquites represent the priests that nourish their hungry gods in an effort to maintain the life of the universe. The mesquites, by emulating the rituals of these ceremonial priests, preserve life and, as a result, the existence of a culture represented by the brown skin of the mestizo.

In addition to its strong connection with Mexican American culture, the mesquite is consistently present in Ibáñez's poems when man experiences individual mental vulnerabilities, as when he feels a lack of moral power and questions his purpose in life ("Sitting Alone") or walks aimlessly through the world meditating over death ("The Walking Man"). Man and tree seem inseparable, both feeding from the shadow of the other. In "Just a Tree" Ibáñez expresses man's desperate

*Advertisement for one of Ibáñez's video productions (courtesy of Ibáñez)*

desire for salvation by trying to find a sense of place in this world. This effort is fruitless, for he soon discovers that the tree is destined to experience a similar fate:

> I wish
> that i could be
> a tree
> a mesquite
> that lives
> like it does.
> But,
> how can i
> say such a thing
> if it too
> searches the heavens
> with its outstretched limbs
> and has nothing
> but its arms.

The poem suggests that the physical body of man offers limitations that are impossible to break. The heavens symbolize the untouched, the overwhelming mystery that remains unsolved, forcing people to accept things that they are incapable of understanding.

Perhaps the most visible cultural aspect of Ibáñez's work is in the language he uses in his poetry. Some poems are written in English, others in Spanish, and many in a combination of both, a style that Ibáñez refers to as "Tex-Mex." Ibáñez believes that the Mexican American who combines the two languages presents his true reality, for he speaks and functions culturally in Spanish and in English.

The use of "Tex-Mex" in Ibáñez's poetry is not necessarily innovative. Many Chicanos, primarily in the 1960s, used such linguistic representations to express their Chicano experience. The poems in which Ibáñez mixes the two languages are written to highlight cultural sensibilities that need to be expressed in Spanish because the cultural message would lose impact in the translation. Many of the untranslated words in Spanish represent Mexican American cultural icons such as *la lechuza* and *la llorona*. Others describe the sort of work traditionally associated with Mexican Americans, such as *el sembrador* (one who seeds the land) and *el piscador* (one who harvests the land). Complete sentences and phrases in Spanish are used to express emotions, usually those relating the long suffering of his people, as in "Las lágrimas de almas lloronas" (the tears of crying souls), "los gritos de aires en batalla" (sounds of battling winds fill the air), "este llorido ensucia las sábanas" (these crying sounds soil the bedspreads). In choosing this kind of bilingual expression, Ibáñez demonstrates a desire to direct his poetry to a selected readership: one that is bilingual and bicultural and can relate intimately to these experiences.

A substantial number of Ibáñez's poems are written entirely in Spanish. This practice creates limitations for many readers, including Chicanos, for many of them are not bilingual. By using Spanish in his poetry,

Ibáñez sends symbolic messages to non-Mexican Americans and to Chicanos. To the non-Mexican American, Ibáñez is demanding to be accepted as he is, demonstrating his unwillingness to lose part of his identity by expressing himself solely in the language of the dominant culture. To the Chicano, Ibáñez tries to emphasize that language is identity and that Spanish is essential to the survival of Chicano culture.

Ibáñez's second collection of poetry, *Wrestling with the Angel* (1997), explores spirituality and man's relationship with God. As with *Midday Shadows,* Ibáñez divides the book into four sections: "The Search," "The First Encounter," "The Struggle–Life, Death," and "The Blessing." In an unpublished interview Ibáñez pointed out that this collection of poems speaks of the joys and sorrows that people encounter in their daily lives:

> We can be moved to tears by a mesmerizing sunset or by the sweet scent of a rose. At those moments, we have no problem believing in a Supreme Being, in God. But then we face times when our heart seems to be torn out by the roots, especially when someone we love dies of AIDS or when we see senseless violence and hate around us. Where is God? Here comes the struggle, the wrestling with the Angel.

Armando Ibáñez is a talented and promising writer whose poetry speaks with an open heart of the existential meaning of life. In his inspiring work he seeks to understand man's relationship with his physical world and his inner self. As he has often stated, his poetry is not filled with "clichés or religious saccharine"; quite the contrary, he believes it is honest and open to a myriad of interpretations. Greatly concerned with a spiritual destiny, Ibáñez presents himself as a poet who, through the magic of the written word, transmits hope to many readers.

# Graciela Limón

*(2 August 1938 – )*

Ellen McCracken
*University of California, Santa Barbara*

BOOKS: *María de Belén: The Autobiography of an Indian Woman* (New York: Vantage, 1990);

*In Search of Bernabé* (Houston: Arte Público, 1993); translated into Spanish by Miguel Angel Aparicio as *En busca de Bernabé* (Houston: Arte Público, 1997);

*The Memories of Ana Calderón* (Houston: Arte Público, 1994);

*Song of the Hummingbird* (Houston: Arte Público, 1996);

*The Day of the Moon* (Houston: Arte Público, 1999).

With the publication of five novels in the 1990s Graciela Limón established herself as one of the key voices in the new Chicana fiction of the post–Chicano Movement period. Her novels cross the literal and figurative borders of the Americas and bring the issues of feminism, social justice, popular religiosity, and cultural identity to the forefront of Chicano letters. They also address larger public concerns about the dynamics of multiculturalism. Her well-crafted, readable experiments with narrative express the postmodernist preoccupation with the erosion of the borders between high and popular culture.

The second of three children and the only girl, Graciela Limón was born in Los Angeles on 2 August 1938, to Mexican immigrants–her father was from Sonora and her mother from Jalisco–who had met in Los Angeles in the 1930s. Her father, Jesús Limón, was a truck driver for the *Los Angeles Herald Express,* and her mother, Altagracia Gómez Limón, worked in a laundry facility. Limón attended Hammel Street School, St. Alphonsus School, and Bishop Conaty High School for Girls. An avid reader since the early years of elementary school, she was particularly attracted in her childhood to history books and narratives about heroic women such as Joan of Arc. She loved school, especially high school, but despite the encouragement of a sister of the Immaculate Heart Order who told Limón she was college material, she was tracked in vocational courses in high school and after graduation was placed, with the school's help, as a stenographer at a stock bro-

*Graciela Limón (Arte Público Press, 1994)*

kerage. In her immigrant family it was inconceivable that a daughter would think about higher education.

Limón saved her money and put herself through college and graduate school, graduating from Marymount College, Palos Verdes, with a B.A. in Spanish literature in 1965. She received an M.A. in the same field from the Universidad de las Americas in Mexico City in 1969 and began teaching at Loyola Marymount University in Los Angeles. In 1975 she received a Ph.D. in Latin American literature from the University of California at Los Angeles with a dissertation on the work of the Mexican writer Juan Rulfo, whom she interviewed in Mexico in 1973. The beauty of Rulfo's prose, marked by his quiet tone and exquisite use of Spanish, was refreshing to Limón in contrast to the verbose and elaborate prose of other Spanish-language writers she had studied; Rulfo came to serve as one of the key models for her creative writing.

Although her grandparents on both sides died before her birth, Limón had a large extended family of uncles, aunts, and cousins. The massive repatriations to Mexico of the 1930s split the family up, with many of Limón's relatives on her mother's side relocating to Guadalajara. She remembers her mother taking her to visit the family there many times throughout her childhood. This connection to Guadalajara is particularly important to her novel *The Day of the Moon* (1999), in which she traces an incident in her own family history: one of her forebears of the 1880s had his wife committed to the insane asylum in Zapopan, near Guadalajara, to punish her for her marital infidelity. Limón visited Zapopan in 1994 to reconstruct this family history. An archivist there showed her photographs of the asylum as it appeared in the late nineteenth century, which inspired the key visual images of the institution that she develops in the novel.

In the late 1980s Limón began to direct her efforts to creative writing, publishing the novel *María de Belén: The Autobiography of an Indian Woman* in 1990. A year of intense research and study of the conquest of Mexico and its colonial period prepared Limón to undertake the writing of the work. Teaching the *crónicas* at Loyola Marymount, Limón was inspired to create an alternative to the master historical narrative that the winners of the wars of conquest had elaborated centuries earlier. In postmodernist fashion Limón merges the ostensibly separate genres of fiction, history, autobiography, *testimonio, crónica,* transcription, and translation. The prologue is narrated by professor Natalia Roldán, the translator of a newly discovered sixteenth-century autobiography dictated by an indigenous woman who witnessed the conquest of Mexico. There are clear correspondences between the information Roldán provides about herself and Limón's biography, and the dates and locations Roldán gives for the writing of her translation, "Los Angeles–11 April 1988" and "Bellalba on Lake Arrowhead / 26 August 1988," match the actual circumstances of the composition of the novel.

The multiple frames around the indigenous woman's narrative self-consciously question the validity of historiography. The fictitious translation reminds readers to question other material outside the main narrative, such as the scholarly endnotes that annotate the main text and other historical narratives that claim to present a truthful account of the events of the conquest. María de Belén's account is intended by the author to call into question the accepted master narratives of the conquest without itself becoming another master narrative.

From 1986 to 1991 Limón participated in demonstrations at the church at La Placita in downtown Los Angeles and the nearby federal building against the involvement of the United States in the civil war in El Salvador. At 6:00 A.M. on Wednesdays, protesters marched with a large cross and sometimes lay down on the sidewalk to make chalk outlines representing the Salvadoran war dead. Limón also worked with Salvadoran refugees who received asylum at La Placita after its pastor, Father Luis Olivares, declared it a sanctuary. Her conversations with refugees inspired Limón's next novel, *In Search of Bernabé,* in which she suggests that the civil war in El Salvador and U.S. involvement in it are of central concern to Chicanos, other minorities, and those in the U.S. mainstream interested in the evolving multiculturalist discourse. After the manuscript for the novel won the University of California, Irvine Chicano Literature Contest in 1991, a UC Irvine professor, María Herrera-Sobek, advised Limón to submit it to the Arte Público Press of Houston. It was published in 1993 and received the Before Columbus Foundation American Book Award in 1994, was named a critic's choice by *The New York Times Book Review,* and was a finalist for the *Los Angeles Times* Ard Seidenbaum Award for First Fiction.

The novel depicts the long civil war as an international conflict in which traditional categories of "good" or "bad" people must be reevaluated; several characters make questionable ethical decisions—not only a military colonel and a rich landowner but an American priest, a Salvadoran seminarian, a dispossessed woman working as a maid, and a leftist guerrilla. Neither the Left nor the Right can be classified as entirely good or entirely evil. A female *coyota* figure, Petra, for example, who transports undocumented refugees and workers into the United States for large sums of money, puts herself at risk trying to get the refugees safely to a Catholic sanctuary center. Limón notes that her conversations with Salvadoran refugees at La Placita caused her to reevaluate her own preconceived notions of the *coyote,* who is generally disliked in Chicano culture.

Liberation theology is central to *In Search of Bernabé* in raising characters' consciousness about issues of social justice in El Salvador as well as determining Limón's narrative strategies. Limón rereads the Bible and religious motifs in terms of the political upheaval in Central America but also brings ethical and moral values to bear on the social turmoil. She demonstrates that politics and religion are inextricably connected and that received moral values need constantly to be reevaluated.

*Cover for Limón's 1993 novel, set in the 1980s and early 1990s, during the civil war in El Salvador*

Bracketed with American news accounts of the 1980 bombing of the funeral procession of assassinated Archbishop Oscar Romero outside the cathedral in San Salvador and the signing of the peace treaty in 1992, *In Search of Bernabé* also pivots centrally on the assassinations in November 1989 of six Jesuit priests, a female employee, and her daughter at the Universidad Centroamericana. In 1990 Limón had gone to El Salvador as part of an international gathering to commemorate the anniversary of the tragic killings. She and the other Loyola Marymount representatives had been invited to travel to a village in Chalatenango to participate in the ceremonies for the renaming of a town in honor of Ignacio Ellacuría, one of the slain Jesuits. Despite having permission papers, the group had frequently been stopped by the Salvadoran military on the journey, and as they tried to sleep on mats in the patio of the rural church after their late-night arrival, they had heard machine guns firing throughout the night. On her return to Los Angeles, Limón had added the first chapter, which recounts Luz Delcano's childhood rape by her grandfather, to *In Search of Bernabé*. Rape, Limón suggests, is an appropriate metaphor for the country's years of civil strife.

Inspired by Zora Neale Hurston's *Their Eyes Were Watching God* (1937), Limón wrote *The Memories of Ana Calderón* in eight weeks in the summer of 1993. In this novel she develops a counternarrative to the conventions of melodrama and soap opera, the Bible, popular cultural beliefs, and the accepted portrayals of the past. The novel follows the rags-to-riches progress of Ana Calderón from her beginnings in a palm-leaf hut in southern Mexico as she rises through adversity to build a multinational corporation from the clothing factory where she started out as a worker. Ana repeatedly saves herself by her own wits, rather than relying on the male hero of traditional melodrama to come to her rescue. After her last, particularly traumatic setback, for example, instead of engaging in the prescribed penitential rites traditionally expected of women in Mexican culture, Ana recuperates an alternate interpretation of the Genesis story of Hagar that she herself had developed twenty years earlier. Through rereading Hagar's story she realizes her own self-worth.

*The Memories of Ana Calderón* uses complementary third- and first-person voices to give the protagonist a more substantive role in the narration. The first-person sections do not merely repeat or amplify events already narrated in the third person; the plot advances in both sections. Ana's double-voiced narrative memoir not only revises the historical narrative of the period from the 1930s to the 1960s but functions as a contestation of her father's curse of Ana and her unborn son ("He swore that only wretchedness and tragedy would fill their empty lives") and the brutal patriarchal authority that undergirds it.

After the publication of *The Memories of Ana Calderón* Limón began to revise *María de Belén* for Arte Público. Deciding after several attempts that the novel was, as she put it in an unpublished 20 March 1998 interview, "like lace—when one part is cut, it all falls apart," she chose instead to rewrite the work completely. The result was her fourth novel, *Song of the Hummingbird* (1996). Like *María de Belén*, *Song of the Hummingbird* draws readers into colonial Latin American history. In the revised novel Limón adapts the multiple voices of the earlier text into a confessional *testimonio* primarily rendered as dialogue, a conversation between eighty-two-year-old Huitzitzilín and a young Franciscan friar, Benito Lara, who has come at her request to hear her last confession. Huitzitzilín tells her story as a *testimonio* rather than following the prescribed rituals of the Catholic sacrament of confession, and thus asserts her superiority over her confessor. The two characters engage in a rhetorical battle between the rubrics of the confession and the alternative mode of dialogue represented by the *testimonio*. This struggle serves as a metaphor for the larger question of who will be allowed to tell the story of the conquest and through what mode.

Huitzitzilín's story gradually begins to transform Father Benito's consciousness. While the religion she practices does not triumph over the Christian beliefs of the conquerors, she enables him to see that the conquerors' rituals were only "mutterings" to the native peoples and that in the name of proper Christian education thousands of young children were taken from their mothers and sent to Spain. The young priest comes to understand Huitzitzilín's transgressions in the context of the everyday violence of the conquest over decades; he ultimately substitutes mercy and forgiveness for his first impulse to judge her for her sins. In effect, Huitzit-

zilín transforms the conqueror's sacrament of confession into a means of obtaining another human being's forgiveness for the wrongs she has done, rather than the forgiveness of the official Catholic deity as the sacrament prescribes. Her story transforms her interlocutor as it draws him in, and he records her unconventional chronicle in the hope that it will similarly transform future generations of readers.

A Spanish translation of *In Search of Bernabé* appeared in 1997; Limón's fifth novel, *The Day of the Moon*, was published two years later. The narrative frame of *The Day of the Moon* begins in Los Angeles in 1965, before the advent of the Chicano Movement, and certain problematic issues of the movement leave their mark on the text, as the novel considers *mestizaje*, or mixed Spanish and Indian heritage, an issue of significance to many Chicanos during the late 1960s and 1970s. The novel moves backward and forward in time, revisiting battles over racial and gender identity in the first half of the twentieth century in Mexico and Los Angeles. Focusing on the painful rather than the celebratory aspects of *mestizaje* for Chicanos and Latinos across the Americas, Limón notes in the preface that the dual heritage is "a condition of anguish, because to be *Mestiza* or *Mestizo* is to dangle between being Spanish and indigenous . . . existing between gratitude and rage. It means choosing white or brown. It means acceptance or denial of color."

Limón positions a series of strong women characters between two opposing male icons who represent the poles of Latino *mestizaje*—a Rarámuri (Tarahumara) tribesman and the Castillan patriarch who defeats him, who, Limón argues, stands as a metaphor for the "*Mestizo*'s white side which denies, and even assaults, the haunting presence of his brown ancestor who dwells inside of him." Shortly before his death in Los Angeles in 1965 Flavio Betancourt, the central patriarch of the novel, recounts his life. Having risen to landed wealth in Mexico by winning property in a card game, Don Flavio has continually rejected the indigenous side of his heritage and contests the efforts of his sister, wife, daughter, and granddaughter to move beyond his patriarchal and racial authority. Flavio consummates his power-consolidating marriage to Velia Carmelita by forcing sex on her but is powerless when she finds love, companionship, and sexual fulfillment with his sister. He is similarly ineffectual in attempting to prevent his daughter and granddaughter from reclaiming the indigenous part of their heritage. Despite Flavio's daughter Isadora's acquiescence to the marriage partner he arranges for her, she later carries on an illicit relationship with a Rarámuri, Jerónimo, whom she has loved since childhood. Although Flavio has Jerónimo murdered and interns Isadora in a mental institution in

"No, Niña. You must live. That is your obligation. It is your father who is cursed by the blood that is on his hands. Do you want the same for yourself?"

Ursula's words nearly unnerved Isadora, who had thought that she was convinced of what to do moments before. The image of a lifetime without Jerómino unfolded in front of her, however, making her return to her resolve.

"Are you going to swear or not?"

"I swear. But..."

Isadora stood and helped Ursula to her feet. It was early morning, and the fire in the hearth had died, but light was trailing in from the entrance to the cave. Isadora looked around, remembering, wondering if she would ever return to the place where she had loved and known happiness.

"I'll return soon, Vieja. Remember, you've taken an oath."

Isadora took nothing with her except a gourd of water. She wore the long dress of the tribeswomen, a huipil to shroud her shoulders, and huaraches to protect her feet. As she made her way out, Ursula took her in her arms; it was an embrace that lasted only a few seconds.

Once on the pathway down toward el llano, Isadora walked briskly, then she trotted, accelerating her speed until she was running. She was sure-footed, and even though she had not eaten or slept, a spirit had possessed her body, energizing it. She was el Rarámuri the distance runner now; her feet were those of the deer. Isadora ran knowing that her strength would hold and that she would reach her destination at sundown.

She was not surprised that when she walked by the stables of her father's hacienda no one stopped her even though many of the Mestizos and other servants saw her. No one ran to tell Don Flavio of what they had

*Page from Limón's revised typescript for* The Day of the Moon, *her 1999 novel (Collection of Graciela Limón)*

Zapopan "where men hide disobedient women," he cannot ultimately suppress the indigenous side of his *mestizaje* heritage: his granddaughter, Alondra, journeys to Mexico after his death in search of her interned mother and finds happiness by returning to her father's Rarámuri village in Chihuahua.

In this novel, written two decades after the Chicano Movement, Limón expands upon the earlier preoccupation of some Chicano writers with the recuperation of their indigenous heritage. Without resorting to stereotyping or romanticizing, Limón links ancient cultural beliefs to richly developed people of past historical moments and inscribes *mestizaje* with key gender issues. On the eve of the movement Alondra returns to Mexico to undergo an epiphanic moment of discovery of her *mestizaje* heritage while listening to nuns chant the Canticles in a convent in Zapopan: "*I am black, but beautiful, O daughters of Jerusalem.* Alondra felt her breath catch in her throat because she had never heard such words before. Her mind raced. She was not black, but she was Rarámuri. She was copper. She was mahogany. She was cacao. She was peyote." Discerning in this moment an invitation to come home to the Rarámuri caves of Chihuahua, where she enters into spiritual communion and dialogue with her mother in their ancestral site, Alondra redresses the grievances of patriarchy and racial repression in ways distinct from those engaged in during the early Chicano Movement.

Limón's five novels represent some of the most important contributions to the renaissance of Chicana fiction in the United States in the late 1980s and 1990s; they have been reviewed in such publications as *The New York Times, The Washington Post,* and *World Literature Today.* Her work is situated in a multicultural experience of the Americas in which the women and men of Central America, Mexico, and Los Angeles come together in political and gender struggles, reexamine their historical past, and plot the course of their future. The accessibility of her prose, indebted to the poetic gracefulness of Rulfo and to the postmodernist experimentation of other contemporary writers of the Americas, invites a wide readership. Limón's novels show her to be a key voice of multiculturalism in the 1990s and will enrich the understanding of the experience of American Latinos in the new century.

### Reference:

Ellen McCracken, *New Latina Narrative: The Feminine Space of Postmodern Ethnicity* (Tucson: University of Arizona Press, 1999), pp. 43–45, 58–62, 66, 84–88, 103, 189–190.

# Josefina López

## (19 March 1969 – )

### Kat Avila

BOOKS: *Real Women Have Curves* (Seattle: Rain City
    Projects, 1992);
*Food for the Dead; La Pinta: Two One-Act Plays* (Woodstock,
    Ill.: Dramatic Publishing, 1996);
*Simply María, or The American Dream: A One-Act Play*
    (Woodstock, Ill.: Dramatic Publishing, 1996);
*Confessions–: A One Woman Show* (Woodstock, Ill.: Dra-
    matic Publishing, 1997);
*Confessions of Women from East L.A.: A Comedy* (Woodstock,
    Ill.: Dramatic Publishing, 1997);
*"My Low Self-Esteem Days" & Other Poetic Thoughts* (Los
    Angeles: Privately printed, 1997);
*Unconquered Spirits: A Historical Play* (Woodstock, Ill.:
    Dramatic Publishing, 1997);
*Yes! You Too Can Be a Chingona* (Los Angeles: Privately
    printed, 1997).

OTHER: *Simply María, or, The American Dream: A One-
    Act Play,* in *Shattering the Myth: Plays by Hispanic
    Women,* edited by Linda Feyder (Houston: Arte
    Público Press, 1992).

PLAY PRODUCTIONS: *Simply María, or The Ameri-
    can Dream,* San Diego, Gaslamp Quarter Theatre
    Company, 13 January 1988; revised, San Juan
    Bautista, El Teatro Campesino, 13 October
    1989;
*Food for the Dead,* San Juan Bautista, El Teatro
    Campesino, 13 October 1989;
*Real Women Have Curves,* San Francisco, El Teatro de la
    Esperanza, 25 May 1990;
*La Pinta,* Los Angeles, Los Angeles Theatre Center, 15
    March 1991;
*Confessions of Women from East L.A.,* workshop production,
    Northridge, California State University, 20 April
    1995;
*Unconquered Spirits,* workshop production, Northridge,
    California State University, 28 April 1995;
*Super Chingona,* Northridge, California State University,
    6 March 1998.

*Josefina López at the time of the 1996 publication of her play* Simply
María, or The American Dream *(1988)*

SELECTED PERIODICAL PUBLICATION–
UNCOLLECTED: "On Being a Playwright," *Ollantay,*
    1 (July 1993): 43–46.

Josefina López, whose first play was produced
when she was eighteen, has become one of the most
widely produced Latina playwrights in the United
States. Her outrageous sense of humor softens the
harsh emotional settings of her Chicana-driven plays.
In her work she reveals the culturally repressed passions and needs of Chicanas in an effort to achieve healing and transformation.

Born on 19 March 1969 in Cerritos, San Luis Potosí, Mexico, María Josefina López is the sixth of eight children. She moved to the Boyle Heights area of Los Angeles when she was about five years old; her mother, Catalina Perales, had to use the birth certificate of an American-born girl to get López across the border. Her father, Rosendo Z. López, already had his green card, as did her mother. Subsequently, López attended Breed Elementary School, Hollenbeck Junior High School, and Roosevelt High School, graduating from the Los Angeles County High School for the Arts in 1987. Later she received her green card under the amnesty provision in the Simpson-Rodino immigration bill.

Aside from her mother, from whom she inherited her storytelling ability, another influential person in López's life has been the playwright and El Teatro Campesino founder Luis Valdez, whose early plays made her aware of the creative value of her bilingual/bicultural background and experiences. Her ambition was to become an actress, but, inspired by Valdez's groundbreaking work, she began writing, knowing that as a Chicana she would have to create her own parts if she ever wanted to be cast in a production. López developed her craft as a member of the Young Playwrights Lab at the Los Angeles Theatre Center from 1985 to 1988; she also worked with Cuban-born playwright María Irene Fornés in a 1988 workshop at the International Arts Relations (INTAR) Hispanic American Arts Center in New York City. She studied dramatic writing at New York University's Tisch School of the Arts in 1988–1989 and theater at the University of California, San Diego, in 1989–1990. She received a B.A. in film and screenwriting in 1993 from Columbia College in Chicago. She also trained at the Warner Brothers Comedy Writing Workshop in 1993.

López wrote *Simply María, or The American Dream* (published in 1992) at the age of seventeen after seeing Valdez's 1986 play, *I Don't Have to Show You No Stinking Badges,* at the Los Angeles Theatre Center. In Valdez's play Connie and Buddy Villa have created a comfortable middle-class lifestyle for themselves by working as Hollywood extras. They have put a daughter through medical school and have supported a son at Harvard for the past two years. A crisis develops when their son unexpectedly returns and announces he is quitting school; he has not reconciled the ambivalence of being Chicano. The internal struggle of the adolescent protagonist in *Simply María* is similar, but complicated by her gender. María is torn between assuming the traditional, subordinate gender role of a working-class Mexican or the modern, career-oriented feminist role available to her as an ethnically self-hating but upward-bound North American. At times the humor has an extraordinarily cruel, blunt edge, exposing the disparate treatment of women in society.

María's parents, Ricardo and Carmen, have forsaken a small Mexican village for greater Los Angeles, not foreseeing that their daughter would grow up with independent qualities including ambition and a questioning of the institution of marriage. At a young age María is told by her father that she can be anything she wants to be in the United States; but later, when she declares she wants to go to college to be an actress, her parents belittle her ambition. Frustrated and emotionally spent, María falls asleep, only to have a nightmare about a marriage in which she fails so abominably at being a good housewife that she is put on trial. Upon awakening from this foreboding dream, she overhears her mother accusing her father of carrying on an affair; the argument provokes her to continue with her college plans.

López sent *Simply María* to the 1987 Young Playwrights Festival of New York; she was a semifinalist, and the play received a reading. On 13 January 1988 the Gaslamp Quarter Theater California Young Playwrights Project in San Diego produced the play with director Luis Torner. In August 1988 José Luis Valenzuela of the Latino Theatre Lab (now the Latino Theatre Company) directed a workshop reading of *Simply María* at South Coast Repertory in Costa Mesa as a part of the annual Hispanic Playwrights Project managed by José Cruz González. The script took second place in the 1989 Chicano/Latino Literary Contest sponsored by the Department of Spanish and Portuguese, University of California, Irvine.

A television production of *Simply María* by the Playwrights Project aired on 17 and 24 September 1989 on KPBS in San Diego. The production won a 1990 Public Television Local Program Award from the Corporation for Public Broadcasting—the Gold Award in the children's category, as well as a Media Award by the National Conference of Christians and Jews and an Emmy for outstanding achievement in an entertainment program.

In October 1989 Valdez's El Teatro Campesino mounted a shorter, touring version of *Simply María* along with López's second play, *Food for the Dead*. Subsequently, El Teatro Campesino toured *Simply María* through 1993 as part of a double bill with such plays as Evelina Fernandez's *How Else Am I Supposed to Know I'm Still Alive?* (1989) and Valdez's *Soldado Razo* (Buck Private, 1971) and *El baile de los gigantes* (Dance of the Giants, 1974). *Simply María* was included in *Shattering the Myth: Plays by Hispanic Women* in 1992 and published separately in 1996.

*Food for the Dead,* a one-act play written in 1989, keeps alive the playwright's questions about a Chicana's place in the community. The play takes place on Halloween night as Candela is concluding a nine-year period of mourning for her late husband, Ruben. His death forced her out of her protective shell: during those nine years she lost weight, went back to school, and finally made the last payment on the house. On this night, as Candela is surrounded by her four children at dinner, Ruben literally climbs out of hell to join her after hearing their son Jesús, with his lover, Fernando, announce his homosexuality. Candela at first meekly obeys the commands of her resurrected, obnoxious husband, a situation that quickly changes after she finds out how Ruben died. Courageously defending her fledgling independence and her son's sexual liberation, recognizing both as natural outgrowths of the same rigorous process of self-examination, Candela finally retires Ruben's stubborn ghost. A Pandora's box has now been opened, however, and Candela's other children have their own surprises to unveil as the play draws to a close. Besides the 1989 tour, *Food for the Dead* was produced in November 1989 at the Teatro de las Americas at the University of California, San Diego, and in May 1993 by Teatro Visión in San Jose. Both productions were directed by Laura Esparza.

*Real Women Have Curves* (published in 1992), a play López wrote when she was nineteen, addresses the body as a site where female experience and history are vividly recorded. The action is set in a small sewing factory with a cast of five female characters. Estela is a twenty-four-year-old factory owner who is under great pressure to complete a clothing order before the end of the week: one hundred pink evening dresses must be sewn for the Glitz Company. Upon their delivery, Estela will be able to pay her employees for their past three weeks of work as well as avoid a lawsuit by paying the outstanding balance on her sewing machines. If she has to go to court, the authorities will find out that she does not have a green card; she has not applied for a card because she thinks that she will be denied legal residency if immigration officials discover that she is involved in a lawsuit. Much is at stake, and the women band together in a race against the clock.

Estela's employees are her mother, Doña Carmen; a younger sister, Ana; and two others, Pancha and Rosali. Because the employees are all women, the sewing factory is a space where they can feel relatively free to be themselves and talk about anything they wish. But this liberated sphere is continually threatened by the outside world in the form of *la migra* (the immigration authorities) and possible closure of the factory if the sewing equipment is repossessed.

Within the factory, the structure of the outside world imposes itself through instruments of measurement and related references. An especially large calen-

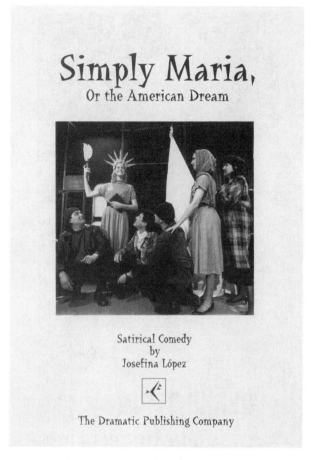

*Cover for the 1996 publication of López's first play, written when she was seventeen*

dar and clock are posted; the date and time are indicated at regular intervals in the dialogue to show the progress of the garment workers as the deadline looms. The overall passage of time in the women's lives is marked by Estela's celebration of her birthday and Carmen's discovery that she is going through menopause.

Cultural expectations are another form of intrusion. Carmen is constantly measuring her daughters against social standards of what is appropriate and inappropriate behavior for young Mexican women, and she pushes them to conform. She does not question whether these expectations should be applied to her daughters, though Estela and Ana resist them.

The most damaging intrusion of the outside world into the women's sphere is the propaganda representing the ideal body size for a woman: the size 7 tailor's mannequin, the pictures of anorexic-looking models wearing the latest fashions, and the fact that there is no size 13/14 for the dress style the garment workers are making. The play makes the point that the societal ideal of the female body bears little resemblance

*Cover of program for a production of López's 1990 play, which focuses on social and cultural expectations of women (courtesy of López)*

to the actual body, which will reflect life experiences: a real body reeks of natural odor, growls for food, aches to be touched, displays stretch marks and scars from Caesarean sections, and goes through biological changes. Real women have bodies that look lived in, López says. In the end, the garment workers triumphantly start on a path of redefining the world to include big women such as themselves.

After some development at INTAR, *Real Women Have Curves* received further work at the 1989 Isadora Aguirre Playwriting Lab led by Mexican playwright Emilio Carballido and sponsored by El Teatro de la Esperanza. In May 1990, El Teatro de la Esperanza presented the world premiere of the play at Mission Cultural Center in San Francisco with director Hector Correa; later, Esperanza director Rodrigo Duarte-Clark took it on tour from spring 1990 through fall 1992. Productions of *Real Women* have collectively grossed more than $1,000,000 in the 1990s. A Spanish-language ver-

sion titled *Las Mujeres de Verdad Tienen Curvas* premiered in August 1994 at the Repertorio Español in New York City. That same month, López held an assistant director-in-residency position at Borderlands Theater in Tucson, Arizona, where she also performed in their production of *Real Women Have Curves*.

López's next efforts included *Unconquered Spirits* and *Confessions of Women from East L.A.* (both published in 1997). The former is a feminist updating of the popular ghost legend of *La Llorona* (The Wailing Woman). Ten-year-old Xochimilco hears one version of the story from her exasperated mother while packing for a trip to the United States to escape the Mexican Revolution. *La Llorona* is an indigenous woman who dares to love a Spaniard, only to be abandoned when he marries a Spanish woman. To spite her unfaithful lover, the spurned woman murders their children. A river swallows the evidence of her misdeed. The woman then kills herself but discovers that there will be no eternal rest for her until she finds the bodies of her children. To this day *La Llorona* continues to haunt the riverbanks of Mexico looking for her children, mournfully wailing, "Ayyy, mis hijos!" (Ohhh, my children!). The legend of *La Llorona* is reinvented each time *Unconquered Spirits* moves into a different set of historical circumstances, from revolutionary Mexico to the devastation of pre-Christian Tenochtitlán to a labor strike at the worksite of a much older, weathered Xochimilco in San Antonio. The text of the play documents the emotional and physical violence against indigenous women and the courageous, albeit reckless, reactions of those women to the abuse of trust and power by men of the ruling order.

*Unconquered Spirits* won an honorable mention in the 1992 TENAZ (Teatros Nacionales de Aztlán) International Quincentennial Playwriting Competition, sponsored by the Guadalupe Cultural Arts Center, and received a public reading at the TENAZ International Festival of Chicano/Latino Theatre in San Antonio in November 1992. *Unconquered Spirits* also was a finalist in the Arizona Theater Company's First Annual Hispanic Playwriting Contest in 1995. The play had its world premiere in April 1995 at California State University, Northridge, directed by Anamarie García.

Also in April 1995 there was a workshop production of *Confessions of Women from East L.A.*, directed by William Alejandro Virchis. In San Diego, Virchis directed another production of the play, presented by Teatro Máscara Mágica and the Fritz Theater, from 25 April through 12 May 1996. The same production traveled to the University of California, Riverside, for a final performance at a fine arts festival on 29 June 1996. "Awake, my *raza*, awake!" exhorts Valentina, the final character in López's parade of proud and different Chicanas who flaunt their comically bittersweet lives in

*Confessions of Women from East L.A.* There is Doña Consepcion, who is glad that her husband is dead because she never liked sex–not because he gave her AIDS; she admits that she is a lesbian. Calletana, the corn vendor, was jailed for street-selling. Yoko Martinez is trying to act and look Japanese, even volunteering to tie up her size 36D breasts if she can get a job at Mrs. Ito's restaurant. Tiffany, the Valley Chicana, is unable to concentrate on her speech against Proposition 187 because she just got into a fight with her boyfriend. Finally, Valentina makes everyone feel uncomfortable with her efforts against racism and other social injustices. If, as López says, she herself is the protagonist in all her plays, Valentina most closely approximates the public persona of the playwright.

López is a member of the Dramatists Guild and the Writers Guild of America West. She has written for television as well as for the stage; her television-writing credits include episodes for *Living Single* (June–October 1993) and *Culture Clash* (October 1993–January 1994) on Fox TV; *The Latino Anthology Series* (October 1994) on HBO/TROPIX; *The Chavez Family* (November 1995), an ABC/Norman Lear/Paramount Television production; *Innercity H.S.T.A.* (September 1995) on NBC; and *La Fiesta* (February 1996) on UPN. She founded a production company with writer/producer Jon Mercedes III in January 1995 to create, develop, and produce film, television, and theater projects; this partnership was dissolved the following year.

On 16 September 1995 López was awarded a Diosa de Plata (Silver Goddess) award in recognition of her contributions to the field of arts and entertainment; the award was presented by the Chicano Federation of San Diego County at their twenty-fifth annual fundraising gala dinner and anniversary celebration. Fellow honorees were Valdez, actress and Bilingual Foundation of the Arts cofounder Carmen Zapata, actor Mario López, and novelist Victor Villaseñor.

**Interviews:**
Jeff Kaliss, "Heavy Topic Handled With Humor: Hispanic playwright looks at body images in Real Women Have Curves," *San Francisco Chronicle*, Datebook section, 20 May 1990, p. 31;
Nancy Churnin, "Simply Josefina López," *Los Angeles Times*, Calendar section, 29 July 1990, pp. 48, 50;
Churnin, "Young Playwright Takes Giant Steps Toward Her Dream," *Los Angeles Times*, Thursday, Nuestro Tiempo section, 20 December 1990, pp. 1, 5;

Todd Salovey, "The Woman Behind *Real Women:* An Interview with Playwright Josefina López," *REP/Lyceum REPorter* (Spring 1994): 1, 4;
Sybil P. Webb, "Josefina López: Real Women Playwright is Real Success," *Latin Style Magazine* (1994): 71–72;
Minerva Canto, "Taking a Chance on The Chavez Family," *Orange County Register,* Show section, Thursday, 7 May 1998, p. 2.

**References:**
Dahlia Aguilar, "Catch Them If You Can," *Hispanic,* 6 (January/February 1993): 102, 104;
Kat Avila, "1992–1993 California Theater Season Summary," *Ollantay,* 1 (July 1993): 54–59;
Melanie Cole, "Thirty Under Thirty," *Hispanic,* 8 (August 1995): 22–30;
Ronie-Richele Garcia-Johnson, "Josefina López," in *Notable Hispanic American Women,* edited by Diane Telgen and Jim Kamp (Detroit: Gale Research, 1993): 232–233;
Jorge Huerta, "Professionalizing Teatro: An Overview of Chicano Theatre During the 'Decade of the Hispanic," *Tonantzin,* 8 (November 1992): 3–6; *TheatreForum* (April 1993): 54–59;
"Josefina López," in *Women Playwrights of Diversity: A Bio-Bibliographical Sourcebook,* edited by Jane T. Peterson and Suzanne Bennett (Westport, Conn.: Greenwood Press, 1997), pp. 220–222;
Tiffany Ann López, "Beyond the Festival Latino: (Re)Defining Latina Drama for the Mainstage," in *Women Playwrights of Diversity: A Bio-Bibliographical Sourcebook,* edited by Jane T. Peterson and Suzanne Bennett (Westport, Conn.: Greenwood Press, 1997), pp. 17–25;
Brian Lowry, "Lear gears up Act III prod'n slate," *Variety,* 10 July 1995, pp. 1, 18;
Teresa Marrero, "Real Women Have Curves: The Articulation of Fat as a Cultural/Feminist Issue," *Ollantay,* 1 (January 1993): 61–70;
Margo Milleret, "Girls Growing Up, Cultural Norms Breaking Down in Two Plays by Josefina López," *Gestos,* 13 (November 1998): 109–125;
Ed Morales, "Shadowing Valdez," *American Theatre,* 9 (November 1992): 14–19.

# Demetria Martínez
*(10 July 1960 –    )*

Gwendolyn Díaz
*Saint Mary's University*

BOOKS: *Three Times a Woman: Chicana Poetry,* by Martínez, Alicia Gaspar de Alba, and María Herrera-Sobek (Tempe, Ariz.: Bilingual Review/Press, 1989);
*MotherTongue* (Tempe, Ariz.: Bilingual Press/Editorial Bilingüe, 1994); republished as *Mother Tongue* (New York: One World, 1996);
*Breathing Between the Lines: Poems* (Tucson: University of Arizona Press, 1997).

Demetria Martínez brings a fresh voice to Chicano literature. Her worldview and experiences center around the social causes and political issues of dispossessed Latinos in general and Central American refugees in the United States in particular. Hers is also a voice of deep spirituality and belief in the power of faith to help overcome social and political strife. In addition to these issues, Martínez explores the world of love and sexuality with genuine insight as well as a refreshing sense of naïveté. Also significant is her view of the Chicano of New Mexico and the search for culture through language, religion, and political commitment.

Demetria Louise Martínez was born in Albuquerque, New Mexico, on 10 July 1960. Her father, Ted, was the first Chicano to be elected to the Albuquerque School Board. Her mother, Dolores, was a kindergarten teacher, and her grandmother and aunt held several county offices. In an unpublished interview in 1994, Martínez said she grew up with the idea that it was normal to challenge the powers that be and to change things that one was not happy with. A shy child, she expressed herself at an early age through writing rather than engaging in teenage social life. She began to write because she felt it would help her come out of her depression, and she learned to associate writing with transcendence. Her grandmother encouraged her to read the Bible, and often they read from the Psalms. Martínez claims that this reading led her to associate the Bible with poetry, with the sacred, with magic, and with healing. The mystical elements of her writing are rooted in her Catholic upbringing as well as in the spirituality of the indigenous cultures of New Mexico.

*Demetria Martínez (photograph by Raechel Maria Running)*

Martínez graduated from Princeton University's Woodrow Wilson School of Public and International Affairs in 1982. While at Princeton she also took courses in religion and ethics and attended poetry workshops. Later she joined a Catholic artists' colony called Sagrada Art Studios in Old Town Albuquerque, where she began to develop and polish her poetry. In the mid 1980s she freelanced as a reporter for the *National Catholic Reporter* and as the religion writer for the *Albuquerque Journal*. During this period she began to write poetry about the plight of Salvadoran refugees fleeing their military government. She reported extensively on these refugees and on the Sanctuary Movement, in which Americans defied U.S. immigration law and transported refugees into the country.

In 1986 Martínez was invited by a Lutheran minister to go with him to the U.S./Mexico border, where he was planning to help two pregnant Salvadoran women cross over into the United States. In 1987 she learned that the U.S. Attorney in New Mexico had indicted both her and the minister. She was charged with conspiracy against the U.S. government and with aiding in the transport of illegal aliens and inducing their entry. The penalty for these charges would have been twenty-five years in prison and $1.25 million in fines. In 1988 Martínez went to trial and was acquitted on the grounds of the First Amendment with the argument that as a reporter she had the right to research the Sanctuary Movement. Her poetry and prose draw extensively on these experiences. Interestingly, her poem "Nativity: For Two Salvadoran Women, 1986–1987," which was based on Martínez's involvement in the incident with the minister, was used as evidence against her in the trial.

This poem is included in *Turning,* a collection of poetry published as part of *Three Times a Woman: Chicana Poetry* (1989). Written while Martínez was in her twenties, *Turning* is divided into five sections and includes poems that revolve around themes of love, politics, and feminism. The first section, "To Keep Back the Cold," consists of an eclectic selection of poems that range in subject from a goddaughter's birthday to an abused undocumented worker. The title piece in this section depicts a series of home scenes, each set against the backdrop of cold weather, strong winds, and blizzards. The frailty of the people in refugee camp tents is juxtaposed with the security of a family in a well-to-do home, yet all are equally victimized by the inclement weather, which does not distinguish between alien or citizen, poor or rich. A sense of frustration with both nature and human-inflicted pain is evident in the last verse: "I will not sing of it / I will not sing. / Feel ashes storm into your eyes, / you will turn and ache / all night forever, longing / to keep back the cold."

In "To My Goddaughter (on her 6th birthday)" Martínez gives a religious twist to the birth of an illegitimate child: "No angel beamed down / to herald your inception, / just a do-it-yourself pregnancy test." By drawing a loose parallel between this child's humble birth and that of Christ's—"Little raisin, you lay in a glass manger"—she elevates this child's worth and at the same time pays tribute to the simplicity of a Christ who comes to save all.

In "Troublemaker" the poetic persona says, "I want to be / a mango seed / that men trip over." The men she refers to are those who hold that economic "progress" in the United States will somehow benefit Third World peoples. The speaker concludes by saying that she intends to be a troublemaker when she grows up, someone who will grow like a tree to trip men such as these in their path.

"An El Paso Street by Night" is a simple yet powerful poem about a Juarez woman who has sex with a man who promises her a job in America. After he has taken advantage of her, she ends up scrubbing sinks in El Paso for slave wages. In "Poem for the Men I Respect" Martínez's feminism leads her to present a variation on the theme of men having their way with women: in this poem a woman is having her way with men, from whom she is only seeking the seed for a child. The woman concludes: "I'll name my baby Sophia Dolores / Because wisdom comes of pain, / You can tell the world she's yours / When I've achieved my fame."

The second section of the collection is titled "Border Wars: 1985," and in these poems Martínez focuses specifically on the Sanctuary Movement and the situation of the Salvadoran refugees. Her lyrical voice combined with her political commitment makes poetry out of fear, violence, and injustice. In "Prologue: Salvadoran Woman's Lament" Martínez introduces a theme that is later expanded in her 1994 novel, *MotherTongue.* In the poem a young Salvadoran man must leave his home and loved ones because he is being threatened by the authorities. His lover laments his loss and foresees that he will meet another woman—an American woman who will want to "take the war out of him," who will "make love to a man and a monster," and who will "rise from the bed / grenades ticking in her."

The poem "Crossing Over" is headed by an epigraph that is a statement from an official of the U.S. Immigration and Naturalization Service, in reference to the Sanctuary Movement: "a sanctimonious band of renegades who advocate open violation of the law." This poem about a baby that has been thrown into the Rio Grande, rescued by Sanctuary members, and brought into the United States underscores the cruelty of the war in El Salvador, the wrongness of North American involvement in it, and the innocence of most of its victims. "Angelo's Story" is headed by an epigraph, taken from an editorial, that serves to indict the position of the U.S. government on the immigration of Salvadorans into the United States: "the migration of illegal aliens to your community . . . greatly increases the cost to taxpayers of welfare and other social programs." The poem gives a human face to the

*Cover for Martínez's 1994 novel, about a young Chicana's love for a Salvadoran refugee*

"illegal alien"; he becomes Angelo, a young man who has to cut his brother from the tree in which he has been hung by government soldiers. Angelo realizes he must flee to the north before the same thing happens to him. A similar situation occurs in "Orlando's Story / The War Persists," in which the Salvadoran Orlando's mother and sister have been murdered by military death squads. He also must flee but suffers from nightmares of "my mother and sister / red mouths and breasts / in circles of blood / dead."

"North American Woman's Lament (for Orlando)" echoes the theme of "Prologue: Salvadoran Woman's Lament." In this poem Orlando has come to the United States and has fallen in love with an American woman. The speaker in the poem is the woman, who loves Orlando not only for himself but also for what he represents—the war, the suffering, the injustice: "but you are history / a date burnt into your chest / by the clit of a cigarette." The poem ends with a poignant view of an America that could possibly shelter such persons in need:

at my palm, the rib
they fractured with a rifle,
the rib, that if taken into the body
of America might make us new,
a country where mercy and nobility
reside, where the bones we have broken
teach us of strength.

The association between Orlando's fractured rib and that of Adam, the new man, brings to light a possible new generation of Americans guided by compassion. The concluding poem of the section, "Grand Jury Indicts 16 in Sanctuary Movement," is based on the first Sanctuary trial in Tucson.

The third section of *Turning,* "Love Notes," consists of a series of love poems, each with the name of a month as the title. In "July" Martínez explores eroticism at the same time as she experiments with concise form and the graphic layout of words. As the two lovers return from a romantic stroll to their "white bed," the female persona states:

```
My
     legs
          open
               like a beak
          bird
     great
   a
Of
```

"September" expresses hope for the dawning of a new day, after war, when there are "No losers or visitors / . . . just survivors / to lay hands / on one another, / to begin again." In "December," a touching poem about the frailty of life, a young woman dies in a car accident; later her father gazes at her dead body with its "fractured face" and whispers "baby wake up."

"Turning," the section that gives its title to the collection, deals with incidents that can cause a turn or a change in one's destiny. This section begins with "Nativity: For Two Salvadoran Women, 1986–1987," which is about the trauma of fleeing one's home. A reporter meets the two pregnant women in a Juarez train station; their blouses are stained with breast milk, and their undergarments, tagged "Made in El Salvador," are stuffed in their purses to hide their origin. The recurring idea that "It is impossible to raise a child / in that country" is interwoven with the motif of the Virgin Mary, who also fled her home to have her child. The poem points out the hypocrisy of a nation where people "sing of a baby in a manger" and at the same time "finance death squads." The final association between the unborn babies and the birth of Christ reflects the idea of salvation and the attempt of these two women to save their children by raising them in a country free of war.

Abortion is the topic of "Hit and Run," in which a woman is abandoned by her lover when he learns she is pregnant. The speaker considers abortion and having the child. She opts for the latter, deciding, "I am the victor here, leaving / the clinic with a pink bundle / of your best features, / your violence washed down the sinkhole / with the placenta." She ends by adding, "touch us and I'll / sink a knife into you, sir."

Divorce is the turning point in both "Divorce" and "Bill of Rights." In the first poem a divorced woman sees herself as someone who "woke / from a coma and remembered / her name." In the second poem the speaker considers the meaning of divorce and finds that she does not approve of violating a pact. Nevertheless, she says, "against all we promised / I choose my life over yours / I have broken the accords / I do not approve."

The poem titled "Turning" is a delightful piece that reflects the carefree attitude of youth. A young woman enjoys her weekend as she walks "in bare feet,

gold earrings, / a Mexican dress that cost fifty cents," samples perfumes at a shop, and goes to Mass with unshaven legs. She ends by laughing over her bright future and thinking she has "so many babies / waiting to be born."

The final section of *Turning* consists of a single long poem, Martínez's self-professed favorite, called "Only Say the Word." This piece is subtitled "A Poem for Three Women's Voices" and was performed in 1984 at the Albuquerque Museum as a poetic drama. The piece is headed by a few paragraphs about the Santuario de Chimayó, a church erected by the Catholics over an area of land that the Pueblo Indians considered to have curative and spiritual powers. The church is visited by the faithful who believe the earth there has healing properties. The poem comprises three dramatic voices: a Guatemalan woman, a North American schoolteacher, and a Chimayó native. The Guatemalan describes an existence in the midst of war and violence. Her husband has been beaten and crippled by soldiers because of his espousal of the ideals of Liberation Theology. This woman has all but lost faith, and she challenges Christ to come down from the cross to help those in need: "You have not lifted your head / in 2,000 years." The North American schoolteacher feels that she has "taught thousands" but has "helped no one." The Chimayó native says she has had a good life: "sadness does not splinter my heart." Yet, the reader learns later that this woman's teenage daughter was killed in an accident. The woman has learned to find hope where there is none, and she exhorts the other two women to do the same. The message of the poem is to face adversity with hope and faith; this theme echoes the poet's religious belief. Since the success of Martínez's novel, *MotherTongue,* this collection of poetry has begun to receive attention from critics and to be considered a good first effort.

*MotherTongue* was published by Bilingual Press/ Editorial Bilingüe in 1994, and it won the Western States Book Award for fiction in that year. The cover features praise from novelist John Nichols, who comments that "Demetria Martínez is one of the best, the most poetic, and the most passionate writers of her generation," and from poet Denise Levertov, who says that Martínez "writes like the poet she is, but also with a novelist's ear and with the authority of her close knowledge of the life of Central American refugees." The novel caught the attention not only of the reading public but also of critics. It received favorable reviews, including those in *The Bloomsbury Review, The Washington Post, The Village Voice,* and *The Los Angeles Times.* Martínez has commented in interviews that the inspiration to write this novel came as she was listening to a reading by Sandra Cisneros. As Cisneros spoke, Martínez heard

*Dust jacket for Martínez's 1997 collection of poems, several of which were begun in Boston at the William Joiner Center for the Study of War and Social Consequences*

a voice say to her: "His nation chewed him up and spat him out like a piñón shell, and when he emerged from an airplane one late afternoon, I knew I would one day make love with him." Those words became the opening line of *MotherTongue* and set the tone for what is one of the freshest and most compelling works in Chicano literature of the 1990s.

Martínez's prose is lyrical above all, but she also develops an effective pace that alternates between passionate excitement and meditative introspection. The title of the novel refers to a recurrent theme: the Latino American's search for identity through the Spanish language and through all of the cultural knowledge that the language holds. As is the case for many members of her generation of Chicanos, Martínez's mother tongue is English; she views Spanish not only with admiration

as a language that opens the doors to a wealth of Hispanic tradition but also with the trepidation of one to whom Spanish is a second language still being learned. In the novel the mother tongue refers to an exploration into the Spanish language and also to taking possession of one's Latino heritage by making that culture a part of one's everyday life.

The protagonist of the work is Mary, a nineteen-year-old Chicana who lives in Albuquerque and is searching for purpose in her life. When Soledad, an activist friend who works in the Sanctuary Movement, asks her to pick up a Salvadoran refugee at the airport, Mary becomes involved in the man's cause. He tells them his name is José Luis Romero; he is a political refugee with a violent past in a war-torn country. As the young woman becomes acquainted with the Salvadoran, her initial attraction to him grows stronger. She takes him to meetings where he tells his story, or "testimonio," in order to educate the American public about the atrocities being committed in El Salvador. Mary's attraction toward José Luis is as much for his romantic past (or her romantic view of his past) and his history of war and liberation as for the man himself. José Luis, on the other hand, is torn between his love for Mary and his desire to go into hiding and continue his dedication to the cause of El Salvador. The novel is both an impassioned account of the plight of refugees in the United States and a love story centered around a woman who searches for love at the same time as she seeks her own identity as a Latina. After José Luis leaves, Mary (now María by her own choice) gives birth to his son, who later learns Spanish and goes with her to El Salvador to search for his father and continue María's pursuit of the mother tongue and the mother culture.

Structurally, the novel is multifaceted, consisting of a series of first-person and third-person narratives; letters (particularly those between Soledad and Mary/María); photograph descriptions that seem to make a moment eternal; newspaper and periodical clippings dealing with the Salvadoran saga; José Luis's speeches or testimonies; poems by politically inclined authors such as Roque Dalton, Pablo Neruda, and Claribel Alegría; and headlines that portray the hypocrisy of the American government and its intervention in Central America. The novel shuns a chronological treatment of time and intersperses the various scenes and narratives with a technique that juxtaposes past, present, and future. This juxtaposition creates the holistic effect of a present that is frozen in time and that includes both its origin and its destination. Much like Gabriel García Márquez in his *Cien años de soledad* (1967; translated as *One Hundred Years of Solitude,* 1970), Martínez begins the novel with a sentence that ties past, present, and future together.

The novel is divided into five parts focusing on different characters and themes. The first part is Mary's story, the story of a naive young woman who comes face to face with the basic questions of existence: who she is, what her purpose in life is, and what her roots and heritage are. She falls in love with a man whose past reflects a life of commitment—to a cause, a nation, and freedom—and who also represents her ideal of a Latino. Mary gives herself to José Luis, to his cause and his goals, and by doing so she begins to find out who she really is. She learns Spanish, becomes an activist, and finally travels to El Salvador. She also learns that her country has been sending millions of dollars to El Salvador to support a dictatorial government that has enslaved its people and against which the people have

rebelled (as José Luis has) to fight for their political and economic freedom. One moment of truth comes when Mary mentions a priest who has just come back from El Salvador with bullet casings imprinted with the name of an American city. Mary remarks that the involvement of American people such as herself in aiding the Salvadorans "were not isolated incidents but formed what became a movement of sorts, of U.S. citizens taking an 'option for the poor,' which Liberation Theologians said was God's way of acting in history." Her romantic worldview and her Catholic upbringing are both part of her compelling persona, and though she is initially naive, she grows, through time, into a spiritually and politically committed woman whose search for authenticity is continued in her son.

Part 2 is José Luis's story. Mary has kept his journal and quotes excerpts from it, allowing readers to see the story from his point of view. José Luis considers himself to be a simple Salvadoran who opposes the regime because it is unjust to the people. Though he had been involved in the opposition, as a seminarian he preferred to resist by studying the Bible and teaching the people: "our cry had been, not by the gun but by the Word made flesh in action." He had been captured by the regime and tortured, finally escaping to the United States to seek refuge. Once in the country, he is sheltered by Soledad and Mary as he works odd jobs, gathers intelligence for the Salvadoran cause, speaks at meetings of the Sanctuary Movement, and tries to decide what to make of his life. Though he loves Mary, he is tormented by the demons of his past, and ultimately he chooses to return to El Salvador. Many years later, Mary receives a letter that José Luis has written from Canada, telling her the reasons he felt he should leave her.

Part 3 takes place when Mary and José Luis's son (also named José Luis) is nineteen years old. She has raised him alone. He is a college student with diverse interests, and he is not particularly inclined to seek his Latino roots. Part 4 is the climactic section in which readers learn another reason why José Luis left. Mary tells her son about the night he was conceived: José Luis had a flashback, lost his senses, and repeatedly hit Mary, thinking that she was the enemy in El Salvador. The beauty of their romance was darkened by the fear and anxiety still alive in José Luis, and he left not long after that. In part 5 Mary travels to El Salvador with her son, who wants to learn more about his father. They are greeted by a nun who takes them to the archdiocese office where records of the war are kept. Mary and her son look through the pictures and find one of José Luis. There is no death date listed for him. They rejoice to learn that he is still alive and that his name is indeed José Luis; he had risked his own safety to tell them that much of his real name. His last name is Alegría (happiness). While in El Salvador, the son becomes interested in the history of the land and meets a young woman whom he plans to come back to visit in the summer. Mary's quest has become his.

Though not exactly autobiographical, *Mother-Tongue* comes from personal experience. It draws considerably from Martínez's own involvement with the Sanctuary Movement and with individual Salvadoran refugees. She has said in interviews that both Mary and Soledad reflect some aspects of herself, and that José Luis is a composite of various refugees with whom she came into contact. Stylistically, the work is a fast-paced narrative imbued with local color and poetic language. In the parts that take place in Albuquerque, particularly in the picturesque Old Town, warm hues of terra-cotta masonry and golden sunrises color the landscape:

> The silence of the golden room with its blue walls and white door frames was astonishing. At most, we whispered to one another. To try to keep the room cool, we kept the door leading outside open. A sarong from Bali, the color of apricot skin and just as thin hung over the screen; it is all that separated us from the din of tourists. Keeping quiet, we read the Braille of one another's bodies.

The neighborhood where Mary lives in a one-hundred-year-old house is described with the beauty and color typical of the Southwest:

> Postcard of Old Town, Albuquerque: eighteenth-century adobe plaza, shops with red chile ristras on door posts like Passover blood, Native Americans selling jewelry under the portal in front of the cantina. The picture must have been taken after the rain. The stucco surfaces of San Rafael Catholic Church are the color of bruised peach.

Martínez's background in poetry is evident not only in the lyrical quality of her prose but also in her meta-phors and similes, which are unusual and captivating: she declares that "Reality is a lump of clay and prayer is the potter's wheel" and describes "San Rafael's bells pecking away at the shell of night." Only occasionally does she use images that do not work and seem a bit awkward. Overall, Martínez has managed to make of her first novel an enticing lyrical journey into the culture, history, and future of modern-day Latinos.

Martínez's work continues to move in the direction of this search for origins and authenticity. She is currently working on a collection of poetry, "The Devil's Workshop," as well as a second novel, called "Mexican Rubies," in which her exploration of language as a source of ethnic knowledge and awareness takes on a new twist. The protagonist, Emma, has an affair with a white reporter who, unlike Emma, speaks perfect Spanish. Set in Santa Fe, the work explores issues of ethnicity and class. Her second book of poetry, *Breathing Between the Lines,* also dealing with themes of love and politics, was published by the University of Arizona Press in 1997. Because of the success of *Mother-Tongue,* One World (an imprint of Ballantine) republished the novel in hardcover in September 1996 and in paperback in August 1997, making it more readily available to a large mainstream audience.

Achieving and maintaining a lyrical quality in her writing is one of Martínez's primary goals. At the same time she is committed to conveying the Chicano experience in her work. Martínez currently lives in Tucson, Arizona, where she gives lectures and readings, practices journalism, and continues her creative writing.

### References:

Patricia Dubrava, "Mother Tongue," *Bloomsbury Review,* 14 (November/December 1994);

Tey Diana Rebolledo, *Women Singing in the Snow: A Cultural Analysis of Chicana Literature* (Tucson: University of Arizona Press, 1995).

# Rubén Martínez

*(9 July 1962 – )*

Salvador C. Fernández
*Occidental College*

BOOK: *The Other Side: Fault Line, Guerrilla Saints, and the True Heart of Rock 'n' Roll* (London & New York: Verso, 1992); republished as *The Other Side: Notes from the New L.A., Mexico City, and Beyond* (New York: Vintage, 1993).

OTHER: "The Beginning," "Untitled," and "Hotel Ontario," in *Invocation L.A.: Urban Multicultural Poetry,* edited by Michelle T. Clinton, Sesshu Foster, and Naomi Quiñónez (Albuquerque: West End, 1989), pp. 109–115;
"East Side Stories: Joseph Rodríguez's Images of East L.A.," in *East Side Stories: Gang Life in East LA,* by Joseph Rodríguez (New York: powerHouse, 1998), pp. 9–33.

SELECTED PERIODICAL PUBLICATION–
UNCOLLECTED: "Salvador Homecoming," *Enclitic,* 10, no. 2 (1988): 54–65.

Rubén Martínez, a poet, performer, and journalist from Los Angeles, represents a new generation of Chicano/Latino writers whose cultural production generally focuses on Southern California. Yet, in his writings he also fuses historical, political, and cultural discourses in order to depict the oppressive conditions that Chicano/Latino communities face in the United States, Mexico, and El Salvador. Martínez is concerned with the representation of marginalized communities that have been displaced, because these communities produce cultural and social dissidents who serve as the voices of the underdogs. Martínez's writings enunciate the voice of the Chicano/Latino community in Los Angeles, which has historically resided in the center of the city but has occupied a peripheral space economically, politically, and culturally. Thus, his writings, emerging from the arena of cultural politics, contest the hegemonic cultural practices that have traditionally excluded his community.

Rubén Martínez, a second-generation Latino, is the son of Rubén Martínez, a Mexican American who

*Rubén Martínez at the time of* The Other Side: Fault Line, Guerrilla Saints, and the True Heart of Rock 'n' Roll
*(photograph by Ted Soqui)*

worked as a lithographer, and Vilma Angula, a Salvadoran psychologist. He was born on 9 July 1962 in Silver Lake, a middle-class neighborhood in Los Angeles. His professional career as a writer began in 1986 when he became a regular contributor to the *L.A. Weekly,* one of the major alternative newspapers of Los Angeles. In 1992 he became an editor for this publication. He has served as the Los Angeles bureau chief for Pacific News Service and as cohost of the PBS-affiliate KCET-TV public-affairs program, *Life and Times.* In addition to his journalistic duties, Martínez has been a member of the faculty at Claremont McKenna College, where he taught a course in journalism. He now lives in Mexico City and Los Angeles.

In 1992 Martínez published his first book, *The Other Side: Fault Line, Guerrilla Saints, and the True Heart of Rock 'n' Roll,* a title that was later changed to *The Other Side: Notes from the New L.A., Mexico City, and Beyond* when the work appeared in paperback. *The Other Side* is a collection of *crónicas* (chronicles) and poetry that documents three geographical and cultural spaces: the United States, Mexico, and El Salvador, each reflecting the author's personal heritage and literary formation. Martínez's personal background as a half Chicano, half *Salvadoreño* indicates a shift in the demographics of urban America. Chicanos still constitute the largest Latino ethnic group, but new communities, such as the *centroamericano,* are acquiring an important role in the representation of the Chicano/Latino community. Thus, as a Chicano, Latino, Mexican, Salvadoran, and Central American, Martínez represents the face of Chicano/Latino culture in the United States, a hybrid and heterogenous product influenced by many cultural traditions.

The identification of a new literary generation is the first topic that Martínez addresses in *The Other Side.* It serves as the nucleus of his introductory chapter, also titled "The Other Side." In an attempt to define his cultural generation, Martínez states:

> Mine is the generation that arrived too late for Che Guevara but too early for the fall of the Berlin Wall. Weaned on a blend of cultures, languages, and ideologies (Anglo/Latino, Spanish/English, individualist/collective), I have lived both in the North and the South over my twenty-nine years, trying to be South in the South, North in the North, South in the North and North in the South. . . . My quest for a true center, for cultural, political and romantic home, is stripped of direction.

The cultural and social revolution of the 1960s and the ensuing triumph of capitalism over communism, epitomized by the fall of the Berlin Wall, establish the historical parameters of this new literary generation. These writers, including Martínez, Luis Alfaro, Marisela Norte, and Guillermo Gómez-Peña, were affected by the changes of the 1960s, but they did not personally participate actively in the political movements. They also experienced the transformation of eastern Europe, but they do not belong to the social generation dubbed "Generation X." Thus, "betweenness" is the social and cultural space that these writers occupy. It is a de-centered space that allows them to cross different borders.

In his first chapter Martínez develops the historical and cultural events that influenced his generation. He identifies political figures, elements of popular culture, and violent images that typified the 1960s, 1970s, and 1980s:

> From Elvis to Fidel to Vietnam to Allende to L.A.'s eternal HOLLYWOOD dream-line to the shell-shocked *barrios* of Central America; and the flames leaping skyward from Watts, and the tear-gas canister that blew off Rubén Salazar's head outside the Silver Dollar Saloon on a hot August East L.A. afternoon when the Chicano Moratorium met its end, and the JFK/RFK assassination scenes playing over and over in my mind . . . shots ringing out, explosions that shook my childhood awake to the ways of the world: dreams are blown away, dreams are blown.

For the Chicano/Latino community Fidel Castro, Salvador Allende Gossens, John F. Kennedy, Robert F. Kennedy, the Watts Riots, the civil war in Central America, Elvis Presley, and Hollywood produce contradictory images of hope and despair, violence and peace, and creative fantasies and destructive realities. This diverse imagery characterizes the Chicano/Latino communities, which are constantly searching for a utopian state but encountering only dystopias.

These binary oppositions also typify the backbone of *The Other Side,* titled "L.A. Journal," which consists of nine fragmented sections integrated throughout the work. An earlier version of these sections was published as a single text in David Reid's anthology, *Sex, Death and God in L.A.* (1992), with the title "La Placita." For Martínez, La Placita, with its architectural landmarks of Chicano/Latino culture, is the most important symbolic space for the Chicano/Latino community in Los Angeles.

The literary depiction of La Placita in *The Other Side* represents an important shift in economic, political, and cultural power. Originally the center of such power during the periods of Spanish and Mexican rule, La Placita now belongs to the periphery in an Anglo-dominant city. La Placita also serves as a geopolitical space that signals new social, political, and cultural movements in Los Angeles. The location of La Placita symbolically represents the dominance of three cultures: Spanish, Mexican, and American. For traditional Anglo Americans, La Placita symbolizes its Spanish heritage; but for the Chicano community, it represents Mexican culture. In the 1980s Father Luis Olivares used the church located in La Placita as a community and resource center for new immigrants and political refugees from Central America. As La Placita established itself geographically and politically as an advocacy center for Central Americans, it acquired a new symbolic

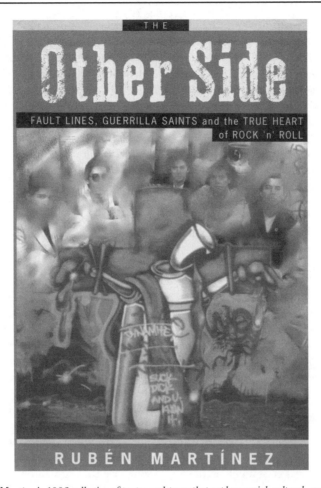

*Dust jacket for Martínez's 1992 collection of poetry and prose that explores social, cultural, and political themes*

and cultural meaning. La Placita became the geographical space where the formation of a Central American social and cultural consciousness began. Thus, La Placita continues to identify the demographic and cultural changes occurring in the Chicano/Latino communities: they are not a constant, homogeneous, and easily identifiable people, but rather a shifting, heterogenous mass of peoples.

La Placita as an urban space also serves as a focal point for the representation of other social problems affecting the community, such as AIDS. The theme of AIDS in *The Other Side* is first associated with Father Olivares, who died from this disease. It is also the principal subject that Martínez addresses in one of the *crónicas,* "A Death in the Family," in which he depicts the marginalization of the Chicano/Latino gay community and challenges the traditional values of Mexican society. This *crónica* traces the relationship between Daniel, a Chicano from Los Angeles, and Sergio, a Mexican, in order to show the discrimination suffered by gay Chicanos at the hands of their own people, who are unable

to accept homosexuality. Martínez narrates: "When Sergio's mother came up from Mexico City to visit her son soon after his AIDS diagnosis, she faced his homosexuality openly for the first time. She told him that she would not speak to him until after he 'changed his lifestyle.'" The irony of this *crónica* is that when Sergio immigrated to Los Angeles from Mexico City, he established his sexual independence but soon found himself at the bottom of the ladder economically, physically, and socially.

The economic and social subordination of the Chicano/Latino community also affects the cultural politics of Los Angeles, which Martínez repeatedly addresses in *The Other Side.* In particular, he is concerned with the political intentions of the Anglo literary establishment, which is represented by Peter Sellars, the organizer of the 1990 Los Angeles Cultural Festival. The analysis of this event depicts the marginalization of minority discourses by the cultural establishment. The festival was officially presented as an artistic multicultural event, but it became an example of what Martínez calls "cultural tourism." The Anglo literary establishment and Sellars invited only a few non-Anglo performers to participate in the festival but then used their presence to obtain funding from the city of Los Angeles. Martínez states: "I also was suspicious of the curatorial slant toward folkloric/traditional expressions at the big free events; the 'masses' were getting mariachis and Eskimo dancers, while the avant-garde remained entrenched at the usual pricy venues." Through his cynical tone Martínez criticizes the subordination of Chicano/Latino art and the dominance of Anglo performers. The peripheral status bestowed on Chicano/Latino artists by the Los Angeles Cultural Festival symbolizes the economic, social, and political suppression of the Chicano/Latino community.

The politics of multiculturalism is the subject of another *crónica* that analyzes the emergence of Tijuana as a multicultural center typifying the hybrid and postmodern city, an issue that has been studied by the anthropologist Néstor García Canclini in his work *Culturas híbridas* (1990). Martínez's literary representation of Tijuana is based on the analysis of a local artistic community—the Nopal group. The Nopal community is integrated by artists including Hugo Sánchez, Marco Vinicio González, Carmela Castrejón, María Eraña, and Angélica Robles. These border artists drafted a manifesto that documents their cultural movement as representative of the modern fin-de-siècle generation. According to Martínez, the Nopal community reflects "the clashing, the melding, the hybridization of culture that is taking place here, virtually invisible to the Northern eye." Martínez identifies himself with the Nopal group because it represents his own cultural generation, which is influenced by multiple literary traditions: Karl Marx and Bertolt Brecht, Juan Rulfo and Carlos Fuentes, and Jack Kerouac and Allen Ginsberg. This fusion is an example of intertextual zones, or what Michel Foucault has called, in *Les mots et les choses* (translated as *The Order of Things*, 1970), heterotopia. These intertextual zones create a hybrid text that challenges the hegemonic cultural practices that deny the artistic space of alternative groups.

The fusion of multiple discourses is also used as a political tool, especially in the *crónicas* in which Martínez presents the physical and political destruction of El Salvador. For instance, in "The Winds of October" Martínez documents the devastation that San Salvador suffered from a 1986 earthquake. The imagery of a natural disaster is compared to the political violence that El Salvador suffered as the result of the civil war. In part, this *crónica* echoes the literary representations of contemporary Mexican writers: Carlos Monsiváis in *Entrada libre: crónicas de la sociedad que se organiza* (Free Entry: Chronicles of a Society in Formation, 1987) and Elena Poniatowska in *Nada, nadie: las voces del temblor* (Nothing, Nobody: The Voices of the Earthquake, 1988), also incorporate political themes into the representation of the 1985 Mexico City earthquake.

Furthermore, Martínez incorporates psychological elements into this physical and political devastation in order to illustrate the suffering caused by political repression in El Salvador. In the *crónica* "Homecoming" Martínez portrays the capital, San Salvador, as a neurotic bazaar—a metaphor that characterizes the psychological instability of the country. This schizophrenic state is represented by Pedro, Martínez's cousin, who has been in and out of the country for political reasons. "Homecoming" also shows the transformation of Salvadorans' political consciousness, through the characterization of Soledad, Pedro's oldest daughter, who works for a human rights organization. Martínez's depictions of Pedro as a political exile and Soledad as a human rights activist are examples of the subaltern and postcolonial images that typify the writings of Central America.

In *The Other Side* Martínez also includes several poems that examine the social and political repression of Chicanos/Latinos in Central America and the United States. These poems provide examples of what has been called resistance literature. In general this type of writing has been done in exile, but in the United States there are also several Chicano and Latino writers who are currently publishing this type of literature. For example, Graciela Limón, a Chicana writer and professor of Spanish, published a novel titled *In Search of Bernabé* (1993), in which she recounts the fragmentation of Luz Delcano's family as caused by the political chaos of El Salvador.

Martínez's poetry is grounded in the literary traditions of Central American poets such as Roque Dalton, Ernesto Cardenal, and Claribel Alegría. The first poem, "There's a War," documents the civil war in El Salvador and depicts the destruction of the speaker's country, his family, and himself. Like Alegría and Cardenal, Martínez employs the landscape and topographical markers in this poem to create literary images that characterize past and present political oppression in El Salvador. For instance, he alludes to the 1932 eruption of the Izalco volcano, which serves as a metaphor for the massacre of peasants that occurred during this historical period. Martínez writes:

> In our ears a
> sledgehammer
> pounds the mountains,
> the insects land
> on the face, the face
> now broken lava, the lava
> running down my mother's

cheek. I am twelve.
I hear machine guns downtown.
I am twenty-four. My grandfather
was born in Guazapa.
1909. Thirty thousand dead.
1932.

These images and references are also present in Alegría's *Flores de volcán/Flowers from the Volcano* (1982). Both writers personify the environment in order to dramatize the violence that their communities have experienced. In their representation of violence Martínez and Alegría seek a utopian world. They employ a nostalgic poetic voice in which the memory of their ancestors becomes a focal point. They write in search of a mythical and peaceful society, but what they find instead is a community torn by violence.

Violence is also a social element that transcends geographical boundaries. In his poem "Manifesto" Martínez depicts the war at home (Los Angeles) and abroad (El Salvador). The structural symmetry of these representations of war parallels the social uprising of the 1960s in the United States created by the antiwar movement. Central Americans flee their countries to escape the chaotic world in which they live, and they come to the United States only to end up fighting oppressive institutions such as the Los Angeles Police Department.

Martínez also published several poems in *Invocation L.A.: Urban Multicultural Poetry* (1989), an anthology edited by Michelle T. Clinton, Sesshu Foster, and Naomi Quiñónez. "Hotel Ontario" is a reference to a downtown hotel in Mexico City that houses political exiles from other Latin American countries. "The Beginning," set in Venice Beach, is divided into four sections that alter-nate between summer and winter. The poem is structured by a binary opposition that symbolizes the conflict between the dream of a perfect world and the destruction of society, which is represented by a storm that turns into a hurricane. This destruction represents the two Americas that characterize Venice Beach: the myth of the promised land and the reality of poverty. Finally, "Untitled" is an earlier version of a poem titled "Generation," which Martínez includes in *The Other Side*. In this poem he associates his cultural generation with carnivalesque, violent, and macabre images. This imagery depicts a world upside-down, staged as a musical performance, established by the sound of bullets that are part of everyday life in urban America and Central America.

Rubén Martínez's *The Other Side* is an example of a postmodern text characterized by representation of communities without borders. His writings are associated with other Chicano/Latino writings that interpret the identity of border cultures–works written by Gloria Anzaldúa (*Borderlands: The New Mestiza/La frontera*, 1987), Guillermo Gómez-Peña (*Warrior for Gringostroika: Essays, Performance Texts, and Poetry*, 1993), and Luis Alberto Urrea (*Across the Wire: Life and Hard Times on the Mexican Border*, 1993). Furthermore, Martínez represents a new generation of Chicano/Latino writers who are identified by the diversity of their community, as well as by their use of multiple literary traditions in order to recount the political, economic, social, and cultural conflicts of their generation.

**Reference:**

Raúl Homero Villa, "Writing on the Border," *Alchemy* (1992): 39–43.

# María Cristina Mena
## (María Cristina Chambers)
### (3 April 1893 – 9 August 1965)

### Luis Leal
*University of California, Santa Barbara*

BOOKS: *The Water-Carrier's Secrets* (London & New York: Oxford University Press, 1942);

*The Two Eagles* (London & New York: Oxford University Press, 1943);

*The Bullfighter's Son* (London & New York: Oxford University Press, 1944);

*The Three Kings* (New York: Oxford University Press, 1946);

*Boy Heroes of Chapultepec: A Story of the Mexican War* (Philadelphia: Winston, 1953);

*The Collected Stories of María Cristina Mena,* edited by Amy Doherty (Houston: Arte Público, 1997).

SELECTED PERIODICAL PUBLICATION–
"Afternoons in Italy with D. H. Lawrence," *Texas Quarterly,* 7 (Winter 1964): 114–120.

Before the recent discovery of romances by María Amparo Ruíz de Burton, the short stories and novels of María Cristina Chambers were considered by literary historians to be the first fiction by a Mexican American woman writer. Chambers's stories began to appear in New York periodicals in 1913. She published initially under her maiden name, María Cristina Mena, and as María Cristina Chambers after her marriage in 1916. Burton and Chambers were ignored by mainstream literary historians and have only recently been rediscovered by scholars interested in reconstructing the history of Chicano literature. These discoveries correct the commonly held assumption that the first novel by a Mexican American was José Antonio Villarreal's *Pocho* (1959).

María Cristina Mena was born on 3 April 1893 in Mexico City, the daughter of a Mexican father and a Spanish mother. In 1907, at the age of fourteen, she moved to New York, where she lived most of her life. As Matthew Hoehn reports in *Catholic Authors* (1948), Mena started to write when she was ten years old. Her first and most successful story, "John of God, the

*María Cristina Mena*

Water-Carrier," appeared in *The Century Illustrated Monthly Magazine* in November 1913. The same month she published "The Gold Vanity Set" in *The American Magazine* in November 1913. Until 1916 she continued to publish short stories and articles in *The Century* and *Cosmopolitan.*

Chambers from the beginning created her own style, as she asserts in a brief note included by Matthew Hoehn in *Catholic Authors:* "I have never read, much less studied, the so-called 'methods' for learning how to write. I do not believe an aspirant for authorship needs any more than to learn from observation and much reading of good authors: that writing is something that is born and grows naturally through much working at it and particularly from one's own original and very personal feeling and thinking."

Chambers's style is distinct not only for her treatment of Mexican themes, customs, and characters but also for her use of Spanish idiom, a practice that magazine editors of the time tried to discourage. When she submitted "John of God" to the editor of *The Century,* Robert Sterling Yard, he suggested deleting Spanish words and some passages related to Mexican customs. *The Century* ultimately cut the story to half its original length. Mena bitterly complained but accepted the cuts. In a letter to Yard written during the fall of 1913 she told him:

> Please forgive my long delay in writing about the curtailed version of "John of God, the Water Carrier." . . . I was perplexed by discovering in the August *Century* a story very much longer than "John of God." . . . Could it be that the water carrier's lowly station in life made him a literary undesirable? Then what of Maupassant's Norman peasants, Kipling's soldiers and low-caste Hindoos, Myra Kelly's tenement children, and many other social nobodies of successful fiction?

In an undated letter accompanying the revised manuscript of her 1915 story "The Son of His Master," which Mena sent to Douglas Zabriskie Doty, Yard's successor at *The Century,* she agrees to "cut out many of the Spanish words—but I must make a special plea for the few that remain, all of them having a definite value of humor, irony, local color, or what not." Ultimately, *The Century* rejected the story, one of the first to address specifically the Mexican Revolution, and it went unpublished until 1931, when it appeared in *Household Magazine* as "A Son of the Tropics."

Another of Mena's stories, "Doña Rita's Rivals," was published in *The Century* in September 1914, in spite of the Spanish names, words, and phrases in the text. The story begins with a depiction of class distinctions in the Mexico of Don Porfirio Díaz, who was the dominant figure in Mexican politics from 1876 to 1911:

> With her packet of love-letters in her hand, Alegría returned to the roof—Alegría Peralta—, the band-master's daughter, who had committed the error of loving above her. She should have known better than to imagine that she would ever be received into a family of hat, she who was of shawl. . . . The females of a family of shawl—*de tápalo*—do not aspire to decorate their heads with millinery, for the excellent reason that God has

not assigned them to the caste *de sombrero.* Their consolation is that they may look down upon those *de rebozo.*

At the same time that Doty discouraged Mena's use of Spanish in her fiction, he was encouraging her to write about Mexican Americans. When he was appointed editor of *The Century,* he wrote a letter to Mena introducing himself and taking the opportunity to praise her work: "I know your work and have read several of the stories that have gone into the magazine, but this one, 'The Vine-Leaf,' is by all odds the best you have done. It is an exquisite thing, worthy of Maupassant, both for style and treatment." He added in a last paragraph: "I am wondering whether you would be interested to consider the idea of transplanting a Spanish character to this country; that is to say, using a Mexican character with an American background."

Mena responded to Doty two days later: "Such praise from you is very precious, and your letter has made me happier than I can tell you. Yes, I would be very glad indeed to make some stories of a Spanish or Mexican character with an American background and many thanks to you for the suggestion." Mena, however, never wrote such a story, or at least did not publish one. Commenting on this exchange of letters, Ernestina N. Eger—whose presentation on the writer at a 19 August 1986 National Endowment for the Humanities (NEH) is the most thorough study of her work—said:

> This unexplainable rejection of the primordial situation of Chicano literature—the conflict between two cultures—must surprise the contemporary reader. It might have been that she did not experience personal ethnic prejudice (or refused to acknowledge it), or that, first, her socio-economic class, and then her literary relations protected her from discrimination, or that she preferred to maintain a conciliatory rather than a conformational attitude; the fact is that Mena, upon confronting Mexican and American characters, never went beyond innocuous encounters among tourists in Mexico in which the American—both in real life and as characters—is eliminated by the cultural relativism of the author.

Mena was not interested in depicting Mexican Americans in her writings. According to Eger, two aspects of her fiction stand out—her desire to interpret Mexico and the Mexican people to the American reader and the plight of the indigenous people of Mexico. In a letter to Robert Sterling Yard, quoted by Eger, she wrote: "I expect to write more stories of Inditos than any other class in Mexico. They form the majority; the issue of their rights and wrongs, their aspirations and possibilities, is at the root of the present situation in my

*Illustration by F. Luis Mora for Mena's story "Doña Rita's Rivals" (from* The Century Illustrated Monthly Magazine, *September 1914)*

unhappy country. . . . I believe that American readers, with their intense interest in Mexico, are ripe for a true picture of a people so near to them, so intrinsically picturesque, so misrepresented in current fiction." This thematic unity, however, does not render her stories and novels monotonous, since she varies her treatment of these subjects considerably. The only exception in her body of work is the last story written during this period, "The Soul of Hilda Brunel" (1916), a tale dealing with reincarnation that does not take place in Mexico or feature Mexican characters.

More than ten years after Mena's marriage in 1916 to Henry Kellett Chambers, a dramatist and the editor of *Literary Digest* from 1920 to 1935, "John of God, the Water-Carrier" was republished in October 1927 in T. S. Eliot's *Monthly Criterion.* The following year the story was selected by Edward J. O'Brien for inclusion in *Best Short Stories of 1928.*

D. H. Lawrence's "Flowery Tuscany" appeared alongside "John of God" in the same issue of *The Criterion,* and Chambers wrote to Lawrence to tell him that she admired his *Mornings in Mexico,* which also appeared in 1927. Chambers was particularly delighted by the essay "El mozo," about an Indian named Rosalino, and told Lawrence that she was Rosalino's godmother. Lawrence, who had lived among the Indians in Taos and Mexico, was surprised at Chambers's characterization of the Indians. In an 11 November 1927 letter to her he wrote of "John of God": "And did you really write the story in *The Criterion?* I wondered very much what woman it was knew the Indian so intimately." The exchange of letters between Chambers and Lawrence lasted for two years and led to her visiting him in Italy just before his death in March 1930.

Chambers's article "Afternoons in Italy with D. H. Lawrence" (1964) gives an excellent description of Lawrence in his last days and affirms his abiding love of Mexican popular culture:

> "Do you know the Mexican song 'Cielito Lindo'?" I asked. Lawrence began to hum it and I began to sing it with him. I had never heard anyone but a Mexican give the perfect turn to the words with the music. But Lawrence did. When he finished he bowed his head over his knees and was silent again.

Chambers's interest in the writings of Lawrence lasted all her life. She actively sought to increase the distribution of his works, particularly *Lady Chatterley's Lover* (1928), which was banned in the United States until 1959. In "Afternoons in Italy with D. H. Lawrence" she relates: "Pino Orioli had agreed to print *Lady Chatterley's Lover* in Italy, when Lawrence had rewritten the novel three times, still couldn't find a publisher, and had almost decided to burn the manuscript. As for me, I had volunteered to take advance orders from friends and foes in the United States." In a 28 September 1929 letter to Chambers, Lawrence suggested to her that she open a bookstore to sell his books: "I wonder if you could have a tiny bookshop. Or better, if someone would let you be a partner in a shop, and you could have a little section for yourself, to deal only with special authors–say me, Norman Douglas, and others of Pino's connection." Although Lawrence acknowledged Chambers's efforts on his behalf, he apparently did not return the admiration she felt for him, as an 8 January 1930 letter to Dorothy Brett indicates: "María Cristina Chambers cabled she would come over in Feb. Frankly, I don't like her very much but don't say so to anybody, as she seems to slave for me–for my books in New York. Not that much is achieved."

Chambers published four novels between 1942 and 1946–*The Water-Carrier's Secrets* (1942), *The Two Eagles* (1943), *The Bullfighter's Son* (1944), and *The Three Kings* (1946)–and another novel in 1953, *Boy Heroes of Chapultepec: A Story of the Mexican War,* all of them about Mexican subjects and intended for young readers. They were each well received by contemporary reviewers. About her first novel, as quoted by Hoehn, she wrote: "I've written this book–my first juvenile–with 'the hand on the heart' as we say in Mexico. It is my small contribution and very large wish for a better

understanding by the youth of the United States–my adopted country–of Mexico–the country of my birth."

Because of her married name, Chambers's writing was generally overlooked in histories of Chicano literature until 1969, when she was mentioned in Lillian Faderman and Barbara Bradshaw's *Speaking for Ourselves: American Ethnic Writing.* In 1978 Raymund Paredes discovered Chambers's early short stories. In "The Evolution of Chicano Literature" he briefly comments on her stories, and his negative evaluation discouraged others from undertaking extensive studies of her fiction. Referring to her by her maiden name, under which she published most of the stories, Paredes criticizes Chambers's condescending attitude toward the Indians of Mexico, the subjects of much of her fiction:

> Mena was a talented story-teller whose sensibility unfortunately tended towards sentimentalism and preciousness. She aimed to portray Mexican culture in a positive light, but with great decorum; as a consequence, her stories seem trivial and condescending. Mena took pride in the aboriginal past of Mexico and she had real sympathy for the downtrodden Indians, but she could not, for the life of her, resist describing how they "washed their little brown faces . . . and assumed expressions of astonishing intelligence and zeal." Occasionally, she struck a blow at the pretensions of Mexico's ruling class, but to little effect; Mena's genteelness simply is incapable of warming the reader's blood.

After briefly discussing "The Vine Leaf" as an example of how Mena strikes a blow at the ruling class, he adds that she "tried to depict her characters within the boundaries of conventional American attitudes about Mexico" and that "she knew what Americans liked to read about Mexico so she gave it to them: quaint and humble *inditos,* passionate *señoritas* . . . a dashing *caballero* or two 'with music in their fingers.'" Paredes finds that Mena's portrayals are "ultimately obsequious, and if one can appreciate the weight of popular attitudes on Mena's consciousness, one can also say that a braver, more perceptive writer would have confronted the life of her culture more forcefully."

In her NEH presentation Eger attempted to qualify the consensus regarding the nature of Chambers's fiction. For her Chambers's writings represent the first examples of the *indigenista* movement in Mexico, which came to fruition in literature and the arts during the 1920s and 1930s. The view of Paredes, however, has dominated opinion on Chambers in contemporary Chicano literary criticism. In *Chicano Literature* (1982) Charles M. Tatum says: "María Cristina Mena is a fine writer whose short stories and sketches appeared early in this century in the *Century* and *American* magazines.

Unfortunately, her talents are undermined by her tendency to create obsequious Mexican characters who fit comfortably within the American reader's expectations. This results in trivial and condescending stories." Carl R. Shirley and Paula W. Shirley, in their *Understanding Chicano Literature* (1988), say: "María Cristina Mena wrote romantic, sentimental, completely idealized and unrealistic stories which she published from 1913 to 1916, principally in the magazine *Century*. It is unfortunate that her work did much to perpetuate among Anglo readers a romanticized stereotype of Mexican-Americans."

Despite her limited thematic repertoire, María Cristina Chambers should be given credit for her success in a demanding literary world where her writings were accepted by the most prestigious literary magazines of the period, an accomplishment that few Mexican American writers, of either gender, were able to attain. In the context of the development of Chicana fiction written in English, Chambers can be considered as the link between Amparo Ruíz de Burton and such writers as Jovita González, Fabiola Cabeza de Baca, Nina Otero, Nellie Sánchez Van de Grift, and Josephina Niggli. In the field of the Mexican American short story written in English she is a pioneer, although, since her stories were not collected until 1997, her influence has been minimal.

**References:**

Lillian Faderman and Barbara Bradshaw, eds., *Speaking for Ourselves: American Ethnic Writing* (Glenview, Ill.: Scott, Foresman, 1969);

Matthew Hoehn, ed., *Catholic Authors: Contemporary Biographical Sketches, 1930–1947* (Newark, N.J.: Mary's Abbey, 1948);

Raymund Paredes, "The Evolution of Chicano Literature," *MELUS,* 5 (Summer 1978): 71–110;

Carl R. Shirley and Paula W. Shirley, *Understanding Chicano Literature* (Columbia: University of South Carolina Press, 1988);

Charles M. Tatum, *Chicano Literature* (Boston: Twayne, 1982).

# José Montalvo

*(9 September 1946 – 15 August 1994)*

Francisco A. Lomelí
*University of California, Santa Barbara*

BOOKS: *Pensamientos capturados: poemas de José Montalvo* (San Antonio, Tex.: Privately printed, 1977);
*¡A mí qué!* (San Antonio, Tex.: Raza Cósmica, 1983);
*Black Hat Poems* (Austin, Tex.: Slough, 1987);
*The Cat in the Top Hat by Dr. Sucio (A.K.A. José Montalvo)* (San Antonio, Tex.: Privately printed, 1990);
*Welcome to My New World* (San Antonio, Tex.: Saddle Tramp, 1992).

OTHER: "Carmen," "Mis hijos," "Perpetuation," "Today," "Contradicciones de acuerdo," "Muerte cruel," "Salmo 8," "Summer of '66," "In memorium a Richard Morales," and "Recuerdos," in *El quetzal emplumece,* edited by Carmela Montalvo, Leonardo Anguiano, and Cecilio García-Camarillo (San Antonio, Tex.: Mexican American Cultural Center, 1976), pp. 142–147;
"Canto a Nuevo México" and "Canción de angustia," in *Flor y Canto IV and V: An Anthology of Chicano Literature from the Festivals Held in Albuquerque, New Mexico, 1977 and Tempe, Arizona, 1978,* edited by José Armas and Justo S. Alarcón (Albuquerque: Pajarito, 1980), pp. 100–101.

SELECTED PERIODICAL PUBLICATIONS– UNCOLLECTED: "Poesía" and "El paseo de marzo en San Antonio," *Caracol,* 1 (March 1975): 13, 14;
"Carta abierta a Cristal," *Caracol,* 2 (November 1975): 15;
"The Shadow of the Frito Bandito," *Caracol,* 2 (May 1976): 17.

José Montalvo is perhaps best described as a social poet. A product of the more militant elements of the Chicano movement of the 1970s, he adapted to the pragmatism of the 1980s without losing sight of his origins, both Mexican and Texan. He resembles Ricardo Sánchez in his penchant for nonconformity and zany iconoclasm, Abelardo Delgado in his lyrical exposition of humanistic ideas, and several other Chicano poets in his blending of nationalism with a pan-Hispanic focus.

*José Montalvo*

As a testimonial poet he speaks about the barrio while offering himself as an example of someone who has reached the state of a "mente concientizada" (socially aware mind), as Cecilio García-Camarillo described it in his introduction to Montalvo's first collection of poetry. Above all, Montalvo sought acceptance and affection in a hostile world.

José Luis Montalvo's worldview was deeply conditioned by the Texas-Mexico border environment in which he was raised. He was born in Piedras Negras in northern Mexico on 9 September 1946. From his working-class parents, Zapopan Villagrán and José Luis Montalvo, who crossed the border regularly, he received what he later termed a "commuter education." He moved with his family permanently to San Antonio in 1959. His grandmother played a central role in his upbringing, introducing him to the world of letters by teaching him how to read and write in Spanish at the age of five. As he recalled in an autobiographical profile in *El quetzal emplumece* (1976), she was "una mujer muy hembra, de poca escuela, pero muy leída, con una filosofía muy liberal y avanzada y de mucho corazón" (a very feminine woman, of little schooling, but well read, with a very liberal and advanced outlook and a lot of heart). Young Montalvo finished elementary school in Mexico in 1959 and later enrolled in Louis W. Fox Vocational and Technical School—which had a student body that was 95 percent Chicano and 5 percent black—where he completed his secondary education in May 1966. In *El quetzal emplumece* he recalled: "Antes de completar los 18 años, mi vida fue simple, normal y sin novedades" (Before I became eighteen years old, my life was simple, normal, and without novelties).

Somewhat lost in terms of goals and motivation and faced with the imminent threat of being drafted for military service in Vietnam, Montalvo joined the U.S. Air Force in 1967 and enrolled in San Antonio College, where he quickly discovered that he was unprepared for university study. On 28 October 1967 he married Carmen Sánchez, with whom he eventually had four children: José Luis, Juan Lorenzo, Canela, and Daniel Tizoc. For part of his tour of duty in the air force Montalvo was stationed at Camp New Amsterdam in the Netherlands; he was transferred to Laredo, Texas, in 1969. He claims that at this time his views on cultural politics crystallized and he was "reborn" a Chicano. A more complete awareness of his cultural self emerged, and the groundswell of civil-rights activism propagated by the Chicano movement helped shape his fervent sense of fairness and justice. During this period he became a spokesperson for disenfranchised Chicanos who were attempting to affirm their cultural identity, choosing poetry as his vehicle by which to move others.

After his honorable discharge in 1971 Montalvo returned to San Antonio College, graduating in 1973 with an A.A. degree. In 1974 he completed a B.A. in political science at St. Mary's University in San Antonio. Montalvo's experiences in the air force and with higher education afforded him the opportunity to master English while further developing his sensibilities in Spanish. After college he held part-time jobs in Austin and San Antonio as a community organizer, a vocational and educational counselor in a halfway house, and an adult-education instructor, and he participated in Chicano student and community organizations. He also became a youth activities counselor for the Texas Youth Commission. At the same time Montalvo

became keenly interested in politics through his affiliation with the Raza Unida (United People) Party. In 1974 he ran for state representative as a self-proclaimed "ultra-nationalist" under the banner of the party. He lost the election but learned useful lessons about racial politics in Texas.

The Spanish language, which Montalvo spoke almost exclusively during his formative years, is always important to his poetry. His love of the language is reflected in the nuances and cadences in all of his writings, but it is especially apparent in his first two collections, *Pensamientos capturados: poemas de José Montalvo* (1977) and *¡A mí qué!* (1983). Although he intersperses Spanish with English in his other collections, *Black Hat Poems* (1987), *The Cat in the Top Hat by Dr. Sucio (A.K.A. José Montalvo)* (1990), and *Welcome to My New World* (1992), they are mostly in English.

In *Pensamientos capturados* (Captured Thoughts) Montalvo pits his poetic voice against the complacency that threatens to halt the social gains made by Chicanos. The collection is divided into two sections, "La onda romántica y soñadora de José Montalvo" (The Romantic and Dreamer Trend of José Montalvo) and "La onda política y cínica de José Montalvo" (The Political and Cynical Trend of José Montalvo), in which the poet offers a loving homage to family—both immediate and cultural—and delves into the socially charged questions of his times. In the process he traces his burgeoning social awareness, as García-Camarillo notes in the introduction to the work: "no son poemas sutiles, poemas bien escultados, sino poemas emocionales que surgen de una manera abrupta, a veces caótica" (they are not subtle poems, nor well-sculptured poems, but rather emotional poems that emerge in an abrupt manner, at times chaotic). Sentiment prevails over craft as Montalvo's way of expounding on issues that concern him: love relationships, idealism, a male-centered sensuality, anger, war, and social criticism. Most of the poems in the first section—lyrical in nature and written in rhyme—allude to the intrigues of romance but also, in poems such as "Mis hijos" (My Children) and "Carmen," identify his family as a fundamental source of poetic inspiration.

The second half of *Pensamientos capturados* assumes a more angry and cynical tone, evoking Chicanismo, a sense of ethnic pride tied to a social conscience. The poet attacks capitalism in "Wampum" and "Poem in Three Sections" and sellouts in "El caballo blanco" (The White Horse), makes an appeal for historical vindication in "Versos chicanos" (Chicano Verses), and deplores militarism and commercialized celebrations in "G.I. José" and "Bicentennial Blues." He particularly mocks assimilated Mexican Americans who sing patriotic songs without fully realizing what they utter, as in

"Bicentennial Blues": "Pendejos—todavía no se dan cuenta [Dumb idiots—they still don't realize] that / This land is not our land; for: / manifest destiny robbed us of it."

¡A mí qué! (What Do I Care!), a collection of thirty-seven poems, shares with *Pensamientos capturados* its testimonial quality. As an ardent nationalist Montalvo first conducts an internal critique of the state of affairs within Chicano cultural circles. For example, in the opening piece, "Amor Chicano" (Chicano Love)—subtitled "A Poem/Play"—a nameless man and woman discuss issues surrounding gender dynamics, such as why the man is macho with his wife but meek with his Anglo boss. The poem stresses the importance of dealing with injustice in a consequential and consistent manner and presents liberation as a shared concept between the sexes. The text articulates other popular Chicano sentiments as a way of recovering cultural pride. Like *Pensamientos capturados* the work is clearly male-centered, although ¡A mí qué! tends to be less categorical in its indictments than his first book. As Ricardo Sánchez states in the introduction, Montalvo functions as a troubadour and town crier: "honesty, earthiness, and rusticity commingle with a darting/penetrating simplicity throughout the book."

¡A mí qué! includes humorous poems—for example, "Oda al jalapeño" (Ode to the Jalapeño) and "Pendejismos sin fronteras" (Platitudes without Boundaries)—as well as commentary on aesthetics, such as "Nosotros los poetas" (We the Poets), in which he stresses the importance of versatility in a poet:

> Pues para ser poeta
> hay que tener conciencia
> y hablar de todas cosas.
> No sólo de belleza
> y sueños muy hermosos
> y rosas rojas rojas.
>
> (Well, to be a poet
> you must have a conscience
> and speak of many things.
> Not just beauty
> and very pretty dreams
> and red red roses.)

Other poems in the collection use street slang as a way of capturing barrio realities. Montalvo no longer delves into conventional rhyme as his basic scheme of expression, opting for free verse and vibrant, flowing language, both English and Spanish. He also explores more international themes in poems such as "Canaan," "Para Nicaragua libre" (For a Free Nicaragua), and "Que nunca nos brille el sol" (May the Sun Never Shine on Us). Throughout, his idealism struggles with his cynical side. In "Tengo el sueño" (I Have a Dream) the

poet envisions his own destiny, which entails neither being boss nor slave. Perhaps the most lyrical poem of this collection, "Canción de angustia" (Song of Anguish) echoes the famous Latin American modernist Rubén Darío, who wrote in eloquent terms of the passing of youth. As a way of capping the many detours and thematic explorations of the collection, Montalvo concludes with "¡A mí qué!," which seems to try to minimize or dismiss the seriousness of the topics covered to that point. He expresses cynicism about the social stagnation afflicting Chicanos but also professes to having success in resisting such a state.

In *Black Hat Poems* Montalvo displays more confidence and flair. The title refers to Montalvo's favorite article of apparel, and the thirty-nine poems in the collection are intended to present a portrait of the poet through his many moods and sentiments. *Black Hat Poems* includes angry social commentary, as in "Why Trying to Be White Liberal Didn't Work For Me!" and "What the Sasquash-Centennial Means to Me!"; nostalgic evocations of family life, as in "Mama" and "An Apology to My Abuela" (Grandmother); and humorous verse ("With All Due Respect, to All the Chicanas Who Don't Look Like Tanya Tucker"). The collection displays poignant lyricism and even sensuality without becoming contrived or overly chauvinistic. The poems are carefully composed and thoughtful, offering heartfelt glimpses into the poet's and others' souls. As reflected in such provocative pieces as "El Barrio Revisited," however, Montalvo does not ignore the social problems that continue to plague Chicanos. The collection achieves a robust mixture of satire, parody, and warmth and eschews self-pity, although disillusionment and a biting mockery are apparent in "What the Sasquash-Centennial Means to Me!" and "Independence Day," with their suggestion that the meaning of these celebrations has become distorted.

In *The Cat in the Top Hat by Dr. Sucio,* a cartoon-filled satire of American institutions and such iconic figures as Uncle Sam, Montalvo's technique verges on the slapstick. The collection is a parody of the children's books by Dr. Seuss, although it is not intended for young readers (*sucio* is Spanish for *dirty*). Its more serious underlying purpose is to trace the development through history of a power-mongering mentality in the United States. Montalvo's customary sardonic tone pervades the collection, but otherwise the work does not fully display his poetic talents.

On 20 July 1990 Montalvo was diagnosed with colorectal cancer and given a few months to live, but he survived for another four years, a circumstance he attributed to the healing properties of aloe vera. His illness clearly influenced the writing of *Welcome to My New World,* a collection of thirty-four poems arranged in four

*Covers for Montalvo's books*

sections that balance form and content without losing a sense of experiential earthiness. The book uses Spanish only minimally and emphasizes a positive focus without succumbing to simple sentimentality. Montalvo is at his most personal, even introspective, although he does not take himself too seriously; yet, his mortality is a central issue, as indicated by "The Death of José Luis Montalvo": "I saw the face of death / And shook her cold, cold hand / I looked her in the eye / But could not understand." Some poems offer pointed criticism at the slow pace of social progress, but Montalvo is more concerned with celebrating life with gusto, as in "Living," in which he asserts: "Living is being at peace with your self."

This sense of spiritual calm saves Montalvo's poetry from becoming mushy or trite. His previous cynicism and contempt give way to a more forgiving tone at the same time that his iconoclasm leads him to lighthearted self-deprecation. A conviction that he has been reborn or received a second chance gives the collection an air of humility. In "I Am Not a Poet," for example, he proclaims himself a "bohemian of my people":

I am a simple *bohemio de mi raza*
who talks about beans and *jalapeños,*
. . . . . . . . . . . . . . . . . . . . . . . . . . . . . . .
I am the *bohemio* who sings about
*grandes ilusiones* and bigger *injusticias.*
I am the one who talks about
long lost loves
and new found dreams.

The repeated phrase "I am not a poet" serves to purge Montalvo's verse of academic baggage so that he can function as a *trobador perverso* (perverse troubadour), his people's conscience:

I am that voice inside of you
that reminds you
that you are not Hispanic,
but an ethnically
dysfunctional Mexican.
For you will never escape your past.
"You will never escape your past."

In other poems Montalvo expresses bitter disappointment, voicing his disenchantment over friends who have usurped his remaining energy, as in "I Am Tired." He recognizes he used to be the "giver of dreams," forgotten by people who at one time needed him. In the fourth section of the book, "Welcome to My New World," however, the poet successfully combines lyricism, ideology, and real-life experience, speaking with humble conviction and mature wisdom. He expresses hope for reconciliation with burdens of the past, embodied in the Spanish-sponsored explorer Christopher Columbus. "Welcome to My New World" addresses—and implicitly challenges—a metaphoric father on behalf of a new social order created by Chicanos, asserting "my soul grows and grows."

Montalvo's poetry was popular at festivals and poetry readings and his collections were well reviewed by critics, but there has been little serious scholarly consideration. His popularity appears to be more a result of his performances instead of his contributions to written culture. In an unpublished 1990 interview with Michael Pina he observed: "When you hear me shout in my poetry, that just doesn't come across in the reading of it. Maybe I should put my poetry on cassettes instead of books." Among the few commentaries on his work are the introductions to his books, by García-Camarillo and by Ricardo Sánchez, who in *¡A mí qué!* discusses Montalvo's verse as a "poetry of a people no longer in control of the past nor in step with modern amerikan [sic] technocracy."

The poetry of José Montalvo offers a tribute to the diversity of his people while striving to right wrongs. His poetry tends to emerge from everyday, even mundane, happenings, and he is particulary adept at observing and deciphering cultural customs. His literary project initially involved channeling his angst about the Chicanos' loss of their political and economic base, but his lyrical tendencies always led him to explore a wide range of themes concerning love relationships, family, and passing anecdotes or fantasies. His last two books, particularly, are dominated by his personal reflections on identity and mortality. *Welcome to My New World,* his most mature work, provides a fitting summary to the author's eclectic thematic explorations.

**References:**

Cecilio García-Camarillo, introduction to *Pensamientos capturados: poemas de José Montalvo* (San Antonio, Tex.: Privately printed, 1977), p. 6;

Ricardo Sánchez, "Earthiness, Honesty, and Rusticity: The Poetry of José Montalvo; an Introduction," in *¡A mí qué!* (San Antonio, Tex.: Raza Cósmica, 1983), pp. 8–10.

# Pat Mora

*(19 January 1942 –   )*

Nicolás Kanellos
*University of Houston*

BOOKS: *Chants* (Houston: Arte Público, 1984);
*Borders* (Houston: Arte Público, 1986);
*Communion* (Houston: Arte Público, 1991);
*A Birthday Basket for Tía* (New York: Macmillan, 1992);
*Nepantla: Essays from the Land of the Middle* (Albuquerque: University of New Mexico Press, 1993);
*Agua, Agua, Agua* (Glenview, Ill.: Goodyear Books, 1994);
*Listen to the Desert/Oye al desierto* (New York: Clarion, 1994);
*Pablo's Tree* (New York: Macmillan, 1994);
*The Desert Is My Mother/El desierto es mi madre* (Houston: Piñata, 1994);
*Agua Santa/Holy Water* (New York: Beacon, 1995);
*The Gift of the Poinsettia/El regalo de la flor de Nochebuena,* by Mora and Charles Ramírez-Berg (Houston: Arte Público, 1995);
*The Race of Toad and Deer* (New York: Orchard, 1995);
*Confetti: Poems for Children* (New York: Lee & Low, 1996);
*Uno, Dos, Tres/One, Two, Three* (New York: Clarion, 1996);
*Tomás and the Library Lady* (New York: Knopf, 1997);
*House of Houses* (Boston: Beacon, 1997);
*Aunt Carmen's Book of Practical Saints* (Boston: Beacon, 1997);
*This Big Sky* (New York: Scholastic, 1998);
*Delicious Hulabaloo/Pachanga deliciosa* (Houston: Piñata, 1998);
*The Rainbow Tulip* (New York: Viking, 1999).

Pat Mora has developed one of the broadest audiences of any Hispanic poet in the United States. Her crisp narrative style and the healing messages in her verse appeal to both adult and young readers. As a result, her poems have been reprinted in many elementary-, middle-, and high-school textbooks. While Mora has often been considered a soft-spoken feminist and a regional poet who celebrates life in the desert, her poetic vision has an all-embracing quality; she has written verse that explores the condition of women not only in the Southwest but also in Third World countries

*Pat Mora (courtesy of Mora)*

such as Pakistan. She has also written deeply humanistic essays and richly diverse children's literature that both encompasses Mexican folk traditions and addresses such modern topics as adoption.

Patricia Estella Mora was born on 19 January 1942 in El Paso, Texas, the daughter of an optician, Raúl Antonio Mora, and Estella Delgado Mora. She attended Catholic schools in El Paso and received her higher education at institutions in the city, graduating with a B.A. from Texas Western College in 1963 and an M.A. in English from the University of Texas at El Paso in 1967. After finishing college in 1963 she worked as an English teacher in the El Paso Independent School District and El Paso Community College; eventually she returned to the University of Texas at El Paso as an instructor and from 1981 to 1989 served as a university administrator and museum director. In 1986 Mora received a Kellogg Fellowship to study cultural conservation issues nationally and internationally. Subsequently, she became a consultant for the W. K. Kellogg Foundation on U.S.-Mexico youth exchanges. In addition to the Kellogg honor, Mora received in 1994 a National Endowment for the Arts fellowship to further the writing of her poetry, which resulted in the publication of *Agua Santa/Holy Water* (1995). With her background in education and in exploring issues of cultural development and conflict, as well as her skill as a reader of her poetry, Mora has become a popular speaker and guest presenter at gatherings of teachers and education professionals around the country.

Mora is the mother of three children, William, Elizabeth, and Cecilia, all from a first marriage to William Burnside. In 1984 she married an archaeologist, Vernon Lee Scarborough, with whom she has traveled extensively. When Scarborough relocated from the University of Texas at El Paso to the University of Cincinnati, Mora made the transition from the West Texas desert to the colder Midwest. Since moving to Ohio, Mora has published several books for children, including *A Birthday Basket for Tía* (1992), *Listen to the Desert/ Oye al desierto* (1994), *Pablo's Tree* (1994), *The Desert Is My Mother/El desierto es mi madre* (1994), and *The Gift of the Poinsettia/El regalo de la flor de Nachebuena* (1995); a collection of autobiographical essays, *Nepantla: Essays from the Land of the Middle* (1993); a family memoir, *House of Houses* (1997); and a volume of religious poems, *Aunt Carmen's Book of Practical Saints* (1997). Mora began publishing poetry in the late 1970s in little magazines such as the *Americas Review* as part of the first wave of the Chicano literary movement. Her first books of poetry clearly indicate her interest in shamanism and biculturalism. *Chants* (1984) and *Borders* (1986) each received the Southwest Book Award, critical acclaim, and a place in college and high-school curricula. Her third book of poetry, *Communion* (1991), solidified her reputation with scholars and general readers.

In *Borders* Mora posits the metaphor that unites most of her work. She is intrigued by borders and interprets them not only in physical but broad philosophical terms. Having dwelled on the border between Mexico and the United States for much of her life, she came to see that Mexican Americans, wherever they resided, lived a type of border existence. While the border can serve to provide a vantage point from which to observe and understand two societies, such a perspective tends to make one feel like an outsider, so that alienation becomes a central condition of the border dweller. Mora has stressed the border as a position of power, a place in which to bridge divisions, heal wounds, and facilitate mutual understanding. This process begins in *Chants,* in which the inhospitable and uninhabitable borderland is envisioned as a mother who nurtures her

Cover for Mora's 1991 collection of poetry, which includes poems inspired by her travels to Cuba, India, and New York City

children: "she: the desert / She: strong mother" ("Mi Madre").

In "Legal Alien" Mora uses the metaphor of the border to represent the outsider status of Mexican Americans:

> an American to Mexicans
> a Mexican to Americans
> a handy token
> sliding back and forth
> between the fringes of both worlds
> . . . . . . . . . . . . . . . . . . . . . . . . . . .
> Of being prejudged
> bilaterally.

She also sees the border in terms of social class and racism: the skin color of Mexicans is a border to Anglos in "Mexican Maid," and class differences separate Mexicans from Mexican Americans in "Illegal Alien." In other poems in *Chants,* such as "Legal Alien," "Abuelita

*Cover for Mora's 1997 memoir*

Magic," and Curandera," however, Mora begins to see the borderland as a center of power in itself. In particular, she personifies the desert in strong, enduring women such as her grandmother who nurtured her when she was growing up. She continually finds the strength in Mexican women, and eventually in herself, to bridge gaps in society, whether by commanding respect in an industry or university boardroom, speaking before an audience of educators, or pursuing relationships with men. Of particular significance in *Chants,* however, is the magical relationship between the poet and Mother Desert; the poet demonstrates shamanistic abilities, tapping into the mysterious power of the desert, its rhythms, its ability to heal with the herbs that grow there, its warmth, and its toughness and strength: "Desert women know / about survival" ("Desert Women"). Behind this idea of the desert being a strong mother is the somewhat romantic idea that women are closer to nature than men.

This identification with the desert provides a great deal of the power that Mora brings to her poetry readings, in which she often evokes the image of a sha-

man or *curandera* (faith healer), another of her alter egos in *Chants.* The image of the Desert Mother is the central conceit in "Mi Madre" and became the basis for one of Mora's books for children, *The Desert Is My Mother,* which won the Stepping Stones Award in 1995.

In *Chants, Borders,* and *Communion* Mora also attempts to negotiate the border between the past and the present, so as to draw upon the strong women who preceded her: her aunt Ygmacia Delgado, whom she and her siblings called Tía Lobo (Aunt Wolf); her grandmother, and her mother, as well as *curanderas* and rebels. In *Nepantla* she adds the Mexican colonial poet and intellectual Sor Juan Inés de la Cruz to her personal pantheon of influences. Mora envisions herself as a link in the tradition of passing on wisdom to her own daughters and to society at large, choosing the best from the past and making what changes are necessary: "To transform our traditions wisely, we need to know them, be inspired and saddened by them, choose for ourselves what to retain. But we can prize the past together, valuing the positive female and Mexican traditions. We can prize the elements of the past as we persist in demanding, and creating, change." Mora rejects the limited roles society has forced on women in the past, especially those that control their sexuality. Such rituals and practices as burying a female child's umbilical cord in the house or placing orange blossoms in the hair of a bride are censured in the poems "Dream" and "Aztec Princess," for example.

In *Borders* Mora's central metaphor broadens considerably to characterize relationships between men and women as well as the cultural and political relationships of Chicanos to the larger society. Again, Mora emphasizes traversing borders and creating understanding. In fact, in 1991 she said in an interview published in *Hispanic Writers:* "I write in part because Hispanic perspectives need to be part of our literary heritage; I want to be part of that validation process."

In *Communion* Mora extends her metaphysics of borders to international politics, to poverty in the Third World, and to a recognition of the similarities between Chicano and other minority cultures in the United States and the marginalized peoples of poor countries around the world. As reflected in the title of the collection, Mora emphasizes coming together, healing rifts, and creating a global community. She states in *Nepantla:* "My community is not only my ethnic community but also all the like-minded souls seeking a more equitable world." In Mora's travels, many of which are documented in *Nepantla,* she has seen race and class differences that bear comparisons with the minority condition in the United States, and in poems such as "Too Many Eyes," "Veiled," and "The Mystery" she identifies the many faces of the patriarchy that suppresses women in various societies.

In *Nepantla* Mora devotes extended attention to the borders she has encountered in her own life and expands upon the themes of her poetry and the lessons she has learned. The style of the book, which oscillates between the poetic and the discursive–at times even becoming preachy and pedagogical–reflects a particular division in her life, the conflict between her work as an administrator and as a poet and writer.

Mora's poetry has attracted the attention of Chicano and feminist scholars and reviewers from smaller journals, who generally appreciate her shamanistic imagery and her idealistic desire to unite and heal. A reviewer of *Chants* in *Dusty Dog Reviews* asserted: "This is richly feminine poetry, in which a healthy womanly sensuality is being continuously awakened like the living dawn that spreads its westward lights across the world, continuously unveiling a physical magic." Anya Achtenberg wrote in *Contact II* (1995), "Healers, those

who restore harmony by bringing together what seems to be separate, often suffer but possess great 'magic,' and Mora's is a healing voice." Jewelle Gómez wrote in *Hurricane Alice* (Spring/Summer 1984) that "Mora has a powerful grasp of the music of everyday language, and she is not afraid of dark, complex feelings. . . . Mora's simplicity and economy create a haunting sense of timelessness." Gómez went on to say that none of the women in *Chants* "have been bowed by the weighty roles chosen for them in this society. To be old, to speak only one language, are not stigmas; they are conditions in a natural transitory order. . . . This collection is rich, spirited, promising."

Bryce Milligan in the *National Catholic Reporter* (10 May 1991) found the poems in *Communion* to be "powerful, imaginative and well crafted. . . . it is clear the poet is giving birth to a new voice." In *Texas Books in Review* (Winter 1991), however, Betsy Colquitt found some of the poems in this new voice to be "more engaged intellectually than emotionally" and suggested that Mora's best poems were still those that related to the Southwest and her bilingual, bicultural identity.

Mora's books for children have been acclaimed almost universally for the sensitive and deft portrayals of Mexican American and Mexican culture. Mary Sarber's assessment of *A Birthday Basket for Tía* in the *El Paso Herald-Post* could be applied equally to all of Mora's picture books: "This is an outstanding addition to the growing body of literature that will help Hispanic children identify with their culture." Mora's writing for children has also helped to bring Hispanic culture to non-Hispanic children.

**References:**

Anya Achtenberg, "Healing with Age," *Contact II* (1985): 31–32;

Linda C. Fox, "From Chants to Borders to Communion: Pat Mora's Poetic Journey to Nepantla," *Bilingual Review/Revista Bilingue* (1996);

Patrick Murphy, "Grandmother Borderland: Placing Identity and Ethnicity," *Interdisciplinary Studies in Literature and Environment* (1993): 35–41;

Kristina Passman, "Demeter, Kore, and the Birth of the Self: The Quest for Identity in the Poetry of Alma Villanueva, Pat Mora, and Cherríe Moraga," *Monographic Review,* 6 (1990): 35–41;

Sonia Saldívar-Hull, "Feminism on the Border: From Gender Politics to Geopolitics," in *Criticism in the Borderlands: Studies in Chicano Literature, Culture, and Ideolog,* edited by Héctor Calderón and José David Saldívar (Durham, N.C.: Duke University Press), pp. 203–220.

# Joe Navarro
*(13 October 1953 –   )*

Luis Leal
*University of California, Santa Barbara*

and

David Conde
*Metropolitan State College of Denver*

BOOKS: *Reflections of an Aztlaneco,* preface by Ramón Del Castillo (Oakland, Cal.: Unity Publications, 1987);
*For the Sisters: A Collection of Poetry* (Denver: Aztlaneco Publications, 1991);
*Rhythmic Rage: A Collection of Poetry* (Denver: Privately printed, 1991);
*Animal Behavior* (Denver: Privately printed, 1991);
*Awakening* (Denver: Privately printed, 1992).

Joseph Lewis Guadalupe ( Joe) Navarro was born on 13 October 1953 in San Francisco, California. Brought up by his mother after the family was abandoned by his father, Navarro was a typical product of the many Chicano families raised mostly on welfare. He was expelled in the eleventh grade for wearing a brown beret, a symbol of Chicano pride and commitment, although his grades had been failing for some time before that.

After his expulsion Navarro launched himself more fully into the Chicano political struggle, helping to found an organization called "Free Los Siete de la Raza," which was named after a successful movement to free seven Latino youths who had been framed by the San Francisco police for killing a police officer; they were finally acquitted of the crime. Navarro went on to work in a foundry and became involved in union politics. In 1975 he was elected president of the International Molders and Allied Workers' Union Local 164, a position he held for six years.

Navarro moved to Denver, Colorado, in 1982 to seek better employment opportunities. In Denver he finished his high-school education and received a B.A. from Metropolitan State College with a major in English and a minor in Spanish. He also received his teaching certification. A *Mechista* (member of MECHA,

*Joe Navarro (courtesy of Navarro)*

a militant Chicano student organization) of long standing, Navarro continued to represent Chicano student concerns on college and university campuses. He was a founder and campaign coordinator of Coloradans for Language Freedom, a group organized in

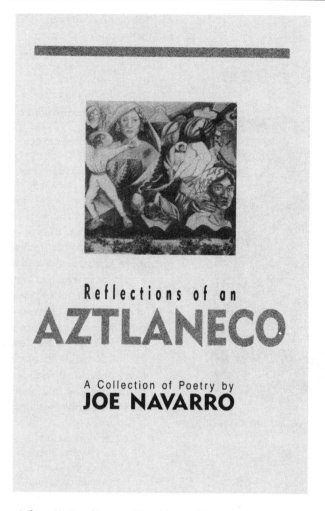

Reflections of an
# AZTLANECO

A Collection of Poetry by
**JOE NAVARRO**

*Cover for Navarro's first collection of poems, which addresses Chicano experiences and Third World concerns*

1988 to fight the "English Only" movement in that state. He also worked in Jesse Jackson's 1984 and 1988 presidential campaigns and was a founder of the Colorado chapter of the National Rainbow Coalition. In 1995 he moved to California, where he was active in opposition to Proposition 227, a ballot initiative to end bilingual education in the public schools in the state.

Working side by side with people of other races and cultures, as well as traveling abroad, gave Navarro a strong multicultural perspective and a sense of identification with all oppressed people of the world. His writing reflects these preoccupations.

In Navarro's poetry published since 1987 traditional Chicano themes predominate: identity, barrio life, racial confrontations, nationalism, drug addiction, gender relations, and Chicano pride. Representative of the pride theme is "Untitled," from the collection *Reflections of an Aztlaneco* (1987):

Where did I come from? You ask.
I came from a great civilization
. . . . . . . . . . . . . . . . . . . . . . .
I am the heir to the traditions of
Cuauhtémoc, Benito Juárez, Emiliano Zapata.

The titles of the six sections of *Reflections of an Aztlaneco*— "Experiences in the Barrio," "La Migra" (Immigration Authorities), "La Familia," "Education and the Media," "Central America," and "South Africa"–indicate Navarro's consistent interest in raising the reader's awareness of major social and historical issues in both the Chicano experience and that of Third World peoples. "Thank You Mexicano" attempts to recognize the contributions of the Mexican immigrant to Chicano life by finding common cause in the struggle to maintain culture and identity in the face of mainstream oppression. "My Chicana Daughter" deals with Chicano parental involvement in the education of their children, particularly when there is a need to correct what the

# Rhythmic Rage

A Collection of Poetry by
**JOE NAVARRO**

*Cover for one of Navarro's 1991 books, which includes poems that
focus on social protest*

teachers are saying about people of color. "Misty Blue Radiation" addresses the desensitized human condition produced by the modern love affair with television. "Sounds So Right to Me" invokes the South African antiapartheid leader Nelson Mandela as a symbol of "justice and liberty." Many of the poems offer slices of everyday life told in a conversational style, much like the scenes depicted in the *costumbrista* (dealing with regional customs) literature of nineteenth-century Spain and Latin America.

"Men and Women" addresses the difficulties of putting intellectual commitment to equality of the sexes into practice after centuries of male chauvinism. Gender relations are also the predominant theme in the five poems collected under the title *For the Sisters* (1991), although these poems are much more personal. The book is dedicated "to all the sisters of Aztlán, my wife, Lucía, and my daughters,

Olivia and Adriana." The poetic voice longs for a harmonious existence between men and women, Chicanas and Chicanos. In "Hermana" (Sister) a Chicana complains about her situation:

> I'm tired of how we're treated
> I want to be equal instead
> . . . . . . . . . . . . . . . . . . . .
> It's bad enough to be oppressed
> By the others
> But it hurts more to be oppressed
> By our own brothers.

Social protest is a major theme in the fifteen poems collected in *Rhythmic Rage* (1991). In the acknowledgments Navarro says: "This book was written to reflect the struggles and aspirations of oppressed people everywhere who are struggling for peace, justice, equality, democracy, and self-determination." Most of the poems have the characteristics of what is known in Chicano literary criticism as "Movimiento poetry," the poetry written during the 1960s and 1970s by authors such as Rodolfo "Corky" Gonzales, Alurista, José Montoya, and Ricardo Sánchez. Chicano cultural motifs predominate. The title poem was inspired by the popular music of Carlos Santana:

> When I first heard
>         Carlos Santana jam
> My pride exploded
> Into a temperamental
>         Rhythmic Rage

Drug abuse is one of the reasons for the poet's rage, as in "Someone Else's Plan":

> Poof! and white powder turns green
>     Selling a self destructive rage
> A rage where hot bodies turn cold
>     By those who can't help it
>         Quick cold cash
>     And quick cold death

Although Navarro's literary production is not extensive, it is rich and varied in themes. His perceptive treatment of social and psychological problems is one of Navarro's strong points, as is his style. What Ramón Del Castillo says in his preface to *Reflections of an Aztlaneco* can be applied to all of Navarro's work: it is "a reaffirmation of our cultural identity as Chicanos. . . . José portrays human emotion as he leads into the past as well as the future with strong images . . . his book is about humanity, brotherhood, and equality."

# Raúl Niño

*(15 March 1961 –   )*

Marc Zimmerman
*University of Illinois at Chicago*

BOOK: *Breathing Light* (Chicago: MARCH/Abrazo, 1991).

OTHER: Carlos Cumpián, ed., *Emergency Tacos: Siete Poets con Picante,* includes poems by Niño (Chicago: MARCH/Abrazo, 1989).

With *Breathing Light* (1991) the Chicago Chicano poet Raúl Niño positioned himself as a writer committed to exploring individual and cultural, as opposed to social and political, concerns. Perhaps the least public and least extroverted of the Mexican poets one could call "Chicano" in Chicago–a group that includes Chicano poets writing mainly in English, recent emigrants from Mexico, and, above all, the self-named *Generacion mojada,* or "Wetback Generation," writing in Spanish–he represents an important dimension of contemporary Chicago and national Chicano writing as it has developed from its more militant roots and uses in the 1960s.

Raúl Niño was born on 15 March 1961 in Monterrey, Mexico, and was raised in southern Texas. In the late 1960s he moved with his mother to the Chicago suburbs where he worked as a domestic.

He graduated from New Trier West High School in 1980. He attended Loyola University for three years; there he met Sandra Cisneros, who encouraged his attempts at writing and introduced him to other writers in Chicago. This series of events eventually led to his introduction to MARCH/Abrazo Press and its editor, Carlos Cumpián, and to the publication of his collection, *Breathing Light,* in 1991.

Few of Niño's early poems have Chicano, Mexicano, or Latino themes, reflecting his sense of disconnectedness, which stems from the discomfort he feels with both English and Spanish. His initial reliance on precise English in his poetry was partly a response to those for whom his spoken English had marked him as an ethnic outsider. His Mexican cultural heritage began to assert itself, however, as he related in July 1994: "I've only gradually brought Spanish into my writing–it's as if it's sought me out and demanded to speak through

*Raul Niño (photograph by Donna Seaman, 1998)*

me, in spite of all my limitations in the language, as if it won't let me go or let English kill it."

*Breathing Light* can be viewed as the poetic autobiography of Niño's experiences as a child and young adult. The collection includes few narrative poems but has a vivid sense of place, evoking the neighborhoods of Chicago and the hills and factories of Monterrey. The volume addresses such topics as love and fantasy, climate, and memory. Niño utilizes a variety of poetic forms but favors slender, short-lined lyrics that convey situations, feelings, and moods with a minimum of words. Chicago winters figure prominently in several

*Cover for Niño's 1991 collection of poetry, which explores his ties to Chicago and Monterrey, Mexico*

poems. In "February on Eighteenth Street," for example, lovers walking through the heart of the city's most recognizable Mexican barrio hold hands as they stare longingly at a map of Mexico in a store window. "February on Eighteenth Street" is one of the few poems in the collection that alludes directly to questions of Mexican or Chicano identity and expressions, however. Instead the poet seems to invert the notion of ethnic identity and dreams of throwing off the burdens of race and class. He is disenchanted with his ancestral culture of sun, sky, and spirit, dominated by conservative norms of arranged relationships, marriage, and stability. These poems suggest a sense of self removed from his Chicano identity, which is tied to negative memories of his birthplace.

"Monterrey Sketches" is a four-part prose poem that meditates on the city Niño loves and hates so acutely. In the first part he establishes the basis of his ambivalence: this city is where his mother was seduced and made into a "woman whose future was becoming

solitude." In part 2 the poet remembers Monterrey's dry winds, sulphurous factories, and shantytowns, far removed from any nostalgic sense of a Mexican paradise. He writes: "I am filled with rage because I have no other means of expression towards you other than meanness. I know that you are ambivalent, what's another expatriate to you? But remember this, though I may be far away, I will always make room for you, between my pain and happiness."

In part 3 of "Monterrey Sketches" the poet crosses "borders backwards in memory." He evokes his mother's border crossings, when she held him as "sleeping contraband tight to her breast." He recalls his "first and only conversation" with his father, whom he met when he was ten: his father gives him some coins and tells him to be good. In part 4 the poet envisions Monterrey as a "mural of muted color and awful beauty," the setting for a dream of a green mountain and of the dog people who "wandered south to the valley, long before the tribes became nations, long before stones were chiseled into pyramids and calendars, long before the sun became ravenous for beating hearts, long before the bearded ones on horses begot my people."

In "Hijo de la Malinche" (Son of la Malinche) the poet affirms his American identity. He reminds his fellow Americans that "We are all immigrants / fallen from the same sky / into a land claimed / long before Columbus." The poem also invokes Niño's mestizo origins and—sounding a theme present in "Monterrey Sketches"–defiantly asserts his status as an "hijo de la chingada" (son of the raped woman): "La historia de mi raza / is older than this colonized nation / my blood runs in rivers / no border can divide, / in me oppressor and the oppressed / drink from the same cup." Pointing to the colonization of Mexican lands, he concludes: "America! / If I am illegal / then we are all illegal!"

In the same poem Niño says that his ancestors passed on to him "the language of the sun in an immigrant's voice." There is no doubt that Niño's English is marked by his original, partially forgotten Spanish–from whence comes the solemnity and formality of his tone, his limited use of contractions, and his syntactic twists and turns. Caught between languages, he devotes the poem "Querido lenguaje mío" (My Beloved Language)to this unease, using images of light and seed to express his sense of a rich Latino identity. The question of identity is posed in Spanish at the beginning of the poem: "Quién soy yo?" (Who am I?). He is not a piñata waiting for a blind swipe, he says, but "maíz" (corn), "frijoles" (beans), "pulque" (a fermented beverage made from maguey plants), and the smell of "velas" (candles) used in prayer. The "hijo de la Malinche" addresses the Spanish language as his mother:

Querido lenguaje,
soy tu hijo
[Beloved language
I am your son]
alone on these English leaves of grass,
my blood refusing to thicken
through the syntax of amnesia
the texture of my voice
clings to you,
from song to silence
in hushed communications
through the din of assimilation.

He considers the origin of languages described in the myth of the Tower of Babel, "the original Word corrupted / tossed into the melting pot / bribed to forget,"

and tells his mother tongue that though some of her sons have forgotten her and some never knew the quality of her intonations, "you are the mirror / I the tone that sinks into you." The poem concludes with a triumphant acceptance of Spanish, despite Niño's insecurity over his fluency:

Esta es la noche y
la voz nos dio la luz
tu eres la tierra y
mis palabras las semillas.

(This is night and
the voice gave us light
you are the earth and
my words the seeds.)

This poem, which links Niño's relationships to his mother, his mother language, his adopted country, and his expressive identity, marks the culmination of the themes of *Breathing Light*. That the book concludes with a rather unfocused poem, "Zeb and His Mistress," raises questions not only about the poet's capacity for self-criticism but also about his ultimate attitude toward the Mexican themes in his work. Ironic allusions to "conquistadores" and "Aztlan" in a poem about a dog who is seen as the "legitimate inheritor / to a race of chiefs" hardly reinforce a sense of deep ethnic commitment and identification. Since publishing *Breathing Light* Niño has been asked to write specifically ethnic and "raza" poems in the manner of "Hijo de la Malinche"; he says that he has sometimes been tempted to do so, although he confesses to difficulty with these themes. He worked on a collection of poems, "The Flowery War," based on Aztec campaigns and struggles, but abandoned the project, feeling that it traded on an affected persona as a Mexican poet in the United States. Niño has also assembled a small body of intimate reveries, meditations and musings, minimalist poems, and poem fragments with the working title "The Book of Mornings," and has drafted other longer-lined, more complex, and visionary prose poems for a collection tentatively titled "Still Life with Hands."

### References:

"Poetry: Raúl Niño," *Howl*, 1 (Summer 1992): 3;

Marc Zimmerman, *U.S. Latino Literature: An Essay and Annotated Bibliography* (Chicago: MARCH/Abrazo Press, 1992), p. 69.

# Marisela Norte

(28 December 1955 – )

## Michelle Habell-Pallán
### University of Washington, Seattle

PLAY PRODUCTIONS: *La Condición Femenina,* by Norte and María Elena Gaitán, Los Angeles, Self Help Graphics, 7 August 1982;

*Exito,* San Francisco, Galeria de la Raza, July 1983.

RECORDINGS: "Lost in Los," on *Black and Tan Club,* New Alliance Records, NAR CD 060, 1991;

*Norte/word,* performed by Norte, New Alliance Records, NAR CD 062, 1991;

"Three Little Words," on *DisClosure: Voice of Women,* New Alliance Records, NAR CD 067, 1992;

"Angel," on *L.A. Photo Journal,* Voyager, 1992.

VIDEO: *Exito,* ASCO, 1985.

OTHER: "Each Street/Each Story," in *201: Homenaje a La Ciudad de Los Angeles: Latino Experience in Literature and Art,* edited by Helena Maria Viramontes (Los Angeles: Los Angeles Writers Association/ Self Help Graphics and Art, 1982), p. 57;

"Baby Sitter Girl," in *Hispanics in the U.S.A.,* edited by Ellen Bick Meier and Birgit Jeng (Transcript of a radio program for Denmark's Radio for Under-visnings-ministeriet, April 1983) p. 17;

"976-LOCA," in *Recent Chicano Poetry/Neueste Chicano-Lyrick,* edited by Heiner Bus and Ana Castillo (Bamberg, Germany: Universitätsbibliothek Bamberg, 1994) pp. 15–30.

SELECTED PERIODICAL PUBLICATIONS–
UNCOLLECTED:

POETRY

"June 24th" and "Pictures," *Milestone Magazine* (1978): 21, 31;

"Salmo Para: Ella," *Corazón de Aztlán,* 1 (March/April 1982): 8–9;

"Las Metropolitanas" and "Peeping Tom Tom Girl," *El Tecolote Literario* (July 1983): 7, 9;

"Se habla inglés," *Raras Avis: Southern California Women Writers,* 6–7 (1983): 89–93;

*Marisela Norte in 1994 (photograph by Saul Picazo)*

"La Bruja y La Señorita," *Electrum,* 30 (Summer 1983): 30–32;

"El Club Sufrimiento 2000," *Rattler: American Poetry and Art,* 4 (1987): 37–42;

"Dolores Fuertes" and "Wind cries mari," *Alchemy,* 1 (1992): 14–16, 32–33;

"Shelf Life," *Caffeine April,* 1, no. 2 (1993): 23–26;

"Misfortune in Woman's Eyes," *(untitled): a literary art journal,* 2 (Fall 1993): 29–32.

NONFICTION

"Harry Gamboa Jr.: No-Movie Maker," *El Tecolote Literario* (July 1983): 3, 12.

Marisela Norte is known for the sharp literary acumen demonstrated in her cinematic depiction of Los Angeles cityscapes. Though Norte constructs sweeping takes of Los Angeles public spaces, her forte lies in her ability to focus her audience's attention on images that less-keen observers usually overlook. Her writing tends to circulate more often in spoken-word form—compact discs, cassettes, and live performances—than as written text; Cynthia Rose describes Norte's performances as "something to behold, her low, sweet voice shifting from English to a passionate, rhythmic *español,* her words capturing contemporary moments as brilliantly as Kodachrome snapshots." Norte's gift of humor and a biting sense of irony combine to capture her audience. She is part of a group of artists who have produced what George Lipsitz calls some "of the most dynamic and innovative forms of youth culture in the postindustrial era." Her prose narratives and plays have also contributed to the ever transforming category of transnational border writing by exploring what D. Emily Hicks calls "the border feminine subject." Her work depicts the tensions many working-class women feel about their lives, specifically the tension generated between the desire for progress in the struggle for economic and social equality and an immobility that seems at times impossible to break.

Marisela Norte was born on 28 December 1955 to Mexican parents who had immigrated to southern California in the late 1930s or early 1940s. Her mother, Eloisa, was a medical office administrator; her father, Armando, a retired film projectionist, worked in various factory jobs. Norte recalls that her father banned English from their home; but growing up during the 1950s and 1960s, she learned to speak impeccable standard English at public schools and from television, radio, and movies, though she retained her fluency in the Spanish language. While trips with her father to the movies and through East Los Angeles neighborhoods left a lasting impression on her, so did group visits with her mother, aunts, and cousins to local museums and rehearsals of the Russian Ballet.

After graduating in 1973 from George M. Shurr High School in Montebello, California, Norte began her travels to Mexico—visits that forever transformed both her worldview and her writing. Upon returning from her first trip to Mexico, she attended East Los Angeles City College and then studied at California State University, Los Angeles, from 1976 to 1978.

Because a mix of Mexican and American news headlines, advertisements, popular song lyrics, and autobiographical experience converge against a backdrop of movie fragments in Norte's writing, her work appeals to a heterogeneous audience—despite publishing practices that tend to exclude Chicana/Latina writers on the basis of their gender and ethnicity. She has been published in several periodicals, and her work has been discussed in magazines such as *Rolling Stone* and *Face.*

Over the years, Norte has written many of her pieces on the downtown bus ride to her various jobs as a waitress, retail clerk, and office worker. Her narratives are as long "as it takes to get from one bus stop to another." In the liner notes to her compact disc, *Norte/word* (1991), she explains:

> I write on the bus, the No. 18 bus especially. . . .That's where so many of the images, the ideas for the work have been born. If I'm lucky, I manage a choice seat by a window where I can write comfortably until someone looks over my shoulder and starts reading whatever it is that I'm writing. That's when I will switch languages depending on who's sitting next to me. It changes everything. I would rather not have anyone know what it is that I do even though I do it in public.

Norte also draws her material from everyday life: family *chisme* (gossip), *chistes* (jokes), *brujerías* (witchery), broken relationships with men, and strained relationships with women. Another important influence on her memory and writing is the movies. Her deep love for the movies was first nurtured by her father's tales about his youthful experiences as a film projectionist in Chihuahua, Mexico. In addition to her father's stories, Norte's imagination was stimulated by images from Hollywood B movies. In her article "Harry Gamboa Jr.: No-Movie Maker" (1983), Norte remembers that "My father used to baby-sit me at the old Center Theater [in East Los Angeles] and spoon-fed me gems like *Blood Feast, The Tingler,* and *Playgirls vs. The Vampires.*" In the liner notes for *Norte/word,* she recalls further:

> I was very much influenced by the black and white bombshells of those B horror films of the 50s and 60s. . . . At the same time I was watching Mexican movies at the Floral Drive-In where I wanted to look like Maria Felix, sing like Lola Beltran and wiggle around in a G-string like Tongolele!

> As a child, I went through a heavy gangster/prison film stage. I would refer to my classmates as "lousy screws," roll up my arithmetic homework into cigarettes and outline the neighborhood kids' bodies in chalk on the sidewalks off of Downey Road. I'd go to Ford Boulevard School with my Brooklyn (and Soto) accent and make sure I lost it by the time I got home.

*Cover for Norte's compact disc of spoken-word performances*

An additional influence on Norte's creative impulse are the published diaries of Anaïs Nin. Though Norte had kept diaries since she was an adolescent, it never occurred to her that the genre would be of interest to the reading public until she devoured Nin's. Over the years, the work of José Montoya, Willa Cather, Truman Capote, Tennessee Williams, Dorothy Allison, and Ana Castillo inspired her to continue writing. In an unpublished July 1995 interview, however, she said that the strongest forces shaping her work so far are "living in L.A. as a single woman and having made choices along the way that I never thought I could."

Since her early narratives focus in part on surviving sexual, racial, and economic violence, some of them—such as "El Club Sufrimiento 2000" (1987), a wry meditation on the violation of women—stirred controversy in both the Chicano/Latino and non-Latino artistic communities. The former found fault with her critique of gender relations, while the latter found themselves perplexed by her femme fatale image and urban imagery that was seemingly "not authentically Mexican."

During the early 1980s, Norte was a part of two of the most productive artist collectives in Los Angeles: the Los Angeles Latino Writers Workshop and ASCO (Nausea). The Los Angeles Latino Writers Workshop continued to expand the space created by the Chicano Movement in the late 1960s and 1970s for literary expression produced by Latinos. Working double shifts as a writer and freelance waitress, Norte published "Each Street/Each Story" in an anthology titled *201: Homenaje a La Ciudad de Los Angeles: Latino Experience in Literature and Art* (1982), a special issue of *Chismearte* (Art of Gossip, or Gossip Art). She later served on the editorial staff of that periodical. According to the introduction in the anthology, the workshop was initiated by noted Chicano writers Ron Arias and Alejandro Morales; original members besides Norte included Luis J. Rodríguez, Helena María Viramontes, Naomi Quiñónez, and Gina Valdés. Norte became part of the workshop after responding to a tiny classified ad the group had placed in the *L.A. Weekly*. In the 1995 interview she recalled that it was a supportive environment for those who attended: "We weren't critical; we were just happy to hear other Chicanos."

ASCO was another artist forum that played an important role in what critics have called the Chicano Cultural Renaissance of the 1970s. The do-it-yourself impulse and the questioning of the status quo that runs through both Chicano and punk aesthetic currents merged in this group. Founding members Harry Gamboa Jr., Gronk, Willie Herrón, and Patssi Valdez recognized the importance of the Chicano Movement and participated in it but decidedly broke away from the indigenous iconography frequently found in Chicano nationalist aesthetics; like Norte, they looked toward urban imagery to comment on sexuality, state violence, and postmodern alienation. Forging a space between Chicano and mainstream art, the group often incorporated members who shared their precarious position within and outside of the art world.

During her tenure with ASCO, Norte wrote and performed a play titled *La Condición Femenina* (The Feminine Condition, 1982) with María Elena Gaitán. The play is a conversation between a homegirl from the barrio and a middle-class Chicano Valley Girl; the two characters come to realize that they share an inferior position in the hierarchy of patriarchal gender relations. The exhibition *ASCO '83* included a performance of Norte's next play, *Exito* (Success). In a review of the 1985 video version of *Exito,* Linda Burnham described the play as "a dialogue with the dead. As a crowd of friends hovered about her body on its bier, the camera switched to a dialog between a live Norte and a fascinated . . . investigator who wanted desperately to prove she had killed herself for love, which she staunchly denied."

Norte's prose narratives, performances, and plays contributed to and benefited from the struggles of the Los Angeles Latinos Writers Workshop and ASCO to maintain both intellectual and physical spaces for Chicano/Latino writers and artists. In the 1995 interview Norte recalled the dearth of performance spaces for Chicanos/Latinos and writers in general: "there weren't coffee-houses on every corner like there is now, or even bookstores. Spoken-word readings weren't as common. Gorky's Cafeteria in downtown L.A. was the meeting place because there was no place else to go." Along with many other Chicano/Latino writers, Norte continued to write despite another serious lack: that of interest in Latino writers on the part of major publishing houses. Norte was able, however, to participate in the first wave of small Chicano journals, publications crucial in the distribution of Chicano/Latino writing.

"Peeping Tom Tom Girl," which first appeared in *El Tecolote Literario* (The Literary Owl) in 1983 and was later modified for *Norte/word,* serves as an excellent introduction to the form and themes of Norte's writing. The speaker describes a bus ride to her job, a ride beginning in her East Los Angeles neighborhood and ending at her final destination downtown. Along the way the speaker travels back and forth in time, peeping at and remembering the faces of working-class single women who live on the economic edge of society. Norte's representation of what she sees happening on the streets of eastern and downtown Los Angeles makes her work compelling. Moving through economically marginalized sections of the city, the speaker in "Peeping Tom Tom Girl" documents an unofficial record of Chicana experiences by proclaiming, "I am a peeping tom, tom girl / and from my seat on the downtown bus / I have been driven through, / been witness to, / invaded by / las vidas de ellas [the women's lives]."

Riding through different Los Angeles neighborhoods, the speaker witnesses the economic stratification of Chicanas/Latinas. She counters the stereotypical images often used to portray Chicanas by forcing her audience to notice "the widow with the gladiolus / who never misses a day of forgiveness" as well as "the countess," who "sleeps in doorways / hefty bag wardrobe / broken tiara / and too much rouge." This countess "counts todos los días en ingles y español [every day in English and Spanish], she is nuestra señora de la reina perdida que cayó en Los Angeles [our lady of the lost queen who fell in Los Angeles]." Using this phrase, the speaker ironically twists the meaning of the original name of Los Angeles, El Pueblo de Nuestra Señora La Reina de los Angeles de Porciúncula (The Town of Our Lady the Queen of the Angels of Porciúncula), in order to comment critically on the living conditions of women surviving in the city.

This pun on the Spanish name of Los Angeles is characteristic of the linguistic strategies Norte uses to articulate social criticism. She gives new meaning to the name, making it describe more accurately the women's lives. The Spanish pastoral myth of the limitless abundance of Los Angeles is contrasted with the dwindling chances of survival for many Chicanas/Latinas in the city. On the same bus ride the speaker shares a different view of the city with a friend named Silent, "who taught a friend of mine how to flick her cigarette out of a window and be so bad in the process / Silent who spends a lot of time in the welfare office now filling out those pink and blue forms / Can't find a baby-sitter, a good man, a job."

Norte began publishing what are presently called transnational borderland narratives in 1982, though it took five more years for that genre to be recognized. An example of such a narrative is "Se habla inglés" (English Is Spoken), which was first published in *Raras Aves: Southern California Women Writers* (1983) and then included on *Norte/word*. This work debunks myths about Latino/Anglo gender relations, romance, and marriage within the context of both Mexican and American patriarchal culture. In the process of depicting the ways in which Latina women are objectified by both the Latino and dominant cultures, "Se habla inglés" also portrays the dreams that Mexicans have about life in the United States. Norte's speaker, from Los Angeles, visits Chihuahua, Mexico, on the eve of her cousin's wedding. As the speaker sits with her cousins and aunts at the kitchen table, making "buñuelos para los olvidados" (this pun refers to Luis Buñuel's 1950 movie *Los Olvidados,* also known as *The Young and the Damned* ) and other sweets for the wedding, her cousins ask questions about "el otro lado" (the other side of the border). Her cousins would like to believe the media misrepresentation of Los Angeles; they imagine that "life is so easy driving from swimming pool to swimming pool."

"Se habla inglés" reveals how the Anglo family objectifies Chicanas/Latinas based on both their gender and ethnicity. The critique is established as the women's preparation of the *buñuelos* for the cousin's wedding is contrasted with the speaker's own affairs:

> "Primero cuentanos que paso con tu 'boyfriend'?"
> [First tell us what happened with your boyfriend?]
>
> "Sí!" They all cheer
> "There are no boyfriends . . ."
> I begin, but there was this man you see
> and I thought he was supposed to be the one
> fter all, I had met the parents
> had that all-important meeting with cold-cuts and Hula
>   punch
> that all-important meeting where I was crowned "Miss
>   Señorita Black Velvet Latina" by them.

The significance of the puns "cold-cuts" and "Hula punch" is twofold. Norte contrasts the *buñuelos* with the cold cuts to indicate that the boyfriend's working-class family is not Latino. "Cold-cuts" and "punch" also convey the speaker's feelings of being put down and excluded. By highlighting the fact that "they crowned" the speaker "Miss Señorita Black Velvet Latina," Norte points to the fact that advertising media often stereotype Latinas—Black Velvet Liquor uses seductive images of women of color to market its product—and those images determine, in part, how non-Latinos will perceive Chicanas/Latinas.

After hearing the speaker's story of "real" failed romance, the cousins are not satisfied. They still want to know more. They beg the speaker to read "en ingles" (in English) from a year-old copy of *Cosmopolitan* magazine. As she reads to her cousins, she calls attention to the contradictions between the idealized *Cosmopolitan*

version of romance—"Keep plenty of scented candles for scrumptious, spontaneous love-making. Your man will love you for it"—and the disappointing reality of working-class Latina relationships. Norte's speaker debunks the myth of magazine romance: "Scented candles? I still live at home. Premeditated sex is about as spontaneous as I ever get / but they too are convinced that things go better en el otro lado [on the other side], home del sueño dorado de coors [of the Coors golden dream] / things are easier, so much easier." The final image of the piece demonstrates the ways in which women, along with men, maintain patriarchal practices. By the end of the story the speaker's cousins assume that the speaker has stepped beyond traditional gender behaviors, which mandate that women remain inexperienced: "they all want to know as they come closer / forming heavy double knit / when was it / when did I stop being a nice girl?" The image of "heavy double knit" illustrates the theme of constraint that runs throughout women's lives as they push against traditions.

Frustrated by the lack of respect for women writers who did not fit stereotypes in both the Chicano/Latino and Anglo artistic communities, Norte took a self-imposed exile from public readings in 1989. Despite her absence from the reading scene, her grass-roots following thrived. While she was working as an administrative assistant at the Los Angeles Medical Association, Harvey Kubernick—well known in Los Angeles for producing spoken-word recordings—asked her to contribute to a compact disc compilation titled *Black and Tan Club* (1991), emphasizing material from African American and Chicano/Latino writers from Los Angeles. Because of the hybrid nature of her narratives—which merge prose and poetry, lyrical and rap forms—as well as her tendency to experiment with and circulate them in the form of live performances, Norte discovered while recording material for Kubernick's compilation that the audio recording was an ideal medium for writing. Later that same year, New Alliance Records released *Norte/word*.

*Norte/word* covers the geography of the extended borderlands, moving among Los Angeles, El Paso, and Mexico City as well as across the geography of collective frustration and ecstasy. In addition to showing that different women share common ground in their struggle to survive economic hardship and gender discrimination, Norte's work illustrates how location in the borderlands shapes Chicana experiences, as Jennifer González and Michelle Habell-Pallán point out. For example, the urban spaces the narrator rides through in "Peeping Tom Tom Girl" are contrasted with the United States–Mexico border-crossing experience in "Act of the Faithless." This narrative articulates one way that women who live and work across national borders negotiate lines purposefully and artificially drawn between national and economic communities:

> . . . It was a Holiday Inn
> downtown El Paso
> where she crossed the line daily
> paso por paso
> mal paso que das
> al cruzar la Frontera
> [step by step
> mis-stepping
> as you cross
> the border]
>
> There was the work permit
> sealed in plastic
> like the smile
> she flashed every morning
> to the same uniformed eyes

Considering that Norte herself travels across unfriendly urban terrain to reach her job at the Museum of Contemporary Art in downtown Los Angeles, it is not surprising that many of her narratives recognize and pay tribute to the lives of the women who must constantly travel the hostile terrain of the United States–Mexico border to earn their wages. Urban experience is significantly different from the woman's border experience: urban dwellers are not required to flash documentation "sealed in plastic" to travel to and from work. However, the woman in the text–later revealed to be the speaker's aunt–travels from Mexico to her job at the Holiday Inn in relative safety compared to those without documentation, those for whom national borders are a site of exclusion and, many times, death.

The aunt has "decorated her home with objects of rejection / souvenirs turistas left behind," illustrating how the demands of the transnational tourist market affect her everyday life. The discarded objects the aunt collects, such as the "Lone Star state of the art back scratchers / all the way from Taiwan," also travel across many borders, arriving at their final destination to be sold to tourists as authentic Texan artifacts.

Though the "uniformed eyes" fail to see the complexity of the aunt's identity, she is more than a "smile" with a work permit. If on the American side she is seen only as labor for the *turistas,* at home she also must serve her husband, who leaves "his laundry / waiting to be washed / cleansed delivered from evil." Though she may not be marginalized by her citizen status in Mexico, she is discriminated against because of her gender.

While watching her aunt clean at the Holiday Inn, the speaker listens to the advice she offers. Handing her niece a pair of women's sunglasses she found in her husband's jacket, the aunt tells her to "cuidate los

ojos" (take care of her eyes), because there is "too much you should see." The aunt's advice is double-edged: she seems to be both warning her young niece to be aware of possibly harmful situations and giving her hope that there is something worth living for. She leaves unspoken exactly what she sees and what the niece "should see."

Their exchange is interrupted by a lounging Holiday Inn tourist. Displaying a complete lack of cultural consciousness, the tourist yells in his American accent: "Excuse me–um–Senorita, can you come over here por favor?" The narrative articulates for the aunt and niece what they cannot say to him directly:

> Señorita
> and the name stings like the sun
> and my Aunt
> she cusses him out real good in Spanish
> under her breath . . . The man in the chair
> is still trying to get her attention
> "Maria . . . Marrria!"
>
> only I can't hear it anymore
> only his lips are moving
> I tug on her arm
> I point at the man
> now gone silent
>
> there is too much to see
> she said
> too much to remember

This concluding segment of "Act of the Faithless" critiques the way the dominant culture narrowly envisions Chicanas/Latinas. The aunt knows that the tourist mistakes her for a servant. Though Maria is not her name, he sees her as he probably sees most Latina women–as a homogeneous, indistinguishable group. Although the aunt's defiant muttering–she cannot "cuss him out" aloud, because if she does, she will jeopardize her job– may not be considered radical, it does demonstrate her self-pride, self-knowledge, and dissatisfaction with the status quo. The narrative ends more realistically than idealistically, however: the tourist remains ignorant of his offensive racist and classist actions, demonstrating that there may be too much "to see."

A reviewer for the *Village Voice* (16 January 1992) particularly commended Norte's narrative titled "Dance in the Shadows" for being "at once angry, defiant ('So many of us are getting pregnant, getting gray hairs, and being lied to') and soothing, seductive ('I keep a full moon in a glass by my bed')." Encouraged by the favorable reviews of *Norte/word,* Norte decided to dedicate herself to her writing; she resigned from the Los Angeles Medical Association, though she continues to volunteer as a crisis intervention counselor for the East Los

Angeles Rape Hot Line and remains active in the pro-choice movement.

Norte considers *Norte/word* to be an ethnography of Los Angeles culture, especially of the young working-class glamour girls–otherwise known as Cha Cha Girls–and their mothers, sisters, and daughters. The subject matter of her work has left an indelible mark on the imaginations of her peers and the subsequent generation of Los Angeles writers, especially women writers who previously have had limited exposure to works written by Chicanas/Latinas. Her participation in workshops for young writers has also helped to nurture a new generation of Chicana/Latina writers.

Norte has made the transformation from the "bad girl poet" of the *ASCO,* as Linda Burnham described her in *High Performance* (1986), to "one who has cut the label out," in Norte's own words. In an untitled narrative written for a performance in *Diva L.A.: A Salute to L.A.'s Latinas in the Tanda Style* (2 July 1995), Norte's speaker lists a series of stereotypical labels used to define Chicanas/Latinas, then turns the list upon its head by boldly undefining them. She asserts:

> For the record
> I am not
> Woman Mujer of power poder
> cactus flower eating
> Goddess of whatever?
> No

The speaker then continues to resist the stereotypical labeling of Chicanas/Latinas by telling several stories that represent the diverse experiences of Chicano/Latinas. Norte's narrative thus offers the possibility of creating new images and new ways of being Chicana/Latina.

Ultimately, the innovative form and content of Norte's writing counters a monolithic vision of Chicana/Latina experience. Instead, by depicting the stratification of the Chicana/Latina population in terms of marital, economic, and citizen status, Norte's writing illustrates why no single image can stand for all Chicanas/Latinas. Because both Chicanas/Latinas and non-Latinas are subject the practices of patriarchal cultures, however, many readers and listeners can recognize experiences in Norte's narratives that resemble their own. The fact that Norte's work represents a shared circumstance without negating her own specific ethnic and local experience indicates its strength and importance. As a cultural worker Norte hopes to mobilize women by utilizing strategies of humor and irony to pose diffi-

cult questions. Yet, few literary scholars have critically investigated the provocative form and context of Norte's work. Such engagement can help readers understand the nature of the transformation that literature and literary studies are undergoing at the end of the twentieth century.

**References:**

Linda Burnham, "Viewpoint: Life: The ASCO Version," *High Performance,* 8 (1985): 66–67;

Burnham, "Marisela Norte," *High Performance,* 35 (1986): 56;

Adam Cruz, "Latin Looker," *Elle,* 3, no. 12 (1988): 38–45;

Harry Gamboa Jr., "Marisela Norte," *La Opinion,* 117, La Comunidad section, 17 October 1982, pp. 10–11;

Gamboa, "ASCO," *Imagine: International Chicano Poets Journal* (Summer–Winter 1986): 64–66;

Holly George-Warren, "New Faces," *Rolling Stone,* 656 (13 May 1993): 27;

Jennifer González and Michelle Habell-Pallán, "Heterotopias: Navigating Social Spaces and Spaces of Identity," *Inscriptions: Enunciating Our Terms,* 7 (1994): 80–104;

Habell-Pallán, "'No Cultural Icon': Marissela Norte," in *Women Transforming Politics: An Alternative Reader,* edited by Kathy Jones, Cathy Cohen, and Joan Tronto (New York: New York University Press, 1997), pp. 256–268;

D. Emily Hicks, *Border Writing: The Multidimensional Text* (Minneapolis: University of Minnesota Press, 1991), pp. 112, 117;

S. Zaneta Kosiba-Vargas, *Harry Gamboa and ASCO: The Emergence and Development of a Chicano Art Group* (Ann Arbor, Mich.: University Microfilms, 1989);

George Lipsitz, "We Know What Time It Is," in *Microphone Fiends: Youth Music & Youth Culture,* edited by Andrew Ross and Tricia Rose (New York: Routledge, 1994), pp. 17–28;

Wilfredo Rosado, "Our Latin Thang," *Interview,* 18 (February 1988): 101;

Cynthia Rose, "Word UP!" *Face,* 51 (December 1991): 23;

Ginger Varney, "Faces in the Crowd," *L.A. Style* (November 1985): 77;

Alan Weizman, "Born in East L.A.," *Los Angeles Times Sunday Magazine,* 27 March 1988, pp. 11–25.

# Nina Otero

*(23 October 1881 – 3 January 1965)*

Clara Lomas
*Colorado College*

BOOK: *Old Spain in Our Southwest* (New York: Harcourt, Brace, 1936).

PERIODICAL PUBLICATIONS: "En N. Mexico las mujeres se han organizado y votarán," *Evolución,* 27 January 1920, p. 1;
"My People," *Survey Graphic* (May 1931): 149–151.

Nina Otero's *Old Spain in Our Southwest* (1936) represents one of the early regional literary responses to Anglo-American economic and sociopolitical domination in New Mexico. A compilation of folkloric vignettes, the work reflects the effort of New Mexican women, originally from a landed gentry, on behalf of their cultural heritage. Similar to the writings of Fabiola Cabeza de Baca and Cleofas Jaramillo, Otero's nostalgic, romanticized narratives praise a utopian Spanish heritage and lament a vanishing way of life. At the same time that these women claim authority through authorship over an irretrievable past, they also bear witness to a present of forced cultural assimilation.

Maria Adelina Isabel Emilia (Nina) Otero was born on 23 October 1881 in La Constancia, New Mexico, along the Río Grande some twenty miles south of Albuquerque. According to Charlotte Whaley, her biographer, Otero's was a distinguished family that traced its origins back to eleventh-century Spain. Her parents, Eloisa Luna and Manuel Basilio Otero, both traced their lineage to the original Spanish conquistadores, of whom she writes in *Old Spain in Our Southwest*. At the age of sixteen Otero moved with her family to Santa Fe, the city she called home until her death at age eighty-three. Otero's life, as Whaley points out in her biography, *Nina Otero-Warren of Santa Fe* (1994), "paralleled the life of Santa Fe itself"; the arrival of the railroads the year of Otero's birth brought vast transformations to the region as "American capitalists gradually began appropriating the land and the livelihood of the early aristocratic *ricos*." Otero's relationship to these new values, which made commodities of the region's natural resources and cultural practices, was

*Nina Otero, circa 1929 (Bergere Family Collection, New Mexico State Records Center and Archives, Santa Fe)*

ambivalent. Whaley characterizes her as a "conservative in many ways, but rarely a conformist," who was to become a pioneer as a suffragist, educator, politician, homesteader, writer, and business entrepreneur.

Otero was educated at Maryville College of the Sacred Heart, a finishing school in St. Louis, Missouri, from 1892 to 1894. In 1908 she married Rawson Warren, a lieutenant in the U.S. Cavalry. Although her marriage failed after a year, she continued to use her married name on occasion. While she had no children of her own, she became the matriarchal figure of her family, caring for nine brothers and sisters as well as some of their offspring after her mother's death. This responsibility did not stop her from becoming actively involved in social, political, and economic matters outside the home.

In 1915 Otero became state chair of the legislative committee for the Federation of Women's Clubs. For the next five years she was a leader in the Congressional Union for Woman Suffrage founded by Alice Paul, which later became the National Women's Party. From 1917 to 1929 she worked as superintendent of public schools in Santa Fe County. During those years she also held other public positions: chair of the State Board of Health in New Mexico, member of the executive board of the American Red Cross, chair of the women's auxiliary board of the New Mexico State Council of Defense in the First Judicial District, chair of New Mexico's Republican Women's Organization, inspector of Indian services for the Department of the Interior, and an interpreter and liaison officer with the Pueblo Land Board. She was also a Republican Party nominee for the U.S. House of Representatives in 1922.

Little of this activist impulse is apparent in *Old Spain in Our Southwest*. Her greatest influence in writing the collection was her close association with a colony of artists and writers who heeded the admonition of historian Charles F. Lummis, author of *The Land of Poco Tiempo* (1893), to preserve the Spanish and Indian ancient traditions of the Southwest. This Santa Fe-based group included Mary Austin, Alice Corbin Henderson, Witter Bynner, John Sloan, Will Shuster, and Gustave Baumann. Austin advised Otero to take a sabbatical from her many activities and record her knowledge of the area's colonial heritage.

In the late 1920s Otero and a friend, Mamie Meadors, purchased 1,257 acres of land outside of Santa Fe. From 1929 through 1932 they homesteaded the property–called "Las Dos" (The Two)–which overlooked the Sangre de Cristo and Jemez mountain ranges and inspired Otero's opening chapter of *Old Spain in Our Southwest*. She completed her writing project in 1935, and the book was published in the spring of 1936 with illustrations by Otero's cousin Aileen Nusbaum. *Old Spain in Our Southwest* quickly went through three printings. By then Otero had returned to education and civil administration: as director of literacy education for New Mexico with the Civilian Conservation Corps and soon after as director of the state's adult literacy program; as director of the Work Conference for Adult Teachers in Río Piedras, Puerto Rico; and from 1942 to 1945 as Santa Fe County director for the Office of Price Administration. Having profited from their land investments, she and Meadors owned and managed Las Dos Realty and Insurance Company from 1947 until Otero's death in 1965.

Although Otero considered herself more of a political activist than a writer, she did receive recognition and praise for *Old Spain in Our Southwest*. The year of its publication Maryville College, her alma mater, awarded her an honorary bachelor of literature degree for her accomplishments as author and educator. During her lifetime reviews lauded the book as a firsthand account of life in nineteenth-century New Mexico. The fact that portions of the book have continued to appear in various anthologies reflects a sustained interest in her portrayal of Spanish customs in the New World.

*Old Spain in Our Southwest* is divided into five sections. The introductory section, "The Wind in the Mountains," situates the first-person narrator in the southwestern country around Santa Fe–"the ancient City of the Holy Faith"–"on my homestead in a small adobe house," watching an approaching storm and reflecting on feelings of "vastness, of solitude, but never of loneliness." The narrator observes the world beyond the window of the adobe house, inhabited by shepherds, Indians, as well as all the other inhabitants of the region from past and present, whose stories fill the pages of the rest of the collection. The following three sections of the book, "An Old Spanish Hacienda," "Day by Day," and "A Little History," compile memories, anecdotes, and simple historical accounts that encapsulate the old Spanish heritage, praise the old social mores and feudal relationships, and attempt to preserve a way of life that belonged to "the Spaniard" of yesteryear and his descendants in the region.

The final section of *Old Spain in Our Southwest*, "Songs and Stories," comprises almost half of the book, gathers scattered vignettes, including folktales submitted by schoolchildren for a contest Otero sponsored while she was superintendent of public schools. Otero, however, does not distinguish between the various narrative voices of these tales and that of her first-person narrator, suggesting instead a collective voice of "our" Southwest that tells stories about rich and misunderstood cultural practices: "Strangers do not understand our hospitality." Many of the stories in the first four sections begin with a statement that the narrator offers as an essential quality of the Spanish American people: "The Spanish descendant of the *Conquistadores* may be poor, but he takes his place in life with a noble bearing, for he can never forget that he is a descendant of the Conquerors"; "The Spaniard is dramatic in his love affairs"; "The Spaniard is not greatly disturbed by an unusual occurrence"; "The Spanish-American woman loves her flowers"; "A Spanish child is taught the religious side of Christmas."

PROCESSIONAL.

Old Spain
in Our Southwest

BY NINA OTERO

ILLUSTRATIONS BY AILEEN NUSBAUM

HARCOURT BRACE AND COMPANY
NEW YORK

*Frontispiece and title page for Otero's only book, published in 1936*

Although marked by rigid class distinctions, the entire community lives in social harmony, united by pride in their family lineages and race. In the story "The Harvest" the narrator maintains that "they cherished their traditions, inherited from Spain and adapted to their new life. Theirs was a part of the feudal age, when master and man, although separate in class, were bound together by mutual interests and a closed community of human sympathy. Much of this form of life remains today." This Spanish heritage is characterized by the social mores and morals of a religious, respectful, dignified, prudent, honorable people who know their place in the world: the grandees proudly "held court" while the peons proudly served their masters. Master and peon share an unconventional, unhurried work ethic, and both are subservient to their feudal lord, the grand hidalgo. The disparate and nearly disappearing memories, tales, anecdotes, "little histories," songs, and narratives of the various descendants of grandees, *patronas,* peons, and shepherds simultaneously familiarize outsiders with this value system and instruct the native

younger generations of the grandeur of the typography, physiognomy, and cultural practices of their "old Spain." The text is a translation of those southwestern cultural practices not valorized by the dominant culture of the period. Subsequently, the text has also become an important cultural document, adopted as a classroom text in New Mexico. While it is clearly intended to contribute to the native cultural esteem of school-age Hispano children, this somewhat positive image is grounded on uncritical and ahistorical essentialism and thus inevitably sends mixed ideological messages.

Accordingly, critical reception of the book has been mixed as well. As part of the cultural preservation effort of the colony of Anglo artists and writers during Otero's lifetime, the book stands as one of the most effective ideological devices of a discursive movement focused on the New Mexican landscape and the exoticism of native cultures. As Genaro Padilla has critically assessed:

However much they may have considered themselves intellectually and socially progressive, these artists and

*The first trustees of the Edward Grisso Scholarship Fund of the University of New Mexico in 1958: W. D. Grisso, Ethel Bond Huffines, Otero, and A. B. Carpenter (Bergere Family Collection, New Mexico State Records Center and Archives, Santa Fe)*

intellectuals who retreated to the southwest to escape the dehumanizing effects of an alienating industrial and urban society on the East Coast often participated in the dehumanization of their subjects, or better put, their objects—Mexicans and Native Americans. . . . Instead of relating to people as social subjects, the "newcomers" mystified and occulted native culturals . . . and reified their social history, as one sees in scores of newspapers, magazines, and books that celebrated the legendary Spanish *conquistadores.*

Because Otero's book, as well as those of Jaramillo and Cabeza de Baca, was the product of a native *hispana,* it helped to legitimize the discourse of this preservation movement that, notwithstanding its intentions, was dehistorizing the Southwest as it created a utopian retreat for nonnatives.

During the political activism of the Chicano movement in the 1970s critics such as Raymund Paredes reproached what he calls the "hacienda" mentality of New Mexican writers of the 1930s, noting that there is "something profoundly disturbing about this body of work. It seems a literature created out of fear and intimidation, a defensive response to racial prejudice, particularly the Anglo distaste for miscegenation and ethnocentrism." While this reading seeks to explicate the romanticized, ahistorical, genteel textual discourse, feminist readings in the 1980s by critics Tey Diana Rebolledo and Genaro Padilla add a further level of complexity by analyzing the historical social text as well. Rebolledo's interpretation reveals conscious "narrative strategies of resistance" on the part of writers such as Otero, who "subverted" the "official text" by subtly allowing dissident "strange occurrences" in their narratives. Rebolledo attests that "close readings will show that the paradise depicted in the beginnings of their books becomes a land of transition and struggle (almost a purgatory) in the early twentieth century."

Taking into account Rebolledo's and Padilla's insights allows one to read Otero's "curious" reaction to the "'wild and dismal' . . . storm that made her feel strangely out of place," as Whaley characterizes it in the introduction to *Old Spain in Our Southwest,* as a reflection of the ideological contradictions Otero was confronting in a time of phenomenal social and economic transitions in her Southwest. Otero identifies her narrator as a homesteader, an observer viewing from behind a window, who somehow cannot feel "in complete tune with the instruments of God" such as the shepherd and the Indian, whose presences contrast sharply with the narrator's: "I, alone, . . . felt a sense of loss that they were closer to nature than I, more understanding of the storm."

The title of the first section, "The Wind in the Mountains," reflects the community's sense that winds of change were blowing through the area. Although fearful, the narrator is nevertheless compelled to record the culture of "old Spain" from the perspective of the dominant Anglo culture. This ambivalence, subtly registered and echoed throughout the collection, testifies to the resilience of the Hispanic people of the Southwest.

## Biography:

Charlotte Whaley, *Nina Otero-Warren of Santa Fe* (Albuquerque: University of New Mexico Press, 1994).

## References:

Joan M. Jensen, "'Disfranchisement is a Disgrace': Women and Politics in New Mexico, 1900–1940," in *New Mexico Women: Intercultural Perspectives,* edited by Jensen and Darlis A. Miller (Albuquerque: University of New Mexico Press, 1986);

Genaro M. Padilla, *My History, Not Yours: The Formation of Mexican American Autobiography* (Madison: University of Wisconsin Press, 1993), pp. 196–227;

Raymund Paredes, "The Evolution of Chicano Literature," in *Three American Literatures,* edited by Houston A. Baker Jr. (New York: Modern Language Association, 1982), pp. 33–79;

Tey Diana Rebolledo, "Narrative Strategies of Resistance in Hispana Writing," *Journal of Narrative Technique,* 20, no. 2 (Spring 1990): 134–146;

Rebolledo, "Tradition and Mythology: Signatures of Landscape in Chicana Literature," in *The Desert Is No Lady: Southwest Landscapes in Women's Writing and Art,* edited by Vera Norwood and Janice Monk (New Haven: Yale University Press, 1987), pp. 96–124;

Rebolledo, *Women Singing in the Snow: A Cultural Analysis of Chicana Literature* (Tucson: University of Arizona Press, 1995), pp. 29–47.

# Américo Paredes

*(3 September 1915 – 5 May 1999)*

Cida S. Chase
*Oklahoma State University*

BOOKS: *Cantos de adolescencia* (San Antonio: Librería Española, 1937);

*"With His Pistol in His Hand": A Border Ballad and Its Hero* (Austin: University of Texas Press, 1958);

*Folk Music of Mexico. Book for the Guitar No. 671,* by Paredes and Joseph Castle (Chicago: M. M. Cole, 1966);

*A Texas-Mexican Cancionero: Folksongs of the Lower Border* (Urbana: University of Illinois Press, 1976);

*George Washington Gómez: A Mexicotexan Novel*, introduction by Rolando Hinojosa (Houston: Arte Público, 1990);

*Between Two Worlds* (Houston: Arte Público, 1991);

*Uncle Remus con chile* (Houston: Arte Público, 1993);

*Folklore and Culture on the Texas-Mexican Border,* edited by Richard Bauman (Austin: University of Texas Center for Mexican American Studies, 1993);

*The Hammon and the Beans and Other Stories* (Houston: Arte Público, 1994);

*The Shadow* (Houston: Arte Público, 1998).

OTHER: "The Love Tragedy in Texas-Mexican Balladry," in *Folk Travelers: Ballads, Tales, and Talk,* edited by Mody C. Boatright, Wilson M. Hudson, and Allen Maxwell, Publications of the Texas Folklore Society no. 25 (Dallas: Southern Methodist University Press, 1953), pp. 110–114;

"The Legend of Gregorio Cortez," in *Mesquite and Willow,* edited by Boatright, Hudson, and Maxwell, Publications of the Texas Folklore Society no. 27 (Dallas: Southern Methodist University Press, 1957), pp. 3–22;

"The Mexican Corrido: Its Rise and Fall," in *Madstones and Twisters,* edited by Boatright, Hudson, and Maxwell, Publications of the Texas Folklore Society no. 28 (Dallas: Southern Methodist University Press, 1958), pp. 91–105;

"The Bury-Me-Not Theme in the Southwest," in *And Horns on the Toads,* edited by Boatright, Hudson, and Maxwell, Publications of the Texas Folklore

*Américo Paredes (Office of Public Affairs, University of Texas at Austin)*

Society no. 29 (Dallas: Southern Methodist University Press, 1959), pp. 88–92;

"Folklore and History" and "On Gringo, Greaser and Other Neighborly Names," in *Singers and Storytellers,* edited by Boatright, Hudson, and Maxwell, Publications of the Texas Folklore Society no. 30 (Dallas: Southern Methodist University Press, 1961), pp. 56–69, 285–290;

Vincente T. Mendoza, "Some Forms of the Mexican 'Canción,'" translated by Paredes, in *Singers and Storytellers,* pp. 46–55;

Edward Larocque Tinker, ed., *Corridos & Calaveras,* includes notes and translations by Paredes (Austin: University of Texas Press, 1961);

"No Estiendo," "La flora y la fauna," and "Moochers," in *Buying the Wind: Regional Folklore in the United States,* edited by Richard M. Dorson (Chicago: University of Chicago Press, 1964), pp. 452–454;

"Pastorela to Celebrate the Birth of Our Lord Jesus Christ" and "Corrido de Jacinto Treviño," translated by Paredes, in *Buying the Wind,* pp. 466–479, 483–485;

Daniel Cosío Villegas, *American Extremes,* translated by Paredes (Austin: University of Texas Press, 1964);

"The Anglo-American in Mexican Folklore," in *New Voices in American Studies,* edited by Ray B. Browne, Donald M. Winkelman, and Allen Hayman (West Lafayette, Ind.: Purdue University Studies, 1966), pp. 113–127;

"Folk Medicine and the Intercultural Jest," in *Spanish-Speaking People in the United States,* edited by June Helm, Proceedings of the Annual Spring Meeting of the American Ethnological Society (Seattle: University of Washington Press, 1968), pp. 104–119;

"Tributaries to the Mainstream: The Ethnic Groups," in *Our Living Traditions: An Introduction to American Folklore,* edited by Tristram P. Coffin (New York: Basic Books, 1968), pp. 70–80;

Mauricio Charpenel, *Las miniaturas en el arte popular mexicano,* edited, with a preface, by Paredes, Latin American Folklore Series no. 1 (Austin: Center for Intercultural Studies in Folklore and Oral History, University of Texas, 1970);

Manuel Dannemann Rothstein, *Bibliografía del folklore chileno, 1952–1965,* edited, with a preface, by Paredes, Latin American Folklore Series no. 2 (Austin: Center for Intercultural Studies in Folklore and Oral History, University of Texas, 1970);

*Folktales of Mexico,* translated and edited, with a preface, by Paredes (Chicago: University of Chicago Press, 1970);

"Folklore e historia: dos cantares de la frontera del norte," in *25 estudios de folklore,* edited by Fernando Anaya Monroy, Estudios de folklore no. 4 (México: Instituto de Investigaciones Estéticas, Universidad Autónoma de México, 1971);

"Mexican Legendry and the Rise of the Mestizo," in *American Folk Legend: A Symposium,* edited by Wayland D. Hand (Berkeley: University of California Press, 1971), pp. 97–107;

*The Urban Experience and Folk Tradition,* edited by Paredes and Ellen J. Stekert (Austin: University of Texas Press, 1971);

Paulo de Carvalho, *The Concept of Folklore,* preface by Paredes (Coral Gables, Fla.: University of Miami Press, 1971), pp. 9–12;

*Toward New Perspectives in Folklore,* edited by Paredes and Richard Bauman (Austin: University of Texas Press, 1972);

*Mexican-American Authors,* edited by Paredes and Raymund Paredes (Boston: Houghton Mifflin, 1972);

"Dichos," in *Mexican-American Authors,* pp. 27–34;

Lily Litvak, *El nacimiento del Niño Dios: A Pastorela from Tarimoro, Guanajuato,* edited, with a preface, by Paredes, Latin American Folklore Series no. 3 (Austin: Center for Intercultural Studies in Folklore and Oral History, University of Texas, 1973);

"The Role of Folklore in Border Relations," in *San Diego/Tijuana—The International Border in Community Relations: Gateway or Barrier?* edited by Kiki Skagen (San Diego: Fronteras, 1976), pp. 17–22;

*Humanidad: Essays in Honor of George I. Sánchez,* edited by Paredes (Los Angeles: Chicano Studies Center Publications, University of California, 1977);

"Jorge Isidoro Sánchez y Sánchez (1906–1972)," in *Humanidad: Essays in Honor of George I. Sánchez,* pp. 120–126;

"The Problem of Identity in a Changing Culture: Popular Expressions of Culture Conflict along the Lower Río Grande Border," in *Views across the Border: The United States and Mexico,* edited by Stanley Ross (Albuquerque: University of New Mexico Press, 1978), pp. 68–94;

"The Folk Base of Chicano Literature," in *Modern Chicano Writers: A Collection of Essays,* edited by Joseph Sommers and Tomás Ybarra-Frausto (Englewood Cliffs, N.J.: Prentice-Hall, 1979), pp. 4–17;

"The Corrido: Yesterday and Today," in *Ecology and Development of the Border Region: Proceedings of the Second Symposium of Mexican and United States Universities on Border Studies,* edited by Ross (Mexico City: Asociación Nacional de Universidades e Institutos de Enseñanza Superior, 1983), pp. 293–297;

"Nearby Places and Strange-Sounding Names," in *The Texas Literary Tradition: Fiction, Folklore, History,* edited by Don Graham and others (Austin: University of Texas College of Liberal Arts, 1983), pp. 130–138.

SELECTED PERIODICAL PUBLICATIONS—
UNCOLLECTED: "The Mexico-Texas Corrido," *Southwest Review,* 27 (1942): 470–481;

*Cover for Paredes's 1990 novel, which depicts life in the Rio Grande Valley during the Great Depression and World War II*

"El corrido de José Mosqueda as an Example of Pattern in the Ballad," *Western Folklore,* 17 (1958): 154–162;

"The University of Texas Folklore Archive," *Folklore and Folk Music Archivist,* 2–3 (Fall 1959): 1–4;

"Gringo," *Western Folklore,* 19 (1960): 277;

"Luis Inclán: First of the Cowboy Writers," *American Quarterly,* 12 (1960): 55–70;

"The Mexican Contribution to Our Culture," *Texas Observer,* 19 August 1960, pp. 6–7;

"Mexican Riddling Wellerisms," *Western Folklore,* 19 (1960): 200;

"Tag You're It," *Journal of American Folklore,* 73 (1960): 157–158;

"Where Cultures Clashed and Merged," *Texas Observer,* 12 August 1960, p. 7;

"Folklore Bibliography for 1960," *Southern Folklore Quarterly,* 25 (March 1961): 1–89;

"Folklore Bibliography for 1961," *Southern Folklore Quarterly,* 26 (March 1962): 1–96;

"El folklore en los Estados Unidos durante la última decada (1953–1962)," *Folklore Americano,* 10 (1963): 256–262;

"The Ancestry of Mexico's Corridos: A Matter of Definitions," *Journal of American Folklore,* 76, no. 301 (1963): 231–235;

"El cowboy norteamericano en el folklore y la literatura," *Cuadernos del Instituto Nacional de Antropología,* 4 (1963): 227–240;

"Texas' Third Man: The Texas-Mexican," *Race: The Journal of the Institute of Race Relations,* 4, no. 2 (1963): 49–58;

"Folklore Bibliography for 1963," *Southern Folklore Quarterly,* 28 (March 1964): 1–94;

"Some Aspects of Folk Poetry," *Texas Studies in Literature and Language,* 6 (Spring 1964): 213–225;

"Vicente T. Mendoza, 1894–1964," *Journal of American Folklore,* 78 (1965): 154–155;

"The Décima Cantada on the Texas-Mexican Border: Four Examples," by Paredes and George Foss, *Journal of the Folklore Institute,* 3 (1966): 91–115;

"The Décima on the Texas-Mexican Border: Folksong as an Adjunct to Legend," *Journal of the Folklore Institute,* 3 (August 1966): 154–167;

"El folklore de los grupos de origen mexicano en los Estados Unidos," *Folklore Americano,* 14 (August 1966): 146–163;

"El folklore en el XXXVII Congreso Internacional de Americanistas," *Folklore Américas,* 26 (1966): 31–33;

"Divergencias en el concepto del folklore y el contexto cultural," *Folklore Américas,* 27 (1967): 29–38;

"Estados Unidos, México y el machismo," *Journal of Inter-American Studies,* 9 (January 1967): 65–84;

"A Selective Annotated Bibliography of Recent Works in Latin American Folklore, 1960–1967," *Handbook of Latin American Studies,* 30, no. 30 (1968): 385–410;

"Concepts about Folklore in Latin America and the United States," *Journal of the Folklore Institute,* 6 (1969): 20–38;

"Proverbs and Ethnic Stereotypes," *Proverbium,* 15 (1970): 95–97;

"The Where and Why of Folklore," *Illinois History,* 23, no. 4 (1970): 75–76;

"El concepto de la 'médula emotiva' aplicado al corrido mexicano 'Benjamín Argumedo,'" *Folklore Americano,* 17 (1972): 138–176;

"José Mosqueda and the Folklorization of Actual Events," *Aztlán,* 4 (1973): 1–30;

"On Ethnography Work among Minority Groups: A Folklorist's Perspective," *New Scholar,* 6 (1977): 1–32;

"Yamashita, Zapata, and the Arthurian Legend," *Western Folklore,* 36 (1977): 160–163;

"El romance de la Isla de Jauja en el suroeste de Estados Unidos," *Logos: Revista de la Facultad de Filosofía y Letras de la Universidad de Buenos Aires,* 13–14 (1977–1978): 399–406;

"Folklore, Lo Mexicano, and Proverbs," *Aztlán,* 13 (1982): 1–11.

Américo Paredes, whose scholarly and creative-writing career began in the early 1950s, has been instrumental in the study of the folklore of the American Southwest, Chicano culture, and Chicano literature. His many publications led the way toward new theoretical and methodological approaches to folklore and to sociohistorical studies of minority groups in the United States. Moreover, Paredes has been an influential Chicano personality, guiding generations of Chicanos toward the pursuit of their literary and academic goals.

Américo Paredes Manzano was born in Brownsville, Texas, on 3 September 1915 to Justo and Clotilde Manzano-Vidal Paredes. His paternal ancestors had settled in that area in the eighteenth century when it was part of the Spanish province of Nuevo Santander. Paredes graduated from Brownsville High School and began his higher education at the local community college. His early poetry appeared between 1936 and 1940 in "Los lunes literarios" (Literary Mondays), a literary section of *La Prensa* of San Antonio, and in the *Brownsville Herald,* which published his articles and poetry in both the English and the Spanish versions of its issues. In addition to his writing activities Paredes spent many of his early years studying music, namely piano and guitar techniques, until the onset of World War II, when he was sent overseas. He became a reporter for *Stars and Stripes* in Japan and served as administrator for the international Red Cross in China and Manchuria. Paredes has married twice, to Consuelo Silva in 1939 and to Amelia Sidzu Nagamine in 1948. He has four children, Américo Jr., Alan, Vicente, and Julia.

In 1951 Paredes obtained a B.A. degree in English and philosophy at the University of Texas and received an M.A. at that institution in 1953. In 1956 he completed his doctorate in English (specializing in folklore) and Spanish, and he joined the English faculty of the University of Texas at Austin in 1957. Paredes was involved in the creation and organization of significant innovative programs at the university, including the organization of folklore archives in 1957 and the creation of the Mexican American Studies Program in

1970. He served as head of the latter and director of the Center for Mexican American Studies between 1970 and 1972.

Paredes began his career in creative writing with the publication of a volume of lyric poetry, *Cantos de adolescencia* (Songs of Adolescence, 1937), when he was twenty-two years old. The poetic voice in the collection is that of an adolescent whose existence as a Hispanic in an Anglo American world compels him to treasure his ancestral roots. He says in the prologue that he began to write poetry at the age of fifteen but composed his verse exclusively in English at that time, the result of his early formal education carried out strictly in the English language. Beginning in 1932, however, he made a conscious effort to convey his innermost feelings in his mother tongue.

*Cantos de adolescencia* is divided into nine sections: "La lira patriótica" (The Patriotic Lyre), "La música" (Music), "La naturaleza" (Nature), "La comedia del amor" (The Comedy of Love), "La tragedia del amor" (The Tragedy of Love), "In Memoriam," "La voz rebelde" (The Rebellious Voice), "Décimas" (Spanish stanzas of ten octosyllabic lines), and "L'envoi" (verses placed at the end of a ballad in praise of someone). The volume includes sixty-one poems plus "Décimas" and the final poem that serves as "L'envoi." One of the initial poems is a hymn dedicated to Mexico and its nature. It consists of two stanzas each having five hendecasyllabic verses in combination with one heptasyllabic line. The first stanza reads:

Canten, aves, desde árboles floridos;
canten, sauces, de cumbre hasta raíz.
Canten, ríos, alegres y movidos;
canten, vientos, que mueven el maíz.
Canten todos, en un cantar unidos,
La beldad de mi país.

(Let the birds sing from the flowering trees;
let the weeping willows sing from their heights to their depths.
Let the joyful, swift rivers sing
Let the wind that moves the corn sing.
Let all sing, in a united song,
The beauty of my native land.)

The poet achieves harmony and a pleasant rhythm in this poem through the use of consonance and the repetition of the term *canten* (sing), which gives the entire poem its vocative tone.

There are also well-conceived love poems in the volume, including some that allude to the celebrated romantic Spanish poet Gustavo Adolfo Bécquer, whose *rimas* (poems) seem to have had a profound impact on young Paredes, as they did on many youths of Spain

Cover for Paredes's 1991 collection of poetry, which includes poems
describing his experiences overseas during World War II

and Latin America. One of Paredes's *rimas* alludes
directly to Bécquer's rima 23:

Un mundo diera él por su mirada,
por su altiva sonrisa diera un cielo;
por sus labios, ¿quién sabe que ofrendara
en el éxtasis loco de su anhelo?

(A world he would give for her glance,
for her haughty smile he would give the sky;
for her lips, who knows what he would offer
in the frantic ecstasy of his longing?)

Paredes concludes his *rima,* however, with a slight touch
of humor when his poetic persona admits that he has
no worlds to give away and least of all skies:

Yo no tengo ni mundos (menos cielos)
y por eso
por un beso, mi vida, yo te ofrezco
otro beso.

(I have no worlds [no hopes for skies]
and thus
for a kiss, my love, I can but offer you
another kiss.)

Although *Cantos de adolescencia* was the first sign of
Paredes's creative talent, the work that brought him
fame is *"With His Pistol in His Hand": A Border Ballad and
Its Hero* (1958). The book inspired a movie adaptation,
*The Ballad of Gregorio Cortez,* which aired on PBS on 29
June 1982. Paredes dedicated the book to the memory
of his father and to all the old men he remembered
from his childhood who sat around on summer nights
and told about border struggles. As Paredes explains in
the introduction, the book "is an account of the life of a
man, of the way that songs and legends grew up about
his name, and of the people who produced the songs,
the legends, and the man. It is also the story of a ballad,
'El corrido de Gregorio Cortez,' of its development out
of actual events, and of the folk traditions from which it
sprang." Paredes sets for himself the task of discussing
all facets of the story of Gregorio Cortez in this book,
and in the process he produces a pioneering study on
Mexican American folklore, the genesis of which he
finds in a prevailing cultural and sociopolitical conflict
between Hispanic Americans and Anglos.

After examining court records and conducting a
series of interviews, including talks with Valeriano
Cortez, a son of Gregorio Cortez, Paredes recon-
structed Cortez's tragic story. He was born on 22 June
1875 "on a ranch between Matamoros and Reynosa on
the Mexican side of the Border." He and his brother
Romaldo were farming a piece of rented land near
Kenedy in Karnes County, Texas, when his altercation
with the law took place. Sheriff Morris and two deputies rode to Cortez's place in pursuit of a horse thief.
Since the sheriff spoke no Spanish, he relied on one of
his deputies for translation. The translator was not suf-
ficiently proficient in Spanish, however, and because of
one or more linguistic errors that led to misunderstand-
ings, the sheriff tried to arrest Cortez and shot his
brother. Cortez shot and killed the sheriff in self-defense
and then fled, knowing that he would not get a fair trial
in that region of Texas. For ten days hundreds of men,
including sheriffs, deputies, Texas Rangers, and several
posses, looked for him. No one could capture him until
a man named Jesús González, alias El Teco, betrayed
him. Paredes explains that during the chase Cortez
"walked at least one hundred twenty miles and rode
more than four hundred on . . . brown . . . and sorrel
mares." Cortez repeatedly crossed back and forth over
the same area in order to confuse the men who were
after him, some of whom were convinced that he was
the head of an entire gang.

Gregorio Cortez became a folk hero for Mexican Americans. Both the legend of Cortez and the ballad emphasize that the Anglo Americans were able to capture him only because he decided to give himself up in order to spare his people any further suffering. Some versions of the incident relate that every man who offered Cortez water had been severely beaten and thrown in jail. Other Mexicans who fed him were hanged from trees because they had refused to tell in what direction Cortez was going. Although some of the details depicted in the ballad and the legend are obviously embellishments, Paredes's research revealed that indeed many Mexicans were victimized because of the Cortez affair. The Anglo American authorities harassed Cortez's mother, wife, and children and put them in jail. In addition, a friend who had helped him, the friend's wife, and their children were also jailed, in some cases after they had received gunshot wounds. The most blatant example of such mistreatment was the case of a thirteen-year-old Mexican boy who, accused of being a member of the nonexistent Cortez gang, was hanged from a tree nearly fatally.

*Folktales of Mexico* (1970) is a collection of tales edited and translated by Paredes. In his introduction Paredes offers a complete history of folklore societies and folklore studies in Mexico. In addition he offers a survey of Mexican and Mexican American folktale collections up to 1970, pointing out those that present genuine folk narratives and those in which the tales are in a dubious folk style. He states that folktale collections should specify where the collector found each item and supply background information on sources. In addition, maintaining the sources' style and providing annotated texts are necessary features that attest to the validity of the collections. "As a translator for this collection," he says, "I have sought to achieve the style of each narrator, without making him sound either like a midwestern American or a B movie Mexican." As sources of the tales he uses different informants and sound recordings made by himself, Joel Gómez, Gabriel Moedano, and Stanley L. Robe. Paredes alerts the reader to make use of the glossary when encountering Spanish or Indian terminology and notes that he has purposely left out overly familiar legends such as "La Llorona" (The Crying Woman). In addition to presenting a glossary and annotations, Paredes completes *Folktales of Mexico* with a list of abbreviations, a bibliography, an index of motifs, and an index of tale types.

The collection presents eighty-five tales divided into five categories: "Legendary Tales," "Animal Tales," "Ordinary Tales," "Jokes and Anecdotes," and "Formula Tales." Paredes supplies a detailed commentary on the types of tales included and remarks on those that are more popular in Mexico: "From my own experience

as a child in northern Mexico, I would say that the communities where I spent the summers and listened to storytelling cultivated the legend to a much greater degree than they did the wonder tale."

Many of the tales in *Folktales of Mexico* are intriguing. The section "Legendary Tales," for example, begins with a story about the biblical flood in which a rabbit advises a man about the imminent danger. The rabbit gets into a box with the man and his family until the flood is over. On getting out of the box the man finds dead cattle, which he cooks on an open fire, while the rabbit eats only herbs. When God sees the smoke rising from Earth, he sends small angels to investigate and orders that they not eat anything. The angels eat some of the meat, however, and are turned into the vultures of the earth. "Animal Tales" contains stories about rabbits, foxes, burros, coyotes, and a billy goat. In one story a burro who is frequently beaten by his owner asks an older burro how old he has to be in order not to suffer so many beatings. He is told that the fate of burros is to be beaten all their lives and that he should pray that men do not make a drum out of him when he dies, "For then they'll keep on beating you on Saturdays and Sundays, even after you are dead."

Several tales located in different sections feature allusions to religion. The section "Ordinary Tales" includes "The Priest Who Had a Small Glimpse of Glory," the story of a priest who, just before saying mass, asks God to allow him to take a glimpse at heaven. He hears a bird sing, looks up, and falls into a deep trance; when he comes to his senses he is standing in an ancient church. He asks what happened, and the people relate to him his own story, about a priest who sought a vision of heaven and disappeared. The storyteller wonders that if a glimpse of heaven can throw a person into ecstasy for years, "what would it be like if he saw God's glory in all its splendor."

The section "Jokes and Anecdotes" includes several examples of tales dealing with the traditional Spanish trickster Pedro de Urdemalas, whose stories form an extensive cycle in Spanish folklore. In "Pedro de Urdemalas and the Gringo" Pedro feeds his burro some coins. Proclaiming that the animal excretes money in his dung, he exchanges it to a greedy gringo for two mules loaded with silver, a horse, and a suit with gold buttons. "Formula Tales" features stories that have delighted Latin American children for generations, such as those of Pérez the mouse, whose troubles include falling into a steaming pot because he did not stir the food with a large spoon as his wife had recommended.

Although Paredes's research centers on Mexican, Mexican American, and southwestern folklore, he has edited several publications on urban folklore reflecting different regions of the United States. *The Urban Experi-*

*Cover for Paredes's 1993 collection of folktales, compiled during a year of field research in the Lower Rio Grande borderlands, 1962–1963*

North American folklorist, like many of his colleagues in the social sciences has looked on theories less as the basis of sound methodologies and more as pronouncements with emotional, if not moral implication. He embraces them fervently when they appear, enshrining their proponents as prophets. Later, when experience shows that they will not answer all his questions, he denounces them *in toto,* casts them into outer darkness, and begins all over again. Perhaps this is the reason meaningful dialogue has been*scarce* in our discipline.

Some of the essays included in this volume develop a performance-oriented perspective and consider folklore as communicative interaction. They also examine methods of preparing oral narrative for literary presentation and the impact of folklore on the development of sociolinguistics.

Paredes's contributions to the development of Chicano studies are significant. In collaboration with Raymund Paredes, he produced one of the earliest Chicano anthologies, *Mexican-American Authors* (1972), offering an overview of twentieth-century Chicano literature in all its genres. It begins with a ballad, "Jacinto Treviño," one of the earliest samples of Mexican American folklore, which Paredes collected and translated into English. The anthology also features Jovita González's short narratives and works by Paredes, Fermina Guerra, Josephina Niggli, Rafael Jesús González, Mario Suárez, Luis Omar Salinas, Amado Muro, Arnulfo D. Trejo, Alfredo Otero y Herrera, Nick C. Vaca, and Richard Olivas.

*A Texas-Mexican Cancionero: Folksongs of the Lower Border* (1976) is one of Paredes's most valuable contributions to the knowledge and preservation of Mexican American ballads and other folk songs. It constitutes a comprehensive anthology and study of traditional songs in the border area. The sixty-six songs featured appear complete with their original lyrics, English translations, and the melody line. The book includes five song categories: "Old Songs from Colonial Days," "Songs of Border Conflicts," "Songs for Special Occasions," "Romantic and Comic Songs," and "The Pocho Appears." Paredes explains in the introduction that he began collecting these songs around 1920: when he was growing up he heard them "on the lips of *guitarreros* and other people of the ranchos and towns."

Paredes says that "The whole of a people's past is reflected in these songs, from the days when they journeyed out of Chichimecaland, mid-eighteenth century pioneers, traveling north until they reached the Rio Grande, drank of its waters, and traveled no more. They settled on the river banks long before there was such a thing as the United States of America." He also explains that these songs "record an important aspect of the Mexican-American's long struggle to preserve [his]

*ence and Folk Tradition* (1971), a collection of essays that he edited with Ellen J. Stekert, is essentially a publication of a special issue of the *Journal of American Folklore.* These essays are the product of a symposium, "The Urban Experience and Folk Tradition," held at Wayne State University on 20–21 May 1968. The book comprises five essays that focus on varied ethnic groups, traditions that these groups brought to the city, and traditions that developed in the city. The collection is of general interest not only to folklorists but also to ethnographers and sociologists. In addition to the essays, it includes prepared comments for each essay and replies to the prepared comments.

*Toward New Perspectives in Folklore* (1972) is a collection of essays edited by Paredes and Richard Bauman featuring innovative approaches to conducting research in folklore. Paredes explains the purpose of this collection, stating in the foreword that the

188

identity and affirm [his] rights as a human being." Paredes also provides valuable insights into the situations in which these songs were sung, recalling folk singers he knew and admired and tracing how border family celebrations became full folklore performances, including not only singing but also sharing oral history and legends and playing games.

Paredes includes insightful introductory essays for each section of the book in which he reveals his findings concerning the origins of the songs as well as the history and legends that surround them. He expands on the predominant role that cultural conflict has had in the production of border ballads, observing that many Mexican border folk songs center on violent encounters with Texas Rangers and other Anglo authorities. The situations portrayed reveal extreme contempt and disdain toward Anglo Americans, a quality missing from songs that feature other folk motifs such as Indians and sheepherders. Paredes uses the song "Los Inditos" to illustrate this point. The song, which refers to an Indian attack, became a favorite among children in the border areas:

> Ahí vienen los inditos
> por el carrizal,
> ahí vienen los inditos
> por el carrizal.
> ¡Ay mamita! ¡Ay papito!
> me quieren matar, . . .
>
> (There come the little Indians
> by the field of reeds,
> there come the little Indians
> by the field of reeds.
> Oh mommy! Oh daddy!
> they want to kill me, . . .)

Paredes explains that the inspiration for this song, a massacring party of Indians, is subdued and disguised by the choice of diction. *Indio* (Indian) becomes *inditos* (little Indians), the use of the Spanish diminutive implying sympathy for the Indians. They were not regarded as enemies, as were Anglo Americans such as the Texas Rangers, the much-despised *rinches*. Paredes points out humorously that there are no songs that refer to *rinchitos* or *gringuitos*, no attempts to encourage Mexican American children to identify with "little Texas Rangers or little Anglo American invaders of the Southwest." On the contrary, Texas Rangers and Anglo-Americans in general are viewed as hypocritical and abusive in Mexican American border folklore. Many songs included in *A Texas-Mexican Cancionero*, including *corridos* such as "Jacinto Treviño," "Gregorio Cortez," and "Los tequileros" (The Tequila Runners), tell of vicious *rinches* who murder Mexicans in cowardly fashion.

*Humanidad: Essays in Honor of George I. Sánchez* (1977) gives evidence of Paredes's contributions to the humanities and to the field of education. The volume includes ten essays dealing with bilingualism and biculturalism, the presence of the Spanish language in the American Southwest, Chicano history, and the works of Mexican intellectuals such as Justo Sierra, Trinidad Sánchez, and Ricardo Flores Magón. Paredes and the other contributors to the volume present George I. Sánchez as a teacher, a scholar, and an advocate of human rights. As early as the 1930s Sánchez's efforts to ensure "equal educational opportunities for the Spanish speaking" were evident. Among Sánchez's many contributions are his findings that IQ tests were culturally biased instruments, which directed the attention of educators to admit that test results among minorities had been misinterpreted for years. The collection comprises essays by Paredes and nine other distinguished scholars, including Ernesto Galarza, the Chicano social scientist, historian, author, and educator.

*George Washington Gómez: A Mexicotexan Novel* (1990) is Paredes's most outstanding contribution to Chicano fiction. As Chicano writer Rolando Hinojosa relates in his introduction to the novel, Paredes began the novel in 1936 and had completed it by 1940. His various activities and his academic career, however, interfered with the final preparation of the manuscript for publication. The novel, Hinojosa says, is authentically "set against the Great Depression, the onset of World War II in Europe, and set also against the over-100-year-old conflict of cultures in the Lower Río Grande Valley of Texas, not far from where the Río Grande empties into the Gulf." It is a portrayal of an era of hardships that left a deep mark on the Chicanos of south Texas.

The novel is divided into five parts: "Los sediciosos" (The Seditionists), "Jonesville-on-the-Grande," "Dear Old Gringo School Days," "La Chilla" (The Squeal), and "Leader of His People." Paredes establishes early the environment, ridden with cultural conflict, in which Guálinto, the central character, develops. The character's father, Gumercindo, appears as an innocent victim of violence on the part of the *rinches*. The Texas Rangers treacherously murder Gumercindo because they erroneously assume that he is linked to the seditionist movement involving Anacleto de la Peña and Lupe García, Gualinto's uncle on his mother's side. The seditionists aim toward the establishment of a Spanish-speaking republic in the Southwest. The bitter tone of the novel also is evident from the onset with the portrayal of fearful Mexicans and Texas Mexicans who are convinced that "a Border Mexican knew that there was no brotherhood of men." As the story progresses, María, Guálinto's mother, moves to Jonesville-on-the-Grande under the protection of her brother Feliciano, who fulfills the paternal role for Guálinto and his two sisters, Carmen and Maruca. The violent environment is evident in the childhood games of the protagonist, who pretends that he is killing *rinches* while stabbing the stalks of the banana plants that form a pleasant, secluded grove in the backyard of his home. Although he does not know the story of his father, the child concludes that since the *rinches* easily murder Mexicans, he must kill all the *rinches* when he grows up.

While the Mexican Revolution rages across the border, Feliciano wages his private war against Anglo-Americans. He explains to Guálinto that his family lost a large portion of land in the early days of the division of the territory. When the child inquires as to the fate of that land, his uncle bitterly alludes to the legendary King Ranch: "The Gringos got it. It's part of the Keene ranch now."

The school system in Jonesville-on-the-Grande appears permeated with prejudice against the Mexican American children. The administration disdainfully places the children in "low" first- and second-grade classes until they learn English and are able to attend regular classes. Guálinto, whose father named him George Washington, is a brilliant child, the hope of his family. The narrator explains that "His mother, his uncle, and even Carmen had come to take it for granted that he would grow up to be a great man as his father had wished. A great man who would help and lead his people to a better kind of life." School life is difficult for Guálinto, however. He suffers the abuses of an insensitive teacher, although in his drive to learn he becomes reminiscent of the child Ernesto in Galarza's autobiography, *Barrio Boy: The Story of a Boy's Acculturation* (1971). One scene, which portrays Guálinto reciting a poem about George Washington in front of the school's Parent-Teacher Association, brings to mind Ernesto's successful public performance during a Cinco de Mayo celebration.

Despite such rewarding moments, Guálinto's school days include unpleasant experiences. On one occasion, his abusive teacher beats him and publicly humiliates him for having written a love note to the girl of his dreams. As a teenager he is unable to attend a school party held at a nightclub because the doorman claims that the establishment does not allow admission to Mexican Americans.

In the section "La Chilla" the eighteen-year-old Guálinto dreams of writing an immortal poem for María Elena Osuna, his childhood sweetheart. Guálinto faces the ravages of the Great Depression, which brings serious consequences to his people, although it arrives late in south Texas. The shipping to Mexico of Mexicans and Mexican Americans who cannot readily produce papers becomes common practice. Mexicans who

had been in the United States since 1915 are made to leave the country and are arrested when they attempt to come back to see their families. Guálinto suffers salary discrimination when he is lucky enough to find a job. "La Chilla" is the phrase characters in the novel use to comment on the slight value the Anglo authorities place on Mexican lives. "Sugar is two cents a pound and men are two cents a dozen, Mexicans half-price. Flour costs a quarter a sack, and a quarter costs all of man's efforts and the little pride he has left. La Chilla."

Guálinto also faces the disintegration of his family when his sister Maruca becomes pregnant, bringing shame and dishonor to the family. The protagonist's anguish becomes more intense when he encounters a wanted man on a dark night and hits him with a brick. The man, who turns out to be the former rebel Lupe García, his mother's brother, later dies of pneumonia. Guálinto learns from Feliciano that García was wanted because he had killed an old *rinche,* the murderer of Guálinto's father.

"Leader of His People," the fifth section of the novel, brings the narrative to an end with an ironic twist. Guálinto, who has become a lawyer and changed his name to George G. Gómez, returns to his hometown just before the United States enters World War II, bringing with him an Anglo American wife. He is a first lieutenant in counterintelligence for the U.S. Army. When his uncle Feliciano learns about his mission, he tells him that he hopes he is "smart enough not to mistake a slant-eyed Indian from southern Texas for a Japanese agent." Guálinto has become a *vendido* (sellout) who has lost faith in his people and has little regard for his cultural heritage.

The creative work of Américo Paredes has also enriched Chicano poetry. His second volume of poetry, *Between Two Worlds* (1991), contains early poems dating from the 1930s and 1940s as well as later compositions. Some of the poems had appeared sporadically in Texas newspapers. Paredes confesses that he has always been writing poetry on small pieces of paper. In 1960 he decided to burn his poems, handwritten on "yellowing pieces of paper of all shapes and sizes." He did not completely destroy his poetic corpus, however, and what remains qualifies him as a forerunner of modern Chicano poetry. Aware of his contribution, Paredes says that he "might compete for the title of Grandpa Moses of Chicano literature."

*Between Two Worlds* presents two main sections. In the first part, containing eighty-four poems, some of which are in English and others in Spanish, the poet develops themes that deal with the nature of man and his universal anguish, as well as themes centering on conflicts arising from the poet's Mexican American identity. In addition to examining the effects of oppos-

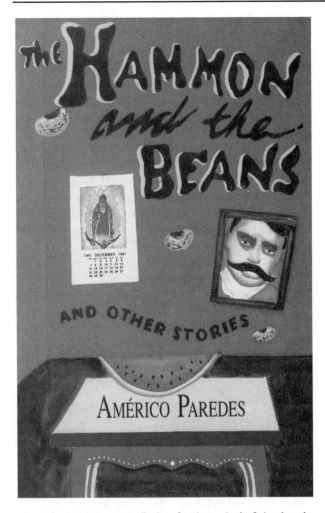

*Cover for Paredes's 1994 collection of stories, set in the fictional south Texas town of Jonesville-on-the-Grande*

poetry, the inner conflicts of the human soul and the anxiety of a dual existence between two worlds. Personalizing the river, the poet seeks emotional comfort from it. He perceives in the river the same turmoil that tortures his soul, however:

> All my pain and all my trouble
> In your bosom let me hide,
> Drain my soul of all its sorrow
> As you drain the countryside,
>
> For I was born beside your waters,
> And since very young I knew
> that my soul had hidden currents,
> that my soul resembled you, . . .

The Spanish version of this poem, "El Río Bravo," which dates from 1936, is included in Paredes's *Cantos de adolescencia.*

Some of Paredes's poetry makes evident his intense reading of Spanish and Latin American poets. A case in point is "Ahí nomás" (Just Over There), from the first part of *Between Two Worlds.* This composition has clear correspondences with "Ahí, no más . . ." (There, no more . . .) from "Notas del alma indígena" (Notes on the Indian Soul), by the Peruvian poet José Santos Chocano. Both Paredes and Santos Chocano praise the physical and inner strength of the New World Indian; both see him as an integral part of their ethnic heritage; and both perceive in the Indian a model to follow. Whereas Santos Chocano's poem is extensive and forms part of a triptych composition, however, Paredes's poem comprises seven stanzas and addresses its theme more directly:

> Long was the road that he had to travel,
> Difficult, rocky his journey was,
> But with a shrug and a smile he answered,
> "Just over there. Sí ahí nomás."
>
> For so the ages have taught the Indian
> To mask his bitterness and despair;
> His way is long but he bravely travels,
> And all his goals are "just over there."

The poet addresses the Indian and admires the fortitude of his spirit, recognizing him as part of his ethnic heritage. He acknowledges the abuse that has afflicted the Indian's life in stanzas 2 and 3. He makes evident, however, that while the Indian has suffered, he continues to move forward, avoiding anger and hopelessness. Hence, the Indian offers a model for the poet to follow as he pursues the path of his existence. In *Between Two Worlds* Paredes offers the reader the poetic work of a lifetime. He ends the volume with a section titled

ing cultural forces on individuals, the poet evokes his experiences overseas during World War II. He offers glimpses of exotic lands, such as Japan, China, and Manchuria. Moreover, he exhibits touches of humor in his depictions of army personnel and military situations. Lyric poetry, in which the poet celebrates love and feminine beauty, also abounds in this first part.

The second part of *Between Two Worlds,* "From Cantos a Carolina (1934–1946)" (From Songs to Caroline), includes ten lyric poems, in which love, beauty, nature, and the intimate thoughts of the poet are the principal topics. The last poem of the book, which serves as the epilogue, is "Canto de la muerte joven" (Song to Early Death). It questions the validity of life's unjustly imposed struggles before the imminent presence of death.

The first poem, "The Río Grande," which dates from 1934, sets the tone for the entire volume and brings forth the most prevalent motifs in Paredes's

"Notes and Random Comments," in which he gives candid insights into his poems.

Paredes the folklorist emerges again in *Uncle Remus con chile* (1993), a collection of 217 interlingual folk texts he obtained in 1962 and 1963, "during a year of fieldwork mostly along the Lower Río Grande border country." Some of the texts date from research endeavors undertaken in the late 1960s and 1970. Besides the many texts that come from the Lower Border area, he includes in this collection materials from northwestern Mexico, the central Mexican plateau, and the Mexican American communities of the Midwest.

Paredes succeeds in rendering a faithful transcription of his sources' vernacular, making the texts valuable interlingual documents as well as samples of folklore. "A device used in some jests," Paredes explains, "is telling most of the story in Spanish and then springing the punch line in English." Although many of the jests included in this collection allude to difficult issues, most of them are humorous and a few are irreverent. After the texts, Paredes provides background comments on the informants, notes on the texts, and a list of references cited.

The source of many of the jests included in this volume is interethnic conflict, and Anglo Americans, tourists, and Texas Rangers especially are the butt of much of the humor in them. However, there are texts that reflect the mistreatment of Mexicans and texts that feature historical characters such as Pancho Villa and Antonio López de Santa Anna. "Los vendidos por Santa Anna," for example, tells how Santa Anna sold the Mexican territory because he did not allow many *rancheros* (ranchers) and *vaqueros* (Mexican cowboys) to fight for their land against the Americans. This treachery is the reason the Mexicans call Mexican Americans "los vendidos por Santa Anna"–"those sold by Santa Anna." "Pagando por Texas" (Paying for Texas) explains why American tourists pay higher prices on the other side of the border: it is because the Mexicans want to make them pay for having stolen Texas.

The topic of racial discrimination emerges in several of the texts. "Los mexicanos güeros" (The Blond Mexicans) tells about blond Mexicans who are amusing themselves in a swimming pool until the manager asks them to leave. When he finds out that they are of German descent, he tells them that they can stay as long as they do not speak Spanish. This same motif of discrimination surfaces humorously in "La discriminación." In a survey of discriminatory practices in Texas, authorities contact the school superintendent at Rio Grande City. The superintendent replies by stating that there is no racial discrimination in that area because "We treat Anglos just like everybody else." Other amusing jests involving racial discrimination are "Dogs Allowed" and "No comía de eso" (He Didn't Eat That). The former tells about a small town in central Texas that has a restaurant featuring the sign "No Dogs or Mexicans Allowed." Down the street, however, there is a Mexican restaurant with a sign that reads "Dogs Allowed. Gringos Too." "No comía de eso" refers to a Mexican who, when told by a waiter that a restaurant does not serve Mexicans, replies, "I don't eat Mexicans."

Paredes the scholar is evident in *Folklore and Culture on the Texas-Mexican Border* (1993), which contains eleven of his most notable essays, first published between 1958 and 1987. These essays are thematically divided into two sections: "The Social Base and the Negotiation of Identity" and "The Folklore Genres: History, Form, and Performance."

In "Folklore of Groups of Mexican Origin in the United States" (1979) Paredes provides an overview of one of his most significant contributions to American folklore, the discovery of the genesis and development of Mexican American folklore out of intercultural conflict. He found the first examples of this folklore in the border ballads portraying men who defended their rights against North American aggressiveness. Rebels such as Juan Nepomuceno Cortina, Aniceto Pizaña, Gregorio Cortez, and Elfego Baca are all subjects of a *corrido*, or ballad. These ballads, which were already in existence at the end of the 1850s, not only constitute the initial genre of Mexican American folklore but also anticipate the emergence of the Mexican *corrido*. Fragments of these early Mexican American ballads are still in existence around the border areas.

Another insightful essay included in *Folklore and Culture* is "On Ethnographic Work among Minority Groups: A Folklorist's Perspective" (1977), in which Paredes addresses the quarrel between Chicanos and anthropology, specifically the Chicano complaint about "ethnographies made of their people by Anglo anthropologists." Based on his years of study, Paredes is led to agree with the Chicanos' opinion. He finds unreal the Mexicans and the Chicanos portrayed in many anthropological studies of the past and asserts that it is difficult for him to understand the false results found in these studies since he knows that the researchers involved "are for the most part liberal in their racial and political views, with real respect for the culture they study."

Paredes states that ethnographers must be aware that when they write about minority groups in the United States they are dealing with people who are their contemporaries and are thus able to formulate a response about their portrayal. This situation differs greatly from that of scholars who write about inhabitants of faraway lands in the distant past. Therefore, ethnographers who work with American minority groups must improve their methodology. More-rigorous methods of gathering information are necessary in order to obtain valid results. Moreover, a thorough knowledge of the language, both standard and dialectal, is an absolute necessity, for example, to undertake a study with Chicanos. What one usually considers to be fluency in a language other than one's own does not equip an ethnographer to interpret accurately people's feelings and attitudes in actual communicative experiences. Unwarranted generalizations may result when an ethnographer misinterprets a colloquial or a metaphorical expression, especially if that ethnographer takes the expression in its standard dictionary meaning. According to Paredes, a skillful jokester can easily mislead an ethnographer, especially if he is an outsider without full command of the language. The essays in *Folklore and Culture* are of paramount importance in comprehending the nature of Paredes's thought and his innovative perspectives in regard to Chicano ethnography and history and border folklore.

*The Hammon and the Beans and Other Stories* (1994) constitutes another dimension of Paredes's role in the development of Chicano letters. Paredes presents seventeen short stories, several of which share with *George Washington Gómez* the south Texas setting of Jonesville-on-the-Grande, under the shadow of Fort Jones. This setting is reminiscent of Brownsville and historic Fort Brown, established in 1846 to house troops during the Mexican-American War and later used to defend the border.

As in the case of the poetry in *Between Two Worlds,* some of these stories were composed in the 1930s and late 1940s. Cases in point are the title story and "Over the Waves Is Out." Although it was written in 1939, "The Hammon and the Beans" was not published until more than twenty years later, in the *Texas Observer* (18 April 1963). "Over the Waves Is Out," written around 1948, did not appear until the summer of 1953 in the *New Mexico Review.* Both of these stories feature child characters who observe but do not fully understand the uneasiness of the adult world of south Texas.

Another story featuring a child character is "A Cold Night." After witnessing a murder, a boy becomes afraid of death and exhibits signs of existential anguish, cursing God and seeking comfort in the colorful image of the Virgen de Guadalupe. Hence the reader sees in this character a forerunner of the central figures in Tomás Rivera's *"... And the Earth Did Not Part"* (1971) and Rudolfo Anaya's *Bless Me Ultima* (1972). Many of the stories with adult narrators center either on the Mexican American experience in the armed forces, particularly in dealing with racism and stereotyping, or simply on the human experience of war.

Américo Paredes is one of the most notable Chicano scholars. His contributions to American and Mexican culture and folklore, Chicano studies, and Chicano literature have been recognized repeatedly. The University of Texas at Austin has established in his honor the Américo Paredes Distinguished Lecture Series, initiated in 1978. His awards have included the Charles Frankel Prize from the National Endowment for the Humanities in 1989 and the Order of the Aztec Eagle from the Government of Mexico in 1990. Paredes died on 5 May 1999.

**References:**

Luis Leal, "Américo Paredes and Modern Mexican American Scholarship," *Ethnic Affairs,* 1 (1987): 1–11;

José Eduardo Limón, *The Return of the Mexican Ballad: Américo Paredes and His Anthropological Text as Persuasive Political Performance* (Stanford, Cal.: Stanford Center for Chicano Research, 1986);

Stanley Rome, "A Border *Cancionero* and a Regional View of Folksong," in *New Directions in Chicano Scholarship,* edited by Ricardo Romo and Raymund Paredes (La Jolla: Chicano Studies Program, University of California at San Diego, 1978), pp. 257–268;

Ramón Saldívar, "The Folk Base of Chicano Narrative; Americo Paredes' *With His Pistol in His Hand* and the Corrido Tradition," in *Chicano Narrative: The Dialectics of Difference* (Madison: University of Wisconsin Press, 1990), pp. 26–42;

Saldívar, "Paredes, Villarreal, and the Dialectics of History," in *Chicano Narrative: The Dialectics of Difference,* pp. 47–60.

# Terri de la Peña

*(20 February 1947 – )*

Salvador C. Fernández
*Occidental College*

BOOKS: *Margins* (Seattle: Seal Press, 1992); republished as *Chicana Blues* (Berlin: Krug & Schadenberg, 1994);
*Latin Satins* (Seattle: Seal Press, 1994);
*Faults* (Los Angeles: Alyson Books, 1999);
*A is for the Americas,* by de la Peña and Cynthia Chin-Lee (New York: Orchard Books, 1999).

OTHER: "A Saturday in August," in *Irvine Chicano Literary Prize, 1985–1987* (University of California, Irvine: Department of Spanish and Portuguese, 1988), pp. 89–99; reprinted in *Finding Courage,* edited by Irene Zahava (Freedom, Cal.: Crossing Press, 1989), pp. 141–150;
"Good-bye Ricky Ricardo, Hello Lesbianism," in *The Coming Out Stories,* edited by Julia Penelope and Susan Wolfe, second edition (Freedom, Cal.: Crossing Press, 1989), pp. 223–233;
"La Maya," in *Intricate Passions: A Collection of Erotic Short Fiction,* edited by Tee Corinne (Austin, Tex.: Banned Books, 1989), pp. 1–10;
"Once a Friend," in *The One You Call Sister,* edited by Paula Martinac (San Francisco: Cleis Press, 1989), pp. 49–62;
"Tortilleras," in *Lesbian Bedtime Stories,* edited by Terry Woodrow (Little River, Cal.: Tough Dove Books, 1989), pp. 83–92;
"Labrys," in *Word of Mouth: Short Stories by Women,* edited by Zahava (Freedom, Cal.: Crossing Press, 1990), pp. 31–32;
"Mariposa," in *Lesbian Bedtime Stories,* edited by Woodrow (Little River, Cal.: Tough Dove Books, 1990), pp. 7–17;
"Sequences," in *Finding the Lesbians: Personal Accounts from Around the World,* edited by Julia Penelope and Sarah Valentine (Freedom, Cal.: Crossing Press, 1990), pp. 162–171;
"Beyond El Camino Real," in *Chicana Lesbians: The Girls Our Mothers Warned Us About,* edited by Carla Trujillo (Berkeley, Cal.: Third Woman Press,

*Terri de la Peña ( photograph by Cheryl Himmelstein)*

1991), pp. 85–94; reprinted in *Lesbian Travels,* edited by Lucy Jane Bledsoe (San Francisco: Whereabouts Press, 1998), pp. 173–185;
"Blue," in *Riding Desire,* edited by Corinne (Austin, Tex.: Banned Books, 1991), pp. 149–153;
"Catnap," in *Cats (and Their Dykes),* edited by Irene Reti and Shoney Sien (Santa Cruz, Cal.: HerBooks, 1991), pp. 105–108;

194

"Desert Quartet," in *Lesbian Love Stories,* edited by Zahava (Freedom, Cal.: Crossing Press, 1991), pp. 154–161;

"Frankie," in *Blood Whispers,* edited by Terry Wolverton (Los Angeles: Silverton Books/The Gay and Lesbian Community Services Center, 1991), pp. 27–28;

"Mujeres Morenas," in *Lesbian Love Stories,* edited by Zahava (Freedom, Cal.: Crossing Press, 1991), pp. 85–93;

"Nullipara, 44," in *Childless by Choice: A Feminist Anthology,* edited by Reti (Santa Cruz, Cal.: HerBooks, 1992), pp. 52–59;

"Chicana, Workingclass and Proud: The Case of the Lopsided Tortilla," in *Out of the Class Closet,* edited by Penelope (Freedom, Cal.: Crossing Press, 1994), 194–206;

"Pajaritos," in *Another Wilderness: Women Writing About the Outdoors,* edited by Susan Fox Rogers (Seattle: Seal Press, 1994), pp. 90–98;

"At Home," in *Dyke Life,* edited by Karla Jay (New York: Basic Books, 1995), p. 27;

"Fiction into Fact," in *Out in the Workplace,* edited by Lourdes Rodríguez and Richard Rasi (Boston: Alyson Press, 1995), pp. 38–51;

"Eco de una amistad/Echo of a Friendship," in *Lesbian Friendships: For Ourselves and Each Other,* edited by Jacqueline S. Weinstock and Esther D. Rothblum (New York: New York University Press, 1996), pp. 31–37;

"Hormonic Convergence: con sangre / sin sangre," in *Off the Rag: Lesbians Writing on Menopause,* edited by Lee Lynch and Akia Woods (Norwich, Vt.: New Victoria Publishers, 1996), pp. 214–220;

"Refugio," in *Night Bites: Vampire Stories by Women,* edited by Victoria A. Brownworth (Seattle: Seal Press, 1996), pp. 165–178;

"Caballito del Diablo," in *Out for More Blood,* edited by Brownworth and Judith M. Redding (Chicago: Third Side Press, 1996), pp. 137–148;

"Blunt Cuts and Permanent Conditions," in *Mom: Candid Memoirs by Lesbians About the First Woman in Their Lives,* edited by Nisa Donnelly (Los Angeles: Alyson Books, 1998), pp. 111–130.

SELECTED PERIODICAL PUBLICATIONS–
UNCOLLECTED: "Palabras," *Sinister Wisdom,* 40 (Spring 1990): 38–39;

"Bouquets," *Matrix Women's Magazine,* 14 (July 1990): 23;

"Tres Mujeres," *Frontiers: A Journal of Women's Studies,* 14 (1990): 60–64;

"An Interview with Gloria Anzaldúa," *Lesbian News,* 16 (1991): 45; complete version published as "On the Borderlands with Gloria Anzaldúa," *Off Our Backs,* 21 (1991): 1–4;

"Finding Out the Secrets: An Interview with Eva Ayala–Mexicana Lesbiana in the U.S.A.," *Sinister Wisdom,* 47 (1992): 11–17;

"Still on the Margins," *Esto no tiene nombre* (Spring 1993): 6–7.

Terri de la Peña, novelist, short-story writer, and fifth-generation Californian, focuses her narratives on the myriad of cultural and social issues that Chicana lesbians face, such as a search for identity, cultural assimilation, class consciousness, historical awareness, internal and external racism, and homophobia. Her writings, therefore, continue a literary tradition and treatment of themes that began with earlier Chicana writers such as Gloria Anzaldúa and Cherríe Moraga.

Mary Theresa de la Peña was born on 20 February 1947 in Santa Monica, California. Her father, Joaquin de la Peña, was a tire repair foreman; her mother, Juanita Escobedo, owned a beauty shop. De la Peña was educated in Santa Monica parochial schools and at Santa Monica Community College, but she is a self-taught writer. She began to write fiction as an adolescent, though her first publication, "A Saturday in August" did not appear until after her fortieth birthday. Her literary success was immediate, as indicated by the number of awards she has received. "A Saturday in August" won third prize in the University of California, Irvine Chicano/Latino Literary Contest (1986). Other awards include a Woman-of-Color Scholarship from the Flight of the Mind Women Writers' Workshop (1988); an Artistic Excellence in Writing Award from VIVA: Lesbian and Gay Latinos in the Arts (1990); Distinguished Recognition for Outstanding Contributions to the Arts, Academia, and the Community, from the National Association of Chicano Studies (1993); and a residency at Cottages at Hedgebrook, a women writers' retreat (1993).

In 1992 de la Peña published her first novel, *Margins,* which narrates the sexual coming-out of Verónica Meléndez, a Chicana graduate student and writer. The development of Verónica's consciousness as a Chicana and a lesbian is the principal theme of the novel. The increasing awareness of her cultural and sexual identity parallels Verónica's physical rehabilitation from an automobile accident in which her first lover, Joanna Núñez, died. Verónica's physical pain reflects the psychological anguish she feels and the social problems she encounters when she identifies herself as a Chicana lesbian. Her recovery begins with a collection of short stories that she writes as an assignment for a professor. Thus, the process of writing serves as a therapeutic

*Cover for de la Peña's first novel (1992), which traces the protagonist's growing awareness of her identity as a Chicana and a lesbian*

device to ease both her physical and emotional suffering. De la Peña also uses the protagonist's storytelling as a means to explore the identity and character of Chicano literature: for example, de la Peña addresses the question of whether works should be written in English or Spanish, choosing in her work to give equal importance to both languages. Another important theme in this novel is the conflict between traditional and nontraditional Chicano families.

*Margins* is structurally divided into three intertwined sections. The first narrates the initial meeting and subsequent intimate relationship between Verónica and Siena Benedetti. The depiction of Verónica's affair with Siena is characterized by an erotic discourse with sexual imagery that exalts the representation of the female body. This relationship represents the protagonist's first phase in her physical and psychological reha-

bilitation. Dreams and flashbacks throughout this section also reconstruct Verónica's prior partnership with Joanna.

The second section narrates the succeeding relationship that Verónica has with René Talamantes, a Texas lesbian and a film student at UCLA. Verónica and René's relationship permits de la Peña to highlight cultural and social differences from the dominant Anglo society and, more importantly, within the Chicano community itself. The relationship between these two women also serves as a means to contrast two families and thus illustrate the different levels of acculturation that typify a Chicano community. René and her mother, Guadalupe, are less assimilated than Verónica and her family. This difference in acculturation is symbolized by objects found in the Talamantes home: the serape on the sofa, the Spanish newspaper they read, and the votive candles lit in homage to El Santo Niño de Atocha and la Virgen de Guadalupe. Languages spoken at home also illustrate the difference: René's family speaks primarily Spanish, Verónica's primarily English. Finally, René also expresses deep pride in her cultural and sexual identity, a feeling Verónica does not voice until the end of the novel.

The third section recounts Verónica's coming out as a lesbian, represented by her increasingly open relationship with René. The process of disclosure begins with a flashback to Verónica's relationship with Siena, when Verónica's nephew, Phil, with whom she is staying, sees Verónica and Siena in an intimate moment and runs out into the street, where he is hit by a car. This episode deeply affects Verónica, and her dreams are filled with violent images, such as Joanna's dead body lying beside her. Phil's accident intensifies Verónica's personal crises and her subsequent relationship with the more open René eventually lead her to disclose her sexual orientation to her family. This coming out signifies personal and social freedom. As a closeted Chicana lesbian, Verónica experienced loneliness and isolation in a close-knit, although sometimes suffocating, Chicano family.

Verónica's coming out also permits de la Peña to criticize repressive sociocultural institutions and ideology that strongly influence the Chicano community (such as the Roman Catholic Church and Chicanismo, the Chicano political movement of the 1960s). Although Verónica is the product of a hybrid culture and acknowledges the diverse influences that have formed her identity, she rejects the oppressive ideological elements that often characterize sociocultural institutions. Verónica's struggles with public and private spaces serve as a stage for de la Peña to attack the sexism inherent in the Chicano community and its rejection of its homosexual population. Thus, Verónica's resolution of her difficulties serves as an answer to those who feel that gays and lesbians taint a family's honor, attack the moral values of society, or hinder the social status of the Chicano community.

Finally, Verónica's self-acceptance and that of her family symbolizes the solidarity of Chicana motherhood and sisterhood. This unity is portrayed when the mothers, Guadalupe Talamantes and Sara Meléndez, sing the popular folk song "De colores" in their daughters' presence. The episode also signifies the collective empowerment of Chicanas that de la Peña advocates throughout her narratives. *Margins* ends with a positive message by presenting two strong Chicana lesbians who resist the repressive societal and cultural boundaries.

De la Peña's second novel, *Latin Satins,* appeared in 1994. The novel narrates the experiences of four Chicana singers, the Latin Satins, who satirize "golden oldies" songs. The main character is their songwriter, Jessica Tamayo, a childcare worker. In addition, Jessica performs in a lesbian chorus and writes music reviews for a lesbian magazine. The Latin Satins advocate social change and celebrate their cultural heritage through their music. The lyrics of their ballads, included in the narrative, highlight the internal and external social problems faced by the Chicano community. Thus, the songs, written in Spanish and English, parallel social issues that de la Peña treats in the novel, such as racism and misrepresentation by the mass media.

Two particularly important issues that *Latin Satins* raises are the racism and discrimination that Chicanas face from their own people as well as from the Anglo and Mexican communities. De la Peña reveals this problem through the social experiences of two children, Yolanda and Angelita. Yolanda attends the childcare center where Jessica works. As a Chicana, Yolanda does not receive the same care and personal attention from the childcare director that the woman gives to Anglo children. Angelita, who is half Chicana and half African American, is the subject of racist comments made by her Chicana friend Xochi—who learned her prejudice from her father, Efraín, a Mexican immigrant. Jessica is also the subject of discrimination at her day care center when two upper-class Anglo mothers try to get her fired for being a lesbian. Thus, de la Peña criticizes upper-class Anglos, Chicanos, and working-class Mexicans in *Latin Satins.* The exploration of these types of discrimination within the Chicano community readily distinguishes de la Peña from other Chicana/Chicano writers.

De la Peña also emphasizes the negative impact that AIDS has had on the Chicano community. Yolanda's father, Danny, a married Chicano homosexual, lives a double life and dies from AIDS. The need for Danny to lead a double life reflects the sexual repression that typifies Mexican and Chicano communities. Because of this same repression, denial, and the lack of AIDS education, the Chicano/Latino community is one of the largest racial groups affected by the disease. One of de la Peña's short stories, "Frankie" (recounting the life of the narrator's childhood friend who dies of AIDS), best exemplifies the impact of this disease on the Chicano community. The emergence of AIDS as a literary theme is also prevalent in the works of young Chicano writers such as Rubén Martínez and Luis Alfaro.

Two additional important themes that de la Peña explores in both *Margins* and *Latin Satins* are the economic transformation of Santa Monica and West Los Angeles, and the importance of Mexican culture for Chicanos. The setting of both novels in her hometown permits de la Peña to develop the first of these themes. Santa Monica and West Los Angeles have changed from residential neighborhoods to commercial areas patronized by yuppies who frequent the art galleries and expensive shops that now characterize the areas. For de la Peña, this urban metamorphosis signifies the displacement or removal of Chicanos from their community. Simultaneously, the urban transformation is juxtaposed with the depiction of another displaced social class—the homeless who relocated to Santa Monica during the 1980s. Thus, the city of Santa Monica includes both the privileged and the displaced.

De la Peña's exploration of the second theme substantiates the importance of Mexican cultural traditions within the Chicano community as a primary source for Chicano literature. De la Peña makes references to pre-Hispanic cultures (the Pyramid of the Sun in Teotihuacán) and important female icons (Tonantzin/Our Lady of Guadalupe and Frida Kahlo, a famous Mexican painter). She also refers to historical events such as Cinco de Mayo, which has become a significant date for the Chicano community, celebrating the victory in Puebla, Mexico, of Benito Juárez's army over the invading French troops of Napoleon III on 5 May 1862. The cultural and historical visions inherent in this type of reference represent a nostalgic view of the past, another characteristic of Chicano literature. These nostalgic feelings are illustrated in *Latin Satins* by Jessica's father, Arturo, who sings in a Cinco de Mayo celebration at the day care center. Arturo dresses in a *charro* suit (an elegant Mexican cowboy outfit), a clear expression of Mexican identity. The use of the *charro* suit symbolizes the nostalgic vision of Chicano culture, which identifies itself with both Mexico and California.

Another significant aspect of de la Peña's work is her place in the evolution of Chicano literature. De la Peña follows a linguistic tradition in Chicano literature

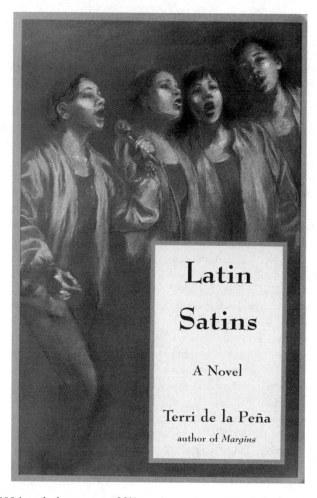

*Cover for de la Peña's 1994 novel, about a group of Chicana singers who use their music to address cultural and social issues*

by advocating the use of bilingual dialogue and code-switching (the alternation between two languages by a single speaker). She also incorporates a new aesthetic element into Chicano literature, erotic discourse, which describes sexual attraction between women, traditionally a taboo topic in Chicano literature. Thus, de la Peña's novels also belong to the lesbian and feminist literary tradition represented by Anzaldúa, Moraga, and Adrienne Rich.

"Territories," a collection of seven short stories, is currently unpublished, although it won first prize in the Chicano/Latino Literary Contest at the University of California, Irvine, in 1992. Some of these stories address women's issues. The first story, "Lonely People" (1980), narrates the struggles of Felicia Montoya, a Chicana feminist organizer who demonstrates against violence in the mass media. A victim of rape, she is rejected by her husband. Later, at a demonstration, she meets a young man who proves to be an unreliable character. The second story, "A Singular Development" (1980), centers on Ramona Quinn, a light-skinned Chi-

cana with a negative body image. Her white boyfriend criticizes her physical appearance, while a Latino praises her beauty. The third story, "Sketches and Silk" (1981), treats the relationship between Cristina Córdova-Vega and her mother. After her parents' divorce, Cristina, a Chicana artist, was raised by her father because her Anglo mother, a clothing designer, moved to the East Coast. Thus, de la Peña analyzes the daughter-mother relationship of two creative women who live in two different worlds.

The next two stories deal with the issues of AIDS and homosexuality in the Chicano/Latino community. In "El Cuñado" (Brother-in-Law, 1990) Mónica Tovar encounters her former brother-in-law, whom she has not seen in twenty-five years, at a gay/lesbian event. In flashbacks, she remembers their relationship and confronts the fact that he now has AIDS. "Ventanas" (Windows, 1992) focuses on the homophobia of a Chicano cop in Santa Monica.

The third group of stories depicts Chicanas and Chicanos in the community and the social problems they face or encounter at critical moments. The principal character in "Territories" (1992) is Rafael Cortés, who also appears in *Latin Satins*. He and Billie Otero relive their past when dealing with a pregnant, runaway teenager. Finally, "Tierra del Fuego" (Land of Fire, 1994) narrates the problems that María de la Luz Fernández faces when she has to evacuate during the Malibu fire of 1993. This story, based on an incident reported by the Los Angeles media, tells of María, a Mexican domestic worker, who is rescued by Cindi Carbajal, a Chicana who works next door. Both characters safely escape the Malibu fire but are left stranded on the beach.

The literary, social, and cultural topics that de la Peña explores in *Margins, Latin Satins,* and the collection "Territories" are also present in her other work. "Good-bye Ricky Ricardo, Hello Lesbianism" (1989) is a coming-out narrative analyzing de la Peña's personal experiences and identity as a Chicana and a lesbian. One of the issues that she examines is her sexual difference, something she felt since childhood. De la Peña employs the *I Love Lucy* television program to illustrate her childhood sexual distinctness. She recounts that as a child she used to play the role of Ricky because she "had the privilege of kissing 'Lucy,' as enacted by Frances, a hazel-eyed, auburn-haired beauty whose familial roots originated in Jalisco."

"Good-bye Ricky Ricardo, Hello Lesbianism" includes several autobiographical elements that appear in de la Peña's other works. One such reference is the recounting of her first date with Rose, a Polish American woman who also comes from a working-class background, an episode developed in two other short stories, "Sequences" (1990) and "Beyond El Camino Real" (1991). Both stories narrate the relationship between Mónica Tovar (the character from "El Cuñado") and Jozie Krozinski as a means to describe the formation of the protagonist's consciousness as a Chicana lesbian. Another personal element is de la Peña's recuperation from a broken heart caused by the marriage of her girlfriend to a Mexican gardener. This experience serves as the primary theme of "Once a Friend" (1989). In this short story de la Peña also treats cultural differences that characterize the Chicano community, such as traditional and nontraditional families, educated and uneducated Chicanas, Mexicans and Chicanos, and monoculturalism and biculturalism. This story further explores the future of Chicanas, exemplified by the characters of Laura Esparza and Toni Dorado. Laura represents the more traditional Chicana who believes that marriage provides security, whereas Toni symbolizes the independent Chicana.

Toni Dorado, at age forty, is also the protagonist of de la Peña's third novel, *Faults* (1999). The prologue,

fifteen chapters, and epilogue of this novel present not only Toni's perspective but also those of the women closest to her: her younger sister, Sylvia; her mother, Adela; Sylvia's teenage daughter, Gabriela; and Toni's former lover, Pat Ramos. In a March 1999 statement, de la Peña explained: "I believe this is the first novel to delve into an elderly Mexican-American mother's feeling about her relationships with her adult daughters, one a lesbian, the other in an abusive marriage. The novel deals with several contemporary issues in the lives of workingclass Mexican-American women in southern California, including the trauma they experience during and after the Northridge earthquake." Characters from *Margins* also appear, although the novels are independent.

In several short stories de la Peña treats the understanding of social issues that affect the Chicano community. In "Tres Mujeres" (Three Women, 1990) de la Peña examines the sociocultural heritage of three generations of Chicanas: Josefina Reyes, her daughter Mariana, and her granddaughter Traci. Mariana, searching for her past, conducts an oral history interview of her mother, who emigrated from Chihuahua, Mexico, and settled in Santa Monica. The interview serves as a narrative device to document the racism and prejudice that each of the women has suffered. Josefina's testimony narrates the social and economic transformation of Santa Monica.

The formation of Chicana cultural heritage is present in "La Maya" (1989) and "Desert Quartet" (1991). In the first story Adriana's love fantasies about Pilar, a tour guide at Mayan ruins, are intertwined with historical references to archaeological monuments found in the Yucatan peninsula, such as Chichén-Itza and Tulum. De la Peña's historical and archaeological references symbolize, once again, a search for a nostalgic past. In "Desert Quartet" de la Peña analyzes cultural contradictions that color the Chicana experience. Marisa Cantú, a mestiza in appearance, recognizes the importance of the Spanish conquistadors but empathizes with the native tribes. She herself is not fluent in Spanish, yet she despises Chicanas who cannot understand the language. She believes in Chicana solidarity, but her lovers are white women.

As a Chicana lesbian, de la Peña also represents in her works a continuous search for private and public space. "A Saturday in August" and "Mujeres Morenas" (Brown-Skinned Women, 1991) illustrate this search. In the first story de la Peña portrays the isolation and alienation that two Chicanas, Alicia Orozco and Marti Villanueva, suffer because of traditional values held by Chicano families. Alicia's family does not approve of her living alone in an apartment because "they believe a Chicana only leaves her parents' home when she mar-

*edited 2/13/88*

Copyright Terri de la Pena 1985

ONCE A FRIEND

Terri de la Pena

She slid in quietly, padding across the living room's russet broadloom, oblivious of our dozing father sprawled on the couch, the evening's Herald Examiner unfurled on his lap. When Mama and I glanced up at her sudden approach, Toni smiled perfunctorily.

"You sure came back fast," I said, helping Mama spread assorted pieces ~~of a~~ (dress pattern) on our rectangular dining room table's surface.

"I have to study." ~~Seeming preoccupied,~~ Toni remained standing, (fiddling with the tousled fringe of her macrame shoulder bag.) "What're you making?" ~~She addeed as an afterthought.~~

"Sylvia's blazer," Mama revealed, expertly pinning the tissue-paper pattern to the ~~soft~~ burgundy ~~fabric.~~ *velvet.*

~~"Velvet?"~~

~~"Yeah.~~ "Isn't it neat?" I grinned, ~~lightly~~ caressing the plushy nap.

"Classy," Toni laconically retorted. "Mama, do you know a Mrs. Luna from church?"

"Oh, ~~si~~ Como no? She's in the Altar Society, *and* ~~j~~Just had a baby, ~~too.~~ *Por que me preguntas?* ~~That reminds me. I should send her a card.~~"

"Laura and I went to visit her in the hospital tonight."

*Page from de la Peña's revised typescript of a story included in the 1989 anthology* The One You Call Sister; *the main character, Toni Dorado, is the protagonist of de la Peña's 1999 novel,* Faults *(Collection of Terri de la Peña)*

ries—or dies." Marti's family considers her a social deviant because she is a lesbian. De la Peña provides an ideal ending for the story—the pairing of two Chicanas who have had to overcome the same personal and social obstacles. This ideal union of Chicanas is further developed to include all Latin Americans or *mujeres morenas,* the theme of "Mujeres Morenas," which recounts the festivities of La Celebración Latina Lesbiana.

Yosemite National Park serves as the setting for two other short stories, "Blue" (1991) and "Mariposa" (Butterfly, 1990). The first recounts an erotic experience between Chic Lozano, a character who appears in *Latin Satins,* and an Anglo woman. This short story explores cultural and sexual differences between women of color and Anglo lesbians, a recurring theme in de la Peña's works. Another persistent theme, the different levels of assimilation occurring in Latino communities, is explored in "Mariposa." In sum, de la Peña's short stories explore the representation of Chicana lesbians who have transgressed societal, cultural, sexual, and personal boundaries.

De la Peña's novels and short stories are concerned with social and cultural problems that Chicanas face within the Chicano community as well as in Anglo society. Her works continue Chicano, feminist, and lesbian literary traditions, and appeal to a wide audience. De la Peña has been the subject of a critical bio-bibliographical entry in *Contemporary Lesbian Writers of the United States. Margins* has been the subject of several critical commentaries and reviews in journals and magazines ranging from *Publishers Weekly* and *Library Journal* to *The Lesbian Review of Books* and *Lambda Book Report.* It was also one of two hundred books selected by *The American Bookseller* for its core list of feminist books. De la Peña continues to expand her literary endeavors:

another 1999 project was *A is for the Americas,* a children's alphabet book that was written with Cynthia Chin-Lee and that is intended to increase the awareness that "Americans" are not just the people who live in the United States. As shown by the positive reception of *Margins* and the appearance of *Latin Satins,* de la Peña's work has become an integral part of the Chicana literary canon.

**Interview:**

"Terri de la Peña: 'I Wrote This Book Because I Wanted to Read it,'" in *Happy Endings: Lesbian Writers Talk About Their Lives and Work,* by Kate Brandt (Tallahassee, Fla.: Naiad Press, 1993), pp. 237–246.

**References:**

Rose Cosme, "One Chicana Lesbiana's View of *Margins,*" *Esto no tiene nombre* (Spring 1993): 7;

Mary Ann Daly, "A Study in Character: Terri de la Peña's Latina Lesbians Light Up the Page," *Lambda Book Report* (July/August 1992): 15;

Donají, "A Closer Look at Terri de la Peña," *Esto no tiene nombre* (Spring 1993): 6;

Ellie Hernández, "A Blind Sided View of *Margins,*" *Esto no tiene nombre* (Spring 1993): 7;

Camille D. Loya, "Terri de la Peña," *Contemporary Lesbian Writers of the United States: A Bio-Bibliographical Critical Sourcebook,* edited by Sandra Pollack and Denise D. Knight (Westport, Conn.: Greenwood Press, 1993), pp. 168–173.

**Papers:**

Terri de la Peña's novel and short-story manuscripts, as well as other materials, are housed in the June L. Mazer Lesbian Archives in West Hollywood, California.

# Cecile Pineda

*(24 September 1942 –     )*

Francisco A. Lomelí
*University of California, Santa Barbara*

BOOKS: *Face* (New York: Viking, 1985);
*Frieze* (New York: Viking, 1986);
*The Love Queen of the Amazon: A Novel* (Boston: Little, Brown, 1992).

PLAY PRODUCTIONS: *Murder in the Cathedral,* adapted from the play by T. S. Eliot, San Francisco, Glide Memorial Church, 1969;
*Vision of the Book of Job,* San Francisco, Sloat Presbyterian Church, 1970;
*After Eurydice,* San Francisco, WABE Theater, Lone Mountain College, 1972;
*The Fool of the World,* by Pineda and Max Pass, San Francisco, Sharon Meadow, Golden Gate Park, 1972;
*The Bear's Bash,* by Pineda and Eric Berne, San Francisco, Sharon Meadow, Golden Gate Park, 1973;
*The Rainbow Caper,* by Pineda and Ben Bayol, San Francisco, Sharon Meadow, Golden Gate Park, 1974;
*Stoneground,* adapted from *Bomarzo,* by Manuel Mujica Laínez, San Francisco, Firehouse Theater, 1974;
*The Trial,* adapted from *Der Prozeß,* by Franz Kafka, San Francisco, All Saints' Episcopal Church, 1975;
*Medea: A Legend for the Theater,* San Francisco, All Saints' Episcopal Church, 1976;
*Threesomes: A Clown Play,* San Francisco, All Saints' Episcopal Church, 1977;
*Time/Piece,* workshop production, San Francisco, All Saints' Episcopal Church, 1978;
*Goya,* workshop production, San Francisco, All Saints' Episcopal Church, 1979.

MOTION PICTURE: *Face,* screenplay by Pineda, Northwood Communications, 1988.

OTHER: "Runes," in *Antología retrospectiva del cuento chicano,* edited by Juan Bruce-Novoa and José Gui-

*Cecile Pineda at the time of* The Love Queen of the Amazon
*(photograph by Marvin Lichtner)*

llermo Saavedra (Mexico City: Consejo Nacional de Población, 1988), pp. 205–207.

SELECTED PERIODICAL PUBLICATIONS–UNCOLLECTED: "Flotsam," *Zyzzyva,* 2 (Fall 1986): 79–82;
"Ocean," *Fire Island Express,* 8 August 1996, p. 29.

Cecile Pineda began her involvement with literature not as a writer of fiction but as the author of several performance pieces originated in collaboration with members of the Theatre of Man, a highly experimental, collaborative ensemble theater company she founded and directed from 1969 to 1981 in the San Francisco Bay area. She operated as an independent theater artist for many years before being recognized and incorporated into Chicano literary circles in 1985 with the publication of her debut novel, *Face*. Performance pieces, short stories, poems, satires, and essays are among her many literary credits.

There are no obvious ethnic overtures in Pineda's creative works, and few knew about her background until Juan Bruce-Novoa discovered her Mexican heritage shortly after the publication of *Face* in 1985. Chicano literature had been gaining a new impetus in trying to surpass the experimentations of the 1970s by promoting new clusters of writers and thereby expanding its definition beyond restrictive nationalist confines. Pineda's emergence coincided with the literary boom of a large group of writers who created what some scholars have called the Chicana Generation. Whether by chance or design, writings by Chicanas came to dominate the general Chicano literary scene in the 1980s, thanks in great part to the experiential resonance of the works of such writers as Ana Castillo, Cherríe Moraga, Pat Mora, Denise Chávez, Gloria Anzaldúa, Margarita Cota-Cárdenas, Sandra Cisneros, Lucha Corpi, Helena María Viramontes, and Naomi Quiñónez. Pineda's work satisfies a need to reevaluate identity, community, and ethnic poetics while exploring other themes that function more aptly at the metaphorical instead of the purely sociological level.

Pineda was born on 24 September 1942 in Harlem in New York City, an unusual point of origin for a Chicano author. Her father, Emilio Rosendo Pineda Galván, along with her grandfather and two uncles, had fled Mexico City for political reasons at the beginning of the 1910–1920 Mexican Revolution. Her father assumed the name Ernesto Pratt to avoid detection from immigration agencies as he journeyed illegally through Brownsville, Texas, and on to New York, where he hoped to pass unnoticed. There he met and married Pineda's mother, Marthe-Alice Henriod, a native of Switzerland.

The immigrant experience left an indelible mark of ambivalence on the family's sense of cultural allegiance. Coming from an educated and patrician background, Pineda's father was accustomed to a privileged existence back in Mexico because of his father's success as a lawyer. Fiercely intellectual and a Renaissance man, Emilio Pineda spoke nine languages and studied at Harvard, Fordham, and Columbia universities at a time when Mexicans had little access to American institutions of higher learning. Except for the dissertation, he completed all requirements at Columbia for a Ph.D. in

linguistics during the 1930s, but after leaving a full-time position at the City College of New York, where he taught Romance languages, he occupied a series of increasingly menial jobs as the young family struggled to survive. In an unpublished 20 April 1995 interview Cecile Pineda explained a key aspect of her father's psyche:

> Although he viewed himself as white, and claimed we were descended from the Spanish explorer, [Alonso de] Pineda, who explored the Gulf of Mexico and mouth of the Natchez river for the Spanish crown in 1521, he deeply feared what he called *La Leyenda Negra* (The Black Legend or an anti-Spanish attitude propagated mainly by the English since the sixteenth century), as he styled American anti-Hispanic prejudice. His aspiration for me, I strongly suspect, was that I not carry my Mexicanness publicly because he was aware of the pervasiveness of racism in the United States.

Pineda's mother, from an aspiring French-Swiss middle-class family (her father built the first automobile in Switzerland), was preoccupied with appearances and fashion. A cold and withholding mother, she ignored the young Cecile, forcing her to fend for herself. Pineda attended Corpus Christi, a parochial school taught by Dominican nuns. Located across the street from Columbia Teachers College, the school afforded her ample opportunities to experience the latest teaching methods in collaborative learning couched within a progressive social agenda. She later studied at Marymount High School and received a full scholarship to Barnard College, from which she graduated with honors in 1964. Her education especially shaped her worldview and sensibilities; her early life was profoundly influenced as well by the family's proximity to Columbia University, Union and Jewish Theological seminaries, the Juilliard School of Music, and other intellectually thriving institutions. In 1966 she married a Frenchman, Felix Leneman, with whom she has two sons.

Pineda was well aware that she was a product of a mixed marriage between two diametrically different immigrant parents situated in a constantly changing social milieu. Her godmother, Jane E. Browne, functioned like a surrogate mother, playing a central role in Pineda's life and intellectual development. Browne instilled in Pineda a deep appreciation for things related to theater, literature, myth and legend, and a love of peasant culture. In another unpublished interview on 23 February 1996, questioned further as to the main factor contributing to her inclination toward literature, Pineda answered succinctly: "Loneliness. The loneliness of being an only child, incredibly unpopular in school, always standing on the sidelines, never partici-

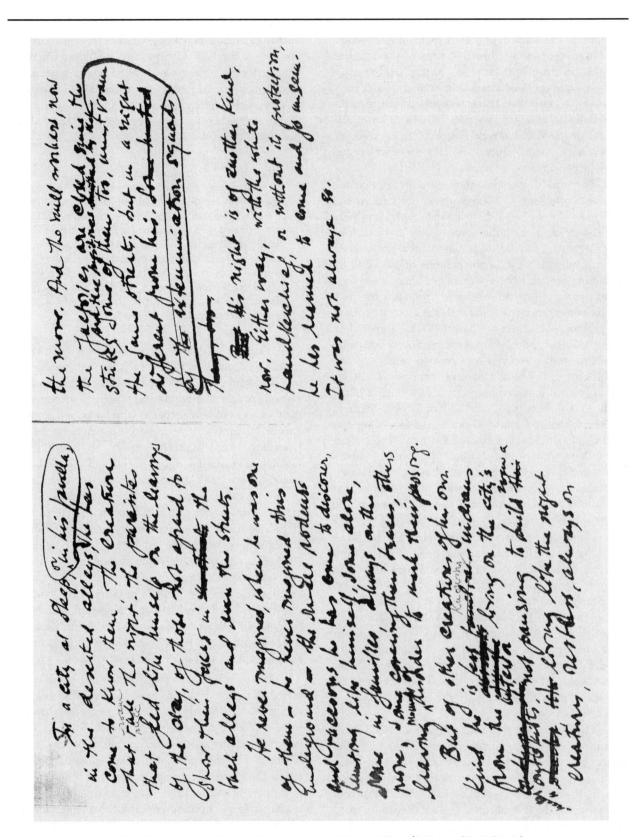

*Pages from the notebook in which Pineda wrote her 1985 novel,* Face *(Collection of Cecile Pineda)*

pating. . . . My interests were different from everyone else's."

Pineda developed her keen intellect through a wide variety of influences; her reading had a particularly international or cross-cultural bent, including the works of Alain Robbe-Grillet, Samuel Beckett, Isaak Babel, Kobo Abe, Eduardo Galeano, and J. M. Coetzee. In the 1995 interview she observed: "My love for the word originates in my involvement already as a high school student in the theater, first as an actress, and only much later, after the birth of my sons, as a director/*metteuse-en-scene*." Prior to her formal involvement in theater she worked as a junior editor at the Commonwealth Fund in New York and later as a line editor at Paul Hoeber, at that time the medical books division of Harper and Row, where she edited a quarterly journal of obstetrics and gynecology. In the late 1960s she began graduate school at San Francisco State University; she received her master's degree in 1970, studying performance under her mentor, Paul Rebillot, whose vision directly contributed to her own concept of theater.

Buoyed by the politics of the 1960s and the renewed idealism for constructing (or at least impacting) a new social order, Pineda founded the Theatre of Man in 1969. She collaborated with visual artists, composers, choreographers, designers, and playwrights from the San Francisco area to create some twelve laboratory works based on her scripts, including three performance works for children. She carried out various functions as director, dramaturgy trainer, publicist, fundraiser, and general driving moral force of the company. Her professional career is also characterized by affiliations with several universities as a creative writer in residence, among them the University of San Antonio (1986), Saidapet University in Madras, India (1987), the University of California at Berkeley (1989), California College of Arts and Crafts in Oakland (1987–1992), San Francisco State University (1992–1993), San Jose State University (1991 to 1994), and Bennington College in Vermont (1995). She taught creative writing in the English department at San Diego State University from 1995 to 1999 and was appointed visiting writer at Mills College from 1999 through 2000.

In the 1995 interview Pineda described the Theatre of Man as a "poet's theater, concerning itself with creating a theatrical language based on archetype, myth, symbol, and dream. Some of my thematic explorations focused on sexual role expectation, totalitarianism, the problem of evil, and the dread of postmodern existence. My training in the craft of writing was acquired by doing." Although her company presented various works of other authors, she also staged several of her original pieces as well as adaptations: *Murder in the Cathedral* (1969), *Stoneground* (1974), and *The Trial* (1975). The original plays *Vision of the Book of Job* (1970), *After Eurydice* (1972), *Medea: A Legend for the Theater* (1976), *Threesomes: A Clown Play* (1977), *Time/Piece* (1978), and *Goya* (1979) were products of collaborative work, somewhat within the mime troupe tradition. The common denominator is experimentalism and a reinterpretation of several canonical archetypes for the sake of pointing out a relevance to contemporary life.

All of these presentations met with critical success, but only two of them, *The Trial* and *Murder in the Cathedral,* were commercial successes as well. Perhaps the most significant piece developed in collaboration with Pineda's ensemble company was *After Eurydice* (*after* intended as a pun in the senses of "following" and "according to"). An investigation of sex-role expectations, the piece took two years to develop. Through carefully elaborated improvisational exercises, the first phase of rehearsal yielded material that was eventually organized into an articulately structured performance score incorporating such elements as original vocal and instrumental music, use of sculptural materials, and movement and dance, as well as material from such disparate sources as the Homeric hymns to Demeter and Fannie Farmer's *Boston Cooking-School Cook Book* (1896).

Through the language of sound and movement, these initial exercises were addressing, in the early 1970s, questions that later became the theoretical ground of gender studies: is there a male language in contrast to a female one? If so, how might it be recognized? What relational qualities might it permit between speakers? In what way might an equitable world exist, from a male or female point of view? In what ways do men's dreams and sexual fantasies differ from women's? These initial explorations were transformed into a series of ritualized events contrasting the imagined and the real, with mythic underpinnings rooted in the story of Orpheus and Eurydice. In an unpublished letter of March 1997 Pineda singled this play out as perhaps the most important in the company's repertoire, particularly in terms of its thematic material and the process of improvisatorial exploration: "It led me to understand that, at least in terms of white heterosexual American society as I recognize it, male and female exist separately as two different cultures, at best fated to enjoy brief moments of shared perception, and even more rarely of intimacy."

Pineda did not begin writing fiction until the early 1980s, when it became clear that curtailment of federal and municipal support for the humanities meant that her theater company could no longer maintain itself. She was finally forced to put the ensemble's assets on the auction block in 1981. As she recalled in the 1996

*Dust jacket for Pineda's second novel (1986), about a master carver who works on the Borobudur temple in Java*

interview, she suddenly found herself in a precarious situation: "I was in effect cutting myself off from my artistic community, and by extension, my society. I recognized that I needed to reinvent a new identity for myself before I could forge another community. I have always looked for family outside traditional ways." Also in 1981 she lost her mother; later her adored godmother became gravely ill, and the urgency to raise money to support her motivated Pineda's switch to fiction. As a self-taught novelist, she was moved by the narrative strategy of *Suna no onna* (translated as *The Woman in the Dunes,* 1964) by Abe; the elliptical narrative of *Le grand cahier* (1986; translated as *The Notebook,* 1988) by Agota Kristof; the plot giveaway of *Crónica de una muerte anunciada* (1981; translated as *Chronicle of a Death Foretold,* 1982) by Gabriel García Márquez; the interpolation of the remembered, dreams, and fantasy material of *Pedro Páramo* (1955) by Juan Rulfo; the notion of catastrophe, elaborated by mathematician René Thom; and the indeterminacy and radical ambiguity of French *nouveau roman* writers such as Robbe-Grillet. An

intrinsic quality appears in all of Pineda's works: an incessant search for, and imagining of, a community. Literature became her way of connecting with others while her immediate personal sphere was jeopardized by the collapse of her marriage and, later, the loss of her theater company.

These traumas resulted in a period of reflection and existential angst from which emerged Pineda's debut novel, *Face.* The book won the Commonwealth Club of California Gold Medal and the Sue Kaufman Prize, awarded by the American Academy and Institute of Arts and Letters; it was also nominated for the American Book Award for first work. It was a response to her need to reconnect with society and to start afresh. A 21 May 1977 article in the *San Francisco Chronicle* titled "A Man Reconstructs His Own Face" had captured her interest: it was the story of Walter Alves Pereira, a thirty-six-year-old barber from Rio de Janeiro whose fall from a cliff resulted in a catastrophic disfigurement, following which he proceeded to reconstruct his face using novocaine, needle and thread, razor blades, and builder's plaster. Pineda reconstitutes that basic plotline around a protagonist named Helio Cara, tracing his steps in the dark underworld of rejection—he is a refugee or exile without a reason, except for his sudden deformity. The simple anecdote reverberates with the meaning and wonder of an existential and philosophical order. It emphasizes the ephemeral quality of physical norms generally taken for granted.

The protagonist experiences a process of alienation that marks his life forever: those close to him, among them his girlfriend, Lula, turn their backs on him; others persecute and ridicule him; and still others burn his shack, forcing him to return to his mother's hovel in the hinterland. There he begins to reconstruct his face, becoming his own surgeon and sculptor of a fleshy mask and, in the process, recovering an identity and dignity that others denied him. Literally, he becomes a creature of the night, wandering among the shadows in the realm of societal nothingness. Others perceive him as an invisible outlaw and marginal enigma: "Finally it seems to him they no longer even see him. More and more, he takes refuge in the night, in darkness, or in the early hours before dawn, before the sun is up." He also scavenges for food and becomes known as a *bruxo* (sorcerer); more importantly, he recovers from a symbolic death of absolute relegation—a condition worse than actual death. Whereas many people might manifest a bitter cynicism in such a situation, at the end Helio Cara displays signs of forgiveness toward the agents of his social alienation as he reincorporates himself, albeit physically reinvented, into the society of Rio de Janeiro.

The simple plot creates suspense and awe while offering a haunting Kafkaesque allegory centering on a person who literally reconstructs his face, stitch by stitch, suggesting either a monstrosity or a miracle worker. He is an elephant-man-like pariah, and his condition offers a multitude of meanings relative to identity, socialization, and individuation. His name *Helio* connotes many things: his given name means "guy" or "everyman" in Portuguese; it may also signify helium, a colorless gas (implying a degree of invisibility or vanishing configuration), or "heliocentric" (the notion of measuring everything in relation to the sun, the source of all life, thus associating his face and the sun as parallel entities necessary for his existence). *Cara* is Spanish for "face," the central focus of his essence. Together, they embody a metaphor of modern man who experiences ostracism and persecution in an amoral world that rejects him for being something other than the norm. Multiple puns emerge: face value, losing face, becoming faceless or lacking an acceptable identity, doing an about-face, or facing the facts of his reality. Helio Cara's predicament entails being judged exclusively by the condition of his face. In other words, since he lacks a face his entire existence is called into question, thus conveying that society judges and values people by external physical characteristics; the precept of inner qualities and attributes is either lost or deemed insignificant.

A social-philosophical criticism is well embedded in the novel with strong symbolic connotations that defy any ethnically specific allusions. The work operates at a metaphorical level to denounce dehumanization at the hands of institutions and so-called friends. Consequently, the journey of the protagonist is a protracted process to reclaim his identity. Although the story seems to be ethnically generic, the process followed is analogous to what any expelled member of society needs to do to recover his humanity. In that sense the novel offers useful lessons for someone of mixed birth who has experienced stigmas, denial, and exile—conditions commonly internalized by ethnic minorities or those who feel they occupy the margins. *Face,* according to a 1994 article by Francisco A. Lomelí, is a Chicana author's configuration of an "invisible minority" syndrome, vicariously and generically placed in Brazil. Such a method emphasizes the universality of the effects.

Depicted as a kind of monster, Helio Cara conjures up many ironies. His expulsion from the unfriendly urban center in Rio de Janeiro into the hinterland becomes both his salvation and his cross to bear. He is forced to resort to his creativity and resourcefulness in order to retain part of what he is, but his condition follows him like a phantasmagoric shadow. He symbolically conducts repeated surgical procedures on himself,

thereby undergoing a metamorphosis equivalent to revamping or recreating his identity. The action of the novel is relatively minimal, because what matters most is the internal process experienced by the protagonist. His journey is one of recovering part of himself while creating a different persona—one that a superficial society can accept. In so doing, he gains a real appreciation for his humanity while reaffirming his dignity.

Much of the narrative centers on flashbacks and dreams, which seem to be stepping-stones to his past or elements by which to define his lived reality. Moreover, his existence is forever marked by the act of remembering—often in an incantatory style—to reconstruct and validate his past:

> He would remember distinctly switching on the light. He would remember sensing that something had changed. He would remember searching the mirror on the wall opposite. He would distinctly remember the sound of the lightswitch. He would remember seeing a mirror in the sudden light. He would remember the first instant of seeing something. He would remember feeling nothing, nothing at all.

His memory is a Cartesian device to remind him of what he is, and it becomes his weapon to fight his own extinction. Most of the novel obsessively concentrates on the moments surrounding his accident, as if that event is a signpost of what he has become; but the work also emphasizes a living and assertive conscience. Helio Cara's entire being seems to be consumed by the shattering consequences of his fall.

Helio Cara exemplifies valor, resourcefulness, and an uncanny knack for survival, despite many overwhelming obstacles. He manages to overcome total negation and in effect becomes his own creator. In the end, he is better prepared to return to Rio de Janeiro, having learned to deal with dehumanizing social forces—especially urban centers—on his own terms. He remarks about his new face, which on the surface may appear generic but actually denotes individuation:

> It is a face; it is not particularly striking, certainly not attractive or handsome. It evokes neither origins nor class. It is unremarkable—like anyone else's. But no. Not like anyone. It is his, his alone. He has built it, alone, sewn it stitch by stitch, with the very thin needle and the thread of gossamer. It has not been given casually by birth, but made by him, by the wearer of it.

Helio Cara, then, triumphs against all odds and ultimately becomes a stronger person, essentially gaining a second chance in a life over which he will now have more control.

Pineda's second novel, *Frieze* (1986), offers a radical departure from the existential quest found in *Face,* but it underscores another kind of exploration with forms–both narrative and architectonic–and an ancient way of life. As the title suggests, the work focuses in part on a cycle of ornate stone reliefs or panels found in the first gallery of the temple of Borobudur, an imposing shrine on the island of Java in Indonesia. This vast Buddhist pyramid from the ninth century is a tribute to the art of stone carving as much as it is a monument to vernacular history, depicting myth and custom as they continue to be celebrated in the Java of the present day. On the surface, the ambience of courtiers and slaves in the novel appears anachronistic, but there are many surprising insights that parallel the modern world; at the same time the work exudes an Eastern spirituality of pantheism and a timeless sense of artistry.

This novel is the lyrical account of an expert frieze maker, Gopal, who dedicates his whole life to his art; the story unfolds within the rigid confines of the social and political mores of his time. Gopal recounts how he is forcibly recruited in India and taken to Java to create "one hundred and twenty friezes carved in stone, friezes to depict the life of the Enlightened One," Siddhartha Gautama, the Buddha. In the process, important glimpses of Gopal's personal life are disclosed, including aspects of his worldview and his relation to his three wives (Maya, the object of desire, Durga, the maid of convenience, and Prenguseng-Poan, the companion of convenience), who mark three stages of his life trajectory. Gopal also chronicles the production of his friezes and the ways his personal history, along with other social-historical elements, influences the mystery of his artistic creation. His story, then, becomes an insider's view of the many struggles involved in producing a magnificent cultural monument that has withstood the test of time.

Gopal contributes to both the creation of the Borobudur temple and what it represents as an instrument of human exploitation by the upper classes and dedication by the artisans. The 120 short chapters correspond to the actual number of friezes comprising the cycle found in the first gallery of the Borobudur shrine, a place initially referred to as a "cosmic mountain, a model of the universe." At the same time, Gopal's life in Java turns into a longing for his earlier personal satisfactions in India, where his artistry has been an end in itself rather than an instrument at the service of the power politics of others.

Various leitmotivs in the novel, such as repeated allusions to darkness, dreams as inner narratives of the subconscious, and fears of blindness, indicate a sense of inevitability. Originally, Gopal works with and learns from Gupta, a master carver who warns him of the dangers of becoming too good at his craft. Another warning comes from his native assistant: "his story of the eyeless carver was clearly meant for me." These words are prophetic. After the completion of his vast project, to which he dedicates more than twenty years, Gopal is blinded by fire to preserve the secrets of the monument he helped create. His life becomes a sacrifice to what the religious shrine presumes to represent: a tribute to the Buddha's eternal value.

Gopal's story appears to exemplify abnegation with respect to religious symbols, but it also reveals the underpinnings of power and hierarchy by those who order the vast army of artisans to execute their grandiose plans. In fact, he feels much like a glorified slave whose every movement, thought, and expression is monitored and regulated: "How easily we accept the yoke!" The novel chronicles human suffering at the hands of rulers bent on a quest for fame and glory in a cyclical struggle for domination. Rulers come and go in their obsession with power, but the poor and the artisans carry the brunt of their burden. For example, the mighty Chola, head of a South Indian dynasty, trades Gopal to another dynasty, the Javanese Sailendra, as a means of balancing power and maintaining an alliance, prompting Gopal to reflect with bitterness: "And what concern was it to him, he who thought of nothing but making war–or peace–when it served him, trading artisans, disrupting whole households merely to decorate a harem wall."

Gopal's commitment to carving the stone is met with nothing but suffering; the implication is that pain is the artist's reward for his dedication to his art. Apparently, artistic perfection must not be repeated; thus his inevitably imposed blindness by those in power:

> Always it astounds me that the face, deprived of eyes, still weeps. I sleep like a stone with no memory of dreaming, yet here the tear lies puddled, trapped in the curve of nose, of cheek, trace of a separate life, closed to my waking. . . . Someone at last, wiping the blood from where it cakes about my eyes. What were once my eyes–hollow now.

The end of Gopal's career as a master carver marks the completion of the religious shrine and caps his devotion to the stone. Irony connects the mundane with the spiritual: his final project portrays Buddha's first sermon, thus indicating life and myth going in opposite directions. Gopal seems to find the secret in the stone, but it is not the secret he has hoped for.

Pineda's third novel, *The Love Queen of the Amazon* (1992), represents another departure, in this case from her aesthetics of an experiential quest for meaning. This delightful antihistorical work, in which actual personages interact with magical-real beings and some caricatures, aims to entertain more than teach, while at the same time it tests all of the senses. It is heavily influenced by the Latin American New Novel and its corresponding cinema, in which multiple dimensions (myth, legend, social realism, eroticism, taboos, landlords versus poor classes, and religion) interact. The light-hearted—and sometimes sardonic—treatment of a wide range of anecdotes satirically evokes the self-conscious seriousness of Peruvian novelist Mario Vargas Llosa (here portrayed as Enrique Vacio-Llares—a pun on his "emptiness"). In some ways, *The Love Queen of the Amazon* resembles the Werner Herzog movie *Fitzcarraldo* (1982) for the unrelenting wish to create an oasis in the midst of a cultural desert. It especially parallels Gabriel García Márquez's *Cien años de soledad* (1967; translated as *One Hundred Years of Solitude,* 1970) with its book-within-a-book internal structure, except that the novelist character Federico Orgaz y Orgaz, who spends his entire time composing "The Love Queen of the Amazon" (supposedly a splendid tapestry of hemispheric history), is a pathetic, class-conscious windbag whose artistic prowess is limited to his perseverance. He imagines that his patrician ego and privilege allow him to buy love in the same way that he might acquire a pet.

The characters' initial blissful innocence becomes transformed into a dubious exploration of freedom from the strict mores of a hierarchical society. The protagonist, Ana Magdalena Arzate de Figueroa, and other characters are involved in the varied constructs of love and end up either rebelling or going their separate ways. At times religiosity gives way to eroticism or a free expression of body and sentiment. Housed in a convent in a dusty Peruvian town called Malyerba (meaning "evil weed"—or marijuana—and evoking García Márquez's Macondo), Ana Magdalena and her fellow students experience the stifling environment of a "stringent oppression," leading to incipient acts of "moral depravity." On a trip to the river to bathe, Ana Magdalena's friend Aurora Constancia displays her provocative, black-laced undergarments to a huddle of spying seminary boys. Later, in an effort to save her friend from drowning, Ana Magdalena sheds her clothing, thereby becoming indecently exposed. Accused of having an unbecoming moral influence on the younger students, both girls are subsequently expelled. Their accuser, Sister Annunciata, clearly demonstrates a myopic inflexibility by casting their acts as impious and dangerous.

On Ana Magdalena's return to her home, she finds her family in deep financial straits, partly because of a vagrant father. Her mother, Andreina, seeks creative ways to earn a living by exploiting the work of her Indian maid, Berta, while maintaining the appearances of a social *doña,* or lady. The mother's pretenses and ambitions are so great that she seizes the opportunity to arrange a marriage between her beautiful daughter and

an older aristocrat, Federico Orgaz y Orgaz, who pontificates about literary creativity but essentially lives in a fantasy world rooted in his social privilege as an impoverished *hacendado* (landowner) barely surviving on his publisher's advance. Although Ana Magdalena attempts to run away rather than comply with such a crude arrangement, her hideout in her great-aunt's brothel facilitates a sexual encounter with Sergio Ballado, a wastrel whom she has always desired, thereby initiating a long but sporadic relationship of fantasy-filled escapades.

A playfulness abounds throughout the narrative, including many puns and tongue-in-cheek allusions, but essentially it is a story of unrequited love between Ana Magdalena—who, like her biblical namesake, is one who is "singularly free of virginal modesty or unnecessary chastity"—and Sergio. Their physical attraction extends throughout the novel until their mutual mercenary interests overtake them; they end up much like the passing ships that Sergio pilots up the Amazon River. Their occasional encounters are temporary flashes of desire, never uncovering the true reason for their attraction. They finish as victims of their own trappings, suggesting that the love they arduously seek does not reflect their real intentions. Love becomes a business arrangement or a simple instrument for their respective games and gains.

Following Aurora Constancia's advice to subscribe to a marriage of convenience with a rich man such as Federico, Ana Magdalena enjoys other romances while her husband becomes a recluse in his own home, producing the great overarching epic novel—bringing to mind Melquíades in *Cien años de soledad.* While oblivious to all the happenings around him, Federico intimates what his young wife is doing as he creates a narrative that somewhat parallels her life. Ana Magdalena's escapades thus inspire a work that otherwise would be devoid of liveliness, sensuality, and expression. She eventually learns the art of becoming a madam from her renegade great-aunt, Ofelia, in a bordello appropriately called La Nymphaea, where real living occurs behind "imposing monastic doors" and where she becomes "The Love Queen of the Amazon." From her great-aunt's original stable she inherits a colorful flock of eight "rainbow girls" who occupy different color-coded rooms, at the service of their clientele. Freed of social restrictions, La Nymphaea is where Ana Magdalena feels fully realized, not so much sexually but as an entrepreneur, exploiting the labor of her girls and thereby gaining control of her life in an otherwise bleakly patriarchal society. She later transfers the defunct brothel to her husband's home, rechristening it Casa Orgaz (a pun on orgasm), while her husband con-

*Dust jacket for Pineda's third novel, the story of an enterprising madam*

fines himself upstairs, pursuing his never-ending "Via Dolorosa of the written word."

Ana Magdalena's ever expanding enterprise includes a courtroom, a torture chamber, a confessional, a classroom, and a hot-air balloon; it becomes a town within a town and a government within a government, to be viewed as either a duplicate or a replacement. Ironic symbolism is heaped upon Federico's home, which eventually eliminates all facades. The "International Fiduciary Fund" (based on the International Monetary Fund) finances brothel improvements; but the ultimate irony occurs when Cardinal Catafalco offers to purchase the business to gain greater profits for the church. Both religion and love are turned into objects of ridicule and profit.

Quite distinct from Pineda's other novels, *The Love Queen of the Amazon* offers an action-packed story filled with intrigue and racy prose that is sometimes poetic but at other times subdued, including many elements of the hyperbole made popular by magical realism: for example, Ana Magdalena witnesses a swarm of bees take over her mother's house and later

literally crystallize her mother by turning her into a human bee- hive, sparking a religious fervor to canonize her. Clemencia, Federico's mother, is clairvoyant and eventually floats away through the Van Allen belt and disappears (satirizing Remedios's ascension in *Cien años de soledad*).

Two as-yet-unpublished novels, "Redoubt" (completed in December 1997) and "Bardo99" (completed in March 1999), locate themselves in a state of imagined consciousness. "Redoubt" takes as its theme the problem of gender, of socialization and sexualization. It was born of questions such as: if the spirit of the present time were to be depicted as pure consciousness, where would it situate itself, how would it find its voice, and what would be the place of woman in such a consciousness? "Bardo99" imagines the twentieth century itself as the protagonist, bound on the journey of the Bardo—a tenet of Tibetan Buddhism, wherein the soul inhabits regions corresponding to hell, purgatory, and paradise before reincarnation as a renewed being. Both works, exploring pure consciousness as they do, represent an abrupt break with her previously published narratives.

Pineda's works have enjoyed critical accolades for their originality and sensitive composition. Her early theatrical productions developed a following by virtue of their experimental nature in conjunction with their social message. Her novels have garnered attention for their distinctive qualities, particularly for her exploration of a human sense of loss in *Face,* a spiritual devotion to craft in *Frieze,* and the exercise of free will in *The Love Queen of the Amazon.* Juan Bruce-Novoa makes the case that Pineda expands the Chicano narrative by incorporating new themes and subjects as she grapples with concerns that are experienced universally, regardless of ethnicity. Marcienne Rocard situates Pineda within a social-movement type of writing even if on the surface her work seems to defy such classification. Lomelí offers a comparative study to uncover analogies and a parallelism between two works that he believes are conditioned by their respective ethnicity, despite their defiance of this effect.

Cecile Pineda is a writer who has insightfully chronicled profound concerns affecting modern times, including identity; power relationships; ephemeral, imagined communities; and the individual's potential to withstand alienating forces. As experiments in assorted narrative strategies, each of her works represents a distinctive attempt to capture an essential quality of the human dilemma. Pineda utilizes art as an instrument to shed greater clarity onto social reality, thus heightening the reader's sense of understanding the many complex facets of existence.

## References:

Juan Bruce-Novoa, "Deconstructing the Dominant Patriarchal Text: Cecile Pineda's Narratives," in *Breaking Boundaries: Latina Writings and Critical Readings,* edited by Asunción Horno-Delgado, Eliana Ortega, Nina M. Scott, and Nancy Saporta Sternbach (Amherst: University of Massachusetts Press, 1989), pp. 72–81;

David E. Johnson, "Face Value: An Essay on Cecile Pineda's *Face,*" *Americas Review,* 19 (Summer 1991): 73–93;

Francisco A. Lomelí, "Cecile Pineda's *Face* and Ralph Ellison's *Invisible Man:* Poetics of Synthesizing an Identity," in *El poder hispano: actas del V Congreso de Culturas Chicanas de los Estados Unidos (Madrid-España, julio 1992),* edited by Alberto Moncala Lorenzo, Carmen Flys Junquera, and José Antonio Gurpegui Palacios (Madrid: Universidad de Alcalá, Centro de Estudios Norteamericanos, 1994), pp. 465–472;

Marcienne Rocard, "Cecile Pineda's *Face:* Reconstructing the Self," dissertation, University of Toulouse, 1994;

Rocard, "Lutte du Chicano sur le plan de l'ecriture: ou la face litteraire du Mouvement Chicano," *Les Langues Modernes,* 80, no. 3 (1986): 45–52.

# Estela Portillo Trambley

*(16 January 1927 – 28 December 1998)*

Paula W. Shirley
*Columbia College of South Carolina*

BOOKS: *Rain of Scorpions and Other Writings* (Berkeley, Cal.: Tonatiuh International, 1975); revised as *Rain of Scorpions and Other Stories* (Tempe, Ariz.: Bilingual Press, 1993);

*Sor Juana and Other Plays* (Ypsilanti, Mich.: Bilingual Press/Editorial Bilingüe, 1983);

*Trini* (Binghamton, N.Y.: Bilingual Press/Editorial Bilingüe, 1986).

PLAY PRODUCTIONS: *Blacklight*, El Paso, Chamizal National Theatre, 1975;

*El Hombre Cósmico,* El Paso, Chamizal National Theatre, 1975;

*Sun Images . . . Los Amores de Don Estufas,* El Paso, Chamizal National Theatre, 1976;

*Isabel and the Dancing Bear,* El Paso, Chamizal National Theatre, 1977;

*The Day of the Swallows,* Los Angeles, California State University, 1979;

*The Labyrinth of Love: Sor Juana Inés de la Cruz,* University Playhouse, 1979.

SELECTED PERIODICAL PUBLICATIONS– UNCOLLECTED: *Day of the Swallows, El Grito,* 4 (Spring 1971): 4–47;

"The Paris Gown," *El Grito,* 6 (Summer 1973): 9–19;

Introduction, excerpt from *Morality Play,* and "After Hierarchy," *Chicanas en la literatura y el arte,* special issue of *El Grito,* 7 (September 1973): 5–6, 7–21, 84;

*Sun Images, Nuevos Pasos: Chicano and Puerto Rican Drama,* edited by Nicolás Kanellos and Jorge A. Huerta, special issue of *Revista Chicano-Riqueña,* 7 (Winter 1979): 19–42.

*Estela Portillo Trambley at the time of* Trini *(photograph by Achilles Studio)*

Estela Portillo Trambley was a Texas writer whose work explores philosophical themes and yet is grounded primarily in the concrete reality of the people she grew up with along the border between El Paso, Texas and Ciudad Juárez, Mexico. Portillo Trambley ventured into many genres, including poetry, prose narrative, and drama. At a time when Chicano literature concentrated on men's experiences, she wrote about women–not silent women who were appendages to their husbands or sons, but strong women who claimed their voices. Critics have focused on Portillo Trambley's feminist stance, which contested traditional feminine stoicism and submissiveness in favor of autonomy and a spiritual, unifying force. To some extent she also located her work outside of Chicanismo and the Chicano Movement. In a 1980 interview with Juan Bruce-Novoa she commented that "The pressure within Chicano literature is a verbal miasma of sameness; it has clung too long to complaint and condemnation. . . . There is certainly a reason for both. . . . Chicano literature will find its own balance. Humanism, detachment, beauty, moderation measure the human condition as Art."

Although some sources list the year of her birth as 1936, Estela Portillo was born on 16 January 1927 in El Paso, Texas, to Delfina and Frank Portillo. Her father was a railroad mechanic, and her mother gave piano lessons. At an early age Estela went to live with her maternal grandparents in the Segundo Barrio of El Paso; after their deaths, when she was twelve, she returned to live with her parents, two brothers, and a sister. Estela Portillo graduated from high school and continued her education at the College of Mines, now part of the University of Texas at El Paso, where she majored in English. In 1947 she married Robert Trambley, with whom she eventually had six children—five daughters and a son. Portillo Trambley taught English at the El Paso Technical High School for several years, serving from 1959 through 1966 as head of the English department.

The Trambleys' only son, a twin, died when less than a year old. In an effort to ease the pain of this loss Portillo Trambley threw herself into reading widely in philosophy and came up with an idea for a book titled "After Hierarchy" that would blend Eastern and Western philosophies. Publishers did not want it, and Portillo Trambley realized that it was a bad book; but in a personal sense it was a success because, as she told Bruce-Novoa, "I found my own solid view-of-my-world."

Portillo Trambley had always loved literature but did not try creative writing until she became active in a bilingual theater group, Chicano Theater, that was established in 1968 by several individuals from the University of Texas at El Paso and the community. They performed Spanish plays as well as Spanish translations of American plays, but the group was not satisfied with the material. Portillo Trambley impulsively offered to write a play for them. In an interview published in the journal *MELUS* in 1982, she said that her first playwriting effort was "the most atrocious play that you could ever imagine. . . . But the bug bit me." She was thrilled by the challenge and excitement of acting, directing, writing music, and doing a myriad of things required to mount a play.

In 1972 Portillo Trambley left high-school teaching for two years to accept an offer to host a talk show for radio station KIZZ in El Paso. Never one to shy away from interesting topics, such as Fidel Castro, Portillo Trambley offered wide-ranging, often controversial discussions that drew many callers, frequently irate ones. She was then asked to write for *Cumbres* (Peaks), a cultural program on television at KROD in El Paso, which she was delighted to accept because she was able to explore freely in the visual and performing arts. She wrote the programs in Spanish. When the grant money that funded the program ran out, Portillo Trambley felt ready to return to a more ordinary personal and work life. After leaving her media shows and a position as resident dramatist at El Paso Community College, Portillo Trambley worked with Special Services in the El Paso public schools as a high-school teacher for the homebound.

Portillo Trambley continued to write theatrical works and was encouraged to submit them for publication, but she was reluctant to do so. A friend sent one play, *The Day of the Swallows,* to Octavio Romano-V., editor of the Chicano literary journal *El Grito* (The Shout). It was accepted and published in 1971, and Trambley began to take her writing more seriously after that.

*The Day of the Swallows* concerns Doña Josefa, a woman who epitomizes virtue and respectability in the Mexican town of San Lorenzo. She is chosen to lead a procession to a lake where the village maidens bathe in an annual ritual that promises to bring them the husbands of their dreams. This ritual represents the collective will of a culture that denies women any future outside of marriage. The perfect lady, Doña Josefa carries a secret: she is a lesbian engaged in a sexual relationship with Alysea, a young woman she has rescued from prostitution. Josefa has created a safe space for herself—a beautiful, orderly home decorated with her exquisite handmade lace. Light streams into the house, creating a magical effect, and her garden is a small paradise. Josefa's tragedy lies in the unreal perception of womanhood that the townspeople have projected onto her. She enjoys their love and fears losing it should they discover who she truly is. As her secret comes unraveled she commits a violent act, then gives in to blackmail. Her desperate actions underscore the difficulty of living contrary to one's being. As a girl, Josefa had refused to participate in the immersion ritual, and instead claimed the moon and the lake as her lovers. When she drowns herself in the lake at the end of the play, she reclaims her true self.

Portillo Trambley enjoyed a great deal of success with *The Day of the Swallows,* although she rewrote it several times. Eventually it was also included in several anthologies. *The Day of the Swallows* is the play that established Portillo Trambley's reputation as a groundbreaking Chicana writer and helped her to win the Quinto Sol Award for literature in 1972.

*Cover for Portillo Trambley's 1983 drama collection. The title play is about a seventeenth-century intellectual and nun.*

Chicano theater during the early 1970s stressed social and political themes largely intended to support the Chicano Movement through grassroots theater productions. In contrast, Portillo Trambley wrote traditional, three-act plays. In addition, *The Day of the Swallows* evoked the language and themes of such well-known Spanish writers as Federico García Lorca and Pedro Calderón de la Barca. Unlike the *actos* (improvised satirical skits using stock characters) of Luis Miguel Valdez and the Teatro Campesino (Farmworkers' Theater), *The Day of the Swallows* represents a kind of theater new to much of the Chicano audience. As Chicano theater scholar Jorge A. Huerta said about the play, "Ms. Portillo has created beautifully developed characters that require careful study and analysis in order to achieve their proper representation on the stage. . . . Employing the well-made play, each scene and act in this *obra* [work] leaves us wanting more, wondering what will happen next."

In writing a character who creates her own mythology, Portillo Trambley showed a kinship with Chicano writers such as Rudolfo A. Anaya, author of the best-selling Chicano novel *Bless Me, Ultima* (1972). Some critics faulted her for not writing more "political" theater, but many recognized the feminist politics of resistance, rebellion, and the desire for personal autonomy in *The Day of the Swallows.* Up to this point, contemporary Chicano literature had been dominated by males. Some Chicanas had published poetry, but Portillo Trambley was a pioneer in drama and later in fiction. She was writing Chicano drama that gives women center stage. Her plays are not rousing calls to action against the oppressive Anglo system, but they exhort Chicanos and Chicanas to examine the issue of identity and to struggle for autonomy against oppression wherever it was found—a call expressed in poetic language and in mythical themes. Janice Dewey, in her article "Doña Josefa: Bloodpulse of Transition and Change" (1989), states that Doña Josefa "is the final sacrificial lamb at the doorstep of aborted change because she is isolated and alone in her attempt to combat the myth of stereotypical lives."

In 1973 Portillo Trambley was invited to be a guest editor of *Chicanas en la literatura y el arte,* a special issue of *El Grito.* This issue was a watershed event that, as Francisco Lomelí explains in "Chicana Novelists in the Process of Creating Fictive Voices" (1985), marked the closure of a "gap that had endured and somehow gone undocumented for a long time." As Chicano writers had been ignored by mainstream publishing houses, Chicana writers had been overlooked as well. Portillo Trambley figured prominently in opening up the literary field to women writers and in validating their view of the world. In the introduction to *Chicanas en la literatura y el arte* she supports the existence of a distinctly feminine view that is personal and also universal.

In addition to the writing and staging of plays, Portillo Trambley was also drawn to writing fiction and published the short story "The Apple Trees" (later included in *Rain of Scorpions and Other Writings* as "The Trees") in the spring of 1972. It is a tragic story of a prosperous family's ruin. The descriptions tend to be overblown and the themes presented in a heavy-handed manner, but the story incorporates literary ideas that Portillo Trambley developed more skillfully in the future.

*Rain of Scorpions and Other Writings,* published in 1975, is considered the first published collection of fiction by a Chicana in the contemporary renaissance of Chicano literature. Comprising nine short stories and a novella, *Rain of Scorpions* exhibits characteristics typical of Portillo Trambley's fiction. The protagonists are usually women struggling with both bread-and-butter issues and questions of spiritual and emotional survival in a world dominated by men. A frequent theme is humanity's relationship to the cosmos. Portillo Trambley admitted in the interview with Bruce-Novoa that "I do sometimes bore you to death by shoving all this philosophy down your throat." A reviewer for *Revista Chicano-Riqueña* (Summer 1977) pointed out the author's often overbearing tendency to explain the symbolism in the stories to the reader but called the collection an "excellent first major effort and a welcomed addition to the growing field of Chicano literature." In 1993 Bilingual Press published a revised edition of *Rain of Scorpions* in its "Clásicos Chicanos" series. This volume includes an introduction titled "Crafting Other Visions: Estela Portillo Trambley's New *Rain of Scorpions*," by Vernon E. Lattin and Patricia Hopkins. Of the original stories only four were retained: "Pay the Criers," "The Paris Gown," "If It Weren't for the Honeysuckle," and "The Burning," as well as the novella, "Rain of Scorpions." Four stories were added: "Leaves," "Looking for God," "Village," and "La Yonfontayn." The revisions were worth the effort, as the stories are much better crafted. The introduction by Lattin and Hopkins is a valuable comparison of the original and revised stories.

"Pay the Criers" keeps the theme and storyline in both editions, but the 1993 version is certainly richer and more enjoyable to read, with leaner language. The age-old tension between a man and his mother-in-law takes on an unusual poignancy here. The principal character is the freedom-loving, irresponsible husband, Chucho, who comes home one day to find his mother-in-law, Refugio, dead. Chucho manipulates his lovestruck wife, Juana, into revealing where Refugio hid the funeral money she had saved for years in order to have a fine ceremony complete with paid mourners, the criers of the title. After spending the money on a binge with his friend Chapo, Chucho returns home only to be overcome by remorse and vows to bury Refugio. The two friends bundle up her now-stinking body, place it in the trunk of the car, and take the old woman on a circuit of the bars in an effort to borrow money from their drinking companions. After failing to scrape together enough money to bury his mother-in-law, Chucho takes her out of town, up a high hill, and buries her, but only after sitting with her until the sun comes up so that she can see one more dawn. Chuco is a foil to his mother-in-law. Their relationship was tempestuous, with an underlying sexual tension. She was a strong character who shared much of the love for life exhibited by her son-in-law.

In "The Paris Gown" Portillo Trambley explores a theme that appears frequently in her work: women's struggle to live autonomous lives. Teresa, a properly raised young university student from Mexico, goes to Paris to visit Clotilde, the grandmother she has never met. Clotilde's name is rarely spoken in Teresa's family because of a long-ago scandal that nobody will talk about. The two women share confidences and their mutual frustrations with patriarchal pressures to conform. Clotilde's youthful desire to study art in Paris was thwarted by her father, who insisted that she marry a rich friend of his. At their engagement party Clotilde made her entrance wearing not the extravagant Paris gown her father had ordered, but nothing. The ensuing scandal that made her an unfit wife in upper-class Mexican society enabled Clotilde to live the life of freedom she craved. The reader is left to assume that the granddaughter will claim the same freedom for herself; the last line describes the two women looking out of a window "at the last full colors of the day."

Like Clotilde in "The Paris Gown," Beatriz, the protagonist of "If It Weren't for the Honeysuckle," is a woman struggling for her freedom. Unlike Clotilde, who comes from a family of wealth and high social position, Beatriz has endured grinding poverty and physical and sexual abuse. Nevertheless, she tenaciously carves out a space for herself, literally building a house alone—a little world that is orderly and peaceful, except when her abuser, Robles, returns. Beatriz decides to kill Robles, not simply to free herself but also to protect Sofía, a young girl whom the brute is intent on adding to his string of "wives." The idea comes to her when she is thinning a patch of honeysuckle and uncovers some poisonous mushrooms. Whereas Clotilde secures her freedom by an act of defiance that breaks the stifling social code, Beatriz kills to obtain freedom. Yet, an act that would normally be considered immoral is seen here as an act of courage and generosity that protects a girl from the brutality visited on Beatriz and the timid Sofía. Beatriz's act violates the patriarchal system within her home as well as the patriarchal institutions of law and church. Yet, she is admirable because by acting she reestablishes a natural harmony that has been violated. In one of the best feminist analyses of this story, Elizabeth J. Ordoñez in "Narrative Texts by Ethnic Women: Rereading the Past, Reshaping the Future" (1982) reads "If It Weren't for the Honeysuckle" as a text that displaces and inverts biblical myths. She comments that "The myth of Eve is inverted; the patriarch alone—not woman—is displaced from the garden. Thus the garden becomes wholly woman's space, its reappropriation signifying a displacement of Biblical myth with a plot shaped and defined by woman herself."

The revised version of "If It Weren't for the Honeysuckle" is a significant improvement in style over the 1975 version. The 1993 version employs more dialogue and less narrative, which makes the language of the

Then she was beside them.

"Here, I'll dig."

She took her billowing skirt and made a knot in front around the knees, ~~She sat~~ on the ground, her long, thick braids touching moist spring grass. After a while, ~~Matilda took~~ a small knife from her apron pocket, ~~and cut~~ into the heart of a bulb. ~~She~~ gripped it, ~~pressing hard~~ to soften the pulp. Then she raised it over her face and held out her tongue to catch the sweet milk. ~~She bit~~ the fruit afterwards.

"Good."

She softened ~~several~~ pochotes for the children. Trini noticed her mother's bare feet in the red, warm earth. ~~her easy laugh, and the tilt of her head that told you she listened to your every word.~~

~~Now the children were telling her about Sabochi's cave. Matilda was listening~~ as she picked a handful of earth and let it pour through her fingers. Matilda and the earth, ~~Matilda,~~ earthcrowned.

~~Trini laughed in acceptance of the feeling.~~

"Why, can't we go, mama, why can't we go to ~~Sabochi's~~ cave?"

"When he comes back..."

That was something to wish for. Sabochi, ~~who was~~ a Tarahumara, took mysterious trips into the Barranca del Cobre ~~and came back with new wisdom.~~ In the shadowed silence of his cave, he ~~would speak about~~ worlds outside of the Valley of Bachotigori.

"He will come soon. I feel it." But ~~she~~ felt something else, pain crossed her face. She tried to stand ~~up~~ with difficulty as Trini ran to help her, ~~Matilda~~ strained and grasped Trini's shoulder for balance.

story more immediate and grounded in human experience. Beatriz's life story is more fleshed out, with a corresponding improvement in her motivation. A new narrative thread in the later edition involves the abuse Beatriz suffered at the hands of a lecherous, old, wealthy, and respected man for whom she worked. One day when he was, as Beatriz puts it, "playing like an idiot with my naked body," he had a heart attack, and Beatriz refused to give him his medicine, letting him die.

"The Burning" is only slightly changed from its original form. It tells the story of Lela, an Indian healer who never gives up her belief in her gods even after living many years among Christians. After she makes little clay gods for everyone in the village as a dying gesture of friendship, the narrow-minded women decide to burn down her home, believing her to be a witch. This narrative depends largely on irony for effect, as the reader discovers that Lela has been praying to be burned after death, in accordance with the tradition of her culture.

"Leaves" and "Looking for God" have young female protagonists, both of whom are lonely and searching for meaning in a world that seems to have none. Thirteen-year-old Isabel in "Leaves" clings to a belief in the miraculous world even though her heroin-addicted mother dies, leaving her to grow up alone. In "Looking for God" Josefa, a girl of ten who lives with her grandmother, feels that God has abandoned the world when she witnesses the senseless killing of swallows in their annual return to San Lorenzo. Portillo Trambley links this story to *The Day of the Swallows,* portraying Doña Josefa as a girl and establishing the childhood trauma that contributes to her development into the woman in *The Day of the Swallows.*

The main character of "Village" is Rico, who appears in "Leaves" and other stories. Portillo Trambley places this character in Vietnam. Many Chicano writers of the 1970s and 1980s exposed the willingness of white politicians to sacrifice Mexican American and African American men to the war in Southeast Asia. Portillo Trambley uses the Vietnamese setting as a moral battleground to expose the indifference of the war machine. When Rico's squad is ordered to kill an entire village that he knows to be full of old men, women, and children, he refuses. He has already observed the similarity between the Vietnamese village and his barrio of Valverde: "It struck him again, the feeling—a bond—that people were all the same everywhere."

The novella "Rain of Scorpions" ties together several themes important in Portillo Trambley's work: the bonds of a community, love, the injustice of the capitalist system, and the centrality of myth to life. Smelter-

town is a community where people breathe the poisoned air emanating from "the second tallest chimney in the world" at the ASARCO plant. The decision to remove all the people from Smeltertown in order to avoid possible lawsuits means the death of the community. This situation provides the impetus for three boys of the town to act on shopkeeper Papá At's stories of El Indio Tolo, who went up into the Guadalupe mountains and encountered Gotallama, "god of waters and fire." Gotallama led El Indio Tolo to the fabled green valley, "where nature gods live." While the boys are away trying to find this valley, a flood brings a wall of mud full of dead scorpions into Smeltertown, threatening their homes.

The boys' search for the green valley is a quest that takes them through a labyrinth of caves, where they finally find the stone map to the valley. The movement is continuously upward: from Smeltertown, up the hill, to a long ascent through the caves, and around a frightening dark abyss called El Hoyo. This mythic ascent brings the three boys into contact with Gotallama, who has been forgotten by most of the people since the advent of Christianity. Upon leaving the mountain the boys wander in the desert before finding a highway and hailing a truck driver willing to take them home. The desert is an ancient symbol of humans' search for spiritual truth, that is, the search for oneself. Its association with the Judeo-Christian tradition establishes the dual traditions that the people of Smeltertown have inherited—the pagan and the Christian. Portillo Trambley juxtaposes the confining emphasis of Christian salvation with the freeing consciousness of the pagan by staging the boys' return in the church, which they enter carrying the stone map. Papá At is the only one capable of deciphering the single word written thereon, "Kear," meaning "you." One of the boys, Miguel, finally understands that "He had journeyed, looking for a place to belong, a place of peace. He found it inside himself. He was the green valley."

"Pilgrimage," one of the stories in the first edition of *Rain of Scorpions* that was not included in the second, also portrays a journey into the desert, a quest for meaning similar to that of the young boys of "Rain of Scorpions." Nan, a wealthy Anglo, is filled with anger and a sense of hopelessness after being left by her husband of sixteen years. Her impetuous decision to accompany her Mexican maid on the latter's annual pilgrimage into the desert to San Juan de los Lagos enables Nan to be reborn in faith and love: "She had found the faith in the desert. She would take it back home and grow with it." María Herrera-Sobek recognizes the mythic structure of both this story and "If It Weren't for the Honeysuckle" in her essay, "La unidad del hombre y el cosmos: Reafirmación del proceso vital en Estela Portillo Trambley" (1982). She comments on the philosophical, metaphysical, and mythical thinking in these stories and the overarching theme of life as an expression of the cosmos. Both stories depict a woman's healing as inseparable from her connection with the earth and a cycle of life greater than her own.

Included in the later edition of *Rain of Scorpions* is a story first published in 1982 in *Revista Chicano-Riqueña*. "La Yonfantayn" is an amusing tale of two romantic manipulators, Alicia and Buti. A wealthy widow who enjoys her freedom and her still considerable charm, Alicia fights aging with all the weapons available to her. To complement her resemblance to the actress Joan Fontaine, she chooses lovers who look like movie stars, and she enjoys maintaining a powerful role in her romantic relationships by making sure that these affairs do not lead to marriage. But when she falls in love with Buti, a man who can manipulate the opposite sex as well as she can, Alicia starts to crumble. Buti wants her money, but he also wants her. Despite Alicia's use of feminine wiles to control her suitor, Buti prevails, and Alicia finally gives in to this Clark Gable look-alike. Its treatment of an aging playboy and an aging coquette, coupled with an ironic and amused tone, sets "La Yonfantayn" apart from the other stories in *Rain of Scorpions*. Hollywood images of wealth and beauty drive the two main characters, yet both find what they want. This tale seems whimsical when compared with the other stories in *Rain of Scorpions* and their themes of violence, loneliness, and struggles to survive. However, Alicia and Buti are part of the fabric of life in Valverde—a life that includes humor.

Throughout the 1970s Portillo Trambley continued to write plays. She told Juan Bruce-Novoa, "Right now I am in the most wonderful, glorious love affair with my new play, *The Labyrinth of Love: Sor Juana Inés de la Cruz*. Right now I am Sor Juana." Portillo Trambley's historical play about the seventeenth-century intellectual, writer, and nun Sor Juana Inés de la Cruz covers the trajectory of the great woman's life in three tightly constructed acts. Two distinct areas of the stage alternately depict scenes from the last two years of her life and previous periods from childhood to young womanhood. Scenes of her early years show that, although raised among the powerful and wealthy, she could not make a good marriage. A prodigious talent, she nevertheless could not be admitted to the university because of her gender. The convent was her only recourse. In the Convent of St. Jerome she was allowed to have books, instruments, and freedom for intellectual and artistic pursuits. But her mentor and occasional antagonist, Father Antonio, scolds Sor Juana for ignoring the rest of the world, where her countrymen live in poverty and oppression. In his essay on Alurista, Piri Thomas,

and Portillo Trambley, "Chicano and Nuyorican Literature–Elements of a Democratic and Socialist Culture in the U.S. of A.?" Dieter Herms observes:

> Antonio's commitment to the victims of feudal exploitation and Sor Juana's all-encompassing spiritual and material humanism are here juxtaposed to show two equally valid variants of a radical plebeian theology. Both of them are mejicana/mejicano versions and visions of a Christian mankind versus the established colonialist Spanish system of Catholicism, whose missionary thrust harmoniously accompanied the European conquest and brutal subjugation of an indigenous people.

In the beginning of her life Sor Juana says that she wants to find God through knowledge. Toward the end she says that "He is all the life around me." Sor Juana died in 1695, two months to the day after Father Antonio's death.

Portillo Trambley always believed, as she said in the *MELUS* interview, that art must "go beyond the social protest." She strove to write theater that could unite people, not just on an emotional level but on an intellectual one. The subject of Sor Juana presented an extraordinary opportunity to explore both levels. By choosing to write about Sor Juana, Portillo Trambley established another link between the Mexican and Mexican American intellectual tradition.

*Puente Negro* (Black Bridge), another play in *Sor Juana and Other Plays* (1983), depicts the dreams of a small band of Mexicans who have just crossed the Rio Grande from Ciudad Juárez to El Paso. Led by La Chaparra, a seasoned guide, the group includes two men who recall the vision of Emiliano Zapata that all Mexicans would one day live with dignity on their own land. Now, this dream has failed and the United States needs cheap labor to maintain its prosperity. Nevertheless, a young brother and sister dance team cling to the notion that they will "make lots of money and become famous." El Topo, the character who initiates the new arrivals into the ways of the United States, has crossed many times and speaks knowledgeably about American culture, where dreams are a commodity and people make pilgrimages to Disneyland. Portillo Trambley vividly conveys the fluid reality of the United States–Mexico border that, despite the illusion of separation, actually brings together people who need each other. The black bridge, an old bridge no longer in use, links an economic power to a culture that still enjoys a living history. As the play ends, El Topo is singing a song about Zapata's return to two immigration officers who have penetrated La Chaparra's hideaway in search of the immigrants.

Portillo Trambley returns to the mythic, indigenous past in *Blacklight* (1979), second-place winner in the 1985 Hispanic-American Playwrights' Competition at the New York Shakespeare Festival. A tragic play of family conflict and a search for transcendence, *Blacklight* illuminates the consequences of cultural erasure. The Chicanos of this drama inhabit a grim world that has separated them from their native roots until Nacho, driven by guilt and anger over his brother's death, erects a pole carved with the faces of Mayan gods. He recites poems from the Mayan sacred text *Chilam Balam* (Secrets of the Soothsayers). Nacho's son, Mundo, suggests another generation's need for the same mythical return by bringing home a large, heavy rock he has painted with various colors. His "mountain" is to be the focal point of a blacklight party with his friends. Images from the stone and the carved post mimic each other. Both Mundo's "mountain" and Nacho's carved post reflect the search for a higher order of being that eludes them. Nacho's daughter, Ixchel, comments that "What we need around here is some kind of faith." After saving Nacho from throwing himself onto the railroad tracks, Mundo ties his father to the post of Itzamná (the supreme Mayan deity) that Nacho had finished carving that night. The play ends with Mundo's murder at the hands of his lover's husband and the birth of Ixchel's child.

Critical attention to Portillo Trambley's plays has focused on her dramas, although she also wrote several comedies. *Autumn Gold,* another play from *Sor Juana and Other Plays,* is a comedy with elements of farce about a group of friends who rebel against the stereotypical behavior expected of aging adults. A philosophy of the eternal life of all things in the universe (One Guy instead of One God) frames the Autumn Gold Society's activities. The principal character, who writes and directs plays, often quotes from Lewis Carroll's *Alice's Adventures in Wonderland* (1865); the group's slogan, "Calloo callay," is a line from the famous children's book. This identification with the upside-down world created by Carroll enhances the comic elements of the fast pace and amusing dialogue in this work. Intergenerational shock is provided by a daughter's horror at her mother's unconventional activities. One especially humorous scene involves a dead body propped up as if asleep in order to fool the daughter's stuffy in-laws.

Although *Autumn Gold* is clearly related to the rest of Portillo Trambley's work in its philosophical theme, it has been largely ignored by critics who have chosen to emphasize her Chicano or border plays. *Autumn Gold* engages none of the themes that are generally associated with Chicano literature. Yet, Portillo Trambley does present a theme that runs through most of her work: the search for meaning and the need for primal

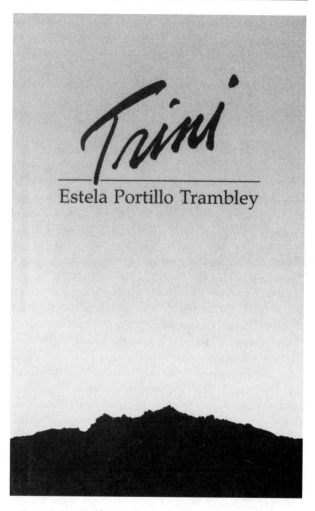

Cover for Portillo Trambley's novel, in which the protagonist feels a powerful connection to the land

connections. By creating Anglo characters rather than Chicano ones, however, she avoids the complexities of biculturalism, bilingualism, and other aspects of Chicano reality.

In the 1976 musical play *Sun Images . . . Los Amores de Don Estufas* Portillo Trambley returns to the locale of the Texas-Mexico border in a comic exploration of life along this fluid line. While this engaging work has farcical moments, it also exposes the economic needs of Mexicans who sometimes go to great lengths to seek the opportunities available on the northern side of the Rio Grande. The action of the play concerns various male-female relationships. Don Estevan, also called Don Estufas behind his back, advertises in Mexico for young women ("I help young girls") whom he then brings across the border to live with him. Convinced that he is still living up to his youthful reputation as a fantastic lover, Don Estevan is actually controlled by the three young Mexican women who manage to keep him at bay with brandy and completely fabricated accounts of his sexual escapades. In fact, they have come in order to work and to pursue their own dreams. A parallel but reverse situation involves a college student, Ana Escobar Smith, who tricks several young men into becoming engaged to her. When she meets a philosophy professor, Refugio Smith, she tries to snare him.

Another parallel relationship is that of Don Estevan and Don Adolfo, the owner of a guitar shop. Both are widowers dealing with loneliness, but the dignified Don Adolfo still finds beauty and hope in life, while the ludicrous Don Estevan tries unsuccessfully to re-create his youth. After his three young women have left, La Melcocha (a name meaning a kind of candy) appears. A Mexican who has crossed the border illegally, she is much older than the women Don Estevan seeks, but her desire to cross over to the United States has driven her to wade across the river in search of the old man who represents a hope of a better life. La Melcocha does not attempt to be a harem girl but rather a wife. The ending suggests that she will stay.

*Sun Images* is a departure from Chicano theater of the 1960s and 1970s because of its lack of political engagement. Armando Miguélez comments that *Sun Images* would have been considered irresponsible Chicano theater in the 1960s because it is entertainment with no political or social value; however, he recognizes that Portillo Trambley's play can help to build a Chicano audience that wants entertainment akin to television comedy. *Sun Images* relies on stock characters to present the vagaries of love and at the same time to demonstrate the economic motives that send many Mexicans north. The proximity to Mexico of the El Paso barrio where Don Estevan and most of the other characters live also suggests the absurdity of the economic differences that figure so strongly in the lives of people living on the border.

For several years Portillo Trambley worked on a novel with the working title of "Woman of the Earth." It was eventually published under the title *Trini* (1986). A compelling novel of a Mexican woman's struggles for survival, *Trini* is rich in myth and magic as well as grim realities that include a rape, the death of the baby born of that violence, and sometimes horrific living conditions. *Trini* displays several themes frequently explored in Chicano literature: the search for economic security, family separation, the ties to the indigenous past, and woman's struggle for autonomy in a sexist culture.

The trajectory of Trini's life is based on a powerful desire to own land, a place where she can live freely. Trini's attachment to the earth originates in a beautiful, fertile valley in Mexico where she lives with her parents, younger brother, and sister. Her mother's death

disturbs a somewhat idyllic existence, and when the mine where her father works closes, the family has to leave the land. The dangerous journey that follows marks a clear separation between the old way of life and the new. Trini's father begins another mining job but develops tuberculosis. The family is separated, plunging Trini into a search to reestablish the happy security of her early years. She lives in a village in northern Mexico, then Chihuahua, Ciudad Juárez, and eventually El Paso. Trini marries but does not experience the loving, devoted marriage her parents had. She struggles to support her five children with an unreliable husband and even crosses into Texas so that her first child can be born in the United States, thereby (she hopes) guaranteeing him some opportunity to live a decent life. Her journey is similar to those depicted in other early novels of Chicano literature that deal with the struggle of survival. Like others before her who wade across the Rio Grande in search of economic opportunity, Trini brings with her a cultural memory of being rooted in the earth and part of all living things.

The first part of the novel establishes an opposition between the values of the indigenous culture and those held by whites: "Long ago the Indians in this valley looked upon the light in the barranca [gorge] as the sacred ground of gods. There was a pure light shooting up from the gash. . . . Turned out to be gold, only gold." Rather than being merely an object of exploitation, for Trini the mountain landscape is a transcendent place where gods live. Although Trini is a mestiza (a person of European and American Indian descent), she is allied with the Tarahumara culture of northern Mexico through her love for Sabochi, a young chief with whom she eventually has a child. This son exhibits insight and intuition associated in Portillo Trambley's work with native culture. A reviewer for *Belles Lettres* (May 1988) commented that "Trini, a mix of the two cultures, is linked to past generations by her steadfast hold on both. Her understanding and respect for each world lets her form alliances that make her unique, a loving woman, in touch with who she is and what she feels." Trini's search ends not only when she finally has her own land but also when she knows who she is; the search and the knowledge are represented by seeds she brings from her first Mexican home to plant someday on her own land. The search motif is analyzed persuasively in the essay by Carmen Salazar Parr and Genevieve M. Ramírez, "The Female Hero in Chicano Literature" (1985). They relate the female hero's journey to a myth described by Joseph Campbell in *The Hero with a Thousand Faces* (1949) and say that "The evolution represented in the journey is paralleled by her [Trini's] mythological identification as mother-earth figure. . . . at the close of the novel [she is] no longer the idealized symbol of selflessness, she is now a human being who will not tolerate what must rightfully be rejected or avenged."

Portillo Trambley continued to work in El Paso throughout the 1990s as a teacher for homebound children with physical, emotional, and learning problems. She was a visiting professor at the University of California, Riverside, and in 1995 she held the Presidential Chair in Creative Writing at the University of California, Davis. She had decided several years earlier not to pursue a doctorate, choosing to spend her time writing plays and fiction. Portillo Trambley showed no aversion to reworking her stories and plays. In addition to the revised version of *Rain of Scorpions* in 1993, she translated *Puente Negro* into Spanish, writing five songs for this version, and she worked on revisions of two earlier stories, "Duende" and "Trees." At the time of her death from cancer on 28 December 1998 she was working on another novel.

Estela Portillo Trambley's short stories, dramas, and novel establish her as a prominent figure in contemporary Chicano literature. At a time when Chicano literature, especially fiction, was predominantly male and concerned with the quest for Chicano identity, Portillo Trambley spoke in a distinctly different voice because, as she said in a video interview at the University of California, Santa Barbara, in 1985, "Women have the unitive values." Portillo Trambley explored ideas that she believed were of importance to all people, but she realized that she wrote from many sources. As she said, "I'm utilizing all the influence of everybody I read, and yet at the same time I'm trying to integrate it into what I am, which is Chicana. And, basically—although I might seem to be very Americanized and you might say I'm not a Chicana, I'm a *gringa*—back there in all those formative years, I was definitely very much Mexican."

## Interviews:

Juan Bruce-Novoa, "Estela Portillo," in *Chicano Authors: Inquiry by Interview* (Austin: University of Texas Press, 1980), pp. 163–181;

Faye Nell Vowell, "A *MELUS* Interview: Estela Portillo Trambley," *MELUS*, 9 (Winter II 1982): 59–66.

## References:

Janice Dewey, "Doña Josefa: Bloodpulse of Transition and Change," in *Breaking Boundaries: Latina Writing and Critical Readings,* edited by Asunción Horno-Delgado, Eliana Ortega, Nina M. Scott, and Nancy Saporta Sternbach (Amherst: University of Massachusetts Press, 1989), pp. 39–47;

Laverne González, "Portillo Trambley, Estela," in *Chicano Literature: A Reference Guide,* edited by Julio A. Martínez and Francisco A. Lomelí (Westport, Conn.: Greenwood Press, 1985), pp. 316–322;

Dieter Herms, "Chicano and Nuyorican Literature–Elements of a Democratic and Socialist Culture in the U.S. of A.?" in *European Perspectives on Hispanic Literature of the U.S.,* edited by Geneviéve Fabre (Houston: Arte Público, 1988), pp. 118–129;

María Herrera-Sobek, "La unidad del hombre y el cosmos: Reafirmación del proceso vital en Estela Portillo Trambley," *La Palabra,* 4/5 (Spring–Fall 1982–1983): 127–141;

Jorge A. Huerta, "From Quetzalcoatl to Honest Sancho: A Review Article of *Contemporary Chicano Theatre,*" *Revista Chicano-Riqueña,* 5 (Summer 1977): 32–49;

Francisco A. Lomelí, "Chicana Novelists in the Process of Creating Fictive Voices," in *Beyond Stereotypes: The Critical Analysis of Chicana Literature,* edited by María Herrera-Sobek (Binghamton, N.Y.: Bilingual Press/Editorial Bilingüe, 1985), pp. 29–46;

Eliud Martínez, "Personal Vision in the Short Stories of Estela Portillo Trambley," in *Beyond Stereotypes: The Critical Analysis of Chicana Literature,* edited by María Herrera-Sobek (Binghamton, N.Y.: Bilingual Press/Editorial Bilingüe, 1985), pp. 71–90;

Armando Miguélez, "Aproximaciones al nuevo teatro chicano de autor único," *Explicación de textos literarios,* 15, no. 2 (1986–1987): 8–18;

Elizabeth J. Ordoñez, "Narrative Texts by Ethnic Women: Rereading the Past, Reshaping the Future," *MELUS,* 9 (Winter 1982): 19–28;

Carmen Salazar Parr and Genevieve M. Ramírez, "The Female Hero in Chicano Literature," in *Beyond Stereotypes,* edited by María Herrera-Sobek (Binghamton, N.Y.: Bilingual Press/Editorial Bilingüe, 1985), pp. 47–60.

## Papers:

Estela Portillo Trambley's papers are in the Benson Latin American Collection, General Libraries, University of Texas at Austin.

# Patricia Preciado Martin

*(6 July 1939 -  )*

## Merrihelen Ponce

BOOKS: *The Legend of the Bellringer of San Agustín: A Bilingual Children's Story / La leyenda del campanero de San Agustín: cuento bilingue para niños* (Albuquerque: Pajarito, 1980);

*Images and Conversations: Mexican Americans Recall a Southwestern Past,* photographs by Louis Carlos Bernal (Tucson: University of Arizona Press, 1983);

*Days of Plenty, Days of Want* (Tempe, Ariz.: Bilingual Review Press, 1988);

*Songs My Mother Sang to Me: An Oral History of Mexican American Women* (Tucson: University of Arizona Press, 1992);

*El Milagro and Other Stories* (Tucson: University of Arizona Press, 1996).

**Edition:** *Days of Plenty, Days of Want* (Tucson: University of Arizona Press, 1999).

*Patricia Preciado Martin at the time of* Songs My Mother Sang to Me *(1992)*

In recent years the many works by Chicano writers of the American Southwest have been a source of interest for students of regional literature in the United States. One common denominator in the works of early Hispanic writers of New Mexico and Texas is the extent to which they brought to their fiction a sense of their immediate environment. Contemporary Chicano writers also situate their fiction and poetry within images of desert landscapes: Gary Soto writes of California's central valley, Denise Chávez evokes New Mexico's dry heat, and the Texas desert gives Pat Mora's poetry its distinctive setting. Likewise, images of old Arizona permeate the works of Patricia Preciado Martin.

Preciado Martin is the author of four books, including children's stories, fiction, photo-essays, and oral histories. Her finely wrought and descriptive works evoke the *mexicano* barrios of "old" Tucson and the desert that was her playground during her formative years. As she recalled in an unpublished interview of May 1994, "the desert . . . awakened in me a lifelong sense of connection to the land and a love of the outdoors."

Patricia Anna Preciado was born on 6 July 1939 to Alfredo and Aurelia Preciado, who lived in Humboldt, a small mining town that lacked a hospital; they were forced to go to nearby Prescott for her birth. She has a sister, Elena, and a brother, Alfredo Jr. She credits her parents as a primary influence in her life. Her father worked in an ore-processing mill until an injury forced his retirement; he was then employed as a salesman. Still, a love of the outdoors led him to buy a small gold mine, which he named the "Little Patricia." A favorite family pastime was to picnic at the mine site. Preciado Martin's love of nature—and its place in her writing—is based on childhood memories of the small town south of Tucson where she grew up. More important, she cites the close relationship with her paternal grandparents—who had owned a ranch in Mexico—as having impacted her life and work.

222

Preciado Martin's mother was a voracious reader who taught Patricia to read at an early age and encouraged her to excel in school. At Salpointe Catholic School in Tucson she was an outstanding student; chemistry, Spanish, and English were her favorite subjects. She graduated in 1956. Later, when Preciado was at the University of Arizona, her mother read and discussed with her the works of William Shakespeare and other classics. She recalls that her mother was beautiful and ladylike and that she excelled in cooking and sewing. Preciado Martin said in May 1994, "para mí, mi madre es una luz en la calle" (for me, my mother is a light in the darkness [literally, "in the street"]).

Preciado Martin majored in elementary education at the University of Arizona, graduating magna cum laude. She never attempted creative writing in school except to meet English requirements. Still, an early love of the fairy tales read to her by her mother and the Mexican legends and myths told within her extended family fired her imagination. Some of her short stories are based on her childhood experiences with these family members. Further, her love of fairy tales has had a broad influence on her writing, imbuing her work generally with a sense of magic.

In 1963 Preciado married D. Jim Martin Jr. They have two children: Elena, born in 1966, and Jim, born in 1969. Preciado Martin's first attempts at children's stories were written for her own children: while on camping trips she made up stories to keep them busy while her husband fished. Her interest in children's literature intensified in the late 1970s and early 1980s when, as part of an oral-history project, she began to collect folktales of interest to young Mexican Americans of the Tucson area. She has written many children's stories, although only one has been published.

*The Legend of the Bellringer of San Agustín* (1980) is the story of a simple man who is revered by his fellow townspeople. It recalls an earlier period in Mexican social history when children were taught to respect and value Mexican traditions. Distinguished by its vivid portrayal of the desert landscape and a strong sense of Catholic spirituality, *The Legend of the Bellringer of San Augustin* tells of a time when "the Bell sang of the purple mountains . . . the first morning light . . . and the clouds and rainbows." Although the book is filled with Arizona history and Mexican folklore, it also reflects Preciado Martin's commitment to old-fashioned storytelling, to drawing on fantasy and imagination to enrich her works.

*Images and Conversations: Mexican Americans Recall a Southwestern Past* (1983), Preciado Martin's second book, is a collaboration with the photographer Louis Carlos Bernal; Preciado Martin wrote the text that accompanies the images of Mexican Americans, among them the

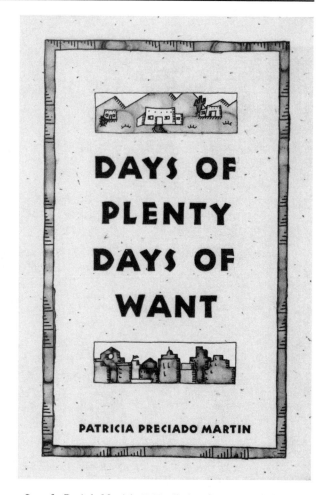

Cover for Preciado Martin's 1988 collection of stories, which describes the lives of Mexicans in an Arizona barrio

old cowboys who brought to Arizona the Mexican *vaquero* tradition. It is a handsome book of photographs and oral histories depicting the lives of those who settled Tucson in the late 1800s; they reminisce about the days prior to Anglo encroachment, when *mexicanos* owned the land that sustained them. The work celebrates Mexican traditions and values and is clearly intended to instill a sense of cultural pride in Mexican Americans of the Tucson area. Published by the University of Arizona Press, where Preciado Martin works as a contract historian, *Images and Conversations* received the Virginia McCormick Scully Award.

According to Preciado Martin, *Images and Conversations* evolved from conversations with elderly Mexican Americans of the Tucson area, who shared their family photographs. While researching the folktales that inspired *The Legend of the Bellringer of San Agustín*, Preciado Martin's informants told her about their lives and about an unspoiled Arizona without borders. She began to document the lives of these *ancianos,* a project that eventually developed into *Images and Conversations.*

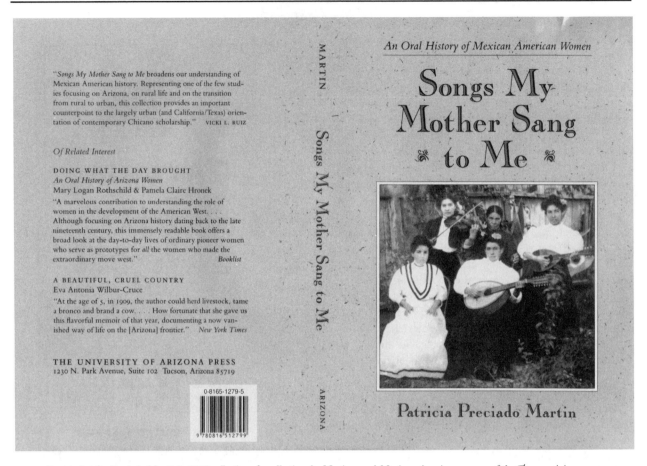

*An Oral History of Mexican American Women*

# Songs My Mother Sang ❧ to Me ❧

"*Songs My Mother Sang to Me* broadens our understanding of Mexican American history. Representing one of the few studies focusing on Arizona, on rural life and on the transition from rural to urban, this collection provides an important counterpoint to the largely urban (and California/Texas) orientation of contemporary Chicano scholarship."   VICKI L. RUIZ

*Of Related Interest*

**DOING WHAT THE DAY BROUGHT**
*An Oral History of Arizona Women*
Mary Logan Rothschild & Pamela Claire Hronek

"A marvelous contribution to understanding the role of women in the development of the American West. . . . Although focusing on Arizona history dating back to the late nineteenth century, this immensely readable book offers a broad look at the day-to-day lives of ordinary pioneer women who serve as prototypes for *all* the women who made the extraordinary move west."   *Booklist*

**A BEAUTIFUL, CRUEL COUNTRY**
Eva Antonia Wilbur-Cruce

"At the age of 5, in 1909, the author could herd livestock, tame a bronco and brand a cow. . . . How fortunate that she gave us this flavorful memoir of that year, documenting a now vanished way of life on the [Arizona] frontier."   *New York Times*

**THE UNIVERSITY OF ARIZONA PRESS**
1230 N. Park Avenue, Suite 102 Tucson, Arizona 85719

0-8165-1279-5

9 780816 512799

Patricia Preciado Martin

*Dust jacket for Preciado Martin's 1992 collection of recollections by Mexican and Mexican American women of the Tucson, Arizona, area*

Preciado Martin's collection of short fiction, *Days of Plenty, Days of Want* (1988), combines her love of oral history and fiction in eight stories that describe the *mexicanos* of an Arizona barrio. Politically subtle, suggestive, and gently critical, two of the stories tell how Anglo politicians instigated the urban renewal that changed forever the lives of Mexican Americans, displacing those with roots in the neighborhood. *Days of Plenty, Days of Want* gives voice to the disenfranchised and calls attention to the destruction of Mexican barrios in the name of modernity, leading to the dislocation of early settlers. In an unpublished August 1995 letter Preciado Martin admitted that some of her works are political: "I try to be subtle—while making a political statement."

*Days of Plenty, Days of Want* depicts a population steeped in Mexican American culture. In "Dreams" the narrator's grandfather Tata Elías is vividly depicted as an old man caught up in his dreams and memories. Preciado Martin skillfully paints a portrait of *un hombre solo* (a lonely man), long past his prime and usefulness, who spends his days brooding about his lost youth and strength—"a man on the run who had changed his name to hide from his deeds and the law."

"María de las Trenzas" (María of the Braids) won the University of California at Irvine's Chicano/Latino Literary Prize in 1989. María is burdened by the expectations placed on her by patriarchal Mexican society, represented by the fact that she must wear her "dark mane of hair" in "two thick braids." She fantasizes about a life different from that of daily chores and obeisance to her elders. In quiet desperation she cuts off her braids, symbolically freeing herself.

Preciado Martin's oral-history collection *Songs My Mother Sang to Me* (1992) again draws its material from the elderly Mexican and Mexican American women of the Tucson area. After conducting many interviews, Preciado Martin's criterion for including stories was that they must be based on the women's personal history and that of their mothers and *abuelas* (grandmothers). Another prerequisite was that the women have a history of commitment to the Mexican American community.

*Songs My Mother Sang to Me* documents the lives of women from different social classes; some were born to privilege and had access to higher education while others lived on *ranchitos* (small ranches), where they worked from dawn to dusk cooking, cleaning, and taking care of large families. The collection recalls the works of Fabiola Cabeza de Baca, author of *We Fed Them Cactus* (1954), which also describes the work-filled days of New Mexican Hispanic *rancho* women.

The reviews of *Songs My Mother Sang to Me* were generally favorable. The *Southwestern Mission Research Center* (March 1993) praised the work's insights into "twentieth-century urban life . . . the words paint pictures of Sonoran ranch life. . . . What emerges is the portrait of tough, resilient men and women." In *The Western Historical Quarterly* (August 1993) María A. Montoya felt that the collection would have benefited from an analysis of interviews by the author and a map of the area to help clarify references in the text. In *The Women's Review of Books* (March 1993) Ruth Behar, a Chicana scholar, thought Preciado Martin edited the women's stories too similarly, thus robbing them of individuality. She acknowledged, however, the importance of recovering Latina voices for American history.

Preciado Martin's narrative style is clear, crisp, and devoid of useless metaphors. Her works echo that of two Spanish women writers: Ana María Matute, author of *El río* (The River, 1963), a work set in Francisco Franco's Spain, and Mercé Rodoreda, author of *La plaça del diamant* (1965; translated as *The Time of the Doves,* 1980). Preciado Martin also cites the influence of other authors she admires, including Mora, Annie Dillard, Janice Bowers, and Luis Alberto Urrea.

Asked in May 1994 which literary genre she preferred to work in, Preciado Martin admitted: "Fiction is an outpouring of my creative self . . . a reflection of my Mexicana culture . . . and all the influences in my life. Oral history is interesting and academic. Ideally, I try to combine both." Her 1996 collection, *El Milagro and Other Stories,* examines cultural colonizations and again affirms the value of stories and traditions passed on by the elders of the Mexican American community. Preciado Martin was named Arizona Author of the Year in 1997. A collection of short stories, "Amor Eterno" (Eternal Love), is scheduled for publication by the University of Arizona Press in February 2000. The importance of the works of Patricia Preciado Martin lies in her ability to give a voice to the Mexican American men and women of Arizona, whom Anglo and Chicano historians have too often omitted from the history of the American Southwest.

# Naomi Quiñónez

*(25 May 1951 – )*

Francisco A. Lomelí
*University of California, Santa Barbara*

BOOKS: *Sueño de colibrí/Hummingbird Dream: Poems* (Los Angeles: West End Press, 1985);

*The Smoking Mirror: Poems* (Albuquerque: West End Press, 1998).

OTHER: "Educators," in *201: Homenaje a la Ciudad de Los Angeles: Latino Experience in Literature & Art,* edited by Helena Viramontes Veloz (Los Angeles: Los Angeles: Latino Writers Association/Self Help Graphics & Art, 1982), p. 55;

"LA Escapade or a Charismatic Love Affair," in *Southern California Anthology* (Santa Barbara: Ross Erikson, 1984), p. 6;

"Jorge With a Sigh," in *Southern California Anthology* (Los Angeles: University of Southern California, 1985), p. 101;

"Ultima II True Blue Eye Shadows of the Past," "My Shattered Sister," and "America's Wailing Wall," in *Invocation L.A.: Urban Multicultural Poetry,* edited by Quiñónez, Michelle T. Clinton, and Sesshu Foster (Albuquerque: West End Press, 1989), pp. 100–106;

"Hesitations," "My Shattered Sister," "People of the Harvest," and "America's Wailing Wall," in *After Aztlán: Latino Poets of the Nineties,* edited by Ray González (Boston: Godine, 1992), pp. 155–161;

"La Llorona" and "The Confession," in *Infinite Divisions: An Anthology of Chicana Literature,* edited by Tey Diana Rebolledo and Eliana S. Rivero (Tucson: University of Arizona Press, 1993);

"Aye Qué María Félix" and "Post-Colonial Contemplations," in *Paper Dance: 55 Latino Poets,* edited by Victor Hernandez Cruz, Leroy V. Quintana, and Virgil Suarez (New York: Persea Books, 1995);

"Ultima II True Blue Eye Shadows of the Past," "The Photograph," "Spousal Rape," "Ay qué María Félix (or María Was No Virgin)," and "La Diosa in Every Woman," in *Chicana Creativity and Criticism: New Frontiers in American Literature,* revised edition, edited by María Herrera-Sobek and Helena

*Naomi Quiñónez (photograph by Alyce Quiñónez)*

María Viramontes (Albuquerque: University of New Mexico Press, 1996), pp. 99–104.

SELECTED PERIODICAL PUBLICATIONS– UNCOLLECTED:
POETRY
"Central Califas," *Chismearte: The Latino Experience in Literature and Art,* no. 9 (September 1983): 17;

"My Shattered Sister," *Forward,* 8 (Spring 1988): 108–
  109;

"The Core," *Guadalupe Review* (October 1991): 255–
  256;

FICTION

"Aurora: Reflections," *Latina Magazine,* 1, no. 3 (1984):
  58.

Naomi Quiñónez is one of an active group of multiculturally diverse artists from Los Angeles who created a grassroots cultural and literary movement. These artists have been motivated by the notion that their social commitment outweighs any individual honors. This group, equivalent to a minority Generation X, views poetry not only as a means of manufacturing innovative images but also as a direct means of engaging an audience or reader in order to instill social change. While crafting imagistic language interests them, their central objective is to achieve a cathartic response through oral performance. For this reason, Quiñónez participated in myriad poetry readings throughout the Southwest, Mexico, and Nicaragua beginning in the 1980s, before she ever became a published writer. From such touring performances she gained a confident poetic voice and provided a testimony of multiethnic Los Angeles, her generation, and her culture as viewed from a feminist standpoint.

Quiñónez is a highly popular poetic performer whose work has appeared in a wide assortment of journals and anthologies. Her first collection of poetry, *Sueño de colibrí/Hummingbird Dream,* was published in 1985; her second, *The Smoking Mirror* (1998), is a ten-year compilation of experimental poetry that offers a critical view of contemporary times while advancing a postcolonial poetics of power relations.

Naomi Helena Quiñónez was born on 25 May 1951 and raised in El Sereno, a part of East Los Angeles that still functions as a source of inspiration. Quiñónez's parents are originally from El Paso, Texas; her grandparents migrated from Mexico during the Mexican Revolution (1910–1920). Her parents, José Quiñónez and Yolanda Castellanos, moved to Los Angeles in the late 1940s and to Pico Rivera, near downtown Los Angeles, in 1950. Shortly thereafter, the family moved to El Sereno, where middle child Naomi and her sisters Roxanne and Yvonne experienced a village type of existence within a sprawling city, surrounded by a large number of Mexican people. Her father had served in World War II as a medic, and after the war he worked as a printer for *The Los Angeles Herald Examiner.* Because of his veteran's benefits, the family was able to afford their own home. Her father worked with the newspaper for a total of twenty years, but the family's sense of stability was shaken when he lost all benefits after a lengthy labor strike.

Quiñónez's home environment was generally nurturing. Her mother was a talented storyteller who could communicate a sense of wonder with descriptions and imagery, and her grandmother reaffirmed that rich oral tradition by also telling folktales. Quiñónez had an early and close affinity to printers such as her grandfather and father and became involved in journalism in high school.

A strong sense of place and time haunt Quiñónez; she grapples with the many facets of Los Angeles, her favorite cultural hub, in order to capture a notion of what the twenty-first century might be like. She particularly enjoys exploring and transcending new boundaries of meaning and cultural expression. The Chicano Movement and the spirit of freedom in the 1960s left a permanent impression on her, and her subsequent move in 1970 to San Jose helped further to develop her social conscience.

She received her entire elementary and secondary education in the Los Angeles area, graduating from Wilson High School in 1969. She then studied for one year at California State University at Los Angeles and later transferred to San Jose State University, where she received a B.A. in English in 1975. In northern California, particularly in Santa Cruz, Quiñónez honed her community activism and administrative skills. She served as chief administrative aide for the Santa Cruz County Board of Supervisors from 1978 until 1980, when she returned to Los Angeles. She then pursued an M.A. in public administration at the University of Southern California, completing the requirements by December 1982. She continued to work for several community-oriented projects and task forces, occupying such administrative posts as consultant for the city of Pasadena in 1983 and director of the L.A.M.P. (Literacy Association of Monterey Park) program from 1983 to 1986.

Quiñónez served as an instructor at La Coalición Migrant Education Project at Watsonville, California (1977–1979), the University of California at Santa Cruz (1979), the University of the Pacific at Stockton (1981), and California State University at Northridge and at Long Beach (1983–1985). In 1996 she completed her Ph.D. at Claremont College in the interdisciplinary field of American Studies and became an assistant professor at California State University at Chico. Quiñónez's teaching and her poetry motivate her to address contemporary issues, racial politics, gender concerns, cultural problems, and the cadences of oral and written language in both Spanish and English. Among her many artistic activities, she has worked on *Caminos Magazine* from 1980 to 1982, joined in the Los

*Cover for Quiñónez's 1985 collection of poems that celebrate women's experiences*

Angeles Barrio Writers Workshop, and participated in several multiethnic and grassroots projects such as the collection *Invocation L.A.: Urban Multicultural Poetry* (1989).

The appearance of *Sueño de colibrí/Hummingbird Dream* coincided with the emergence of a highly experimental generation of Chicana writers, including Denise Chávez, Sandra Cisneros, Helena María Viramontes, Cecile Pineda, Margarita Cota-Cárdenas, and Cherríe Moraga. With an intensely poetic flair, they explore and theorize about family, genre, gender, identity, and social questions, expanding the Chicano literary landscape. At the same time, they offer a feminist-oriented view of the world in contrast to the previously dominant Chicano male discourse.

This collection of forty-three poems, along with her other published works, clearly marks the trajectory of a poet, educator, and activist concerned with the inherent contradictions of society, including social and spiritual transformation. Her poetry offers critically provocative reflections about women at home or in the workplace. Quiñónez attempts to give a testimony of women's lives and their unacknowledged existence in a patriarchal society—not to put them on a pedestal but simply to give their experience faces, names, and substance. Divided into eight sections—"Woman Words," "Insects," "The Fifth Movement," "Cantos de Califas," "Notes of Discord," "Harmony Grits," "Birth Poems," and "The Glass Coffee Shop"—the book chronicles a wide range of moods and contemplations ranging from the nationalistic to the intimately personal.

Quiñónez dissects false notions, debunks stereotypes, and deciphers traditional constraints while appealing to the fancy of imagination and self-realization. In "International Women's Day," she notes: "The Feminine is no farce, you see. / Only a grave misconception / on the part of those / who cannot conceive." She later adds: "The woman inside you is waiting. . . . / The woman inside you is a spirit longing for freedom." In "A Woman Walking," an echo of the Chilean poet laureate Pablo Neruda's famous existentialist poem "Walking Around," the poetic voice questions why a woman must face anonymity on a daily basis, always invisible or at least unacknowledged. Despair, however, does not overtake the poetry; instead, the urgent need to recognize women as contributing to society and as generators of culture and history is communicated.

The heartfelt poems of *Sueño de colibrí/ Hummingbird Dream* are interspersed with nationalistic imagery and symbolism, affirmations of gender empowerment, and remembrances of sensuality and short-circuited love relationships. Throughout, Quiñónez shows a special affection for Los Angeles, which in the poem "L.A.–A Face Only a Mother Could Love," she refers to as a "layered Babylon / of space and time." Quiñónez is interested in communicating ideas without overdecorating them with metaphors or an abundance of images. Her calm, confidential tone mixes well with the seductive orality of a poet dedicated to eliciting a new world order. Consequently, most of the poems focus on imagining alternative solutions and changing attitudes in a quest for fundamental social change for the common good. Quiñónez effectively combines strands of Chicano Movement poetics with a lyrical sense of her surroundings and a postmodern bent.

By design, the first section of *Sueño de colibrí/Humingbird Dream,* "Woman Words," lays the groundwork for seeking a new direction while depicting women within a Mexican female mythology and a backdrop of the history of suffering women: "suspended in time / I wait in suspense / for the mirror to reveal / a forgotten woman." Quiñónez sets out to celebrate women as a sociocultural presence while redefining and reinterpreting such male-constructed myths as Eve, Malinche (supposedly Hernán Cortés's Indian mistress who served as translator and accomplice in destroying the Aztec empire), and Helen of Troy. For example, the poet emphasizes the figure of Coatlicue, the Aztec representation of Mother Earth and the Aztec concept of cosmogony, over Quetzalcóatl, an Aztec male god of high culture and art. She underscores men's scapegoating of women by deriving a lesson for the ages: "perhaps today / we can learn to accept / ourselves." La Llorona–the Wailing Woman, a strong Mexican cultural symbol of loss and family violence–becomes the model of renewal and metamorphosis for modern Chicanas who wish to rid themselves of imposed demons. The poet renders a revisionist view of such figures, explaining them in human terms rather than as archetypes, and seeking to disengage Chicana women from a long tradition that ultimately inhibits discovery and growth.

The section "The Fifth Movement" displays a strong political spirit by alluding to a Chicano Movement consciousness of hope and regeneration. Yet, a tone of disillusionment persuades the poetry of this section, along with the recognition that traditional politics for poor folk will never adequately address their needs. In "Educators"–a poem that brings to mind Abelardo Delgado's "Stupid America" (1969)–Quiñónez addresses the negative effect of the traditional educational system on Chicano children. The technique of incantation and alliteration is used throughout as in the lives, "There is temptation / for co-optation / . . . before total assimilation." Quiñónez expands her themes by including other Latinos beyond Chicanos, such as El Salvadorans torn by revolution and social strife. Her poetry consequently acquires a Third World perspective.

The section titled "Cantos de Califas" (Chants of California) captures images and scenes from various cities throughout California. In "Chile Jalapeño Night" and other poems Quiñónez evokes the psyche of the culture by depicting common folk celebrating the ordinary things. In "L.A.–A Face Only A Mother Could Love," the poet highlights the quirkiness and glitzy qualities of the city while expressing her affection for its trendy strangeness.

In the last four sections of the book Quiñónez concentrates on highly personalized confessional experiences in poems tinged with regret. Two leitmotifs are silence, suggestive of the emptiness experienced by the poet, and rebirth, which indicates that these deeply personal experiences have left permanent scars on the poet's worldview. These sections include more poems in Spanish than the other sections, reaffirming the confessional mode. The last poem, "Con Safos," caps an exploratory trajectory of themes and concerns.

The twenty-nine poems of Quiñónez's *The Smoking Mirror* were written during a ten-year period. Francisco A. Lomelí observes a "mature eloquence" and "ingenious word-making" in the poetry. Divided into four parts–"Worldwides," "Mothertongue," "Post-Colonial Contemplations," and "Corazón Sin Razón" (A Senseless Heart)–Quiñónez begins with the personal in the first section, probes into womanhood in the second, addresses the philosophical-political issues of the times in the third, and explores belonging and culture in the last section.

Quiñónez writes to make "shadows burn / and silence loud, / to enter the mouths of the hungry / and feed the muse." Although she speaks of "mystical incantations," she is concerned with the social role of the poet and often ponders her own solitude or others' marginalized conditions. In the poem "Mystic Mangos Roll on L.A. Freeways" the word *mangos* is used in a ritualistic litany that juxtaposes the sensuality of the fruit and the coldness of cement structures. The poet proposes new considerations for social frameworks by combining

Mejicle

①

I would have loved to dance
in the plaza at Mitla
Rumbaed around
these thick columns
Reworked in corners
that zig zagged on the walls
these geometric ~~and~~ intersections
of ~~memories~~ space
I would have loved to dance
~~in~~ with my black dress swirling
in the heated wind~~s past~~
my red face upwards towards the sun
my dance, my offering to death.
and rebirth of things.
I would have loved to dance
atop the pyramid of the moon
Undulating torso and
captivating movements
a rythmic search for
the ~~soul of~~ the lingering voice
of the mother

*Page from the manuscript for "Mejicles," a poem included in Quiñónez's 1998 collection,* The Smoking Mirror *(Collection of Naomi Quiñónez)*

"Africano soul and jazz 'n' funk" with Latino textures, smells, and tastes.

In *The Smoking Mirror* Quiñónez inserts women into all realms of human experience, from the abstract to the quotidian. In "La Diosa [the goddess] in Every Woman," myth and common roles merge: "This is an altar of women, / a woman's altar, / where the shy goddess speaks / in voices more powerful / than the laments of our / mutilated histories." It is a poem of redemption in which a woman's worth as a healer and a source of strength is acknowledged while it is emphasized that no woman should have to sacrifice herself for others. Such a perspective contributes toward expanding the "smoking mirror" metaphor of the title. While the self-reflective act of looking into the mirror is crucial to establishing an identity, at the same time one must consciously burn away one's sense of contrived roles and prescribed limitations. The central image of the mirror thus suggests a process of purgation that allows for the creation of a more accurate picture of women in history, myth, and society.

In the final section Quiñónez writes, "What the world lacks is not love / or honest politicians, / is not passion or its ensuing / premonitions, is not morality / or its consequential inhibitions, / but simply an act of heartfelt awe / at the life that strikes us in the face." She finds meaning in a vicarious dance with an atavistic Mexico (referred to as "Mejicles") from long ago, as the indigenous world seems to call and soothe her. The book concludes on a note of redemption as the poet finds an inner peace in the indigenous world that nourishes and focuses on the Quinto Sol (Fifth Sun), thus implying regeneration. Quiñónez finds relevance in a worldview—generally overlooked or dismissed—that combines the past with the future.

Quiñónez's poems have been anthologized throughout her career, at least partly because of her ability to capture experiences that are traditionally cloaked in silence, such as the family violence in "Spousal Rape" (1996). Although her work has been included in noteworthy collections such as Ray González's *After Aztlán: Latino Poets of the Nineties* (1992) it has received scant scholarly attention. Only Lomelí and M. Linda Apodaca have examined her work in detail. Lomelí argues that the poet instills a sense of orality and epic celebration in her written poetry. Apodaca summarizes Quiñónez's themes.

Throughout her work, Naomi Quiñónez struggles to stay true to her art in its original form and above all to its oral nature. She debunks conventional attitudes in order to propose a more egalitarian society in which women can share equally without having to sacrifice anything essential to their identities.

### References:

M. Linda Apodaca, "Naomi Quiñónez: Images in Cultural Politics and Gender," in *Proceedings of the 1st Annual International Conference on the Emerging Literature of the Southwest Culture: October 28-30, 1995, El Paso, Texas* (El Paso: University of Texas at El Paso, 1996), pp. 9–13;

Francisco A. Lomelí, "*Ars Combinatoria* in Naomi Quiñónez: From *Trobadora* to Anti-Word Synthesizer," in *Confrontations et Metissage,* edited by Elyette Benjamin-Labarthe, Yves-Charles Grandjeat, and Christian Lerat (Bordeaux: Editions le Maison Des Pays Ibériques, 1995), pp. 261–270.

# Manuel Ramos

*(6 March 1948 –     )*

## María Teresa Márquez
*University of New Mexico*

BOOKS: *The Ballad of Rocky Ruiz* (New York: St. Martin's Press, 1993);
*The Ballad of Gato Guerrero* (New York: St. Martin's Press, 1994);
*The Last Client of Luis Montez* (New York: St. Martin's Press, 1996);
*Blues for the Buffalo* (New York: St. Martin's Press, 1997).

OTHER: "His Mother's Image," in *Southwest Tales: A Contemporary Collection,* edited by Alurista and Xelina Rojas-Urista (Colorado Springs: Maize, 1986), pp. 103–111.

SELECTED PERIODICAL PUBLICATIONS–
UNCOLLECTED: "White Devils and Cockroaches," *Westword,* 9 (January 1986): 8;
"Kite Lesson," *Upper Larimer Arts & Times,* 3 (August 1987): 12;
"A Name on the Wall," *Pearl Street Press,* 2 (February 1989): 14;
"The Truth Is," *Pearl Street Press,* 2 (March 1989): 14;
"Doing 40 on Highway 50," *Rocky Mountain Arsenal of the Arts,* 4 (September 1990): 14;
"The Smell of Onions," *Rocky Mountain Arsenal of the Arts,* 4 (September 1990): 9;
"The Scent of Terrified Animals," *Saguaro,* 6 (1990): 23–28.

*Manuel Ramos (courtesy of Ramos)*

The publication of his novel *The Ballad of Rocky Ruiz* (1993) launched Manuel Ramos's literary career as a major writer and contributor to the Chicano/Latino mystery genre. His mystery novels, beginning with *The Ballad of Rocky Ruiz* and including *The Ballad of Gato Guerrero* (1994), *The Last Client of Luis Montez* (1996), and *Blues for the Buffalo* (1997), all feature the same protagonist, Luis Montez, a lawyer disillusioned over the path his life has taken since the days of the Chicano Movement of the 1970s.

Ramos's literary success was influenced by the University of California at Irvine Chicano/Latino Literary Contest award he received in 1991. In 1986 Ramos received second prize in the *Westword* Fiction Contest for "White Devils and Cockroaches," a short story. In 1993 he was nominated for an Edgar Allan Poe Award by the Mystery Writers of America in the category of best first novel. In 1994 Ramos won the Colorado Book Award presented by the Colorado Center for the Book. Most recently, Ramos was the recipient of the Law Alumni Award for Distinguished Achievement from the University of Colorado School of Law in 1996 and the Jacob V. Shaetzel Award from the Colorado Bar Association in 1998.

Manuel Anthony Ramos was born in Florence, Colorado, on 6 March 1948. His father, Henry, a native of Zacatecas, Mexico, was the director of a training school for the International Laborers Union until his retirement; Ramos's mother, Emma, was born in the mining community of Chandler, Colorado. Ramos is the eldest of three sons; his two brothers are Michael and Richard.

Ramos attended public schools in Florence and Colorado Springs. He received a B.A. with honors in political science from Colorado State University in 1970 and a law degree from the University of Colorado in 1973. On 23 September 1983 he married Florence Hernandez, and they have one son, Diego. Ramos is the deputy director and litigation director for the Legal Aid Society of Metropolitan Denver. Except for the year he was involved in union organizing in a factory, his career has focused on legal services to the less fortunate. He has used his trial and appellate experience to teach a course in trial practice at the University of Denver College of Law. He also teaches courses in Chicano literature at Metropolitan State College of Denver.

Motivated to provide "the best in Chicano and Latino literature," Ramos started a mail-order business, SouthWest Tales, in 1993. He also reviews books for KUVO, a public-radio jazz station in Denver, and writes about books for the *Denver Post* and the *Bloomsbury Review*. Ramos's legal experience provides background for his Luis Montez novels, but in an interview with Camille Martinez in *La Voz Hispana de Colorado* (4 August 1993) Ramos stated "the parallels between fiction and reality ended there."

*The Ballad of Rocky Ruiz* is set in Denver and narrated by Montez, a middle-aged lawyer who has lost the ideals for which he fought in the 1970s. Montez recounts the turbulent times as experienced by him and his fellow Chicano revolutionaries, Los Guerrilleros: Héctor García, now a respected judge; Tino Pacheco, manager of an apartment complex; and Orlie Martínez, a longtime community activist.

Some twenty years before Montez and Los Guerrilleros attempted to change the social conditions of the time and to make known the presence of Chicanos in the community at large. Rocky Ruiz, the leader of Los Guerrilleros, was murdered one night, and the crime was never solved. The deed was attributed to hooded men, members of a group opposed to Chicano activists and the Chicano Movement. Rocky's young wife left town with their baby daughter and was never heard from again by Montez or his fellow Guerrilleros, which disbanded after Rocky's death.

Since his revolutionary days Montez has become a burned-out case; he attends baseball games, his favorite pastime, whenever possible, but mostly he spends his time in bars in attempts to drink away his troubles related to his former wives, children, mounting bills, and diminishing law practice. Montez makes a subsistent living hustling cases, defending clients too poor to afford other legal counsel and criminals who know the juridical principles as well as the lawyers and judges.

When a young lawyer named Teresa Fuentes enters Montez's life, he immediately falls for her, harboring a small hope that she will be his salvation. Teresa, however, has other plans. She is hired, with the help of Judge García, by a high-powered law firm and finds shelter in the apartment complex managed by Tino Pacheco. Shortly after Teresa arrives in the city and makes contact with the former Guerrilleros, suspicious events occur: Orlie begins receiving threatening telephone calls; Tino is found dead; the judge apparently commits suicide; and Teresa disappears. Tino's death, the judge's suicide, and Orlie's increasing anxiety over the mysterious phone calls lead Montez to investigate the circumstances surrounding Rocky's untimely death. Montez's trip to rural Texas in search of Teresa and answers to questions about his friend's murder becomes a search for his old ideals and his self-worth.

*The Ballad of Rocky Ruiz* is more than a tale of murder, greed, and politics. Ramos recounts the attempts of those in the Chicano Movement to change the social and political status quo of the time. His depiction of the events of the 1970s indicates that the movement made some differences, although the economic, social, and political interests of the select few remain dominant. Through Montez, however, Ramos seems to project optimism about life and the opportunities to effect change.

In *The Ballad of Gato Guerrero* Montez has successfully turned his life around, reviving his law practice and leading a relatively normal life. Trouble, however, follows the lawyer as he becomes entangled in the conundrums of an old friend's life. Montez's friend, Felix "Gato" Guerrero, a Vietnam veteran with financial and alcoholic problems, lost his only child in an elevator accident and his wife to suicide. Gato's father-in-law, Edwin Talmage, a wealthy and well-connected man, blames Gato for his family's tragedies and seeks revenge. Talmage's major business associate, Trini Anglin, is a criminal gang leader whose wife is involved in an adulterous affair with Gato. Trini also seeks revenge. Gato and Elizabeth, Trini's wife, seek Montez's help to escape from Trini and his thugs. Elizabeth was one of Montez's high-school classmates, a beautiful Chicana who was often the subject of his fantasies. The lovers' escape becomes more problematic when Gato is charged with the murder of Cuginello, Trini's main henchman.

*Dust jacket for Ramos's 1993 novel, which introduced his detective hero, Luis Montez*

A subplot in the novel involves Victor, a juvenile Chicano gang leader, and Jenny, his tough mother, well known to the Denver police. Jenny hires Montez to represent her in a lawsuit against the police for a severe beating that sent her to the hospital. Victor, the subject of a drug investigation, is apprehended by the police after a shootout with a rival gang that results in the death of his best friend. Attempting to help Victor and to lead him away from crime, prison, and possibly an early death, Montez assumes personal responsibility for the young thug.

Montez's efforts to cope with Victor, work on the lawsuit against the police force, and save the condemned lovers lead him from the barrios and urban centers of Denver and the peaceful San Luis Valley in southern Colorado to Española and Santa Fe in New Mexico. Montez is beaten, shot at, and threatened, but he never gives up.

Ramos sets his story of murder and suspense against the clash of different cultural worlds that manage to coexist. He draws miniature portraits of Chicano and Latino life in the barrios, urban centers, and rural areas of Colorado, Texas, and New Mexico. In *The Ballad of Gato Guerrero,* as in *The Ballad of Rocky Ruiz,* Ramos declines to resolve all of the elements of the mystery. In *The Ballad of Rocky Ruiz* Montez is never able to confirm that Teresa Fuentes is responsible for the murders that take place. The reader is left with conjectures about the exact nature of Teresa's involvement. In *The Ballad of Gato Guerrero,* Montez successfully solves the murderous connection between Anglin and Talmage, but he does not know the final fate of Gato and Elizabeth. Ramos implies the fates of his main characters but leaves the ending hopefully ambiguous.

Both *The Ballad of Rocky Ruiz* and *The Ballad of Gato Guerrero* examine the social divisions between those who are economically and politically established and those who are not. For example, those who are less well-off usually live in barrios or in poor rural communities. Though Ramos's characters may lack personal control over their destinies, they are not entirely without opportunities to change and overcome life's challenges, as indicated by Montez's decision to accept responsibility for the quality and direction of his life. Ramos's plots involve the dignity of individuals, the family, and the impact of poverty and racism on society. In the barrio and less economically stable rural towns, his characters suffer the effects of low incomes, unemployment, and second-class status.

Ramos develops urban settings in which his characters struggle to survive the daily grind of city life: crime, gangs, corruption, political maneuvering, unemployment, drugs, and homelessness. Antithetical to urban centers, Ramos depicts rural areas as places where his main characters find spiritual healing and solace. Furthermore, the rural settings are where Ramos's Chicano characters are close to nature and where they find the strength to survive the harshness of life in economically depressed areas.

Ramos's interest in the family and family values is evident in his work. Montez is developed as a son, husband, and father. Even though he is portrayed as a divorced man, he still attempts to be a father to his sons, and a son to his father, a cantankerous man with a soft heart. Ramos depicts single-parent families in the barrio, faced with urban challenges and struggling to remain a family unit. Middle-class Chicano families, comfortable and secure, are also confronted with tragedy and the disruption of the family unit in his novels. Ramos develops his families as microscopic communities that withstand disappointments and reversals of fortunes and confront the future with optimism.

*The Last Client of Luis Montez* begins with Montez at a professional high point. He defends James Esch, a wealthy young client, in a drug case and gets the case thrown out on appeal. Soon after, however, Esch is brutally killed and his sister vanishes, and Montez is arrested and charged with Esch's murder. At the same time he must contend with his father's critical illness, and his brother's return to Denver reignites sibling rivalries. Montez becomes a fugitive, hitchhiking to San Diego to find the former police officer who may know the truth about Esch's murder. Along the way he encounters a variety of offbeat characters, used by Ramos to create a vision of 1990s America as spinning out of control. By the end of the novel Ramos has solved the murder of his client and his reputation is restored, but his search has exacted a physical and psychological toll from which he may not recover.

At the beginning of *Blues for the Buffalo* Montez is in Mexico convalescing from the injuries he received during the Esch murder investigation. He meets Rachel Espinoza, a writer who immediately inspires in him a sense of foreboding. He returns to the United States to begin the process of resuscitating his law practice but is soon confronted by a private investigator from California, Conrad Valdez, who has been hired by Rachel's father because the woman has disappeared in Mexico. Animosity quickly develops between Montez and the younger man, not only because of Valdez's suspicions about him but also because of their cultural differences. A fully assimilated American, Valdez has no use for the Chicano cultural and political activism that has played such a role in Montez's life. To Montez, Valdez represents the European bloodline within the Chicano people. The two men form a grudging partnership, however, in order to solve Rachel's disappearance. They discover that the solution to the mystery is bound up in the real-life disappearance in 1974 of Oscar Zeta Acosta, a writer and radical Chicano activist perhaps best known for his association with journalist Hunter S. Thompson.

Each of Ramos's novels successfully combines engaging thriller elements with insightful social commentary. Through his serial protagonist Ramos depicts the direction that Chicano culture has taken in the years since its activist high point in the 1970s; Montez also serves to reflect Ramos's sense of the resiliency and future promise of the Chicano people. Though they are usually characterized as mysteries, Ramos's novels can thus fruitfully be read as social documents as well.

**References:**

Peter Handel, "Latino Noir," *Armchair Detective,* 27 (Spring 1994): 220–221;

Betsy Rothstein, "The Haunting, Mysterious Words of Manuel Ramos," *El Semanario,* 29 July 1993, p. 12.

# Joe D. Rodríguez

*(4 November 1943 –     )*

### Roberto Cantú
*California State University, Los Angeles*

BOOK: *Oddsplayer* (Houston: Arte Público, 1989).

OTHER: "Oscar Z. Acosta" and "Orlando Romero," in *Chicano Literature: A Reference Guide,* edited by Julio A. Martínez and Francisco A. Lomelí (Westport, Conn.: Greenwood Press, 1985), pp. 3–16, 346–351;

"United States Hispanic Autobiography and Biography: Legend for the Future," in *Handbook of Hispanic Cultures in the United States: Literature and Art,* edited by Lomelí (Houston: Arte Público, 1993), pp. 268–290;

"Chicano Literature and German Science: Some Notes on the Limitations of Meaning and Common Sense," in *Gender, Self, and Society: Proceedings of the IV International Conference on the Hispanic Cultures of the United States,* edited by Renate von Bardeleben (Frankfurt am Main: Peter Lang, 1993), pp. 371–381.

SELECTED PERIODICAL PUBLICATIONS– UNCOLLECTED: "The Chicano Novel and the North American Narrative of Survival," *Denver Quarterly,* 16 (Fall 1981): 64–70;

"Chicano Poetry: Mestizaje and the Use of Irony," *Campo Libre: Journal of Chicano Studies,* 1 (Summer 1981): 229–235;

"God's Silence and the Shrill of Ethnicity in the Chicano Novel," *Explorations in Ethnic Studies,* 4 (July 1981): 14–21;

"The Sense of Mestizaje in Two Latino Novels," *Revista Chicano-Riqueña,* 12 (Spring 1984): 57–63;

"Oscar Zeta Acosta and the Challenge of Epistemic Literacy," *Hispanorama* (1990): 13–16.

Joe D. Rodríguez is a novelist, literary critic, war veteran, licensed vocational nurse, and university professor. He has also been a janitor, a construction worker, and a homeless person living on the streets of San Diego. Rodríguez's critical and narrative works are an attempt to make his life experiences communicable.

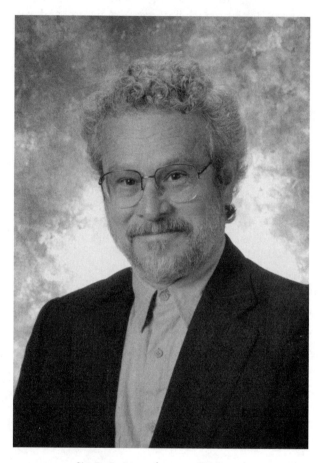

*Joe D. Rodríguez (courtesy of Rodríguez)*

Joe Domingo Rodríguez Jr. was born in Hawaii on 4 November 1943. His paternal grandfather, a Mexican from Durango, had been born with the surname Saavedra but had received the name Rodríguez when he was adopted. The grandfather married an Indian woman who is remembered by Rodríguez as beautiful, with raven-black hair. Their marriage mirrors the emblematic Mexican union of the Spanish male and the native woman that is historically associated with the

*Rodríguez's parents in Guam, 1949 (courtesy of Rodríguez)*

Spanish conquest. His grandparents' marriage was the source of Rodríguez's understanding of *mestizaje* (cultural admixture) and ethnicity as "mixed legacies" and an "extended sense of self."

Rodríguez's father was a Mexican American *Tejano* (Texan) who, in spite of his light complexion, grew up aware of prejudice toward Mexicans. Rodríguez Sr. had a career in the navy, serving in the Pacific during World War II and in Korea. The author's mother, Julia Fernández de Rodríguez, was born in Maui to Puerto Rican parents who had migrated to Hawaii at the turn of the century to work in the sugarcane fields. According to Rodríguez, his parents met at Pearl Harbor; he is the eldest of their five children.

Because of his father's military career, Rodríguez moved from one city or country to another every two or three years and had to adapt to contrasting landscapes, languages, and friends. As he said in a 1997 interview in *(untitled)*, "I come from a family of migrant workers, but dad always had the same job. What happened is that he moved with his job all over the world,

and when we were lucky we were able to follow him. In these unsettled circumstances, your family is your ground of being, and the nexus among members can be both secure and stifling." Rodríguez's brother Frank Louis Rodríguez was an army officer who wanted to follow in their father's footsteps by making a career of the military but died in combat in Vietnam. The loss stunned the family because Frank had been the favorite; his charisma and friendly personality had made him the mediator in the family's conflicts. "Our family was never the same," said Rodríguez; "I loved him, dedicated *Oddsplayer* [1989] to his memory and carry him with me still."

Rodríguez attended Stanford Ballard Dole, a junior high school in Oahu, in the ninth grade; for the tenth grade he transferred to Long Beach Polytechnic High School. He graduated from North Chicago Community High School in 1961 and received a Naval Reserve Officer Training Corps Scholarship to study at the University of Texas at Austin, where he majored in microbiology (premed). Rodríguez attended the univer-

157

seriously

The last of the wounded was evacuated by helicopter. The dead

remained. The direct hit on the dispensary was still ringing in his

ears. While Kirsch was unconscious from the blast, Isaacs bled to death.

Kirsch and Hartman moved his litter and the medic smoothed Isaacs' body

bag because his hands would not keep still. Hartman looked like he would

never go home.

Kirsch didn't know if Priest had a chance. Hendrick was wounded

bad but would live.

"Where is he?" Lieck demanded. "He's here somewhere gathering

flies."

Lieck jerked back a blanket. "Half his head is blown away. A

Sergeant's pay." Lieck spat in Talbot's face.

"I made it clean," Lieck told them. "Not a scratch and the aid

station took a direct hit. Talbot and Isaacs are wasted. Hendrick is in

parts. That fucking Priest went over the enemy."

"Deserter? You low life," Hartman was reaching for his weapon.

"No more," Kirsch said, "or it will never stop." Talbot was

brought in with many wounds, he was already dead. No questions. The

attack came from everywhere.

"Priest is no deserter," Kirsch told Lieck. "He's MIA. He'll find

his way back."

The horizon was seeping red and in the distance Four-Miles was

burning from napalm and artillery. The bodies in the dust, people

wounded and lost, and all around the wire. Brooding over the devastation

was a profound sense of loss.

*Front and back of a leaf from Rodríguez's revised typescript for* Oddsplayer, *his 1989 novel (Collection of Joe D. Rodríguez)*

"No more," Kirsch said, "or it will never stop." Talbot
was carried in with many fatal wounds. The litter
bearers who brought in the remains didn't say a
word. No questions. The attack came from everywhere.
"Priest is no deserter," Kirsch told Lieck. "He'll find his way back."
The horizon is seeping red, and in the distance,
a village burns from napalm and artillery. There are
bodies next to fired shells, and people wounded or and
lost.. All around runs barbed wire, and all bets are
off. The light gathers the morning as if some presence
brooding over the metal strands. No one thinks
of playing odds. Dust swirls over the devastation.

The horizon is seeping red, and in the distance, Four Miles
a village is burning from napalm and artillery. There are bodies
next to fired shells and people wounded or lost. All around runs barbed
wire, and all bets are off. No one plays odds. Dust
swirls over the devastation.

sity for only one academic year, returning to Hawaii in 1962. Hawaii and Texas were worlds apart; the former was a multicultural environment, while the latter seethed with anti-Mexican attitudes and practices.

Rodríguez enrolled at the University of Hawaii, received a Regents Scholarship, and got married. Finding the scholarship insufficient to meet his growing expenses, he took part-time jobs as a janitor and a construction worker. He changed majors several times, from microbiology to religion, psychology, and finally philosophy. In 1964 he dropped out and moved with his wife and daughter, Nikki, to San Diego. There he worked as a short-order cook and later in a plastics factory in Escondido. In 1965 he was divorced and became homeless, working temporary jobs to make enough money to survive.

After several months of living in the streets, Rodríguez joined the navy and served in Vietnam in 1965–1966 as a medical corpsman. Rodríguez became a medic because he "did not want to be shooting at anybody in Vietnam." *Oddsplayer* is an attempt to reconstruct his experiences while serving with a Marine detachment in a rear-guard station at Da Nang. The racism he encountered there revived long-repressed memories of his experiences in Austin. "The racism was so pervasive and venomous my skin crawled. After all, I am Mexican. I came to ethnic consciousness with flares lighting the skies after nightfall." He began working on *Oddsplayer* six months after he returned from Vietnam, but it took fifteen years to write.

Rodríguez returned to San Diego and married a second time; his son, Bruce David, was born in 1966. After finishing his B.A. in philosophy at San Diego State University in 1967 he served as a probation officer, then enrolled at the University of California, San Diego, where he majored in English. While studying for his doctorate, Rodríguez supplemented his veteran's benefits by working a night shift as a nurse. At the university he met Ed Fussell, an English professor and the author of a book on Nathaniel Hawthorne's vision of the frontier. Although he never enrolled in one of Fussell's courses, Rodríguez remembers that the professor "took me through sentence by sentence in my doctoral dissertation; if it hadn't been for Fussell, I wouldn't have made it through." The dissertation is titled "Aspects of Internal Conflict in Certain Early Tales and Sketches from Hawthorne." Rodríguez earned his Ph.D. in 1977 and was hired to teach in the department of Mexican American studies at San Diego State University. During his first year of teaching he enrolled in a summer program in Cuernavaca, Mexico, where he studied Spanish and immersed himself in the culture.

In his 1993 article "United States Hispanic Autobiography and Biography: Legend for the Future" Rodríguez writes:

> Hispanics have to construct their sense of "reality" in the United States and also negotiate their identity. Hispanics are the product of distinct cultural legacies which include Iberian, Native American and African, as well as other groups of people including the Anglo. Hispanics can blend their different legacies or choose some and not others. In some circumstances, a Hispanic can reject them all or create a hybrid culture which is unprecedented.

Rodríguez dramatizes this sudden awareness of multiple cultural backgrounds in a passage in *Oddsplayer* in which Pérez, a Mexican American, experiences an epiphany in the midst of destruction:

> The fire made him recall the Indians' destroyed codices, skull racks with whitened skulls and the pioneers who seized a continent. He was mestizo and each one of his cultural backgrounds was a legacy of doom. An Asian war, the Indios' blood sacrifice to feed the sun, the Spaniard's bloody cross. . . . History was written in blood. All the past was part of the sheeted fire. He was at point zero.

While writing *Oddsplayer,* Rodríguez could not bring himself to read any books on Vietnam or see any movies about it; he used Joseph Conrad's *Heart of Darkness* (1899) as a textual point of reference, unconsciously making the same choice made by Michael Herr in *Dispatches* (1977) and by Francis Ford Coppola in the 1979 motion picture *Apocalypse Now.* Rodríguez said, "My experience with the men I knew in Vietnam is that most were decent people who did their duty—but once in country we spiraled off the edge of the earth. There were authentic psychos though—warped and malignant people" like his character Sergeant John Talbot.

*Oddsplayer* is divided into three chapters, with chapter 1 beginning at dawn ("an unseen sun bled into morning"), chapter 2 moving toward high noon, and chapter 3 taking place under "twilight's blued gun-metal sky". The narrative condenses the drama of the Vietnam War through a Judeo-Christian imagery of Armaggedon mixed with pre-Columbian symbols of human sacrifice.

*Oddsplayer* has a diverse cast of characters, including Anglo Americans, Latinos, and African Americans, brought together to fight in Vietnam. Contrary to the usual portrayal of the Vietnam veteran driven crazy by the war, *Oddsplayer* depicts the conflicting backgrounds of several characters—Talbot, Lieck, Priest, Pérez—to suggest that the cause of their inner turmoil is not Viet-

Cover for Rodríguez's novel, about Latino, Anglo, and African American soldiers in Vietnam

nam but unresolved past experiences. There are two major groups: officers and noncombatant personnel, usually Anglos, and the mostly minority "grunts" who do the fighting and dying for their country. Fernández, a Puerto Rican soldier, asks with humor bordering on cynicism: "What do politicians do with a Rican who wants to get ahead: They make a war and teach him how to disappear. Domino War." In the second chapter Kirsch—Rodríguez's version of Conrad's Kurtz—is musing over humankind's history of self-destruction and concludes: "What do you call your top sergeant in civilian clothes? The Grim Reaper. . . . Splitters of the atom, we cannot escape the oldest of evils."

The catalyst of dissent and displaced anger is Talbot, an authoritarian and neurotic officer who sends to the northern battlefields—hence, to die—anyone who is a "bleeding heart" or questions his orders. Talbot has an officer's nostalgia for the illusory days of heroic valor, world dominance, and national glory. Just prior to his death, Talbot reflects on the progressive decay in the moral fiber of the enlisted men:

> What was happening to the Corps? Punks with faces like a baby's ass, that liked loud music and that had to question everything were his replacements. How could they stand up under fire? A man had to be raised hungry to be willing to fight. A Marine goes for the balls or throat and kicks at the head when his man is down. What did the future matter to him? Everything was falling apart: the country, the people, and especially the pukes who would take his place. The world was wobbling on its axis like a top running down. When the earth stopped spinning, everything would collapse into rubbish.

Such passages keep *Oddsplayer* from being a novel with simplistic good/evil oppositions. Lieck, Slater, and Dibbs, like Talbot, act on evil impulses, but in each case Rodríguez provides background details—Talbot's memories of a sadistic mother or Lieck's prostitute mother, for example—so that most of these characters are made understandable. Rodríguez presents the viewpoints of the "bad guys" to such an extent that the reader ends up appreciating the strong and memorable portrayals of Talbot, Priest, and Lieck, while the characters who appear to be Rodríguez's favorites, Pérez and Kirsch, are merely sketched. Rodríguez seems to empathize with Priest, who is caught "in a crossfire of generations and values" and "was wounded before he came to combat"; Hendrick, the black youth from north Chicago, a former short-order cook who plans to go to college after Vietnam; Kirsch, a navy enlisted man assigned as hospital corpsman to the Marines; the idealistic Isaacs (the direct opposite of Talbot), whose dream is to become a missionary in Peru; Pérez, the Mexican American from East Los Angeles who is influenced by a college Chicana, María, who plants in his mind the seeds of Chicanismo before his enlistment; and Fernández, the Puerto Rican who becomes Pérez's closest friend in the battlefields of northern Vietnam.

Rodríguez was disappointed that the few reviews of Oddsplayer focused on its fragmentary nature. To readers familiar with Latin American narrative, such as works by Juan Rulfo or Julio Cortázar, fragmentation is an anticipated quality. Rodríguez's selection of fragments underscore the metaphor implicit in the title of the novel, the view of life as a game. Cortázar's Rayuela

(1963; translated as Hopscotch, 1966) and Ana Castillo's The Mixquiahuala Letters (1986)—which is dedicated to Cortázar, "the master of the game"—are narratives arranged under the same concept. There is a direct reference to the title term almost at the end of Rodríguez's novel, as Isaacs thinks of God's absence from the world: "The Oddsplayer made faith a melodramatic wager. War and uncertainty were house odds, banked to the Oddsplayer. With a gambler's grasp of fear, the Player wagered for belief."

Rodríguez is working on a novel based on the life of American anthropologist John Peabody Harrington, who attempted to salvage Indian cultures. In addition, he has completed two other, yet-to-be-published novels. "Words Unspoken Things Unseen" is a riches-to-rags saga of the American Dream that re-envisions Henry Adams's autobiography in terms of a multicultural United States. According to Rodríguez, "The Man Who Moved the Weather" is "about a Golden Boy oceanographer who is framed for murder and who disguises himself as a piñata salesman and runs for his life."

**Interview:**

Roberto Cantú, "Eat Fear and Shower in the Dust: An Interview with Joe Rodríguez," (untitled), 4 (Winter–Spring 1997), pp. 25–29.

# Luis J. Rodríguez
*(9 July 1954 –    )*

Dina G. Castillo
*Santa Barbara City College*

BOOKS: *Poems Across the Pavement* (Chicago: Tía Chucha Press, 1989);

*The Concrete River* (Willimantic, Conn.: Curbstone Press, 1991);

*Always Running: La Vida Loca, Gang Days in L.A.* (Willimantic, Conn.: Curbstone Press, 1993); translated into Spanish by Ricardo Aguilar Melantzón and Ana Brewington as *La vida loca: El testimonio de un pandillero en Los Angeles* (New York: Simon & Schuster, 1996); translation republished as *Siempre corriendo: La vida loca o los días de la ganga en L.A.* (Mexico, D. F.: Planeta, 1996);

*América Is Her Name* (Willimantic, Conn.: Curbstone Press, 1998); translated into Spanish by Tino Villanueva as *La llaman América* (Willimantic, Conn.: Curbstone Press, 1998);

*Trochemoche: Poems* (Willimantic, Conn.: Curbstone Press, 1998);

*It Doesn't Have to Be This Way: A Barrio Story* (San Francisco: Children's Book Press, 1999).

OTHER: "Sometimes You Dance With A Watermelon," in *Best New Chicano Literature,* edited by Julian Pally (New York: Bilingual Review Press, 1986);

"The Blast Furnace," "Tomatoes," "Juchitan," and "Every Breath A Prayer," in *After Aztlán: Latino Poetry of the Nineties,* edited by Ray González (New York: Godine, 1992), pp. 176–178;

"We Never Stopped Crossing Borders," "Speaking With Hands," and "Fire," in *Unsettling America: An Anthology of Contemporary Multicultural Poetry,* edited by Maria Mazziotti Gillan and Jennifer Gillan (New York: Penguin, 1994), pp. 131–137;

"My Nature is Hunger," in *Power Lines: A Decade of Poetry at Chicago's Guild Complex,* edited by Rodríguez, Julie Parson-Nesbitt, and Michael Warr (Chicago: Tía Chucha Press, 1999).

SELECTED PERIODICAL PUBLICATIONS–
UNCOLLECTED: "Hey Louie, Get Up," *Chismearte,* 6 (February 1980): 26;

*Luis J. Rodríguez (photograph © 1997 by Donna DeCesare)*

"Always Running," *Chismearte,* 9 (September 1983): 24–25;

"Electoral Fraud Chronicle," *Crítica: A Journal of Critical Essays,* 2 (Spring 1985): 12–16;

"Running to America," *Americas Review,* 3–4 (Fall–Winter 1989): 63–65;

"The Old Woman of Merida," *Guadalupe Review,* 1 (October 1991): 277–280;

"Smoke & Ash: A Latino Writer Looks Back at the 1992 Los Angeles Uprising," *Centro de Estudios Puertorriqueños Bulletin,* 2 (Spring 1992): 35;

"Wanting to Belong. The Story of Un Vato de La Gerathy Loma," *Puerto del Sol,* 1 (Spring 1992): 223–227;

"Throwaway Kids: Turning Youth Gangs Around," *Nation* (21 November 1994): 605–609;

"The Rabbi and the Cholo," *Forkroads: A Journal of Ethnic American Literature,* 1 (Fall 1995): 52;

"Treating L. A.'s Gang Problem: We Need 'Root' Doctors," *Los Angeles Times,* Sunday, 9 February 1997, p. M6;

"Hearts and Hands: A New Paradign for Work with Youth and Violence," *Social Justice,* 24 (Winter 1997): 7–20;

"Behind *la vida loca:* How stereotypes perpetuate violence in our boy's lives," *Latina* (January 1999): 102–103.

Luis J. Rodríguez is an award-winning poet, journalist, and critic. With the publication in 1993 of his highly acclaimed memoir, *Always Running: La Vida Loca, Gang Days in L.A.,* Rodríguez established himself as an accomplished author. Among the awards he has received for *Always Running* are the Carl Sandburg Literary Award for nonfiction in 1993 and the *Chicago Sun-Times* Book Award for nonfiction in 1994. In addition, the book was chosen as a Notable Book by *The New York Times Book Review* in 1993. Rodríguez's distinctive development of imagery and themes in his poetry has also won him accolades. For his first collection, *Poems Across the Pavement* (1989), he was presented with the Poetry Center Book Award from San Francisco State University. In 1991 he received the P.E.N. West/Josephine Miles Award for Literary Excellence for *The Concrete River,* published that year. He has been honored with prestigious fellowships, grants, and public recognitions in and out of the United States: in 1994, for instance, he was selected by the University of California, Berkeley, as the 1994–1995 Regent's Lecturer. In 1998 he received the Hispanic Heritage Award for literature, presented at the John F. Kennedy Center for the Performing Arts in Washington, D.C. In his poetry and his prose Rodríguez is dedicated to making Americans aware of youth gang problems and their possible solutions.

Luis Javier Rodríguez was born in El Paso, Texas, on 9 July 1954, but lived in Ciudad Juárez, Mexico, for two years until his family settled in the Watts community of Los Angeles in 1956. His mother, Maria Estela Jimerez, worked as a seamstress; his father, Alfonso Rodríguez, held various jobs, retiring as a laboratory custodian. Rodríguez has three siblings, Jose Rene, Ana Virginia, and Gloria Estela, and three half-siblings, Seni, Mario, and Alberto. The family moved to San Gabriel Valley in East Los Angeles in 1962, and his teenage years were spent in the streets of the barrios. In an unpublished interview in February 1996 Rodríguez said that being the son of Mexican immigrants made him a target of harassment by Anglo children and the Los Angeles Police Department in the late 1960s and early 1970s. He acknowledges that in a misguided effort to find friends and achieve a sense of empowerment and protection, he joined the gangs that had operated in the neighborhood for years. Finally, he found sanctuary in education and political activism at the height of the Chicano Movement. Books, Rodríguez has said, saved his life. In a 1995 interview with Aaron Cohen, Rodríguez stated: "I think I found refuge in books when I was real young because I was a shy, broken-down little kid. They were fairytale books, Walt Disney books, whatever. I would kind of go inside and hide myself in books and not have to worry about the yelling and screaming and bullets flying."

At thirteen Rodríguez took part in school walkouts to protest against prejudice in the educational system. His creative endeavors began when he was fifteen, after he dropped out of school. Even when he was heavily involved in gang activity he was writing verses that were often based on his experiences. In 1972 he was selected as a recipient of a Quinto Sol Literary Award of $250 and a trip to Berkeley, California. He returned to school following his incarceration for protesting against the Vietnam War during the Chicano Moratorium on 29 August 1970. After graduation he held several blue-collar jobs, such as blast-furnace operator, carpenter, truck driver, steelworker, and chemical-refinery mechanic. In 1980 he became a professional writer and a journalist/photographer for several East Los Angeles newspapers; in 1982 he was a daily reporter for the *San Bernardino Sun* newspaper but was blacklisted by the Republican editor of the paper for being a communist advocate. In the early 1980s Rodríguez also served as director of the Los Angeles Latino Writers Association and published *Chismearte,* a Latino literary and art magazine in which budding Chicano artists and writers such as Jimmy Santiago Baca, Mary Helen Ponce, Marisela Norte, and Jim Sagel first saw their work in print. Rodríguez has two children, Ramiro Daniel (born 1975) and Andrea Victoria (1977), with his first wife, Camila; no children with his second wife, Paulette; and two sons, Rubén Joaquín (1988) and Luis Jacinto (1944), with his present wife, Maria Trinidad ("Trini").

Rodríguez worked as a public affairs associate for the American Federation of State, County, and Municipal Employees from 1982 to 1984, then moved to Chicago and became the editor of the *People's Tribune,* a weekly revolutionary publication with ties to various community-based struggles throughout the country.

Rodríguez conducts poetry workshops in shelters for the homeless, among gang members, in prisons and migrant camps, and with Spanish-speaking children and their parents. He is also the founder/director of a publishing house, Tía Chucha Press, the publishing wing of the Guild Complex, a nonprofit multicultural arts center in Chicago. He was a regular contributor to the poetry newspaper *Letter eX* (now defunct) and has been a featured reader in the Chicago bar-and-café poetry scene.

Rodríguez's freelance publications range from essays, reviews, and lectures to reportage (published and broadcast) and recordings. Several anthologies have included his poetry, as well as excerpts from *Always Running*. His work can be found in magazines, newspapers, and literary journals, including *The Nation, Los Angeles Times, U.S. News & World Report, Utne Reader, Los Angeles Weekly, Philadelphia Inquirer Magazine, Santa Barbara News & Review, The Chicago Reporter,* and *Poets & Writers*. Rodríguez's work has been translated into German, French, Arabic, and Spanish; exposure to international audiences has led to travel in France, England, Germany, Austria, Italy, Holland, Canada, Mexico, El Salvador, Nicaragua, and Puerto Rico. He is frequently interviewed in Spanish and English for local radio, television, and print media in cities across the United States on the topics of gang life and poetry. He has also become somewhat of a spokesperson on behalf of the deported L.A. gang members that populate El Salvador and other Latin American countries.

When asked about his influences, Rodríguez acknowledges the autobiographical works of outspoken Latino and African American authors who were popular when he was beginning to write. In particular, he found that Alex Haley's *The Autobiography of Malcolm X* (1965), Claude Brown's *Manchild in the Promised Land* (1965), and Piri Thomas's *Down These Mean Streets* (1967) affected him with their portrayals of the downtrodden. Other influences obviously come from well-known social realists from the United States, Latin America, England, and Spain. He cites writers such as Walt Whitman, William Wordsworth, Pablo Neruda, and Federico García Lorca. As he told Cohen, "I find it very exciting to make connections with my Spanish-language tradition, and the English and American poets."

The thematic concerns in his first poetry collection, *Poems Across the Pavement* (1989), attest to the influences of the writers he read. Rodríguez focuses on life in America, but his America is one that relatively few people want to acknowledge: an environment fraught with economic oppression, racism, cultural alienation, class battles, industrial displacement, strained human relations, and street turmoil in Los Angeles and Chicago. The collection is full of tonal changes that give the

*Dust jacket for Rodríguez's 1993 memoir, which he wrote to help his eldest son and other teenagers comprehend the horror of gang life*

poems their distinctiveness and modernity and take readers on an emotional roller coaster; the poems depict the dehumanized urban experience at its worst. This experience is clearly seen in "Rosalie Has Candles," "'Race' Politics," "Alabama," "Tombstone Poets," and "No Work Today."

Rodríguez presents the alienated population with a sensitivity and respect that affords them faces and identities. This empathy is expressed in "Tomatoes," "Walk Late Chicago," and "Running to America." In this last poem Rodríguez exposes the struggles of undocumented immigrants as they attempt to establish a life in the United States:

> They are night shadows
> violating borders;
> fingers curled through chain-link fences,
>
> . . . . . . . . . . . . . . . . . . . . . . . . . . . . . .

They leave familiar smells,
warmth and sounds
as ancient
as the trampled stone

. . . . . . . . . . . . . . . . .

escaping the blood of a land
that threatens to drown them,
they have come,
running to America.

In "The Calling" Rodríguez describes his discovery of his poetic voices. Though the poem was written when Rodríguez was sixteen and under the spell of "night captors / in street prisons," the metaphors express a certain timelessness:

Until then I waited silently,
a deafening clamor in my head,
but voiceless to all around me;
hidden from America's eyes,
A brown boy without a name. . . .

Sexual love is another motif in this collection of nineteen poems. "Lucinda" is a lyrical piece in which the speaker reminisces about his love for a woman with "a crystalline smile." This woman is not spared the effects of her environment; she becomes as hard as the pavement she walks on: "Oh, Lucinda, / of the smooth music, / . . . Of bottles smashed over heads, / knife scars / and stretch marks / you tried so hard to hide."

In *The Concrete River* (1991) Rodríguez further explores the topics he introduced in his first collection. The works in this volume are longer and more varied in thematic range and genre, including both poetry and prose. Rodríguez continues his examination of modern life in general and his own experiences in particular, including American urban realities such as killings, addictions, police abuse, race/class issues, and gender conflicts. In a manner similar to Jimmy Santiago Baca's in *Martín and Meditations on the South Valley* (1987), Rodríguez traces his family's past, his childhood, his existence in Watts and East Los Angeles, and his trek to Chicago.

*The Concrete River* is divided into five sections, each devoted to a theme. In the seven poems of the first section, "Prelude to a Heartbeat," the poet highlights his upbringing in Watts and the events that later molded his outlook on life: "Watts bleeds / on vacant lots / and burned-out buildings— / temples desolated by a people's rage. / Where fear is a deep river. / Where hate is an overgrown weed."

"Dancing On a Grave" is the second section, including nine compositions dealing with the poet's adolescence and dangerous flirtation with death. He is depicted in conflict with the police, his family, and himself as he abandons his life to violence and drugs. In "The Concrete River" he combines reality with fantasy to illustrate what his life had become up to that point: "Come back! Let me swing in delight / To the haunting knell, / To pierce colors of virgin skies. / Not here, along a concrete river, / But there—licked by tongues of flame!"

In the third section, "Always Running," Rodríguez includes eight poems, one of which shares the section title. In this part of the book he explores his relationship with his first wife and the demise of that relationship because of the effects of their troubled past. The conclusion of the poem hints at Rodríguez's subsequent development of motifs that express a desire to escape from urban realities: "When all was gone, / the concrete river / was always there / and me, always running."

In the eight poems of "Music of the Mill," the fourth section, the poet reminisces on his life as a blue-collar worker and his struggle to distance himself from his troubled youth. Fate works against him as he is nearly rendered blind in an industrial accident on his first day at a new job. Vivid descriptions and direct language bring to life for the reader the daily challenges of a highly alienated population that labors from daybreak to sunset without much recognition. Rodríguez humanizes his fellow workers; poems such as "The Blast Furnace" reveal their monotonous and menial existence:

A foundry's stench, the rolling mill's clamor,
the jackhammer's concerto leaving traces
between worn ears. Oh sing me a bucket shop blues
under an accordion's spell
with blood notes cutting through the black air
for the working life, for the rotating shifts,
for the day's diminishment and rebirth. . .

In the final section of eleven poems, "A Harvest of Eyes," the poet's focus becomes his new life and experiences away from the city that almost destroyed him. In this last segment Rodríguez also pays tribute to the person he considers his "savior" and his role model when it comes to writing: Piri Thomas. "Mean Streets" unifies the two poets in perpetual communion; Rodríguez says that he relied on Thomas's work for inspiration:

And your seven long times
was a long night for me,
but I knew you, compadre,
you, steady companion down the alleyways,
barrio brother,
father
partner . . . teacher.

The poem is a heartfelt tribute to a man who walked a path similar to Rodríguez's and who also turns to his past for poetic inspiration.

Rodríguez uses the motifs of concrete and pavement to represent all that has limited him in the past but that nevertheless became the source of his literary creativity. In essence, life is produced from a hardened environment. He views poetry as the water that runs through the concrete river, cleansing and restoring life.

In *Always Running: La Vida Loca, Gang Days in L.A.* Rodríguez uses powerful, expressive language to chronicle his gang life in Watts, East Los Angeles, and the San Gabriel Valley during the 1960s and early 1970s. In the February 1996 unpublished interview he said that his aim was to provide an encompassing view of the gang experience in an objective manner so as "not to glorify them, nor demonize them." The book is dedicated to twenty-five contemporaries who were victims of gang violence.

While some critics have called the book a memoir, others have qualified it as a novel of redemption because of its fictional/poetic qualities. Rodríguez himself has defined it as a combination of both. He told Cohen that it is factual but that he used some "fictionalization," such as changing some characters' names to avoid hurting people. He also "synthesized events and reorganized the material so that it would work as literature [fiction] but still maintain the truth and reality of the situation."

Rodríguez begins with a brief account of his family's life in Mexico, where conditions were difficult. Even as a school principal, his father did not make enough money to provide for his family. The family's troubles deepened with their immigration to Watts in south central Los Angeles. The children, as well as the parents, struggled with the language, insignificant jobs, economic despair, inadequate housing, hopelessness, and racism: "Our first exposure in America stays with me like a foul odor. It seemed a strange world, most of it spiteful to us, spitting and stepping on us, coughing us up, us immigrants, as if we were phlegm stuck in the collective throat of this country."

In *Always Running* Rodríguez shows the reader the conditions that cause gang life. The epilogue reveals that the author's son Ramiro had begun replicating his father's earlier estrangement by joining a gang and rebelling against his family. Rodríguez recognizes the ironic twist. Father and son have found themselves, in effect, "always running":

> It never stopped, this running. We were constant prey, and the hunters soon became big blurs: The police, the gangs, the junkies, the dudes on Garvey Boulevard who took our money, all smudge into one. Sometimes

*Rodríguez and his son Ramiro in Chicago, 1993 (courtesy of Rodríguez)*

they were teachers who jumped on us Mexicans as if we were born with a hideous stain. We were always afraid. Always running.

Rodríguez wrote the book to help Ramiro comprehend the pain and horrors of gang activity. Despite his father's efforts, Ramiro was sentenced to prison in 1998 for attempted murder; but as Rodríguez told Patrick Sullivan in a 1999 interview, "He did leave the gang, by the way. He made a terrible mistake, and he will pay the consequences. But I don't think he should be written off."

With straightforward language and touches of dreamy surrealism reminiscent of Alejandro Morales's *Caras viejas y vino nuevo* (1975; translated as *Old Faces and New Wine,* 1981), Rodríguez delves into stoicism as he recounts his daily childhood contact with violence. The tone is indicated by two phrases employed often in his testimony: "con safos" (nobody can mess with this) and "whatever," as if to show that his existence in this world mattered little: "Anyone can bounce me. Mama. Dad . . . Schools. Streets. I'm a ball. Whatever."

Often poetic, the narration is nevertheless a straight presentation of life as it was for Rodríguez. Readers witness childhood and adult behavior that is surprising for its violence. When Rodríguez was a child, his older brother pushed him off a roof, tied a rope around his neck, dragged him around the yard, and left him hanging by his feet from a fence. When Rodríguez hid in the closet, his mother, belt in hand, chased him from the house to "play" with his brother. Gang life is vividly depicted as a cruel, animalistic world: "For a long time, I observed the beatings as if I were outside of everything, as if a moth of tainted wings floating over the steamed sidewalk."

*Always Running* is composed of ten chapters framed by a preface, an epilogue, and a useful glossary of Spanish and street slang. It is a telling account of disintegration and salvation, a bildungsroman in which the protagonist learns about life and becomes a mature and wiser man. As a child he goes from gang to gang and becomes calloused by his surroundings. The body count rises page by page. The incidents become increasingly bizarre and perversely engaging, making readers cringe at the thought of what lies ahead. Rodríguez is jailed for attempted murder, then released. He participates in the fire bombing of a home. He robs stores. He experiments with hard drugs and sex, pushing his existence to the limit: "Everything lost its value for me: Love, Life and Women. Death seemed the only door worth opening, the only road toward a future."

Finally, during the height of the Chicano Movement, Rodríguez came into contact with two individuals who helped him pull himself out of that life. One was Chente, a charismatic and self-confident Chicano recreational leader at a youth center; the other was Mrs. Baez, a caring high-school counselor. Chente encouraged Rodríguez to research Mexican history; he established discussion sessions aimed at the youths to instill self-esteem in them as they explored Chicano thought. Mrs. Baez taught Rodríguez to become a student leader and to take pride in his culture. His life began to change. By the age of nineteen he was a "veterano," an old man among the new generation of "cholos" (one of the types of barrio youth).

*Always Running* presents raw truths about gangs. Some critics found fault with this bluntness, though they admired Rodríguez's narrative qualities and human touches. Poet Gary Soto said in *The New York Times Book Review* (14 February 1993): "While flawed by occasional lapses into sociological diatribe, especially in the epilogue, where the author outlines his wish list for urban pathologies, Mr. Rodríguez's account of his coming of age is vivid; raw and, as he distances himself from the barrio warfare, even tender toward the destruction." This tenderness is evident as the story concludes outside a party. Rodríguez, by chance, meets Chava, a former gang member from a rival group who survived a vicious head injury and eight stab wounds

that have left him with a colostomy bag at his waist. Chava is ready to kill Rodríguez because, he says, someone must pay; but as Rodríguez convinces his attacker to put the gun down, he confronts himself, his past, his present, and his possible future:

> I hold Chava as if he were cornmeal in my arms, then pity overwhelms me, this complicated affection which cuts across the clearcut states of being we'd rather seek: Here's friend, here's enemy; here's sadness, here's happiness; here's right, here's wrong. Pity draws from all these opposing elements and courses through me like an uncooked stew, mixing and confusing the paradoxes, because now this man I once admired, if not revered, I once feared, if not hated, stands here, a fragment of the race, drunk, agonized, crushed, and I can't hate him anymore; I can't see him as the manifestation of craziness and power he once possessed; he's a caricature, an apparition, but also more like me, capable of so much ache beneath the exterior of so much strength. Pity links us in a perverted way, transcending our veneers, joining us in our vulnerability, and at the same time distancing us from one another. I want to escape from Chava's tired perplexed and tattered face, to run away from how something so beautiful, in its own way, can become so odious.

Such sentiments contrast with the cruel reality at hand; recognizing himself in Chava, Rodríguez realizes that violence, sex, and drugs were the wrong vehicles through which to search for happiness and a sense of identity and group cohesiveness. When he hugs Chava, he establishes his identity, reclaiming himself from the mean streets of Los Angeles: "I hear the final tempo of the crazy life leave my body, the last song before the dying, lapsing forever out of mind as Chava disappears."

*Always Running* has become a focus of controversy: in June 1996 it was banned along with sixteen other books by the Rockford, Illinois, school district, and in July 1998 school use of the book was restricted by the board of education in Santa Rosa, California. School boards in Fremont, San Jose, and San Diego struggled over whether to keep it in the libraries. Opponents claim that the book, with its graphic descriptions, will encourage the violent and criminal activities it chronicles instead of providing a deterrent. In the interview with Sullivan, Rodríguez said that the book "does not glorify or demonize gang involvement. Both views distort reality." He argued that although what he wrote might be violent, "What the kids are living is even worse." He concluded, "I actually hope that my book will lose its validity some day, that there isn't a need for a book like *Always Running*. . . . But right now that's not the case. The book is very relevant, and as long as

10

and names of girlfriends or favorite songs. For homeboys—~~as well as bikers,~~

~~convicts, and other so-called fringe cultures~~—the tattoos externalize trauma, draw

wounds to the surface.

After ~~several minutes [how many?]~~ *about 15 minutes*, the meeting was declared over. The

participants had agreed to send a representative to one of several larger meetings

between *La Eme* and various L.A. barrios. In the tiny but well-kept apartment,

Triste, Cartoon, Scoobie, Boxer, Rascal, Clever, Silent, Negro, and Psycho—

gang members between the ages of thirteen and eighteen—sat around on a

carpeted floor. A ~~young woman and a baby lay on a bed in the living room,~~

~~watching a Spanish-language television station.~~ ~~Spirits were good.~~ Strong

Salvadoran accents punctuated the air, sprinkled with Chicano slang: *placaso*

(one's gang name, usually chosen by other members), *torcido* ("to be

incarcerated"), and *ruca* ("old lady," or any woman). *Insert VII*

"Now we can hang out without worrying about being shot," said Rascal.

"I feel happy for the families." They were the innocents who had made up ~~the~~ *many*

~~majority~~ of *the* victims in the crossfire, who were said to have been the impetus for

the decree. *(They were not the majority)*


A trash-strewn vacant lot at the corner of Frances Street and Westmoreland is the

main MS hangout, unless the police make it ~~too~~ hot to be seen here more than

two at a time. A truck on the corner sells fruit and vegetables, many native to El

Salvador. Since the no-drive-by pact, ~~there~~ *MS members* are out in greater numbers, talking *MS members*

*A warm August night in 1993*

*Page from Rodríguez's revised typescript for "The Endless Dream-Game of Death," an article that appeared in* Grand Street Magazine *in 1995
(Collection of Luis. J. Rodríguez)*

that's the case, then we should make sure that people can get access to it."

With *América Is Her Name* (1998) Rodríguez produced a sensitive story for young children. He focuses his work once more on urban themes and the aching memories of growing up as a poor immigrant child. The setting, however, changes from the mean streets of Los Angeles to a Chicago ghetto. América Soliz, a Mixteca Indian girl from Oaxaca, Mexico, endures poverty and hopelessness but holds on to her desire and determination to be a poet, much as the author did when he searched for his own poetic voice in the midst of a chaotic environment. Though it is especially appropriate for young Latinos, the story is for children from all backgrounds. *América Is Her Name* invites children to write, to be poets, and to become part of their communities. Rodríguez published another children's story, *It Doesn't Have to Be This Way: A Barrio Story,* in 1999.

Rodríguez's poetry collections have yet to receive the attention they deserve, though critics have recognized them as well-crafted portrayals of the human condition. Writing about *The Concrete River* for *American Poetry Review* (1991), one reviewer said: "What makes Rodríguez's poetry attractive is . . . the lyrical beauty that suddenly emerges at unpredictable moments. There are lines that bloom like the flowers he is always making reference to." Rodríguez's 1998 collection, *Trochemoche,* is another example of his talent for producing exacting images that re-create the life of the barrio. Recovery and personal growth continue to be part of his concerns in *Trochemoche*. In Spanish *trochemoche* (or *troquemoche*) means "helter-skelter," and this collection fur-

ther exposes the turmoil of barrio life, urban youth, and neglected communities while also exploring the power of poetry and the richness of Rodríguez's ancestry. His incursions into street talk and the speech of the social outcast take him a step beyond the work in his first two collections. In *Trochemoche* Rodríguez draws on more than ten years of poems, offering new meters, meanings, and paradigms, blurring genres in a postmodern form of expression.

In the February 1996 unpublished interview Rodríguez said that he considers himself primarily a poet, and though he has had many offers to write a screenplay for a movie version of *Always Running,* he will continue to develop the genre that he considers his salvation. "Poetry," Rodríguez told Cohen, "is the foundation of everything I do. It's poetry with a sense of social engagement. The written, powerful expressive language of poetry is the springboard for everything that I want to write."

**Interviews:**

Aaron Cohen, "An Interview with Luis J. Rodríguez," *Poets & Writers Magazine* (January/February 1995): 50–55;

"La Vida Loca: Joseph Rodríguez and Luis J. Rodríguez on 'The Crazy Life,'" in *East Side Stories: Gang Life in East LA,* by Joseph Rodríguez (New York: powerHouse Books, 1998), pp. 175–185;

Patrick Sullivan, "Class War: Luis Rodríguez Casts a Skeptical Eye on Attempts to Ban His Autobiography," *Sonoma County Independent,* 4–10 February 1999, pp. 21–22.

# María Amparo Ruiz de Burton

*(3 July 1832? – 12 August 1895)*

Beatrice Pita
*University of California, San Diego*

BOOKS: *Who Would Have Thought It?* anonymous (Philadelphia: Lippincott, 1872);

*Don Quixote de la Mancha: A Comedy, in Five Acts, Taken from Cervantes' Novel of That Name* (San Francisco: Carmany, 1876);

*The Squatter and the Don: A Novel Descriptive of Contemporary Occurrences in California,* as C. Loyal (San Francisco: Carson, 1885).

**Editions:** *The Squatter and the Don,* edited by Rosaura Sánchez and Beatrice Pita (Houston: Arte Público, 1992);

*Who Would Have Thought It?* edited by Sánchez and Pita (Houston: Arte Público, 1995).

The relative dearth of information on nineteenth-century Latino/Chicano literary history is slowly being remedied by the discovery of long-neglected texts such as those written by María Amparo Ruiz de Burton. These texts will undoubtedly have a central place in the growing canon of Latino/Chicano literature. Ruiz de Burton was a writer with a powerful voice who addressed crucial issues of ethnicity, power, gender, class, and race. As an acculturated Californio writing for publication in English, Ruiz de Burton utilizes contemporary nineteenth-century discourses—political, juridical, economic, commercial, and literary—to voice the bitter resentment of the Californios faced with Anglo American domination in the aftermath of annexation to the United States. Seen in this light, Ruiz de Burton is clearly a precursor of Chicano literature whose novels investigate issues at the core of Chicano history and literature. As a woman writer her work is of special significance because it offers the perspective of one who was in a position to be simultaneously inside and outside of U.S. culture and who minced no words in voicing the subaltern's critique of dominant society.

María Amparo Ruiz was born in Loreto, Baja California, on 3 July 1832 (1835 in some accounts). She was the granddaughter of Don José Manuel Ruiz, commander of the Mexican northern frontier in Baja California and, from 1822 to 1825, governor of the state.

Her great-grandmother was Doña Isabel Carrillo Millar, and Ruiz was related by blood or marriage to several leading Californio families, including the Vallejos, the Guerra y Noriegas, the Carrillos, the Pachecos, the Ortegas, and the Estradas. Ruiz's more immediate family history is obscure. María del Amparo Ruiz Arango, as her name is given on her marriage certificate, was the daughter of Isabel Ruiz Maytorena and sister to Federico Maytorena. Her father's identity remains unclear. Why her father's surname—presumably "Arango" —differs from her mother's is uncertain.

The granddaughter of the former governor met Capt. Henry S. Burton of the U.S. Army when an expedition of New York Volunteers under his command arrived at La Paz in July 1847 to take possession of Baja California while Gen. Winfield Scott marched on Mexico City. By the time Burton arrived La Paz had surrendered and many of its citizens had signed articles of capitulation that allowed them to retain their own officials and laws and granted them U.S. citizenship. A few months after Burton's arrival, however, U.S. troops faced armed resistance at San José, Todos Santos, and La Paz. By the time the peninsula was again under American control, Mexico and the United States had signed the Treaty of Guadalupe Hidalgo, which excluded Baja California and granted Alta California and the rest of the Southwest to the invaders. In view of promises that had been made to residents of Baja California, when the U.S. ships left the area in the fall of 1848 two vessels were reserved as refugee transports. A total of 480 Baja Californians left for Monterey in Upper California, among them María Amparo Ruiz, then sixteen years old, and her mother Doña Isabel. Some of the refugees returned to Baja California, but others remained in the north around San Francisco, gaining with the other residents and native Californios full U.S. citizenship. María Amparo was among the latter, staying to marry Captain Burton, then twenty-eight years old and a widower.

The two were wed in 1849 in Monterey, California, before Samuel Wiley, a Presbyterian minister. The love story of Burton and María Amparo Ruiz, which includes the intervention of a rejected suitor, became

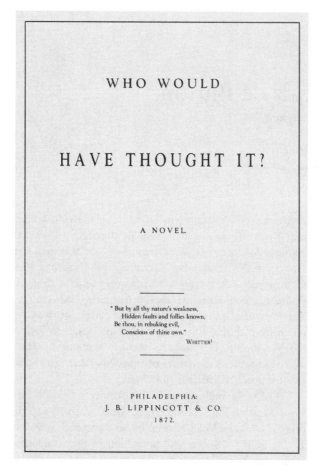

WHO WOULD

HAVE THOUGHT IT?

A NOVEL

"But by all thy nature's weakness,
Hidden faults and follies known,
Be thou, in rebuking evil,
Conscious of thine own."
WHITTIER[1]

PHILADELPHIA:
J. B. LIPPINCOTT & CO.
1872.

*Title page for Ruiz de Burton's first novel, which satirizes the hypocrisy of Northern abolitionists prior to and during the Civil War*

part of local California lore and was later recounted by Hubert Howe Bancroft in his *California Pastoral* (1888) and by Winifred Davidson, who in the 1930s wrote several articles for the *San Diego Union* and the *Los Angeles Times* about the Burton-Ruiz love story. Davidson reports that Ruiz is believed to have been the maiden referred to in the anonymous ballad "The Maid of Monterey," sung by veterans of the Mexican War in the early days of California. Davidson describes their love affair in her article "Enemy Lovers," which was published in the 16 October 1932 issue of *The Los Angeles Times Sunday Magazine,* as the union of "natural enemies," given their difference in religion, nationality, and age and the state of war between their countries. Those interviewed who still remembered Ruiz de Burton in the early part of the twentieth century recalled her beauty and aristocratic air but only a few mention her work as a writer. There is little information on her education in La Paz before she sailed for Alta California, but the family's position of prestige would have doubtlessly afforded some privileges for the governor's children and grandchildren; upon arriving in Monterey

with her mother she is said to have entered school, where she mastered the English language. Her novels and extensive correspondence in both Spanish and English with a wide range of people indicate a strong background in the classics, English, Spanish, and American literature, and European and American history.

After their marriage Captain Burton was assigned first to Monterey, then to San Diego, where the family lived for ten years. In 1859, with the outbreak of civil war imminent, Burton was ordered east, where he was promoted first to major and then brevetted brigadier general in the Union Army. While fighting in the South during the Civil War, Burton contracted malaria; he died in 1869 in Rhode Island. Ruiz de Burton, who had accompanied him to the East Coast, was left a thirty-seven-year-old widow with two children. This ten-year period spent in the East as an army general's wife was a crucial period in Ruiz de Burton's life; moving in the highest military, political, and social circles, an intimate friend of Mary Todd Lincoln and privy to an insider's view of the scandals, corruption, and inner workings of capital life at the time, she drew heavily on this experience for her representations and critiques of U.S. society. Her first novel, *Who Would Have Thought It?* (1872), deals pointedly and precisely with the hypocrisy, greed, and moral turpitude of Northern abolitionists, clergymen, and politicians.

Ruiz de Burton's most ambitious undertaking was neither her literary production nor the various enterprises she attempted at her Jamul Ranch—including a cement plant, a commercial-scale castor bean factory, and a reservoir—nor even her mining interests in Baja California. Rather, it was her attempt to claim the whole of the Ensenada tract of land in Baja California, which she tried for many years to have recognized as her own, envisioning a large-scale colonization and development project. Although a U.S. citizen after 1848, Ruiz de Burton responded as a Mexican against foreign investors backed by American businessmen seeking to colonize the Baja California area. Her efforts turned her mother and brother against her, led her to write newspaper articles against the colonization companies, and eventually took her to Mexico to fight both American and British companies in court. When she died impoverished in Chicago in 1895, she had recently returned from Mexico City and was preparing a new legal appeal. She had a strong sense of her Latino roots and was willing to do battle with powerful adversaries.

Ruiz de Burton was an exceptional woman, as her friend Mariano Guadalupe Vallejo acknowledged in the prologue to his unpublished five-volume history of California. She is the only woman he mentions as having been instrumental in the writing of the history: "erudita y culta dama, celosa de la honra y tradiciones de su patria, valiosa esposa, cariñosa madre y leal amiga" (a learned and cultured lady, concerned with the honor and traditions of her land, worthy wife, loving mother and loyal friend). While Ruiz de Burton was willingly acculturated into U.S. society, she always held on to her Latino culture and made it a point in her writings to counter the prevailing derogatory portrayals of Mexicans and Latinos. Resentment of the racism directed at Californio Mexicanos and their mistreatment and betrayal by both individuals and official U.S. policy clearly fuels the critiques in both her novels, *Who Would Have Thought It?* and *The Squatter and the Don: A Novel Descriptive of Contemporary Occurences in California* (1885).

*Who Would Have Thought It?* was not Ruiz de Burton's first literary work. While living in San Diego, where her husband was stationed in the 1850s, she wrote and produced a five-act stage adaptation of *Don Quixote;* in 1876 she had the play published. *Who Would Have Thought It?* was published by J. B. Lippincott with no author credited on the title page, although the book is listed under H. S. Burton and Mrs. Henry S. Burton by the Library of Congress. Ruiz de Burton never published the novel under her own name—perhaps as much to conceal her gender as her Latin background—and, considering the content of the novel, one can understand why. The work satirizes a prominent scandal of the day involving the Rev. Henry Ward Beecher and the wife of one of his friends and reveals the hypocrisy, pettiness, and racism of a Northern abolitionist family and community.

The outsider's perspective is provided by María Delores Medina, a Mexican child whose aristocratic mother has been kidnapped by Indians. Lola, as the child is known, is rescued by James Norval, a Yankee geologist exploring near the banks of the Gila River, and brought east to live with his family on the eve of the Civil War. Despite the family's abolitionist rhetoric, Mrs. Norval demonstrates nothing but racism and class prejudice toward Lola, whom she considers "black," and her immediate reaction is to send the girl to the kitchen and to sleep with the Irish servants, who are also considered inferior. Lola "whitens" as the pigment her mother used to protect her among the Indians wears off, but attitudes toward her remain unchanged; cultural racism continues to consign her to the social margins.

History and romance are bound up together in the narrative; the love story between Lola and the geologist Norval's son, Julian, is played out against the backdrop of the Civil War, detailing the moral and political transgressions and corruption of the self-righteous Easterners. Ruiz de Burton's novel is an allegory in which the fall of "republican motherhood," that is, of the moral authority of a Yankee matron, represents the fall of a romantic conception of politics, the unmasking of corrupt liberal democratic ideologies. In *Who Would*

*Have Thought It?* Norval has to go into exile to avoid arrest for criticizing the suspension of habeas corpus with the outbreak of the war. Julian, an officer in the Union army, faces dismissal and loss of rank without a court martial when his father's comments are attributed to him. He is saved, not by constitutional guarantees and protections, but by the intervention of political and financial supporters, reinforcing the point that the system works for those with power. Ruiz de Burton thus counters idealized views of the United States as a democratic nation. It is a place, she insists, where dissent is not tolerated, where justice works for the economically powerful telegraph and railroad monopolies, and where the electoral system is for sale to the highest bidder.

Although Ruiz de Burton has no basic quarrel with patriarchal values, her representations of women, their roles, and their capacity for reasoning and agency are particularly noteworthy in *Who Would Have Thought It?* Especially striking is her depiction of Mrs. Norval, a nuanced portrait of feminine psychology and nineteenth-century social norms. In this regard Ruiz de Burton's work is significant not only within minority literatures in the United States but also in relation to that of women writers such as Harriet Beecher Stowe and Lydia Maria Child.

*The Squatter and the Don* can be seen as a fictional account of the fortunes of many Californio families; it is a composite account of various cases of land loss to squatters and litigation, including that of Ruiz de Burton's friend Vallejo, whose Soscol rancho is mentioned in the novel, and the author's own legal problems with the Jamul Ranch in San Diego County. Published after her return with her two children, Nellie and Harry, to San Diego, where she and her husband had earlier purchased the ranch, *The Squatter and the Don* appeared under the pseudonym "C. Loyal," a reference to *Ciudadano Leal* (Loyal Citizen), a common closing for official government correspondence in Mexico during the nineteenth century. The work is severely critical of American political structures.

Ruiz de Burton had begun working on the novel in 1880 and by 1884 had developed the story into a full-length narrative. The novel was clearly a commercial venture, as she was living on a meager army widow's pension while engaged in costly litigation to validate her claim to Jamul Ranch. She was determined to pay the cost of printing the novel herself, knowing that whoever controlled its publication would benefit from its sales. Her correspondence relates the obstacles she faced in getting the work published, given her perilous personal financial situation, which continued until her death.

Like her first novel, *The Squatter and the Don* is an historical romance; it details the repercussions of the Land Act of 1851 after the U.S. invasion of California and the rapid rise of the railroad monopoly in the state.

THE SQUATTER

AND

THE DON

———

A NOVEL DESCRIPTIVE OF COMTEMPORARY OCCURRENCES

IN CALIFORNIA

———

C. LOYAL

SAN FRANCISCO
1885

*Title page for Ruiz de Burton's second novel, the first English-language account of the U.S. annexation of California told from the perspective of the displaced Mexicans*

The novel is unusual in that it is told from the perspective of the conquered Californio population, which, despite being promised all rights of citizenship under the Treaty of Guadalupe Hidalgo, was by 1860 a subordinated minority. The narrative builds on the tension between the romantic and the historical, reconstructing conflicts between Californios of Mexican descent and the invading Anglo squatters by focusing on two families: that of Don Mariano Alamar, owner of a 47,000–acre ranch in the San Diego area, and that of William Darrell, one of the squatters on the Alamar ranch. The action roughly covers the period from 1872 to 1885 and traces the trials of the lovers Mercedes Alamar and Clarence Darrell. While the romantic plot is resolved happily, the historical issues posed, especially in relation to dispossession of the Californios and the rise of corporate monopolies and their power over government policy, are not as easily reconciled.

While the novel focuses on the demise of the heroic aristocratic/feudal Californios, it differs from other nineteenth-century historical romances in that it is not written from the perspective of the conquerors, with the usual portrayal of a backward people constrained by an outmoded feudal system. On the contrary, Ruiz de Burton questions whether the new order brought progress to the region and deplores the reprehensible treatment of the conquered, who the novel shows were willing to accommodate to the new structures. From the invasion of Californio lands Ruiz de Burton goes on to address similar incursions into the economic and political culture of the region. By the end of the novel the victims of Anglo domination are not only the Californios but also the city of San Diego and, in the long run, the entire population of California, which is subject to the tyranny of the railroad monopoly. While both her novels thus focus on matters of race and ethnicity, Ruiz de Burton widens the scope of her denunciations by taking to task the ostensible superiority of the Anglo, the ignominious state of internal U.S. politics, and the travesties of justice taking place in the halls of Congress, in the prisons and hospitals of the Civil War, in the boardrooms of the railroad monopolies, and in the bedrooms of the wealthy of New York.

*The Squatter and the Don* is not the only novel about the righteous dispossessed of nineteenth-century California or the voracity of the Railroad Trust: Frank Norris's *The Octopus* (1901) describes the trust as "an iron-hearted monster of steel and steam, implacable, insatiable, huge—its entrails gorged with the life blood that it sucked from an entire commonwealth." Although Ruiz de Burton's novel does not focus on the dispossession of farmers in the San Joaquin Valley, as does Norris's novel, it does, years before Norris's account, provide a critical portrayal of the railroad monopoly that thwarted the construction of the Texas and Pacific Railroad to San Diego and ends with a reference to the Mussel Slough massacre of 1880, which provides a subtext in *The Octopus.* Unlike Norris's novel, in which the Spanish-Mexicans are described as "decayed, picturesque, vicious and romantic," Ruiz de Burton presents a capable, cultured, even heroic people who were robbed of their territory, economically strangled, linguistically oppressed, and politically marginalized after 1848. The author rails against the cultural defamation of Mexicans and Californios as much, perhaps, as against their material dispossession.

Ruiz de Burton attacks corporate monopolies and government collusion in her novels but not the capitalist system per se; underlying her critiques is a defense of earlier entrepreneurial competitive capitalism, which is seen as jeopardized by the political power of monopoly capitalism and the latter's political power. Ruiz de Burton calls for a return to a more principled capitalism but sees that unless the trusts are checked by immediate political action no reform is possible. Consequently, while in *Who Would Have Thought It?* she satirizes the hypocrisy of U.S. society and the debasement of its government, in *The Squatter and the Don* she exhorts her readers to act while there is still time, to take matters into their own hands, to divest monopoly of its stranglehold on the government:

> It seems now that unless *the people of California take the law into their own hands,* and seize the property of those men and confiscate it, to re-imburse the money due *the people,* the arrogant corporation will never pay. They are so accustomed to appropriate to themselves what rightfully belongs to others, and have so long stood before the world in defiant attitude, that they have become utterly insensible to those sentiments of fairness animating law-abiding men of probity and sense of justice.

While referring specifically to the power of the railroad monopoly and its domination of transportation in California, the passage clearly conveys the disenfranchised social and political position of the Californios in the period after annexation to the United States and resentment against the invaders and usurpers. Ruiz de Burton is not devoid of class, racial, and patriarchal prejudices; she is less than generous in her assessment of the Chinese and other immigrants and on occasion falls back on stereotypical portrayals of Jews, Indians, and blacks. Further, as a strategy to counter anti-Latino cultural biases, Ruiz de Burton argues for the superiority of Latino peoples. Still, despite her own ideological blinders, Ruiz de Burton attempts to articulate a resistance to what she terms "the hydra-headed monster" in both its economic and cultural manifestations.

Ruiz de Burton analyzes these problems as systemic, issuing her critique at the level of policy and politics, profit and propaganda. Mexico's loss of the Southwest and the treatment of its people stand out in her mind and work as a watershed event, a caveat of the threats posed by monopoly capitalism. The new order that Ruiz de Burton sees consolidating itself economically and politically in the last quarter of the nineteenth century is constructed around the ideology of American expansionism and corporate greed. Ruiz de Burton judges the United States, despite its early potential and promise, as a nation in decay.

In both of her historical romances Ruiz de Burton also depicts male agency as handicapped or truncated by the forces of decay and corruption. Thus, the Californio men in *The Squatter and the Don* fall victim to accidents or debilitating illness, in addition to suffering land loss and ignominy at the hand of squatters and the government; and in *Who Would Have Thought It?* the Norval

men find their authority circumscribed as a result of the machinations of male and female villains in collusion with the government. In both novels the romance genre allows for the requisite felicitous union of the lovers; the historical plane, however, is so fraught with contradictions that no such happy ending is envisioned.

*The Squatter and the Don* is probably the first published narrative written in English from the perspective of the conquered Californio population. A writer who witnessed the disappearance of the old order and the consequent disruption of traditional everyday life, shifts in power relations, and the rapid capitalist development of the territory, Ruiz de Burton questions the dominant Anglo American ideology on which such changes were built. Unwilling to adopt a position of resignation or to ensconce herself in nostalgia for the past, she used her novels to forthrightly denounce the despoliation of the Californios and satirize the presumed superiority of the Anglo Americans. She wrote and published her historical romances at a time when the few histories narrated by Californios existed only in manuscript form and were collecting dust in archives. The recovery of these texts thus has an important role to play in tracing the literary and ideological historiography of the Southwest.

## References:

José F. Aranda Jr., "Contradictory Impulses: María Amparo Ruiz de Burton, Resistance Theory, and the Politics of Chicano/a Studies," *American Literature,* 70 (September 1998): 551–580;

Anne E. Goldman, "'Who Ever Heard of a Blue-eyed Mexican?': Satire and Sentimentality in María Amparo Ruiz de Burton's *Who Would Have Thought It?*" in *Recovering the U.S. Hispanic Literary Heritage,* volume 2, edited by Erlinda Gonzales-Berry and Chuck Tatum (Houston: Arte Público Press, 1996);

John M. González, "Romancing Hegemony: Constructing Racialized Citizenship in María Amparo Ruiz de Burton's *The Squatter and the Don,*" in *Recovering the U.S. Hispanic Literary Heritage,* volume 2;

Beatrice Pita, "Engendering Critique: Race, Class and Gender in Ruiz de Burton and Martí," in *José Martí's "Our América": From National to Hemispheric Cultural Studies,* edited by Jeffrey Belnap and Raúl Fernández (Durham: Duke University Press, 1998);

José David Salívar, "Nuestra América's Borders: Remapping American Cultural Studies," in *José Martí's "Our América"*;

Rosaura Sánchez, "Dismantling the Colossus: Martí and Ruiz de Burton on the Formation of Anglo América," in *José Martí's "Our América."*

# Benjamin Alire Sáenz

*(16 August 1954 –   )*

Theresa Meléndez
*University of Texas at El Paso*

BOOKS: *Calendar of Dust* (Seattle: Broken Moon, 1991);

*Flowers for the Broken* (Seattle: Broken Moon, 1992);

*Dark and Perfect Angels* (El Paso: Cinco Puntos, 1995);

*Carry Me Like Water* (New York: Hyperion, 1995);

*The House of Forgetting* (New York: HarperCollins, 1997);

*A Gift from Papa Diego* (El Paso: Cinco Puntos, 1998);

*Grandma Fina and Her Wonderful Umbrellas* (El Paso: Cinco Puntos, 1999).

OTHER: "Born in the U.S.A.," in *Unknown Texas,* edited by Jonathan Eisen and Harold Straughn (New York: Macmillan, 1988), pp. 389–404;

"I Want to Write an American Poem: On Being a Chicano Writer in America," in *Without Discovery: A Native Response to Columbus,* edited by Ray Gonzalez (Seattle: Broken Moon, 1992), pp. 127–143.

SELECTED PERIODICAL PUBLICATIONS-
UNCOLLECTED: "The Ruins of Prieto's Barrio" and "Alejandro's Funeral," *Saguaro,* 4 (1987): 79–85;

"On Telling My Catholic Mother I Was Leaving the Priesthood" and "Abuelita," *Chiricu,* 5, no. 2 (1988): 82–86;

"City of the Conquered," *Rio Grande Review,* 7 (Summer 1988): 5–19;

"Portrait of My Father," *Bilingual Review,* 14 (September–December 1989): 77–78;

"Poem: For My Brother," *Puerto Del Sol,* 24 (Summer 1989): 214–217;

"Workers," *Poetry East,* 31 (Fall 1990): 129–131;

"City of the Dying," *Saguaro,* 6 (1990): 58–67;

"A Full Moon for Daniel," *Seattle Review,* 14 (Fall 1991): 72–86.

*Benjamin Alire Sáenz at the time of* The House of Forgetting
*(photograph by Cynthia Farah)*

Benjamin Alire Sáenz's first book, *Calendar of Dust* (1991), won the American Book Award of the Before Columbus Foundation in 1992, and a year later he received the prestigious Lannan Poetry Fellowship. He has received many other awards, prizes, and fellowships since he first began writing, among them the Wallace E. Stegner Fellowship in creative writing from Stanford University for two consecutive years, 1988 and 1989. Sáenz writes poetry, essays, short stories, and novels about Chicanos and other peoples of the Southwest and their struggles with the cultural and economic imperialism of the dominant classes. His writing stresses the violence of American society, as well as the determination and spirit of resistance among its disenfranchised people.

Sáenz was born on 16 August 1954 in Old Picacho, a farming community outside Las Cruces, New Mexico. He was the fourth of seven children of Eloisa Chavez Alire and Juan Villanueva Sáenz. Sáenz's parents originally worked as seasonal cotton pickers but eventually found less nomadic occupations: his father worked as a cement finisher and his mother as a cook. At home he spoke Spanish, while at public school he learned to speak and write in English. He entered the seminary in 1972 and graduated from the University of Louvain in Belgium with a master's degree in theology in 1980. The next year he was ordained a Catholic priest. Later, he left the priesthood and entered the University of Texas at El Paso, where he received an M.A. in creative writing in 1988. He also studied at the University of Iowa and then, under the Stegner Fellowship, at Stanford University, where he pursued but did not complete his doctorate in English. He teaches at the University of Texas at El Paso in the bilingual M.F.A. program. In 1994 Sáenz married Patricia Macias.

*Calendar of Dust* opens with a quotation from Walt Whitman's "Song of Myself" (1855): I bequeath myself to the dirt to grow from the grass I love"; the homage to the poet of American place and its varied identities is appropriate, since *Calendar of Dust* commemorates the Southwest and its natives. In the three sections of the collection, "Exiles," "Lamentations," and "Resurrections," the poet acknowledges the migrations of the peoples who have inhabited the borderland: Native American, Mexican, Spanish, Anglo, and Asian. Through this collage of identities Sáenz presents the imprint of imperialism and exploitation, depicting the civilization of the Southwest as having been created from the blood and on the backs of the oppressed. The migrations, which entail both a difficult separation from the familiar and a subsequent incorporation into the unknown, focus on the transitory journeys of people at war with each other and themselves.

The first poem, "Creation," narrates in geologic as well as historical time the significance of the new age that began with the explosion of the first atomic bomb, a "new incense" that heralds the arrival of a coming darkness and the destruction of all that is holy. This advent sets the tone for the other poems of exile in this section, which tell of the forced travels of the displaced and the homeless, domestic and agricultural workers, and warriors and war survivors, all "condemned to carry what is left / of ourselves into exile."

The second section of the collection looks more particularly at the individual lives of those affected by racism and economic exploitation, from farmworkers suffocated in a boxcar to a grandmother worn by poverty and hard work. Each of them participates in the "ring of life–to fight again–to give again– / To love–

and die again." After these sorrowful poems the third section reminds the reader that what is shattered can be re-created and transformed. The poet explores a series of mainly personal events that celebrate the strength of human will in the face of darkness. Like the Navajo in "The Return," the reader is drawn by the "gravity of home."

*Flowers for the Broken* (1992), a collection of short stories, is framed by a prologue and epilogue that emphasize the unusual status of those who live on the border between the United States and Mexico and whose quotidian existence is defined by this boundary. The border creates a cultural, economic, political, and personal divide that undermines the historical and environmental unity of the area. Its natural elements, river, desert, and mountains, are intimately valued as "sacraments of belonging" but offer no respite for the political reality that separates and disinherits its natives. The first story of the collection is "Cebolleros" (The Onion Workers), which depicts a young boy's entry into the life of a fieldworker, with its grueling labor, social stigmatization, and family discord.

In each of the short stories the Chicano protagonists struggle for enlightenment both personally and politically in a world plagued with strife. Generational conflicts are at issue in most of the stories, such as "A Silent Love," "The Idol Worshippers," and "Holy Week." Fathers and sons, mothers and daughters, husbands and wives, all work at resolving their misplaced resentments toward one another as well as their own conflicted notions regarding appropriate race and gender roles. Anger of another kind fuels the actions of Ricardo (also known as Richard) in "Kill the Poor." Richard has worked quietly in a university library for ten years, attempting to escape both his culture and the world through books, but the violent death of a young nephew and the conflicts of a nation at war as well as among the privileged university students cause him to unleash his contained rage. His anger is at both "the enlightened immaculate moralities" of the bourgeoisie and at his own internalized acceptance of "a race he had to win but could not win, and knowing he could not win, he ran it faster not only to forget he could not win, not only to forget that his feet were tired and weak, but to forget that he was even running a race." The geopolitics are broader in "Alligator Park" and "In London There Is No Summer," which focus on refugees of national oppression and poverty and on those activists who work with them to confront the discordance of social inequalities. In this collection only the earth and its elements draw no lines and ask for no assertions of identity.

In his second poetry collection, *Dark and Perfect Angels* (1995), Sáenz eulogizes dead friends, relatives,

*Dust jacket for Sáenz's 1995 novel, about twelve people whose lives are touched by AIDS*

I write in English, dream
in Spanish, listen to Latin chants.
I like streets where
Chicanos make up words.
. . . . . . . . . . . . . . . . . . .
I want to feel words
swimming in my throat
like fighting fish
that refuse to be hooked
on a line.

In spite of the many lives and deaths that have created this need to validate and to re-create their worlds, however, the poet himself longs to merge like river waters into the oceans: "I am tired of my name. / I am crooked from this yoke: from the heavy borders of 'I am.'"

Sáenz's novel *Carry Me Like Water* (1995) follows the intertwining lives of twelve urban characters who, like the apostles of Jesus, go forth into the world to teach and to learn. Their names reverberate with biblical allusions: there are three Marys, an Elizabeth, two Johns, a Joachim (Joaquin), a James (Diego), two Jacobs, and two Jesuses (Reymundo and Salvador). These characters, living in El Paso or in San Francisco, closely examine the nature of their identities and relationships. Elizabeth experiences a visitation when a dying man at an AIDS hospice bequeaths her the gifts of prophecy and the ability of out-of-body flight. These gifts create the possibility of the characters' coming together as Elizabeth unites lost siblings, creates friendships, and moves friends from California to Texas.

Most of the characters live in exile from their histories or are in flight from themselves, a diaspora from family roots. "Don't be afraid of your blood," says one character to another, who responds, "Am I my blood?" Their various struggles—against sexual abuse, racism, disabilities, homophobia, AIDS, abandonment, poverty—have isolated each of them in a solipsistic despair. Yet, the narrative rings with comic irony as the friends find small blessings in their daily lives: *cholo* (gang member) pallbearers in their low-rider cars, the bag lady who declares herself the Virgin Mary, or Elizabeth's out-of-body chaperoning of her friends' absent husbands. Like Diego, who has not killed himself only because he is unsatisfied with his suicide note, the characters yearn for a completion they do not know how to achieve. As they travel in and around the desert of the Southwest, separately and in various combinations, their sufferings and pilgrimages form a Jacob's ladder that takes them from rage to compassion and from apathy to commitment. The novel ends with the embittered and aloof Jacob encountering hatred once again but offering compassion nonetheless, saying, "Today I committed an act of kindness." Living communally near the border, the group of friends invites a homeless,

and strangers whose hardships and joys have marked his perspective on the world. The four sections of the book, "Winter," "Novena for a Lost Ancestor," "Prayers for the Holy and the Dead," and "Summer," chronicle the responses of the poet to the violence and the difficulties of the American social experience. "I am drunk remembering," he says. Memories, both grateful and mournful, surface as wounds and scars, ghosts and angels, tombstones and altars, all monuments to those who maintained their vitality amid desolation and ruin. Family history is interspersed with national wars, border conflicts, racism, viral diseases, and alcoholism but is treated with affection, humor, spirituality, strength, and grace. The merging of these conflicting realities has shaped the poet's contemplative stance; his "prayers" are dark meditations on the state of the living. Present throughout is the elemental force of the southwestern desert: "You taught me how to live without the rain. / You are thirst and thirst is all I know." The most telling feature of these poems is the concerted need to document the histories of his people:

homophobic junkie with AIDS to enter their circle. This act becomes a form of inheritance, an action like that of the biblical Jacob's descendants, that marks the first step in conquering the Promised Land. Jacob's turning away from alienation toward engagement signals the beginning of this new age of promise.

An equally prominent feature of the novel is the symbolism of earth, sky, and water in the numinous desert of the borderlands. As the author frequently underscores, the narrative is situated in the location of the historical struggle of impoverished Mexicans. The desert becomes a double metaphor of the desolation of the spirit in the face of racism and oppression but also of the regenerative power of the will through human agency and community. The desert appears to be a wasteland but offers solace to those who understand and search out its hidden fertility. In the same way the characters must learn to risk being vulnerable by reaching out to another: "the world conspires to keep us all separate from each other. We have to fight to belong to those we love—maybe that's all we can hope for." Like the transformative power of rain in the desert, the characters come to life as they accept their fears and their wounds—in other words, their pasts. Survival in the desert, as in life, means to endure hardships, to understand the dangers, and to celebrate the minor miracles that are offered one.

Sáenz's work is set firmly in the tradition of Chicano literature of displacement, utilizing American themes of questioned identity, familial conflict, reverence for place, and class conflict. In his poetry Sáenz alludes to Whitman and T. S. Eliot, while his prose at times purposely reflects Ernest Hemingway, F. Scott Fitzgerald, and William Faulkner. Readers may also observe the influence of Latin Americans Alejo Carpentier and Gabriel García Márquez in Sáenz's use of fragmented narrative and elements of magic realism. Sáenz utilizes these forms and styles to provide subtle commentary on his varied literary heritage, as a means to explore new definitions of the role of the writer in recreating and inventing realities. As he says in his preface to *Dark and Perfect Angels*, "to work with words is to work with community property," and he acknowledges "the community of workers who have labored at my side," a belief in literary production as cultural artifact and not merely individual effort.

*The House of Forgetting* (1997) represents a foray into genre fiction—specifically, the psychological thriller. At the same time, however, it is an allegorical exploration of the effects of colonialism on an oppressed people. The novel opens with the revolt of the thirty-year-old Gloria Santos against her kidnapper, an esteemed professor of humanities, who stole her from the streets of El Paso when she was seven years old. She has been

*Dust jacket for Sáenz's 1997 novel, about the relationship between a young Chicana woman and her mysterious mentor*

kept in a kind of "humanistic" captivity in his Chicago home, educated broadly, and given all the accoutrements of an upper-class upbringing. Her escape brings her in touch with a lawyer, Jenny Richard, and a police lieutenant, Alexander Murphy, who befriend her. The novel examines the psychological trauma experienced by the oppressed and the oppressor as Gloria works out her love-hate relationship with the professor and tries to recover her lost culture.

Sáenz's themes encompass the alienation and estrangement of modernity but are underlined by a strong commitment to the spiritual power of Mexican culture in overcoming them. Folk Catholicism, Chicano style, underlies the many rituals within his stories—blessings of water, lighting of candles, prayers to the saints, reverence for the dead, and the acceptance of the preternatural—all framed ironically, sometimes humorously, but always with the understanding that ceremony and rite in whatever form are necessary elements of culture. Spirituality, in Sáenz's hands, becomes an affirmation of the people's resistance to the hegemonic culture of the mainstream. It is an identification of an ethnically based poetics that refuses to turn away from its formative symbols and that embraces the contradictions of its histories to reformulate and reconceptualize a living tradition.

The strengths and weaknesses of Chicano family life are perhaps the strongest undercurrents in all Sáenz's work: the complex web of love and resentment, the ties that bind through blood and guilt, the weave of generations, the commitment, albeit unwillingly at times, to family above all other concerns. Family is the Chicano ideology of community, a local politics of hope that risks envisioning a utopic future. In all his work, but especially in *Carry Me Like Water,* Sáenz deconstructs the American family to reveal its untidy secrets and then redefines the family in its largest context: the extended family that includes friends, street people, dead relatives, God, the urban poor, and those who find themselves in need of family and are willing to accept its responsibilities. His Chicano characters are multidimensional and reflect the heterogeneous circumstances of Mexicans in the United States, including recent immigrants, acculturated American citizens, *puro Mexicanos,* gays, and militant activists. Sáenz has a strong sense of Chicano discourse that comes through most successfully in the dialogue between characters and that is articulated often through the interplay of his comic vision with his mordant evaluation of middle-class sensibilities, but he also reveals lyrical tendencies in his moving descriptions of love, death, and the desert.

His strongest trope, in fact, is the borderland desert, which he uses to critique national identities and to analyze Chicano history. It is the presence of the expansive desert that subverts the arguments of artificial borders between peoples, of the xenophobic beliefs of closed societies, and of the possibility of surviving in a troubled world without encountering otherness. The border landscape is not a margin, boundary, or periphery but is the *frontera,* the frontier to the newly expanded world. The desert and the border signify the liminal spaces of the potential, in Sáenz's words, for exile and redemption.

# Saúl Sánchez

*(16 June 1943 –    )*

## Luis Leal
### *University of California, Santa Barbara*

BOOKS: *Hay Plesha Lichans Tu Di Flac* (Berkeley, Cal.: Editorial Justa, 1977);
*Desalojos: Versos a la soledad* (San Antonio: M & A, 1982).

OTHER: "Tres dimensiones en la narrativa chicana contemporánea," in *Canto al Pueblo: An Anthology of Experiences,* edited by Leonardo Carrillo and others (San Antonio: Penca, 1978), pp. 93–98;
"Folklore and Life Experience," in *The Tejano Community, 1836–1900,* by Arnoldo De Leon (Albuquerque: University of New Mexico Press, 1982).

SELECTED PERIODICAL PUBLICATION-
UNCOLLECTED: "La incipiente narrativa chicana: un espejo de telarañas," *Cuadernos Hispanoamericanos,* 390 (December 1982): 641–645.

*Saúl Sánchez (courtesy of Sánchez)*

Although fiction about poor immigrants and migrant Americans has long been an important feature of American literature, and Chicano migrant workers have been part of American life since the nineteenth century, the first fiction that directly addresses the plight of Mexican and Chicano migrants did not appear until the late 1940s in the works of such authors as Mario Suárez and Luis Pérez. Early experiences by migrants are also chronicled in many *corridos* (ballads) of the time. In 1971 the first novel dedicated entirely to the life of the Chicano migrant people, Tomás Rivera's *"... y no se lo tragó la tierra"/"...and the Earth Did Not Part,"* appeared, providing a prototype for this subgenre of Chicano literature. The followers of Rivera are many, among them Rolando Hinojosa, author of *Klail City y sus alrededores* (1976), and Saúl Sánchez, who also in 1976 began publishing sections of his novelette, *Hay Plesha Lichans Tu Di Flac,* which appeared the following year in a bilingual edition.

One of seven children of Julián and Manuela Sánchez, Saúl Sánchez was born on 16 June 1943 in Crystal City, Texas, about forty-five miles east of Eagle Pass on the Mexican border. Rivera was born in the same town eight years earlier. Sánchez's grandparents came to Crystal City during the Mexican Revolution. Like many Chicanos along the Texas border, the Sánchezes became migrant workers, first in the cotton fields of the Rio Grande Valley and then in the sugar beet fields of the Midwest. Sánchez has said that he was a third-generation migrant worker. If the families had not migrated from April to November each year, thus

*Cover for Sánchez's 1977 novel, which chronicles the unhappy life of a young Chicano and his death in the Vietnam War*

national University), Sánchez was offered a position at Wichita State University. In 1973 he moved to Angelo State University. In 1975 he was appointed assistant to the vice president for academic affairs, a position he still held in 1977, the year he published *Hay Plesha Lichans Tu Di Flac.*

The novelette is made up of ten unnumbered chapters, each of which is a self-contained story. Six of the chapters follow a Chicano boy from his first day in school to his funeral after he has been killed in Vietnam. The other four chapters place his life in context.

In "The First Day of School" the traumatic experiences of a young Chicano are graphically presented. The boy, attending an Anglo school and not knowing a word of English, hears the pledge of allegiance being recited by the other students. He mumbles the sounds he thinks he hears: "Hay plesha lichans to de flac, off de june aires taste off America; an to de reepablic for huish eet estans, guan nayshon, andar got, wits liverty an yastes for oll." This humorous episode is not representative of the general tone of the novelette, which is otherwise a grim portrayal of the conditions under which border Chicanos live and the struggles they undergo to survive. In the first story the boy cannot eat lunch at school because he does not have the twenty-five cents he needs to buy it. The students who cannot read English are not helped but punished, which makes them hate the teacher, usually an Anglo woman, and the school. After a pushing match among students during recess, the principal, Mr. Ray, orders the boys to put on boxing gloves and fight it out to solve the conflict. When the protagonist is promoted from third to fourth grade, "the only thing was that they really didn't change rooms because third and fourth grade classes were held in the same room; the same teacher taught both grades at the same time except that one of the groups sat on one side of the room and the other group sat on the other side." Conflicts with the other children, who first ignore then persecute him, lead him to stay away from school in the third story, "He Didn't Want to Go to School Anymore." No less denigrating are the experiences he undergoes as a migrant with his family, related in "The Field Next to the Golf Course." As they work in the field, the Anglo golfers stare at them as if they were monkeys in a zoo.

In the eighth story, "Nothing Was the Same Anymore," the family returns to Crystal City: "But when they got back to Texas and enrolled in school there again, things were not the same anymore. Everything had changed." Many students had dropped out of school, while others "wanted only to chase girls and they went around dressed differently and even wore their hair different, with duck tails and lots of grease smeared on it. Then too they would argue with the

interrupting their children's education, they could not have survived. (In the chapter "The Field Next to the Golf Course" in *Hay Plesha Lichans Tu Di Flac* a girl who is working in the field along with other members of the family tells her father that she wants to go back to Texas. He replies, "And just what are we going to do back there? Eat lizards?") Sánchez, however, was able to break away from the migrant life by obtaining an education. He completed high school in 1963 in Crystal City and, following in Rivera's steps, enrolled at Southwest Texas State Junior College at Uvalde, forty-five miles north of Crystal City. In 1967 he received a B.A. in Spanish with a minor in English from Southwest Texas State University in San Marcos. That same year he married and began to teach junior high school in Bakersfield, California; he and his wife, Marta, have two children, Yvette and Saúl Jr. He continued his education by attending the University of Oklahoma, where he received a doctorate in 1971. After a summer teaching at Laredo State University (now Texas A&M Inter-

teachers when they were told to button up their shirts or to get their hair cut shorter." When the protagonist and his brother start dressing similarly, their father tells them that "only Pachucos dressed that way and that he was not going to let them become clowns." In "The Trip to California" he goes to Los Angeles, where he takes a series of odd jobs. He soon finds himself out of work and homesick, and he expresses his loneliness in a letter to his sweetheart, Sonia. Unwilling to return to the backbreaking field work, he decides, according to the postscript of the letter, to join the army. In "The Funeral" he returns home in a casket. At the end of the ceremony a soldier, after reciting the pledge of allegiance, delivers the American flag to his parents. "It was hard to tell if the Mother and the Father understood why or for what purpose they had given it to them. The flag, I mean. The Anglo soldier who folded it was saying something when he was handing it over to them but it didn't look like they understood at all what he was trying to tell them."

The remaining stories are "The Arab," "The Barracks," "Esperanza and 'Turo," and "The Elections." The title character of "The Arab" is a mysterious old man who lives in a shack in the barrio and passes his time collecting junk along the railroad tracks. Over the course of the story he obtains mythical proportions and becomes a bogeyman, a kind of masculine "La Llorona" (The Wailing Woman). Mothers tell their children that if they do not behave, the Arab "would come and throw 'em into his dirty knapsack that he always carried with him and then he'd carry them far way along the tracks and then no one would ever find them again." One day the Arab's shack burns down, and he disappears forever.

The title of "The Barracks" refers to a boarding house in the barrio where workers live while waiting to be contracted for day labor or farm work. "There were families there from Crystal City, from Eagle Pass, from San Antonio, from The Valley, and even from as far away as Monterrey." Although the inhabitants of the barracks are transients, one day they organize a dance and begin to form the rudiments of a community. "Esperanza and 'Turo" is a love story that ends in tragedy. In "The Elections" some card players discuss the tricks that the Anglo politicians use to keep them from voting, such as nominating a Chicano candidate who has no chance of winning. Although the Anglo population in the town is between 15 and 20 percent, the Chicano and Mexican population is kept away from the polls by a poll tax that most of them cannot pay and by holding the elections in April, when the people have gone north. Some criticism is directed at the older Mexican generation, as represented by the old armchair revolutionary Don Florentino, who does not want to get involved in order to change the system.

In 1982 Sánchez published *Desalojos: Versos a la soledad* (Displacement: Verses to Solitude), which comprises twenty-two poems, nineteen in Spanish and three in English. The Spanish poems are divided into three groups: "Versos a la soledad," "Delicias amargas" (Bitter Delights), and "Tanteos en rima" (Essays in Rhyme). The central theme of the poems is the poet's desolation over an absent or lost love. Some of the shorter poems are quite rhythmical, as can be seen in a stanza from "Hoja . . . sin par" (Leaf without Peer), one of the few poems in which love is not the theme:

Muerte de muertes
muerte sin par
muerte de frío . . .
hoja que pierdo
hoja que cae.
(Death of deaths
death without peer
cold death . . .
lost leaf
falling leaf.)

Today Sánchez teaches full time at Laredo Community College. He occasionally teaches at Texas A&M International University and is an adjunct professor at Texas Lutheran University in Seguin.

**References:**
Carl R. Shirley and Paula W. Shirley, *Understanding Chicano Literature* (Columbia: University of South Carolina Press, 1988), pp. 148–149;

Charles M. Tatum, *Chicano Literature* (Boston: Twayne, 1982), pp. 84–85.

# Arthur Tenorio

*(5 June 1924 –    )*

Nasario García
*New Mexico Highlands University*

BOOK: *Blessing from Above* (Las Vegas, N.Mex.: West Las Vegas Schools' Press, 1971).

OTHER: "Mexican Americans," in *In Praise of Diversity,* edited by Milton Gold, Carl A. Grant, and Harry N. Rivlin (Washington, D.C.: Teacher Corps, Association of Teacher Education, 1977), pp. 176–190.

SELECTED PERIODICAL PUBLICATIONS–UNCOLLECTED: "Methadone Treatment of Heroin Dependence," by Tenorio and Julius L. Wilson, M.D., *Rocky Mountain Medical Journal,* 71, no. 9 (1974): 516–518;
"La idioma del norte," *Seers,* 23 April 1976, p. 15;
"Slang of the Pachucos Still Here," *Seers,* 23 April – 7 May 1976, p. 21.

As a science-fiction writer, Arthur Tenorio has displayed a penchant for exploring the unknown, a capacity for curiosity, and esoteric tendencies. He is an unassuming person deeply preoccupied with man's inhumanity to man and the future welfare of the planet. He adheres tenaciously to three basic Christian tenets: the brotherhood of man, good will unto others, and peace on earth.

Arthur Tenorio was born on 5 June 1924 in Las Vegas, New Mexico, on Ninth Street, known then as *el Barrio de Chihuahuita.* His parents were divorced when he was five years old, and he was raised by his maternal grandparents, Sósimo and Candelaria Lucero. His grandfather owned rental properties, and often Tenorio accompanied him on visits to his tenants. On these ventures Tenorio found playmates who have remained his lifelong friends.

Tenorio's grandparents, who were economically well-to-do even during the Great Depression, fostered independence and self-reliance in their grandson. As he said in an unpublished 31 December 1994 interview, "My grandparents were wealthy, but they never gave me any money, so as a consequence I didn't have good

*Arthur Tenorio in 1995 ( photograph by Nasario García )*

clothes or money. I could have if they had given it to me, but they never did, and I never asked them either, so that was that."

Tenorio's lifelong thirst for knowledge first became evident in elementary school. Although he stresses that the home environment is of paramount importance in creating an awareness regarding the virtues of education, he believes that in the final analysis the sole responsibility for one's own educational destiny rests with the individual. As he noted in the December 1994 interview, "My grandfather was a businessman.

264

He sent my mother to town from Sapelló [thirteen miles north of Las Vegas] to get educated. My great-grandfather was sent to Durango, México to be educated way back in the nineteenth century. I have some of his letters. He quotes Aristotle, but in all that—knowing that, nobody inspired me. I did it by myself."

Tenorio attended public schools in Las Vegas, where in 1930 he was enrolled in Douglas Elementary School. He remembers vividly that, by the time he started school, he was able to read, write, and speak in both Spanish and English; tell time; and count to one thousand. Classes at the school were segregated, with Hispanic children (mostly from poor families) in one classroom and Anglo children (mainly middle class) in another. This segregation, according to Tenorio, was based on the policy of an all-Anglo school board, which had decided that Hispanic students must learn English in grades one through five before intermingling with Anglo children in the sixth grade. The same policy existed at Castle Elementary School, where he transferred in the fourth grade. All but one of Tenorio's teachers from elementary through high school were Anglos. His first-grade teacher was Hispanic (and she had red hair and blue eyes).

In 1941, after finishing the eleventh grade at the age of seventeen, Tenorio enlisted in the U.S. Navy. His first tour of duty took him to the South Pacific. He was stationed at Pearl Harbor when the Japanese attacked on 7 December. On his second tour, also in the South Pacific, he was sent to Guadalcanal and the Solomon Islands, where he served in ordnance, delivering ammunition and supplies from one island to another after each successful invasion. By age eighteen he had fought in three major naval battles, and he was involved in one more before World War II came to an end. Tenorio spent a total of forty months in the South Pacific before being discharged from the navy in 1945.

After a short stay in Oakland, California, with his mother and stepfather, Tenorio returned home to Las Vegas. Having completed a correspondence course to earn the one credit he needed for high-school graduation, he enrolled at New Mexico Highlands University in March 1946. His venture into higher education at the time was by happenstance, even though he always intended to seek further education. In the December 1994 interview, Tenorio recalled the episode with bittersweet emotions:

If you're under battle stress and conditions for seven months, you crack up. I had been in it forty months, and I wasn't cracked up, but I was close to it. I was drunk for about maybe sixty days, day and night. And then I finally bumped into a friend of mine who came out of the navy, who didn't have as much battle experi-

ence as I did and he said, "Arthur, tomorrow I'll go for you. We will start school."

By 1949, under the auspices of the G.I. Bill, Tenorio had earned a B.S. degree in sociology and psychology with minors in history and business. In 1950 he was awarded a master's degree in clinical psychology, also from Highlands University, where he taught for a short while. Subsequently he taught in Mora, north of Las Vegas, and then in Trementina, a rural village forty-six miles southeast of Las Vegas. Later he was awarded a fellowship to pursue his Ph.D. in anthropology and sociology at Washington University in St. Louis. He finished all requirements for the degree, including his dissertation, but various circumstances prevented him from returning for the dissertation defense. By that time he was employed as chief psychologist at the Boys' School in Springer, New Mexico.

Tenorio next went to work as a psychologist under the guidance of Edwin Swope, a highly respected judge from Albuquerque and a defender of children's rights. In 1958 Judge Theodore Scoggin named Tenorio psychologist for the delinquent and criminal courts in Las Cruces. Tenorio held this position until 1960, when he was appointed director of guidance and counseling for the Bernalillo public-school system, which included Bernalillo and five Indian pueblos. In 1963 he returned to Las Vegas, as counselor at the West Las Vegas public schools, where he implemented or inherited the National Youth Association Program, Head Start, and other bilingual programs. He was determined not to become involved in public-school administration "because I always felt that an administrator was a politician first, and an educator second." Yet, in 1978 he was appointed superintendent of the West Las Vegas schools, serving until his retirement in 1980.

Tenorio still lives in Las Vegas, where he continues to be involved in local social issues, particularly those involving minorities and young people. While his personal idealism remains strong, it is tempered with caution based on past experiences: "I would like to see a stable society. I'd love to see people learn. In World War II they told us we were fighting for a better society for our families, for peace, and for progress. The thing I fear the most now is drugs because I think that drugs will destroy our country."

Francisco A. Lomelí and Donaldo W. Urioste have labeled Tenorio's *Blessing from Above* (1971) "the first known Chicano science fiction novel." Before he began writing the book in 1968, Tenorio had read a wide range of science fiction—from Buck Rogers, Superman, and Flash Gordon in the comic strips to classic science-fiction writers such as Jules Verne and Robert A. Heinlein. For him science fiction has always been ahead

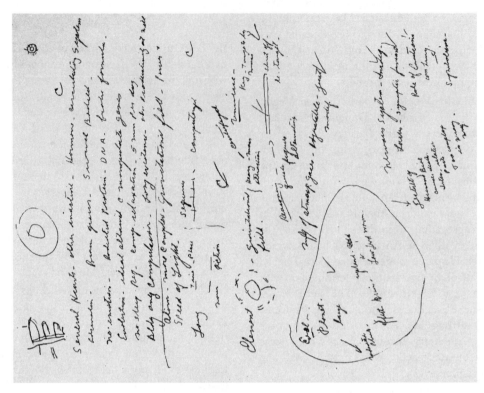

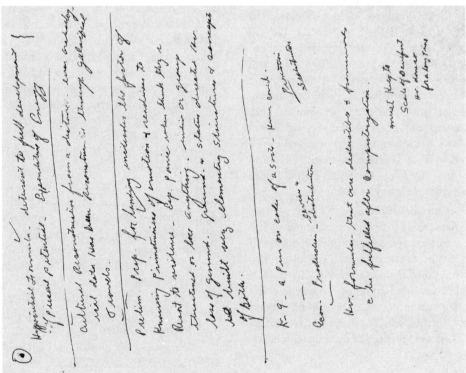

*Notes for Tenorio's* Blessing from Above, *his 1971 science-fiction novel (Collection of Arthur Tenorio)*

of true science: yesterday's science fiction is today's reality.

Tenorio wrote *Blessing from Above* to counter the growing belief that UFOs carrying aliens with hostile intentions were hovering over the United States. His novel suggests that if superior beings from another planet were to descend to Earth, it might be to bring a message of goodwill rather than to provoke war. He set his novel in Africa, hoping to create a picture of peaceful coexistence among peoples and races that would serve as an example of racial harmony for the rest of the world.

The novel starts by introducing a white missionary, Zebulah Fullson, and his wife, Dilia, a generous and "unselfish couple" who "worked as a team" to help others. Their goodwill toward all humanity sets the tone that prevails throughout *Blessing from Above*.

The principal purveyor of goodwill is the protagonist, Nifty. Dropping inconspicuously from outer space and emerging from the bush, he is adopted by the Fullsons, who act as his foster parents until he becomes self-reliant. Nifty is an intellectual genius who also is endowed with great physical prowess. He adapts rather quickly to life on Earth and is initiated into the Mesani tribe in a series of ritualistic ceremonies. Tribe members greet him with open arms:

> Great god of the Mesani,
> we present to you and do avow
> a new member to join the ranks.
> To you great Zulili,
> this young man to fulfill
> his duties and tend to your will
> we offer him as one of the Mesani.

A series of scientific experiments with cross-pollination, seed radiation, and plant genetics brings Nifty recognition among some prominent scientists in the fictitious African nation of Morunda. His discoveries are fundamental for improving the quality and quantity of crops to feed the people of Morunda and perhaps the entire continent, thus alleviating the temptation of the powerful populations to dominate the weaker ones. Tenorio underscores the tendency for the strong to victimize the weak by creating another fictitious country, Purpolia, the "cesspool of creation," which one day found itself "over packed, over eroded, barren and impoverished" and victimized by its leader, Rajatupa, who thrives on his people's misery. In their minds he is their "mythical prince" and "corporal deity incarnate,"

but he is a scoundrel bereft of concern for his own citizenry.

The conflict between haves and have-nots comes to a climax when Rajatupa deploys his troops to attack Morunda and exploit its potential wealth. Led by Megalion, Morunda is on the verge of an unprecedented economic breakthrough that will ensure economic stability and wealth, thanks to careful planning by Megalion's advisers and Nifty's revolutionary discoveries. One of his experiments results in the development of the electrical pulsar, a weapon that has the capability of knocking an enemy unconscious or into a stupor without killing him. This weapon is used to defeat Rajatupa and his army. Underscoring the message that superior beings from another planet are messengers of goodwill and charitable tidings, air vehicles and glistening objects land in Veronica, the capital of Columboland, a fictitious nation in the Western Hemisphere. Machon, the leader of the extraterrestrial clan from Uranus, conveys a message of goodwill, but not without chastising the people of Earth: "Your terrestrial mind," says Machon, "is similar to the majority of people with whom you dwell. . . . you are a by-product of a million years of wrong doing. . . . your inherent hostility and aggression is being projected upon myself and what I represent. . . . For you see, we bring you blessings from above."

The message of *Blessing from Above* is one of peace, love, honor, kindness, and respect toward all humankind, with the ultimate aim of enticing everyone to build and not to destroy. Nifty spearheads this philosophy during his stay on Earth and leaves his message behind as he ascends into the heavens to return to Uranus. He bids farewell to Perfecta, his lover on Earth, who appears distraught and in a state of hopelessness as he departs. Perhaps Tenorio was attempting to convey the viewpoint he expressed in 1994: "Life is a struggle, day in, day out. There's no let up. Everything is a struggle. To be alive, even when you have it all, it's a struggle. You still have to breathe, you still have to compete, you still have problems that arise daily for all reasons. My attitude is that you better be prepared for all of it, and the worst, too."

**Reference:**

Francisco A. Lomelí and Donaldo W. Urioste, "Tenorio, Arthur. *Blessing from Above*," in their *Chicano Perspectives in Literature: A Critical and Annotated Bibliography* (Albuquerque: Pajarito Publications, 1976), p. 48.

# Luis Alberto Urrea

*(20 August 1955 – )*

César A. González-T.
*San Diego Mesa College*

BOOKS: *Frozen Moments* (La Jolla: University of California at San Diego Print Co-Op, 1977);

*Across the Wire: Life and Hard Times on the Mexican Border* (New York: Anchor, 1993);

*In Search of Snow: A Novel* (New York: HarperCollins, 1994);

*The Fever of Being: Poems* (Albuquerque: West End Press, 1994);

*By the Lake of Sleeping Children: The Secret Life of the Mexican Border* (New York: Anchor, 1996);

*Ghost Sickness* (El Paso: Cinco Puntos, 1997);

*Nobody's Son: Notes from an American Life* (Tucson: University of Arizona Press, 1998);

*Wandering Time: Western Notebooks* (Tucson: University of Arizona Press, 1999).

PLAY PRODUCTION: *Un Puño de Tierra/A Handful of Dust,* San Diego, Teatro Máscara Mágica, 22 February 1991.

OTHER: "canción al final de un día de sombras," "la primavera nunca llega," and "prima," in *Literatura Fronteriza: Antología del Primer Festival San Diego-Tijuana, Mayo 1981,* edited by Alurista (San Diego: Maize Books, 1982), pp. 57–61;

*Fragmentos de Barro: The First Seven Years,* edited by Urrea and González-T. (San Diego: Tolteca Publications, Centro Cultura de la Raza, 1987);

"Mr. Mendoza's Paintbrush," in *Mirrors Beneath the Earth: Short Fiction by Chicano Writers,* edited by Ray González (Willimantic, Conn.: Curbstone, 1992), pp. 301–311;

"Down the Highway With Edward Abbey," in *Resist Much, Obey Little: Remembering Ed Abbey,* edited by James R. Hepworth and Gregory McNamee (San Francisco: Sierra Club Books, 1996);

"None of Them Talks About Their Dreams," in *The Late Great Mexican Border,* edited by Bobby Byrd and Susannah Mississippi Byrd (El Paso: Cinco Puntos, 1996), pp. 64–79;

*Luis Alberto Urrea (photograph by Terri H. Fensel)*

*A World of Turtles: A Literary Celebration,* edited by Urrea and McNamee (Boulder, Colo.: Johnson, 1997).

SELECTED PERIODICAL PUBLICATIONS–UNCOLLECTED: "Wet Streets Shining," *Vision Magazine* (November 1978): 53–54, 56–57, 68;

"Volcano Nights: 1. Gunrunners, 2. Carmen, 3. Volcano Nights" and "Living in the USA," *Maize,* 3 (Fall–Winter 1979–1980): 80–84;

"Evidence of Life on Earth: Introduction," *Imagine: International Chicano Poetry Journal,* 2 (Winter 1985): vii–xviii;

"Ring of Fire," *Cedar Rock,* 10 (Spring 1985): 12;

*Cover for Urrea's 1993 collection of essays about the lives of poor people in Tijuana*

"First Light," *Long Story,* 4 (Spring 1986): 147–172;

"Here's the Dream," *The Mind's Eye,* 1 (September 1986): 43;

"The Sunday Drive," *Agni Review,* 33 (Spring 1991): 50–52;

"Bid Farewell to Her Many Horses," *Blue Mesa Review,* 4 (Spring 1992): 61–70;

"I Tried to Write a Poem about This Once a Year for Thirteen Years," *Agni Review,* 35 (Fall 1992): 63–65.

Luis Alberto Urrea made a strong debut in 1993–1994 with two books brought out by mainstream commercial publishers. His sustained naturalism, exciting imagery, and confessional tone appear in a variety of genres, including essays, long and short fiction, poetry, and journalism. The themes he treats in his writing are also reflected in his graphic art. "My art work," he said of his collage and pen-and-ink pieces that appeared in the special Summer/Winter 1986 art issue of Tino Villanueva's *Imagine: International Chicano Poetry Journal,* "is a

chronicle of a longing–perhaps for God, perhaps for shelter, I cannot say. Everybody there is looking for home."

The response to his work was immediate, affirmative, and sustained. The comments of writer and critic Arthur Salm in *The San Diego Union-Tribune* (17 April 1994) are typical. After calling for some improvement in the structure of Urrea's first novel, *In Search of Snow* (1994), Salm conceded that in the end, the author successfully makes everything come together "with a fine cataclysmic/comedic ending, even suggesting the possibility of The Further Adventures of Mike and Bobo in the only possible place left for them–California. They'd be most welcome, as would, come to think of it, just about anything from Luis Alberto Urrea, One Terrific Writer."

The painful events of his life, Urrea claims, have deeply affected his writing. In an unpublished 1993 autobiographical sketch he says that "most everything I write ends up being tragicomic. Even when I don't mean to, I often write the saddest comedies in town."

He was born in Tijuana, Mexico, on 20 August 1955 and registered with the United States government as an "American Citizen Born Abroad." His mother, Phyllis Dashiell, was originally from Staten Island, New York; his father, Alberto Urrea Murray, was from Rosario, Sinaloa, Mexico. Both were educated people and were frustrated with their economic lot. Urrea was a sickly child; as an infant he contracted scarlet fever, German measles, and tuberculosis.

Because his parents commuted daily to San Diego, where his father worked in a tuna cannery and his mother in a department store, Urrea spent his days in the care of Mexican women; hence, the first language he spoke was Spanish. His mother did not speak Spanish, and according to family history he told relatives, "Mami está loca" (Mommy's crazy), because she would come home and make strange sounds–English–that sounded like babbling to him.

In 1958 the Urreas moved to the black and Mexican barrio of Logan Heights in south San Diego. Life there was violent and frightening, both outside and within their apartment. In his autobiographical sketch Urrea remembers his parents' marriage as "dreadfully painful and vindictive. The general tone of resentment and hysteria spilled over onto me." He was sexually abused by members of his extended family. He writes:

> Life in our home was an emotional minefield. These are ghosts that haunt me to this day. I mention this in passing because it affects my writing. You will find these matters discussed overtly in my two books of poetry, *The Fever of Being* [1994] and *Ghost Sickness* [1997]. They are also hugely evident in the narrative drive of *In Search of Snow* and, finally, in nonfictional form in *Nobody's Son: Notes from an American Life* [1998]. I suppose that these childhood pains even affected my writing of *Across the Wire* [: *Life and Hard Times on the Mexican Border,* 1993]. Certainly, I have an eye for the pain of others.

His writings are, he says, "in some ways the scars of those things, and in others, their blossoming."

What Urrea refers to as the most enduring blessing of his childhood were the days he spent in the home of his godparents, Abelino and Rosario García, who are fictionalized in the final third of *In Search of Snow* and also appear in *The Fever of Being*. He says they made it possible for him to believe in love. "They gave me," he says, "the hope to continue." Because the boy had tuberculosis, it was a struggle for his parents to find anybody to care for him during the day. Abelino García worked with Urrea's father at the cannery and offered to take the boy into his home. Every morning Alberto Urrea dropped his son off with the García family and returned in the evening to take the boy home. Urrea

recalls life in the cannery in his poem "La Tere Smelled of Fish":

> Day shift's closing bells
> stilled conveyer belts: *La Tere*
> and the other women
> stepped away from eighteen-year-old bald spots worn
> into the factory floor,
>
> . . . . . . . . . . . . . . . . .
>
> Up at four, silent
> in the silent rooms, three
> tortillas with butter, a little tuna:
> then she went alone into the fish-belly dawn,
> and when one day she didn't come back
> from Starkist, they sealed her house
> like a can.

Abelino García was the head of a household of women. There were the twins Quela and Fina and "La Nina," the ninety-eight-year-old María Moreno. "But the most important person on earth," Urrea says in his autobiographical sketch, was "Mamá Chayo, *Rosario García,* Abelino's wife and my godmother."

Urrea attributes his keen sense of the numinous to his godmother:

> All I know of God and angels I know because of her. Not from preaching. I'm not even sure she wasn't still a pagan, for she was an Indian woman, pouchy in the belly and small of stature, with slanted cat-eye glasses and big flat feet that slapped the floor in decrepit slippers. She wore her hair in a braided bun at the back of her head, and once, when I saw it loose, it formed a curtain all across her shoulders and over her back.

All around the house grew herbs–*telimón* (lemon grass), *canela* (cinnamon), and *yerba buena* (mint). The Garcías used their herbal knowledge to cure Urrea and they used their wizardry in the kitchen to bring him back from the brink of malnourishment. "In this house," Urrea says, "I was healed."

Until he entered the first grade, Urrea spent every day with the Garcías. Afterward, he spent most of his weekends there, from Friday night to Sunday afternoon. He was always sent home with a multicourse supper cooked by the women and wrapped in soft white cotton cloths for his mother: "*una cena pa' doña Filis* (a little dinner for Mrs. Phyllis)."

Urrea attended a Catholic elementary school, St. Jude's Academy. When he was in the second grade, he decided to become a priest. His father, believing that a man who did not desire women was a homosexual, began a campaign of "toughening" in an attempt to break Urrea of this ambitious obsession. This boot-camp situation added to the stress of his early years.

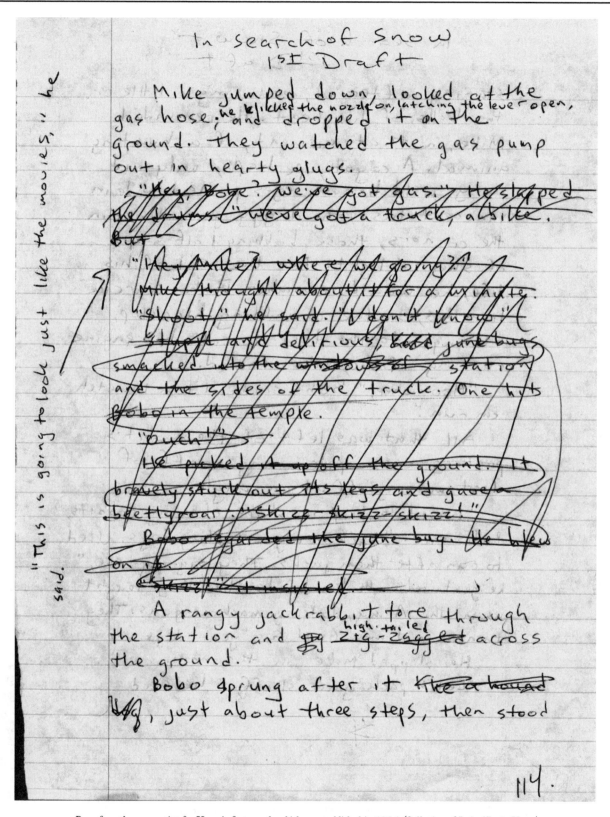

In search of snow
1st Draft

Mike jumped down, looked at the
gas hose; he clicked the nozzle on, latching the lever open,
and dropped it on the
ground. They watched the gas pump
out in hearty glugs.

"Hey, Bobo. We've got gas." He slapped
the ~~truck~~. "We've got a truck, a bike.
But

"Hey Mike, where we going?"
Mike thought about it for a minute.
"Shoot," he said. "I don't know."
~~stupid and delirious~~, bobo june bug,
smacked into the ~~windows of~~ station
and the sides of the truck. One hits
Bobo in the temple.

"Ouch!"

He picked it up off the ground. It
bravely stuck out its legs and gave a
beetly roar. "Skizz-skizz-skizz!"

Bobo regarded the june bug. He blew
on it.

"Skizz!" it insisted.

A rangy jackrabbit tore through
the station and ~~by~~ high-tailed zig-zagged across
the ground.

Bobo sprung after it ~~like a house~~
~~fly~~, just about three steps, then stood

"This is going to look just like the movies," he said.

114.

*Page from the manuscript for Urrea's first novel, which was published in 1994 (Collection of Luis Alberto Urrea)*

In 1965, the family left the barrio and moved to Clairemont, then a predominantly white suburb. English became for him "a tool, music, anchor, and thought." Reminiscent of a character in the Chicano writer Arturo Islas's novels who evolves from "Ricardo" to "Richard" and, finally, to "Dick" as he is assimilated by corporate America, Urrea was transformed into "Louis" or "Lou" in junior high and high school. No Anglos called him "Luis" until he entered the University of California at San Diego in 1973. The pronunciation of his name, he emphasizes, had a great impact on his sense of his identity.

As a senior at UCSD, Urrea took part in a writing workshop led by the science-fiction writer Ursula K. Le Guin. For his senior thesis he wrote and illustrated a book of short fiction and poetry. Titled *Frozen Moments,* it appeared in 1977 in an edition of 1,500 copies, its publication paid for by a special grant from the university.

Urrea graduated from UCSD in 1977. The following year he began to work in Tijuana with "Pastor Von" (E. G. Von Treutzchler III) and a missionary group, Spectrum Ministries, based at Clairemont Emmanuel Baptist Church. *Across the Wire* grew out of these experiences. In 1978 he became a teacher's aide and tutor in the Chicano Studies department at San Diego Mesa College. There he began editing *Fragmentos de Barro,* a literary journal, with César A. González-T.

What Urrea calls his first publications of merit began at this time. The Chicano poet Alurista presented some of Urrea's poetry and artwork in a new journal, *Maize.* Urrea sold the poem "Father Returns from the Mountain" to Le Guin for *Edges,* her 1980 Pocket Books anthology, and was also publishing in such magazines and journals as *Burnt Sienna, Hollywood Drama-Logue, Roadwork,* and *Vision Magazine.*

In June 1982, Urrea accepted an offer to teach expository writing at Harvard. He had come, he reflected in an unpublished interview, from a dirt street in Tijuana "to teach English to the most powerful *gringitos* (little Yankees) in the country." Soon he was teaching creative writing in the summer sessions, as well. At Harvard, Urrea became friends with Villanueva, and they made the initial plans for *Imagine* over beers at a pizza parlor. Urrea served as associate editor from 1984 until he left New England in 1990. From 1986 to 1990 he taught and served as special assistant to the president at Massachusetts Bay Community College. He was married in 1987.

Urrea's father had died in 1977; when his mother died in 1990 he returned to California to settle her affairs. He began publishing fragments of *Across the Wire,* which had been rejected by every major publisher (by some of them twice), in the *San Diego Reader.* "The need

to clarify for readers alien to each story," he explains, "served to distill the essential stories."

Urrea and his wife moved to Colorado in June 1991, separated in 1992, and divorced in 1993, the year *Across the Wire* was finally published by Anchor Books. The work successfully responds to the challenge of dealing with shocking material with compassionate detachment. While championing the cause of the poor, Urrea attains a narrative tone free of judgmental editorializing. The structure of the book is simple. He circles from the Tijuana city dump as it existed in the 1980s through the region and back to the dump. Each chapter is a self-contained account of events or a portrait of a person. In 1991 Urrea joined with the Chicano theater scholar and director Jorge Huerta and his Teatro Máscara Mágica to write, rehearse, stage, produce, and tour a full stage play in six weeks. The play, *Un Puño de Tierra/A Handful of Dust,* was directed by Jose Luis Valenzuela and based on the opening chapter of *Across the Wire,* "Sifting Through the Trash."

Urrea knew that in dealing with such poverty, crime, and disease he ran the risk of reinforcing negative stereotypes of Mexicans. "Still," he says in his autobiographical sketch, "the writer at some point has to trust his materials and his readers. It was my job to tell the stories with respect, and those who had the eyes to see would accept these people, would learn to see them perhaps with a little compassion."

*In Search of Snow,* Urrea's first novel, endured an initial fate similar to that of *Across the Wire:* it was rejected by a series of publishers (eighteen in this case). Urrea cut the manuscript by half and gave the first part new shape and depth, and HarperCollins published the work in 1994. The "snow" that protagonist Mike McGurk seeks is love. After the death of his mother, seven-year-old Mike drifts with his redneck, small-time boxer father, Texaco Turk McGurk, across the Southwest until Turk buys a gas station miles off the main highway northwest of Tucson. Years later, returned from World War II, Mike continues to work for his father until Turk dies of a heart attack in the mid 1950s after a final demonstration boxing brawl. Taking to the road, Mike encounters love in its varied forms: erotic and romantic love, love of place, love of God, love of ethnicity and race, fraternal love, and finally, the complex and intricate loves of a healthy and happy family, a fictionalized portrait of the García family that took Urrea in as a boy. Mike's pain is laid bare when he goes home with his friend Bobo and Mr. García, Bobo's father, limps out to meet them:

"M'ijo [my son]," the old man said, and stepped forward. They shook hands. Then Bobo threw his arms around his father in a fierce *abrazo* [embrace] that

*Cover for Urrea's 1994 collection of semi-confessional poems*

knocked the old man's hat off. And the old man twisted his face around and kissed Bobo on the cheek.

It was the kiss that did Mike in.

Tears filled his eyes. He couldn't hold them back. His eyes burned as the heartbreak overcame him. He sobbed, and it boomed in the cab of the truck, and they all turned to stare at him. . . . He heard himself saying "Tu-hur-hurk!" and "Mo-ho-hom!"

"*Rraccatta-rracatta,*" they were saying to him. Soft women's hands were laid on him.

"*Pobrecito* [poor little thing]," Mamá said.

Mike, like Urrea in his childhood, is nourished by the Garcías. Pots bubble "around and behind the tortilla pan. The smell of coffee, beans, and sauces fill the house." Even the Garcías' canaries, "pondering the sight of Mike first thing in the morning," smell like bread. Mike would have enjoyed keeling over right there at the table and being buried out under Mr. García's *membrillo* [quince] tree." His announcement that

he wants to be a Mexican is "greeted with several translations and an outburst of joy."

Ray González, reviewing *In Search of Snow* in *The Nation* (18 July 1994), compares it to Rudolfo A. Anaya's *Bless Me, Ultima* (1972) as frames or "bookends in the historical and psychic shape of the Mexican-American experience." He explains that these two novels demonstrate that "this literature is succeeding in encompassing the choices we have as a culture, as writers, and as a people coming from the same landscape to redefine our spiritual and familial needs." If Anaya's novel "represents the rich, psychic garden of regeneration," Urrea's "echoes the realistic, brutal turn off-course many Mexican-Americans feel they have taken as we coast into the next century." González praises Urrea's "flair for creating strong characters and bringing them alive in a blend of drama, slapstick comedy and cinematic technique." While he criticizes Urrea's "almost too short chapters" as reflecting a trend in current fiction that results in "short books that potentially have greater and deeper stories to tell than their structure allows," he adds that "Urrea has written a story that captures the development of the male psyche in this fractured time, and also shows how far Chicano writers have come and how much they have learned from Rudolfo Anaya."

Urrea is part of a second generation of Chicano writers who, early in their careers, are enjoying the attention of mainstream publishers. Chicano literature has historically moved from barrio newspapers to the university presses and small Chicano publishing houses. Now, in the era of multiculturalism, there is money to be made, and commercial publishers are interested. Urrea, however, refuses to limit himself to marketable ethnic themes. Urrea insists that writers and scholars must develop an alternative literature that challenges the traditional canon.

*The Fever of Being,* Urrea's 1994 book of poems, which won the prestigious Western States Book Award before it was published, cannot be classified as Chicano poetry, though there are some barrio vignettes, and a classic elegiac Chicano quality is strongly in evidence. Several poems seem Mexican in nature, such as "Prima," "Sombra," and "Abelino García"; the rest are firmly in the modern American voice. In the long poem "Horses," which takes up the middle of *The Fever of Being,* Urrea fashions a lament for the American West; readers face the deaths of rivers, of the gunfighter Tom Horn, and of the Apache chief Geronimo. Regarding the rest of the text, Urrea explains in the 1993 autobiographical sketch:

> Elsewhere, I write of the gradual death of my own family, of my childhood, and of an innocence I mourn even today. The epigraph that begins that book laments the loss of life while we have slept, so afraid of waking up. I sense the time beginning to rush, and I have not lived enough. This book comes bursting out of my troubled history.

*Across the Wire* was joined by another volume of essays, *By the Lake of Sleeping Children: The Secret Life of the Mexican Border,* in 1996. Carolyn Alessio, reviewing the book in the 15 December 1996 *Chicago Tribune,* called Urrea "an immersion journalist in the most literal and convincing form." *Ghost Sickness,* another book of poems, was published in 1997 and has been excerpted in *The Best American Poetry* (1996), edited by Adrienne Rich. *Nobody's Son,* Urrea's autobiography, appeared in 1998. *Wandering Time: Western Notebooks* (1999), is a book of nature writing that is deeply influenced by the Zen outlook of the Haiku poets Issa, Buson, Onitsura, and Basho.

Urrea's great-aunt, Teresita Urrea, "La Santa de Cabora" (The Saint of Cabora) who died in 1906 at age thirty-three, was a near-mythical *curandera* (healer) and miracle worker in Sonora and the American Southwest and came to be known as the "Queen of the Yaquis." Undergoing a resurgence in popularity and devotion among Chicanos, Native peoples, and what Urrea calls "New Age wannabe Indians" in the 1990s, Teresita is the subject of several years of research that he hopes to turn into an historical novel. He and his second wife, Cindy, an investigative reporter, have two children, Eric and Megan.

As Tom Auer, publisher of *The Bloomsbury Review,* has said, "Regardless of the form he chooses, Urrea writes beautifully and sensitively about difficult political and sociological issues on both sides of the U.S. and Mexican border." It is Luis Alberto Urrea's plan to continue to explore forms and genres as he moves farther away from the expected parameters of Chicano literature. "All I want to accomplish," he finally says, "is to know at the end of the day that I told the truth."

### Reference:

Tom Auer, "Young Writers to Watch," *Bloomsbury Review* (January/February 1997): 17.

# Richard Vásquez

*(11 June 1928 – )*

Joe D. Rodríguez
*San Diego State University*

BOOKS: *Chicano* (Garden City, N.Y.: Doubleday, 1970);
*The Giant Killer* (Davenport, Fla.: Coral Reef, 1977);
*Another Land* (New York: Avon, 1982).

SELECTED PERIODICAL PUBLICATIONS–UNCOLLECTED: "Palos estillados," "La peluquería del maestro," "El difunto pititos," "El pan nuestro de cada día," ". . . a la muerte," and "The Wedding," *Revista Chicano-Riqueña,* 1 (Winter 1974): 26–30;
"Barrio Book Trade: It Doesn't Lose a Thing in Translation," *Los Angeles Times,* 8 May 1977, p. 3;
"'Zoot Suit' Image Raises Chicano Consciousness," *Los Angeles Times Calendar,* 22 April 1979, pp. 73–75;
"Bronson vs. Floodtide of Illegals in 'Borderline,'" *Los Angeles Times Calendar,* 27 January 1980, pp. 3–4;
"Reliving the Panic at 'Borderline,'" *Los Angeles Times Calendar,* 5 October 1980, p. 3;
"'Mojado Power': A Boost for Illegal Aliens," *Los Angeles Times Calendar,* 22 February 1981, p. 41;
"Disney Dubbed into Spanish," *Los Angeles Times Calendar,* 12 April 1981, p. 4.

OTHER: "Chicano Studies: Sensitivity for Two Cultures," in *The Chicanos: Mexican American Voices,* edited by Ed Ludvig and James Santibanez (Baltimore: Penguin, 1971), pp. 205–211.

*Richard Vásquez at the time of* Chicano

The writing of Richard Vásquez straddles the realms of journalism and fiction, Mexico and the United States, and fact and fantasy. His contributions as a writer must be considered in terms of the explosive development of the city of Los Angeles and the growing importance of the United States–Tijuana border corridor. In both his fiction and his reporting Vásquez examines the impact of people of Mexican descent on Southern California, from U.S. citizens of Mexican heritage to newly arrived, undocumented workers drawn across the border by the hope of better wages. Vásquez is best known for his three novels: *Chicano* (1970), among the first sagas about a Chicano family to be published by a mainstream press; *The Giant Killer* (1977), an adventure novel about a Mexican American reporter who uncovers a conspiracy to create separate homelands for different ethnic groups in the United States; and *Another Land* (1982), a romantic fantasy involving two immigrant lovers hounded by a vengeful criminal.

Vásquez was born in the community of Southgate near downtown Los Angeles on 11 June 1928.

Southgate was a bustling, blue-collar area that grew with the greater city. He was one of ten children raised in the San Gabriel Valley outside of Los Angeles and has lived in many locations throughout the city. Vásquez incorporates his family's story into *Chicano,* part of which traces the patriarch Héctor Sandoval's immigration and settling of his family in Los Angeles between 1910 and 1930, during the time it was transformed from a city of roughly 350,000 inhabitants to a metropolis with more than 1.2 million residents.

Vásquez's writing encompasses distinct cultural points of view, different generations, and various historical periods. He often utilizes irony and paradox to call a single, dominant point of view into question. Vásquez struggles to come to terms with the Anglo, Chicano, and Mexican aspects of his *mestizaje* heritage, granting to no single one of these cultural perspectives an absolute claim to the truth. His novels assert the futility of simply clinging to Mexican traditions in the United States, where change is constant and dramatic, but also reject sacrificing mixed cultural legacies in favor of becoming Anglo American. His writing is fundamentally concerned with the question of how *mestizos,* or people from mixed cultural backgrounds, negotiate their identity. Vásquez has devoted his career as a writer and journalist to chronicling the historical and demographic significance of *mestizaje* ancestry in the southwestern United States.

In addition to writing novels Vásquez has served as a reporter for the *Santa Monica Independent,* the *San Gabriel Valley Daily Tribune,* and the *Los Angeles Times.* In 1963, while he was with the *Tribune,* he received a Sigma Delta Chi award for an exposé about the city government of Irwindale, which his grandparents helped settle. After police killed the *Los Angeles Times* reporter Rubén Salazar in 1970 during the Chicano Moratorium protesting the Vietnam War, Vásquez began writing for that newspaper.

In *Chicano* the rapid changes in the Sandoval household reflect the dramatic growth of Los Angeles. Electricity, indoor plumbing, and other conveniences improve life for the first generation of immigrants but also lead to clashes with their Americanized offspring over traditional folkways and modern standards of behavior. Héctor Sandoval is struck by how houses in the United States are designed to ensure privacy indoors and to trumpet individual achievement to the world outside. Further, the Mexican tradition of primogeniture is challenged by siblings and modified over the four generations of family history covered in the novel.

Another striking feature of *Chicano* is its depiction of the way relationships between people of Mexican descent and Anglo Americans are undermined by ethnocentrism and discrimination, as in the opening of the novel, when Héctor witnesses "a young tattered man wearing a sombrero" gunned down by Anglo lawmen. Vásquez draws upon his experience as a journalist to document how prejudice flourishes in segregated communities and the barrios. Chicanos and Anglos live apart and turn into enemies, and even reasonable and well-intentioned members of both groups distrust and resent one another. *Chicano* suggests that neither group wants trouble in the schools between Anglo teachers and growing numbers of Mexican students or clashes between homeowners from different ethnic backgrounds in the new suburbs that spring up after World War II. People are inculcated with mistrust for those who are from different cultures, however, and share the pessimistic notion that "you can't teach ideas out of people," as one Anglo character in the novel observes.

Each of Vásquez's novels is attentive to the significance of skin color and to the difficulties it poses regarding a *mestizo's* efforts to assimilate. In *Chicano* every generation bears the "stigma" of *mestizaje:* one family member is born *moreno* or *prieto* (dark) and another is born *güero* or *rubio* (fair). Those who are light-skinned can pass for Anglo and are accepted more easily than their counterparts. Fair skin becomes a source of irony in Vásquez's novels, however, when Anglo characters attempt to compliment the Chicano protagonists by observing that they are "not like other Mexicans." Such comments invariably have the opposite of the intended effect, making Chicanos uncomfortably aware of prejudice and stereotypes. Such passages reflect Vásquez's sense of the ambiguous place of Chicanos in American society: even if they are the third generation born in the United States, *mestizos* must still negotiate between Mexican and Anglo points of view.

Pete Sandoval, grandson of Héctor and the most developed character in *Chicano,* shares many of Vásquez's life experiences. He is an ambitious former serviceman who uses his military service during World War II as a way to learn a trade in construction. As a token of his Americanization he begins calling himself Pete instead of Pedro. Pete buys into the rags-to-riches myth of American success popularized by Horatio Alger. By dint of hard work, *ganas,* and good luck he becomes a cement mason and helps build the Los Angeles freeway system, reflecting Vásquez's own experience in the building trade pouring and finishing cement. Pete makes more money than he ever dreamed of and can afford a life that is better than that of an Anglo family who resides in the East Los Angeles barrio as well. The myth of the American dream mocks Vásquez's Chicano characters, however: Pete's son, Sammy, hates such talk about success—it reminds him of his failings and inferiority.

Pete's life in *Chicano* is a paean to assimilation; when Sammy begins to fall behind in Anglo-dominated schools, Pete decides to move out of the barrio into a whites-only suburb. In doing so he sows the seeds of a family catastrophe. The novel ends with his daughter, Mariana, dying of a septic abortion and Sammy, now a heroin addict, being sent to prison. The fates of both Pete's offspring are precipitated by his acquaintance with David Stiver, an upper-class snob from the East who dabbles in college and the promotion of racial tolerance. Stiver wants to help reduce the high dropout rate for Chicanos in local schools. What begins as his sociology project contributes to the termination of a family line when Mariana becomes pregnant by him, lending to her botched abortion. Thus the novel concludes with a bitter portrayal of the devastation that can be wrought by good intentions. To some extent *Chicano* is written for people like Stiver, who have good intentions about tolerating cultural differences and combatting ingrained prejudices about race, but who lack self-awareness.

Pete and his family are obsessed with class, which they perceive as an indefinable quality of good taste and mannered civility that indicates having arrived in American society. They learn, however, that class is not a commodity that attaches to income level or place of residence but a code of privilege spoken by a cabal of initiates. Only acceptance fosters social polish, and *Chicano* offers no hope that Anglo Americans will treat Latinos as equals. Pete's traditional notions of respectability and gender roles lead him to insist that Mariana attend business school instead of college, even though she is a good student. At the end of the novel Stiver agonizes over the possibility that if his family and peers had understood that Mariana was descended from a venerable, land-owning Spanish family, they would have accepted her. His self-serving delusion lends another level of irony to Mariana's tragedy, however, since the Sandovals are Mexican and not Spanish. *Chicano* closes with a sense of hopelessness and despair that troubled many critics, and their negative response likely influenced Vásquez's decision to contrive happy endings for his two following novels.

One of the most dramatic scenes in *Chicano* occurs just before Héctor Sandoval dies of a bleeding ulcer caused by alcohol and stress. His son, Neftalí, decides to visit a brothel and discovers his two sisters working there. "It . . . it would have been better had we stayed in Mexico," he exclaims. "Like hell it would," they respond. "Don't you remember, brother, the hunger, the nothing we had, no clothes, beans and corn everyday, a big occasion when we had a chicken?" Although some readers find such sentiments stereotypical, others find this passage a harsh but true-to-life assessment of

what drives many undocumented immigrants across the border.

Nostalgia and the memory of Mexico as a lost Eden are shown to be bankrupt ideas in *Chicano*. When Neftalí considers his false U.S. birth certificate, guilt and longing for the old country are less important than the fear of appearing like a hypocrite in the eyes of his children. Unlike in José Antonio Villarreal's *Pocho* (1959), the first mainstream novel about a Mexican American family, the hope of going back to Mexico has little force in *Chicano*. The few characters in each generation who succeed hitch their dreams to the future of the United States. There is sadness over the loss of traditions that bind together extended families and small Mexican communities. All around the characters in the novel, however, Los Angeles rushes toward the future, and those who look back are left behind.

Perhaps the sense of disjunction in *Chicano,* the detachment from traditional Mexican values and folkways, helps account for its mixed reception. Chicano critics tended to favor more powerful statements of activism and social cohesion in works such as Tomás Rivera's "*. . . y no se lo tragó la tierra*"/"*. . . And the Earth Did Not Devour Him*" (1971) and Oscar Zeta Acosta's *Revolt of the Cockroach People* (1973), both of which present a vision far different from the cynicism and despair of Vásquez's novel. Carlota Cárdenas de Dwyer, in her dissertation "Chicano Literature 1965–1975" (1976), makes an important point when she observes that "*Chicano* displays almost every Anglo caricature of Chicanos, from the sad-eyed, silent, and mustached villagers at the beginning to the articulate but humble Mariana Sandoval at the end." Many other critics, including Rafael F. Grajeda in his 1979 essay "José Antonio Villarreal and Richard Vásquez: The Novelist against Himself," find the novel flawed because the author appears to be writing at odds with his ethnic identity. The attempt of the *mestizo* to find acceptance in American society becomes not only a narrative issue but an authorial dilemma.

Although the critics Francisco A. Lomelí and Donald W. Urioste characterize *Chicano* as technically well written, they find the protagonists flat and one-dimensional. One possible explanation for the constrained development of the main figures is that coping with *mestizaje* ancestry is primarily an intellectual struggle, and Vásquez's characters are not deep thinkers like the protagonists of *Pocho* and "*. . . y no se lo tragó la tierra.*" Judy Salinas finds an exception in Mariana, who is "bright, sharp, intelligent, and wise to the ways of the Anglo-Chicano community." She is killed off so quickly that she appears more like a foil to Stiver than a developed character, however. Similarly, Sammy can only partially articulate the confusion he feels over his iden-

*Dust jacket for Vásquez's 1970 novel, which follows four generations of the Sandoval family in Los Angeles*

tity. As Grajeda observes, Sammy feels trapped in limbo wherever he is, caught between cultures. In Tijuana he "noticed the American tourists taking him for granted as part of the scenery, while natives spotted him for a tourist."

Critics such as Teresa McKenna, Martin Levin, Philip Ortego, E. M. Guiney, and Lomelí and Urioste are correct when they fault the novel for various shortcomings in characterization and technique but are also justified in acknowledging its literary importance. One way of assessing its value is that the issue of *mestizaje* and weaving an identity out of mixed cultural legacies continue to inspire works such as Sandra Cisneros's *House on Mango Street* (1983), Gloria Anzaldúa's *Borderlands/La Frontera: The New Mestiza* (1987), and Richard Rodriguez's *Days of Obligation* (1992). In the years since *Chicano* was published in 1970, however, the discussion of *mestizaje* has grown symbolically richer. Vásquez is thwarted by assuming that a Chicano has to be either Mexican or American, while his successors consider how to be both in some contexts and neither in others.

Vásquez's novels share an ironic perspective on group loyalty and the extended sense of self that defines

ethnic awareness. The *mestizos* in his novels are compelled to decide how to mix and match their distinct legacies in order to forge bonds with people like themselves. The irony is compounded when a character is operating in one cultural framework and hears the echo of another. The protagonist of *The Giant Killer,* Ray García, is a Mexican American reporter who believes in assimilating into Anglo American culture and has struggled to be more than a token Mexican covering the barrio. When a congressman is set up with pornography planted in his car, García decides to investigate. He seeks information about the case from Jesús Serrano, an activist journalist from East Los Angeles. After meeting with Serrano, García muses about why he did not go to work for him: "While I admired him, and thought all he did was good and needed doing, I was convinced that ultimately the Chicano must integrate into the dominant society. I'm not so sure now."

Ray García's given name is Ramón, and when he "hears" his Mexican name, he experiences a jolt of memory about the past. Ray set aside a part of his mixed cultural legacy in order to find a place in the newspaper business. On the other hand, Serrano does not believe that assimilation is in the best interest of Chicanos. Serrano is stabbed and dies just before he can tell García about the conspiracy that seeks to establish separate homelands in the United States for Anglo-Americans and "others."

By the end of the novel García has tied up all the loose ends of the plot, including a rigged election and murder, and although he still does not "know who or what I was," he intends to return to the woman he loves, Sidney Voight, who works in an art museum. The themes of racial conflict and ethnic separatism, the scene with Serrano, and García's questions about who he is underscore the issues concerning *mestizaje* and identity that occupy *Chicano.*

*The Giant Killer* has not received much literary notice except for brief reviews. Roberto Serros and Julio A. Martínez in *Chicano Literature: A Reference Guide* (1985) comment that the novel "possesses a crisp narrative style reminiscent of Mickey Spillane's and portrays colorful characters capable of holding the attention of the average reader."

A similarly ironic tone pervades Vásquez's most recent novel, *Another Land.* For example, when the macho protagonist, Margarito, or "Rito," is almost netted in a sweep for illegal aliens by the Immigration and Naturalization Service, he imagines what the INS agents are thinking and, switching cultural perspectives, adopts their point of view. The officers are on the lookout for people with Mexican features, so he takes the arm of an Anglo woman and strolls from the restaurant as if he were a U.S. citizen. Vásquez builds the scene carefully, but while technically well constructed, it strains credulity. The escape is in keeping, however, with the fairy-tale tone of the novel. Rito's childhood sweetheart, Anastacia Herrera, finds sanctuary as a housekeeper in the Los Angeles mansion of a wealthy woman of French descent. She is reunited with Rito after he is cleared of murder and she obtains her U.S. citizenship.

*Another Land* is set in Los Angeles, the Baja Peninsula of Mexico, and the border region and ends with Anastacia's affirmation of the area's distinct cultural legacies: "I still have my apartment here. I have a home in Baja. You see, we can cross the border any time we want, as often as we want. Just like you always could. None of you will ever really understand about that." While this passage refers literally to Anglo Americans owning the border region, it also alludes to the *mestizo's* ability to negotiate identity across different cultures. Anastacia and Rito have been forced to immigrate from Baja by poverty and the machinations of a murderous pimp. In the United States Rito is framed for murder and Anastacia is threatened with deportation. Because of her charm and connections, however, all ends happily.

While Vásquez's fantasy/romance/crime novel at times loses touch with reality, its fairy-tale quality can be understood as an attempt to deal with issues concerning immigration and the persistent theme of negotiating identity in terms of multiple cultural legacies. Undeniably, however, a series of unbelievable coincidences and such fantastic devices as a magic talisman tend to deflect hard questions about the place of Mexicans in U.S. society. For example, Anastacia's wealthy mistress, Mrs. De Beauclair, has supported a senator in his election campaign and persuades him to help her undocumented immigrant housekeeper. The head of the Immigration and Naturalization Service in Los Angeles is so taken with Anastacia that he agrees to try to apprehend Rito before the police shoot him as a wanted fugitive.

The most believable figure in the novel is Ben Garza, a starving law student who barely keeps himself alive doing private investigative work. He struggles with his hand-to-mouth existence, trying not to be too mindful of the "spic haters" he regularly encounters. He too is touched by the fabulous good luck that characterizes the novel: although he has not yet passed the bar exam, he represents Anastacia during immigration proceedings and does such an impressive job that he attracts the professional interest of one of the most powerful attorneys in Los Angeles.

The novel ends with congratulations to Garza, Anastacia, and Rito from the head of INS after they fend off deportation in legal proceedings. Garza smil-

ingly asks the official to leave because parking attendants are afraid to approach a car with the emblem of the Immigration and Naturalization Service on the door. "Wilder looked puzzled only for a moment, and then Garza heard him roar with laughter as the car pulled away. Ben turned to join the others, and as if by magic two smallish, dark men came scurrying toward them saying 'Teekets? Give me teekets.' He looked at Anastacia and Margarito. They too were observing the attendants seriously, and it was impossible to tell what they were thinking, whether they were happy or sad."

The implied answer is that they are both happy *and* sad, although *Another Land* does not plumb these feelings, opting instead for what seems to be an unqualified happy ending. Aside from brief reviews of the novel in the *Los Angeles Times* and *Publishers Weekly,* critical commentary is sparse. Serros and Martínez write that "while most average readers will enjoy this action-packed novel, it lacks the moving and trenchant qualities of *Chicano.* Vásquez's claim to fame continues to rest on his earlier literary opus."

In his reporting Vásquez does not try to solve dilemmas over assimilation and how a *mestizo* juggles multiple cultural orientations and outlooks. The ambiguous position of Chicanos in Los Angeles does not consume him as a journalist. He presents both sides of issues cogently, then steps back and lets readers make their own judgments. Not only is his writing focused and clear, but there is a studied air of personal detachment. In his review of Luis Valdez's play *Zoot Suit* (1978), for example, he presents a range of responses to the jitterbugging Mexican youth in the Los Angeles barrios: some audience members welcomed the play about racial violence against pachucos, while others considered the pachucos to be bad role models and a discredit to Mexican people.

These pieces are clear and immediate, offering a window to Vásquez's interests in barrio life and the field of Chicano studies. His newswriting explains Mexican American topics of interest to an Anglo audience. Three of Vásquez's newspaper articles deal with illegal immigrants. He has a knack for bracketing this topic in terms of discrete points of view and letting these perspectives speak for themselves. In two articles about the motion picture *Borderline* (1980), which stars Charles Bronson as a U.S. Border Patrol guard, the perspectives of undocumented workers who risk their lives crossing the *frontera* between the United States and Mexico are juxtaposed with the perspectives of INS officials who served as paid consultants for the movie. In a 12 April 1981 article about *Bambi* (1942) and other animated Disney movies translated into Spanish, Vásquez mutes his own opinions and quotes an educator who asserts, "the availability of the Disney-type classics is a boon to Hispanic acculturation."

One of Vásquez's most significant journalistic pieces, "Chicano Studies: Sensitivity for Two Cultures," was reprinted in the anthology *The Chicanos: Mexican American Voices* (1971). The essay begins with a dialogue between college chums Jim and Ramón—one of Scandinavian descent, the other Mexican—after Ramón takes an ethnic studies course. Vásquez documents why an old friendship ends because of ethnocentrism and recrimination uncovered by taking the course. "Many persons today are angered by such deliberate confrontations, which seemingly create antagonism. But a great number of Chicano faculty members and administrators agree such a confrontation is a fundamental step in the studies."

Vásquez's short poems underscore the reality of death, the enervating grind of daily life, and the ways people deceive themselves with false dreams. He uses the barrio as a stage to offer readers sad reminders of life's illusions. Of all his work these poems are his most personal, and Vásquez's use of *caló,* a barrio dialect of Spanish, and his switching from Spanish to English are powerful. Like his essay on Chicano studies, these poems invite the question of how to improve the quality of barrio life. Given the fact that Vásquez is a wordsmith, one obvious possibility is to use ideas to create a better vision of existence.

The time is appropriate for a reappraisal of Vásquez's body of work, especially with the current critical interest in cultural groups. Vásquez's writing is best understood against the growth of Los Angeles as a major city and the development of the Tijuana-Baja corridor as one of the busiest border crossings in the world. The United States–Mexico border shakes Anglocentric assumptions about cultural homogeneity and is a powerful reminder of cultural diversity and the place of multiple legacies in the development of the United States. For his explorations of the history and sociopolitical development of southern California, Vásquez has earned a significant place in Chicano and U.S. letters. In terms of his work as a journalist, Vásquez has to be considered with a cohort of newspaper contributors, including Rúben Salazar and Frank del Olmo, who have helped transform the complexion of journalism in Los Angeles and its surroundings.

Vásquez's novelistic voice is as distinct as that of his contemporary, Villarreal. Like Villarreal's *Pocho,* Vásquez's best-known novel, *Chicano,* grapples with the spiritual and philosophical challenges of being *mestizo,* of claiming Mexican descent in a sometimes hostile Anglo American environment. If *Chicano* falters, it is because the novel fails to offer an answer regarding how individuals of mixed cultural legacies can create an integrated self-awareness and a satisfying sense of group identity.

## References:

Carlota Cárdenas de Dwyer, "Chicano Literature 1965–1975: The Flowering of the Southwest," dissertation, State University of New York at Stony Brook, 1976, pp. 125–126;

Sergio Elizondo, "Una nota sobre la estructura de *Chicano* de Richard Vásquez," in *Festival de Flor y Canto: An Anthology of Chicano Literature,* edited by Alurista and others (Los Angeles: University of Southern California, 1976), pp. 16–19;

Francine Ginsburg, "*Chicano* Revisited/*Chicano* se visita de nuevo," *Entrelíneas,* 4 (Spring–Summer 1975): 7, 10;

Rafael F. Grajeda, "José Antonio Villarreal and Richard Vásquez: The Novelist against Himself," in *The Identification and Analysis of Chicano Literature,* edited by Francisco Jiménez (New York: Bilingual Press, 1979), pp. 329–357;

Francisco A. Lomelí and Donald W. Urioste, *Chicano Perspectives in Literature: A Critical and Annotated Bibliography* (Albuquerque: Pajarito Publications, 1976), p. 48;

Ted Lyons, "Loss of Innocence in Chicano Prose," in *The Identification and Analysis of Chicano Literature,* pp. 254–262;

Joel C. Micelson, "The Chicano Novel Since World War II, *La Luz,* special literary edition, 6 (April 1977);

Judy Salinas, "The Role of Women in Chicano Literature," in *The Identification and Analysis of Chicano Literature,* pp. 191–240;

Roberto Serros and Julio A. Martínez, "Richard Vásquez," in *Chicano Literature: A Reference Guide,* edited by Martínez and Lomelí (Westport, Conn.: Greenwood Press, 1985), pp. 404–413.

# Alfredo Véa Jr.

*(28 June 1950 –   )*

Roberto Cantú
*California State University, Los Angeles*

BOOKS: *La Maravilla* (New York: Dutton, 1993);
*The Silver Cloud Café* (New York: Dutton, 1996);
*Gods Go Begging* (New York: Dutton, 1999).

SELECTED PERIODICAL PUBLICATION–
UNCOLLECTED: "Caliban and Prospero No More,"
*(untitled),* 3 (Winter–Spring 1997), pp. 58–65.

Alfredo Véa Jr. is a criminal-defense lawyer who
has been in private practice in San Francisco since
1986. In 1989, while Véa was working on a death-penalty case in a small town in the central valley ("an
incredibly racist place," he recalled in an unpublished
June 1995 interview with María Teresa Márquez), a
judge commented that he was not aware that Mexican
lawyers existed. Sensing a need for "something that
endures, something to touch," Véa turned his controlled anger toward a constructive end: he rented a
trailer for the duration of the trial and began writing the
novel *La Maravilla* (The Wonder), which was published
in 1993. "I began to write about ancestry," Véa says,
"about archetypes that were not European, about forms
that persist. I began with the most remarkable image in
my possession: the image of my grandmother, in a
mourning dress, playing her upright piano in front of
her cardboard house."

Véa's writing is driven by a desire to raise questions not necessarily answered by historical reflections on
the alleged contradiction between European and Native
American civilizations. Shifting his focus away from
notions of cultural synthesis, Véa considers Indian ancestry in opposition to European, which is often associated
with the modern and the new, that is to say, with imper-
manence and historical amnesia. Véa's critique of
Europe is moral and epistemological, a sort of genealogical reflection that focuses on values, on the limits of language, and, ultimately, on the relative nature of
knowledge itself. Europe turns into a metaphor for hier-
archies of violence and authoritarian assumptions of universal truth.

*Alfredo Véa Jr. (photograph © by Jerry Bauer)*

Interpreted in the context of Chicano literature,
Véa's critique of modernization as a global project
seems to undermine the ideological tendencies of the
New Novel–such as José Antonio Villarreal's *Pocho*
(1959)–or notions of cultural synthesis, as in the novels
of Rudolfo A. Anaya. Véa's political art returns to questions generally concealed under class differences and
often ignored in the name of progress; hence his choice
to write on behalf of those left behind, no matter what
gender or race. Véa told John Boudreau in 1993: "I'm
writing for all these poor people in my life whom I love,
all those farm workers, Hindus, Koreans, Filipinos,

everybody—so they finally have one of their own who has the discipline and energy to say who they are."

Véa was born in the Arizona desert near Phoenix, in a place called Buckeye Road (not the town known by the same name today). In his 1995 interview with Márquez, Véa said that he was born "around 1950; nobody knows." On the copyright page of *La Maravilla*, Véa's year of birth is given as 1952; during another unpublished interview, he settled for 28 June 1950. Véa affirms that *La Maravilla* is autobiographical, with close parallels between himself and Beto (Alberto), the young protagonist who does not know the identity of his father and who, through the theme of ancestry, dramatizes modern conflicts related to sociocultural identity and maturation. Véa's Mexican mother, Lorenza, of Yaqui and Spanish ancestry, was abandoned by her husband shortly after Véa's birth; she was only thirteen years old. When Véa reached the age of six, his mother decided to leave Buckeye Road, entrusting her son to the care of her parents while she became a farm laborer in California, migrating from one crop to the next. "It was in these camps," Véa recalled, "that my mother met the fathers of my brothers" (he has three half brothers and one half sister).

Véa acknowledges that the most important influences on his personal growth were his maternal grandparents, Manuel Carvajal and Josephina Castillo de Carvajal:

> Through their stories and their religious arguments I became aware, even as a child, of the ancient forces that converged there in the manzanita and cactus. Though both were ostensibly Catholic, their beliefs had an undercurrent of magic and mysticism that flowed from the Moors and the Gypsies of Spain and from the Rio Yaqui and the ancient Olmecs of Mexico. My days with my grandparents were filled with spirits. The nights were filled with ghosts.

Véa's first English lessons involved listening to his grandmother's favorite singers: Sarah Vaughan, the Ink Spots, and Dinah Washington. His grandmother's appreciation of African American musical artists, particularly Duke Ellington, Count Basie, and Louis Armstrong, remains with Véa. Because Véa's Yaqui grandfather had married a Spanish woman, he was excommunicated by the Yaqui tribe; "so he was living in the outskirts of Phoenix by himself, but his tribe would come and see him. He didn't like modern America, he didn't like television."

Véa's grandfather was fluent in Yaqui, Spanish, and English; in addition, his many years as a railroad man brought him close to Irish workers from whom he learned Gaelic. Véa's early youth in the Arizona desert was thus influenced by a polyglot household that instilled a "worldly" sensibility as well as a sense of Yaqui heritage. Through his grandfather's eyes, Véa claims, he had a vision of Aztlán, the homeland, before he ever saw Arizona; he learned about peyote tea when he was nine years old (corresponding to Beto's Yaqui initiation in *La Maravilla*), thus undergoing the kind of "mind-expanding" experiences that became pivotal for his generation.

When Véa was ten years old, his mother took him away from Buckeye Road and into a life of seasonal farmwork in California. His grandparents had given him the foundation for a polycultural worldview. In Brawley, Mexican *braceros* (day laborers) taught him how to fistfight, and his Filipino friends in Stockton taught him how to read and write. He also recalls taking apart the radios of these friends, a curiosity that developed into an interest in electronics. Véa also met French Canadian *braceros* in the northern California fields; as a result of these early friendships, Véa chose to study French in Livermore High School in Alameda County, California. Years later, in a speech published in 1997 as "Caliban and Prospero No More," Véa identified himself as Mexican-Yaqui-Filipino-American.

While still a teenager and in high school, Véa was entrusted with the care of his younger siblings. He worked, studied, and bought his first home, with the help of his high-school teacher Jack Beery. Véa dedicated *La Maravilla* to the memory of this Irish-German mentor and friend ("the best high school teacher there ever was") who, according to Boudreau, "had instructed Véa and his brothers in everything from academics to how to use a fork and knife." Beery died in 1992, one year before the publication of *La Maravilla*.

Véa enrolled at the University of California at Berkeley, taking a leave of absence in 1967 because of financial pressures. He remembers that he was picking brussels sprouts in Arizona when he received notification of being drafted by the army. Véa at first identified himself as a conscientious objector (CO) and went to court but lost his case because he refused to base his request for CO status on a belief in a supreme being. Véa was drafted into military service in 1967, and in the following year he found himself in Vietnam in the midst of the Tet Offensive. "They didn't give me CO status," Véa told Márquez, "but they stuck me in radio school and then I ended up being shot at anyway." Before entering the service, Véa got on his motorcycle and drove to the heartland of the eight Yaqui pueblos in Sonora, Mexico, spending time in Ciudad Obregón, Potam, and Cokoim (the ancient Yaqui name for modern-day Cócorit). Véa was not traveling as a tourist; he was going back to his grandfather's homeland before going to war. His grandfather had died in 1964, and his grandmother died in 1967, shortly after Véa's entry into the army.

During his military service, Véa was active as a radio telephone operator (RTO), working with portable radio communications in the demilitarized zone and carrying radios for an infantry unit. Véa told Boudreau what he learned about war:

> In order to survive, you can kill an entire family, including the children; you are given the license, the uniform and every weapon under the sun. You could get away with anything, and that's when you find out who you are. You realize that kindness and gentility are acts of will. You have to choose a side.

Véa returned home knowing that Vietnam had been a crucial experience: "I never again," he told Márquez, "had any respect for tall white men with gray hair telling me everything was going to work just fine. It gave me a real belief, I think, in myself, because that was all that was left of me." Although *La Maravilla* touches on Vietnam only briefly, it is considered an important contribution to a developing literary subgenre, the Chicano novel of the Vietnam War. Joe D. Rodríguez's novel, *Oddsplayer* (1989) shares with Véa's a similar vision of that military conflict.

After being discharged from the army in 1969, Véa worked temporarily as a truck driver and as a forklift operator. In 1970 he decided to move to France; he lived in Paris for one year in an Armenian hotel close to the Louvre. He read widely, spent many hours at the museum, and worked as a janitor to make a living. He returned to the United States in 1971 speaking fluent French and having decided to complete his university education.

Véa was an undergraduate at the University of California at Berkeley from 1971 to 1975. To earn a living he took jobs as a construction worker and later as a carnival mechanic doing repairs on the Tilt-A-Whirl and the Mad Mouse. After earning a B.A. in English and physics, Véa entered the law school at the university, receiving his law degree in 1978.

According to Véa, he had always wanted to be a criminal-defense lawyer. Unlike many of his Chicano classmates—who claimed they would eventually work for *la huelga* (the social struggle), social welfare, or social services but ended up working for corporations—he immediately volunteered to work for the United Farm Workers. In 1979 he began working for the Centro Legal de la Raza (Legal Center of the People), and the following year he joined the San Francisco Public Defender's Office, where he worked until 1986. He has been in private practice since then, specializing in death-penalty homicide cases. "As far as I know," Véa says, "I

*Dust jacket for Véa's first novel (1993), about the maturation of Beto, an autobiographical character*

am the only Mexicano-Chicano doing that kind of thing in the state."

Véa told Márquez that he wrote *La Maravilla* "in a way that an English reader could read it and understand what it felt like to have a childhood in Spanish." He wanted his novel to be "an argument that cultural maintenance and cultural difference, and especially language, are the engines of society." Organized into a prologue and sixteen chapters, the narrative weaves together various anecdotal threads, including flash-backs (shamanic "visions"), flash-forwards, the life histories of three women in love with deceased husbands or lovers, and the character development of a Mexican American youth.

The prologue of the novel is narrated with playful intelligence by the long-deceased Josephina Valenzuela de Castillo, Beto's grandmother; it is an omniscient and ironic account of selected events that take place in the novel. Josephina also reveals how she manages to "guide" the writing of *La Maravilla:* "My grandson, Beto, finds these moments in his dreams and in his memory and sets them down." Readers familiar with Chicano literature will make connections between this novel and Arturo Islas's *The Rain God* (1984) and Eliud Martínez's *Voice-Haunted Journey* (1990), novels that reverberate with analogous relationships and with similar ideas regarding the recollection of a family's (or a region's) historical past through the act of writing.

The focus of the narrative never departs from Beto's education in Buckeye Road. Beto's Yaqui peyote-tea rite serves a crucial purpose in his maturation; for in a hallucinatory "voyage" back to Cócorit (Beto's ancestral Yaqui birthplace), he discovers a "meeting place" with his grandfather and ancestors and learns as well of his grandfather Manuel's approaching death. This death occurs in chapter 13 with the fulfillment of a sign: Apache, Manuel's dog, returns to serve as guide to *Mictlan* (the land of the dead, according to pre-Columbian mythology). The last three chapters conclude the narrative with several events: a flood—that washes away most of Buckeye Road—a symbolic "end of the world" through water, a Yaqui mythical element; an ingenious narrative fast-forward into Beto's adulthood as he, now a Vietnam veteran, returns to his grandparents' graves; Josephina's transference of her powers to young Norma Paz, her chosen successor as *curandera* (healer); and the final account of Beto's departure as he is driven away by his mother in her new boyfriend's dark Oldsmobile "with the blinding light in the backseat."

*La Maravilla* is a complex yet illuminating narrative that revolves around themes of the voyage, epiphany, and spectacle, thus making altered forms of consciousness—such as the dream, the vision, and the nightmare—a trope for reading the novel as satire, hence the possible rethinking of the "costs" of the American Dream. *La Maravilla* endorses diversity in cultural expressiveness, encourages reflection on man's cognitive limits ("Most mortals have a mind-closing function that works so much better than the mind-opener," says Josephina in the prologue), and exhorts the reader to accept the multiform—the apparently disconnected—as a substantial representation of the protean qualities of the world. The result is a narrative amalgam that includes love stories, "visions" (particularly Beto's Yaqui rite of initiation), and folk healers, all displayed through a setting in the "wasteland" of Phoenix, on a city dump awaiting the cleansing fires and the new life-forms that shall rise from their own ashes.

*La Maravilla* presents a neo-Romantic vision of love, stressing "transgressive" love between people of different ethnic or racial backgrounds, thus challenging social ideas of segregation. Recurring references to the poetry of Andrew Marvell, particularly to the poem "To His Coy Mistress"—with its emphasis on carnal love and the dread of the grave—suggest the presence of a carpe-diem undercurrent throughout the novel.

When Márquez asked him how he approaches the act of writing, Véa answered: "I sit down and write what I feel like writing. . . . And I keep doing that and something in the subconscious knows that it is going to fit together and it is only when the work takes shape that I become obsessively focused on certain parts of the work and in making the interstitial connections." Speaking of authors who influenced his writing, Véa revealed his love for Herman Melville, Fyodor Dostoyevsky, T. S. Eliot, William Faulkner, Gabriel García Márquez, Theodore Roethke, Dylan Thomas (whose poem "A Process in the Weather of the Heart" provides an epigraph for *La Maravilla*), William Butler Yeats, and Octavio Paz. Véa acknowledges the writing of Refugio Zavala, a Yaqui poet.

The reviews of *La Maravilla* called it "astonishing" and "enchanting and powerful." Novelist Sam Harrison, reviewing *La Maravilla* for *The Washington Post* (27 April 1993), judged Véa's novel "sometimes brilliant, sometimes frustrating, always rich and extravagant." Despite Véa's "fascinating cultural information," Harrison found the "random jumping from present to past to future" in the novel too demanding, for it is either "ultimately frustrating" or "preachy and out of context." The reviewer for *The Los Angeles Times* (10 May 1993) declared *La Maravilla* "beautifully written" and "thematically vital for our times." Boudreau comments that the publication of *La Maravilla* was indeed a marvel, given Véa's past: "Teachers told him he would never attend college because he came from the fields."

The main contributions of *La Maravilla* to the enrichment of the Chicano novel are its historical breadth and the scope of its polycultural world; just as significant are its unabashed celebration of a monogamous eroticism and its open disdain toward any form of minimalism or standardization of life. Also noteworthy are Véa's views on contemporary "market" culture and his critique of consumption, as exhibited by Beto's mother, Lola, a Chicana who has fallen under the "commodity lust" engendered by the American Dream ("the best thing to learn is the value of a dollar"). Véa told Márquez that people diminish their sense of honor "by demanding that we all act the same, by allowing ourselves to generate a market morality where things are sold," and by creating a world in which "in order to belong there are certain things that must be owned, not things that must be believed or concepts that must be overcome, or rites of passage, or thoughts that must be cleaved on to, but rather things that must be owned."

Véa's second novel, *The Silver Cloud Café*, was published in 1996. "It's about migrant farm workers," Véa told Márquez, "both earthly and unearthly, and their harvest is both of this world and out of this world." In an unpublished 1995 interview Véa explained that symbolic elements in this novel include Enoch, the son of Cain; the town of San Rafael de Ocumichu (Michoacán), known in Mexico for its clay "devils"; and the name of the "Silver Cloud Café," a bar in Albuquerque patronized by Mexican laborers, both documented and undocumented. Véa told Márquez that his editor's initial reaction to this book was that it was "too complicated, it's not like anything she's ever read, but I think that's the kind of thing that needs to be written. She wants me to write something a little bit more marketable."

*The Silver Cloud Café* raises, for the first time in Chicano literature, questions related to Spanish and American imperial histories. The narrative combines an account of farmworkers (Mexican, Hindu, and Filipino), a murder mystery, a Gothic tale, and an historical essay. *The Silver Cloud Café* interconnects Santo Paulo and Baguio (the Philippines), Michoacán (Mexico), and Stockton and San Francisco (California) in an intricate web of religious conflicts, fractured loves, and extravagant lives. The cast of characters includes Faustino, a homosexual in love with the poetry of Constantine Cavafy; Teodoro, a hunchback who pines for the love of a beautiful Irish-Mexican dancer; Bambino Reyes, an earthly parody of Christ; Raphael Viajero, a peripatetic man of visionary powers (only when far from his home in Ocumicho, Michoacán); and Zeferino, an autobiographical character. The narrative sequence is nonlinear and driven by flashbacks.

With his third novel, *Gods Go Begging* (1999), Véa depicts the pain of the Vietnam War while avoiding the usual anecdotal tales of combat. It is a novel about the true source of war: desire. Véa interconnects the destinies of various characters (including an Army chaplain, a high-ranking North Vietnamese infantry officer, and an African American sergeant) who dwell in an increasingly violent and commodified world, deaf to the subtlety of irony and focused only on what the protagonist defines as desires stripped of humanity. Véa provides historical depth through Jesse Pasadoble, a Chicano criminal-defense attorney whose Vietnam flashbacks serve as a basis for the reconstruction of a personal history, resulting in a layered narrative with various spatial and temporal planes. As a long meditation on death and violence—with scenes of napalm and burnt bodies in Vietnam, American urban violence, and the increasing racism and xenophobia in American cities—*Gods Go Begging* articulates its critical vision of the modern world in a death-defying story of three hills: one in Laos, one in Chihuahua, and one in San Francisco.

*Dust jacket for Véa's third novel (1999), about the relationship between war and desire*

Véa's approach to life—as a lawyer and as a novelist—derives from the heterogeneity of his own personal past. His first marriage ended in divorce. He has no children and is married to Carole Conn. Véa, once a licensed contractor, likes to build stereo speakers and amplifiers; he also builds furniture and rebuilds antique cars. He is working on another novel, which will focus on a central subject in Chicano history: the Mexican-American War. Unlike writers who need "deepest, profoundest silence," Véa admits to being content with some music and a bottle of wine within reach while writing. In "Caliban and Prospero No More," Véa says that culture "is a translation of the human experience in the way that wine is a translation of the soil, the seed and the water. Like wine, it remembers the wood that encased it, the bottle that bound it; the taste of freedom."

**Reference:**
John Boudreau, "In Celebration of All Americans," *Los Angeles Times*, 28 June 1993, p. E2.

# Edit Villarreal

*(7 September 1944 –     )*

## Kat Avila

PLAY PRODUCTIONS: *The Fat Man Likes Poached Eggs,* New York, Theatre for the New City, 12 June 1983;

*Crazy from the Heart,* New Haven, Yale Repertory Theatre, Winterfest VI, 9 January 1986;

*My Visits with MGM (My Grandmother Marta),* San Jose, San Jose Repertory Theatre, 17 January 1992;

*The Language of Flowers,* Seattle, Contemporary Theatre, 19 October 1995;

*Marriage Is Forever,* San Diego, San Diego Repertory Theatre, 2 April 1999.

TELEVISION: *La Carpa,* script by Villarreal and Carlos Avila, *American Playhouse,* PBS, 16 June 1993;

*Mangas,* script by Villarreal and Bennett Cohen, PBS, 15 October 1997;

*The Fix,* script by Villarreal and Cohen, PBS, 22 October 1997.

OTHER: *My Visits with MGM (My Grandmother Marta),* in *Shattering the Myth: Plays by Hispanic Women,* selected by Denise Chávez and edited by Linda Feyder (Houston: Arte Público, 1992), pp. 143–208.

SELECTED PERIODICAL PUBLICATIONS–UNCOLLECTED: "El Teatro Ensemble de UCSD: First International Tour," *Americas Review,* 17 (Summer 1989): 73–83;

*The Language of Flowers* [excerpts], in *Ollantay,* forthcoming, 1999.

*Edit Villarreal (from* Southwest Magazine, *Summer 1993)*

Edit Villarreal's bilingual/bicultural plays have been presented successfully before both Latino and non-Latino audiences, an unusual accomplishment given the limited access that Latino theater professionals have had to important performance spaces. Part of her success is attributable to the fact that she writes for a crossover audience. In an unpublished 1 April 1996 letter she explains:

I tend to want to introduce one group of people to another–the Mexican immigrant to mainstream audiences, the Latina to mainstream audiences, the middle-class Chicano to mainstream audiences. In this sense, I am not writing particularly to Latinos. I'm writing about Latinos to mainstream audiences. I believe this is very important work to do. I want to tear down stereotypical attitudes held by non-Latinos about Latinos. At the same time, I do not want to reinforce stereotypical attitudes Latinos have about themselves; so I have no desire to write to the converted, so to speak.

The drawback in not writing especially for Latinos and not using the confrontational manner some playwrights employ toward the mainstream is that Villarreal's work is sometimes overlooked by reviewers and scholars in favor of the work of Latino-intellectual-crowd-pleasing writers such as Josefina López and Cherríe Moraga. On the other hand, theater critic Richard Scaffidi, critiquing Villarreal's 1992 play, *My Visits with MGM (My Grandmother Marta)*, for *Drama-Logue* magazine (28 May – 3 June 1992), supports her strategy:

What may be most refreshing about Edit Villarreal's comedy . . . is that it emphasizes character-driven humor rather than cultural/political correctness. . . . what best serves "the cause" is not indulgent or strident speechifying but honest, accessible and *universal* theatre.

It is the rare playwright who is as comfortable or as adventuresome moving between cultural settings and views as Villarreal; with her craft she demonstrates how to create new cultural material and survive within a Eurocentric theater paradigm. Her distinctiveness as a Latina playwright stems partially from the intersection of her Ivy League training with her practical upbringing in a Texas border town.

Edit Emili Villarreal was born on 7 September 1944 in the bilingual town of Brownsville, on the Rio Grande at the southernmost point in Texas. She is a fourth-generation Chicana on her mother's side and the eldest of four children; she has two sisters and a brother. Her mother, Elba Cortinas, a registered nurse, was born in Brownsville, and her father, Emilio Villarreal, was also born in Matamoros, Mexico, just across the border. He died in November 1944 while serving in the U.S. Army Air Corps during World War II. A bold and curious child, Villarreal loved the hurricanes that frequently hit the town; disregarding warnings, she would sit by a window to watch things blow past in the wind. Her widowed mother eventually remarried.

Until the age of six Villarreal was looked after by her maternal grandmother, Marta Garza, who had been born on a ranch in Monterrey in the Mexican state of Nuevo León. The feisty, pragmatic character of Marta Grande from *My Visits with MGM* was based largely on Garza, a Methodist who immigrated to the United States when she was fifteen as a ward of the Baptist Church. She came with her younger sister during a great dispersion northward caused by the Mexican Revolution of 1910 to 1920. Stubbornly postponing marriage until she was twenty-four, Garza eventually wed the American-born Juan Cortinas.

Villarreal went to Catholic elementary schools in San Antonio, even though she was not Catholic, because those schools offered the best education in the area. Her family then moved from Brownsville to Los Angeles for better work and educational opportunities. In California, Villarreal attended public schools because her family could no longer afford Catholic ones. In 1962 she graduated from Arroyo High School in El Monte.

Like many talented Latino playwrights, Villarreal studied under the influential Cuban-born dramatist María Irene Fornés at the International Arts Relations (INTAR) Hispanic American Arts Center in New York City; from January to June 1981 she was a participant in the Hispanic Playwrights Laboratory there. She earned a B.A. at the University of California, Berkeley, in 1967 and an M.F.A. in playwriting at Yale University in 1986. After graduation she started teaching at the University of California, Los Angeles, where she is presently a professor in the School of Theater, Film and Television. In September 1988 Villarreal married Los Angeles-born writer Bennett Cohen, whom she met while both were working at Berkeley Stage Company; the couple has no children.

Besides being active as a playwright and dramaturge, Villarreal is a theater critic and book reviewer, with published articles in *Theatre Journal*, the *San Jose Mercury News*, and *The Washington Post*. She has been an artist in residence in several places, including the Yaddo Arts Colony in 1986 and the University of California, Riverside, New Plays Festival in 1993. She served as a panelist and text evaluator for the National Endowment for the Arts 1993 Opera–Musical Theatre Program and as a juror for the 1994 P.E.N. West Award in playwriting and the 1994–1995 Minneapolis Playwrights Center Jerome Fellowship Awards. Her professional affiliations include membership in the Writers Guild of America.

Villarreal's piece *The Fat Man Likes Poached Eggs* was performed at a United Nations rally in Central Park in 1983. Her first full-length play, *Crazy from the Heart,* was performed as part of Winterfest VI at Yale Repertory Theatre in 1986. Malcolm L. Johnson, writing for *The Hartford Courant* (24 January 1986), called *Crazy from the Heart* "the most original of the Winterfest plays" that year. The play has had several public readings since then and has been performed in workshops.

*Crazy from The Heart* dramatizes a Native American gambling game, called variously the Hand Game or the Stick Game or the Grass Game. One team guesses in which hand or hands an opposing player has hidden the marked bone or bones. When a team is in possession of the bones, they sing gambling songs as a group to help their player fool the opposing team. With every

*Scene from a 1993 Milwaukee Repertory Theatre production of Villarreal's 1992 play,* My Visits with MGM (My Grandmother Marta), *with Maricela Ochoa as Marta Feliz, Renee Victor as Marta Grande, and Feiga M. Martinez as Florinda ( photograph by Jay Westhauser)*

correct call of the bones a team loses one or more of their sticks. The game ends when one team has all the sticks and all the bones. Games can easily last a full day, and usually go on even longer.

The setting is a private game, played in traditional Indian style, in which possessions, not money, are bet. Participants from various tribes have converged in the sparse northern Nevada desert, not far from a powwow taking place on the other side of Pyramid Lake. It is Minnie's game, and on her heels is George, who hopes to learn all of her gambling secrets. Minnie forces George to become partners with Lawrence, who declares that this game is his last and that he is moving to Los Angeles. Minnie teams up with the brash Bodie. Matt and Roseanne, a married white couple, have to settle for side betting because they are non-Indian.

Tension builds as the gamblers, bet by bet, remove from their treasure bags what they are willing to risk for the game. A fascinated Matt, who has studied Minnie's game for four years, explains to a proportionately disinterested Roseanne, who tagged only along to keep watch on her husband, how to play: "Keep betting, Rosie, keep betting

until you cut through to something you really care about. Find the dearest thing you love and risk it, Rosie."

Roseanne, encouraged on by Matt to reexamine their marriage and her values, learns her lessons only too well. In the end she rises above the gibes of the group to teach Matt a thing or two about the game and about what it means to love someone fully. Roseanne is actually a cardsharp, but she has been pushed into the biggest game of her life naive and unprepared. Their marriage is on the rocks; Matt has known this fact for some time but has been unable to resolve the situation. Subconsciously or not, aching for a return to simpler times, he makes Roseanne strip herself of all their material possessions.

The play belongs to Roseanne, but it also focuses on presenting Native Americans humanistically on the stage in a culturally relevant setting. *Crazy from the Heart* is innovative in its portrayal of Native Americans; it is a refreshing encounter with their courage and unapologetic sense of humor.

The widely produced *My Visits with MGM (My Grandmother Marta)* evolved from a twenty-five-page poem, "Boogie to Grandma," written on Mother's Day 1983, three years after Marta Garza's death from an intestinal obstruction. During winter break 1988, Villarreal rewrote the poem as a play. An experiment with magical realism, *My Visits with MGM* was intended to be not only an homage to Villarreal's grandmother but also a comedy about assimilation and a critique of the powerful Roman Catholic Church.

*My Visits with MGM* depicts the ways in which three generations of women discover what it means to act on behalf of the self and to have the courage to live a life compatible with a woman's personal rhythms and truths, unswayed by the tiresome opinions of society. It pays tribute to the protective mantle of knowledge and guidance one Chicana grandmother bequeathed to her granddaughter.

The play is prefaced by "Marta Grande's Poem," a *corrido* (ballad) with English and Spanish lyrics informing the audience that the historical starting point for *My Visits with MGM* is the Mexican Revolution, from which many a Chicano has inherited a story. The ballad tells of fifteen-year-old Marta Grande and her thirteen-year-old sister, Florinda, leaving behind a crowded family of brothers and sisters for a fresh start in the United States. As the play begins both women have died; the blackened, burned-out shell of Marta Grande's home dominates the stage. Granddaughter Marta Feliz has come back to Texas from California to inspect the destruction. Recollections come flooding back and propel her into an altered state of consciousness in which her grandmother, grandaunt, grandfather, mother, and best friend rise phoenixlike from the shadows to re-create scenes from her memory. At the end of the play, the audience's attention is returned to the fire-scarred house. When Marta Feliz departs from the burnt house for the last time, her snapshot images of Marta Grande and Florinda have been restored.

Just as Marta Grande's life began when she left her family cocoon in Mexico, her granddaughter Marta Feliz's life changed dramatically after a priest and friend, the comical Father Ernesto, persuaded her to leave her native Texas for California. Both women leave familiar surroundings to risk all they have for better lives elsewhere, on their own terms, repeating an intimate and courageous part of the American experience. The grandaunt, Florinda, represents the sad side of that experience, of immigrants who never adjust. The Church becomes Florinda's crutch; she clings to it in direct proportion to her perceived alienation in the United States. The ghostly Marta Chica, Marta Feliz's mother, represents the strong work ethic and culture-erasing assimilation that first-generation Americans inculcate in their sons and daughters for survival and success.

José Cruz González, project director at South Coast Repertory in Costa Mesa, California, selected Villarreal's script for further development and a public reading as part of the annual Hispanics Playwrights Project (HPP) in summer 1989. In an interview with Chuck Graham in the *Tuc-*

son (Ariz.) *Citizen* (5 July 1990), González spoke about directing *My Visits with MGM*:

> I've never been so personally involved with a play in my life. . . . [Villarreal] has such a strong sense of these characters. The writing is so real. And to be honest, it sounded so much like the way I grew up.

Within three years there were three equity productions of *My Visits with MGM*. In January 1992 the play was fully produced by San Jose Repertory Theatre in California directed by Peggy Shannon. Months later, the Bilingual Foundation of the Arts (BFA) in Los Angeles produced a Spanish-language version of *My Visits with MGM* (translated by Lina Montalvo) as well as the English version. Strong ticket sales prompted the BFA to move the production from their regular performance space to a larger downtown facility. In September 1993 the play was produced at the Milwaukee Repertory Theatre with Norma Salvador directing. It was also performed for radio station KCRW at the Los Angeles Theatreworks in June 1992.

*My Visits with MGM* was included in the anthology *Shattering the Myth: Plays by Hispanic Women* (1992); its publication led to more than twenty subsequent productions, including performances at Borderlands Theatre in Arizona, La Compania de Teatro de Albuquerque in New Mexico, Teatro Vision in California, Teatro del Pueblo in Minnesota, Miracle Theatre Group in Oregon, and Different Stages in Texas. The version published was the fourth or fifth draft; the play has gone through at least eight additional drafts since then, and some of the Spanish has been deleted.

*The Language of Flowers* (1995), Villarreal's adaptation of William Shakespeare's romantic tragedy *Romeo and Juliet* (circa 1595–1596), makes great literature palatable and relevant to Latinos who might be discouraged from perusing the original version because it represents a drastically different cultural reality separated from them by time, geography, and dialect. José Cruz González, who was teaching at California State University, Los Angeles, had approached Villarreal about adapting one of Shakespeare's plays for his students, and *Romeo and Juliet* seemed the perfect choice. Villarreal transformed fifteenth-century Verona, Italy, into twentieth-century Los Angeles; she toned down the family feud to avoid writing another *West Side Story* (1957) and placed the action during the holiday period of *El Día de Los Muertos* (The Day of the Dead) to take advantage of the carnival atmosphere. The young star-crossed lovers, Romeo Martinez and Juliet Bosquet, become secondary to a larger dialogue about the impact of the boundaries created by assimilation and economic status within the Latino community.

In *The Language of Flowers* Julian Bosquet, a wanna-be-Anglo banker, has arranged for his non-Spanish-speaking daughter Juliet to marry fully assimilated Ruben Gutierrez, a law school student. An illegal immigrant belonging to the working class, Romeo would normally not have the opportunity to meet someone like Juliet; but Romeo and his American-born cousin, Benny Martinez, plan on crashing Julian's Halloween party. Benny, inspecting a list of guests, notes: "He's inviting the entire United Nations but nobody south of the border." At the party Romeo is captivated by Juliet's beauty; later his life is threatened by Juliet's maladjusted cousin, Tommy Bosquet.

From this point in the play through Juliet's taking the sleeping potion, Villarreal follows Shakespeare's plot fairly faithfully. With the death of Romeo, however, Villarreal's adaptation and Shakespeare's original drama diverge widely. In Villarreal's version, Romeo is killed during a drive-by shooting, witnessed metaphysically by the ghost of his dead American-born cousin, Benny Martinez. After Juliet finds Romeo dead on the street, she kills herself with a knife, similar to Shakespeare's play. Immediately after Juliet's death, though, Villarreal has the star-crossed lovers resurrected and reunited in the tradition of the Day of the Dead. As the young lovers enter an Aztec textured afterlife, they become flowers, echoing the title of the play as well as Mesoamerican imagery. The presence of *calaveras* (skeletal figures) throughout the play foreshadows the untimely deaths of the two young lovers. Their spiritual reunion and ascension into Aztec heaven, however, keeps *The Language of Flowers* from being completely tragic.

*The Language of Flowers,* under an early working title of "R and J," had a public reading during the 1991 Hispanic Playwrights Project. On 19 October 1995 it premiered at A Contemporary Theatre in Seattle under Norma Saldivar's direction and with music by Germaine Franco.

In 1996 Villarreal wrote two plays, both commissioned by major theaters in the Los Angeles area. *Marriage Is Forever,* her return to comedy writing, was commissioned by the Latino Theatre Initiative at The Mark Taper Forum under the leadership of Luis Alfaro and Diane Rodriguez. It was produced at the San Diego Repertory Theatre on 2 April 1999 under the direction of Sam Woodhouse. Another new play, *Chicago Milagro,* was commissioned by the South Coast Repertory Theatre, where it received a staged reading under the title *Tracks* in 1996. *Chicago Milagro* takes place in Chicago from 1905 to 1910 and follows the spiritual journey of Horacio Alvarez, an educated Mexican who travels to Chicago shortly before the Mexican Revolution. He becomes a healer in Back of the Yards, an Irish ghetto in Chicago, and never returns to war-ravaged Mexico. Today, Back of the Yards has a large Mexican population.

In Villarreal's plays the occasional use of Spanish dialogue could have caused problems for mainstream audiences, but she writes in such a way that non-Spanish speakers are able to grasp the emotional subtext and movement of the drama. She tries to avoid expressing something in Spanish and then repeating it in English, because for a bilingual audience the constant interruptions would soon become wearisome. Instead, when she uses Spanish dialogue, she makes sure that the response in English includes enough hints about what was said to make it understandable. Still, Villarreal readily admits that if audience members understand Spanish they will better appreciate certain moments in the plays, especially the comedy.

Through her writings Villarreal has helped to make Latino culture accessible and understandable to mainstream audiences. She has accomplished this goal without losing her original base of supporters while challenging them to view and interpret the Mexican American experience from different perspectives, as she has.

**Interviews:**

Robert Koehler, "To Grandmother's House She Returns," *Los Angeles Times,* 30 May 1992, p. F10;

Thomas O'Connor, "Chicano Playwrights Take Spotlight," *Orange County Register,* 6 August 1989, p. K24.

**References:**

Kat Avila, "1992–1993 California Theater Season Summary," *Ollantay,* 1 (July 1993): 54–59;

Avila, "The Genesis of Edit Villarreal's *MGM,*" *Ollantay,* 4, no. 1 (1996): 52–57;

Jorge Huerta and Carlos Morton, "Chicano Theatre in the Mainstream: Milwaukee Rep's Production of a Chicana Play," *Gestos,* 16 (November 1993): 149–159;

Huerta, "Professionalizing Teatro: an Overview of Chicano Dramaturgy since *Zoot Suit,*" *Ollantay,* 4, no. 1 (1996): 91–102;

Huerta, "Professionalizing Teatro: An Overview of Chicano Theatre During the 'Decade of the Hispanic,'" *Tonantzin,* 8 (November 1992): 3–6; *TheatreForum* (April 1993): 54–59;

Tiffany Ann López, "Beyond the Festival Latino: (Re)Defining Latina Drama for the Mainstage," in *Women Playwrights of Diversity: A Bio-Bibliographical Sourcebook,* edited by Jane T. Peterson and Suzanne Bennett (Westport, Conn.: Greenwood Press, 1997), pp. 17–25;

Susan Mason, "Romeo and Juliet in East L.A.," *Theatre,* Yale School of Drama, 23 (Spring 1992): 88–92;

Ed Morales, "Shadowing Valdez," *American Theatre,* 9 (November 1992): 14–19;

John J. O'Connor, "Cultures Clash on 'American Playhouse,'" *New York Times,* 16 June 1993, p. B4;

John Villiani, "'My Visits With MGM' Borrows from Life of Rich Latino Culture," *Santa Fe* (N.M.) *Pasatiempo,* 14 May 1993, p. 29.

# Victor Villaseñor

### (11 May 1940 –   )

### Nicolás Kanellos
*University of Houston*

BOOKS: *Macho!* (New York: Bantam, 1973);
*Jury: The People vs. Juan Corona* (New York: Little, Brown, 1977);
*Rain of Gold* (Houston: Arte Público, 1991); translated into Spanish as *Lluvia de oro* (Mexico City: Editorial Planeta Mexicana, 1993);
*Walking Stars: Stories of Magic and Power* (Houston: Arte Público/Piñata Books, 1994);
*Wild Steps of Heaven* (New York: Delacorte Press, 1996).

MOTION PICTURE: *The Ballad of Gregorio Cortez*, screenplay by Villaseñor, Embassy Pictures, 1982.

Victor Villaseñor is a novelist and screenwriter whose novel of immigration, *Macho!* (1973), and epic saga of his family, *Rain of Gold* (1991), have helped bring Chicano literature to a wide readership. His screenplay for the television movie *The Ballad of Gregorio Cortez* (1982), adapted from Américo Paredes's *"With His Pistol in His Hand": A Border Ballad and Its Hero* (1958), introduced Mexican and Chicano concerns to a broad viewing audience.

Victor Edmundo Villaseñor was born on 11 May 1940 in Carlsbad, California, to Mexican immigrants Salvador and Lupe Villaseñor. He was raised on a ranch in Oceanside with his brother and three sisters. Having started school as a Spanish-speaker and, unknown to his family and teachers, a dyslexic, he experienced learning difficulties in school. As he recalled in an unpublished interview, "Both my parents are from Mexico and I grew up in a house where there were no books. When I started school, I spoke more Spanish than English. I was a D-student and every year of school made me feel more stupid and confused—many of these feelings had to do with being Chicano. In my junior year of high school, I told my parents I had to quit school or go crazy." He dropped out of high school and worked on his family's ranch, other farms, and construction sites. After attempting college at the University of San Diego for a brief period, he dropped out and went to live in Mexico, where he discovered

*Victor Villaseñor at the time of* Wild Steps of Heaven

books and learned to take pride in his identity and cultural heritage. "I felt good about myself. I wanted to stay in Mexico and never return to the United States where I felt ashamed of being Mexican. But my parents came for me and after weeks of arguments I agreed to go back home for awhile." Villaseñor did return to Southern California but recalls that he found himself "feeling like a bombshell, ready to explode and kill anyone who made me feel ashamed."

Back in California, Villaseñor overcompensated for his problems with reading and writing by working at the art of writing fiction, even begging to be allowed to audit English and creative-writing classes at the University of California at Los Angeles. "I would write," he resolved. "Instead of killing or bashing people's brains out, I would change their minds." During ten years of supporting himself as a construction worker, he completed nine novels and sixty-five short stories, all of which were rejected for publication some 260 times—until *Macho!* launched his professional writing career in 1973.

Although his first novel was published by Bantam, the largest paperback publisher in the world, it did not lead to national success. The publisher's treatment of his novel instead set him on a path of repeated conflict and disillusionment with commercial publishing in the United States. When *Macho!* was not as heavily promoted as other titles on the Bantam list, Villaseñor took to the road himself and promoted his novel with sales representatives and booksellers. Sales of the book eventually reached sixty thousand copies, but Bantam pulled it from circulation.

*Macho!*, the tale of the young Mexican Indian Roberto García's illegal entry into the United States to find work, proceeds along the familiar lines of the novel of immigration. Roberto, a Tarascan teenager from the state of Michoacán, finds work in the agricultural fields of California and becomes caught up in the farm-labor movement led by César Chávez. He becomes the victim of culture shock, discrimination, and exploitation and decides to go back to his village. The novel departs from the model, however, when Roberto reaches his hometown in central Mexico. Finding that he has been forever changed and is unable to accept the traditional social code, especially in regard to *machismo,* he refuses to take blood vengeance on the man who killed his father. In *Macho!* Villaseñor drew on his firsthand experience with field work and the conflicts of biculturalism.

*Macho!* was well received by critics. The reviewer for the *Los Angeles Times* (23 September 1973) compared the novel to the best work of John Steinbeck, saying *Macho!* was "poetic in its devotion to realistic detail and classic spareness of style. . . . The relentless, spare detail is stunning, the descriptions of violent encounters among men trying to get across the border in any way possible are terrifying." Jerry Belcher in the *San Francisco Examiner* (6 November 1973) stated, "It rings true. His sentences and his characters have the smell of rich earth and honest sweat about them. His story, too, is direct and exciting."

Villaseñor encountered further difficulties with publishers over his next work, the nonfiction *Jury: The People vs. Juan Corona* (1977). Villaseñor's sensitivity to sensational, negative stereotypes of Mexicans in the media drew his interest to the case, and he set out to find out the truth about Juan Corona, to document his trial, and to follow up with the jurors after the case. The book received an enthusiastic review from Tom Wicker on the front page of *The New York Times Book Review* (1 May 1977), but Villaseñor's publisher, Little, Brown, was unable to get copies of the book into stores around

the country until weeks later, when the impact of the positive early reviews had dissolved.

*Jury* is an investigative report of the trial of a labor contractor who was convicted in 1973 of murdering twenty-five derelicts and drifters. On the basis of several months of interviews, Villaseñor reconstructs the eight days of emotionally charged deliberations that led the jury from an original majority favoring acquittal to a unanimous verdict of guilty. The reviewer for the *San Diego Union* (29 May 1977) declared that *Jury* provides "one of the finest insights into the conflicts and emotions of twelve ordinary people deciding the fate of one of their peers that has probably ever been published" and called the work "a powerful book to read carefully and thoroughly and, probably, never to forget." The *Sacramento Bee* (15 May 1977) asserted that although Villaseñor's book is nonfiction it "reads like a fast-paced suspense novel." The *Portland Oregonian* (15 May 1977) concluded that *Jury* was "one of the most thorough and authoritative reports on just what a juror in a major case is called upon to do and the great importance of what the jury does."

When Villaseñor attempted to publish his monumental family autobiography, *Rain of Gold,* he once again ran into barriers in commercial publishing. Receiving reports that there was little enthusiasm among booksellers for *Rain of Gold,* Putnam decided—over Villaseñor's protests—to edit the book, repackage it as fiction, and change the title to "Rio Grande." In response, Villaseñor took the unusual step of buying back his contract and withdrawing the book from publication. Unable to find another publisher in New York, he took *Rain of Gold* to Arte Público Press, a modest-sized noncommercial publisher at the University of Houston and the largest U.S. publisher of Hispanic literature. Despite the limited resources of Arte Público for marketing and distribution, *Rain of Gold* became a hardcover best-seller in the West and brought renewed national attention to Villaseñor. The paperback edition, published by Dell in 1992, was a national best-seller.

*Rain of Gold* is the saga of generations of Villaseñor's family. The book chronicles how the clan survived the Mexican Revolution and eventually immigrated to the United States, establishing themselves in California. It is narrated in a style that evokes respect for spiritualism, myths, and oral traditions, reflective of Villaseñor's upbringing in an extended working-class family. In addition to drawing on family lore in preparing the book, Villaseñor conducted years of interviews and research.

The focus of *Rain of Gold* is divided between the families of Villaseñor's paternal grandparents, eventually becoming unified as they meet, court, and get married. The book begins in 1911 in mountainous northwest Mexico, in a secluded box canyon where the gold mine "Lluvia de Oro" (Rain of Gold) indirectly provides an impoverished living for Villaseñor's grandmother, Lupe Gómez, and her family. This hard life amid a beautiful, almost magically lush setting is periodically interrupted by seasonal floods and the encroaching Mexican Revolution. Surprise raids by marauding soldiers happen with growing frequency. The main force behind the family's strength is Lupe's mother, Doña Guadalupe, who through her intelligence and cunning manages to keep her children together, to see her eldest daughters marry, to save her son from execution, and to accept her husband back into the family after years of forced absence. At age eleven a mature Lupe and her family are able to leave the canyon and the war-torn gold mine for an arduous journey to the United States.

Part 2 of *Rain of Gold* begins when eleven-year-old Juan Villaseñor, his mother, and sisters are making their way north to cross the Río Grande into the United States. They travel on foot until they are crowded into boxcars with thousands of other starving refugees of the revolution. Doña Margarita, Juan's mother, never despairs and, despite her temporary blindness and Juan's wild and sometimes dangerous antics, keeps the family together and manages to lead them to the border. At the border the situation is so desperate that Doña Margarita, a grand dame educated in Mexico City, is forced to beg on the streets so that her family can survive.

They cross the border, and members of the family become separated. Juan serves time in prison and escapes to Montana, where he becomes a gambler and adventurer, but later he rejoins the family in California. In California, Juan becomes aware of the widespread exploitation of and discrimination against Mexicans. He finds it impossible to work for others under such circumstances and sets to create his own businesses, first as a bootlegger during Prohibition and later in more legitimate enterprises.

Lupe's family follows the stream of migrant farm laborers up and down the length of California. Lupe has grown into a breathtaking beauty who captures Juan's heart. Somewhat repulsed by the tough and marginally criminal Juan, however, Lupe vows that she will never marry a man who has anything to do with liquor, violence, or cards. It takes Juan months to work out a strategy to win over Lupe while hiding his illicit bootlegging business, the enterprise that allows him to build a grand house like the one the family had to leave in Mexico. Despite many reversals and barriers, Juan and his family eventually win over Lupe and her family. The women of the families make the decisions, consolidating their strength to forge the new Villaseñor clan. The book ends as Juan and Lupe have the largest and

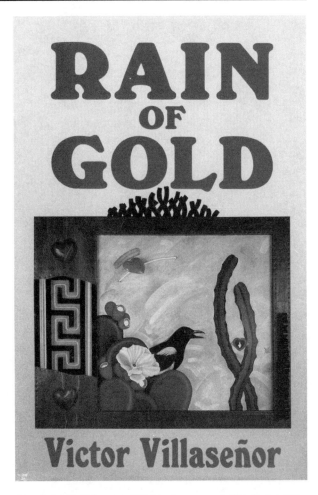

*Dust jacket for Villaseñor's 1991 book, an account of his family's history*

most expensive wedding the barrio has ever seen—a celebration of both their mothers, great women who have survived war, starvation, and dislocation.

*Rain of Gold* was greeted with almost unanimously positive reviews when it appeared. *Publishers Weekly* (1 February 1991) called Villaseñor "a born storyteller, and this the Latino *Roots* . . . a gripping inspirational epic full of wild adventure, bootlegging, young love, tragedies, murder and triumph over cultural barriers." *Kirkus Reviews* stated that the book was "an inspiring, fast-paced tale with a simple, fable-like quality that's often surprisingly moving." *The New York Times* (8 September 1991) called it "a grand and vivid history," and *The Washington Post* (12 September 1991) asserted that it was "a story that deserves to be told, bringing to life a cultural heritage of all Americans." Tom Miller, writing in *The New York Times Book Review* (8 September 1981), assessed the work as not only well written but also historically significant:

*Dust jacket for Villaseñor's 1996 sequel to* Rain of Gold

The immigrant experience has always been integral to the American adventure. What makes the Mexican ordeal different is that they arrived on foot rather than by airplane or in steerage. The Villaseñor and Gómez families came in the first wave of mass migration from Mexico, in the early 20th century. Villaseñor had been hearing stories from his family's older generations about the arduous journey, descriptions of cruelty and hardship that strained credulity and obsessed him with the desire to squeeze every memory from his elders. . .

Like many other critics, Miller underlines the importance of oral tradition to the work. Not only does the style of narration owe a great deal to the culture and worldview of working-class people, but the spirituality and faith that undergird the saga of survival derive from a folk culture connected to the earth as well as to pre-Columbian and Catholic conceptions of God and nature.

An exception to the general acclaim accorded *Rain of Gold* was Juan Bruce-Novoa's review in *World Literature Today* (September 1992), in which he judged the work to be trite and cliché-ridden. Misidentifying it as a

work of fiction, Bruce-Novoa asserted that "*Rain of Gold* is not the great Chicano novel. The tale . . . repeats many clichés of U.S. immigration writing, from victimization by warring factions in the homeland, to the perils of exodus, to the culture shock in the States, with struggles for economic and spiritual survival in the face of anti-foreigner and racial prejudice." He labels Villaseñor's "claim that everything told is true, gleaned from the family oral tradition" as a variety of "ethnic schtick." More often, however, the reviewers echoed Alan Ryan, who wrote in *USA Today* (9 January 1992) that "Villaseñor has written my family history, too. And yours. *Rain of Gold* is one of the best—and most American—books of this or any other year."

Following the success of *Rain of Gold* Villaseñor became a sought-after speaker nationally, was offered the opportunity to write for television, and began negotiating movie and television rights for his books. Despite having signed a contract to produce a sequel to *Rain of Gold* for Delacorte Press—it appeared in 1996 as *Wild Steps of Heaven*—he remained faithful to the publishing house that had previously supported him. Arte Público published Villaseñor's next book, *Walking Stars: Stories of Magic and Power* (1994), a collection of young-adult stories related to *Rain of Gold*.

In the title story and throughout the collection, Villaseñor revisits the spirituality and magical world of his parents when they were children amid the dangers of revolutionary Mexico. Full of anecdotes and wisdom handed down through oral tradition, *Walking Stars* offers engrossing stories on topics such as the uncanny ability of dogs to know when their masters die, the indomitable spirit of Villaseñor's father when he was young, and the power of witches, as well as a bloodcurdling depiction of how two children set out to kill a tyrant.

Again the critics commended Villaseñor's work. *Publishers Weekly* concluded that *Walking Stars* was "both original and moving," while the *Booklist* identified the collection as "an exquisite example of quality literature that helps explain diverse cultures and beliefs while unifying us all within the human family."

Villaseñor's works have brought to millions of Americans the family stories of the social, economic, and political struggles that resulted in Mexican immigration to the United States, where new stories of racism, discrimination, and the occasional triumph over these barriers continues to develop the epic of Mexican American life. Villaseñor has expressed his intention to create other sequels to *Rain of Gold* and to develop motion picture adaptations of the saga and of *Macho!*

# Chicano Literature: A Bibliography

Donaldo W. Urioste
*California State University, Monterey Bay*

Chicano literature has flourished since the 1970s, and tracking all of the material being published is a difficult task. This checklist identifies the main corpus of the literature; it is intended not only as a source of information for the general reader interested in Chicano literature but also as a research tool for literary scholars and critics. The list is divided according to genre (novels, poetry, short fiction, theater, nonfiction narratives, anthologies, and criticism) and arranged by author. This bibliography includes only literary texts and critical studies published as books, chapbooks, or monographs.

## NOVELS

Acosta, Adalberto Joel. *From Common Clay*. New York: Maryland Books, 1978.

Acosta, Oscar Zeta. *The Autobiography of a Brown Buffalo*. San Francisco: Straight Arrow Books, 1972.

Acosta. *The Revolt of the Cockroach People*. San Francisco: Straight Arrow Books, 1973.

Ainslie, Jorge. *Los Pochos*. Los Angeles: Latin Publishing, 1934.

Alarcón, Justo S. *Crisol: Trilogía*. Madrid: Editorial Fundamentos, 1984.

Alarcón. *Los siete hijos de la Llorona*. Mexico: Alta Pimaría Pro Arte y Cultura, 1986.

Alcalá, Kathleen. *The Flower in the Skull*. San Francisco: Chronicle Books, 1998.

Alcalá. *Spirits of the Ordinary: A Tale of Casas Grandes*. San Francisco: Chronicle Books, 1997.

Anaya, Rudolfo A. *Alburquerque*. Albuquerque: University of New Mexico Press, 1992.

Anaya. *Bless Me, Ultima*. Berkeley, Cal.: Quinto Sol Publications, 1972. Translated into German by Horst Tonn as *Segne mich, Ultima: Roman*. Frankfurt, Germany: Nexus Verlag, 1984. Translated into Spanish by Alicia Smithers as *Bendíceme, Ultima*. México City: Editorial Grijalbo, 1992.

Anaya. *Heart of Aztlán*. Berkeley, Cal.: Editorial Justa Publications, 1976.

Anaya. *Jalamanta: A Message from the Desert*. New York: Warner, 1996.

Anaya. *The Legend of La Llorona*. Berkeley, Cal.: Tonatiuh-Quinto Sol International, 1984.

Anaya. *Lord of the Dawn: Legend of Quetzalcóatl*. Albuquerque: University of New Mexico Press, 1987.

Anaya. *Rio Grande Fall*. New York: Warner, 1996.

Anaya. *Shaman Winter*. New York: Warner, 1999.

Anaya. *Tortuga*. Berkeley, Cal.: Editorial Justa Publications, 1979.

Anaya. *Zia Summer*. New York: Warner, 1995.

Apodaca, Rudy S. *The Waxen Image*. Mesilla, N.Mex.: Titan Publishing, 1977.

Aranda, Charles. *Dudes or Duds*. Albuquerque: Carlo Press, 1984.

Arellano, Juan Estevan. *Inocencio: ni pica ni escarda, pero siempre se come el mejor elote*. Miguel Hidalgo, México: Editorial Grijalbo/Paso del Norte Press, 1992.

Arias, Ron. *The Road to Tamazunchale*. Reno, Nev.: West Coast Poetry Review, 1975.

Arias. *The Castle*. Jamaica, N.Y.: Bilingual Press, 1976.

Barrio, Raymond. *The Plum Plum Pickers*. Sunnyvale, Cal.: Ventura Press, 1969.

Beltrán Hernández, Irene. *Across the Great River*. Houston: Arte Público, 1989.

Beltrán Hernández. *Heartbeat, Drumbeat*. Houston: Arte Público, 1992.

Beltrán Hernández. *The Secret of Two Brothers*. Houston: Piñata Books, 1995.

Betancourt, T. Ernesto. *The Me Inside Me*. Minneapolis: Lerner Publications, 1985.

Brawley, Ernest. *The Alamo Tree*. New York: Simon & Schuster, 1984.

Brawley. *The Rap*. New York: Atheneum, 1974.

Brawley. *Selena*. New York: Atheneum, 1979.

Brito, Aristeo. *El diablo en Texas*. Tucson, Ariz: Editorial Peregrinos, 1976. Translated by David William Foster as *The Devil in Texas*. Tempe, Ariz.: Bilingual Press/Editorial Bilingüe, 1989.

Bruce-Novoa, Juan. *Only the Good Times*. Houston: Arte Público, 1995.

Cabeza de Baca Gilbert, Fabiola. *We Fed Them Cactus*. Albuquerque: University of New Mexico Press, 1954.

Cabeza de Baca, Manuel. *Historia de Vicente Silva, sus cuarenta bandidos, sus crímenes y retribuciones*. Las Vegas, N.Mex.: La Voz del Pueblo, 1896.

Candelaria, Antonio Serna. *Juan Cíbola: A Tale of Spanish Swords, Missionary Padres, and Lost Aztec Gold*. Riverside, Cal.: Jim Gallegos, Anthony Lithographers & Printers, 1983.

Candelaria. *Unscaled Fortress*. Alamagordo, N.Mex.: Bennett Printing, 1966.

Candelaria, Nash. *Inheritance of Strangers*. Binghamton, N.Y.: Bilingual Press/Editorial Bilingüe, 1985.

Candelaria. *Leonor Park*. Tempe, Ariz.: Bilingual Press/Editorial Bilingüe, 1991.

Candelaria. *Memories of the Alhambra*. Palo Alto, Cal.: Cíbola Press, 1977.

Candelaria. *Not by the Sword*. Ypsilanti, Mich.: Bilingual Press/Editorial Bilingüe, 1982.

Cano, Daniel. *Pepe Rios*. Houston: Arte Público, 1991.

Cano. *Shifting Loyalties*. Houston: Arte Público, 1995.

Cantú, Norma Elia. *Canícula: Snapshots of a Girlhood en la Frontera*. Albuquerque: University of New Mexico Press, 1995.

Cárdenas, Leo. *Return to Ramos*. New York: Hill & Wang, 1970.

Castillo, Ana. *The Mixquiahuala Letters*. Binghamton, N.Y.: Bilingual Press/Editorial Bilingüe, 1986.

Castillo. *Peel My Love Like an Onion*. New York: Doubleday, 1999.

Castillo. *Sapogonia: An Anti-Romance in 3/8 Meter*. Tempe, Ariz.: Bilingual Press/Editorial Bilingüe, 1990.

Castillo. *So Far From God*. New York: Norton, 1993.

Chacón, Eusebio. *El hijo de la tempestad / Tras la tormenta la calma: Dos novelitas originales*. Santa Fe: El Boletín Popular, 1892.

Chambers, María Cristina [Mena]. *Boy Heroes of Chapultepec: A Story of the Mexican War*. Philadelphia: Winston, 1953.

Chambers. *The Bullfighter's Son*. London & New York: Oxford University Press, 1944.

Chambers. *The Three Kings*. New York: Oxford University Press, 1946.

Chambers. *The Two Eagles*. London & New York: Oxford University Press, 1943.

Chambers. *The Water Carrier's Secrets*. London & New York: Oxford University Press, 1942.

Chávez, Denise. *Face of an Angel*. New York: Farrar, Straus & Giroux, 1994.

Chávez. *The Last of the Menu Girls*. Houston: Arte Público, 1986.

Chávez, Fray Angélico. *La Conquistadora: The Autobiography of an Ancient Statue*. Paterson, N.J.: St. Anthony Guild, 1954.

Chávez. *The Lady From Toledo*. Fresno, Cal.: Academy Guild, 1960.

Cisneros, Sandra. *The House on Mango Street*. Houston: Arte Público, 1983. Translated into Spanish by Elena Poniatowska as *La Casa en Mango Street*. New York: Vintage, 1994.

Corpi, Lucha. *Cactus Blood: A Mystery Novel*. Houston: Arte Público, 1995.

Corpi. *Delia's Song*. Houston: Arte Público, 1989.

Corpi. *Eulogy for a Brown Angel: A Mystery Novel*. Houston: Arte Público, 1992.

Corpi. *Where Fireflies Dance*. San Francisco: Children's Books Press, 1997.

Cota-Cárdenas, Margarita. *Puppet: A Chicano Novella*. Austin: Relámpago Press, 1985.

De Casas, Celso A. *Pelón Drops Out*. Berkeley, Cal.: Tonatiuh International, 1979.

De Flores, Packard J. *The Last of the Dons.* New York: Vantage, 1964.

Del Fuego, Laura. *Maravilla.* Encino, Cal.: Floricanto Press, 1989.

De la Garza, Beatriz. *Pillars of Gold and Silver.* Houston: Piñata Books, 1997.

Delgado, Abelardo. *Letters to Louise.* Berkeley, Cal.: Tonatiuh-Quinto Sol International, 1982.

Díaz, Debra. *The Red Camp.* Houston: Arte Público, 1996.

Duarte-Valdez, Octavio. *El perro.* Watsonville, Cal., 1993.

Durán, Miguel. *Don't Spit on My Corner.* Houston: Arte Público, 1992.

Elizondo, Sergio. *Muerte en una estrella.* México: Tinta Negra Editores, SA, 1984.

Elizondo. *Suruma.* El Paso: Dos Pasos, 1990.

Encinias, Miguel. *Two Lives for Oñate.* Albuquerque: University of New Mexico Press, 1997.

Escamill, Edna. *Daughter of the Mountain: Un Cuento.* San Francisco: Aunt Lute Books, 1991.

Espinosa, Aurelio Macedonio. *Conchita Argüello: Historia y novela Californiana.* New York: Macmillan, 1938.

Espinoza, Máximo. *Fronteras.* Los Angeles: Holloway House, 1980.

Fernández, Roberta. *Intaglio: A Novel in Six Stories.* Houston: Arte Público, 1990.

Flores-Williams, Jason. *The End of the West.* San Francisco: Caught Inside Press, 1996.

Flores-Williams. *The Last Stand of Mr. America.* San Francisco: Caught Inside Press, 1998.

Flores-Williams. *A Postmodern Tragedy.* Prague: Orpheus Press, 1991.

Fontes, Montserrat. *First Confession.* New York: Norton, 1991.

Fontes. *Dreams of the Centaur.* New York: Norton, 1996.

Galarza, Ernesto. *Barrio Boy.* Notre Dame, Ind.: University of Notre Dame Press, 1971.

Gallegos, Sallie. *Stone Horses.* Albuquerque: University of New Mexico Press, 1996.

García, Guy. *Obsidian Sky.* New York: Simon & Schuster, 1994.

García. *Skin Deep.* New York: Farrar, Straus, & Giroux, 1988.

García, Lionel G. *Hardscrub.* Houston: Arte Público, 1990.

García. *Leaving Home.* Houston: Arte Público, 1985.

García. *A Shroud in the Family.* Houston: Arte Público, 1987.

García. *To a Widow with Children.* Houston: Arte Público, 1994.

García Robinson, Louie. *The Devil, Delfina Varela and the Used Chevy: Which Examines Delfina Varela's Puzzling Pact With the Devil, the Plaintive Love Story of Ruiz Lopez Mondragon, and the Doomed Hispanic Political Dream of Manuel Caballos.* New York: Anchor Books, 1993.

Gilb, Dagoberto. *The Last Known Residence of Mickey Acuña.* New York: Grove, 1994.

Gómez-Peña, Guillermo. *Friendly Cannibals.* San Francisco: Artspace Books, 1996.

Gonzales, Laurence. *Jambeaux.* New York: Harcourt Brace Jovanovich, 1979.

Gonzales. *The Last Deal.* New York: Atheneum, 1981.

Gonzales. *The Still Point.* Fayetteville: University of Arkansas Press, 1989.

Gonzales. *El Vago.* New York: Atheneum, 1983.

Gonzales-Berry, Erlinda. *Paletitas de guayaba.* Albuquerque: El Norte Publications, 1991.

Gonzales-Bertrand, Diane. *Alicia's Treasure.* Houston: Arte Público/Piñata Books, 1996.

Gonzales-Bertrand. *Sweet Fifteen.* Houston: Arte Público/Piñata Books, 1995.

González, Genaro. *Rainbow's End.* Houston: Arte Público, 1988.

González de Mireles, Jovita. *Dew on the Thorn.* Edited by José E. Limón. Houston: Arte Público, 1997.

González de Mireles and Eve Raleigh. *Caballero: A Historical Novel.* Edited by José E. Limón and María Cotera. College Station: Texas A&M University Press, 1996.

Grattan-Domínguez, Alejandro. *The Dark Side of the Dream.* Houston: Arte Público, 1995.

Griego, Alfonso. *Panchita: A Romantic Adventure of a Young Girl's Climb From Rags to Riches Through Honesty and Faith in God.* Albuquerque: A. V. Griego, 1987.

Hinosoja-Smith, Rolando. *Becky and Her Friends.* Houston: Arte Público, 1990. Translated as *Los amigos de Becky.* Houston: Arte Público, 1991.

Hinosoja-Smith. *Claros varones de Belken / Fair Gentlemen of Belken County.* Translated by Julia Cruz. Tempe, Ariz.: Bilingual Press/Editorial Bilingüe, 1986.

Hinosoja-Smith. *Estampas del valle y otras obras / Sketches of the Valley and Other Works.* Translated by Gustavo Valadez and José Reyna. Berkeley, Cal.: Quinto Sol Publications, 1973. Republished as *The Valley: A Recreation on Narrative Prose of a Portfolio of Etchings, Engravings, Sketches, and Silhouettes by Various Artists in Various Styles, Plus a Set of Photographs from a Family Album.* Ypsilanti, Mich.: Bilingual Press/Editorial Bilingüe 1983.

Hinosoja-Smith. *Klail City y sus alrededores.* Havana, Cuba: Casa de las Américas, 1976. Republished in a bilingual edition as *Generaciones y semblanzas.* Translated by Rosaura Sánchez. Berkeley, Cal.: Editorial Justa Publications, 1977. Republished and translated by Rolando Hinojosa-Smith as *Klail City.* Houston: Arte Público, 1987. Republished as *El condado de Belken–Klail City.* Tempe, Ariz.: Bilingual Press/Editorial Bilingüe, 1993.

Hinosoja-Smith. *Mi querido Rafa.* Houston: Arte Público, 1981. Revised and translated by Hinosoja-Smith as *Dear Rafe.* Houston: Arte Público, 1985.

Hinosoja-Smith. *Partners in Crime: A Rafe Buenrostro Mystery.* Houston: Arte Público, 1985.

Hinosoja-Smith. *Rites and Witnesses: A Comedy*. Houston: Arte Público, 1982.

Hinosoja-Smith. *The Useless Servants*. Houston: Arte Público, 1993.

Hinosoja-Smith, trans. *This Migrant Earth*. By Tomás Rivera. Houston: Arte Público, 1987.

Islas, Arturo. *Migrant Souls*. New York: Morrow, 1990.

Islas. *La Mollie and the King of Tears*. Edited by Paul Skenazy. Albuquerque: University of New Mexico Press, 1996.

Islas. *The Rain God: A Desert Tale*. Palo Alto, Cal.: Alexandrian Press, 1984.

Jaramillo, Cleofas M. *Romance of a Little Village Girl*. San Antonio: Naylor, 1955.

Jaramillo, Stephan. *Going Postal*. New York: Berkley Publishing Group, 1997.

Jiménez, Francisco. *La mariposa*. Boston: Houghton Mifflin, 1998.

Juárez, Tina. *Call No Man Master*. Houston: Arte Público, 1995.

Juárez. *South Wind Come*. Houston: Arte Público, 1998.

Lachtman, Ofelia Dumas. *Call Me Consuelo*. Houston: Arte Público, 1997.

Lachtman. *The Girl from Playa Blanca*. Houston: Arte Público/Piñata Books, 1995.

Lachtman. *Leticia's Secret*. Houston: Arte Público/Piñata Books, 1997.

Lachtman. *A Shell for Angela*. Houston: Arte Público/Piñata Books, 1996.

Limón, Graciela. *The Day of the Moon*. Houston: Arte Público, 1999.

Limón. *In Search of Bernabé*. Houston: Arte Público, 1993. Translated into Spanish by Miguel Angel Aparicio as *En busca de Bernabé*. Houston: Arte Público, 1997.

Limón. *María de Belén: The Autobiography of an Indian Woman*. New York: Vantage, 1990.

Limón. *The Memories of Ana Calderón*. Houston: Arte Público, 1994.

Limón. *Song of the Hummingbird*. Houston: Arte Público, 1996.

Limón, Martin. *Buddha's Money*. New York: Bantam, 1998.

Limón. *Jade Lady Burning*. New York: Soho, 1992.

Limón. *Slicky Boys*. New York: Bantam, 1997.

López, Tomás. *The Aguila Family*. Sacramento, Cal.: Mexican-American Press, 1980.

López. *Chicano Go Home!: The Life of Alfonso Rodríguez*. Hicksville, N.Y.: Exposition Press, 1976.

López-Medina, Sylvia. *Cantora*. Albuquerque: University of New Mexico Press, 1992.

López-Medina. *Siguiriya*. New York: HarperCollins, 1997.

Martínez, Demetria. *MotherTongue*. Tempe, Ariz.: Bilingual Press/Editorial Bilingüe, 1994.

Martínez, Eliud. *Voice-Haunted Journey*. Tempe, Ariz.: Bilingual Press/Editorial Bilingüe, 1990.

Martínez, Floyd. *Spirits of the High Mesa*. Houston: Arte Público/Piñata Books, 1997.

Martínez, Max. *Layover*. Houston: Arte Público, 1997.

Martínez. *A Red Bikini Dream*. Houston: Arte Público, 1990.

Martínez. *Schoolland*. Houston: Arte Público, 1988.

Martínez. *White Leg*. Houston: Arte Público, 1996.

Martínez, Ricardo A. *The Healing Ritual*. Berkeley, Cal.: Tonatiuh-Quinto Sol International, 1983.

Martínez, Víctor. *A Parrot in the Oven: Mi Vida*. New York: HarperCollins, 1996.

Medina, Robert C. *Fabián no se muere: Novela de Amor*. Las Cruces, N.Mex.: Bilingüe Publications, 1978.

Medina. *Two Ranges*. Las Cruces, N.Mex.: Bronson Printing, 1974.

Meléndez, Rudolph R. *Pachuco Mark*. New York: Grossmont Press, 1976.

Méndez M., Miguel. *Peregrinos de Aztlán*. Tucson, Ariz.: Editorial Peregrinos, 1974. Translated by David William Foster as *Pilgrims in Aztlán*. Tempe, Ariz.: Bilingual Press/Editorial Bilingüe, 1992.

Méndez M. *El sueño de Santa María de las Piedras*. Guadalajara, Jalisco, Mexico: Universidad de Guadalajara, 1986. Translated by David William Foster as *The Dream of Santa Maria de las Piedras*. Tempe, Ariz.: Bilingual Press/Editorial Bilingüe, 1989.

Monreal, David Nava. *Cinco de Mayo: An Epic Novel*. Encino, Cal.: Floricanto Press, 1993.

Mora, Pat. *Tomás and the Library Lady*. New York: Knopf, 1997.

Morales, Alejandro. *The Brick People*. Houston: Arte Público, 1988.

Morales. *Caras viejas y vino nuevo*. México, D. F.: Joaquín Mortiz, 1975. Translated by Max Martínez as *Old Faces and New Wine*. San Diego: Maize Press, 1981. Translated by Francisco A. Lomelí as *Barrio on the Edge*. Tempe, Ariz.: Bilingual Press/Editorial Bilingüe, 1998.

Morales. *The Rag Doll Plagues*. Houston: Arte Público, 1992.

Morales. *Reto en el paraíso*. Ypsilanti, Mich.: Bilingual Press/Editorial Bilingüe, 1983.

Morales. *La verdad sin voz*. México, D. F.: Joaquín Mortiz, 1979. Translated by Judith Ginsberg as *Death of an Anglo*. Tempe, Ariz.: Bilingual Press/Editorial Bilingüe, 1988.

Murray, Yxta Maya. *Locas*. New York: Grove, 1997.

Nava, Michael. *The Burning Plain*. New York: Putnam, 1997.

Nava. *The Death of Friends*. New York: Putnam, 1996.

Nava. *Golden Boy.* Boston: Alyson Publications, 1988.

Nava. *The Hidden Law.* New York: HarperCollins, 1992.

Nava. *How Town: A Novel of Suspense.* New York: Harper & Row, 1990.

Nava. *The Little Death.* Boston: Alyson Publications, 1986.

Nava, ed. *Finale.* Boston: Alyson Publications, 1989.

Niggli, Josephina. *Mexican Village.* Chapel Hill: University of North Carolina Press, 1945. Selections published as *Un pueblo mexicano.* Translated and edited by Justina Ruiz-de-Conde. New York: Norton, 1949.

Niggli. *A Miracle for Mexico.* Greenwich, Conn.: New York Graphic Society Publishers, 1964.

Niggli. *Step Down, Elder Brother.* New York: Rinehart, 1947.

Ornelas, Berta. *Come Down from the Mound.* Phoenix: Miter Publishing, 1975.

Ortiz y Pino III, José. *Curandero: A Cuento.* Santa Fe: Sunstone Press, 1983.

Ortiz y Pino III. *Don José, the Last Patrón.* Santa Fe: Sunstone Press, 1981.

Ortiz Taylor, Sheila. *Coachella.* Albuquerque: University of New Mexico Press, 1998.

Ortiz Taylor. *Faultline.* Tallahassee, Fla.: Naiad Press, 1982.

Ortiz Taylor. *Slow Dancing at Miss Polly's.* Tallahassee, Fla.: Naiad Press, 1989.

Ortiz Taylor. *Southbound: A Sequel to Faultline.* Tallahassee, Fla.: Naiad Press, 1990.

Ortiz Taylor. *Spring Forward, Fall Back.* Tallahassee, Fla.: Naiad Press, 1985.

Paredes, Américo. *George Washington Gómez: A Mexicotexan Novel.* Houston: Arte Público, 1990.

Paredes. *The Shadow.* Houston: Arte Público, 1998.

de la Peña, Terri. *Faults.* Los Angeles: Alyson Books, 1999.

de la Peña. *Latin Satins.* Seattle: Seal Press, 1994.

de la Peña. *Margins.* Seattle: Seal Press, 1992. Republished as *Chicana Blues.* Berlin, Germany: Krug & Schadenberg, 1994.

Pérez, Emma. *Gulf Dreams.* Berkeley, Cal.: Third Woman Press, 1996.

Pérez, Luis. *El Coyote, The Rebel.* New York: Holt, 1947.

Pérez. *The Girls of the Pink Feather.* North Hollywood, Cal.: Frimac Publications, 1963.

Pimentel, Ricardo. *House With Two Doors.* Tempe, Ariz.: Bilingual Press/Editorial Bilingüe, 1997.

Pineda, Cecile. *Face.* New York: Viking, 1985.

Pineda. *Frieze*. New York: Viking, 1986.

Pineda. *The Love Queen of the Amazon*. New York: Little, Brown, 1992.

Ponce, Mary Helen. *The Wedding*. Houston: Arte Público, 1989.

Portillo Trambley, Estela. *Trini*. Binghamton, N.Y.: Bilingual Press/Editorial Bilingüe, 1986.

Quintana Ranck, Katherine. *Portrait of Doña Elena*. Berkeley, Cal.: Tonatiuh-Quinto Sol International, 1982.

Ramírez, Sharon. *Brinktown*. Chapel Hill, N.C.: Carolina Wren Press, 1981.

Ramos, Manuel. *The Ballad of Gato Guerrero*. New York: St. Martin's Press, 1994.

Ramos. *The Ballad of Rocky Ruiz*. New York: St. Martin's Press, 1993.

Ramos. *Blues for the Buffalo*. New York: St. Martin's Press, 1997.

Ramos. *The Last Client of Luis Montez*. New York: St. Martin's Press, 1996.

Rechy, John. *Bodies and Souls*. New York: Carroll & Graf, 1983.

Rechy. *City of Night*. New York: Grove, 1963.

Rechy. *The Fourth Angel*. New York: Viking, 1972.

Rechy. *Marilyn's Daughter*. New York: Carroll & Graf, 1988.

Rechy. *The Miraculous Day of Amalia Gómez*. New York: Arcade Publishing, 1991.

Rechy. *Numbers*. New York: Grove, 1967.

Rechy. *Our Lady of Babylon*. New York: Arcade Publishing, 1996.

Rechy. *Rushes*. New York: Grove, 1979.

Rechy. *This Day's Death*. New York: Grove, 1969.

Rechy. *The Vampires*. New York: Grove, 1971.

Rico, Armando B. *Three Coffins for Niño Lencho*. Berkeley, Cal.: Tonatiuh-Quinto Sol International, 1984.

Ríos, Isabella. *Victuum*. Ventura, Cal.: Diana-Etna, 1976.

Rivera, Rick P. *A Fabricated Mexican*. Houston: Arte Público, 1995.

Rivera, Tomás. *". . . y no se lo tragó la tierra" / ". . . And The Earth Did Not Part."* Translated by Herminio Ríos-C. Berkeley, Cal.: Quinto Sol Publications, 1971.

Rodríguez, Dennis. *Pachuco*. Los Angeles: Holloway Publishing, 1980.

Rodríguez, Luis J. *América Is Her Name*. Willimantic, Conn.: Curbstone Press, 1996. Translated into Spanish by Tino Villanueva as *La llaman América*. Willimantic, Conn.: Curbstone Press, 1996.

Rodríguez. *It Doesn't Have to Be This Way: A Barrio Story*. San Francisco: Children's Book Press, 1999.

Rodríguez, Joe D. *Oddsplayer*. Houston: Arte Público, 1989.

Romero, Danny. *Calle 10*. San Francisco: Mercury House, 1996.

Romero, Orlando. *Nambé–Year One*. Berkeley, Cal.: Tonatiuh International, 1976.

Ruíz, Reynaldo, ed. *Encuentro con Estanislao Eckermann*. Summerville, N.J.: SLUSA Press, 1989.

Ruíz, Ronald L. *Giuseppe Rocco*. Houston: Arte Público, 1998.

Ruíz. *Happy Birthday Jesús*. Houston: Arte Público, 1994.

Ruíz de Burton, María Amparo, as C. Loyal. *The Squatter and the Don: A Novel Descriptive of Contemporary Occurrences in California*. San Francisco: Samuel Carson, 1885. Republished, edited by Rosaura Sánchez and Beatrice Pita. Houston: Arte Público, 1992.

Ruíz de Burton. *Who Would Have Thought It?* Philadelphia: Lippincott, 1872. Republished, edited by Rosaura Sánchez and Beatrice Pita. Houston: Arte Público, 1995.

Sáenz, Benjamin Alire. *Carry Me Like Water*. New York: Hyperion, 1995.

Sáenz. *The House of Forgetting*. New York: HarperCollins, 1997.

Salas, Floyd. *Lay My Body on the Line*. Berkeley, Cal.: Y'Bird, 1978.

Salas. *State of Emergency*. Houston: Arte Público, 1996.

Salas. *Tattoo the Wicked Cross*. New York: Grove, 1967.

Salas. *What Now My Love?* New York: Grove, 1969.

Sálaz-Márquez, Rubén [Rubén Darío Sálaz]. *I am Tecumseh!: Book 1*. Albuquerque: Fine Line, 1980.

Sálaz-Márquez. *I Am Tecumseh!: Book 2*. Albuquerque: Cosmic House, 1985.

Sánchez, Joseph P. *The Aztec Chronicles: The True History of Christopher Columbus, as Narrated by Quilaztli of Texcoco*. Berkeley, Cal.: Tonatiuh-Quinto Sol International, 1995.

Sánchez, Phil. *Don Phil-O-Meno si la Mancha*. Alamosa, Colo.: Phil Sánchez, 1977.

Santos, E. D. *On the Road, Too. . . .* Hondo, Tex.: La Sombra Publishing, 1986.

Soto, Gary. *Boys at Work*. New York: Delacorte, 1995.

Soto. *Buried Onions*. San Diego: Harcourt Brace, 1997.

Soto. *Crazy Weekend*. New York: Scholastic Press, 1994.

Soto. *Jesse*. San Diego: Harcourt Brace, 1994.

Soto. *Off and Running*. New York: Delacorte, 1996.

Soto. *Pacific Crossing*. San Diego: Harcourt Brace Jovanovich, 1992.

Soto. *The Pool Party*. New York: Delacorte, 1993.

Soto. *The Skirt*. New York: Delacorte, 1992.

Soto. *Snapshots from the Wedding*. New York: Putnam, 1996.

Soto. *Summer on Wheels*. New York: Scholastic Press, 1995.

Soto. *Taking Sides*. San Diego: Harcourt Brace Jovanovich, 1991.

Tenorio, Arthur. *Blessing From Above*. Las Vegas, N.Mex.: West Las Vegas Schools' Press, 1971.

Torres-Metzgar, Joseph V. *Below the Summit*. Berkeley, Cal.: Tonatiuh International, Inc., 1976.

Trujillo, Charley. *Dogs From Illusion*. San Jose: Chusma House Publications, 1994.

Urrea, Luis Alberto. *In Search of Snow*. New York: HarperCollins, 1994.

Valdés, Gina. *There Are No Madmen Here*. Edited by Herbert Espinoza and others. San Diego: Maize Press, 1981.

Vásquez, Diego. *Growing Through the Ugly*. New York: Norton, 1997.

Vásquez, Richard. *Another Land*. New York: Avon, 1982.

Vásquez. *Chicano*. Garden City, New York: Doubleday, 1970.

Vásquez. *The Giant Killer*. New York: Manor Books, 1978.

Véa, Alfredo Jr. *Gods Go Begging*. New York: Dutton, 1999.

Vea. *La Maravilla*. New York: Dutton, 1993.

Véa. *The Silver Cloud Café*. New York: Dutton, 1996.

Velásquez, Gloria. *Juanita Fights the School Board*. Houston: Arte Público/Piñata Books, 1994.

Velásquez. *Maya's Divided World*. Houston: Arte Público/Piñata Books, 1995.

Velásquez. *Tommy Stands Alone*. Houston: Arte Público/Piñata Books, 1995.

Venegas, Daniel. *Las aventuras de Don Chipote, o, cuando los pericos mamen*. Mexico City: Secretaría de Educación Pública, 1984.

Villanueva, Alma Luz. *Naked Ladies*. Tempe, Ariz.: Bilingual Press/Editorial Bilingüe, 1994.

Villanueva. *The Ultraviolet Sky*. Tempe, Ariz.: Bilingual Press/Editorial Bilingüe, 1988.

Villarreal, José. *Out of the Wilderness*. Denver: Opus Dei Press, 1969.

Villarreal, José Antonio. *Clemente Chacón*. Binghamton, N.Y.: Bilingual Press/Editorial Bilingüe, 1984.

Villarreal. *The Fifth Horseman*. Garden City, N.Y.: Doubleday, 1974.

Villarreal. *Pocho*. Garden City, N.Y.: Doubleday, 1959.

Villarreal, Rosa Martha. *Doctor Magdalena*. Berkeley, Cal.: TQS Publications, 1995.

Villaseñor, Victor. *Macho!* New York: Bantam, 1973.

Viramontes, Helena María. *Under the Feet of Jesus*. New York: Dutton, 1995.

Ybarra, Ricardo Means. *Brotherhood of Dolphins*. Houston: Arte Público, 1997.

Ybarra. *The Pink Rosary*. Pittsburgh: Latin American Literary Review Press, 1993.

Younis, Vincent. *Shine Boys: A Story about Santa Fe*. Taos, N.Mex.: Blinking Yellow Books, 1995.

## POETRY

Adame, Leonard. *Cantos pa' la memoria*. San Jose: Mango Publications, 1979.

Adame, Omar Salinas, Gary Soto, and Ernesto Trejo. *4 Entrance: Chicano Poets*. New York: Greenfield Review Press, 1975.

Aguila, Pancho. *Anti-gravity*. Berkeley, Cal.: Aldebaran Review, 1976.

Aguila. *Clash*. San Francisco: Poetry for the People, 1980.

Aguila. *Dark Smoke: Poems*. San Francisco: Second Coming Press, 1977.

Aguila. *11 Poems*. San Jose: Mango Publications, 1977.

Aguilar Melantzón, Ricardo. *Caravana enlutada*. Mexico City: Pájaro Cascabel, 1975.

Aguilar. *En son de la lluvia*. Mexico City: Editorial Trasterra, 1980.

Aguilar-Henson, Marcella. *Figura cristalina*. San Antonio: M & A Editions, 1983.

Alarcón, Francisco X. *Body in Flames / Cuerpo en llamas*. Translated by Francisco Aragón. San Francisco: Chronicle Books, 1990.

Alarcón. *De amor obscuro / Of Dark Love*. Translated by Francisco Aragón. Santa Cruz, Cal.: Moving Parts Press, 1991.

Alarcón. *From the Bellybutton of the Moon and Other Summer Poems / Del ombligo de la luna y otros poemas de verano*. San Francisco: Children's Book Press, 1998.

Alarcón. *Laughing Tomatoes and Other Spring Poems / Jitomates risueños y otros poemas de primavera*. San Francisco: Children's Book Press, 1997.

Alarcón. *Lomo Prieta*. Santa Cruz, Cal.: We Press, 1990.

Alarcón. *No Golden Gate for Us*. Santa Fe: Pennywhistle Press, 1993.

Alarcón. *Poemas zurdos*. Naucalpan de Juárez, Estado de México: Editorial Factor, 1992.

Alarcón. *Quake Poems*. Santa Cruz, Cal.: We Press, 1989.

Alarcón. *Snake Poems: An Aztec Invocation*. San Francisco: Chronicle Books, 1992.

Alarcón. *Tattoos*. Oakland, Cal.: Nomad Press, 1985.

Alarcón, Rodrigo Reyes, and Juan Pablo Gutiérrez. *Ya vas, Carnal*. San Francisco: Humanizarte, 1985.

Alarcón, and Lorna Dee Cervantes, eds. *Chicanos y Chicanas en diálogo*. Santa Cruz: Porter College/University of California, Santa Cruz, 1989.

Alarcón, Justo S. *Poemas en mí menor*. Mexico: Alta Pimería Pro Arte y Cultura, 1991.

Alurista. *A'nque*. San Diego: Maize Publications, 1979.

Alurista. *Et tú . . . Raza?* Tempe, Ariz.: Bilingual Press/Editorial Bilingüe, 1996.

Alurista. *Floricanto en Aztlán*. Los Angeles: Chicano Studies Center of UCLA, 1971.

Alurista. *Nationchild Plumaroja, 1969–1972*. San Diego: Toltecas en Aztlán, Centro Cultural de La Raza, 1972.

Alurista. *Return: Poems Collected and New*. Ypsilanti, Mich.: Bilingual Press/Editorial Bilingüe, 1982.

Alurista. *Spik in Glyph?* Houston: Arte Público, 1981.

Alurista. *Timespace Huracán: Poems, 1972–1975*. Albuquerque: Pajarito Publications, 1976.

Alurista. *Tremble Purple: Seven Poems*. Oakland, Cal.: Unity Publications, 1987.

Alurista. *Z Eros*. Tempe, Ariz.: Bilingual Press/Editorial Bilingüe, 1995.

Alurista, and others, eds. *Trece Aliens: Chicano Poetry Anthology*. Austin: Casa Publications, 1978.

Alvarado de Ricord, Elise, Lucha Corpi, and Concha Michel. *Fireflight: Three Latin American Poets*. Translated by Catherine Rodríguez-Nieto. Berkeley, Cal.: Oyez Press, 1976.

Anaya, Rudolfo A. *The Adventures of Juan Chicaspatas*. Houston: Arte Público, 1985.

Arellano, Anselmo, ed. *Los pobladores nuevo mexicanos y su poesía, 1889–1950*. Albuquerque: Pajarito Publications, 1976.

Arellano, Juan Estevan. *Palabras de la vista / Retratos de la pluma: memorias*. Albuquerque: Academia Publications, 1984.

Arteaga, Alfred. *Cantos*. San Jose: Chusma House Publications, 1991.

Artola-Allen, Adela, and Marco Antonio Jerez. *Lágrimas Chicanas: Haikus trágicos*. Tucson: University of Arizona Mexican American Studies & Research Center, 1982.

Baca, Jimmy Santiago. *Black Mesa Poems*. New York: New Directions, 1989.

Baca. *Immigrants in Our Own Land*. Baton Rouge: Louisiana State University Press, 1979. Reprinted as *Immigrants in Our Own Land and Selected Early Poems*. New York: New Directions, 1990.

Baca. *Jimmy Santiago Baca*. Santa Barbara, Cal.: Mudborn Press, 1978.

Baca. *Martin & Meditations on the South Valley*. New York: New Directions, 1987.

Baca. *Poems Taken from My Yard*. Fulton, Mo.: Timberline Press, 1986.

Baca. *Swords of Darkness*. San Jose: Mango Publications, 1981.

Baca. *What's Happening*. Willimantic, Conn.: Curbstone Press, 1982.

Badikian, Beatriz. *Akewa is a Woman*. Chicago, Ill.: MARCH/Abrazo Press, 1982.

Baptiste, Víctor N. *Unos pasos*. Hollywood, Cal.: Ediciones de la Frontera, 1968.

Barrios, Gregg. *Puro rollo (a colores)*. Los Angeles: Posada Press, 1982.

Beltrán, Carmen Celia. *Remanso lírico*. Privately Published, n.d.

Benavídez, Max. *The Stopping of Sorrow*. Santa Monica, Cal.: Momentum Press, 1985.

Bernal, Juan Manuel. *Diaridad*. N.p.: n.d.

Bernal. *La cocina en huelga de hambre / The Kitchen on a Hunger Strike*. N.p., 1987.

Bernal, Vicente J. *Las primicias*. Dubuque, Iowa: Telegraph-Herald, 1916.

Blea, Irene I. *Celebrating, Crying and Cursing*. Pueblo, Colo.: Pueblo Poetry Project, 1980.

Blea. *Damn, Sam I Want to Share My Life But I Need to Be Alone: Poetry*. Denver: Baculite Publishing, 1989.

Bobian, Arturo Silvano, David García, and Roberto "Chips" Portales. *And This Is What We Said*. Lubbock, Tex.: Trucha Publications, 1975.

Bornstein, Miriam. *Bajo cubierta*. Tucson, Ariz.: Scorpion Press, 1976.

Bornstein. *Donde empieza la historia*. Sacramento, Cal.: Spanish Press, 1993.

Bruce-Novoa, Juan. *Inocencia perversa / Perverse Innocence*. Phoenix: Baleen Press, 1977.

Burciaga, José Antonio. *Drink Cultura Refrescante*. San Jose: Mango Publications, 1979.

Burciaga. *Restless Serpents: Poetry and Drawings*. Menlo Park, Cal.: Diseños literarios, 1976.

Burciaga. *Undocumented Love /Amor Indocumentado: A Personal Anthology of Poetry*. San Jose: Chusma House Publications, 1992.

Burciaga and Emy López. *Versos para Centroamérica*. Menlo Park, Cal.: Diseños Literarios, 1981.

Burk, Ronnie. *En el Jardín de los Nopales: Poems 1976–1977*. San Jose: Mango Publications, 1979. Revised, San Antonio: Ganesha Head Stand, 1983.

Burk. *Father of Reason, Daughter of Doubt*. San Francisco: Saturn's Clock, 1996.

Burk. *Indios Verdes*. San Francisco: Centaur Productions, 1998.

Burk. *Man-Of-War*. San Francisco: Hekate's Gallery, 1999.

Burk. *Mutations*. San Francisco: Centaur Productions, 1998.

Cabello-Argandoña, Roberto. *Cinco de Mayo: A Symbol of Mexican Resistance*. Edited and translated by Luis A. Torres. Encino, Cal.: Floricanto Press, 1993.

Campbell, Roberto. *Poems From My Notebook*. San Antonio: M & A Editions, 1978.

Calderón, Tomás M. *Think of This Situation*. Santa Barbara, Cal.: Alternative Press, 1977.

Candelaria, Cordelia. *Arroyos to the Heart*. Santa Monica, Cal.: Santa Monica College Press, 1993.

Candelaria. *Ojo de la cueva / Cave Springs*. Colorado Springs, Colo.: Maize Press, 1984.

Cantú, Reynaldo. *Being a Thing in Drunken Time*. Santa Fe: Sleeping Fox Enterprises, 1974.

Carrasco, José A. *Thoughts Wander Thru. . . . and Other Verse to Linger Too*. Menlo Park, Cal.: Markgraf Publications Group, 1989.

Cárdenas, Reyes. *Anti-Bicicleta Haiku*. San Antonio: Caracol, 1976.

Cárdenas. *Chicano Territory*. Seguin, Tex.: Rifan, 1975.

Cárdenas. *I Was Never a Militant Chicano*. Austin: Relámpago, 1986.

Cárdenas. *Survivors of the Chicano Titanic*. Austin: Place of Herons, 1984.

Carlson, Lori M., ed. *Cool Salsa: Bilingual Poems on Growing Up Latino in the United States*. New York: Holt, 1994.

Castaño, Wilfredo Q. *Small Stones Cast Upon the Tender Earth*. San Francisco: Second Coming Press, 1981.

Castellano, Olivia. *Blue Horse of Madness*. Sacramento, Cal.: Crystal Clear Printers, 1983.

Castellano. *Blue Mandolin, Yellow Fever*. Berkeley, Cal.: Tonatiuh-Quinto Sol International, 1980.

Castellano. *Spaces that Time Missed*. Sacramento, Cal.: Crystal Clear Printers, 1986.

Castillo, Ana. *I Close My Eyes (To See)*. Pullman: Washington State University, 1976.

Castillo. *The Invitation*. Chicago, 1979. Revised edition, San Francisco: La Raza Graphics, 1986.

Castillo. *My Father Was a Toltec*. Novato, Cal.: West End Press, 1988. Revised as *My Father Was a Toltec and Selected Poems 1973–1988*. New York: Norton, 1995.

Castillo. *Otro canto*. Chicago: Alternativa Publications, 1977.

Castillo. *Women Are Not Roses*. Houston: Arte Público, 1984.

Catacalos, Rosemary. *Again For the First Time*. Santa Fe: Tooth of Time, 1984.

Catacalos. *As Long as it Takes*. Springfield, Mo.: Iguana, 1984.

Cervantes, Irma H. *The Gifts*. Scottsdale, Ariz.: Five Windmills, 1984.

Cervantes. *Sparks, Flames, and Cinders*. Scottsdale, Ariz.: Five Windmills, 1982.

Cervantes. *Wings of Love: Poetry*. Scottsdale, Ariz.: Five Windmills, 1984.

Cervantes, Lorna Dee. *Emplumada.* Pittsburgh: University of Pittsburgh Press, 1981.

Cervantes. *From the Cables of Genocide: Poems of Love and Hunger.* Houston: Arte Público, 1991.

Chacón, Felipe Maximiliano. *Obras de Felipe Maximiliano Chacón, "El Cantor Mexicano": Poesía y prosa.* Albuquerque: Felipe M. Chacón, 1924.

Chávez, Fray Angélico. *Clothed With the Sun.* Santa Fe: Writer's Editions, 1939.

Chávez. *Eleven Lady-Lyrics, and Other Poems.* Paterson, N.J.: St. Anthony Guild, 1945.

Chávez. *Selected Poems: With an Apologia.* Santa Fe: Press of the Territorian, 1969.

Chávez. *The Single Rose; the Rose Unica and Commentary of Fray Manuel de Santa Clara.* Santa Fe: Los Santos Bookshop, 1948.

Chávez. *The Virgin of Port Lligat.* Fresno, Cal.: Academy Library Guild, 1959.

Chávez, Mario. *When it Rains in Cloves.* San Jose: Mango Publications, [1980].

Cisneros, Sandra. *Bad Boys.* San Jose: Mango Publications, 1980.

Cisneros. *Loose Woman.* New York: Knopf/Random House, 1994.

Cisneros. *My Wicked, Wicked Ways.* Bloomington, Ind.: Third Woman Press, 1987.

Corpi, Lucha. *Palabras de mediodía / Noon Words.* Translated by Catherine Rodríguez-Nieto. Berkeley, Cal.: El Fuego de Aztlán Publications, 1980.

Corpi. *Variaciones sobre una tempestad / Variations on a Storm.* Translated by Catherine Rodríguez-Nieto. Berkeley, Cal.: Third Woman Press, 1990.

Cortéz, Carlos. *Crystal-Gazing the Amber Fluid & Other Wobbly Poems.* Chicago: Charles H. Kerr, 1990.

Cortéz. *De Kansas a Califas & Back to Chicago: Poems & Art.* Chicago: MARCH/Abrazo Press, 1992.

Cortéz. *Where Are the Voices? & Other Wobbly Poems.* Chicago: Charles H. Kerr, 1997.

Cota-Cárdenas, Margarita. *Marchitas de mayo (Sones pa'l pueblo): poesia chicana.* Austin: Relámpago Books, 1989.

Cota-Cárdenas. *Noches despertando in conciencias.* Tucson, Ariz.: Scorpion Press, 1977.

Cuadros, Gil. *City of God.* San Francisco: City Lights, 1994.

Cuéllar Ximénez, Ben. *Gallant OutCasts.* San Antonio: Naylor, 1963.

Cuervoazul. *Earth Spirit:* N.p.: Cristal Clear Printers, 1983.

Cumpián, Carlos. *Armadillo Charm.* Chicago: Tía Chucha Press, 1996.

Cumpián. *Coyote Sun.* Chicago: MARCH/Abrazo Press, 1990.

Cumpián. *Latino Rainbow: Poems about Latino Americans.* Chicago: Childrens Press, 1994.

Curiel, Barbara Brinson, as Bárbara Brinson-Pineda. *Nocturno.* Berkeley: University of California, Chicano Studies, 1978.

Curiel. *Speak to Me From Dreams.* Berkeley, Cal.: Third Woman Press, 1989.

Curiel, as Bárbara Brinson-Pineda. *Vocabulary of the Dead.* Oakland, Cal.: Nomad Press, 1984.

De France, Gary. *Seascapes.* San Jose: Mango Publications, 1979.

De la Junta, Paco. *1983 Chicano Engagement Calendar: A Year of Poetry de Paco de la Junta, Frank Trujillo and Carlotta Espinoza.* Denver: Bread & Butter, 1982.

De La Torre, Alfredo. *Caracoleando: Poems.* San Antonio: M & A Editions, 1979.

De León, Nephtalí. *Chicano Poet: With Images and Visions of the Poet.* Lubbock, Tex.: Trucha Publications, 1973.

De León. *Coca-Cola Dream.* Lubbock, Tex.: Trucha Publications, 1973.

De León. *Guadalupe Blues.* San Antonio: Privately printed, 1985.

De León. *Hey, Mr. President, Man!: On the Eve of the Bicentennial.* Lubbock, Tex.: Trucha Publications, 1975.

De León. *I Color My Garden.* Shallowater, Tex.: Tri-County Housing, 1973.

De León. *I Will Catch the Sun.* Lubbock, Tex.: Trucha Publications, 1973.

Del Castillo, Ramón. *Broken Concrete: Poetry and a Short Story.* Oakland, Cal.: Unity Publications, 1988.

Del Castillo. *From the Corazón of a Bato Loco.* Denver: Rubén Sosa Villegas Publications, 1994.

Del Castillo. *When the Owl Can't See at Night.* Edited by Brenda Romero. Denver: Printed by Denver School Press, 1994.

Delgado, Abelardo. *Bajo el sol de Aztlán: 25 soles de Abelardo.* El Paso: Barrio Publications, 1973.

Delgado. *Chicano: 25 Pieces of a Chicano Mind.* Denver: Barrio Publications, 1969.

Delgado. *Here Lies Lalo: 25 Deaths of Abelardo.* Salt Lake City: Barrio Publications, 1977.

Delgado. *It's Cold: 52 Thought Poems of Abelardo.* Salt Lake City: Barrio Publications, 1974.

Delgado. *Mortal Sin Kit.* El Paso: Barrio Publications, n.d.

Delgado. *A Quilt of Words: 25 Quilts by Abelardo.* N.p.: Barrio Publications, 1976?

Delgado. *Reflexiones . . .* Lubbock, Tex.: Trucha Publications, n.d.

Delgado. *Reflexiones: 16 Reflections of Abelardo.* Salt Lake City: Barrio Publications, 1976.

Delgado. *A Thermos Bottle Full of Self Pity: 25 Bottles by Abelardo.* Arvada, Colo.: Barrio Publications, 1975?

Delgado. *Toton Caxihuitl, a Laxative: 25 Laxatives of Abelardo.* Arvada, Colo.: Barrio Publications, 1981.

Delgado. *Under the Skirt of Lady Justice: 43 Skirts of Abelardo.* Denver: Barrio Publications, 1978.

Delgado. *Unos Perros con Metralla: 25 Dogs of Abelardo*. Arvada, Colo.: Barrio Publications, 1982.

Delgado, Holly. *The Junk City Journal: Poems and Illustrations*. Albuquerque: Holly Delgado, 1977.

Delgado, Juan. *Green Web*. Athens: University of Georgia Press, 1994.

Delgado. *El Campo*. Santa Barbara, Cal.: Capra Press, 1998.

Delgado. *Working On It*. Berkeley, Cal.: Chicano Chapbook Series, 1997.

Delgado, Raymundo Perez, Ricardo Sánchez, and Juan Valdez. *Los Cuatro: Poémas y reflecciones de cuatro chicanos con alms brotando el desmadrazgo, duelo, orgullo, corage, y alegría en esto de ser hechizos de la raza de bronce . . . . más que coplas . . .* Denver: Barrio Publications, 1970.

Domínguez, Marco A. *Sol-Edad*. Los Angeles: N.p., 1981.

Durán, Roberto Tinoco. *Reality Ribs*. Tempe, Ariz.: Bilingual Review/Editorial Bilingüe, 1993.

Elizondo, Sergio. *Libro para batos y chavalas chicanas*. Translated by Edmundo García Girón. Berkeley, Cal.: Editorial Justa Publications, 1977.

Elizondo. *Perros y antiperros: una épica chicana*. Berkeley, Cal.: Quinto Sol Publications, 1972.

Estupinián, Rafael. *A Tostón: Reminiscences of a Mexican American*. San Diego: San Diego State University Press, 1973.

Fernández, Armando. *Dedicated to You*. Sacramento, Cal.: J. Rad Publications, 1985.

Flores, Gloria Amalia. *And Her Children Lived*. San Diego: Toltecas in Aztlán Publications, Centro Cultural de la Raza, 1974.

Flores, José. *Mesqui + tierra*. Albuquerque: Pajarito Publications, 1977.

Foster, C. S. *Some Poems for My People*. N.p.: El Güero Vaquetón Press, 1988.

Gaitán, Marcella T. *Chicano Themes: Manita Poetry*. Minneapolis: Chicano Studies Department, University of Minnesota, 1975.

Galarza, Ernesto. *Kodachromes in Rhyme*. Notre Dame, Ind.: University of Notre Dame, 1982.

Galarza. *Thirty Poems*. Jamaica Estates, N.Y.: Year-Long School, 1935.

Galaz, María L. *Gris*. Los Angeles: 1938.

Galván, Roberto. *Poemas en español: escritos por un méxico-americano*. San Antonio: Mexican American Cultural Center Press, 1977.

Gálvez, Javier. *Encanto Chicano*. Claremont, Cal.: 1971.

Gallegos, Robert. *Amador*. Grants, N.Mex.: Vanadium Partners Research, 1980.

Gallegos, and Jim Sayre. *Carnero*. Thoreau, N.Mex.: Carol Sayre Gallery, n.d.

Gamboa, Manuel. *Born into a Felony*. Syracuse, N.Y.: Pulp Art Forms Unlimited, 1977.

Gamboa. *Divergencias.* Boulder, Colo.: Backstage Books, 1976.

Gamboa, Reymundo. *Madrugada del '56 / Morning of '56: Selected Poems.* La Jolla, Cal.: Lalo Publications, 1978.

Gamboa, and Ernesto Padilla. *The Baby Chook and Other Remnants: Selected Poems.* Tempe, Ariz.: Other Voices, 1976.

García, Arnoldo. *Un macehual en Madrid.* Seattle: Editorial Ce Atl, 1981.

García, José Inés. *Castillos en el aire.* Trinidad, Colo.: El Faro Press, 1925.

García. *Dedicatoria monumental a Don Francisco Durán y María Dolores Durán a los 66 años de Casados, Weston, Colorado.* Trinidad, Colo.: El Faro Press, 1932

García. *¡Sería rata!* Trinidad, Colo.: El Faro, 1930.

García. *El sombrero es pagador.* Trinidad, Colo.: El Faro Press, n.d.

García, Luis. *Beans.* N.p.: Oyez, 1976.

García. *The Mechanic.* N.p.: White Rabbit Press, 1970.

García. *Mister Menu.* San Francisco: Kayak, 1968.

García. *Two Pears.* N.p.: House of Four Press, 1982.

García, Richard. *The Flying Garcías.* Pittsburgh: University of Pittsburgh Press, 1993.

García. *Selected Poetry.* Berkeley, Cal.: Quinto Sol Publications, 1973.

García-Camarillo, Cecilio. *Black Horse on a Hill.* Albuquerque: Mano Izquierda Books, 1988.

García-Camarillo. *Borlotes mestizos.* Albuquerque: Mano Izquierda Books, 1984.

García-Camarillo. *Burning Snow.* Albuquerque: Mano Izquierda Books, 1984.

García-Camarillo. *Cacetines embotellados.* Albuquerque: Mano Izquierda Books, 1982.

García-Camarillo. *Calambola.* Albuquerque: Mano Izquierda Books, 1982.

García-Camarillo. *Crickets.* Albuquerque: Mano Izquierda Books, 1992.

García-Camarillo. *Cuervos en el Río Grande.* Albuquerque: Mano Izquierda Books, 1983.

García-Camarillo. *Double-Face.* Albuquerque: Mano Izquierda Books, 1982.

García-Camarillo. *Dream-Walking.* Albuquerque: Mano Izquierda Books, 1994.

García-Camarillo. *Ecstasy and Puro Pedo.* Albuquerque: Mano Izquierda Books, 1981.

García-Camarillo. *Fotos.* Albuquerque: Mano Izquierda Books, 1993.

García-Camarillo. *Hang a Snake.* Albuquerque: Mano Izquierda Books, 1981.

García-Camarillo. *The Line.* Albuquerque: Mano Izquierda Books, 1984.

García-Camarillo. *Soy pajarita*. Albuquerque: Mano Izquierda Books, 1986.

García-Camarillo. *Winter Month*. Albuquerque: Mano Izquierda Books, 1982.

García-Camarillo. *Zafa'o*. Albuquerque: Mano Izquierda Books, 1992.

García-Camarillo, Carmen Tafolla, and Reyes Cárdenas. *Get Your Tortillas Together*. San Antonio: Cultural Distribution Center, 1976.

García-Camarillo, ed. *Nahualliandoing: Poetry in Español/Nahuatl/English*. San Antonio: Caracol, 1977.

Garza, Cheo. *Capirotada*. San Antonio: Trucha Publications, 1980.

Garza, Juan Manuel. *13 Realities / 13 Realidades: Poemas y Plays*. San Antonio: Xochitl Publications, 1978.

Garza, Mario. *Un paso más / One More Step*. Lansing, Mich.: El Renacimiento Publications, 1976.

Gaspar, Tomás. *North Side Story*. Berkeley, Cal.: El Fuego de Aztlán, 1978.

Gaspar de Alba, Alicia, María Herrera-Sobek, and Demetria Martínez. *Three Times a Woman: Chicana Poetry*. Tempe, Ariz.: Bilingual Press/Revista Bilingüe, 1989.

Gómez-Quiñones, Juan. *5th and Grande Vista: Poems 1960–1973*. New York: Editorial Mensaje, 1974.

Gonzales, Gloria Luz. *Another View From My Porch*. Ribera, N.Mex.: Good Friends, 1995.

Gonzales. *The View From my Porch*. Santa Fe: SFHS Technical, 1990.

Gonzales, Rebecca. *Slow Work to the Rhythm of the Cicadas*. Fort Worth: Prickly Pear Press, 1985.

Gonzales, Rodolfo. *I am Joaquin / Yo soy Joaquín*. Denver: Crusade for Justice, 1967.

González, Beatriz. *The Chosen Few*. San Antonio: M & A Editions, 1984.

González, David J. *A Journey to the Third World*. Venice, Cal.: Indígena Publications, 1979.

González, Rafael Jesús. *El hacedor de juegos / The Maker of Games*. San Francisco: Casa Editorial, 1977.

González, Ray. *Apprentice to Volcanoes*. Fort Collins, Colo.: Leaping Mountain Press, 1986.

González. *Cabato Sentora*. Rochester, N.Y.: BOA Editions, 1999.

González. *From the Restless Roots*. Houston: Arte Público, 1986.

González. *The Heat of Arrivals*. Brockport, N.Y.: BOA Editions, 1996.

González. *Twilights and Chants*. Golden, Colo.: James Andrews, 1987.

González-T., César A. *Unwinding the Silence: A Supplement of Translations: Fifteen Poems*. La Jolla, Cal.: Lalo Press, 1987.

Hernández, Alfonso C. *Arrullos de la revelación: Manantiales, paradojas, anatemas / Lullabies of Revelation: Springs, Paradoxes, Anathemas*. Guadalajara, México: Editorial Summa, 1978.

Hernández, Armand. *Police Make House Calls*. Tempe, Ariz.: Bilingual Press, 1991.

Hernández, David. *Rooftop Piper*. Chicago: Tía Chucha Press, 1991.

Hernández, Leo, and Marty Hernández. *Padre y hijo / Father and Son: Chicano Thoughts*. Cerrillos, N.Mex.: San Marcos Press, 1974.

Hernández-Ávila, Inés, as Inés Hernández Tovar. *Con razón, corazón*. San Antonio: Caracol, 1977. Enlarged. San Antonio: M & A Editions, 1987.

Herrera, Juan Felipe. *Akrílica*. Translated by Stephen Kessler and Sesshu Foster with Dolores Bravo and others. Santa Cruz, Cal.: Alcatraz Editions, 1989.

Herrera. *Border-Crosser with a Lamborghini Dream*. Tucson: University of Arizona Press, 1999.

Herrera. *Exiles of Desire*. Fresno, Cal.: Lalo, 1983.

Herrera. *Facegames*. Berkeley, Cal.: As Is/So & So, 1987.

Herrera. *Laughing Out Loud, I Fly: Poems in English and Spanish*. New York: HarperCollins, 1998.

Herrera. *Love After the Riots*. Willimantic, Conn.: Curbstone Press, 1996.

Herrera. *Memoria(s) From an Exile's Notebook of the Future*. Santa Monica, Cal.: Santa Monica College Press, 1983.

Herrera. *Night Train to Tuxtla*. Tucson: University of Arizona Press, 1994.

Herrera. *187 Reasons Why Mexicanos Can't Cross the Border: An Emergency Poem by Juan Felipe Herrera*. Fresno, Cal.: Borderwolf Press, 1995.

Herrera. *Rebozos of Love we have woven sudor de pueblos on our back*. San Diego: Toltecas en Aztlán, 1974.

Herrera. *The Roots of a Thousand Embraces: Dialogues*. San Francisco: Maniac-D Press, 1994.

Herrera. *Zenjosé: Scenarios*. San Jose: Hot Colors, 1988.

Hinojosa, Rolando. *Korean Love Songs: From Klail City Death Trip*. Berkeley, Cal.: Editorial Justa Publications, 1978.

de Hoyos, Angela. *Arise, Chicano!: and Other Poems*. Bloomington, Ind.: Backstage Books, 1975.

de Hoyos. *Chicano Poems for the Barrio*. Bloomington, Ind.: Backstage Books, 1975.

de Hoyos. *Selecciones*. Xalapa, México: Universidad de Veracruz, 1976.

de Hoyos. *Woman, Woman*. Houston: Arte Público, 1985.

de Hoyos. *Selected Poems / Selecciones*. San Antonio: Dezkalso Press, 1979.

Huerta, Gregorio. *Poesías*. Chicago: Gregorio Huerta, 1984.

Ibáñez, Armando P. *Midday Shadows*. New York: Vantage Press, 1980.

Ibáñez. *Wrestling with the Angel: A Collection of Poetry*. Los Angeles: Pluma Productions, 1997.

Kirack, Alex, as Gallo. *Space Flutes & Barrio Paths*. San Diego: Centro de Estudios Chicanos, 1972.

*Lágrimas, pistolas y ombligos.* Seattle: Centro de Estudios Chicanos, University of Washington, Monograph Series, 1974.

Lazo, William. *The Ching Poems.* Denver: Baculite Publishing Company, 1990.

Lomelí, Francisco A., ed. *Morena.* Santa Barbara, 1980.

Luera, Yolanda. *Solitaria J.* La Jolla, Cal.: Lalo, 1986.

Luna Robles, Margarita. *Triptych: Dreams, Lust and Other Performances.* Santa Monica, Cal.: Santa Monica College Press/ Lalo Literature Division, 1993.

Maciel, Olivia. *Más salado que dulce / Saltier Than Sweet.* Chicago: MARCH/Abrazo Press, 1995.

Maciel, ed. *Shards of Light / Astillas de luz.* Chicago: Tía Chucha Press, 1998.

Maldonado, Jesús María. *Sal, pimienta y amor.* Seattle: Endless Despair Press, 1976.

Manazar Gamboa, Manuel. *Jam Session: Twenty Poems and One Short Story.* Los Angeles: Olmeca Press, 1983.

Mares, E. A. *There Are Four Wounds.* N.p.: Trilobite Poetry Chapbook, 1994.

Mares. *The Unicorn Poem.* Cerrillos, N.Mex.: San Marcos Press, 1980.

Mares. *The Unicorn Poem & Flowers and Songs of Sorrow.* Albuquerque: West End Press, 1992.

Martínez, Carla. *Letting the Ghosts Out.* Santa Barbara, Cal.: Woodie Press, 1980.

Martínez, Demetria. *Breathing Between the Lines.* Tucson: University of Arizona Press, 1997.

Martínez, Lorri. *Where Eagles Fall.* Brunswick, Maine: Blackberry, 1982.

Martínez, María. *Sterling Silver Roses.* San Luis Obispo, Cal.: La Morenita, 1981.

Martínez, Víctor. *Caring for a House.* San Jose: Chusma House, 1992.

Méndez M., Miguel. *Los criaderos humanos (épica de lo desamparados) y Sahuaros.* Tucson, Ariz.: Editorial Peregrinos, 1975.

Mirandé, Alfredo, ed. *Alma Abierta: Pinto Poetry, Mayo de CRC.* Riverside: University of California, Chicano Publications Series, 1980.

Molina, Juan Bilcen. *Emotions of a Mexican American.* New York: Vantage, 1980.

Mondragón, Jerry and Elena Avila. *Amantes Sin Casa.* Río Rancho, N.Mex.: Tú y Yo Productions, 1994.

Monreal, Art. *Los Angeles and Other Tragedies.* Glendale Cal.: Great Western, 1981.

Montalvo, José. *¡A mí qué!* San Antonio: Raza Cósmica, 1983.

Montalvo. *Black Hat Poems.* Austin: Slough Press, 1987.

Montalvo. *The Cat in the Top Hat by Dr. Sucio (A.K.A. José Montalvo).* San Antonio: José Montalvo, 1990.

Montalvo. *Pensamientos capturados: poemas de José Montalvo.* San Antonio: Privately published, 1977.

Montalvo. *Welcome to My New World*. San Antonio: Saddle Tramp Publications, 1992.

Montaño Salazar, Barbara. *Life, Don't Hold It In*. New York: Vantage Press, 1984.

Montejano, Diana L. *Nebulous Thoughts*. Albuquerque: Mano Izquierda Books, 1987.

Montoya, José. *Information: 20 Years of Joda*. San Jose: Chusma House, 1992.

Montoya. *El Sol y los de Abajo and Other R.C.A.F. Poems*. San Francisco: Ediciones Pocho-Che, 1972.

Mor, Barbara, and others. *Fired Up With You: Poems of a Niagara Vision*. Edited by Will Inman and Robert Volbrecht. Naco, Ariz.: Border, 1977.

Mora, Pat. *Agua Santa / Holy Water*. Boston: Beacon, 1995.

Mora. *Aunt Carmen's Book of Practical Saints*. Boston: Beacon, 1997.

Mora. *Borders*. Houston: Arte Público, 1986.

Mora. *Chants*. Houston: Arte Público, 1984.

Mora. *Communion*. Houston: Arte Público, 1991.

Mora. *Confetti: Poems for Children*. New York: Lee & Low, 1996.

Mora. *The Desert Is My Mother / El desierto es mi madre*. Houston: Arte Público/Piñata Books, 1994.

Mora. *Listen to the Desert / Oye al desierto*. New York: Clarion, 1994.

Mora, Ricardo. *The Black Sun*. Lubbock, Tex.: Trucha, 1973.

Moraga, Cherríe. *Loving in the War Years: lo que nunca pasó por sus labios*. Boston: South End Press, 1983.

Moreno, Dorinda. *La mujer es la tierra: la tierra da vida*. San Francisco: Casa Editorial, 1975.

Morton, Carlos. *White Heroine Winter*. El Paso: One Eye Press, 1971.

Muñoz, Arthur. *From a Cop's Journal and Other Poems*. San Antonio: Corona, 1984.

Muñoz. *In Loneliness*. San Antonio: Naylor, 1975.

Murguía, Alejandro. *Oración a la mano poderosa*. San Francisco: Ediciones Pocho-Che, 1972.

Murguía. *Farewell to the Coast*. San Francisco: Heirs Press, 1980.

Navarro, Joe. *Animal Behavior*. Denver: Privately printed, 1991.

Navarro. *Awakening*. Denver: Privately printed, 1992.

Navarro. *For the Sisters*. Denver: Aztlaneco, 1991.

Navarro. *Reflections of an Aztlaneco*. Oakland, Cal.: Unity Publications, 1987.

Navarro. *Rhythmic Rage*. Denver: Privately printed, 1991.

Niño, Raúl. *Breathing Light.* Chicago: MARCH/Abrazo Press, 1991.

Ochoa, Jesús B. *A Soft Tongue Shall Break Hardness.* El Paso: American Printing Company, 1973.

Olvera, Enrique "Joe." *Voces de la gente.* El Paso: Mictla, 1972.

Ortega, Adolfo. *Caló Tapestry.* Berkeley, Cal.: Editorial Justa, 1977.

Ortega. *A Turn of Hands.* San Jose: Mango Publications, 1981.

Ortega, Koryne. *Proud Ones: Poems by Koryne Ortega.* Barstow, Cal.: Esotérica Press, 1988.

Palomo Acosta, Teresa. *Passing Time.* Austin, 1984.

Padilla, Ernesto. *Cigarro Lucky Strike.* San Francisco: MediammiX, 1986.

Paredes, Américo. *Between Two Worlds.* Houston: Arte Público, 1991.

Paredes. *With His Pistol in His Hand: A Border Ballad and Its Hero.* Austin: University of Texas Press, 1958.

Pérez, Genaro Jesse. *Prosapoemas.* Odessa: University of Texas of the Permian Basin, 1980.

Pérez, Raymundo "Tigre." *Free, Free at Last.* Denver: Barrio Publications, 1970.

Pérez. *Phases.* Corpus Christi, Tex., 1971.

Pérez. *The Secret Meaning of Death.* Lubbock, Tex.: Trucha, 1972.

Pérez, Raymundo "Tigre," and Esidro Ortega. *Ich Bin Das Gesicht Das Hinter Den EinschusslÖchern: Gedichte aus dem indianischen Widerstand.* Basel, Switzerland: Nachtmaschine, 1982.

Pigno, Antonia Quintana. *La Jornada.* Coffeyville, Kans.: Zauberberg Press, 1987.

Pigno. *Old Town Bridge.* Coffeyville, Kans.: Zauberberg Press, 1987.

Pigno. *Unas poesías de "la jornada": A Chapbook.* Barstow, Cal.: Esotérica Press, 1988.

Pino, Frank. *Paseos y peregrinaciones.* San Antonio: Munguía Printers, 1979.

Ponce-Montoya, Juanita. *Grief Work.* Hicksville, N.Y.: Exposition Press, 1978.

Quiñónez, Naomi. *The Smoking Mirror: Poems.* Albuquerque: West End Press, 1998.

Quiñónez. *Sueño de Colibrí / Hummingbird Dream.* Los Angeles: West End Press, 1985.

Quintana, Leroy. *Hijo del Pueblo: New Mexico Poems.* Las Cruces, N.Mex.: Puerto del Sol Publications, 1976.

Quintana. *The History of Home.* Tempe, Ariz.: Bilingual Review, 1993.

Quintana. *Interrogations.* Chevy Chase, Md.: Burning Cities Press, 1990.

Quintana. *My Hair Turning Gray Among Strangers.* Tempe, Ariz.: Bilingual Press/Editorial Bilingüe, 1996.

Quintana. *Sangre.* Las Cruces, N.Mex.: Prima Agua Press, 1981.

Ramírez, Orlando. *Speedway*. San Jose: Mango Publications, Chicano Chapbook Series, 1979.

Ramírez, Sharon. *Eve Grown Wise*. Berkeley, Cal.: Thorpe Spring Press, 1972.

Rangel, Rubén. *Bajo la sombra de la maquinaria*. Seattle: Editorial Ce Atl, 1980.

Raulrsalinas. *East of the Freeway (Reflections de mi pueblo)*. Austin: Red Salmon Press, 1995.

Raulrsalinas. *Un Trip through the Mind Jail y otras excursions*. San Francisco: Editorial Pocho-Che, 1980.

Raulrsalinas. *Viaje/Trip*. Providence, R.I.: Hellcoal Press, 1973.

Ríos, Alberto. *Elk Heads on the Wall*. San Jose: Mango Publications, Chicano Chapbook Series, 1979.

Ríos. *Five Indiscretions: A Book of Poems*. Riverdale-on-Hudson, N.Y.: Sheep Meadow Press, 1985

Ríos. *The Lime Orchard Woman*. Riverdale-on-Hudson, N.Y.: Sheep Meadow Press, 1988.

Ríos. *Sleeping on Fists*. Story, W.Va.: Dooryard Press, 1981.

Ríos. *Teodoro Luna's Two Kisses*. New York: Norton, 1990.

Ríos. *The Warrington Poems*. Tempe: Pyracantha Press, Arizona State University School of Art, 1989.

Ríos. *Whispering to Fool The Wind*. New York: Sheep Meadow Press, 1982.

Ríos, Isabella. *A Dance with Eucalyptus*. Lahaina, Maui, Hawaii: Whale Watch Publications, 1995.

Rivera, Marina. *Mestiza*. N.p.: Gilded Flowers, 1977.

Rivera. *Sobra*. San Francisco: Casa Editorial, 1977.

Rivera, Tomás. *Always and Other Poems*. Sisterdale, Tex.: Sisterdale Press, 1973.

Rivera. *The Searchers: Collected Poetry*. Houston: Arte Público, 1990.

Rocha, Rina G. *Eluder*. Chicago: Alexander Books, 1980.

Rodríguez, Alfonso. *Levantando la palabra*. Buenos Aires: Ayala Palacio, Editores Universitarios, 1991.

Rodríguez, Estevan Antonio., ed. *Agua Fresca: An Anthology of Raza Poetry*. Tucson, Ariz.: Oreja Press/Pajarito Publications, 1979.

Rodríguez, Luis J. *The Concrete River*. Willimantic, Conn.: Curbstone Press, 1991.

Rodríguez. *Poems Across the Pavement*. Chicago: Tía Chucha Press, 1989.

Rodríguez. *Trochemoche*. Willimantic, Conn.: Curbstone Press, 1998.

Rodríguez Ramón, Andrés. *Alma y perfil de Santa Bárbara*. Santa Barbara, Cal.: Schauer Printing Studio, 1956.

Rodríguez Ramón. *Anchura a la esperanza*. Santa Barbara, Cal.: Schauer Printing Studio, 1957.

Rodríguez Ramón. *Luces*. Santa Bárbara, Cal.: Schauer Printing Studio, 1957.

Romero, Levi. *In the Gathering of Silence.* Albuquerque: West End Press, 1996.

Romero, Leo. *Agua negra.* Boise, Idaho: Ahsahta Press, 1981.

Romero. *Celso.* Houston: Arte Público, 1985.

Romero. *Desert Nights.* Santa Fe: Fish Drum Press, 1989.

Romero. *During the Growing Season.* Tucson, Ariz.: Maguey Press, 1978.

Romero. *Going Home Away Indian.* Boise, Idaho: Ahsahta Press, 1990.

Romero, Lin. *Happy Songs, Bleeding Hearts.* San Diego: Toltecas en Aztlán Publications, 1974.

Roybal, Rose Marie. *From la Llorona to Envidia . . . A Few Reflections.* Denver: Southwest Clearing House for Minority Publications, 1973.

Sáenz, Benjamín Alire. *Calendar of Dust.* Seattle: Broken Moon Press, 1991.

Sáenz. *Dark and Perfect Angels.* El Paso: Cinco Puntos Press, 1995.

Saiz, Flor. *Sentidavida: Thru the Eyes of Flor.* Denver: La Chicana Publications, 1984.

Salas, Floyd. *Color of My Living Heart.* Houston: Arte Público, 1996.

Salas. *To My Wife to Tell Her Boss What I Do All Day.* Poems Needing Print Series Number 23. Berkeley, Cal.: Crosscut Saw, n.d.

Sálaz, Fernando. *Cornerstone in Rhythm.* Belen, N.Mex.: Alpha Printing, 1981.

Sálaz. *Un día y una vida.* Boulder, Colo.: Pruett, 1977

Salinas, Luis Omar. *Afternoon of the Unreal.* Fresno, Cal.: Abramas Publications, 1980.

Salinas. *Crazy Gypsy.* Fresno, Cal.: Orígenes Publications, 1970.

Salinas. *Darkness Under the Trees / Walking Behind the Spanish.* Berkeley: Chicano Studies Library, University of California, 1982.

Salinas. *Follower of Dusk.* Chico, Cal.: Flume Press, 1991.

Salinas. *I Go Dreaming Serenades.* San Jose: Mango Publications, 1979.

Salinas. *Prelude to Darkness.* San Jose: Mango Publications, 1981.

Salinas. *The Sadness of Days.* Houston: Arte Público, 1987.

Sánchez, Carol Lee. *Conversations From the Nightmare.* San Francisco: Casa Editorial, 1975.

Sánchez. *Excerpts from a Mountain Climber's Handbook: Selected Poems, 1971–1984.* San Francisco: Taurean Horn Press/ Out West Limited, 1985.

Sánchez. *From Spirit to Matter: New and Selected Poems, 1969–1996.* San Francisco: Taurean Horn Press, 1997.

Sánchez. *Message Bringer Woman*. San Francisco: Taurean Horn Press, 1977.

Sánchez. *She) Poems*. Goshen, Conn.: Chicory Blue Press, 1995.

Sánchez, Elba Rosario. *Tallos de luna / Moon Shoots*. Santa Cruz, Cal.: Moving Parts Press, 1992.

Sánchez, Pilar. *Symbols*. San Francisco: Casa Editorial Publications, 1974.

Sánchez, Ricardo. *Amerikan Journeys / Jornadas Americanas*. Iowa City: Rob Lewis, 1994.

Sánchez, Ricardo. *Amsterdam Cantos y poemas pistos*. Austin: Place of Herons, 1983.

Sánchez. *Bertrand & the Mehkqoverse: A Xicano Filmic Nuance*. Austin: Slough Press, 1989.

Sánchez. *Brown Bear Honey Madnesses: Alaskan Cruising Poems*. Austin: Slough Press, 1982.

Sánchez. *Canto y grito mi liberación (y lloro desmadrazgos . . .)*. El Paso: Mictla Publications, 1971.

Sánchez. *Eagle Visioned / Feathered Adobes: Manito Sojourns & Pachuco Ramblings October 4th–24th, 1981*. El Paso: Cinco Puntos Press, 1990.

Sánchez. *Hechizospells: Poetry/Stories/Vignettes/Articles/Notes on the Human Condition of Chicanos & Pícaros, Words & Hopes Within Soulmind*. Los Angeles: Chicano Studies Center, University of California, 1976.

Sánchez. *The Loves of Ricardo*. Chicago: Tía Chucha Press, 1997.

Sánchez. *Milhuas Blues and Gritos Norteños*. Milwaukee: Spanish Speaking Outreach Institute, University of Wisconsin, 1978.

Sánchez. *Selected Poems*. Houston: Arte Público, 1985.

Sánchez, Saúl. *Desalojos: Versos de soledad*. San Antonio: M & A Editions, 1982.

Sánchez, Trinidad Jr. *Authentic Chicano Food is Hot!* Detroit: N.p., n.d.

Sánchez. *Poems by Trinidad Sánchez*. Lansing, Mich.: Renaissance Publications, 1984.

Sánchez. *Why Am I So Brown?* Chicago: MARCH/Abrazo Press, 1991.

Santana, Francisco. *Amanecer*. Santa Cruz: Third World Teaching Resource Center / University of California, 1974.

Santana. *¡Pos aquí estamos!* N.p., 1979.

Santana. *Tristealegría*. Tempe, Ariz.: Bilingual Press/Editorial Bilingüe, 1991.

Sapia, Yvonne. *Valentino's Hair*. Boston: Northeastern University Press, 1987.

Serritos, Ken. *Saturn Calling*. Chicago: MARCH/Abrazo Press, 1981.

Serros, Michele M. *Chicana Falsa and Other Stories of Death, Identity, and Oxnard*. Valencia, Cal.: Lalo Press, 1993.

Sierra, Michael. *In Their Father's Time*. San Jose: Mango Publications, 1981.

Silva, Beverly. *The Second Street Poems*. Ypsilanti, Mich.: Bilingual Press/Editorial Bilingüe, 1983.

Solórzano, Stephanie, ed. *Whispering Images*. Santa Barbara: University of California, Santa Barbara, 1984.

Somoza, Joseph. *Backyard Poems*. El Paso: Cinco Puntos Press, 1986.

Somoza. *Greyhound: A Poem Sequence*. Sacramento, Cal.: Grande Ronde Press, 1968.

Somoza. *Olive Woman: Poems*. Cerrillos, N.Mex.: San Marcos Press, 1976.

Somoza. *Out of This World: Poems*. El Paso: Cinco Puntos Press, 1990.

Somoza. *Sojourner, So To Speak*. Albuquerque: La Alameda Press, 1997.

Soto, Gary. *Black Hair*. Pittsburgh: University of Pittsburgh Press, 1985.

Soto. *Canto familiar*. San Diego: Harcourt Brace, 1995.

Soto. *Como arbustos de niebla*. Translated by Ernesto Trejo. San Jose: Mango Publications / Mexico, D.F.: Editorial Latitudes, 1980.

Soto. *The Elements of San Joaquin*. Pittsburgh: University of Pittsburgh Press, 1977.

Soto. *Father is a Pillow Tied to a Broom*. Pittsburgh: Slow Loris Press, 1980.

Soto. *A Fire in My Hands: A Book of Poems*. New York: Scholastic Press, 1990.

Soto. *Home Course in Religion: New Poems*. San Francisco: Chronicle Books, 1991.

Soto. *Junior College*. San Francisco: Chronicle Books, 1997.

Soto. *Neighborhood Odes*. San Diego: Harcourt Brace, 1992.

Soto. *New and Selected Poems*. San Francisco: Chronicle Books, 1995.

Soto. *The Sparrows Move South: Early Poems*. Berkeley, Cal.: Bancroft Library Press, 1995.

Soto. *The Tale of Sunlight*. Pittsburgh: University of Pittsburgh Press, 1978.

Soto. *Where the Sparrows Work Hard*. Pittsburgh: University of Pittsburgh Press, 1981.

Soto. *Who Will Know Us?: New Poems*. San Francisco: Chronicle Books, 1990.

Tafolla, Carmen. *Curandera*. San Antonio: M & A Editions, 1983.

Tafolla. *Sonnets to Human Beings and Other Selected Works*. Edited by Ernesto Padilla. Santa Monica, Cal.: Lalo Press, 1992.

Talamántez, Luis. *Life Within the Heart Imprisoned: The Collected Poems of Luis Talamántez*. San Jose: Fidelity Printing, 1976.

Tapia, John R. *Shadows of Ecstacy and Other Poems*. New York: Vantage Press, 1971.

Tejeda, Juan. *Enamorado en la guerra y reconociendo la tierra: Aztlán '76-'78*. San Antonio: M & A Editions, 1980.

Terán, Heriberto. *Espejo de alma y corazón: A Collection*. Denver: La Familia Terán, 1975.

Terán. *Vida de ilusiones.* Corpus Christi, Tex.: El Tercer Bookstore, 1971.

Tijerina, Louis L., ed. *Poetas del barrio de la misión.* San Francisco: Casa Editorial, 1973.

Trejo, Ernesto. *The Day of the Vendors.* Fresno, Cal.: Calavera Press, 1977.

Trejo. *El día entre las hojas.* Mexico City: Fondo de Cultura Económica, 1984.

Trejo. *Entering a Life.* Houston: Arte Público, 1990.

Trejo. *Instrucciones y señales.* Mexico City: La Máquina Eléctrica, 1977.

Trejo. *Los nombres propios.* Mexico City: Editorial Latitudes, 1978.

Turcotte, Mark. *The Feathered Hat.* Chicago: MARCH/Abrazo Press, 1995.

Ulibarrí, Sabine R. *Al cielo se sube a pie.* Madrid: Ediciones Alfaguara, 1966.

Ulibarrí. *Amor y Ecuador.* Madrid: Ediciones José Porrúa Turranzas, 1966.

Urrea, Luis Alberto. *The Fever of Being.* Albuquerque: West End Press, 1994.

Urrea. *Frozen Moments.* La Jolla: University of California at San Diego Print Co-Op, 1977.

Urrea. *Ghost Sickness.* El Paso: Cinco Puntos Press, 1997.

Valdés, Gina. *Comiendo lumbre / Eating Fire.* Colorado Springs: Maize Press, 1986.

Valdés. *Puentes y fronteras: Coplas chicanas.* Los Angeles: Castle Lithograph, 1982. Translated by Valdés and Katherine King as *Puentes y fronteras / Bridges and Borders.* Tempe, Ariz.: Editorial Bilingüe, 1996.

Valdez, Luis. *Pensamiento serpentino: A Chicano Approach to the Theatre of Reality.* N.p.: Cucaracha Publications, El Centro Campesino Cultural, 1973.

Valle, Víctor Manuel. *Calendar of Souls, Wheel of Fire.* Irvine, Cal.: Pacific Writers Press, 1991.

Valle-Santíes, Raquel. *Yo soy como soy y qué!* San Antonio: M & A Publications, 1996.

Vallejo, Armando. *Luna llena: Ocho años de poesía Chicana, 1971–1979.* Santa Barbara, Cal.: Ediciones Aztlán, 1979.

Vallejo. *Para morir en tus brazos y compromiso.* Santa Barbara, Cal.: Xalmán, 1989.

Vallejo. *Poemas de un emigrante / Poems of an Immigrant.* Santa Barbara, Cal., 1990.

Vargas, Roberto. *Nicaragua: Yo te Canto besos, balas y sueños de libertad.* San Francisco: Ediciones Pocho-Che, 1980.

Vargas. *Primeros Cantos.* San Francisco: Ediciones Pocho-Che, 1971.

Vásquez, Robert. *At the Rainbow.* Albuquerque: University of New Mexico Press, 1995.

Velásquez, Gloria. *I Used to Be a Superwoman.* Houston: Arte Público, 1997.

Verastique, Bernardino. *Yellow Luna.* N.p.: 1977.

Vigil-Piñón, Evangelina. *The Computer is Down*. Houston: Arte Público, 1984.

Vigil-Piñón. *Nade y nade: A Collection of Poems*. San Antonio: M & A Editions, 1979.

Vigil-Piñón. *Thirty an' Seen a Lot*. Houston: Arte Público, 1982.

Villanueva, Alma. *Bloodroot*. Austin: Place of Herons Press, 1977.

Villanueva. *Desire*. Tempe, Ariz.: Bilingual Press/Revista Bilingüe, 1998.

Villanueva. *Life Span*. Austin: Place of Herons, 1984.

Villanueva. *Mother, May I?* Pittsburgh: Motheroot Publications, 1978.

Villanueva. *Planet, with Mother, May I?* Tempe. Ariz.: Bilingual Press/Revista Bilingüe, 1993.

Villanueva, Tino. *Crónica de mis años peores*. La Jolla, Cal.: Lalo Press, 1987. Translated by James Hoggard as *Chronicle of My Worst Years*. Evanston, Ill.: TriQuarterly Books, 1994.

Villanueva. *Hay Otra Voz: Poems (1968–1971)*. New York: Editorial Mensaje, 1972.

Villanueva. *Scene From the Movie Giant*. Willimantic, Conn.: Curbstone Press, 1993.

Villanueva. *Shaking Off the Dark*. Houston: Arte Público, 1984. Revised. Tempe, Ariz.: Bilingual Press/Editorial Bilingüe, 1998.

Xelina. *Ku: Poemas*. La Jolla, Cal.: Xelina, 1970.

Zamora, Bernice. *Restless Serpents*. Menlo Park, Cal.: Diseños Literarios, 1976.

Zamora. *Releasing Serpents*. Tempe, Ariz.: Bilingual Press/Revista Bilingüe, 1994.

Zepeda, Ofelia. *Ocean Power: Poems from the Desert*. Tucson: University of Arizona Press, Sun Tracks Series, 1995.

## SHORT FICTION

Acosta Torres, José. *Cachito mío,* with English translation by Herminio Rios-C. Berkeley, Cal.: Quinto Sol Publications, 1973.

Aguilar Melantzón, Ricardo. *Aurelia*. Ciudad Juárez, Mexico: Universidad Autónoma de Ciudad Juárez, Programa Cultural de las Fronteras, Consejo Nacional para la Cultura y las Artes, 1990.

Aguilar. *Madreselvas en flor*. Xalapa, Mexico: Universidad Veracruzana, 1987.

Alcalá, Kathleen. *Mrs. Vargas and the Dead Naturalist*. Corvallis, Ore.: Calyx Books, 1992.

Alarcón, Justo S. *Chulifeas fronteras: cuentos*. Albuquerque: Pajarito Publications, 1981.

Alarcón. *Los dos compadres: Cuentos breves del barrio*. Mexico: Alta Pimería Pro Arte y Cultura, 1993.

Alurista. *Colección Tula y Tonán: Textos generativos*. 9 volumes. San Diego: Toltecas en Aztlán, 1973.

Alurista, and Xelina Rojas-Urista, eds. *Southwest Tales: A Contemporary Collection*. Colorado Springs: Maize Press, 1986.

Anaya, Rudolfo A. *The Silence of the Llano*. Berkeley, Cal.: Tonatiuh-Quinto Sol International, 1982.

Anaya, and Antonio Márquez, eds. *Cuentos Chicanos*. Albuquerque: New America, 1980. Revised as *Cuentos Chicanos: A Short Story Anthology*. Albuquerque: University of New Mexico Press, 1984.

Anaya, and José Griego y Maestas. *Cuentos: Tales from the Hispanic Southwest: Based on Stories Originally Collected by Juan B. Rael*. Santa Fe: Museum of New Mexico Press, 1980.

Aragón, Clyde James. *The PC Affair: A Comic Mystery of Murder, Mayhem, and Data Processing*. Albuquerque: Cliff Zone Books, 1996.

Aragón. *Tales of Delight and Shame*. Albuquerque: Cliff Zone Books, 1996.

Atencio, Paulette. *Cuentos from My Childhood: Legends and Folktales of Northern New Mexico*. Translated by Rubén Cobos. Santa Fe: Museum of New Mexico Press, 1991.

Avendaño, Fausto. *El sueño de siempre y otros cuentos*. Ciudad Juárez, Mexico: Universidad Autónoma de Ciudad Juárez, 1996.

Avila, Alfred. *Mexican Ghost Tales of the Southwest*. Houston: Arte Público/Piñata Books, 1994.

Ballesteros, Jeannie. *Paco con Priscilla*. N.p: J. Ballesteros, 1985.

Brito, Aristeo. *Cuentos i poemas*. Washington, D.C.: Fomento Literario, 1974.

Bruce-Novoa, Juan, and José Guillermo Saavedra, eds. *Antología retrospectiva del cuento Chicano*. Mexico, D. F.: Consejo Nacional de Población, 1988.

Campbell, Trini. *Canto indio mexicano*. New York: Abra Ediciones, n.d.

Candelaria, Nash. *The Day the Cisco Kid Shot John Wayne*. Tempe, Ariz.: Bilingual Press/Editorial Bilingüe, 1988.

Candelaria. *Uncivil Rights and Other Stories*. Tempe, Ariz.: Bilingual Press/Editorial Bilingüe, 1998.

Cárdenas, Leo. *Return to Ramos*. New York: Hill & Wang, 1970.

Castañeda, Jesús. *Cuentecitos*. Albuquerque: 1970.

Castillo, Ana. *Loverboys*. New York: Norton, 1996.

Castillo, Rafael C. *Distant Journeys*. Tempe, Ariz.: Bilingual Press/Editorial Bilingüe, 1991.

Chacón, Felipe Maximiliano. *Short Stories*. Translated by Julián J. Vigil. Las Vegas, N.Mex.: Editorial Telaraña, 1980.

Chávez, Fray Angélico. *From an Altar Screen / El retablo: Tales from New Mexico*. New York: Farrar, Straus & Cudahy, 1957. Republished as *When the Santos Talked: A Retablo of New Mexico Tales*. Santa Fe: W. Gannon, 1977.

Chávez. *New Mexico Triptych; Being Three Panels and Three Accounts: 1. The Angel's New Wings; 2. The Penitente Thief; 3. Hunchback Madonna*. Paterson, N.J.: St. Anthony Guild, 1940.

Chávez. *The Short Stories of Fray Angélico Chávez*. Edited by Genaro M. Padilla. Albuquerque: University of New Mexico Press, 1987.

Chávez. *The Song of Francis*. Flagstaff, Ariz.: Northland Press, 1973.

Cisneros, Sandra. *Woman Hollering Creek and Other Stories.* New York: Random House, 1991. Translated into Spanish by Liliana Valenzuela as *El arroyo de la Llorona y otros cuentos.* New York: Vintage, 1996.

Contreras, Juan A. *Morningsing. . . . Mañanitas.* El Paso: Education Systems Development, 1987.

De la Garza, Beatriz. *The Candy Vendor's Boy and Other Stories.* Houston: Arte Público, 1994.

Díaz Bjorkquist, Elena. *Suffer Smoke.* Houston: Arte Público, 1996.

Elizondo, Sergio. *Rosa, la flauta.* Berkeley, Cal.: Editorial Justa Publications, 1980.

Forté-Escamilla, Kleya. *The Storyteller with Nike Airs, and Other Barrio Stories.* San Francisco: Aunt Lute Books, 1994.

Gaspar de Alba, Alicia. *The Mystery of Survival and Other Stories.* Tempe, Ariz.: Bilingual Press/Editorial Bilingüe, 1992.

Gilb, Dagoberto. *The Magic of Blood.* Albuquerque: University of New Mexico, 1993.

Gilb. *Winners on the Pass Line and Other Stories.* El Paso: Cinco Puntos Press, 1985.

Gómez, Alma, Cherríe Moraga, and Mariana Romo-Carmona, eds. *Cuentos: Stories by Latinas.* New York: Kitchen Table/Women of Color Press, 1983.

González, Genaro. *Only Sons.* Houston: Arte Público, 1991.

González, Ray, ed. *Mirror Beneath the Earth: Short Fiction by Chicano Writers.* Willimantic, Conn.: Curbstone Press, 1992.

Gutiérrez, Stephen D. *Elements.* Normal, Ill.: FC2, Unit for Contemporary Literature, 1997.

Hayes, Joe. *The Day it Snowed Tortillas: Tales from Spanish New Mexico Retold by Joe Hayes.* Santa Fe: Mariposa Publishing, 1982.

Jaramillo, Cleofas M., compiler. *Cuentos del hogar (Spanish Fairy Tales).* El Campo, Tex.: Citizen Press, 1939.

Jiménez, Francisco. *The Circuit: Stories From the Life of a Migrant Child.* Albuquerque: University of New Mexico Press, 1997.

Keller, Gary D. *Tales of El Huitlacoche.* Colorado Springs: Maize Press, 1984.

Keller. *Zapata Rose in 1992 and Other Tales.* San Luis Obispo, Cal.: Maize Press, 1992.

Martínez, Max. *The Adventures of the Chicano Kid and Other Stories.* Houston: Arte Público, 1982.

Martínez. *Monologue of the Bolivian Major: Cuento.* San Antonio: M & A Editions, 1978.

Martínez. *A Red Bikini Dream.* Houston: Arte Público, 1990.

Martínez-Serros, Hugo. *The Last Laugh and Other Stories.* Houston: Arte Público, 1988.

Mayo, Wendell. *Centaur of the North.* Houston: Arte Público, 1996.

Mena, María Cristina [María Cristina Chambers]. *The Collected Stories of María Cristina Mena.* Edited by Amy Doherty. Houston: Arte Público, 1997.

Méndez M., Miguel. *Cuentos para niños traviesos / Stories for Mischievous Children*. Translated by Eva Price. Berkeley, Cal.: Editorial Justa Publications, 1979.

Méndez M. *Cuentos y ensayos para reír y aprender*. Hermosillo, Mexico: Miguel Méndez M., 1988.

Méndez M. *De la vida y del folclor de la frontera*. Tucson: Mexican American Studies and Research Center, University of Arizona Press, 1986.

Méndez M. *Los muertos también cuentan*. Ciudad Juárez, Mexico: Universidad Autónoma de Ciudad Juárez, 1995.

Méndez M. *Tata Casehua y otros cuentos*. Berkeley, Cal.: Editorial Justa Publications, 1980.

Monreal, David Nava. *The New Neighbor and Other Stories*. Translated by Eva Price, Leo Barrow, and Marco Portales. Irvine, Cal.: Pacific Writers Press, 1987.

Murguía, Alejandro. *Southern Front*. Tempe, Ariz.: Bilingual Press/Editorial Bilingüe, 1989.

Navarro, J. L. *Blue Day on Main Street*. Berkeley, Cal.: Quinto Sol Publications, 1973.

Ochoa, Esperanza. *Siete del Valle / Seven Valley Stories*. Edinburg: University of Texas-Pan American Press, 1995.

Paredes, Américo. *The Hammon and the Beans and Other Stories*. Houston: Arte Público, 1994.

Paredes. *Uncle Remus con chile*. Houston: Arte Público, 1993.

Paredes, ed. *Folktales of Mexico*. Translated by Paredes. Chicago: University of Chicago Press, 1970.

Peña, Abe M. *Memories from Cíbola: Stories from New Mexico Villages*. Albuquerque: University of New Mexico Press, 1997.

Pino, Cecilia, and Ricardo Aguilar Melantzón, eds. *El cuento chicano, (Antología)*. Montevideo, Uruguay: Editorial Signos, 1991.

Ponce, Mary Helen. *Recuerdo: Short Stories of the Barrio*. Tujunga, Cal.: Adame and Associates, 1983.

Ponce. *Taking Control*. Houston: Arte Público, 1987.

Portillo Trambley, Estela. *Rain of Scorpions and Other Writings*. Berkeley, Cal.: Tonatiuh International, 1975. Revised as *Rain of Scorpions and Other Stories*. Tempe, Ariz.: Bilingual Press/Editorial Bilingüe, 1993.

Preciado Martin, Patricia. *Days of Plenty, Days of Want*. Tempe, Ariz.: Bilingual Press/Editorial Bilingüe, 1989.

Preciado Martin. *El Milagro and Other Stories*. Tucson: University of Arizona Press, 1996.

Rael, Juan B., ed. *Cuentos españoles de Colorado y de Nuevo Méjico / Spanish Tales from Colorado and New Mexico*. Stanford, Cal.: Stanford University Press, 1957.

Ramos, Luis Alberto. *Siete veces el sueño*. San Antonio: M & A Editions, 1976.

Reveles, Daniel. *Enchiladas, Rice and Beans*. New York: Ballantine, 1994.

Reveles. *Salsa and Chips: Tales from Tecate*. New York: One World Press, 1997.

Ríos, Alberto Alvaro. *The Iguana Killer: Twelve Stories of the Heart.* Lewiston, Idaho: Blue Moon and Confluence Press, 1984.

Ríos. *Pig Cookies and Other Stories.* San Francisco: Chronicle Books, 1995.

Rivera, Tomás. *The Harvest / La Cosecha.* Houston: Arte Público, 1988.

Rodríguez, Armando Rafael, ed. *The Gypsy Wagon: Un sancocho de cuentos sobre la experiencia Chicana.* Los Angeles: Aztlán Publications/University of California, 1974.

Romero, Leo. *Rita and Los Angeles.* Tempe, Ariz.: Bilingual Press/Editorial Bilingüe, 1995.

Sáenz, Benjamin Alire. *Flowers for the Broken.* Seattle: Broken Moon Press, 1992.

Sálaz, Rubén Darío. *Heartland: Stories of the Southwest.* Santa Fe: Blue Feather, 1978.

Sánchez, Ramón. *How to Meet the Devil and Other Stories.* San Jose: Chusma House Publications, 1995.

Sánchez, Rosaura, ed. *Requisa treinta y dos: colección de cuentos.* La Jolla: Chicano Research Publications, University of California, 1979.

Sánchez, Saúl. *Hay Plesha Lichans Tu Di Flac.* Berkeley, Cal.: Editorial Justa Publications, 1977.

Santos, E. D. *Mesquite Sighs: A Collection of Short Stories.* Hondo, Tex.: La Sombra Publishing, 1992.

Sauvageau, Juan, ed. *Stories That Must Not Die.* Austin: Oasis Press, 1978.

Silva, Beverly. *The Cat and Other Stories.* Tempe, Ariz.: Bilingual Press/Editorial Bilingüe, 1986.

Simmen, Edward, ed. *The Chicano: From Caricature to Self Portrait.* New York: Mentor Books, New American Library, 1971.

Simmen, ed. *Gringos in Mexico: One Hundred Years of Mexico in the American Short Story.* Fort Worth: Texas Christian University Press, 1988.

Simmen, ed. *North of the Río Grande: The Mexican American Experience in Short Fiction.* New York: Penguin, 1992.

Somoza, Oscar U., ed. *Nueva Narrativa Chicana.* Mexico City: Editorial Diógenes, 1983.

Soto, Gary. *Baseball in April and Other Stories.* San Diego: Harcourt Brace, 1990.

Soto. *The Cat's Meow.* San Francisco: Strawberry Hill Press, 1987.

Soto. *Living Up the Street: Narrative Recollections.* San Francisco: Strawberry Hill Press, 1985.

Soto. *Local News.* San Diego: Harcourt Brace, 1993.

Soto. *Petty Crimes.* San Diego: Harcourt Brace, 1998.

Soto. *Small Faces.* Houston: Arte Público, 1986.

Soto, ed. *California Childhood: Recollections and Stories of the Golden State.* Berkeley, Cal.: Creative Arts Books, 1988.

Soto, ed. *Pieces of the Heart: New Chicano Fiction.* San Francisco: Chronicle Books, 1993.

Treviño, Jesús Salvador. *The Fabulous Sinkhole & Other Stories*. Houston: Arte Público, 1995.

Ulibarrí, Sabine. *The Best of Sabine Ulibarrí: Selected Stories*. Edited by Dick Gerdes. Albuquerque: University of New Mexico Press, 1993.

Ulibarrí. *El Cóndor and Other Stories / El cóndor y otros cuentos*. Houston: Arte Público, 1988.

Ulibarrí. *El gobernador Glu Glu y otros cuentos / Governor Glu Glu and Other Stories*. Tempe, Ariz.: Bilingual Press/Editorial Bilingüe, 1988.

Ulibarrí. *Mi abuela fumaba puros y otros cuentos de Tierta Amarilla / My Grandmother Smoked Cigars and Other Stories of Tierra Amarilla*. Berkeley, Cal.: Quinto Sol Publications, 1977.

Ulibarrí. *Primeros encuentros / First Encounters*. Ypsilanti, Mich.: Bilingual Press/Editorial Bilingüe, 1982.

Ulibarrí. *Sueños / Dreams*. Edinburg: University of Texas-Pan American Press, 1994.

Ulibarrí. *Tierra Amarilla: Cuentos de Nuevo México*. Quito, Ecuador: Editorial Casa de la Cultura Ecuatoriana, 1964. Translated by Thelma Campbell Nason as *Tierra Amarilla: Stories of New Mexico / Cuentos de Nuevo México*. Albuquerque: University of New Mexico Press, 1971.

Vigil, Angel. *The Corn Woman: Stories and Legends of the Hispanic Southwest / La Mujer de Maíz: Cuentos y leyendas del sudoeste hispano*. Translated by Jennifer Audrey Lowell and Juan Francisco Marín. Englewood, Colo.: Libraries Unlimited, 1994.

Villanueva, Alma Luz. *Weeping Woman / La Llorona and Other Stories*. Tempe, Ariz.: Bilingual Press/Editorial Bilingüe, 1994.

Villaseñor, Victor. *Walking Stars: Stories of Magic and Power*. Houston: Arte Público/Piñata Books, 1994.

Viramontes, Helena María. *The Moths and Other Stories*. Houston: Arte Público, 1985.

Weigle, Marta, ed. *Two Guadalupes: Hispanic Legends and Magic Tales from Northern New Mexico*. Santa Fe: Ancient City Press, 1987.

## THEATER

Alemán, Alfredo, Nephtalí De León, and Carlos González. *El segundo de Febrero: A Historical Play for Young People*. San Antonio: Centro Cultural Aztlán, 1983.

Avedaño, Fausto. *El Corrido de California*. Berkeley, Cal.: Editorial Justa Publications, 1979.

Barrio, Raymond. *The Devil's Apple Corps: A Trauma in Four Acts*. Guerneville, Cal.: Ventura, 1976.

Campa, Arthur León, ed. *Los Comanches: A New Mexican Folk Drama*. Albuquerque: University of New Mexico Press, 1942.

Campa. *Spanish Religious Folk Theatre in the Spanish Southwest (First Cycle)*. Albuquerque: University of New Mexico Press, 1934.

Campa. *Spanish Religious Folk Theatre in the Spanish Southwest (Second Cycle)*. Albuquerque: University of New Mexico Press, 1934.

Castro, Sister M. Celeste. *The Story of Our Lady of Guadalupe.* San Antonio: Mexican American Cultural Center, 1978.

Chávez, Denise and Linda Macías Feyder, eds. *Shattering the Myth: Plays by Hispanic Women.* Houston: Arte Público, 1992.

Dávila Flores, Olivia. *Qué, cómo y cuándo.* Irvine, Cal.: Ediciones Teatrales de Gestos, 1987.

De León, Nephtalí. *5 Plays.* Denver: Totinem Publications, 1972.

De León. *Tequila Mockingbird, Or the Ghost of Unemployment.* San Antonio: Trucha Publications, 1979.

Domínguez, Sylvia Maída. *La comadre María: Una comedia.* Austin: American Universal Artforms, 1973.

Garza, Roberto J., ed. *Contemporary Chicano Theatre.* Notre Dame, Ind.: Notre Dame University Press, 1976.

Hernández, Alfonso. *The False Advent of Mary's Child and Other Plays.* Berkeley, Cal.: Editorial Justa Publications, 1979.

Huerta, Jorge A., *Necessary Theatre: Six Plays About the Chicano Experience.* Houston: Arte Público, 1989.

Huerta, ed. *El teatro de la Esperanza: An Anthology of Chicano Drama.* Goleta, Cal.: El Teatro de la Esperanza, 1973.

Huerta, and Nicolás Kanellos, eds. *Nuevos Pasos: Chicano and Puerto Rican Drama.* Special issue of *Revista Chicano-Riquena,* 7 (Winter 1979).

Jones, David Richard, ed. *New Mexico Plays.* Albuquerque: University of New Mexico Press, 1989.

Latins Anonymous. *Latins Anonymous: Two Plays.* Houston: Arte Público, 1996.

López, Josefina. *Confessions—: A One Woman Show.* Woodstock, Ill.: Dramatic Publishing, 1997.

López. *Confessions of Women from East L.A.: A Comedy.* Woodstock, Ill.: Dramatic Publishing, 1997.

López. *Food for the Dead; La Pinta: Two One-Act Plays.* Woodstock, Ill.: Dramatic Publishing, 1996.

López. *Real Women Have Curves.* Seattle: Rain City Projects, 1992.

López. *Simply María, or The American Dream: A One-Act Play.* Woodstock, Ill.: Dramatic Publishing, 1996.

López. *Unconquered Spirits: A Historical Play.* Woodstock, Ill.: Dramatic Publishing, 1997.

Mares, E. A. *I Returned and Saw Under the Sun: Padre Martínez of Taos.* Albuquerque: University of New Mexico Press, 1989.

Monreal, David Nava. *Cellmates.* Edited by Juan Villegas and Julie Foraker. Irvine, Cal.: Ediciones Teatrales de Gestos, 1987.

Moraga, Cherríe. *Giving up the Ghost: Teatro in Two Acts.* Los Angeles: West End Press, 1986.

Moraga. *Heroes and Saints & Other Plays.* Albuquerque: West End Press, 1994.

Morton, Carlos. *Los Dorados.* Studio City, Cal.: Players Press, 1991.

Morton. *Los Fatherless.* Studio City, Cal.: Players Press, 1997.

Morton. *El Jardín*. Studio City, Cal.: Players Press, 1991.

Morton. *Johnny Tenorio*. Studio City, Cal.: Players Press, 1988.

Morton. *Johnny Tenorio and Other Plays*. Houston: Arte Público, 1992.

Morton. *The Many Deaths of Danny Rosales and Other Plays*. Houston: Arte Público, 1983.

Morton. *The Miser of Mexico*. Studio City, Cal.: Players Press, 1993.

Morton. *Pancho Diablo*. Studio City, Cal.: Players Press, 1993.

Morton. *Rancho Hollywood*. Studio City, Cal.: Players Press, 1991.

Morton. *The Savior*. Studio City, Cal.: Players Press, 1993.

Najera, Rick. *The Pain of the Macho and Other Plays*. Houston: Arte Público, 1997.

Niggli, Josephina. *Mexican Folk Plays*. Edited by Frederick H. Koch. Chapel Hill: University of North Carolina Press, 1938.

Portillo Trambley, Estela. *Sor Juana and Other Plays*. Ypsilanti, Mich.: Bilingual Press/Editorial Bilingüe, 1983.

Romano-V, Octavio I., and Herminio Ríos-C., eds. *Chicano Drama*. Berkeley, Cal.: Quinto Sol Publications, 1974.

Rufus. *The Last Taco in Pérez: A Comic Tragedy*. Los Angeles: Pachuco Publishing, 1975.

Seller, Maxine Schwartz, ed. *Ethnic Theatre in the United States*. Westport, Conn.: Greenwood Press, 1983.

Soto, Gary. *Novio Boy*. San Diego: Harcourt Brace, 1997.

Teatro de la Esperanza. *Guadalupe: An Original Script*. Goleta, Cal.: Teatro de la Esperanza, 1973.

Teatro del Piojo. *Tortilla Curtain: A Collective Play*. Edited by Rubén Rangel. Seattle: Editorial Ce Atl, 1980.

Teatro Libertad. *Teatro Libertad Presenta "Los Peludos": An Original Bilingual Play*. Tucson, Ariz.: Teatro Libertad, 1978.

Valdez, Luis. *Luis Valdez–Early Works: Actos, Bernabé and Pensamiento serpentino*. Houston: Arte Público, 1990.

Valdez. *The Shrunken Head of Pancho Villa*. San Juan Bautista, Cal.: Cucaracha Press, 1974.

Valdez. *Zoot Suit and Other Plays*. Houston: Arte Público, 1992.

Valdez and El Teatro Campesino. *Actos*. San Juan Bautista, Cal.: Cucaracha Press, 1971.

Vigil, Angel. *Teatro! Hispanic Plays for Young People*. Englewood, Colo.: Teacher Idea Press, 1996.

Villegas, Robert. *The Resurrection: A Short Play*. Indianapolis: Lion Enterprises, 1978.

## NONFICTION NARRATIVES:
## (AUTO)BIOGRAPHIES; DIARIES; MEMOIRS; ESSAYS; JOURNALS

Acosta, Adalberto Joel. *Chicanos Can Make It*. New York: Vantage, 1971.

Alvarado, Arturo Rocha. *Crónica de Aztlán: A Migrant's Tale.* Berkeley, Cal.: Quinto Sol Publications, 1977.

Alvarez, Everett Jr. and Anthony S. Pitch. *Chained Eagle.* New York: D. I. Fine, 1989.

Alvarez, and Samuel A. Schreiner Jr. *Code of Conduct.* New York: D. I. Fine, 1991.

Anaya, Rudolfo A. *A Chicano in China.* Albuquerque: University of New Mexico Press, 1986.

Anaya and Francisco A. Lomelí. *Aztlán: Essays on the Chicano Homeland.* Albuquerque: Academia/El Norte Publications, 1989.

Anaya, Juan Esteban Arellano, and Denise Chávez. *Descansos: An Interrupted Journey.* Albuquerque: Academia/El Norte Publications, 1995.

Anzaldúa, Gloria. *Borderlands / La Frontera: The New Mestiza.* San Francisco: Spinsters/Aunt Lute, 1987.

Anzaldúa and others, eds. *This Bridge Called My Back: Writings by Radical Women of Color.* Watertown, Mass.: Persephone Press, 1981.

Arellano, Juan Estevan. *Palabras de la vista: retratos de la pluma; memorias.* Albuquerque: Instituto del Río Grande/Publicaciones Academia, 1984.

Arias, Ron. *Five Against the Sea: A True Story of Courage and Survival.* New York: New American Library, 1989.

Armas, José. *La Familia de la Raza.* Albuquerque: Pajarito Publications, 1972.

Arteaga, Alfred. *House with the Blue Bed.* San Francisco: Mercury House, 1997.

Augenbraum, Harold, and Ilan Stavans, eds. *Growing Up Latino: Memoirs and Stories.* Boston: Houghton Mifflin, 1993.

Baez, Joan. *And a Voice to Sing With: A Memoir.* New York: Summit Books, 1987.

Baez. *Daybreak.* New York: Dial Press, 1968.

Baca, Jimmy Santiago. *Working in the Dark: Reflections of a Poet of the Barrio.* Santa Fe: Red Crane Books, 1992.

Barrios de Márquez, Guadalupe. *Amor a la vida.* El Paso: G. Barrios de Márquez, 1990.

Benavidez, Roy P., and John R. Craig. *Medal of Honor: A Vietnam Warrior's Story.* Washington, D.C.: Brassey's, 1995.

Benavidez, and Oscar Griffin. *The Three Wars of Roy Benavidez.* San Antonio: Corona, 1986.

Burciaga, José Antonio. *Drink Cultura: Chicanismo.* Santa Barbara: Capra Press, 1993.

Burciaga. *Spilling the Beans: Lotería Chicana.* Santa Barbara: Joshua Odell Editions, 1995.

Burciaga. *In Few Words: A Compendium of Latino Folk Wit and Wisdom: A Bilingual Collection / En Pocas Palabras.* San Francisco: Mercury House, 1997.

Burciaga. *Weedee Peepo: A Collection of Essays / Una colección de ensayos.* Edinburg, Tex.: Pan-American University Press, 1988.

Cabeza de Baca Gilbert, Fabiola. *The Good Life: New Mexico Food.* Santa Fe: San Vicente Foundation, 1949.

Cabeza de Vaca, Alvar Núñez. *The Account: Alvar Núñez Cabeza de Vaca's Relación*. Edited and translated by José Fernández and Martín A. Favata. Houston: Arte Público, 1993.

Carey-Herrera, Patrick. *Chicanismo: Hypothesis, Thesis and Argument*. Torrence, Cal.: Martin Press, 1983.

Carranza, Elihu. *Pensamientos on los Chicanos: A Cultural Revolution*. Berkeley, Cal.: California Book Co., 1969.

Castillo, Ana. *Massacre of the Dreamers: Essays on Xicanisma*. Albuquerque: University of New Mexico Press, 1994.

Castillo, ed. *Goddess of the Americas / La Diosa de las Américas: Writings on the Virgin of Guadalupe*. New York: Riverhead Books, 1996.

Castro, Tony. *Chicano Power: The Emergence of Mexican America*. New York: Saturday Review Press, 1974.

Cedeño, María E. *César Chávez: Labor Leader*. Brookfield, Conn.: Millbrook Press, 1993.

Chávez, Fray Angélico. *But Time and Chance: The Story of Padre Martínez of Taos, 1793–1867*. Santa Fe: Sunstone Press, 1981.

Chávez. *Chávez: A Distinctive American Clan of New Mexico*. Santa Fe: W. Gannon, 1989.

Chávez. *Coronado's Friars*. Washington, D.C.: Academy of American Franciscan History, 1968.

Chávez. *My Penitente Land: Reflections on Spanish New Mexico*. Albuquerque: University of New Mexico Press, 1974.

Chávez. *Origins of New Mexico Families in the Spanish Colonial Period. In Two Parts: The Seventeenth (1598–1693) and the Eighteenth (1693–1821)*. Santa Fe: Historical Society of New Mexico, 1954. Revised as *Origins of New Mexico Families: A Genealogy of the Spanish Colonial Period*. Santa Fe: Museum of New Mexico Press, 1992.

Chávez. *Our Lady of the Conquest*. Santa Fe: Historical Society of New Mexico, 1948.

Chávez. *Très Macho—He Said: Padre Gallegos of Albuquerque, New Mexico's First Congressman*. Santa Fe: W. Gannon, 1985.

Chávez, John R. *The Lost Land: The Chicano Image of the Southwest*. Albuquerque: University of New Mexico Press, 1984.

Chávez, Linda. *Out of the Barrio: Toward a New Politics of Hispanic Assimilation*. New York: Basic Books, 1991.

De la Fuente, Mario, with Boye de Mente. *I Like You, Gringo, But!* Phoenix: Phoenix Books, 1972.

De la Torre, Adela, and Beatríz M. Pesquera, eds. *Building With the Hands: New Directions in Chicano Studies*. Berkeley: University of California Press, 1993.

De León, Nephtalí. *Chicanos: Our Background and Our Pride*. Lubbock, Tex.: Trucha Publications, 1972.

Del Castillo, Adelaida, ed. *Between Borders: Essays on Mexicana/Chicana History*. Los Angeles: Floricanto Press, 1990.

Delgado, Abelardo. *The Chicano Movement: Some Not Too Objective Observations*. Denver: Totinem Publications, 1971.

Elsasser, Nan, Kyle MacKenzie, and Yvonne Tixier y Vigil, eds. *Las Mujeres: Conversations from a Hispanic Community*. Old Westbury, N.Y.: Feminist Press, 1980.

Flores, Bettina. *Chiquita's Cocoon: The Latina Woman's Guide to Greater Power, Love, Money, Status and Happiness*. Granite Bay, Cal.: Pepper Vine Press, 1990.

Frias, Gus. *Barrio Warriors: Homeboys of Peace*. Los Angeles: Diaz Publications, 1982. Revised as *Barrio Patriots: Killing and Dying for America*. Los Angeles, 1989.

Galarza, Ernesto. *Alviso: The Crisis of a Barrio*. San Jose: Mexican American Community Service Agency, 1973.

Galarza. *The Case of Bolivia*. Washington, D.C.: Pan American Union, 1949.

Galarza. *Farm Workers and Agri-Business in California, 1947–1960*. Notre Dame, Ind.: University of Notre Dame Press, 1977.

Galarza. *La industria eléctrica en México*. Mexico City: Fondo de Cultura Económica, 1941.

Galarza. *Merchants of Labor: The Mexican Bracero Story: An Account of the Managed Migration of Mexican Farm Workers in California, 1942–1960*. Charlotte, N.C.: McNally, 1964. Republished in Spanish as *Los braceros y mercaderes del trabajo*. Mexico: SEP, 1972.

Galarza. *Report on the Farm Labor Transportation Accident at Chualar, California, September 17, 1963*. Washington, D.C.: U.S. Congress, House Committee on Education and Labor, 1963. Republished as *Tragedy at Chualar: El crucero de las treinta y dos cruces*. Santa Barbara: McNally & Loftin, 1977.

Galarza. *Spiders in the House and Workers in the Field*. Notre Dame, Ind.: University of Notre Dame Press, 1970.

Galarza. *Strangers in Our Fields*. Washington, D.C.: Joint United States–Mexico Trade Union Committee, 1956.

Galarza, Herman Gallegos, and Julian Samora. *Mexican-Americans in the Southwest*. Santa Barbara: McNally & Loftin, 1969.

Gallegos, María Magdalena, ed. *Auraria Remembered*. Denver: Community College of Denver, 1991.

García, Alma M., ed. *Chicana Feminist Thought: The Basic Historical Writings*. New York: Routledge, 1997.

García, Andrew. *Tough Trip through Paradise, 1878–1879*. Edited by Bennett H. Stein. Boston: Houghton Mifflin, 1967.

García, John A., Teresa Córdova, and Juan R. García, eds. *The Chicano Struggle: Analyses of Past and Present Efforts*. Binghamton, N.Y.: Bilingual Press/Editorial Bilingüe, 1984.

García, Lionel G. *I Can Hear the Cowbells Ring*. Houston: Arte Público, 1994.

García, Mario T. *Memories of Chicano History: The Life and Narrative of Bert Corona*. Berkeley: University of California Press, 1994.

García, Nasario. *Abuelitos: Stories of the Rio Puerco Valley*. Albuquerque: University of New Mexico Press, 1992.

García. *Comadres: Hispanic Women of the Rio Puerco Valley*. Albuquerque: University of New Mexico Press, 1997.

García. *Más antes: Hispanic Folklore of the Rio Puerco Valley*. Santa Fe: Museum of New Mexico Press, 1997.

García. *Recuerdos de los viejitos: Tales of the Río Puerco*. Albuquerque: University of New Mexico Press, 1987.

García, ed. *Tata: A Voice from the Río Puerco*. Albuquerque: University of New Mexico Press, 1994.

Gómez-Peña, Guillermo. *The New World Border: Prophesies, Poems, & Loqueras for the End of the Century*. San Francisco: City Lights, 1996.

Gómez-Peña. *Warrior for Gringostroika: Essays, Performance Texts, and Poetry*. St. Paul, Minn.: Graywolf Press, 1993.

Gómez-Peña, and Roberto Sifuentes. *Temple of Confessions: Mexican Beasts and Living Santos With Texts by Phillip Brookman . . . et al*. New York: powerHouse Books, 1996.

Gonzales, Sylvia Alicia. *La chicana piensa: The Social-Cultural Consciousness of a Mexican American Woman*. N.p.: Sylvia A. Gonzales, 1974.

González, Doreen. *Cesar Chavez: Leader for Migrant Farm Worker*s. Springfield, N.J.: Enslow Publishers, 1996.

González, Ray, *Memory Fever: A Journey Beyond El Paso del Norte*. Seattle: Broken Moon Press, 1993.

González, ed. *Muy Macho: Latino Men Confront their Manhood*. New York: Doubleday/Anchor Books, 1996.

Griswold del Castillo, Richard, and Richard A. García. *Cesar Chávez: A Triumph of Spirit*. Norman: University of Oklahoma Press, 1995.

Guerrero, Andrés G. *A Chicano Theology*. Maryknoll, N.Y.: Orbis Books, 1987.

Gutiérrez, José Angel. *A Gringo Manual on How to Handle Mexican*s. Crystal City, Tex.: Wintergarden Publishing House, 1974?

Herrera, Juan Felipe. *Calling the Doves / El canto de las palomas*. San Francisco: Children's Book Press, 1995.

Herrera. *Mayan Drifter: Chicano Poet in the Lowlands of America*. Philadelphia: Temple University Press, 1997.

Jaramillo, Cleofas M. *Shadows of the Past / Sombras del pasado*. Santa Fe: Seton Village, 1941.

Keefe, Susan E., and Amado M. Padilla. *Chicano Ethnicity*. Albuquerque: University of New Mexico Press, 1987.

Larralde, Carlos. *Carlos Esparza: A Chicano Chronicle*. San Francisco: R & E Research Associates, 1977.

Lomas-Garza, Carmen. *In My Family: Paintings and Stories by Carmen Lomas Garcia as Told to Harriet Rohmer / En mi familia: cuadros y relatos de Carmen Lomas Garza*. Translated by Francisco X. Alarcón. Edited by David Schecter. San Francisco: Children's Book Press, 1996.

López, Arcadia H. *Barrio Teacher*. Houston: Arte Público, 1992.

López-Stafford, Gloria. *A Place in El Paso: A Mexican-American Childhood*. Albuquerque: University of New Mexico Press, 1996.

Maciel, David R., ed. *El México olvidado: La historia del pueblo Chicano*. Ciudad Juárez, México: Universidad Autónoma de Ciudad Juárez; El Paso: University of Texas at El Paso, 1996.

Maciel, ed. *La Otra Cara de México, el pueblo Chicano*. Mexico City: Ediciones El Caballito, 1977.

Maciel, and José Guillermo Saavedra, eds. *Al norte de la frontera: El pueblo Chicano*. Mexico City: Consejo Nacional de Población, 1988.

Maciel, and Patricia Bueno, eds. *Aztlán, historia del pueblo Chicano, 1848–1910: Ensayos*. Translated by Roberto Gómez Ciriza. Mexico City: SepSetentas, 1975.

Maciel, and Isidro D. Ortiz, eds. *Chicanas/Chicanos at the crossroads: social, economic, and political change*. Tucson: University of Arizona Press, 1996.

Maíz, Apaxu. *Xicano: An Autobiography*. Revised. Lansing, Mich.: Sun Dog Clan Press, 1996.

Mares, E. A., and Alex Traube. *Las Vegas, New Mexico: A Portrait*. Albuquerque: University of New Mexico Press, 1984.

Marroquín, Sol. *Part of the Team: Story of an American Hero*. Mission, Tex.: Río Grande Printers and Publishers, 1979.

Martínez, Al. *Ashes in the Rain: Selected Essays*. Berkeley, Cal.: TQS Publications, 1989.

Martínez. *City of Angeles: A Drive-By Portrait of Los Angeles*. New York: St. Martin's Press, 1996.

Martínez. *Dancing Under the Moon*. New York: St. Martin's Press, 1992.

Martínez. *Jigsaw John*. Los Angeles: J. P. Tarcher, 1975.

Martínez. *Rising Voices: Profiles of Hispano-American Lives*. New York: New American Library, 1974.

Martínez, Reynel. *Six Silent Men: 101 LRP/Rangers: Book One*. New York: Ivy Books, 1997.

Martínez, Rubén. *The Other Side: Fault Lines, Guerrilla Saints and the True Heart of Rock 'n Roll*. New York: Verso, 1992. Reprinted as *The Other Side: Notes from the New L.A., Mexico City, and Beyond*. New York: Vintage, 1993.

Melville, Margarita B., ed. *Twice a Minority: Mexican American Women*. St. Louis, Mo.: Mosby, 1980.

Méndez M., Miguel. *Entre letras y ladrillos: Autobiografía novelada*. Tempe, Ariz.: Bilingual Press/Editorial Bilingüe, 1996.

Mirandé, Alfredo. *Hombres y machos: Masculinity and Latino Culture*. Boulder, Colo.: Westview Press, 1997.

Mirandé, Alfredo and Evangelina Enríquez, eds. *La Chicana: The Mexican American Woman*. Chicago: University of Chicago Press, 1979.

Mora, Pat. *House of Houses*. Boston: Beacon, 1997.

Mora. *Nepantla: Essays from the Land in the Middle*. Albuquerque: University of New Mexico Press, 1993.

Moraga, Cherríe. *The Last Generation: Prose and Poetry*. Boston: South End Press, 1993.

Moraga. *Waiting in the Wings: Portrait of a Queer Motherhood*. Ithaca, N.Y.: Firebrand Books, 1997.

Morales, Dionicio. *A Life in Two Cultures*. Houston: Arte Público/Piñata Books, 1997.

Moreno, Dorinda. *The Image of the Chicana, and La Raza Woman*. Stanford, Cal.: Moreno Press, 1975.

Morin, Raúl. *Among the Valiant: Mexican-Americans in WWII and Korea*. Los Angeles: Borden, 1963.

National Association for Chicano Studies. *Chicana Voices: Intersections of Class, Race, and Gender*. Austin: Center for Mexican American Studies, University of Texas, 1986.

Navarrette, Rubén Jr. *A Darker Shade of Crimson: Odyssey of a Harvard Chicano*. New York: Bantam, 1993.

Orozco, E.C. *The Chicano Labyrinth of Solitude: A Study in the Making of the Chicano Mind and Character*. Dubuque, Iowa: Kendall/Hunt, 1996.

Ortiz Taylor, Sheila. *Imaginary Parents*. Albuquerque: University of New Mexico Press, 1996.

Otero, Miguel Antonio. *My Life on the Frontier, 1864–1882: Incidents and Characters of the Period when Kansas, Colorado, and New Mexico Were Passing Through the Last of Their Wild and Romantic Years.* New York: Press of the Pioneers, 1935.

Otero. *My Life on the Frontier, 1882-1897: Death Knell of a Territory and Birth of a State.* New York: Press of the Pioneers, 1939.

Otero. *My Nine Years as Governor of the Territory of New Mexico, 1897-1906.* Edited by Marion Dargan. Albuquerque: University of New Mexico Press, 1940.

Otero, Nina. *Old Spain in Our Southwest.* New York: Harcourt, Brace, 1936.

Palomares, José Francisco. *Memoirs of José Francisco Palomares.* Translated by Thomas Workman Temple II. Los Angeles: G. Dawson, 1955.

Paredes, Américo, ed. *Humanidad: Essays in Honor of George I. Sánchez.* Los Angeles: Chicano Studies Center Publications, UCLA, 1977.

Patoski, Joe Nick. *Selena: Como la flor.* Boston: Little, Brown, 1996.

Pérez, Ramón "Tianguis." *Diary of an Undocumented Immigrant.* Translated by Dick J. Reavis. Houston: Arte Público, 1991.

Pérez, Frank. *Dolores Huerta.* Austin: Raintree Steck-Vaughn, 1996.

Ponce, Mary Helen. *Hoyt Street: An Autobiography.* Albuquerque: University of New Mexico Press, 1993. Republished as *Hoyt Street: Memories of a Chicana Childhood.* Translated by Mónica Ruvalcoba as *Calle Hoyt: recuerdos de una juventud Chicana.* New York: Anchor, 1995.

Preciado Martin, Patricia. *Images and Conversation: Mexican Americans Recall a Southwestern Past.* Tucson: University of Arizona Press, 1983.

Preciado Martin. *Songs My Mother Sang to Me: An Oral History of Mexican American Women.* Tucson: University of Arizona Press, 1992.

Prieto, Jorge. *Harvest of Hope: The Pilgrimage of a Mexican-American Physician.* Notre Dame, Ind.: Notre Dame University Press, 1989. Translated as *Cosecha de esperanzas: La peregrinacion de un médico Mexico-norteamericano.* Notre Dame, Ind.: University of Notre Dame Press, 1997.

Prieto. *The Quarterback Who Almost Wasn't.* Houston: Arte Público, 1994.

Quinn, Anthony. *The Original Sin: A Self Portrait.* Boston: Little, Brown, 1972.

Quinn, with Daniel Paisner. *One Man Tango.* New York: HarperCollins, 1995.

Ramos, George and Frank Sotomayor, eds. *Southern California's Latino Community: A Series of Articles Reprinted from the Los Angeles Times.* Los Angeles: Los Angeles Times, 1983.

Rechy, John. *The Sexual Outlaw: A Documentary; A Non-fiction Account, With Commentaries, of Three Days and Nights in the Sexual Underground.* New York: Grove, 1977.

Rivas, Rafael Alberto. *Survival: My Life in Love and War.* Hicksville, N.Y.: Exposition Press, 1977.

Rodríguez, Consuelo. *Cesar Chavez.* New York: Chelsea House, 1991.

Rodríguez, Jeanette. *Our Lady of Guadalupe: Faith and Empowerment Among Mexican American Women.* Austin: University of Texas Press, 1994.

Rodríguez, Luis J. *Always Running: La Vida Loca: Gang Days in L.A.* Willimantic, Conn.: Curbstone Press, 1993. Translated into Spanish by Ricardo Aguilar Melantzón and Ana Brewington as *La vida loca: El testimonio de un panderillo en Los Angeles.* New York: Simon & Schuster, 1996. Translation republished as *Siempre corriendo: La vida loca o los días de la ganga en L.A.* Mexico, D. F.: Editorial Planeta, 1996.

Rodriguez, Richard. *Days of Obligation: An Argument With My Mexican Father.* New York: Viking, 1992.

Rodriguez. *Hunger of Memory: The Education of Richard Rodriguez: An Autobiography.* Boston: Godine, 1981.

Rojas, Arnold R. *California Vaquero.* Fresno, Cal.: Academy Library Guild, 1953.

Rojas. *Last of the Vaqueros.* Fresno, Cal.: Academy Library Guild, 1960.

Rojas. *Lore of the California Vaquero.* Fresno, Cal.: Academy Library Guild, 1958.

Rojas. *The Vaquero.* Charlotte, N.C.: McNally & Loftin, 1964.

Rojas. *Vaqueros and Buckeroos.* Shafter, Cal., 1979.

Rojas. *These Were the Vaqueros: Collected Works by Arnold R. Rojas.* Shafter, Cal.: A. R. Rojas, 1974.

Romano-V., Octavio I. *Geriatric Fu: My First Sixty-five Years in The United States.* Berkeley, Cal.: TQS Publications, 1990.

Rosales, F. Arturo. *Chicano!: The History of the Mexican American Civil Rights Movement.* Houston: Arte Público, 1996.

Ruiz, Mona, and Geof Boucher. *Two Badges: The Lives of Mona Ruiz.* Houston: Arte Público, 1997.

de Ruiz, Dana Catharine, and Richard Larios. *La Causa: The Migrant Farmworkers' Story.* Austin: Raintree Steck-Vaughn, 1993.

Saiz, Flor. *La Chicana: Preliminary Booklet.* N.p., 1973.

Salas, Floyd. *Buffalo Nickel: A Memoir.* Houston: Arte Público, 1992.

Sálaz, Rubén Darío. *Cosmic: The La Raza Sketch Book.* Santa Fe: Blue Feather Press, 1975.

Sálaz. *The Cosmic Reader of the Southwest for Young People: A History of the Hispanic Southwest for Young Readers/ La lectura cósmica del suroeste para los jóvenes: historia del suroeste hispánico para lectores jóvenes.* Albuquerque: Fine Line Press, 1976.

Salazar, Rubén. *Rubén Salazar, Border Correspondent: Selected Writings 1955–1970.* Edited by Mario T. García. Berkeley: University of California Press, 1995.

Salazar. *Rubén Salazar: A Selection of Columns Reprinted from the Los Angeles Times.* Los Angeles: Los Angeles Times, 1970.

Saldívar, José David. *Border Matters: Remapping American Cultural Studies.* Berkeley: University of California Press, 1997.

Sánchez, George J. *Becoming Mexican American: Ethnicity and Identity in Chicano Los Angeles, 1900–1945.* New York: Oxford University Press, 1994.

Sánchez, Rosaura, comp. *Telling Identities: The Californio Testimonio.* Minneapolis: University of Minnesota Press, 1996.

Sánchez, and Rosa Martínez Cruz, eds. *Essays on la Mujer.* Los Angeles: Chicano Studies Center Publications, University of California, 1977.

Shorris, Earl. *Latinos: A Biography of the People.* New York: Norton, 1992.

Simmen, Edward, ed. *Pain and Promise: The Chicano Today.* New York: New American Library, 1972.

Soto, Gary. *Lesser Evils: Ten Quartets.* Houston: Arte Público, 1988.

Soto. *A Summer Life.* Hanover, N.H.: University Press of New England, 1990.

Stavans, Ilan. *Bandido: Oscar 'Zeta' Acosta and the Chicano Experience.* New York: Icon Editions, 1995.

Stavans. *The Hispanic Condition: Reflections on Culture and Identity in America.* New York: HarperCollins, 1995.

Strachwitz Chris, and James Nicolpulos, chroniclers. *Lydia Mendoza: A Family Autobiography.* Houston: Arte Público, 1993.

Tafolla, Carmen. *To Split a Human: Mitos, Machos y la Mujer Chicana.* San Antonio: Mexican American Cultural Center, 1985.

Torres, Olga Beatriz. *Memorias de mi viaje / Recollections of My Trip.* Translated by Juanita Luna-Lawhn. Albuquerque: University of New Mexico Press, 1994.

Trujillo, Carla, ed. *Living Chicana Theory.* Berkeley, Cal.: Third Woman Press, 1998.

Trujillo, Charley, ed. *Soldados: Chicanos in Viet Nam.* San Jose: Chusma House Publications, 1990.

Ulibarrí, Sabine R. *El alma de la Raza.* Albuquerque: University of New Mexico Cultural Awareness Center, 197?

Ulibarrí. *Mayhem Was Our Business: Memorias de un Veterano.* Tempe, Ariz.: Bilingual Press/Revista Bilingüe, 1997.

Ulica, Jorge. *Crónicas diabólicas (1916–1926) de "Jorge Ulica."* Compiled by Juan Rodriguez. San Diego: Maize Press, 1982.

Urrea, Luis Alberto. *Across the Wire: Life and Hard Times on the Mexican Border.* New York: Anchor, 1993.

Urrea. *By the Lake of Sleeping Children: The Secret Life of the Mexican Border.* New York: Anchor/Doubleday, 1996.

Urrea. *Nobody's Son: Notes from an American Life.* Tucson: University of Arizona Press, 1998.

Urrea. *Wandering Time: Western Notebooks.* Tucson: University of Arizona Press, 1999.

Vélez-Ibáñez, Carlos G. *Border Visions: Mexican Cultures of the Southwest United States.* Tucson: University of Arizona Press, 1996.

Vigil, James Diego. *Barrio Gangs: Street Life and Identity in Southern California.* Austin: University of Texas Press, 1988.

Vigil. *From Indians to Chicanos: A Sociocultural History.* St. Louis, Mo.: Mosby, 1980.

Villaseñor, Victor. *Jury: The People vs. Juan Corona.* Boston: Little, Brown, 1977.

Villaseñor. *Rain of Gold.* Houston: Arte Público, 1991. Translated as *Lluvia de oro.* Mexico, D. F.: Editorial Planeta, 1993.

Villaseñor. *Wild Steps of Heaven*. New York: Delacorte, 1996.

Villegas de Magnón, Leonor. *The Rebel*. Edited by Clara Lomas. Houston: Arte Público, 1994.

Wilbur-Cruce, Eva Antonia. *A Beautiful, Cruel Country*. Tucson: University of Arizona Press, 1987.

Zúñiga, José. *Soldier of the Year: The Story of a Gay American Patriot*. New York: Pocket Books, 1994.

## ANTHOLOGIES

Aguilar Melantzón, Ricardo, Armando Armengol, and Oscar Somoza, eds. *Palabra nueva: Cuentos chicanos*. El Paso: Texas Western Press, 1984.

Aguilar, Armengol, and Sergio Elizondo, eds. *Palabra nueva: Cuentos chicanos II*. El Paso: Dos Pasos Editores, 1987.

Aguilar, Armengol, and Elizondo, eds. *Palabra nueva: Poesía chicana*. El Paso: Dos Pasos Publications, 1985.

Alarcón, Justo S., Juan Pérez Aldape, and Lupe Cárdenas. *Canto al pueblo: antología / Anthology*. Mesa: Arizona Canto al Pueblo, 1980.

Alarcón, Norma, Ana Castillo, and Cherríe Moraga, eds. *The Sexuality of Latinas*. Berkeley, Cal.: Third Woman Press, 1993.

Albi, F. E., and Jesús G. Nieto, eds. *Sighs and Songs of Aztlán: New Anthology of Chicano Literature*. Bakersfield, Cal.: Universal Press, 1975.

Alurista, Jorge González, and others, eds. *El Ombligo de Aztlán: An Anthology of Chicano Student Poetry*. San Diego: Centro de Estudios Chicanos Publications, San Diego State College, 1972.

Alurista, and others, eds. *Festival de Flor y Canto: An Anthology of Chicano Literature*: Los Angeles: University of Southern California Press, 1976.

Alurista, and others, eds. *Literatura fronteriza: Antología del primer festival San Diego-Tijuana, mayo 1981*. San Diego: Maize Press, 1982.

Anaya, Rudolfo A. *The Anaya Reader*. New York: Warner Books, 1995.

Anaya, ed. *Voces: An Anthology of Nuevo Mexicano Writers*. Albuquerque: El Norte Publications, 1987.

Anaya, and Simon Ortiz. *A Ceremony of Brotherhood, 1680–1980*. Albuquerque: Academia, 1981.

Anzaldúa, Gloria, ed. *Making Face, Making Soul / Haciendo Caras: Creative and Critical Perspectives by Feminists of Color*. San Francisco: Aunt Lute Foundation Books, 1990.

Armas, José, ed. *La Cosecha / The Harvest: The Chicana Experience*. Special issue of *De Colores: A Bilingual Quarterly Journal of Chicano Expression and Thought,* 4, no. 3 (1978).

Armas, ed. *Mestizo: Anthology of Chicano Literature*. Special double issue of *De Colores: Journal of Chicano Expression and Thought,* 4 (1978).

Armas, Justo S. Alarcón, and others, eds. *Flor y Canto IV and V: An Anthology of Chicano Literature from the Festivals Held in Albuquerque, New Mexico, 1977, and Tempe, Arizona, 1978*. Albuquerque: Pajarito Publications, 1980.

Augenbraum, Harold, and Margarite Fernández Olmos, eds. *The Latino Reader: An American Literary Tradition From 1542 to the Present.* New York: Houghton Mifflin, 1997.

Becerra, David, Juan Manuel Bernal, and Ivón Gordon-Vailakis, eds. *Bajo la piel / Under The Skin.* Translated by Ramón Oceguera. Irvine: University of California, 1987.

Benavides, Rosamel, ed. *Antología de cuentistas chicanas: Estados Unidos de los '60 a los '90.* Santiago, Chile: Editorial Cuarto Propio, 1993.

Benjamin-Labarthe, Elyette, ed. *Vous Avez Dit Chicano: Anthologie Thèmatique de Poésie Chicano.* Bordeaux, France: Editions de la Maison des Sciences de l'Homme d'Aquitane, 1993.

Binder, Wolfgang, ed. *Contemporary Chicano Poetry: An Anthology.* Nuremberg, Germany: Erlag Palm and Enke Erlander, 1986.

Boza, María del Carmen, Beverly Silva and Carmen Valle, eds. *Nosotras: Latina Literature Today.* Binghamton, N.Y.: Bilingual Press/Editorial Bilingüe, 1986.

Bruce-Novoa, Juan, and José Guillermo Saavedra, eds. *Antología retrospectiva del cuento Chicano.* Mexico City: Consejo Nacional de Población, 1988.

Bus, Heiner, and Ana Castillo, eds. *Recent Chicano Poetry / Neueste Chicano-Lyrik.* Bamberg, Germany: Universitätsbibliothek Bamberg, 1994.

*Cantoleo '76: Anthology of Literature, Music, and Theatre Documenting a Festival held in Austin, Texas, December, 1976.* Austin: CASA (Chicanos Artistas Sirviendo a Aztlán) Publications, 1977.

Cárdenas de Dwyer, Carlota. *Chicano Voices.* Boston: Houghton Mifflin, 1975.

Carrillo, Leonard, and others, eds. *Canto Al Pueblo: An Anthology of Experiences.* San Antonio: Penca Books, 1978.

Castillo-Speed, Lillian, ed. *Latina: Women's Voices From the Borderlands.* New York: Simon & Schuster, 1995.

Catañeda-Shular, Antonia, Tomás Ybarra-Frausto and Joseph Sommers, eds. *Literatura Chicana: texto y contexto / Chicano Literature: Text and Context.* Englewood Cliffs, N.J.: Prentice-Hall, 1972.

Cavazos, David Sergio, and others, eds. *Ta Cincho.* Austin: CASA Publications, 1977.

*Cenzontle: Chicano Short Stories and Poetry. Fifth Chicano Literary Prize, 1978–1979.* Irvine: Department of Spanish and Portuguese, University of California, 1979.

*Cenzontle: Chicano Short Stories and Poetry. Sixth Chicano Literary Prize, 1979–1980.* Irvine: Department of Spanish and Portuguese, University of California, 1980.

*Cenzontle: Chicano Short Stories and Poetry. Seventh Chicano Literary Prize, 1980–1981.* Irvine: Department of Spanish and Portuguese, University of California, 1981.

Chávez, Albert C., ed. *Yearnings: Mexican American Literature.* West Haven, Conn.: Pendulum Press, 1972.

*(First) Chicano Literary Prize, Irvine, 1974–1975.* Irvine: Department of Spanish and Portuguese, University of California, 1975.

*(Second) Chicano Literary Prize, Irvine, 1975–1976.* Irvine: Department of Spanish and Portuguese, University of California, 1976.

*(Third) Chicano Literary Prize, Irvine, 1976–1977.* Irvine: Department of Spanish and Portuguese, University of California, 1977.

*(Fourth) Chicano Literary Prize, Irvine, 1977–1978.* Irvine: Department of Spanish and Portuguese, University of California, 1978.

Christian, Karen, ed. *Irvine Chicano Literary Prize 1988–1989 / 1989–1990.* Irvine: Department of Spanish and Portuguese, University of California, 1991.

Clinton, Michelle T., Sesshu Foster, and Naomi Quiñónez, eds. *Invocation L.A.: Urban Multicultural Poetry.* Albuquerque: West End Press, 1989.

Cota-Cárdenas, Margarita, and Eliana S. Rivero, eds. *Siete Poetas.* Tucson, Ariz.: Scorpion Press, 1978.

Cruz, Victor Hernández, Leroy V. Quintana, and Virgil Suarez. *Paper Dance: 55 Latino Poets.* New York: Persea Books, 1995.

Cumpián, Carlos, ed. *Emergency Tacos: Seven Poets con Picante.* Chicago: MARCH/Abrazo Press, 1989.

Daydí-Tolson, Santiago, ed. *Five Poets of Aztlán.* Binghamton, N.Y.: Bilingual Press/Editorial Bilingüe, 1985.

De la Fuente, Patricia, ed. *RiverSedge: Chicano Issue: A Journal of Art, Poetry, and Prose.* Special issues of *RiverSedge,* 2 (1980), 4 (1982).

Di-Bella, José Manuel, and others, eds. *Literatura de la frontera méxico-norteamericana: cuentos / U.S. Mexican Border Literature: Short Stories.* Mexicali: Universidad Autónoma de Baja California; Calexico, Cal.: San Diego State University, 1989.

Durán, Roberto, Judith Ortiz Cofer, and Gustavo Pérez Firmat, eds. *Triple Crown: Chicano, Puerto Rican and Cuban American Poetry.* Tempe, Ariz.: Bilingual Press/Editorial Bilingüe, 1987.

Empringham, Toni, ed. *Fiesta in Aztlán: An Anthology of Chicano Poetry.* Santa Barbara: Capra Press, 1982.

Fernández, José B., and Nasario García, eds. *Nuevos horizontes: Cuentos Chicanos, puertorriqueños y cubanos.* Lexington, Mass.: D. C. Heath, 1982.

Fernández, Roberta, ed. *In Other Words: Literature by Latinas of the United States.* Houston: Arte Público, 1994.

*Festival Flor y Canto II: An Anthology of Chicano Literature from the Festival Held March 12–16, 1975, Austin, Texas.* Albuquerque: Pajarito Publications, 1975?.

Fisher, Dexter, ed. *The Third Woman: Minority Women Writers of the United States.* Boston: Houghton Mifflin, 1980.

Flores, Joseph A., ed. *Songs and Dreams.* West Haven, Conn.: Pendulum Press, 1972.

Frumkin, Gene, and Stanley Noyes, eds. *The Indian Río Grande: Recent Poems from 3 Cultures.* Cerrillos, N.Mex.: San Marcos Press, 1977.

Galindo, Mary Sue, María Limón, and Jesse Johnson. *Merienda Tejana.* Austin: Relámpago Books, 1985.

Gaona, María Eugenia, ed. *Antología de la literatura chicana.* Mexico City: Centro de Enseñanza Para Extranjeros, UNAM, 1986.

Gillan, María Mazziotti, and Jennifer Gillan, eds. *Unsettling America: An Anthology of Contemporary Multicultural Poetry*. New York: Viking/Penguin, 1994.

González-T., Cesar, and Luis Alberto Urrea, eds. *Fragmentos de Barro: The First Seven Years*. San Diego: Tolteca Publications, Centro Cultura de la Raza, 1987.

González-T. *Fragmentos de Barro/Pieces of Clay VIII*. San Diego: San Diego Mesa College, MECHA/Chicano Studies, 1991.

González, Ray, ed. *After Aztlán: Latino Poets of the Nineties*. Boston: Godine, 1992.

González, ed. *Crossing the River: Poets of the Western U.S.* Sag Harbor, N.Y.: Permanent Press, 1987.

González, ed. *Currents From the Dancing River: Contemporary Latino Fiction, Non-fiction and Poetry*. New York: Harcourt Brace, 1994.

González, ed. *Inheritance of Light: Contemporary Poetry from Texas*. Denton: University of North Texas Press, 1996.

González, ed. *Mirrors Beneath the Earth: Short Fiction by Chicano Writers*. Willimantic, Conn.: Curbstone Press, 1992.

González, ed. *Touching the Fire: Fifteen Poets of Today's Latino Renaissance*. New York: Anchor/Doubleday, 1998.

González, ed. *Under the Pomegranate Tree: The Best New Latino Erotica*. New York: Washington Square Press, 1996.

González, ed. *Without Discovery: A Native Response to Columbus*. Seattle: Broken Moon Press, 1992.

Gordon-Vailakis, Ivón, ed. *Irvine Chicano Literary Prize, 1985–1987* [*Cenzontle*: Twelfth Chicano Literary Prize, 1985–1986; Thirteenth Chicano Literary Prize, 1986–1987]. Irvine: Department of Spanish and Portuguese, University of California, 1988.

Guerra, Víctor, ed. *El camino de la cruz: Una antología chicana*. Austin: Tejidos Publications, 1981.

Harth, E. Dorothy, and Lewis M. Baldwin, eds. *Voices of Aztlán: Chicano Literature Today*. New York: New American Library, 1974.

Hermans, Hub and Francisco Lasarte, eds. *Literatura chicana*. Amsterdam & Atlanta: Rodopi, 1995.

Hernández, Lisa, and Tina Benítez, eds. *Palabras Chicanas: An Undergraduate Anthology*. Berkeley: Mujeres en Marcha, University of California, Berkeley, 1988.

Hernández-Gutiérrez, Manuel de Jesús and David Foster. *Literatura Chicana 1965–1995: An Anthology in Spanish, English, and Caló*. Hamden, Conn.: Garland, 1997.

Herrera-Sobek, María, ed. *Cenzontle: Chicano Writing of the 80's. Eighth Chicano Literary Prize, Irvine 1981–1982*. Irvine: Department of Spanish and Portuguese, University of California, 1982.

Herrera-Sobek, and Helena María Viramontes, eds. *Chicana Creativity and Criticism: Chartering New Frontiers in American Literature*. Houston: Arte Público, 1988. Revised and expanded. Albuquerque: University of New Mexico Press, 1996.

Herrera-Sobek and Viramontes, eds. *Chicana (W)rites: On Word and Film*. Berkeley, Cal.: Third Woman Press, 1995.

Hintz, Joy, ed. *Anthology of Ohio Mexican American Writers*. Tiffin, Ohio: Heidelberg College, 1974.

Hintz, ed. *Mexican American Anthology II: Poetry, Prose, Essays, Stories, Songs, Dichos, Corridos, Art.* Lansing, Mich:. El Renacimiento Press, 1976.

Jiménez, Francisco, comp. *Mosaico de la vida: Prosa chicana, cubana y puertorriqueña.* New York: Harcourt Brace Jovanovich, 1981.

Jiménez, and Gary Keller, eds. *Hispanics in the United States: An Anthology of Creative Literature.* Ypsilanti, Mich.: Bilingual Review Press, 1982.

Joysmith, Claire, ed. *Las formas de nuestras voces: Chicana and Mexicana Writers in Mexico.* Mexico City: UNAM, 1995.

Kanellos, Nicolás, ed. *A Decade of Hispanic Literature: An Anniversary Anthology.* Special issue of *Revista Chicano-Riqueña* 10 (Winter-Spring, 1982).

Kanellos, ed. *Short Fiction by Hispanic Writers of the United States.* Houston: Arte Público, 1993.

Kanellos, and Luis Dávila, eds. *Latino Short Fiction.* Special issue of *Revista Chicano-Riqueña,* año 8, no. 1 (Winter 1980).

Kanellos and Dávila, eds. *Los Tejanos: A Texas-Mexican Anthology.* Special issue of *Revista Chicano-Riqueña,* año 8, no. 3 (Summer 1980).

Keller, Gary D., and Francisco Jiménez, eds. *Hispanics in the United States: An Anthology of Creative Literature.* Ypsilanti, Mich.: Bilingual Review Press/Editorial Bilingüe, 1980.

Lomelí, Francisco A., ed. *Nuevos horizontes de 15 mundos.* Santa Barbara: Chicano Studies Creative Writing, University of California, 1979.

López, Tiffany Ann, ed. *Growing Up Chicana/o: An Anthology.* New York: Morrow, 1993.

Lowenfels, Walter, ed. *From the Belly of the Shark: A New Anthology of Native Americans; Poems by Chicanos, Eskimos, Hawaiians, Indians, Puerto Ricans in the U.S.A. with Related Poems by Others.* New York: Vintage, 1973.

Ludwig, Ed, and James Santibáñez, eds. *The Chicanos: Mexican American Voices.* Baltimore: Penguin, 1971.

Martín-Rodríguez, Manuel M., ed. *La Voz Urgente: Antología de Literatura Chicana en Español.* Madrid, Spain: Editorial Fundamentos, 1995.

*Mexican American Literature.* Englewood Cliffs, N.J.: Globe Book Co., 1993.

Milligan, Bryce, Mary Guerrero Miligan, and Angela de Hoyos, eds. *Daughters of the Fifth Sun: A Collection of Latina Fiction and Poetry.* New York: Riverhead Books, 1995.

Montalvo, Carmela, Leonardo Anguiano, and Cecilio García-Camarillo, eds. *El quetzal emplumece.* San Antonio: Mexican American Cultural Center, 1976.

Morales, Arcadio, and Brian Martínez, eds. *Every Other Path.* Santa Barbara: Chicano Studies, University of California, 1982.

*Nosotros Anthology.* Special issue of *Revista Chicano-Riqueña,* año 5, no. 1 (Winter 1977).

Oliphant, Dave and Luis Ramos-García, eds. *Washing the Cow's Skull: Texas Poetry in Translation / Lavando la Calavera de la vaca: poesía texana en traducción.* Fort Worth, Tex.: Prickly Pear, Studia Hispánica Editors, 1981.

Olivares, Julián, and Evangelina Vigil-Piñón, eds. *Decade II: An Anniversary Anthology.* Houston: Arte Público, 1993.

Ortego, Philip D., ed. *We are Chicanos: An Anthology of Mexican American Literature*. New York: Washington Square Press, 1973.

Palley, Julian, ed. *Best New Chicano Literature 1986* [*Cenzontle:* Ninth Chicano Literary Prize, 1982–1983]. Tempe, Ariz.: Bilingual Press/Editorial Bilingüe, 1986.

Palley, ed. *Best New Chicano Literature 1989* [*Cenzontle:* Tenth Chicano Literary Prize, 1983–1984; Eleventh Chicano Literary Prize, 1984–1985]. Tempe, Ariz.: Bilingual Press/Editorial Bilingüe, 1989.

Paredes, Américo, and Raymund Paredes, eds. *Mexican-American Authors*. Boston: Houghton Mifflin, 1972.

Polkinhorn, Harry, ed. *Border Literature/literatura fronteriza: A Binational Conference: Proceedings of a Seminar Held in October 1986, La Jolla, California*. San Diego: Institute for Regional Studies of the Californias, San Diego State University, 1987.

Rebolledo, Tey Diana, Erlinda Gonzales-Berry, and Teresa Márquez, eds. *Las mujeres hablan: An Anthology of Nuevo Mexicana Writers*. Albuquerque: El Norte Publications, 1988.

Rebolledo and Eliana S. Rivero, eds. *Infinite Divisions: An Anthology of Chicana Literature*. Tucson: University of Arizona Press, 1993.

Rivera, Tomás. *Tomás Rivera: The Complete Works*. Edited by Julián Olivares. Houston: Arte Público, 1991.

Romano-V., Octavio I., ed. *El Espejo/The Mirror: Selected Chicano Literature*. Berkeley, Cal.: Quinto Sol Publications, 1969. Revised and edited by Romano-V. and Herminio Ríos-C. Berkeley, Cal.: Quinto Sol Publications, 1972.

Romano-V., ed. *The Grito de Sol Collection, Winter 1984: An Anthology*. Berkeley, Cal.: TQS Publications, 1984.

Romano-V., ed. *Voices: Selected Readings from El Grito, a Journal of Contemporary Mexican American Thought, 1967–1971*. Berkeley, Cal.: Quinto Sol Publications, 1971. Revised and expanded as *Voices: Readings from El Grito, a Journal of Contemporary Mexican American Thought, 1967–1973*. Berkeley, Cal.: Quinto Sol Publications, 1973.

Romano-V., and Herminio Ríos-C., eds. *Chicanas en la literatura y el arte*. Berkeley, Cal.: Quinto Sol Publications, 1973.

Sagel, Jim, ed. *Resiembra: An Anthology of Writings*. Española, N.Mex.: Conjunto Cultural Norteño, 1982.

Salas, Floyd, Glenn Kraski, and Claire Ortalda, eds. *Stories and Poems from Close to Home*. Berkeley, Cal.: Ortalda & Associates, 1986.

Salinas, Luis Omar, and Lillian Faderman, eds. *From the Barrio: A Chicano Anthology*. San Francisco: Canfield Press, 1973.

Sánchez, Rita, ed. *Vision*. San Diego: San Diego State University, 1976.

Somoza, Oscar U., ed. *Chicano Literature*. Special issue of *Denver Quarterly*, 16 (Fall 1981).

Spargo, Edward, ed. *Voices from the Bottom: Selections by and about the American Indian, the Chicano, and the Puerto Rican*. Providence, R.I.: Jamestown Publishers, 1982.

Stavans, Ilan, ed. *Oscar "Zeta" Acosta: The Uncollected Works*. Houston: Arte Público, 1996.

Tashlik, Phyllis, ed. *Hispanic, Female and Young: An Anthology*. Houston: Arte Público/Piñata Books, 1994.

Tatum, Charles M., ed. *Mexican American Literature*. Orlando, Fla.: Harcourt Brace Jovanovich, 1990.

Tatum, ed. *New Chicana / Chicano Writings 1*. Tucson: University of Arizona Press, 1992.

Tatum, ed. *New Chicana / Chicano Writings 2*. Tucson: University of Arizona Press, 1993.

Tatum, ed. *New Chicana / Chicano Writings 3*. Tucson: University of Arizona Press, 1993.

Torres, Luis A. *California Poetry, 1855–1881*. Volume 1 of *The World of Early Chicano Poetry, 1846–1910*. Encino, Cal.: Floricanto Press, 1992.

Trujillo, Carla, ed. *Chicana Lesbians: The Girls My Mother Warned Us About*. Berkeley, Cal.: Third Woman Press, 1991.

Ulibarrí, Sabine R., and Flora Orozco, eds. *La fragua sin fuego / No Fire for the Forge: Stories and Poems in New Mexican Spanish and English Translation*. Translated by Ulibarrí. Cerrillos, N.Mex.: San Marcos Press, 1971.

Valdez, Luis, and Stan Steiner, eds. *Aztlán: An Anthology of Mexican American Literature*. New York: Knopf, 1972.

Vigil-Piñón, Evangelina, ed. *Woman of Her Word: Hispanic Women Write*. Houston: Arte Público, 1983.

Villanueva, Tino, comp. *Chicanos: Antología histórica y literaria*. Mexico: Fondo de Cultura Económica, 1980. Abridged as *Chicanos: selección*. Mexico, D.F.: Fondo de Cultura Económica, 1985.

Villegas, Juan, and Julie Foraker, eds. *Irvine Chicano Literary Prize, 1987–1988* [*Cenzontle*: Fourteenth Chicano Literary Prize]. Irvine: Department of Spanish and Portuguese, University of California, 1988.

Zamora, Bernice, and Linda Morales Armas, eds. *The Best of Chicano Fiction*. Special issue of *De Colores: Journal of Chicano Expression and Thought*, 5, nos. 3–4 (1981).

## CRITICISM

Aguilar-Henson, Marcella. *The Multi-faceted Poetic World of Angela de Hoyos*. Austin: Relámpago Press Books, 1985.

Alarcón, Justo S., and Lupe Cárdenas. *El espacio literario de Juan Bruce-Novoa y la literatura Chicana: un análisis metacrítico del texto/ Juan Bruce-Novoa's Theory of Chicano Literary Space: A Metacritical Analysis of the Text*. Translated by Cárdenas. San Diego: Marín Publications, 1994.

Alarcón, Norma, and others, eds. *Chicana Critical Issues*. Berkeley, Cal.: Third Woman Press, 1993.

Armas, Linda Morales, Sue Molina, and Teresa Márquez. *La Cosecha: Literatura y la Mujer Chicana*. Special issue of *De Colores: Journal of Emerging Raza Philosophies*, 3, no. 3 (1977).

Arteaga, Alfred. *Chicano Poetics: Heterotexts and Hybridities*. Cambridge & New York: Cambridge University Press, 1997.

von Bardeleben, Renate, Dietrich Briesemeister, and Juan Bruce-Novoa, eds. *Missions in Conflict: Essays on U.S.-Mexican Relations and Chicano Culture*. Tübingen, Germany: Gunter Narr Verlag, 1986.

Bleznick, Donald William. *A Sourcebook for Hispanic Literature and Language: A Selected, Annotated Guide To Spanish and Spanish American Bibliography, Literature, Linguistics, Journals, and Other Source Material*. Philadelphia: Temple University Press, 1974. Expanded as *A Sourcebook for Hispanic Literature and Language: A Selected, Annotated Guide To Spanish, Spanish-American, and Chicano Bibliography, Literature, Linguistics, Journals and Other Source Material*. Metuchen, N.J.: Scarecrow Press, 1983. Expanded again as *A Sourcebook for Hispanic Literature and Language: A Selected, Annotated Guide to Spanish, Spanish-American, and United States Hispanic Bibliography, Literature, Linguistics, Journals, and Other Source Materials*. Lanham, Md.: Scarecrow Press, 1995.

Balassi, William, John F. Crawford and Annie O. Eysturoy, eds. *This is About Vision: Interviews with Southwestern Writers.* Albuquerque: University of New Mexico Press, 1990.

Binder, Wolfgang, ed. *Partial Autobiographies: Interviews with 20 Chicano Poets.* Erlangen, Germany: Palm & Enke, 1985.

Broyles-González, Yolanda. *El Teatro Campesino: Theatre in the Chicano Movement.* Austin: University of Texas Press, 1994.

Bruce-Novoa, Juan. *Chicano Authors: Inquiry by Interview.* Austin: University of Texas Press, 1980.

Bruce-Novoa. *Chicano Poetry: A Response to Chaos.* Austin: University of Texas Press, 1982.

Bruce-Novoa. *La literatura chicana a través de sus autores.* Mexico City: Siglo Veintuno Editores, 1983.

Bruce-Novoa. *RetroSpace: Collected Essays on Chicano Literature, Theory, and History.* Houston: Arte Público, 1990.

Calderón, Hector and José David Saldívar, eds. *Criticism in the Borderlands: Studies in Chicano Literature, Culture and Ideology.* Durham, N.C.: Duke University Press, 1991.

Candelaria, Cordelia. *Chicano Poetry: A Critical Introduction.* Westport, Conn.: Greenwood Press, 1986.

Candelaria, ed. *Chicanas en el ambiente nacional / Chicanas in the National Landscape.* Special edition of *Frontiers: A Journal of Women Studies.* 5 (Summer 1980).

Candelaria, ed. *Multiethnic Literature of the United States: Critical Introductions and Classroom Resources.* Boulder: University of Colorado, 1989.

Chabram, Angie C., and Rosalinda Fregoso, eds. *Chicana/o Cultural Representations: Reframing Alternative Critical Discourses.* Special issue of *Cultural Studies,* 4 (1990).

Chávez, John R. *The Lost Land: The Chicano Image of the Southwest.* Albuquerque: University of New Mexico Press, 1984.

Christian, Karen. *Show and Tell: Identity as Performance in U.S. Latina/o Fiction.* Albuquerque: University of New Mexico Press, 1997.

Corpi, Lucha, ed. *Máscaras.* Berkeley, Cal.: Third Woman Press, 1997.

Duke Dos Santos, María I. and Patricia De la Fuente, eds. *Sabine R. Ulibarri: Critical Essays.* Albuquerque: University of New Mexico Press, 1995.

Eger, Ernestina N. *A Bibliography of Criticism of Chicano Literature.* Berkeley: Chicano Studies Library Publications, University of California, 1980.

Elam, Harry J. Jr. *Taking it to the Streets: The Social Protest Theater of Luis Valdez and Amiri Baraka.* Ann Arbor: University of Michigan Press, 1997.

*El Teatro Campesino: The Evolution of America's First Chicano Theatre Company, 1965–1985.* San Juan Bautista, Cal.: El Teatro, 1985.

Eysturoy, Annie O. *Daughters of Self-Creation: The Contemporary Chicana Novel.* Albuquerque: University of New Mexico Press, 1996.

Fabre, Genevieve, ed. *European Perspectives on Hispanic Literature of the United States.* Houston: Arte Público, 1988.

Farah, Cynthia. *Literature and Landscape: Writers of the Southwest.* El Paso: Texas Western Press, 1988.

Fisher, Dexter, ed. *Minority Language and Literature: Retrospective and Perspective.* New York: Modern Language Association, 1977.

Flores, Arturo Conrado. *El Teatro Campesino de Luis Valdez 1965–1990.* Madrid: Editorial Pliegos, 1990.

García, Eugene E., Francisco A. Lomelí and Isidro D. Ortiz, eds. *Chicano Studies: A Multidisciplinary Approach.* New York: Teachers College Press, 1984.

Gish, Robert Franklin. *Beyond Bounds: Cross-Cultural Essays on Anglo, American Indian, and Chicano literature.* Albuquerque: University of New Mexico Press, 1996.

Gonzales-Berry, Erlinda, ed. *Pasó por aquí: Critical Essays on the New Mexican Literary Tradition, 1542–1988.* Albuquerque: University of New Mexico Press, 1989.

Gonzales-Berry, and Chuck Tatum, eds. *Recovering the U.S. Hispanic Literary Heritage,* volume 2. Houston: Arte Público, 1996.

González, María C. *Contemporary Mexican-American Women Novelists: Toward a Feminist Identity.* New York: Peter Lang, 1996.

González-T., César, ed. *Rudolfo A. Anaya: Focus on Criticism.* La Jolla, Cal.: Lalo Press, 1990.

Güereña, Salvador, and Raquel Quiroz González. *Luis Leal: A Bibliography with Interpretive and Critical Essays.* Berkeley: Chicano Studies Library Publications, University of California, 1988.

Gurpegui, José Antonio, ed. *Alejandor Morales: Fiction Past, Present, Future Perfect.* Tempe, Ariz.: Bilingual Press/Editorial Bilingüe, 1996.

Gutiérrez, Ramón and Genaro Padilla, eds. *Recovering the U.S. Hispanic Literary Heritage.* Houston: Arte Público, 1993.

Gutiérrez-Jones, Carl. *Rethinking the Borderlands: Between Chicano Culture and Legal Discourse.* Berkeley, Cal.: University of California Press, 1995.

Hernández, Guillermo. *Chicano Satire: A Study in Literary Culture.* Austin: University of Texas Press, 1991.

Hernández y Gutiérrez, Manuel de Jesús. *El colonialism interno en la narrativa Chicano: El barrio, el anti-barrio y el exterior.* Tempe, Ariz.: Bilingual Press/Editorial Bilingüe, 1992.

Herrera-Sobek, María, ed. *Beyond Stereotypes: The Critical Analysis of Chicana Literature.* Binghamton, N.Y.: Bilingual Press/Editorial Bilingüe, 1985.

Herrera-Sobek. *The Bracero Experience: Elitelore versus Folklore.* Los Angeles: University of California, UCLA Latin American Center, 1979.

Herrera-Sobek, and Helena María Viramontes, eds. *Reconstructing a Chicano/a Literary Heritage: Hispanic Colonial Literature of the Southwest.* Tucson: University of Arizona Press, 1993.

Huerta, Jorge A. *Chicano Theatre: Themes and Forms.* Ypsilanti, Mich.: Bilingual Press/Editorial Bilingüe, 1982.

Huerta. *A Bibliography of Mexican Dance, Drama and Music.* Oxnard, Cal.: Colegio Quetzalcoatl, 1972.

Ibáñez, Armando P. *Mesquites Never Die—A Theology of Poetry.* Oakland, Cal.: Pluma Productions, 1993.

Jiménez, Francisco, ed. *The Identification and Analysis of Chicano Literature*. New York: Bilingual Press/Editorial Bilingüe, 1979.

Kanellos, Nicolás. *Hispanic Firsts: 500 Years of Extraordinary Achievement*. Detroit: Gale Research, 1997.

Kanellos. *Hispanic Theatre in the United States*. Houston: Arte Público, 1984.

Kanellos. *A History of Hispanic Theatre in the United States: Origins to 1940*. Austin: University of Texas Press, 1990.

Kanellos, ed. *The Hispanic-American Almanac: A Reference Work on Hispanics in the United States*. Detroit: Gale Research, 1993.

Kanellos, ed. *The Hispanic Literary Companion*. Detroit: Visible Ink Press, 1996.

Kanellos, ed. *Mexican American Theatre: Legacy and Reality*. Houston: Arte Público, 1987.

Kanellos, ed. *Mexican American Theatre: Then and Now*. Houston: Arte Público, 1983.

Kanellos. *Two Centuries of Hispanic Theatre in the Southwest*. Houston: Arte Público, 1982.

Keller, Gary D., ed. *Miguel Méndez in Aztlán: Two Decades of Literary Production*. Tempe, Ariz.: Bilingual Press/Editorial Bilingüe, 1995.

Keller, Gary D., Rafael J. Magallán, and Alma M. García. *Curriculum Resources in Chicano Studies: Undergraduate and Graduate*. Tempe, Ariz.: Bilingual Review Press, 1989.

*Latin American Literary Review*. Special issue of *Chicano Literature*, 5 (Spring–Summer 1977).

Lattin, Vernon E., ed. *Contemporary Chicano Fiction: A Critical Survey*. Binghamton, N.Y.: Bilingual Press/Editorial Bilingüe, 1986.

Lattin, Rolando Hinojosa-Smith, and Gary D. Keller, eds. *Tomás Rivera, 1935–1984: The Man and His Work*. Tempe, Ariz.: Bilingual Press/Editorial Bilingüe, 1989.

Leal, Luis. *Aztlán y México: Perfiles literarios e históricos*. Binghamton, N.Y.: Bilingual Press/Editorial Bilingüe, 1985.

Leal. *No Longer Voiceless*. San Diego: Marin Publications, 1995.

Leal, Luis, Fernando de Necochea, Francisco A. Lomelí, and Roberto G. Trujillo, eds. *A Decade of Chicano Literature (1970–1979): Critical Essays and Bibliography*. Santa Barbara: Editorial La Causa, 1982.

Lee, Joyce Glover. *Rolando Hinojosa and the American Dream*. Denton: University of North Texas Press, 1997.

Lensink, Judy Nolte. *Old Southwest / New Southwest: Essays on a Region and its Literature*. Tucson, Ariz.: Tucson Public Library, 1987.

Lewis, Marvin A. *Introduction to the Chicano Novel*. Milwaukee: University of Wisconsin, Spanish-Speaking Outreach Institute, 1982.

Limón, José E. *Dancing with the Devil: Society and Cultural Poetics in Mexican-American South Texas*. Madison: University of Wisconsin Press, 1994.

Limón. *Mexican Ballads, Chicano Poems: History and Influence in Mexican American Social Poetry*. Berkeley: University of California Press, 1992.

Lomelí, Francisco A., ed. *Handbook of Hispanic Cultures in the United States,* volume 1: *Literature and Art.* Houston: Arte Público / Madrid, Spain: Instituto de Cooperación Iberoamericana, 1993.

Lomelí, and Donaldo W. Urioste. *Chicano Perspectives in Literature: A Critical and Annotated Bibliography.* Albuquerque: Pajarito Publications, 1976.

Lomelí and Urioste, eds. *Chicano Literature and Criticism.* Special issue of *De Colores,* 3, no. 4 (1977).

López-González, Aralia, Amelia Malagamba and Elena Urrutia, eds. *Mujer y literatura: Mexicana y Chicana: culturas en contacto.* Mexico City: Colegio de México, Programa Interdisciplinario de Estudios de la Mujer / Tijuana, B.C., Mexico: Colegio de la Frontera Norte, 1988.

Maier, Annette. *Dark, Distinct, and Excellently Female?: die Sexualität der Frauen in ausgewählten werken der modernen Chicana-Literatur.* Frankfurt am Main & New York: Peter Lang, 1996.

Maldonado, Jesús (el flaco). *Poesía chicana: Alurista, el mero chingón.* Seattle: Centro de Estudios Chicanos, University of Washington, 1971.

Martín-Rodríguez, Manuel M. *Rolando Hinojosa y su "cronicón" Chicano: Una novela del lector.* Sevilla, Spain: Secretariado de Publicaciones de la Universidad de Sevilla, 1993.

Martínez, Julio A., and Francisco A. Lomelí, eds. *Chicano Literature: A Reference Guide*: Westport, Conn.: Greenwood Press, 1985.

McKenna, Teresa. *Migrant Song: Politics and Process in Contemporary Chicano Literature.* Austin: University of Texas Press, 1997.

Meléndez, A. Gabriel. *So All is Not Lost: The Poetics of Print in Nuevomexicano Communities, 1834–1958.* Albuquerque: University of New Mexico Press, 1997.

Meyer, Doris. *Speaking for Themselves: Neomexicano Cultural Identity and the Spanish Language Press, 1820–1920.* Albuquerque: University of New Mexico Press, 1996.

Miller, Beth, ed. *Women in Hispanic Literature: Icons and Fallen Idols.* Berkeley: University of California Press, 1983.

Morales, Phyllis S. *Fray Angélico Chávez: A Bibliography of His Published Writings, 1925–1978.* Santa Fe: Lightning Tree Press, 1980.

National Association for Chicano Studies, eds. *The Chicano Struggle: Analyses of Past and Present Efforts.* Binghamton, N.Y.: Bilingual Press/Editorial Bilingüe, 1984.

Olivares, Julián, ed. *International Studies in Honor of Tomás Rivera.* Houston: Arte Público, 1986.

Ortego, Phillip D., and David Conde, eds. *The Chicano Literary World 1974. Proceedings of the National Symposium on Chicano Literature and Critical Analysis, November, 1974.* Las Vegas: New Mexico Highlands University, 1975.

Padilla, Genaro M. *My History, Not Yours: The Formation of Mexican American Autobiography.* Madison: University of Wisconsin Press, 1993.

Paredes, Américo. *Folklore and Culture on the Texas-Mexican Border.* Edited by Richard Bauman. Austin: CMAS Books, Center for Mexican American Studies, University of Texas at Austin, 1993.

Peck, David R. *American Ethnic Literatures: Native American, African American, Chicano/Latino, and Asian American Writers and Their Backgrounds: An Annotated Bibliography.* Pasadena, Cal.: Salem Press, 1992.

Pérez-Torres, Rafael. *Movements in Chicano Poetry: Against Myths, Against Margins.* Cambridge: Cambridge University Press, 1995.

Piller, Walter. *Der Chicano-Roman: Stufen seiner Entwicklung.* Bern, Germany & New York: Peter Lang, 1991.

Quintana, Alvina Eugenia. *Homegirls: Chicana Literary Voices.* Philadelphia: Temple University Press, 1996.

Rahner, Christiane. *Chicano-Theater zwischen Agitprop und Broadway: die Entwicklung des Teatro Campesino (1965–1985).* Tübingen, Germany: G. Narr, 1991.

Ramos, Luis Arturo. *Angela de Hoyos, A Critical Look: lo heroico y lo antiheroico en su poesía.* Albuquerque: Pajarito Publications, 1979.

Rebolledo, Tey Diana. *Women Singing in the Snow: A Cultural Analysis of Chicana Literature.* Tucson: University of Arizona Press, 1995.

Robinson, Cecil. *No Short Journeys: The Interplay of Cultures in the History and Literature of the Borderlands.* Tucson: University of Arizona Press, 1992.

Robinson. *Mexico and the Hispanic Southwest in American Literature.* Tucson: University of Arizona Press, 1977.

Robinson. *With the Ears of Strangers: The Mexican in American Literature.* Tucson: University of Arizona Press, 1963.

Rocard, Marcienne. *The Children of the Sun: Mexican-Americans in the Literature of the United States.* Translated by Edward G. Brown Jr. Tucson: University of Arizona Press, 1989.

Rodríguez del Pino, Salvador. *La novela Chicana escrita en español: Cinco autores comprometidos.* Ypsilanti, Mich.: Bilingual Press/Editorial Bilingüe, 1982.

Rojas, Guillermo, ed. *Toward a Chicano/Raza Bibliography: Drama, Prose, Poetry.* Special issue of *El Grito,* 7 (December 1973).

Romo, Ricardo, and Raymund Paredes, eds. *New Directions in Chicano Scholarship.* Special issue of *New Scholar,* 6 (1977).

Rudin, Ernst. *Tender Accents of Sound: Spanish in the Chicano Novel in English.* Tempe, Ariz.: Bilingual Press/Editorial Bilingüe, 1996.

Ruiz, Reynaldo. *The Detroit Poets: Cultural Pride and Social Conditions.* East Lansing: Julián Samora Research Institute, Michigan State University, 1990.

Saldívar, José David. *Border Matters: Remapping American Cultural Studies.* Berkeley: University of California Press, 1997.

Saldívar. *The Dialectics of Our America: Genealogy, Cultural Critique, and Literary History.* Durham, N.C.: Duke University Press, 1991.

Saldívar, ed. *The Rolando Hinojosa Reader: Essays Historical and Critical.* Houston: Arte Público, 1985.

Saldívar, Ramón. *Chicano Narrative: The Dialectics of Difference.* Madison: University of Wisconsin Press, 1990.

Sánchez, Marta Ester. *Contemporary Chicana Poetry: A Critical Approach to an Emerging Literature.* Berkeley: University of California Press, 1985.

Sánchez, Rosaura. *Chicano Discourse: Socio-historic Perspectives.* Rowley, Mass.: Newberry House, 1983.

Schon, Isabel. *A Hispanic Heritage, Series III: A Guide to Juvenile Books about Hispanic People and Cultures.* Metuchen, N.J.: Scarecrow Press, 1988.

Shirley, Carl R., and Paula W. Shirley. *Understanding Chicano Literature.* Columbia: University of South Carolina Press, 1988.

Sommers, Joseph and Tomás Ybarra-Frausto, eds. *Modern Chicano Writers: A Collection of Critical Essays.* Englewood Cliffs, N.J.: Prentice-Hall, 1979.

Somoza, Oscar Urquídez, ed. *Narrativa chicana contemporánea: principios fundamentales.* Mexico City: Casa Editorial Signos, 1983.

Tatum, Charles. *Chicano Literature.* Boston: Twayne, 1982.

Tatum. *La literatura chicana.* Translated by Víctor Manuel Velarde. Mexico City: Secretaría de Educación Pública, 1986.

Tatum. *A Selected and Annotated Bibliography of Chicano Studies.* Manhattan, Kans.: Society of Spanish and American Studies, 1976.

Tessarolo Bondolfi, Lia. *Dal mito al mito: la cultura di espressione Chicana: dal mito originario al mito rigeneratore.* Milan, Italy: Jaca Books, 1988.

Tonn, Horst. *Zeitgenössische Chicano-Erzählliteratur in englischer Sprache: Autobiographie und Roman.* Frankfurt am Main & New York: Peter Lang, 1988.

Trejo-Fuentes, Ignacio. *De acá de este lado: una aproximación a la novela Chicana.* Mexico City: Consejo Nacional para la Cultura y las Artes, 1989.

Trujillo, Roberto G. and Andrés Rodríguez. *Literatura Chicana: Creative and Critical Writings Through 1984.* Oakland, Cal.: Floricanto Press, 1985.

Vassallo, Paul, ed. *The Magic of Words: Rudolfo A. Anaya and His Writings.* Albuquerque: University of New Mexico Press, 1982.

Walter, Roland. *Magical Realism in Contemporary Chicano Fiction.* Frankfurt, Germany: Vervuert Verlag, 1993.

Zimmerman, Marc. *U.S. Latino Literature: The Creative Expression of a People: An Essay and Annotated Bibliography.* Chicago: Chicago Public Library, 1990. Revised as *U.S. Latino Literature: An Essay and Annotated Bibliography.* Chicago: MARCH/Abrazo Press, 1992.

# Contributors

Kat Avila . . . . . . . . . . . . . . . . . . . . . . . . . . . . . . . . . . . . . . . . . . . . . . *Irvine, California*

Nuria Bustamante . . . . . . . . . . . . . . . . . . . . . . . . . . . . . . . . *Los Angeles Harbor College*

Dina G. Castillo . . . . . . . . . . . . . . . . . . . . . . . . . . . . . . . . . *Santa Barbara City College*

Roberto Cantú . . . . . . . . . . . . . . . . . . . . . . . . . . . *California State University, Los Angeles*

Angie Chabram-Dernersesian . . . . . . . . . . . . . . . . . . . . . . *University of California, Davis*

Cida S. Chase . . . . . . . . . . . . . . . . . . . . . . . . . . . . . . . . . . *Oklahoma State University*

David Conde . . . . . . . . . . . . . . . . . . . . . . . . . . . . . *Metropolitan State College of Denver*

Gwendolyn Díaz . . . . . . . . . . . . . . . . . . . . . . . . . . . . . . . . . . *Saint Mary's University*

Salvador C. Fernández . . . . . . . . . . . . . . . . . . . . . . . . . . . . . . . . . . *Occidental College*

Nasario García . . . . . . . . . . . . . . . . . . . . . . . . . . . . . *New Mexico Highlands University*

César A. González-T. . . . . . . . . . . . . . . . . . . . . . . . . . . . . . . *San Diego Mesa College*

Michelle Habell-Pallán . . . . . . . . . . . . . . . . . . . . . . . . *University of Washington, Seattle*

Inés Hernández-Ávila . . . . . . . . . . . . . . . . . . . . . . . . . . *University of California, Davis*

Nicolás Kanellos . . . . . . . . . . . . . . . . . . . . . . . . . . . . . . . . . . . *University of Houston*

Enrique R. Lamadrid . . . . . . . . . . . . . . . . . . . . . . . . . . . . . *University of New Mexico*

Luis Leal . . . . . . . . . . . . . . . . . . . . . . . . . . . . . *University of California, Santa Barbara*

Clara Lomas . . . . . . . . . . . . . . . . . . . . . . . . . . . . . . . . . . . . . . . . *Colorado College*

Francisco A. Lomelí . . . . . . . . . . . . . . . . . . . . . *University of California, Santa Barbara*

Miguel R. López . . . . . . . . . . . . . . . . . . . . . . . . . . . . *Southern Methodist University*

María Teresa Márquez . . . . . . . . . . . . . . . . . . . . . . . . . . . . *University of New Mexico*

Ellen McCracken . . . . . . . . . . . . . . . . . . . . . . . *University of California, Santa Barbara*

Theresa Meléndez . . . . . . . . . . . . . . . . . . . . . . . . . . *University of Texas at El Paso*

Beatrice Pita . . . . . . . . . . . . . . . . . . . . . . . . . . . . *University of California, San Diego*

Merrihelen Ponce . . . . . . . . . . . . . . . . . . . . . . . . . . . . . . . . . *Sunland, California*

Alfonso Rodríguez . . . . . . . . . . . . . . . . . . . . . . . . . . . *University of Northern Colorado*

Joe D. Rodríguez . . . . . . . . . . . . . . . . . . . . . . . . . . . . *San Diego State University*

Jesús Rosales . . . . . . . . . . . . . . . . . . . . . . . *Texas A&M University–Corpus Christi*

Ramón Sánchez . . . . . . . . . . . . . . . . . . . . . . . . . . . . . . . . . . . . . . . . *Olivet College*

Paula W. Shirley . . . . . . . . . . . . . . . . . . . . . . *Columbia College of South Carolina*

Eddie Tafoya . . . . . . . . . . . . . . . . . . . . . . . . . . . . . *New Mexico Highlands University*

Donaldo W. Urioste . . . . . . . . . . . . . . . . . . . . *California State University, Monterey Bay*

Marc Zimmerman . . . . . . . . . . . . . . . . . . . . . . . . . . *University of Illinois at Chicago*

# Cumulative Index

*Dictionary of Literary Biography,* Volumes 1-209
*Dictionary of Literary Biography Yearbook,* 1980-1998
*Dictionary of Literary Biography Documentary Series,* Volumes 1-19

# Cumulative Index

**DLB** before number: *Dictionary of Literary Biography,* Volumes 1-209
**Y** before number: *Dictionary of Literary Biography Yearbook,* 1980-1998
**DS** before number: *Dictionary of Literary Biography Documentary Series,* Volumes 1-19

# G

ISBN 0-7876-3103-5

90000

9 780787 631031